Suzuki DL650 V-Strom & SFV650 Gladius
Service and Repair Manual

by Matthew Coombs

Models covered

(5643 - 336 - 2AQ1)

DL650 V-Strom 2004 to 2013
DL650A V-Strom 2007 to 2013
SFV650 Gladius 2009 to 2013
SFV650A Gladius 2009 to 2013

© **Haynes Publishing 2017**

ABCDE
FGHIJ
KLMNO
PQR

A book in the **Haynes Service and Repair Manual Series**

All rights reserved. No part of this book may be reproduced or
transmitted in any form or by any means, electronic or mechanical,
including photocopying, recording or by any information storage
or retrieval system, without permission in writing from the
copyright holder.

ISBN 978 1 78521 394 6

British Library Cataloguing in Publication Data
A catalogue record for this book is available from the British Library

Library of Congress Control Number 2013944855

Printed in Malaysia

Haynes Publishing
Sparkford, Yeovil, Somerset BA22 7JJ, England

Haynes North America, Inc
859 Lawrence Drive, Newbury Park, California 91320, USA

*Printed using NORBRITE BOOK 48.8gsm (CODE: 40N6533) from NORPAC; procurement system certified under Sustainable Forestry Initiative
standard. Paper produced is certified to the SFI Certified Fiber Sourcing Standard (CERT - 0094271)*

Contents

Contents

REPAIRS AND OVERHAUL

Engine, transmission and associated systems

Chassis components

Electrical system

Wiring diagrams

REFERENCE

Index

Suzuki
Every Which Way

by Julian Ryder

From Textile Machinery to Motorcycles

Suzuki were the second of Japan's Big Four motorcycle manufacturers to enter the business, and like Honda they started by bolting small two-stroke motors to bicycles. Unlike Honda, they had manufactured other products before turning to transportation in the aftermath of World War II.

In fact Suzuki has been in business since the first decade of the 20th-Century when Michio Suzuki manufactured textile machinery.

The desperate need for transport in post-war Japan saw Suzuki make their first motorised bicycle in 1952, and the fact that by 1954 the company had changed its name to Suzuki Motor Company shows how quickly the sideline took over the whole company's activities. In their first full manufacturing year,

Suzuki made nearly 4500 bikes and rapidly expanded into the world markets with a range of two-strokes.

Suzuki didn't make a four-stroke until 1977 when the GS750 double-overhead-cam across-the-frame four arrived. This was several years after Honda and Kawasaki had established the air-cooled four as the industry standard, but no motorcycle epitomises the era of what came to be known as the Universal

The T500 two-stroke twin

50 cc racer won six of the eight world titles chalked up by Suzuki during the 1960s as well as providing Mitsuo Itoh with the distinction of being the only Japanese rider to win an Isle of Man TT. Mr Itoh still works for Suzuki, he's in charge of their racing program.

Europe got the benefit of Suzuki's two-stroke expertise in a succession of air-cooled twins, the six-speed 250 cc Super Six being the most memorable, but the arrival in 1968 of the first of a series of 500 cc twins which were good looking, robust and versatile marked the start of mainstream success.

So confident were Suzuki of their two-stroke expertise that they even applied it to the burgeoning Superbike sector. The GT750 water-cooled triple arrived in 1972. It was big, fast and comfortable although the handling and stopping power did draw some comment. Whatever the drawbacks of the road bike, the engine was immensely successful in Superbike and Formula 750 racing. The roadster has its devotees, though, and is now a sought-after bike on the classic Japanese scene. Do not refer to it as the Water Buffalo in such company. Joking aside, the later disc-braked versions were quite civilised, but the audacious idea of using a big two-stroke motor in what was essentially a touring bike was a surprising success until the fuel crisis of the mid-'70s effectively killed off big strokers.

The same could be said of Suzuki's only real lemon, the RE5. This is still the only mass-produced bike to use the rotary (or Wankel) engine but never sold well. Fuel consumption in the mid-teens allied to frightening complexity and excess weight meant the RE5 was a non-starter in the sales race.

One of the later GT750 'kettle' models with front disc brakes

Japanese motorcycle better than the GS. So well engineered were the original fours that you can clearly see their genes in the GS500 twins that are still going strong in the mid-1990s. Suzuki's ability to prolong the life of their products this way means that they are often thought of as a conservative company. This is hardly fair if you look at some of their landmark designs, most of which have been commercial as well as critical successes.

Two-stroke Success

Early racing efforts were bolstered by the arrival of Ernst Degner who defected from the East German MZ team at the Swedish GP of 1961, bringing with him the rotary-valve secrets of design genius Walter Kaaden. The new Suzuki 50 cc racer won its first GP on the Isle of Man the following year and winning the title easily. Only Honda and Ralph Bryans interrupted Suzuki's run of 50 cc titles from 1962 to 1968.

The arrival of the twin-cylinder 125 racer in 1963 enabled Hugh Anderson to win both 50 and 125 world titles. You may not think 50 cc racing would be exciting - until you learn that the final incarnation of the thing had 14 gears and could do well over 100 mph on fast circuits. Before pulling out of GPs in 1967 the

Suzuki's GT250X7 was an instant hit in the popular 250 cc 'learner' sector

The GS400 was the first in a line of four-stroke twins

Development of the Four-stroke range

When Suzuki got round to building a four-stroke they did a very good job of it. The GS fours were built in 550, 650, 750, 850, 1000 and 1100 cc sizes in sports, custom, roadster and even shaft-driven touring forms over many years. The GS1000 was in on the start of Superbike racing in the early 1970s and the GS850 shaft-driven tourer was around nearly 15 years later. The fours spawned a line of 400, 425, 450 and 500 cc GS twins that were essentially the middle half of the four with all their reliability. If there was ever a criticism of the GS models it was that with the exception of the GS1000S of 1980, colloquially known as the ice-cream van, the range was visually uninspiring.

They nearly made the same mistake when they launched the four-valve-head GSX750 in 1979. Fortunately, the original twin-shock version was soon replaced by the 'E'-model with Full-Floater rear suspension and a full set of all the gadgets the Japanese industry was then keen on and has since forgotten about, like 16-inch front wheels and anti-dive forks. The air-cooled GSX was like the GS built in 550, 750 and 1100 cc versions with a variety of half, full and touring fairings, but the GSX that is best remembered is the Katana that first appeared in 1981. The power was provided by an 1000 or 1100 cc GSX motor, but wrapped around it was the most outrageous styling package to come out of Japan. Designed by Hans Muth of Target Design, the Katana looked like nothing seen before or since. At the time there was as much anti feeling as praise, but now it is rightly regarded as a classic, a true milestone in motorcycle design. The factory have even started making 250 and 400 cc fours for the home market with the same styling as the 1981 bike.

Just to remind us that they'd still been building two-strokes for the likes of Barry Sheene, in 1986 Suzuki marketed a road-going version of their RG500 square-four racer which had put an end to the era of the four-stroke in 500 GPs when it appeared in 1974. In 1976 Suzuki not only won their first 500 title with Sheene, they sold RG500s over the counter and won every GP with them - with the exception of the Isle of Man TT which the works riders boycotted. Ten years on, the RG500 Gamma gave road riders the nearest

The GS750 led the way for a series of four cylinder models

Later four-stroke models, like this GSX1100, were fitted with 16v engines

experience they'd ever get to riding a GP bike. The fearsome beast could top 140 mph and only weighed 340 lb - the other alleged GP replicas were pussy cats compared to the Gamma's man-eating tiger.

The RG only lasted a few years and is already firmly in the category of collector's item; its four-stroke equivalent, the GSX-R, is still with us and looks like being so for many years. You have to look back to 1985 and its launch to realise just what a revolutionary step the GSX-R750 was: quite simply it was the first race replica. Not a bike dressed up to look like a race bike, but a genuine racer with lights on, a bike that could be taken straight to the track and win.

The first GSX-R, the 750, had a completely new motor cooled by oil rather than water and an aluminium cradle frame. It was sparse, a little twitchy and very, very fast. This time Suzuki got the looks right, blue and white bodywork based on the factory's racing colours and endurance-racer lookalike twin headlights. And then came the 1100 - the big GSX-R got progressively more brutal as it chased the Yamaha EXUP for the heavyweight championship.

And alongside all these mould-breaking designs, Suzuki were also making the best looking custom bikes to come out of Japan, the Intruders; the first race replica trail bike, the DR350; the sharpest 250 Supersports, the RGV250; and a bargain-basement 600, the Bandit. The Bandit proved so popular they went on to build 1200 and 750 cc versions of it. I suppose that's predictable, a range of four-stroke fours just like the GS and GSXs.

A Bike of its Time

Suzuki have always been clever at this sort of thing. In many ways they are the most conservative of the big four Japanese companies, but they occasionally like to surprise everyone with something right on the cutting edge. Think GSX-R and RG models in the 1980s. The GSX-R is still with us and is still on the cutting edge of performance, but times have changed. The economic climate, insurance costs, and changes in riders' priorities have seen to that. Sports bikes are not the be-all and end-all of a model range.

In 1995, back before the credit crunch closed in on us all, Suzuki had got in a bit of practice with a bike called the Bandit. They took an older GSX-R motor and put in it a steel tubular frame – no fairing – and bolted a few low-spec bits on. The result was cheap thrills for everyone and a bike that succeeded far beyond anyone's expectations.

A few years later '90s they produced another bike for everyman, although this time they didn't go to the spare-parts bin they started from scratch. The result was the SV650, a versatile and universally praised V-twin. It could commute, tour and even race in the Mini-Twins class. In the spirit of the

The very first DL650 V-Strom appeared in 2004

Bandit, you got an excellent engine but not much in the way of creature comforts – no slipper clutch or multi-adjustable suspension. None of which stopped the SV from being, like the Bandits, a major sales success over a model life of ten years.

With the credit crunch well and truly making itself felt, Suzuki's next target was the adventure-tourer market, rapidly becoming the boom sector with BMW's GS series as the leading light. Suzuki's challenger, the V-Strom DL1000, arrived in 2002. The factory insisted the V-Strom was the first of a new class of motorcycle they called Sport Enduro Tourer, although that does seem like a subdivision too far. However, the road biased big trail bike, or whatever they should be called, was definitely a class on the up.

In 2004 Suzuki used the 650cc V-twin to produce the first middleweight V-Strom. As usual, the motor was slightly modified and wrapped in cycle parts that while perfectly adequate were not state of the art. But as the price tag was again kept down to very reasonable levels there were few complaints. In fact, the reaction was universally positive, verging on the ecstatic. In any review that considered the question of value for money, the 650 V-Strom was up with the front runners. And when the 2011 facelift model came out the approval ratings went even higher. It was already a good bike but the improvement

The V-Strom is sold with factory-fitted luggage in certain markets – 2010 DL650A model shown

in every department , especially styling and finish, made it even better. Here was a motorcycle so versatile you could do anything on it, with the help of a well thought-out range of accessories. V-Stroms have been ridden to the furthest reaches of the Earth, they've been used to commute in big cities, and they've been used for every purpose in between. It's not just that the bike does these things but that it does it so well. One American magazine thought it might be 'shockingly competent', while another found it 'hard to imagine another machine with a competitive versatility-per-dollar ratio'. In Europe the V-Strom twice won top German magazine Motorrad's trans-Alpine comparison test, while the UK's Daily Telegraph thought it might be 'Perhaps the ultimate all-round machine'.

It would be difficult to find a bike with such accolades in any class, let alone a middleweight twin with a surprisingly small price tag.

The Gladius (latin word for sword), whilst using the same engine but in a steel trellis style frame, is aimed at a different type of rider. The F in its SFV model stands for Fun!

The Gladius was available in this retro Heron Suzuki Barry Sheene paint scheme and with a belly pan in 2012

Acknowledgements

Our thanks are due to Bridge Motorcycles of Exeter, Bransons Motorcycles of Yeovil, Speed Superbikes of Exeter and Fowlers of Bristol, who supplied the machines featured in the illustrations throughout this manual. We would also like to thank NGK Spark Plugs (UK) Ltd for supplying the colour spark plug condition photographs, the Avon Rubber Company for supplying information on tyre fitting and Draper Tools Ltd for some of the workshop tools shown.

Thanks are also due to Julian Ryder who wrote the introduction 'Suzuki – Every which way', and to Suzuki (GB) Ltd. who supplied model photographs.

About this Manual

The aim of this manual is to help you get the best value from your motorcycle. It can do so in several ways. It can help you decide what work must be done, even if you choose to have it done by a dealer; it provides information and procedures for routine maintenance and servicing; and it offers diagnostic and repair procedures to follow when trouble occurs.

We hope you use the manual to tackle the work yourself. For many simpler jobs, doing it yourself may be quicker than arranging an appointment to get the motorcycle into a dealer and making the trips to leave it and pick it up. More importantly, a lot of money can be saved by avoiding the expense the shop must pass on to you to cover its labour and overhead costs. An added benefit is the sense of satisfaction and accomplishment that you feel after doing the job yourself.

References to the left or right side of the motorcycle assume you are sitting on the seat, facing forward.

We take great pride in the accuracy of information given in this manual, but motorcycle manufacturers make alterations and design changes during the production run of a particular motorcycle of which they do not inform us. No liability can be accepted by the authors or publishers for loss, damage or injury caused by any errors in, or omissions from, the information given.

Professional mechanics are trained in safe working procedures. However enthusiastic you may be about getting on with the job at hand, take the time to ensure that your safety is not put at risk. A moment's lack of attention can result in an accident, as can failure to observe simple precautions.

There will always be new ways of having accidents, and the following is not a comprehensive list of all dangers; it is intended rather to make you aware of the risks and to encourage a safe approach to all work you carry out on your bike.

Asbestos

● Certain friction, insulating, sealing and other products - such as brake pads, clutch linings, gaskets, etc. - contain asbestos. Extreme care must be taken to avoid inhalation of dust from such products since it is hazardous to health. If in doubt, assume that they do contain asbestos.

Fire

● Remember at all times that petrol is highly flammable. Never smoke or have any kind of naked flame around, when working on the vehicle. But the risk does not end there - a spark caused by an electrical short-circuit, by two metal surfaces contacting each other, by careless use of tools, or even by static electricity built up in your body under certain conditions, can ignite petrol vapour, which in a confined space is highly explosive. Never use petrol as a cleaning solvent. Use an approved safety solvent.

● Always disconnect the battery earth terminal before working on any part of the fuel or electrical system, and never risk spilling fuel on to a hot engine or exhaust.
● It is recommended that a fire extinguisher of a type suitable for fuel and electrical fires is kept handy in the garage or workplace at all times. Never try to extinguish a fuel or electrical fire with water.

Fumes

● Certain fumes are highly toxic and can quickly cause unconsciousness and even death if inhaled to any extent. Petrol vapour comes into this category, as do the vapours from certain solvents such as trichloro-ethylene. Any draining or pouring of such volatile fluids should be done in a well ventilated area.
● When using cleaning fluids and solvents, read the instructions carefully. Never use materials from unmarked containers - they may give off poisonous vapours.
● Never run the engine of a motor vehicle in an enclosed space such as a garage. Exhaust fumes contain carbon monoxide which is extremely poisonous; if you need to run the engine, always do so in the open air or at least have the rear of the vehicle outside the workplace.

The battery

● Never cause a spark, or allow a naked light near the vehicle's battery. It will normally be giving off a certain amount of hydrogen gas, which is highly explosive.

● Always disconnect the battery ground (earth) terminal before working on the fuel or electrical systems (except where noted).
● If possible, loosen the filler plugs or cover when charging the battery from an external source. Do not charge at an excessive rate or the battery may burst.
● Take care when topping up, cleaning or carrying the battery. The acid electrolyte, evenwhen diluted, is very corrosive and should not be allowed to contact the eyes or skin. Always wear rubber gloves and goggles or a face shield. If you ever need to prepare electrolyte yourself, always add the acid slowly to the water; never add the water to the acid.

Electricity

● When using an electric power tool, inspection light etc., always ensure that the appliance is correctly connected to its plug and that, where necessary, it is properly grounded (earthed). Do not use such appliances in damp conditions and, again, beware of creating a spark or applying excessive heat in the vicinity of fuel or fuel vapour. Also ensure that the appliances meet national safety standards.
● A severe electric shock can result from touching certain parts of the electrical system, such as the spark plug wires (HT leads), when the engine is running or being cranked, particularly if components are damp or the insulation is defective. Where an electronic ignition system is used, the secondary (HT) voltage is much higher and could prove fatal.

Remember...

✗ **Don't** start the engine without first ascertaining that the transmission is in neutral.
✗ **Don't** suddenly remove the pressure cap from a hot cooling system - cover it with a cloth and release the pressure gradually first, or you may get scalded by escaping coolant.
✗ **Don't** attempt to drain oil until you are sure it has cooled sufficiently to avoid scalding you.
✗ **Don't** grasp any part of the engine or exhaust system without first ascertaining that it is cool enough not to burn you.
✗ **Don't** allow brake fluid or antifreeze to contact the machine's paintwork or plastic components.
✗ **Don't** siphon toxic liquids such as fuel, hydraulic fluid or antifreeze by mouth, or allow them to remain on your skin.
✗ **Don't** inhale dust - it may be injurious to health (see Asbestos heading).
✗ **Don't** allow any spilled oil or grease to remain on the floor - wipe it up right away, before someone slips on it.
✗ **Don't** use ill-fitting spanners or other tools which may slip and cause injury.

✗ **Don't** lift a heavy component which may be beyond your capability - get assistance.
✗ **Don't** rush to finish a job or take unverified short cuts.
✗ **Don't** allow children or animals in or around an unattended vehicle.
✗ **Don't** inflate a tyre above the recommended pressure. Apart from overstressing the carcass, in extreme cases the tyre may blow off forcibly.
✔ **Do** ensure that the machine is supported securely at all times. This is especially important when the machine is blocked up to aid wheel or fork removal.
✔ **Do** take care when attempting to loosen a stubborn nut or bolt. It is generally better to pull on a spanner, rather than push, so that if you slip, you fall away from the machine rather than onto it.
✔ **Do** wear eye protection when using power tools such as drill, sander, bench grinder etc.
✔ **Do** use a barrier cream on your hands prior to undertaking dirty jobs - it will protect your skin from infection as well as making the dirt easier to remove afterwards; but make sure your hands aren't left slippery. Note that long-term contact with used engine oil can be a health hazard.
✔ **Do** keep loose clothing (cuffs, ties etc.

and long hair) well out of the way of moving mechanical parts.
✔ **Do** remove rings, wristwatch etc., before working on the vehicle - especially the electrical system.
✔ **Do** keep your work area tidy - it is only too easy to fall over articles left lying around.
✔ **Do** exercise caution when compressing springs for removal or installation. Ensure that the tension is applied and released in a controlled manner, using suitable tools which preclude the possibility of the spring escaping violently.
✔ **Do** ensure that any lifting tackle used has a safe working load rating adequate for the job.
✔ **Do** get someone to check periodically that all is well, when working alone on the vehicle.
✔ **Do** carry out work in a logical sequence and check that everything is correctly assembled and tightened afterwards.
✔ **Do** remember that your vehicle's safety affects that of yourself and others. If in doubt on any point, get professional advice.
● If in spite of following these precautions, you are unfortunate enough to injure yourself, seek medical attention as soon as possible.

Coolant level

> ⚠️ **Warning: DO NOT remove the pressure cap from the radiator to add coolant. Topping up is done via the coolant reservoir tank filler. DO NOT leave open containers of coolant about – it is poisonous.**

Before you start:

✔ On 2004 to 2006 DL models the coolant reservoir is located between the frame and the rear cylinder head on the left-hand side; a forward extension of the reservoir allows the coolant level to be viewed through the frame but topping up requires the fuel tank to be raised.

✔ On 2007-on DL models the coolant reservoir is located under the fuel tank – to view the level lines remove the seat (see Chapter 7), and if topping up is required raise the fuel tank (see Chapter 4).

✔ On SFV models the coolant reservoir is located between the frame and the rear cylinder head on the left-hand side – the lower level line is visible with the left-hand side cover in place, but remove it if the marks are unclear (see Chapter 7). If topping up is required raise the fuel tank (see Chapter 4).

✔ Check the coolant level when the engine is cold.

✔ Support the motorcycle upright, making sure it is on level ground.

Bike care:

● Use only the specified coolant mixture of 50% distilled water and 50% corrosion inhibited ethylene glycol anti-freeze – ready-mixed coolant is available in one litre containers. It is important that the correct proportion of anti-freeze is used in the system all year round, and not just in the winter. Do not top the system up using only water unless absolutely necessary, as the system will become too diluted. If water is used check and correct the mixture as soon as possible. If distilled water is not available, and you are in an area that has hard water, the system should be drained and refilled using the correct coolant mixture as soon as possible.

● Do not overfill the reservoir tank. If the coolant is significantly above the F line at any time, the surplus should be siphoned or drained off to prevent the possibility of it being expelled out of the overflow hose.

● If the coolant level falls steadily check the system for leaks (see Chapter 1). If no leaks are found and the level continues to fall, it is recommended that the machine is taken to a Suzuki dealer for a pressure test.

2004 to 2006 DL MODELS

1 The coolant must be between the FULL and LOW level lines (arrowed).

2 Remove the reservoir filler cap.

3 Top up the reservoir with the recommended coolant mixture to the FULL level line.

2007-on DL MODELS

1 The coolant must be between the FULL and LOW level lines on the right-hand side of the reservoir (arrowed).

2 Remove the reservoir filler cap.

3 Top up the reservoir with the recommended coolant mixture to the FULL level line – use a funnel if required.

SFV MODELS

1 The coolant must be between the FULL and LOW level lines (arrowed).

2 Remove the reservoir filler cap.

3 Top up the reservoir with the recommended coolant mixture to the FULL level line.

Suspension, steering and drive chain

Suspension and steering:
● Check that the front and rear suspension operates smoothly without binding (see Chapter 1).
● Check that the suspension is adjusted as required (see Chapter 5).
● Check that the steering moves smoothly from lock-to-lock.

Final drive:
● Check that the chain isn't too loose or too tight, and adjust it if necessary (see Chapter 1).
● If the chain looks dry, lubricate it (see Chapter 1).

Legal and safety checks

Lighting and signalling:
● Take a minute to check that the headlights, tail and brake lights, licence plate light, instrument lights and turn signals all work correctly.
● Check that the horn sounds when the button is pressed.
● A working speedometer, graduated in mph, is a statutory requirement in the UK.

Safety:
● Check that the throttle grip rotates smoothly when opened and snaps shut when released, in all steering positions. Also check for the correct amount of cable freeplay (see Chapter 1).
● Check that the brake lever and pedal, clutch lever and gearchange lever operate smoothly. Lubricate them at the specified intervals or when necessary (see Chapter 1).
● Check that the engine shuts off when the kill switch is operated. Check the starter safety circuit (see Chapter 1).
● Check that the stand return springs hold the stand(s) up securely when retracted.

Fuel:
● This may seem obvious, but check that you have enough fuel to complete your journey. If you smell fuel or notice signs of fuel leakage, rectify the cause immediately.
● Ensure you use the correct grade fuel – see Chapter 4 Specifications.

Brake fluid levels

> ⚠ *Warning: Brake hydraulic fluid can harm your eyes and damage painted surfaces – use extreme caution when handling and pouring it, and cover surrounding surfaces with rag. Do not use fluid that has been standing open for some time as it is hygroscopic (absorbs moisture from the air) – old fluid can cause a dangerous loss of braking effectiveness.*

Before you start:

✔ The front brake fluid reservoir is on the right-hand handlebar. The rear brake fluid reservoir is located behind the right-hand side cover.
✔ Make sure you have the correct hydraulic fluid – DOT 4.
✔ Wrap a rag around the reservoir being worked on to ensure that any spillage does not come into contact with painted surfaces.
✔ To check the fluid in the front reservoir turn the handlebars so the reservoir is level.
✔ To check the fluid in the rear reservoir support the motorcycle upright on level ground.

Bike care:

● The fluid in the front and rear brake master cylinder reservoirs will drop as the brake pads wear down. If the fluid level is low check the brake pads for wear (see Chapter 1), and replace them with new ones if necessary (see Chapter 6).
● If either fluid reservoir requires repeated topping-up there is a leak somewhere in the system. Check for signs of fluid leakage from the hydraulic hoses and/or brake system components – if found, rectify immediately (see Chapter 6).
● Check the operation of both brakes before taking the machine on the road; if there is evidence of air in the system (spongy feel to lever or pedal), it must be bled (see Chapter 6).

FRONT

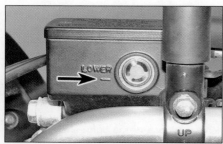
1 The front brake fluid level is visible through the window in the reservoir body – it must be above the LOWER level line (arrowed).

2 If the level is on or below the LOWER line, undo the reservoir cover screws and remove the cover, diaphragm plate and diaphragm.

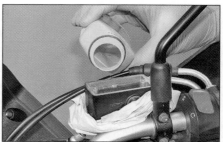
3 Top up with new clean DOT 4 hydraulic fluid, until the level is up to the upper level line cast inside the reservoir. Do not overfill and take care to avoid spills (see **Warning** above).

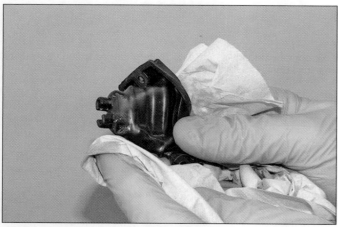
4 Wipe any moisture off the diaphragm with a tissue.

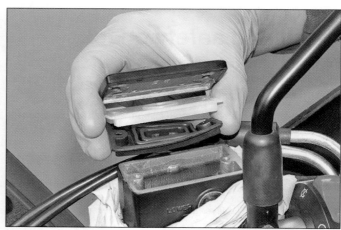
5 Make sure that the diaphragm is correctly seated before fitting the plate and cover. Secure the cover with its screws.

REAR

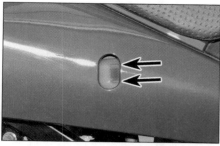

1 Rear brake fluid reservoir UPPER and LOWER level lines (arrowed) – 2004 to 2011 DL models

2 Rear brake fluid reservoir UPPER and LOWER level lines (arrowed) – 2012-on DL models

3 Rear brake fluid reservoir UPPER and LOWER level lines (arrowed) – SFV models

4 If the level is on or below the LOWER line, remove the side cover (see Chapter 7). Undo the reservoir cover screws and remove the cover, diaphragm plate (SFV models only), and diaphragm.

5 Top up with new clean DOT 4 hydraulic fluid, until the level is up to the UPPER line. Do not overfill and take care to avoid spills (see **Warning** on page 0•12).

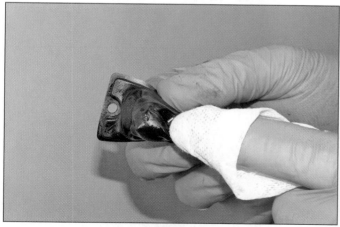

6 Wipe any moisture off the diaphragm with a tissue.

7 Make sure that the diaphragm is correctly seated before fitting the plate (SFV models) and cover.

Engine oil level

Before you start:

✔ Start the engine and let it idle for 3 to 5 minutes.
✔ The oil level inspection window is located on the right-hand side of the engine. If necessary wipe the window so that it is clean.
✔ Support the motorcycle upright, making sure it is on level ground.
Caution: Do not run the engine in an enclosed space such as a garage or workshop.
✔ Stop the engine and allow the oil level to stabilise for 2 to 3 minutes.

Bike care:

● If you have to add oil frequently, check whether you have any oil leaks from the engine joints, oil seals and gaskets. If not, the engine could be burning oil, in which case there will be white smoke coming out of the exhaust (see *Fault Finding*).

The correct oil

● Modern, high-revving engines place great demands on their oil. It is very important that the correct oil for your bike is used.
● Always top up with a good quality oil of the specified type and viscosity and do not overfill the engine.
Caution: Do not use chemical additives or oils labelled "ENERGY CONSERVING". Such additives or oils could cause clutch slip.

Oil type	API grade: SF, SG or higher JASO T 903 grade: MA
Oil viscosity*	SAE 10W40

*If you are using the motorcycle constantly in extreme conditions of heat or cold, other more suitable viscosity ranges may be used – refer to the viscosity table to select the oil best suited to your conditions.

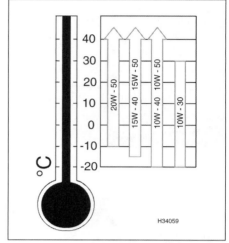

Select the oil best suited to the conditions

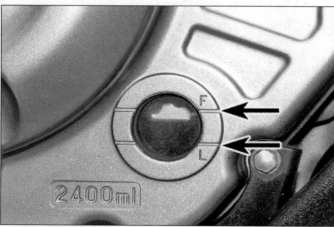

1 With the motorcycle vertical, the oil level should lie between the F and L marks (arrowed).

2 If the level is on or below the L mark unscrew the oil filler cap.

3 Top up the engine with the recommended grade and type of oil to bring the level almost up to the F mark on the inspection window. Do not overfill.

4 Make sure the filler cap O-ring (arrowed) is in good condition and correctly seated before fitting the cap.

Tyres

The correct pressures:

● The tyres must be checked when **cold**, not immediately after riding. The pressure inside the tyre will increase when the tyre is hot. Note that tyre pressure will also change from one day to the next as air temperature changes.

● Correct tyre pressure will increase tyre life and provide maximum stability and ride comfort. Incorrect pressure will cause abnormal tread wear and unsafe handling. Low tyre pressures may cause the tyre to slip on the rim, or in extreme cases come off it.

● Use an accurate pressure gauge. Many forecourt gauges are wildly inaccurate. If you buy your own, spend as much as you can justify on a quality gauge.

Tyre care:

● Check the tyres carefully for cuts, tears, embedded nails or other sharp objects and excessive wear. Operation of the motorcycle with excessively worn tyres is extremely hazardous, as traction and handling are directly affected.

● Pick out any stones or nails that may have become embedded in the tyre tread. If left, they will eventually penetrate through the casing and cause a puncture.

● Make sure a dust cap is fitted. If tyre deflation occurs and it is not due to a slow puncture the valve core may be loose or it could be leaking past the seal. If a core tightening tool is incorporated in the dust cap check the valve is tight. Otherwise refer to Section 11 in Chapter 1.

● If tyre damage is apparent, or unexplained loss of pressure is experienced, seek the advice of a tyre fitting specialist without delay.

Tyre tread depth:

● At the time of writing UK law requires that tread depth must be at least 1 mm over 3/4 of the tread breadth all the way around the tyre, with no bald patches. Many riders, however, consider 2 mm tread depth minimum to be a safer limit. Suzuki recommends a minimum of 1.6 mm for the front tyre and 2 mm for the rear. German law requires a minimum of 1.6 mm for each tyre.

● Most tyres incorporate wear indicators in the tread. Identify the location marking on the tyre sidewall to locate the indicator bar and replace the tyre if the tread has worn down to the bar.

DL models

		Front	Rear
Rider only		33 psi (2.25 Bar)	36 psi (2.5 Bar)
Rider and pillion		33 psi (2.25 Bar)	41 psi (2.8 Bar)

SFV models

		Front	Rear
Rider only		33 psi (2.25 Bar)	36 psi (2.5 Bar)
Rider and pillion		33 psi (2.25 Bar)	36 psi (2.5 Bar)

1 Remove the dust cap from the valve. Do not forget to fit the cap after checking the pressure.

2 Check the tyre pressures when the tyre is **cold**.

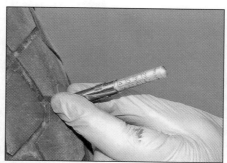

3 Measure tread depth at the centre of the tyre using a depth gauge.

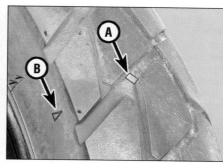

4 Tyre tread wear indicator (A) and its location marking (B) on the edge or sidewall (according to manufacturer).

Frame and engine numbers

The frame number is stamped into the right-hand side of the steering head. The engine number is stamped into the left-hand side of the crankcase. Both of these numbers should be recorded and kept in a safe place so they can be given to law enforcement officials in the event of a theft.

The frame number and engine number should also be kept in a handy place (such as with your driver's licence) so they are always available when purchasing or ordering parts for your machine.

Within the manual models are identified by their model prefix (DL or SFV), along with the production year(s) where necessary, and/or by using the suffix A to denote those with ABS. The tables below show the extended model codes and the production year(s) they relate to.

The frame number is stamped into the right-hand side of the steering head

DL650/A V-Strom	Year
DL650K4	2004
DL650K5	2005
DL650K6	2006
DL650K7/AK7	2007
DL650K8/AK8	2008
DL650K9/AK9	2009
DL650L0/AL0	2010
DL650L1/AL1	2011
DL650AL2	2012
DL650AL3	2013

SFV650/A Gladius	Year
SFV650K9/AK9	2009
SFV650L0/AL0	2010
SFV650L1/AL1	2011
SFV650L2/AL2	2012
SFV650L3/AL3	2013

The engine number is stamped into the left-hand side of the crankcase

Buying spare parts

Once you have found all the identification numbers, record them for reference when buying parts. Since the manufacturers change specifications, parts and vendors (companies that manufacture various components on the machine), providing the ID numbers is the only way to be reasonably sure that you are buying the correct parts for your model.

Whenever possible, take the worn part to the dealer so direct comparison with the new component can be made. Along the trail from the manufacturer to the parts shelf, there are numerous places that the part can end up with the wrong number or be listed incorrectly.

The two places to purchase new parts for your motorcycle – the franchised or main dealer and the parts/accessories store – differ in the type of parts they carry. While dealers can obtain every single genuine part for your motorcycle, the accessory store is usually limited to normal high wear items such as chains and sprockets, brake pads, spark plugs and cables, and to tune-up parts and various engine gaskets, etc. Rarely will an accessory outlet have major suspension components, camshafts, transmission gears, or engine cases.

Used parts can be obtained from breakers for roughly half the price of new ones, but you can't always be sure of what you're getting. Once again, take your worn part to the breaker for direct comparison, or when ordering by mail order make sure that you can return it if you are not happy.

Whether buying new, used or rebuilt parts, the best course is to deal directly with someone who specialises in your particular make.

The VIN label (arrowed) is clearly visible on the frame (DL position shown)

DL650 V-Strom

The DL650 V-Strom was launched in 2004, and is very much the younger sibling of the DL1000 V-Strom.

The V-Twin engine is from the SV650, with revised tuning to improve mid-range power. Drive to the double overhead camshafts that actuate the four valves per cylinder is by chain. The clutch is a conventional wet multi-plate unit actuated by cable, and the gearbox is 6-speed. Drive to the rear wheel is by chain and sprockets.

A fuel injection system supplies fuel and air to the engine via 39mm throttle bodies and two intake valves per cylinder, with exhaust gases exiting via another two valves per cylinder into a two-into-one exhaust system with closed-loop catalytic converter. An electronic engine management system controls both the injection system and the ignition system.

The engine hangs from an aluminium twin-spar diamond frame and acts as a stressed member.

Front suspension is by oil-damped 43mm forks with adjustable pre-load. Rear suspension is by swingarm through a rising rate linkage to a single shock absorber with adjustable spring pre-load and rebound damping.

The hydraulic braking system has two twin piston sliding calipers at the front, and a single piston sliding caliper at the rear.

In 2007 the cylinder heads were changed to hold two spark plugs. An automatic idle speed control system replaced the manual adjuster on earlier models, and a new fuel pump and starter motor were fitted. A longer swingarm was fitted. The DL650A, with an anti-lock braking system, was launched.

In 2012 there was a major update. Engine modifications include a different oil cooler and a modified clutch release mechanism, along with different engine covers. Changes were also made to the instruments, fairing and bodywork, fuel tank, headlights and tail lights.

Model options include the Adventure, Grand Tourer (GT) and Tourer versions, with availability varying according to country and year, and incorporating features such as fitted panniers, top box, tank bag, hand guards, crash bars, sump guard, centrestand and touring windshield, according to model.

SFV650 Gladius

The SFV650 Gladius was launched in 2009, and is the successor to the unfaired SV650.

The V-Twin engine is basically the same as the twin-spark head unit fitted in the DL650 from 2007, but with a different oil cooler and a modified clutch release mechanism, along with different engine covers. Drive to the double overhead camshafts that actuate the four valves per cylinder is by chain. The clutch is a conventional wet multi-plate unit actuated by cable, and the gearbox is 6-speed. Drive to the rear wheel is by chain and sprockets.

A fuel injection system supplies fuel and air to the engine via 39mm throttle bodies and two intake valves per cylinder, with exhaust gases exiting via another two valves per cylinder into a two-into-one exhaust system with closed-loop catalytic converter. An electronic engine management system controls both the injection system and the ignition system.

The engine hangs from a steel trellis frame and acts as a stressed member.

Front suspension is by oil-damped 41mm forks with adjustable pre-load. Rear suspension is by swingarm through a rising rate linkage to a single shock absorber with adjustable pre-load.

The hydraulic braking system has two twin-piston sliding calipers at the front, and a single piston sliding caliper at the rear. SFV650A models have an anti-lock braking system (ABS).

Bike spec

Chassis

Frame type	
DL models	Aluminium, twin-spar
SFV models	Steel, trellis
Rake and trail	
DL models	26°, 110 mm
SFV models	25°, 106 mm
Fuel tank capacity (including reserve)	
DL models – 2004 to 2011	22 litres
DL models – 2012-on	20 litres
SFV models	14.5 litres
Front suspension	
Type	
DL models	Oil-damped 43 mm telescopic forks
SFV models	Oil-damped 41 mm telescopic forks
Travel	
DL models	150 mm
SFV models	125 mm
Adjustment	Spring pre-load
Rear suspension	
Type	Single shock absorber, rising rate linkage, aluminium swingarm
Travel (at axle)	
DL models	150 mm
SFV models	130 mm
Adjustment	
DL models	Spring pre-load and rebound damping
SFV models	Spring pre-load
Wheels	
DL models	19 inch front, 17 inch rear, 3-spoke alloy
SFV models	17 inch 5-spoke alloy
Tyres – DL models	
Front	110/80-R19M/C (59H) tubeless
Rear	150/70-R17M/C (69H) tubeless
Tyres – SFV models	
Front	120/70-ZR17M/C (58W) tubeless
Rear	160/60-ZR17M/C (69W) tubeless
Front brake	Twin floating discs with twin piston sliding calipers
Rear brake	Single disc with single piston sliding caliper

Engine

Type	Four-stroke V-twin
Capacity	645 cc
Bore	81.0 mm
Stroke	62.6 mm
Compression ratio	
DL models – 2004 to 2011	11.5 to 1
DL models – 2012-on, all SFV models	11.2 to 1
Camshafts	DOHC, chain-driven
Clutch	Wet multi-plate, cable
Transmission	Six-speed constant mesh
Final drive	Chain and sprockets
Lubrication system	Wet sump, trochoid pump
Cooling system	Liquid cooled
Fuel system	Fuel injection
Ignition system	Computer-controlled digital transistorised with electronic advance

Dimensions and weights

Note: *For California models add 1kg to weight*

DL models – 2004 to 2006

Overall length	2290 mm
Overall width	840 mm
Overall height	1390 mm
Wheelbase	1540 mm
Ground clearance	165 mm
Seat height	820 mm
Dry weight	190 kg

DL models – 2007 to 2011

Overall length	2290 mm
Overall width	840 mm
Overall height	1390 mm
Wheelbase	1555 mm
Ground clearance	165 mm
Seat height	820 mm
Dry weight	
DL650	194 kg
DL650A	197 kg
Wet weight	
DL650	217 kg
DL650A	220 kg

DL models – 2012-on

Overall length	2290 mm
Overall width	835 mm
Overall height	1405 mm
Wheelbase	1560 mm
Ground clearance	175 mm
Seat height	835 mm
Wet weight	214 kg

SFV models

Overall length	2130 mm
Overall width	760 mm
Overall height	1090 mm
Wheelbase	1445 mm
Ground clearance	135 mm
Seat height	785 mm
Wet weight	
SFV650	202 kg
SFV650A	205 kg

Chapter 1
Routine maintenance and servicing

Contents

Degrees of difficulty

Easy, suitable for novice with little experience		**Fairly easy,** suitable for beginner with some experience		**Fairly difficult,** suitable for competent DIY mechanic		**Difficult,** suitable for experienced DIY mechanic		**Very difficult,** suitable for expert DIY or professional	

Specifications

Engine

Cylinder numbering	
No. 1 cylinder	Front
No. 2 cylinder	Rear
Spark plugs	
2004 to 2011 DL models	
Standard type	NGK CR8E or DENSO U24ESR-N
Cold type (for very hot climates or constant high speed)	NGK CR9E or DENSO U27ESR-N
Hot type (for very cold climates)	NGK CR7E or DENSO U22ESR-N
Electrode gap	0.7 to 0.8 mm
2012-on DL models and SFV models	
Standard type	NGK CR8EIA-9 or DENSO IU24D
Cold type (for very hot climates or constant high speed)	NGK CR9EIA-9 or DENSO IU27D
Hot type (for very cold climates)	NGK CR7EIA-9
Electrode gap	0.8 to 0.9 mm
Engine idle speed	1200 to 1400 rpm
Valve clearances (COLD engine)	
Intake valves	0.1 to 0.2 mm
Exhaust valves	0.2 to 0.3 mm

Cycle parts

Drive chain
  Slack . . . . 20 to 30 mm (bike on sidestand)
  Stretch limit (21 pin length – see text) . . . . 319.4 mm
Clutch cable freeplay . . . . 10 to 15 mm at lever end
Throttle cable freeplay . . . . 2 to 4 mm
Tyre pressures (cold) . . . . see *Pre-ride checks*

Lubricants and fluids

Engine oil type . . . . SAE 10W40, API grade SF, SG or higher, JASO MA, motorcycle oil
(see *Pre-ride checks* for further information on oil grades for extreme temperatures).

Engine oil capacity
  2004 to 2011 DL models
    Oil change . . . . 2.3 litres
    Oil and filter change . . . . 2.7 litres
    Following engine overhaul – dry engine, new filter . . . . 3.1 litres
  2012-on DL models and SFV models
    Oil change . . . . 2.4 litres
    Oil and filter change . . . . 2.75 litres
    Following engine overhaul – dry engine, new filter . . . . 3.0 litres
Coolant type . . . . 50% distilled water, 50% silicate-free corrosion inhibited ethylene glycol anti-freeze

Coolant capacity
  2004 to 2011 DL models
    Radiator and engine . . . . 1.65 litres
    Reservoir . . . . 0.25 litre
  2012-on DL models
    Radiator and engine . . . . 1.70 litres
    Reservoir . . . . 0.25 litre
  SFV models
    Radiator and engine . . . . 1.60 litres
    Reservoir . . . . 0.25 litre
Drive chain . . . . Aerosol chain lubricant suitable for O-ring and X-ring chains
Brake fluid . . . . DOT 4
Brake caliper slider pins and boots . . . . Silicone grease
Clutch lever pivot . . . . Lithium based multi-purpose
Front brake lever pivot and master cylinder pushrod end . . . . Silicone grease
Footrest pivots . . . . Lithium based multi-purpose grease
Gearchange lever and linkage pivots . . . . Lithium based multi-purpose grease
Rear brake pedal pivots . . . . Lithium based multi-purpose grease
Shock absorber pivot bearing and seals . . . . Lithium based multi-purpose grease
Stand pivots . . . . Lithium based multi-purpose grease
Steering head bearings . . . . Lithium based multi-purpose grease
Suspension linkage pivot bearings and seals . . . . Lithium based multi-purpose grease
Swingarm pivot bearings and seals . . . . Lithium based multi-purpose grease
Throttle twistgrip . . . . Lithium based multi-purpose grease
Throttle cables . . . . Aerosol cable lubricant
Throttle and clutch cable ends . . . . Lithium based multi-purpose grease
Wheel bearing seal lips . . . . Lithium based multi-purpose grease

Torque settings

Cooling system drain bolt . . . . 13 Nm
Crankshaft end cap . . . . 11 Nm
Engine oil drain bolt . . . . 21 Nm
Engine oil filter . . . . 20 Nm
Fork clamp bolts (top yoke) . . . . 23 Nm
Rear axle nut . . . . 100 Nm
Spark plugs . . . . 11 Nm
Steering stem nut . . . . 90 Nm
Timing inspection cap . . . . 23 Nm

Note: *The Pre-ride checks outlined in the owner's manual cover those items that should be inspected before every ride.* *Also perform the pre-ride inspection at every maintenance interval (in addition to the procedures listed). The intervals listed* *below are the intervals recommended by the manufacturer for the models covered in this manual.*

Pre-ride
☐ See 'Pre-ride checks' at the beginning of this manual

After the initial 600 miles (1000 km)
Note: *This check is performed by a Suzuki dealer after the first 600 miles (1000 km) from new. Thereafter, maintenance is carried out according to the following intervals of the schedule.*

Every 600 miles (1000 km)
☐ Check, adjust, clean and lubricate the drive chain (Section 1)

Every 4000 miles (6000 km) or 12 months
☐ Check the brake pads for wear (Section 2)
☐ Check the brake system and brake light switch operation (Section 2)
☐ Check the clutch (Section 3)
☐ Check and clean the air filter element (Section 4)
☐ Check the spark plugs (Section 5)
☐ Check the fuel system, PAIR system, crankcase breather and EVAP system (Section 6)
☐ Change the engine oil (Section 7)
☐ Check engine idle speed (Section 8)
☐ Check the throttle cables and adjust if necessary (Section 9)
☐ Check the cooling system (Section 10)
☐ Check the condition of the wheels, wheel bearings and tyres (Section 11)
☐ Check the stands and starter safety circuit (Section 12)
☐ Lubricate the clutch, gearchange and brake levers, brake pedal, stand pivots, and the throttle cables (Section 13)
☐ Check the tightness of all nuts, bolts and fasteners (Section 14)
☐ Check the battery (Section 15)

Every 8000 miles (12,000 km) or 2 years
Carry out all the items under the 4000 mile (6000 km) check, plus the following:
☐ Fit new spark plugs (Section 5)
☐ Check and adjust throttle body synchronisation (Section 16)
☐ Check the front and rear suspension (Section 17)
☐ Check the steering head bearings and adjust if necessary (Section 18)

Every 12,000 miles (18,000 km) or 3 years
Carry out all the items under the 4000 mile (6000 km) check, plus the following:
☐ Fit a new air filter element (Section 4)
☐ Fit a new engine oil filter (Section 7)

Every 16,000 miles (24,000 km) or 4 years
Carry out all the items under the 8000 mile (12,000 km) check, plus the following:
☐ Re-grease the swingarm, shock absorber and suspension linkage bearings (Section 17)
☐ Re-grease the steering head bearings (Section 18)
☐ Check the valve clearances and adjust if necessary (Section 19)

Every two years
☐ Change the brake fluid (Section 2)
☐ Change the coolant (Section 10)

Every four years
☐ Fit new brake hoses (Section 2)
☐ Fit new fuel system hoses (Section 6)
☐ Fit new cooling system hoses (Section 10)

Component locations – DL 2004 to 2011 right side

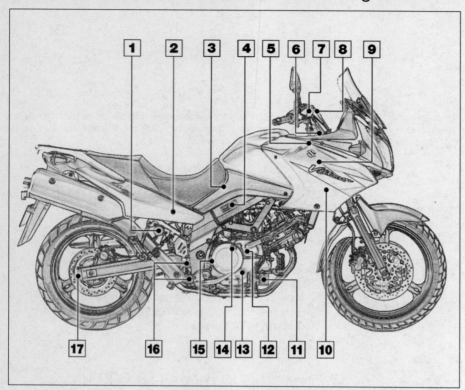

1 Rear shock pre-load adjuster
2 Rear brake fluid reservoir
3 Coolant reservoir – 2007 to 2011 models
4 VIN label
5 Steering head bearing adjuster
6 Front fork pre-load adjuster
7 Front brake fluid reservoir
8 Throttle cable freeplay adjuster
9 Frame number
10 Cooling system pressure cap
11 Engine oil filter
12 Coolant drain bolt
13 Engine oil level inspection window
14 Engine oil filler cap
15 Rear brake light switch
16 Rear brake pedal height adjuster
17 Drive chain adjuster

Component locations – DL 2004 to 2011 left side

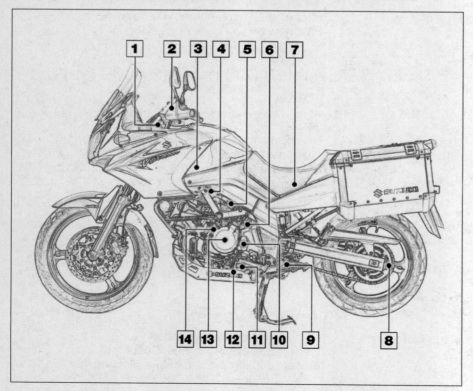

1 Front fork pre-load adjuster
2 Clutch cable adjuster at lever
3 Air filter element
4 Engine idle speed adjuster – 2004 to 2006 models only
5 Coolant resevoir level markings – 2004 to 2006 models
6 Clutch cable lower adjuster
7 Battery
8 Drive chain adjuster
9 Rear shock damping adjuster
10 Clutch release mechanism adjuster
11 Engine number
12 Engine oil drain bolt
13 Crankshaft end cap for engine turning
14 Timing mark inspection cap

Component locations – DL 2012-on right side

1 Rear shock pre-load adjuster
2 Rear brake fluid reservoir
3 Coolant reservoir
4 VIN label
5 Steering head bearing adjuster
6 Front fork pre-load adjuster
7 Front brake fluid reservoir
8 Throttle cable freeplay adjuster
9 Frame number
10 Cooling system pressure cap
11 Engine oil filter
12 Coolant drain bolt
13 Engine oil level inspection window
14 Engine oil filler cap
15 Clutch release mechanism adjuster
16 Rear brake light switch
17 Rear brake pedal height adjuster
18 Drive chain adjuster

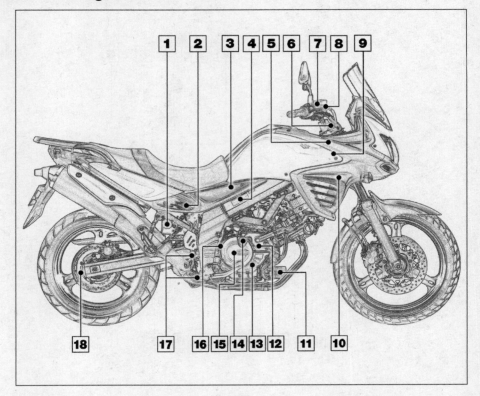

Component locations – DL 2012-on left side

1 Front fork pre-load adjuster
2 Clutch cable in-line adjuster
3 Clutch cable adjuster at lever
4 Air filter element
5 Battery
6 Drive chain adjuster
7 Rear shock damping adjuster
8 Engine number
9 Engine oil drain bolt
10 Crankshaft end cap for engine turning
11 Timing mark inspection cap

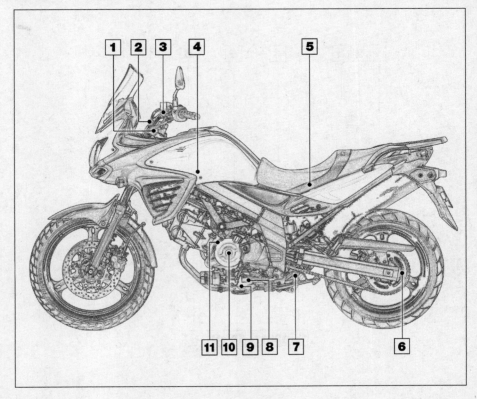

Component locations – SFV right side

1 Rear brake fluid reservoir
2 Steering head bearing adjuster
3 Front fork pre-load adjuster
4 Front brake fluid reservoir
5 Throttle cable freeplay adjuster
6 Frame number
7 Cooling system pressure cap
8 Engine oil filter
9 Coolant drain bolt
10 Engine oil level inspection window
11 Engine oil filler cap
12 Clutch release mechanism adjuster
13 Rear brake light switch
14 Rear brake pedal height adjuster
15 Drive chain adjuster

Component locations – SFV left side

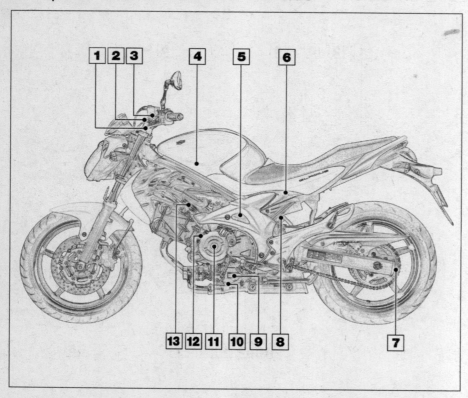

1 Front fork pre-load adjuster
2 Clutch cable in-line adjuster
3 Clutch freeplay adjuster at lever
4 Air filter element
5 Coolant reservoir level markings
6 Battery
7 Drive chain adjuster
8 Rear shock pre-load adjuster
9 Engine number
10 Engine oil drain bolt
11 Crankshaft end cap for engine turning
12 Timing mark inspection cap
13 VIN label

1 This Chapter is designed to help the home mechanic maintain his/her motorcycle for safety, economy, long life and peak performance.

2 Deciding where to start or plug into the routine maintenance schedule depends on several factors. If your motorcycle has been maintained according to the warranty standards and has just come out of warranty, start routine maintenance as it coincides with the next mileage or calendar interval. If you have owned the machine for some time but have never performed any maintenance on it,

start at the nearest interval and include some additional procedures to ensure that nothing important is overlooked. If you have just had a major engine overhaul, then start the maintenance routine from the beginning. If you have a used machine and have no knowledge of its history or maintenance record, combine all the checks into one large service initially and then settle into the specified maintenance schedule.

3 Before beginning any maintenance or repair, clean the machine thoroughly, especially around the oil filter, oil drain plug, drive chain,

suspension, wheels, etc. Cleaning will help ensure that dirt does not contaminate the engine and will allow you to detect wear and damage that could otherwise easily go unnoticed. If you use a pressure washer make sure you do not direct the jet at wheel bearing and suspension seals and at the steering head, or at any electrical/ignition components and connectors.

4 Certain maintenance information is sometimes printed on labels attached to the motorcycle. If the information on the labels differs from that included here, use the information on the label.

1   Drive chain and sprockets

Check

1 A neglected drive chain won't last long and will quickly damage the sprockets. As the chain stretches with wear it will become slack and every so often it needs to be tightened (see below). Routine chain adjustment and lubrication isn't difficult and will ensure maximum chain and sprocket life.

2 To check the chain place the bike on its sidestand and shift the transmission into neutral. Make sure the ignition switch is OFF.

3 Push up on the bottom run of the chain and measure the slack midway between the two sprockets, then compare your measurement to that listed in this Chapter's Specifications **(see illustration)**. Since the chain will rarely wear evenly, roll the bike forward so that another section of chain can be checked (having an assistant to do this makes the task a lot easier); do this several times to check the entire length of chain, and mark the tightest spot.

Caution: Riding the bike with a chain that is too tight or too loose could lead to damage.

4 In some cases where lubrication has been neglected, corrosion and dirt may cause the links to bind and kink, which effectively shortens the chain's length and makes it tight

(see illustration). Thoroughly clean and work free any such links, then highlight them with a marker pen or paint. Take the bike for a ride.

5 After the bike has been ridden, repeat the measurement for slack in the highlighted area. If the chain has kinked again and is still tight, replace it with a new one (see Chapter 6). A rusty, kinked or worn chain will damage the sprockets and a tight chain can damage transmission bearings. If in any doubt as to the condition of a chain, it is far better to fit a new one than risk damage to other components and possibly yourself.

6 Check the entire length of the chain for damaged rollers, loose links and pins, and missing O-rings and replace it with a new one if necessary. **Note:** *Never fit a new chain onto old sprockets, and never use the old chain if*

you fit new sprockets – replace the chain and sprockets as a set.

Adjustment

7 Move the bike so that the tightest point of the chain is at the centre of its bottom run, then put it on the sidestand.

8 Where fitted remove the split pin from the rear axle nut.

9 Slacken the rear axle nut **(see illustrations)**.

10 Turn each adjuster bolt evenly until the amount of freeplay specified at the beginning of the Chapter is obtained at the centre of the bottom run of the chain **(see illustration)** – if the chain was slack turn the bolts clockwise; if the chain was tight turn them anti-clockwise, then move the wheel forwards in the swingarm to take up the gap.

1.3 Push up on the chain and measure the slack

1.4 Neglect has caused the links in this chain to kink

1.9a Rear axle nut (arrowed) – DL

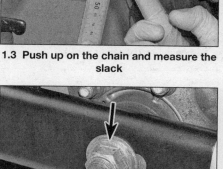

1.9b Rear axle nut (arrowed) – SFV

1.10 Turn the adjuster bolt on each side as required

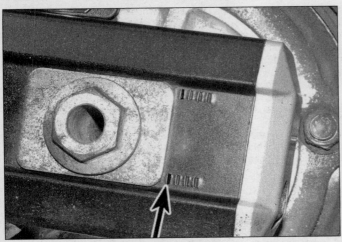

1.11a On DL models make sure the rear edge of the adjustment marker is in the same position each side relative to the index lines on the swingarm

1.11b On SFV models make sure the index lines on the adjuster are in the same position each side relative to the slot in the swingarm

11 Following adjustment, check that each adjustment marker is in the same position in relation to the swingarm **(see illustrations)**. It is important the position is the same on each side otherwise the rear wheel will be out of alignment with the front. Always make sure that each adjuster is butted against the end of the swingarm. If there is a difference in the positions, adjust one side so that its position is exactly the same as the other. Check the chain freeplay again and readjust if necessary.

12 When adjustment is complete tighten the axle nut to the torque setting specified at the beginning of the Chapter **(see illustration 1.9a or b)**. Recheck the adjustment. Where removed fit a new split pin through the nut and bend its ends round.

Cleaning and lubrication

13 If required, wash the chain using a dedicated aerosol cleaner, or in paraffin (kerosene) or a suitable non-flammable or high flash-point solvent that will not damage the O-rings, using a soft brush to work any dirt out if necessary **(see illustration)**. Wipe the cleaner off the chain and allow it to dry. If the chain is excessively dirty remove it from the machine and allow it to soak in the paraffin or solvent (see Chapter 6).

Caution: Don't use petrol (gasoline), an unsuitable solvent or other cleaning fluids that might damage the internal sealing properties of the chain. Don't use high-pressure water to clean the chain. The entire process shouldn't take longer than ten minutes, otherwise the O-rings could be damaged.

14 The best time to lubricate the chain is after the motorcycle has been ridden. When the chain is warm, the lubricant will penetrate the joints between the sideplates better than when cold. **Note:** *Use a heavy engine oil, SAE 80 to SAE 90 gear oil, or an aerosol chain lube that is suitable for O-ring chains; do not use any other chain lubricants – the solvents could damage the O- rings.* Apply the lubricant to the area where the sideplates overlap – not the middle of the rollers **(see illustration)**.

> **HAYNES HiNT** *Apply the lubricant to the top of the lower chain run, so centrifugal force will work the oil into the chain when the bike is moving. After applying lubricant, let it soak in for a few minutes before wiping off any excess.*

⚠ *Warning: Take care not to get any lubricant on the tyres or brake caliper. If any of the lubricant inadvertently contacts them, clean it off thoroughly using a suitable solvent or dedicated brake cleaner before riding the machine.*

Wear and stretch check

15 Chain stretch is assessed by measuring several sections of the chain with it taut. Refer to the adjustment procedure above and turn the adjusters evenly until the chain is taut, but do not strain it.

16 Measure along the bottom run the length of 21 pins (from the centre of the 1st pin to the centre of the 21st pin) and compare the result with the service limit specified at the beginning of the Chapter **(see illustration)**. Rotate the rear wheel so that several sections of the chain are measured, then calculate the average. If the chain stretch measurement exceeds the service limit it must be replaced with a new one (see Chapter 6).

17 If the chain is good, reset the adjusters to the correct amount of freeplay and tighten the axle nut as described above.

1.13 Using a chain cleaning brush

1.14 Apply the lubricant to the overlapping sections of the sideplates

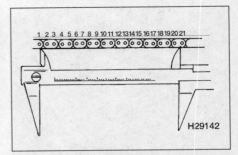

1.16 Measure the distance between the 1st and 21st pins as shown to determine the amount of stretch

1.18a Check the sprocket teeth...

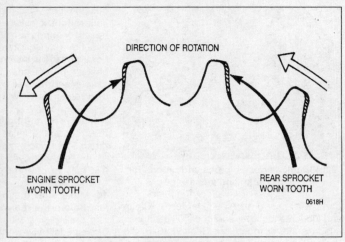

1.18b ...in the areas indicated

Sprocket check

18 Remove the front sprocket cover (see Chapter 6). Check the teeth on the front and rear sprockets for wear **(see illustrations)**. If the teeth are worn excessively, replace the chain and both sprockets with a new set. Check all sprocket fasteners are tight (see Chapter 6).

19 With the sprocket cover removed check the chain slider around the front of the swingarm **(see illustration)** – if the rubbing surfaces of the slider are excessively worn or are damaged remove the swingarm and replace the slider with a new one (see Chapter 5).

2 Brake system

Brake pad wear check

1 Each brake pad has a wear indicator in the form of a cut-out in the friction material **(see illustration)** – if the pads are worn to the beginning of the cut-out, they must be replaced with new ones (see Chapter 6). **Note:** *Some after-market pads may use different indicators to those on the original equipment.*

2 The cut-outs, particularly on the front brake pads, may be difficult to see, especially if they are filled with dirt (using a mirror will help), but the amount of friction material remaining is easily visible, and the pads need replacing when the material is down to about 1 mm **(see illustration)**.

3 Check for uneven wear across the pads in each front caliper, which indicates a sticking or seized piston. If uneven wear is found, the caliper(s) must be overhauled (see Chapter 6).

4 If the pads are dirty or if you are in doubt as to the amount of friction material remaining, remove them for inspection (see Chapter 6). If the pads are excessively worn, check the brake discs (see Chapter 6).

Brake system check

5 A routine general check of the brake system will ensure that any problems are discovered

1.19 Check the amount of wear on the slider (arrowed)

and remedied before the rider's safety is jeopardised.

6 Check the brake pads for wear (see above) and make sure the fluid level in each reservoir is correct (see *Pre-ride checks*).

7 Check the brake lever and pedal pivots for sloppy or rough action, excessive play, bends, and other damage. Replace any damaged

2.1 Brake pad wear indicator cut-outs (arrowed – rear pads shown)

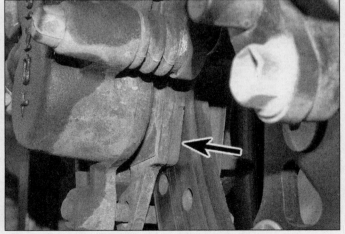

2.2 You can easily see the friction material (arrowed) on the front brake pads

2.8 Check all hoses, pipes and unions for cracks and leaks

parts with new ones (see Chapter 5). Clean and lubricate the lever and pedal pivots if their action is stiff or rough (see Section 13). If the lever or pedal is spongy, bleed the brakes (see Chapter 6).

8 Look for leaks at the hose and pipe connections and check for cracks in the hoses, pipes (ABS models), and unions **(see illustration)**. If leakage or cracked or damaged hoses or pipes are found, fit new ones as described in Chapter 6. Make sure all brake hose and pipe fasteners are tight. Similarly check for any signs of fluid leakage from the caliper and master cylinder – overhaul and seal replacement will be necessary if found (see Chapter 6).

9 Make sure the brake light operates when the front brake lever is pulled in. The front brake light switch, mounted on the underside of the master cylinder, is not adjustable. If it fails to operate properly, check it (see Chapter 8).

10 Make sure the brake light is activated just before the rear brake takes effect. The rear brake light switch is mounted above the brake pedal between the clutch cover and the frame on DL models, and behind the footrest bracket on SFV models **(see illustrations)**. If adjustment is necessary, hold the switch body and turn the adjuster nut until the brake light is activated when required – do not turn the switch itself. If the brake light comes on too late or not at all, turn the ring clockwise so the switch is drawn up out of its bracket. If the brake light comes on too soon or is permanently on, turn the ring anti-clockwise so the switch is drawn down into the bracket. If the switch doesn't operate the brake light, check it (see Chapter 8).

11 The front brake lever has a span adjuster that alters the distance of the lever from the handlebar. Each setting is identified by a number on the adjuster ring aligning with the triangle on the lever – push the lever away from the handlebar and turn the adjuster ring to alter the span as required, making sure that the number specific to the desired setting is aligned with the triangle **(see illustrations)**. Do not set the adjuster between the defined settings.

12 The end of the rear brake pedal should be between 20 to 30 mm (2004 to 2011 DL models), 23 to 33 mm (2012-on DL models)

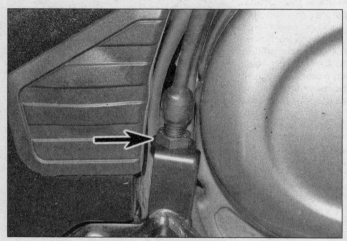

2.10a Rear brake light switch adjuster nut (arrowed) – DL

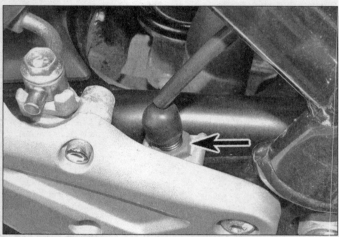

2.10b Rear brake light switch adjuster nut (arrowed) – SFV

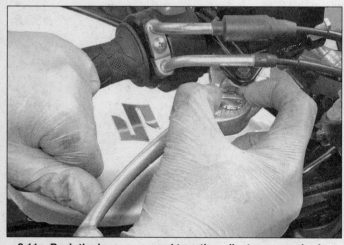

2.11a Push the lever away and turn the adjuster as required...

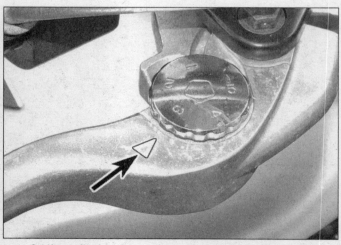

2.11b ...aligning the number with the triangle (arrowed)

or 45 to 55 mm (SFV models) below the top of the footrest when measured as shown **(see illustration)**. It can be adjusted within the specified limits to suit the rider's preference – slacken the master cylinder pushrod locknut, then turn the pushrod using a spanner on the hex section at the top of the rod until the pedal is at the desired height **(see illustrations)**. On completion tighten the locknut. Adjust the rear brake light switch after adjusting the pedal height (see Step 10).

Brake fluid change

13 The brake fluid should be changed every two years. Refer to Chapter 6 for details. Ensure that all the old fluid is pumped from the hydraulic system and that the level in the fluid reservoir is checked and the brakes tested before riding the motorcycle.

Brake hose change

14 The hoses will deteriorate with age and

should be replaced with new ones every four years regardless of their apparent condition (see Chapter 6).
15 Always replace the banjo union sealing washers with new ones when fitting the new hoses. Refill the system with new fluid and bleed the system as described in Chapter 6.

Brake master cylinder and caliper seals

16 Master cylinder and caliper seals will deteriorate over a period of time and lose their effectiveness, leading to sticky operation of the master cylinder or piston(s), or fluid loss. Although seal replacement is not subject to a specific time or mileage interval, it is advised after a high mileage has been covered and particularly if fluid leakage or poor brake action is apparent.
17 A rebuild kit for each master cylinder and caliper is available (see Chapter 6).

3 Clutch

1 Check that the clutch lever operates smoothly and easily.
2 If the lever operation is heavy or stiff, remove the cable (see Chapter 2) and lubricate it (see Section 13). If the cable is still stiff, replace it with a new one. Install the lubricated or new cable (see Chapter 2).
3 With the cable operating smoothly, check that it is correctly adjusted. Periodic adjustment is necessary to compensate for wear in the clutch plates and stretch of the cable. Check that the amount of freeplay at the clutch lever end is within the specifications listed at the beginning of the Chapter **(see illustration)**.
4 If adjustment is required, it can be made both at the lever end of the cable and at the

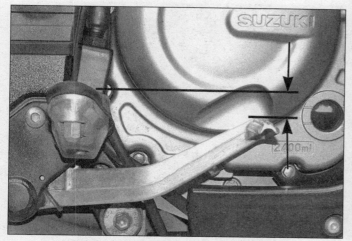
2.12a Rear brake pedal height measurement

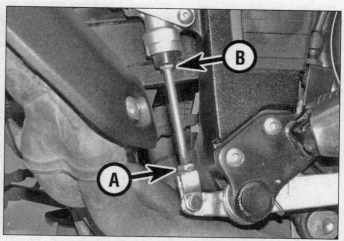
2.12b Locknut (A) and pushrod hex (B) – DL

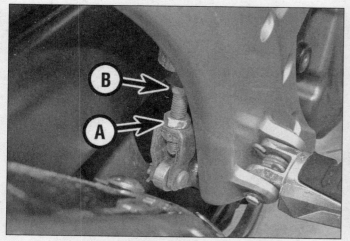
2.12c Locknut (A) and pushrod hex (B) – SFV

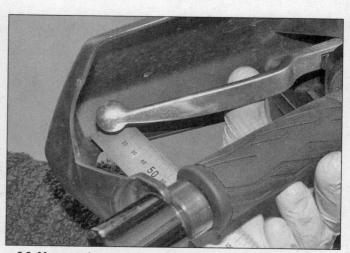
3.3 Measure the amount of freeplay at the clutch lever end as shown

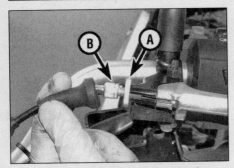

3.4 Pull the boot back, slacken the lockring (A) and turn the adjuster (B) as required

clutch end, but start the procedure at the lever end. Pull back the rubber boot covering the adjuster **(see illustration)**. Loosen the adjuster lockring, then turn the adjuster in or out until the required amount of freeplay is obtained. To increase freeplay, thread the adjuster into

the lever bracket. To reduce freeplay, thread the adjuster out of the bracket.

5 Make sure that the slot in the adjuster and the lockring, are not aligned with the slot in the lever bracket – these slots are to allow removal of the cable, and if they are all aligned while the bike is in use the cable could jump out. Also make sure the adjuster is not threaded too far out of the bracket so that it is only held by a few threads – this will leave it unstable and the threads could be damaged. Tighten the lockring and fit the rubber boot on completion.

6 If all the adjustment has been taken up at the lever, thread the adjuster all the way into the bracket to give the maximum amount of freeplay, then back it out one turn – this resets the adjuster to its start point.

7 Now set the freeplay as follows, according to model.

8 On 2004 to 2011 DL models remove the front sprocket cover (see Chapter 6). Slacken the locknut on the release mechanism adjuster screw, then undo the adjuster screw

two turns **(see illustration)**. Now counter-hold the locknut and turn the adjuster screw in until resistance is felt, then back it off 1/4 turn. Counter-hold the adjuster screw to prevent it turning and tighten the locknut. Slacken the locknuts securing the cable in the bracket on the crankcase, then turn the adjuster until the amount of freeplay at the lever end is correct, then tighten the locknuts **(see illustration)**.

9 On 2012-on DL models and all SFV models remove the clutch cover (see Chapter 2). Slacken the locknut on the release mechanism adjuster screw, then undo the adjuster screw two turns **(see illustration)**. Now counter-hold the locknut and turn the adjuster screw in until resistance is felt, then back it off 1 turn. Now counter-hold the adjuster screw to prevent it turning and tighten the locknut. Slacken the locknut on the cable adjuster near the top yoke, then turn the adjuster until the amount of freeplay at the lever end is correct, then tighten the locknut **(see illustration)**.

10 Install the sprocket cover or clutch cover, according to model.

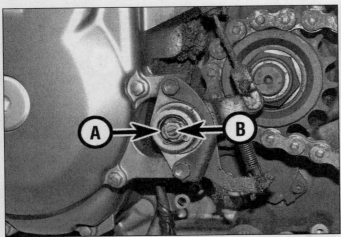

3.8a Slacken the locknut (A) and turn the adjuster screw (B) as described

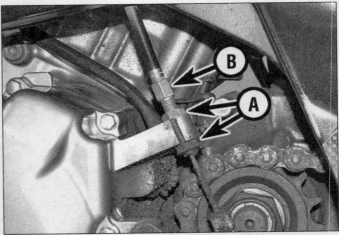

3.8b Slacken the nuts (A) and turn the cable adjuster (B) as described

3.9a Slacken the locknut and turn the adjuster screw as described

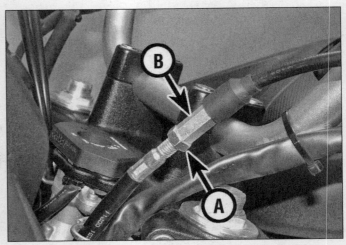

3.9b Slacken the nut (A) and turn the cable adjuster (B) as described

4.2a Undo the screws...

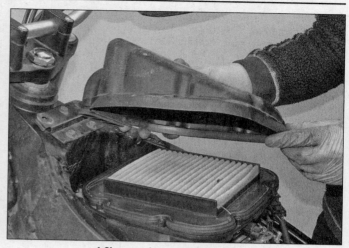

4.2b ...and remove the cover...

4 Air filter

Caution: If the machine is continually ridden in wet or dusty conditions, the filter should be replaced more frequently.

1 Raise or remove the fuel tank (see Chapter 4).
2 Undo the air filter cover screws and remove the cover (**see illustrations**).
3 Remove the filter element from the housing (**see illustration**).
4 Either clean the element as described in Step 5 or replace it with a new one, according to service interval.
5 To clean the filter tap it on a hard surface to dislodge any dirt trapped between the folds, then if available use compressed air to blow through it, directing the air in the opposite way to normal flow, i.e. from the underside (**see illustrations**). Do not use any solvents or cleaning agents on the element. If the element

is excessively dirty or is damaged replace it with a new one.
6 Make sure the seal around the rim of the filter is in good condition and correctly seated. Fit the filter, making sure it seats correctly (**see illustration 4.3**). Fit the cover (**see illustration 4.2b**).
7 Check for any deposits in the air filter housing drain collector, located in the bottom of the housing on the right-hand side on 2004 to 2006 DL models, and on the left on all others. If there are any, clean the collector with some absorbent rag or tissue.
8 Fit the fuel tank (see Chapter 8).

5 Spark plugs

Check

Note: *2004 to 2006 DL models have single spark ignition with one spark plug in the top of*

4.3 ...and the filter element

each head. All other models have dual spark ignition with two plugs per head, one in the top and one on the side, and are fitted with iridium plugs that must be treated differently to conventional ones.
Special tools: *Make sure your spark plug socket is the correct size before attempting to remove the plugs – a suitable one is supplied*

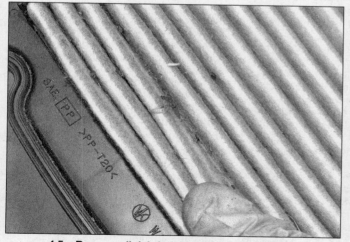

4.5a Remove all debris from between the folds...

4.5b ...and blow through from the underside using compressed air

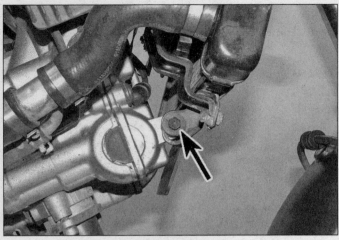

5.1 Unscrew the bolt (arrowed)

5.2 Pull the cap off the plug

5.4a Unscrew the plug...

5.4b ...and lift it out with the tool – the rubber insert should grip around the plug top

in the motorcycle's tool kit (stored under the seat). On 2004 to 2006 DL models either a wire gauge or feeler gauge set is necessary for measuring the spark plug gap. On all other models only a wire gauge should be used to measure the gap.

1 To access the front cylinder plug(s), on SFV models remove the radiator covers (see Chapter 7), and on all models unscrew the radiator lower mounting bolt and pivot the bottom of the radiator forward **(see illustration)**. To access the rear cylinder plug(s) raise the fuel tank (see Chapter 4).

2 Pull the cap off the plug **(see illustration)**.

3 Clean around the base of the plug to prevent any dirt falling into the combustion chamber.

4 Using either the plug removing tool supplied in the bike's toolkit or a spark plug socket, unscrew and remove the plug **(see illustrations)** – lay the plugs out in order so you know which cylinder each comes from.

Conventional plugs – 2004 to 2006 DL models

5 Refer to the colour spark plug chart on the inside rear cover and compare the firing end of each plug to those shown, identifying any abnormal condition and assessing its cause if necessary.

6 Clean the electrodes using a soft wire brush – if any deposits do not come off replace the plugs with new ones. Cleaning spark plugs by sandblasting is fine as long as you blow them with compressed air and clean them with a high flash-point solvent afterwards. Also clean any deposits off the white ceramic body of the plug.

7 Check the condition of the cleaned electrodes. Both the centre and side electrodes should have square edges and the side electrodes should be of uniform thickness. Check for evidence of a cracked or chipped insulator around the centre electrode. Check the plug threads, the washer and the ceramic insulator body for cracks and other damage.

8 If the plugs can be re-used check the gap

between the electrodes with a feeler gauge or wire type gauge **(see illustrations)**. The gap should be as given in the Specifications at the beginning of this chapter. If the electrodes have worn and the gap is wider than it should be, or for some reason the gap is narrower than it should be (if the plug has been dropped for instance) carefully bend the outer electrode as required to restore the correct gap – wire gauges have a special adjuster incorporated **(see illustration)**.

Irridium plugs – 2007-on DL and all SFV models

9 Check the condition of the electrodes, referring to the spark plug reading chart on the inside rear cover if signs of contamination are evident. Note that contaminated iridium plugs should not be cleaned – discard them and install new ones.

10 Examine the pointed iridium-tipped centre electrode – it should have a sharp point; if the tip has rounded off, the plug is worn **(see illustration)**. Measure the gap between the

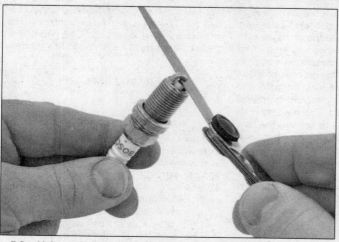

5.8a Using a feeler blade to measure the spark plug electrode gap

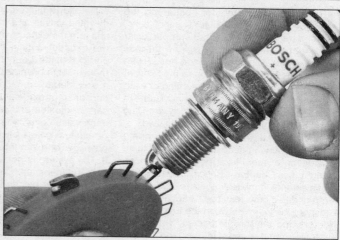

5.8b Using a wire gauge to measure the spark plug electrode gap

5.8c Adjusting the gap using the adjuster on a wire gauge

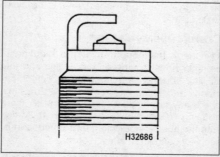

5.10 If the tip is not sharp replace the plug with a new one

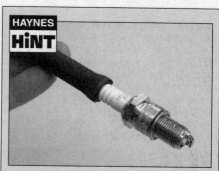

HAYNES HINT

Slip a short length of hose over the end of the plug to use as a tool to thread it into place. The hose will grip the plug well enough to turn it, but will start to slip if the plug begins to cross-thread in the hole – this will prevent damaged threads.

two electrodes with a wire type gauge only **(see illustration 5.8b)** – do not use blade type feeler gauges because the iridium tip might be damaged. The gap should be as given in the Specifications at the beginning of this chapter; if the electrodes have worn and the gap is wider than specified, or for some reason the gap is narrower (if the plug has been dropped for instance) a new plug must be installed. Do not bend the outer electrode to adjust the gap.

11 Check the threads, the washer and the ceramic insulator body for cracks and other damage.

All models

12 If in doubt concerning the condition of the plugs, replace them with new ones.

13 Fit the plug into the end of the tool, then use the tool to insert the plug **(see illustration 5.4b)**. Alternatively there are dedicated plug insertion tools, or you can use some hose (see **Haynes Hint**). Thread the plugs as far as possible into the head turning the tool or hose by hand, making sure they do not cross-thread. Once the plugs are finger-tight, tighten them using a spanner on the tool

supplied or a socket drive **(see illustration 5.4a)**. If a torque wrench can be applied, tighten the spark plugs to the torque setting specified at the beginning of the Chapter. Otherwise, if new plugs are being used tighten them by 1/2 a turn after the washer has seated, and if the old plugs are being reused tighten them by 1/8 to 1/4 turn after they have seated, according to feel. Do not over-tighten them.

14 Fit the cap onto the plug and push it down so it is fully seated **(see illustration 5.2)**.

15 Fit the radiator bolt and fuel tank.

HAYNES HINT

Stripped plug threads in the cylinder head can be repaired with a thread insert – see 'Tools and Workshop Tips' in the Reference section.

Renewal

16 At the prescribed interval, whatever the condition of the existing spark plugs, remove the plugs as described above and install new ones.

6 Fuel and emission control systems

⚠ *Warning: Petrol (gasoline) is extremely flammable, so take extra precautions when you work on any part of the fuel system. Don't smoke or allow open flames or bare light bulbs near the work area, and don't work in a garage where a natural gas-type appliance is present. If you spill any fuel on your skin, rinse it off immediately with soap and water. When you perform any kind of work on the fuel system, wear safety glasses and have a fire extinguisher suitable for a Class B type fire (flammable liquids) on hand.*

1 Raise the fuel tank (see Chapter 4).

Fuel system

2 Check the fuel tank, the fuel supply hose,

the tank drain and breather hoses and the throttle body vacuum hoses for signs of leaks, cracks, deterioration or damage. In particular check that there are no leaks from the fuel hose(s) or hose unions. Replace hoses with new ones as required, referring to the relevant section in Chapter 4. Note the routing of each hose and how it is secured – it is advisable to make a sketch of the hoses before removing them to ensure they are correctly installed.

3 Check the joint between the fuel pump assembly mounting plate and the tank. If there is evidence of fuel leakage, check the bolts are tight (see Chapter 4 Specifications for the torque setting). If the leak persists, remove the pump and fit a new seal (see Chapter 4).

4 Inspect the joints between the fuel rails, the injectors and the throttle bodies. If there are any leaks, remove the injectors and fit new seals and O-rings (see Chapter 4).

5 Fuel filter renewal is not a service item. The filter is in the fuel pump assembly, and there is a strainer in the pump pick-up. If fuel starvation is experienced, and all other possibilities have been checked, a blocked strainer or filter could be the cause; in this event remove the pump and check the strainer and filter (see Chapter 4).

6 Make sure the air filter housing ducts are in good condition and the clamps are tight on the throttle bodies. Make sure the intake ducts between the throttle bodies and the cylinder heads are in good condition and that the clamps and bolts are tight.

PAIR system – 2004 to 2011 DL models

7 To reduce the amount of unburned hydrocarbons released in the exhaust gases, a pulse secondary air supply (PAIR) system is fitted. The system consists of the control valve (mounted on the underside of the air filter housing on the right-hand side), the reed valves (one in each valve cover) and the hoses linking them. The control valve is actuated electronically by the ECU.

8 Under certain operating conditions, the valve allows filtered air to be drawn through the reed valves and cylinder head passages and into the exhaust ports. The air mixes with the exhaust gases, causing any unburned particles of the fuel in the mixture to be burnt in the exhaust port/pipes. This process changes a considerable amount of hydrocarbons and carbon monoxide into relatively harmless carbon dioxide and water. The reed valve in each valve cover is fitted to prevent the flow of exhaust gases back up the cylinder head passages and into the air filter housing.

9 The system is not adjustable and requires little maintenance. Check that the hoses are not kinked or pinched, are in good condition and are securely connected at each end. Replace any hoses that are cracked, split or generally deteriorated with new ones. Make sure the control valve wiring connector is securely connected and no wires or terminals are loose or corroded.

10 Refer to Chapter 4 for further information on the system and for checks if it is believed to be faulty.

Crankcase breather

11 Check the condition of the crankcase breather hose(s) between the engine and the air filter housing (see illustration). Check for cracks and splits and replace it with a new one if any are evident – remove the air filter housing to do this (see Chapter 4). Make sure the hose is not kinked or trapped, and is securely connected at each end.

EVAP system (California models)

12 Visually inspect all the system hoses between the fuel tank, the shut-off valve, the canister, the control valve and the throttle bodies for kinks and splits and any other damage or deterioration. Make sure that the hoses are securely connected with a clamp on each end. Replace any hoses that are damaged or deteriorated.

13 Check the EVAP canister for cracks or other damage.

14 Refer to your dealer for further information and tests on the system. Note that there is an emission control system hose routing diagram on a label under the seat on DL models and on the left-hand side of the frame on SFV models.

7 Engine oil and filter

Special tool: *A filter removal tool is necessary to remove the filter. You can purchase one as a Suzuki spare part (No. 09915-40610 for 2004 to 2011 DL models, and 09915-40620 for all other models), or alternatively there are several after-market options (see Step 5).*

⚠️ **Warning: Be careful when draining the oil, as the exhaust, the engine, and the oil itself can cause severe burns.**

1 Consistent routine oil and filter changes are the single most important maintenance procedure you can perform. The oil not only lubricates the internal parts of the engine, transmission and clutch, but it also acts as a coolant, a cleaner, a sealant, and a protector. Because of these demands, the oil takes a terrific amount of abuse and should be replaced often with new oil of the recommended grade and type. The oil filter must be changed with every third oil change, but as the cost of a filter is minimal consider doing it with every second oil change, or even with every change.

2 Before changing the oil, warm up the engine so the oil will drain easily. The oil drain bolt is on the underside of the engine on the left, and the filter is on the front. Where fitted remove the sump guard (see Chapter 7).

3 Position a large clean drain tray below the engine so it is under both the drain bolt and the filter (if being changed), or use two small ones if a large enough one is not available. Unscrew the oil filler cap to vent the crankcase and to act as a reminder that there is no oil in the engine (see illustration).

4 Unscrew the drain bolt and allow the oil to

6.11 Crankcase breather hoses (arrowed) – early DL shown, later DL and SFV have one hose

7.3 Unscrew the oil filler cap to act as a vent

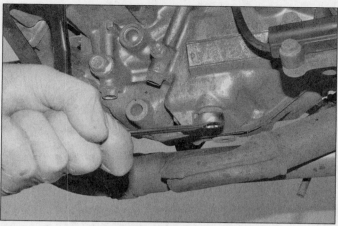

7.4a Unscrew the oil drain bolt...

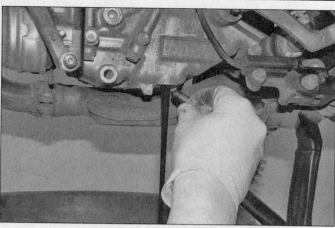

7.4b ...and allow the oil to completely drain

flow into the tray (see illustrations). Remove the sealing washer from the bolt – you may have to lever it off using a small screwdriver, or cut it off. A new washer must be used.

5 If changing the filter unscrew it using a filter socket (see above), filter pliers, or a filter removing strap or a chain-wrench, and tip any residual oil into the drain tray (see illustrations). The filter socket is preferable because it provides a means of tightening the new filter properly.

6 Clean the magnetic tip of the drain bolt. When the oil has completely drained, fit a new sealing washer onto the bolt, then fit the bolt and tighten it to the torque setting specified at the beginning of the Chapter (see illustrations). Do not overtighten it as the threads are easily damaged.

7 If the filter was changed, remove any cellophane

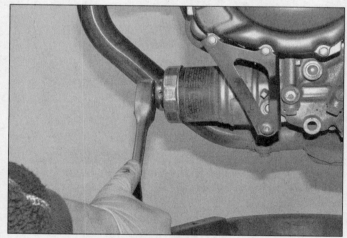

7.5a Unscrew the filter using a filter removing socket or strap...

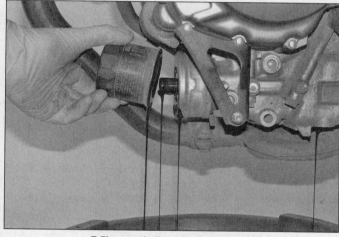

7.5b ...and allow the oil to drain

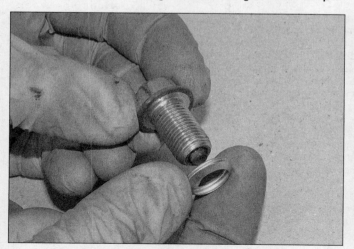

7.6a Fit a new sealing washer...

7.6b ...and tighten the bolt to the specified torque

7.7a Smear clean oil onto the seal...

7.7b ...then fit the filter and tighten it as described

7.8a Add the specified type and amount of oil...

7.8b ...so the level is almost up to the F mark

from the end of the new filter. Smear clean engine oil onto rubber seal (see illustration). Thread the filter onto the engine until the seal contacts the surface (see illustration). From there tighten it two full turns, either by hand or using the filter socket, or to the specified torque setting if you have a torque wrench. Note: *Do not use a strap or chain-type filter removing tool to tighten the filter as you will damage it.*

8 Refill the engine using the recommended

7.8c Make sure the O-ring (arrowed) is in good condition and correctly seated

type and amount of oil (see Specifications) until the level is almost up to the F mark on the inspection window with the motorcycle vertical (see illustrations). Do not overfill. Check the condition of the O-ring on the cap and replace it with a new one if it is damaged or worn (see illustration). Fit the cap.

9 Start the engine and let it run for two or three minutes (make sure that the oil pressure light extinguishes after a few seconds). Shut it off, wait a few minutes, then check the oil level again. If necessary, add more oil to bring the level close to the F mark, but do not go above it.

10 Check around the drain bolt and the filter for leaks. If leaks are evident, and the bolt and filter are correctly tightened using a new washer and a lubricated seal, there is another cause (such as dirt or corrosion) that must be investigated before riding the bike.

11 The old oil drained from the engine cannot be re-used and should be disposed of properly. Check with your local refuse disposal or recycling facility to see whether they will accept the used oil for recycling. Don't pour used oil into drains or onto the ground.

HAYNES HiNT *Check the old oil carefully – if it is very metallic coloured, then the engine is experiencing wear from break-in (new engine) or from insufficient lubrication. If there are flakes or chips of metal in the oil, then something is drastically wrong internally and the engine will have to be disassembled for inspection and repair. If there are pieces of fibre-like material in the oil, the clutch is experiencing excessive wear and should be checked.*

OIL CARE FOLLOW THE CODE

Note: It is illegal and anti-social to dump oil down the drain. To find the location of your local oil recycling bank in the UK, call 03708 506 506 or visit www.oilbankline.org.uk

8 Engine idle speed

2004 to 2006 DL models

1 Check and adjust the idle speed before and after the throttle bodies are synchronised (balanced), after checking the valve clearances, and when it is obviously too high or too low. Before adjusting the idle speed, make sure the valve clearances were checked at the previous prescribed interval, and the spark plugs are in good condition and their gaps are correct, and the air filter is clean. Also, turn the handlebars back-and-forth and see if the idle speed changes as this is done. If it does, the throttle cables may not be adjusted or routed correctly, or may be worn out. This is a dangerous condition that can cause loss of control of the bike. Be sure to correct this problem before proceeding.

2 Warm up the engine to normal running temperature.

3 The idle speed adjuster is located on the left-hand side of the bike **(see illustration)**. With the engine idling, turn the adjuster until the speed listed in this Chapter's Specifications is obtained.

4 Snap the throttle open and shut a few times, then recheck the idle speed. If necessary, repeat the adjustment procedure.

5 If a smooth, steady idle cannot be achieved, the throttle bodies may need synchronising (Section 16). Also check the intake manifold rubbers for cracks that will cause an air leak, resulting in a weak mixture.

2007-on DL and all SFV models

6 Idle speed is controlled automatically by the idle speed control valve. If idle speed is not as specified at the beginning of the Chapter, refer to Chapter 4.

8.3 Idle speed adjuster (arrowed)

9.2 Throttle cable freeplay is measured in terms of twistgrip rotation

9 Throttle cables

1 Make sure the throttle grip rotates smoothly and freely from fully closed to fully open with the front wheel turned at various angles. The grip should return automatically from fully open to fully closed when released. If the throttle sticks, check and lubricate the cable and twistgrip as described below.

Cable freeplay check

2 Check for a small amount of freeplay in the cables, measured in terms of the amount of twistgrip rotation before the throttle opens, and compare the amount to that listed in this Chapter's Specifications for your model **(see illustration)**. If it's incorrect, adjust the cables to correct it as follows according to model.

Cable freeplay adjustment

2004 to 2011 DL models

3 The upper cable in the housing is the opening cable, and the lower is the closing cable. Slide the rubber sleeve off each adjuster. Loosen the locknut on the closing cable adjuster and turn the adjuster fully in **(see illustration)**. Now loosen the locknut on the opening cable adjuster and turn the adjuster until the specified amount of freeplay is obtained (see this Chapter's Specifications), then retighten the locknut. Now hold the throttle closed and turn the closing cable adjuster out until a resistance can just be felt – at this point all the freeplay has been taken up. Do not turn the adjuster out any further than the point at which the resistance is felt. Tighten the locknut.

4 If the top end cable adjusters have reached their limit, or if major adjustment is required, adjust the cables at the throttle body end as follows. First reset the top end adjusters so that the freeplay is at a maximum (i.e. the adjusters are fully turned in). Remove the air filter housing (see Chapter 4). The upper cable in the bracket is the closing cable, and the lower is the opening cable. Slacken the adjuster locknuts **(see illustration)**. Turn the closing cable adjuster out until a resistance can just be felt – at this point all the freeplay has been taken up. Tighten the locknut. Now turn the opening cable adjuster out until the specified amount of freeplay is obtained (see Step 2), and tighten the locknut. Install the air filter housing.

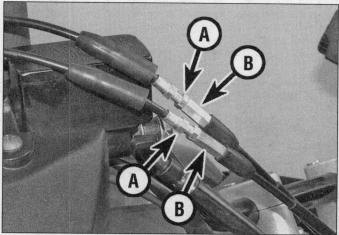

9.3 Slacken the adjuster locknuts (A) and turn the in-line adjusters (B) as described

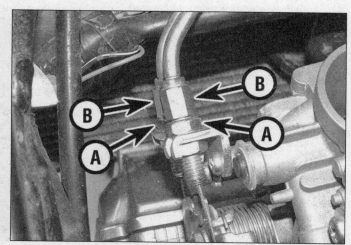

9.4 Slacken the adjuster locknuts (A) and turn the adjusters (B) as described at the throttle body end

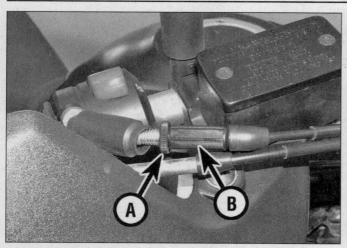

9.6 Throttle cable adjuster lockring (A) and adjuster (B)

9.9 Undo the screw (arrowed) to free the end-weight and twistgrip – note how the hand-guard locates on DL models

5 Subsequent adjustments can now be made at the upper end. If the cables cannot be adjusted as specified, install new ones (see Chapter 4). Check that the throttle twistgrip operates smoothly and snaps shut quickly when released.

2012-on DL models and SFV models

6 Adjust freeplay using the adjuster in the throttle opening cable where it leaves the throttle pulley housing on the handlebar. Slide the rubber sleeve off the adjuster. Loosen the lockring and turn the adjuster in or out as required until the specified amount of freeplay is obtained (see this Chapter's Specifications), then retighten the lockring **(see illustration)**.

7 If the cables cannot be adjusted as specified, install new ones (see Chapter 4). Check that the throttle twistgrip operates smoothly and snaps shut quickly when released.

⚠️ *Warning: Turn the handlebars all the way through their travel with the engine idling. Idle speed should not change. If it does, the cables may be routed incorrectly. Correct this condition before riding the bike.*

Cable and twistgrip lubrication

8 If the throttle sticks, this is probably due to a cable fault. Detach the cables from the throttle pulley (see Chapter 4) and lubricate them (see Section 13). Check that the inner cables slide freely and easily in the outer cables. If not, replace the cables with new ones.

9 With the cables removed, make sure the throttle twistgrip rotates freely on the handlebar – dirt combined with a lack of lubrication can cause the action to be stiff. If necessary undo the end-weight screw and remove the weight and the twistgrip from the handlebar, moving the hand-guard aside where fitted **(see illustration)**. Clean any old grease from the bar and the inside of

the tube. Smear some multi-purpose grease onto the bar, then refit the twistgrip and end-weight.

10 Install the cables, making sure they are correctly routed (see Chapter 4). If this fails to improve the operation of the throttle, the cables must be replaced with new ones. Note that in very rare cases the fault could lie in the throttle bodies. Remove the fuel tank and check the action of the throttle pulley and linkage (see Chapter 4).

10 Cooling system

Check

⚠️ *Warning: The engine must be cool before beginning this procedure.*

1 On 2004 to 2011 DL models remove the fairing side panels (see Chapter 7). On 2012-on DL models remove the complete fairing assembly (see Chapter 7). On SFV models remove the radiator covers (see Chapter 7).

2 Check the coolant level in the reservoir (see *Pre-ride checks*).

3 Examine each rubber coolant hose along its entire length. Look for cracks, abrasions and other damage. Squeeze each hose at various points to see whether they are dried out or hard **(see illustration)**. They should feel firm, yet pliable, and return to their original shape when released. If necessary, replace them with new ones (see Chapter 3).

4 Check for evidence of leaks at each cooling system hose connection, around the pump on the right-hand side of the engine, at the outlet union on each cylinder head, and from the thermostat housing. Tighten the hose clips carefully to prevent future leaks. If the pump is leaking around the cover, check that the bolts are tight. If they are, remove the cover and replace the O-rings with new ones (see Chapter 3).

5 To prevent leakage of coolant from the cooling system to the lubrication system and vice versa, two seals are fitted on the pump shaft. The coolant seal on the water pump side is of the mechanical type and bears on the rear face of the impeller. The oil seal, which is mounted behind the mechanical seal, is of the normal feathered lip type. On the underside of the pump there is a drain **(see illustration)**. If

10.3 Check all the coolant hoses as described

10.5a Water pump drain hose...

either seal fails, the drain allows the coolant or oil (or both) to escape via a hose connected to a union on the bottom **(see illustration)**. If on inspection the hose shows signs of leakage, particularly with the engine running, remove the pump and fit new seals (see Chapter 3).

6 Check the radiator for leaks and other damage. Leaks leave tell-tale scale deposits or coolant stains on the outside of the core below the leak. If leaks are noted, remove the radiator (see Chapter 3) and have it repaired or replace it with a new one – do not use a liquid leak-stop compound to try to repair leaks.

7 Check the radiator fins for mud, dirt and insects, which may impede the flow of air through. If the fins are dirty, remove the radiator (see Chapter 3) and clean it using water or low pressure compressed air directed through the fins from the inner side. If the fins are bent or distorted, straighten them carefully with a small screwdriver. If the airflow is restricted by bent or damaged fins over more than 20% of the radiator's surface area, replace the radiator with a new one.

⚠️ *Warning: Do not remove the pressure cap when the engine is hot. It is good practice to cover the cap with a heavy cloth and turn the cap slowly anti-clockwise. If you hear a hissing sound (indicating that there is still pressure in the system), wait until it stops, then continue turning the cap until it can be removed.*

8 Remove the pressure cap from the filler neck by turning it anti-clockwise until it reaches the stop. If you hear a hissing sound (indicating there is still pressure in the system), wait until it stops. Now press down on the cap and continue turning it until it can be removed **(see illustration)**.

9 Check the condition of the coolant in the system. If it is rust-coloured or if accumulations of scale are visible, drain, flush and refill the system with new coolant (see below). Check the antifreeze content of the coolant with an antifreeze hydrometer – a 50% content should give a reading of 1.084 at 5°C to 1.074 at 25°C, varying accordingly in between. The system must have the correct coolant mixture (see Specifications) – if the coolant is weak (too little anti-freeze) there will not be adequate protection against freezing and corrosion, and if it is too strong the ability to cool the engine is reduced. If the hydrometer indicates an incorrect mixture, drain, flush and refill the system (see below).

10 The function of the pressure cap is crucial to the correct running of the cooling system. Check the cap seal for cracks and other damage. If the coolant level consistently drops and/or the bike overheats, and no evidence of leaks can be found, have the cap pressure checked by a Suzuki dealer, or just fit a new one – the expense is minimal. If a new cap does not cure the problem have the entire system pressure checked by a dealer.

11 Fit the cap by turning it clockwise until it reaches the first stop then push down on it and continue turning until it can turn no further. Start the engine and let it reach normal operating temperature, then check for leaks again. As the coolant temperature increases, the electric fan (mounted on the back of the radiator) should come on automatically and the temperature should begin to drop. If not, refer to Chapter 3 and check the fan and fan circuit.

12 Check the oil cooler on the front of the engine for any signs of damage and leakage. On 2004 to 2011 DL models check the cooler fins (see Step 7). On 2012-on DL models and all SFV models check that the coolant hoses are secure on the unions. If there is leakage refer to Chapter 2.

Coolant change

⚠️ *Warning: Allow the engine to cool completely before performing this maintenance operation. Also, don't allow anti-freeze to come into contact with your skin or the painted surfaces of the motorcycle. Rinse off spills immediately with plenty of water. Anti-freeze is highly toxic if ingested. Never leave anti-freeze lying around in an open container or in puddles on the floor; children and pets are attracted by its sweet smell and may drink it. Check with local authorities (councils) about disposing anti-freeze – many have collection centres that dispose it safely. Anti-freeze is also combustible, so don't store it near open flames.*

Draining

13 Support the bike upright on level ground. On 2004 to 2011 DL models remove the right-hand fairing side panel (see Chapter 7). On 2012-on DL models remove the complete fairing assembly (see Chapter 7). On SFV models remove the right-hand radiator cover (see Chapter 7).

14 Remove the pressure cap from the filler neck by turning it anti-clockwise until it reaches a stop **(see illustration 10.8)**. If you hear a hissing sound (indicating there is still pressure in the system), wait until it stops. Now press down on the cap and continue turning the cap until it can be removed. Also remove the coolant reservoir cap.

15 Position a suitable container beneath the

10.5b ...check the end of the hose (arrowed) for signs of leakage

10.8 Remove the pressure cap as described

10.15a Unscrew the bolt (arrowed)...

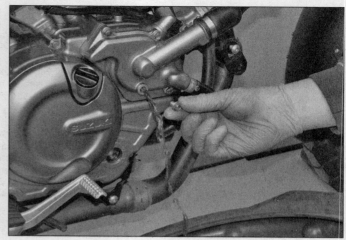

10.15b ...and allow the coolant to drain

water pump on the right-hand side of the engine. Unscrew the drain bolt and allow the coolant to completely drain **(see illustrations)**. A new sealing washer is needed.

16 Draw the coolant out of the reservoir using a hand pump if available, or displace the reservoir (see Chapter 3) and tip the coolant out.

17 Mop up any spilt coolant.

Flushing

18 Flush the system with clean tap water by inserting a hose in the filler neck. Allow the water to run through the system until it is clear and flows out cleanly. If the radiator is extremely corroded, remove it (see Chapter 3) and have it cleaned by a specialist.

Refilling

19 Fit the drain bolt using a new sealing washer and tighten it to the torque setting specified at the beginning of the Chapter **(see illustration)**.

20 Fill the system to the base of the filler neck with the proper coolant mixture (see this Chapter's Specifications) **(see illustration)**. **Note:** *Pour the coolant in slowly to minimise the amount of air entering the system. When full carefully wiggle the bike from side to side, squeeze the hoses and tap the thermostat housing to dislodge any trapped air. Fill the reservoir to the FULL level line (see Pre-ride checks).*

21 Start the engine and allow it to idle for 2 to 3 minutes. Flick the throttle twistgrip part open 3 or 4 times, so that the engine speed rises to approximately 4000 rpm, then stop the engine. Any air trapped in the system should bleed back to the radiator filler neck.

22 If necessary top up the coolant level to the base of the filler neck and top up the reservoir to the FULL level line, then fit the pressure cap and reservoir cap.

23 Start the engine and allow it to reach normal operating temperature, then shut it off. Let the engine cool then remove the pressure cap as described in Step 14. Check that the coolant level is still up to the base of the upper radiator filler neck. If it's low, add the specified mixture until it reaches the base of the filler neck. Refit the cap.

24 Check the coolant level in the reservoir and top up if necessary. Check the system for leaks.

25 Install the fairing side panel, fairing or radiator cover, according to model.

26 Do not dispose of the old coolant by pouring it down the drain. Instead pour it into a heavy plastic container, cap it tightly and take it into an authorised disposal site or service station – see **Warning** on page 1•21.

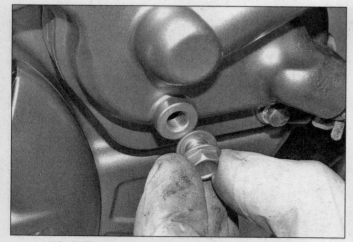

10.19 Fit a new sealing washer onto the drain bolt

10.20 Fill the system as described

11.6 Checking for play in the wheel bearings

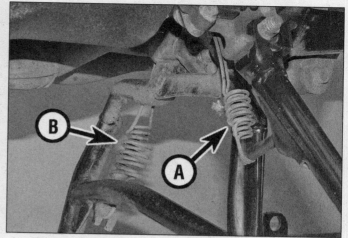

12.1 Check the sidestand springs (A), and on DL models where fitted the centrestand springs (B)

11 Wheels, tyres and wheel bearings

Wheels

1 Cast wheels are virtually maintenance free, but they should be kept clean and checked periodically for cracks and other damage. Never attempt to repair cast wheels – if damaged they must be replaced with new ones. Also check wheel run-out and alignment (see Chapter 6). Check that the wheel balance weights are fixed firmly to the wheel rim. If you suspect that a weight has fallen off, have the wheel rebalanced by a motorcycle tyre specialist.

Tyres

2 Check the tyre condition and tread depth thoroughly – see *Pre-ride checks*.
3 Make sure the valve cap is in place and tight. Check the valve for signs of damage. If tyre deflation occurs and it is not due to a slow puncture the valve core may be loose or it could be leaking past the seal – remove the cap and make sure the core is tight; if it is tight then it could be leaking – unscrew the core from the valve housing using a core removal tool (sometimes incorporated in the valve cap) and thread a new one in its place. A tool can be made quite easily by cutting a slot into the threaded end of a bolt using a hacksaw – the bolt must fit inside the valve housing and the slot must be the correct thickness to fit over the top of the core.

Wheel bearings

4 Wheel bearings will wear over a considerable mileage and should be checked periodically to avoid handling problems.
5 Support the bike using an auxiliary stand so that the wheel being checked is off the ground.
6 Check for any play in the bearings by pushing and pulling the wheel against the hub **(see illustration)**. When checking the front wheel turn the handlebars to full lock on one side and hold the wheel against the lock. Also rotate the wheel and check that it turns smoothly and without any grating noises (bearing in mind that the brakes and drive chain make some noise – do not confuse them).
7 If any play is detected in the hub, or if the wheel does not rotate smoothly (and this is not due to brake or transmission drag), remove the wheel and check the bearings for wear or damage (see Chapter 6).

12 Sidestand and starter safety circuit

Sidestand

1 Check the stand springs for damage and distortion **(see illustration)**. The springs must be capable of retracting the stand fully and holding it retracted when the motorcycle is in use. If a spring is sagged or broken it must be replaced with a new one.
2 Lubricate the stand pivots regularly (see Section 13).
3 Check the stands and mounts for bends and cracks. Stands can often be repaired by welding.

Starter safety circuit

4 Check the operation of the circuit as follows: make sure the transmission is in neutral, then retract the stand and start the engine. Pull in the clutch lever and select a gear. Keeping the clutch lever pulled in, extend the sidestand. The engine should stop as the sidestand is extended.

5 If the circuit does not operate as described, check the sidestand switch, sidestand relay and diodes, gear position switch and clutch switch, and the wiring and connectors between them (see Chapter 8).

13 Pivot points and cable lubrication

Pivot points

1 As the clutch and brake lever pivots, footrest pivots, brake pedal, gearchange lever pivots and linkage, and stand pivots are exposed to the elements, they should be checked and lubricated at the specified service interval to ensure safe and trouble-free operation.
2 In order for the lubricant to be applied where it will do the most good, the component should be disassembled and cleaned (see Chapter 5). The lubricant recommended by Suzuki for each application is listed at the beginning of the Chapter. If an aerosol lubricant is being used, it can be applied to the pivot joint gaps and will usually work its way into the areas where friction occurs, so less disassembly of the component is needed (however it is always better to do so and clean off all corrosion, dirt and old lubricant first). If motor oil or light grease is being used, apply it sparingly as it may attract dirt (which could cause the controls to bind or wear at an accelerated rate). **Note:** *An alternative lubricant for the control lever pivots is a dry-film lubricant (available from many sources by different names).*

Cables

Special tool: *A cable lubricating adapter is necessary for this procedure.*
3 Disconnect the throttle cables from the twistgrip (see Chapter 4) and the clutch cable from the handlebar lever (see

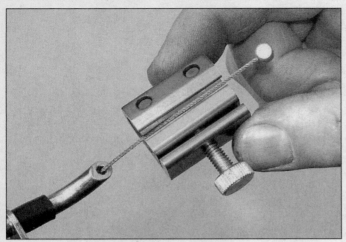

13.3a Fit the cable into the adapter...

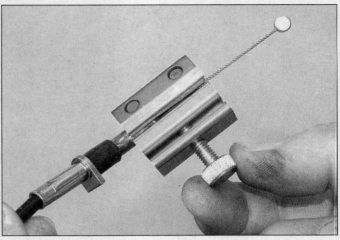

13.3b ...and tighten the screw to seal it in...

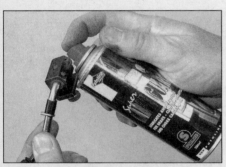

13.3c ...then apply the lubricant using the nozzle provided inserted in the hole in the adapter

Chapter 2). Lubricate them with a pressure adapter and aerosol cable lubricant as shown **(see illustrations)**.

14 Nuts and bolts

1 Since vibration of the machine tends to loosen fasteners, all nuts, bolts, screws, etc. should be periodically checked for proper tightness.
2 Pay particular attention to the following, referring to the relevant Chapter:

Spark plugs
Engine oil drain bolt
Lever pivot bolts/nuts
Footrest bracket and stand bolts/nuts
Front and rear sprocket nuts
Engine mounting bolts/nuts
Shock absorber, suspension linkage and swingarm pivot bolts/nuts
Handlebar bolts/nuts (according to model)
Front fork clamp bolts (top and bottom yoke) and fork top bolts

Steering stem nut
Front wheel axle and axle clamp bolt
Rear wheel axle nut
Brake caliper and master cylinder mounting bolts
Brake hose banjo bolts and caliper bleed valves
Brake disc bolts
Exhaust system bolts/nuts
Battery terminals

3 If a torque wrench is available, use it along with the torque settings given at the beginning of this and other Chapters.

15 Battery

1 All models covered in this manual are fitted with a sealed MF (maintenance free) battery. **Note:** *Do not attempt to remove the battery caps to check the electrolyte level or battery specific gravity. Removal will damage the caps, resulting in electrolyte leakage and battery damage.* All that should be done is to check that the terminals are clean and tight and that the casing is not damaged or leaking. See Chapter 8 for further details.
2 If the machine is not in regular use, disconnect the battery and give it a refresher charge every month to six weeks (see Chapter 8).

16 Throttle body synchronisation

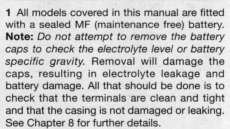

⚠ *Warning: Petrol (gasoline) is extremely flammable, so take extra precautions when you work on any part of the fuel system. Don't smoke or allow open flames or bare light bulbs*

near the work area, and don't work in a garage where a natural gas-type appliance is present. If you spill any fuel on your skin, rinse it off immediately with soap and water. When you perform any kind of work on the fuel system, wear safety glasses and have a fire extinguisher suitable for a Class B type fire (flammable liquids) on hand.

⚠ *Warning: Do not allow exhaust gases to build up in the work area; either perform the check outside or use an exhaust gas extraction system.*

Special tool: *A set of vacuum gauges or a manometer is necessary for this job.*

2004 to 2006 DL models

Note: *Suzuki specify that the throttle bodies should be synchronised with the air filter housing removed. As there is obviously a danger of dirt being drawn into the throttle bodies it is advisable to obtain an old pair of tights or similar and secure a section of the material over the intake with an elastic band to form a barrier without obstructing airflow.*

1 Throttle body synchronisation ensures each throttle body passes the same amount of fuel/air mixture to each cylinder. This is done by measuring the vacuum produced in each throttle body. Throttle bodies that are out of synchronisation will result in increased fuel consumption, higher engine temperature, less than ideal throttle response and higher vibration levels. Before synchronising the throttle bodies, make sure that the air filter is clean or a new one has been fitted (according to service interval), idle speed is properly adjusted (Section 8) and that the valve clearances were checked at the previous prescribed interval, or if they are due to be done check them before synchronisation (Section 19).
2 To synchronise the throttle bodies, you will need a manometer, such as the Morgan Carbtune Pro, or a pair of vacuum gauges, with

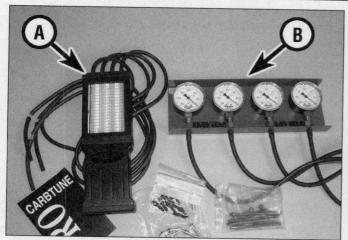

16.2 The Carbtune manometer (A) and a set of vacuum gauges (B), and the various adapters that come with them – each set is available in twin format

16.5 Front throttle body vacuum take-off blanking cap (arrowed)

the necessary hoses and adapters (if required) to fit the take-off points (see illustration). When using such equipment always read the instructions supplied. The hoses usually have some form of restrictor in them for damping the movement of the manometer rod or gauge needle – make sure these are fitted correctly if not already in place otherwise it will be difficult to get an accurate reading, and that in the case of the Carbtune the hoses are connected with the restrictors closest to the take-off points on the throttle bodies.

3 Start the engine and let it run until it reaches normal operating temperature, then shut it off. Raise the fuel tank and remove the air filter housing (see Chapter 4).

4 Remove the intake air temperature and intake air pressure sensors from the air filter housing and reconnect them to the wiring loom (see Chapter 4). Connect the vacuum hose to the IAP sensor. Remove the PAIR

control valve from the air filter housing and reconnect the wiring connector and hose (see Chapter 4).

5 Remove the blanking caps from the vacuum take-off stubs (see illustration). Connect the gauge hoses to the stubs – make sure the No. 1 gauge is attached to the No. 1 (front cylinder) throttle body.

6 Start the engine and let it idle, making sure the speed is still correct. If the gauges are fitted with damping adjustment, set this so that the needle flutter is just eliminated but so that they can still respond to small changes in pressure.

7 The vacuum readings for both cylinders should be the same, or at least within 10 mmHg of each other (see illustration). If the vacuum readings vary, adjust the butterfly valve linkage by turning the synchronising screw on the right-hand side of the rear throttle body until the readings are the same

(see illustration). Note: Do not press hard on the screw whilst adjusting it, otherwise a false reading will be obtained.

8 After each adjustment, open and close the throttle quickly two or three times to settle the linkage, and recheck the gauge readings, readjusting if necessary. When the adjustment is complete check and adjust the idle speed (see below).

9 Remove the gauges and fit the blanking caps (see illustration 16.5). Refit the sensors and PAIR valve to the air filter housing, then install the air filter housing and fuel tank (see Chapter 4).

2007-on DL and all SFV models

10 Throttle body synchronisation on these models can only be done with the Suzuki diagnosis system (SDS) tools and software connected to the ECM. Take the bike to a Suzuki dealer that has this equipment.

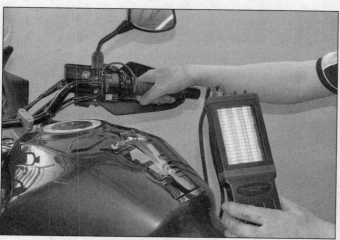

16.7a Checking throttle body synchronisation

16.7b Synchronisation adjuster screw (arrowed)

17 Suspension

1 The suspension components must be maintained in top operating condition to ensure rider safety. Loose, worn or damaged suspension parts decrease the motorcycle's stability and control.

Front suspension check

2 While standing alongside the motorcycle (and with it off the stand), apply the front brake and push on the handlebars to compress the forks several times **(see illustration)**. See if they move up-and-down smoothly without binding. If binding is felt, the forks should be disassembled and inspected (see Chapter 5).
3 Inspect each fork inner tube for scratches, corrosion and pitting in the area of travel through the seals, which will cause seal failure, and for oil leakage, which means the seal has failed **(see illustration)**. If corrosion damage is excessive, new inner tubes should be fitted (see Chapter 5), or the fitted ones must be re-chromed by a specialist company using hard chrome. If leakage is evident, the seals must be replaced with new ones (see Chapter 5).
4 Carefully lever the dust seal out using a flat-bladed screwdriver and inspect the area around the oil seal **(see illustration 17.3)**. If there is evidence of corrosion on the oil seal and/or its retaining ring, spray the area with a penetrative lubricant. If the seal is corroding (from water getting under the rubber) it must be replaced with a new one (see Chapter 5). Press the dust seal back into the outer tube on completion.

Rear suspension check

5 Inspect the rear shock absorber for fluid leakage. If leakage is found, the shock must be replaced with a new one (see Chapter 5).
6 With the aid of an assistant to support the bike, compress the rear suspension several times by pushing down on the back of the bike using the grab handles. It should move up-and-down freely without binding. If any binding is felt, the worn or faulty component must be identified and checked. The problem could be due to either the shock absorber, the suspension linkage bearings, or the swingarm bearings.
7 Place the motorcycle on a stand so that the rear wheel is off the ground. Grab the swingarm and rock it from side-to-side **(see illustration)** – there should be no discernible movement at the rear.
8 Next, grasp the swingarm ends and pull upwards **(see illustration)** – there should be no discernible freeplay before the shock absorber begins to compress.
9 If there's a little movement or a slight clicking can be heard, check the tightness of the swingarm pivot and the shock absorber and suspension linkage mounting bolts/nuts, referring to the procedure in Chapter 5, and

17.2 Pump the front suspension to check its action

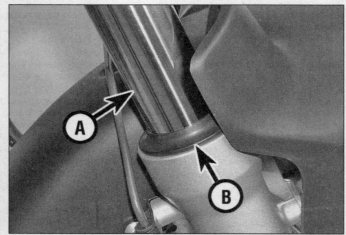

17.3 Check each inner tube (A) for pitting and signs of oil leakage. Dust seal (B)

17.7 Checking for play in the swingarm bearings

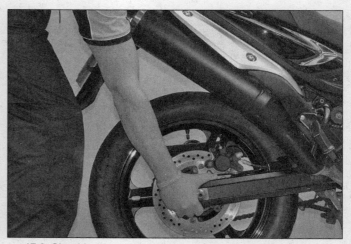

17.8 Checking for play in the rear shock mountings and the linkage bearings re-check for movement. If there is still some noise or freeplay after everything has been correctly tightened then there is either a worn bush in the shock absorber top mount, or worn swingarm bearings, or worn linkage bearings. The worn components must be identified and replaced with new ones (see Chapter 5).

10 You can make a more accurate assessment by isolating the swingarm from the linkage – remove the rear wheel (see Chapter 6) and the bolt securing the linkage to the swingarm (see Chapter 5).

11 Grasp the rear of the swingarm with one hand and place your other hand at the junction of the swingarm and the frame. Try to move the rear of the swingarm from side-to-side. Any wear (play) in the bearings should be felt as movement between the swingarm and the frame at the front. If there is any play, the swingarm will be felt to move forward and backward at the front (not from side-to-side). Next, move the swingarm up and down through its full travel. It should move freely, without any binding or rough spots. If there is any play in the swingarm or if it does not move freely, remove the bearings for inspection (see Chapter 5).

12 With the linkage detached check the bearings for corrosion and wear and failure of the seals, referring to Chapter 5 for details, and clean and re-grease or replace components as required.

Front fork oil change

13 Although there is no set interval for changing the fork oil, the oil will degrade over a period of time and lose its damping qualities. Refer to Chapter 5 for details of front fork removal, oil draining and refilling. The forks do not need to be completely disassembled to change the oil.

Rear suspension bearing lubrication

14 Over a considerable mileage, and if the bike is often ridden in wet conditions (or through incorrect use of jet washers) the seals may fail and allow dirt and water to get in, in which case the grease in the bearings will be washed out or will harden.

15 At the specified service interval remove the shock absorber, linkage and swingarm and clean and re-grease the bearings (see Chapter 5).

18 Steering head bearings

Freeplay check and adjustment

1 Steering head bearings can become dented, rough or loose during normal use of the machine. In extreme cases, worn or loose steering head bearings can cause steering wobble – a condition that is potentially dangerous.

Check

2 Place the motorcycle on a stand so the front wheel is off the ground. Always make sure that the bike is properly supported and secure.

3 Point the front wheel straight-ahead and slowly move the handlebars from lock to lock. Any dents, tightness or roughness in the bearing races will be felt – if the bearings are too tight the bars will not move smoothly and freely. Again point the wheel straight-ahead, and tap the front of the wheel to one side. The wheel should 'fall' under its own weight to the limit of its lock, indicating that the bearings are not too tight (take into account the restriction that cables, hoses and wiring may have). Check for similar movement to the other side.

4 Next, grasp the bottom of the forks and gently pull and push them forward and backward and side-to-side (see illustration). Any looseness or freeplay in the steering head bearings will be felt as front-to-rear or side-to-side movement of the forks. If play is felt, adjust the bearings as described below.

5 If a spring balance (graduated 100 to 600 grams) is available, the bearing loading can be checked by applying a measured pull on the handlebar ends. Attach one end of the balance to the outer end of a handlebar grip (not the end weight) and set the front wheel in the straight-ahead position. Now pull on the balance, making sure it is at right angles to the handlebar (see illustration). If the bearing is adjusted correctly, the steering should start to turn when between 200 and 500 grams register on the balance scale. Connect the balance to the other handlebar and check the loading again – the result should be the same. If the loading is not within the specified range adjust the bearings – if the reading is below 200 grams, the steering head is too loose, if the reading is above 500 grams the steering head is too tight.

> **HAYNES HiNT** *Make sure you are not mistaking any movement between the bike and stand, or between the stand and the ground, for freeplay in the bearings. Do not pull and push the forks too hard – a gentle movement is all that is needed. Freeplay between the fork tubes due to worn bushes can also be misinterpreted as steering head bearing play – do not confuse the two.*

Adjustment

Special tool: *Either the Suzuki special tool (part No. 09910-60611), equivalent suitably sized C-spanner, or a suitable punch/drift is necessary for this procedure – see Step 9.*

6 As a precaution against accidental damage, on 2004 to 2011 DL models remove the fairing side panels and instrument surround (see Chapter 7), on 2011-on DL models remove the complete fairing assembly (see Chapter 7), and on all models remove the fuel tank (see Chapter 4).

18.4 Feeling for play in the steering head bearings

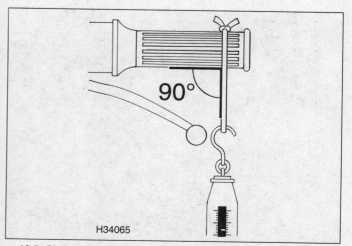
18.5 Checking steering head bearing pre-load using a spring balance

18.7a Slacken the steering stem nut (arrowed)…

18.7b …and the fork clamp bolt (arrowed) on each side

18.8 Slacken the locknut

> **HAYNES HINT**
> *Protect the finish of the steering stem nut by sticking a layer of making tape around it.*

7 Wrap a layer of masking tape around the steering stem nut to prevent marking it. Slacken the nut **(see illustration)**. Slacken the fork clamp bolts in the top yoke **(see illustration)**.
8 On DL models slacken the bearing adjuster locknut (the upper of the two nuts) using a suitable C-spanner or a drift located in one of the notches of the nut **(see illustration)**.
9 Using a suitable C-spanner or a drift located in one of the notches of the adjuster nut, slacken the nut slightly until pressure is just released, then tighten it until all freeplay is removed, yet the steering is able to move freely as described in Steps 3 and 4 **(see illustrations)**. The object is to set the adjuster nut so that the bearings are under a very light loading, just enough to remove any freeplay, but not so much that the steering does not move freely from side to side as described in the check procedure above. If you have the spring balance, set the adjuster nut so that

the steering starts to move at a load of around 350 grams.
Caution: Take great care not to apply excessive pressure because this will cause premature failure of the bearings.
10 If the bearings cannot be correctly adjusted, disassemble the steering head and check the bearings and races (see Chapter 6).
11 On DL models tighten the adjuster locknut.
12 Tighten the steering stem nut, then the fork clamp bolts **(see illustrations 18.7a and b)** – if you have a torque wrench apply the torque settings specified at the beginning of the Chapter, but note that you will have to displace the handlebars from the yoke and move them forwards to get on the stem nut (see Chapter 5 – there is no need to remove any of the assemblies from the bars or disconnect any cables, hoses or wiring).
13 Check the bearing adjustment as described above and re-adjust if necessary.

18.9a Adjusting the bearings on DL models

18.9b Adjusting the bearings on SFV models

14 Install the handlebars if displaced (see Chapter 5), and the fuel tank (see Chapter 4) and fairing panels (see Chapter 7) if removed.

Lubrication

15 Over a considerable time the grease in the bearings will be dispersed or will harden allowing the ingress of dirt and water.

16 At the specified service interval remove the steering stem and clean and re-grease the bearings (see Chapter 5).

19 Valve clearances

Special tool: *A set of feeler gauges is necessary for this job (see illustration 19.7).*

1 The engine must be completely cool, so let the machine sit overnight before beginning.

2 Remove the valve covers (see Chapter 2).

3 Remove the spark plugs (see Section 5).

4 Unscrew the crankshaft end cap and the timing mark inspection cap from the alternator cover **(see illustration)**. Note that a new O-ring and sealing washer should be used.

5 Make a chart or sketch of all valve positions so that a note of each clearance can be made against the relevant valve.

6 Start with the front cylinder. Turn the engine using a 17 mm socket on the alternator rotor bolt, turning it in an anti-clockwise direction only until the line next to the 'F' mark on the rotor is in the centre of the inspection hole **(see illustrations)**. At this point make sure that the cylinder is at TDC (top dead centre) on the compression stroke (and not the exhaust stroke) by checking the positions of the camshaft lobes – they should be pointing away from each other. If not, turn the engine anti-clockwise through one full turn (360°) until the 'F' line again is in the centre of the hole. The camshaft lobes will now be correctly positioned.

7 With the engine in this position all the valves will be closed. Check the clearances on the front cylinder intake and exhaust valves by inserting a feeler gauge of the same thickness as the correct valve clearance (see Specifications, noting that there is a difference between intake and exhaust) between the base of each camshaft lobe and the top of the cam follower on each valve and check that it is a firm sliding fit – you should feel a slight drag when the you pull the gauge out **(see illustration)**. If not, use the feeler gauges to obtain the exact clearance. Record the measured clearance on the chart.

8 To check the rear cylinder valve clearances rotate the engine 270° (3/4 turn) anti-clockwise

19.4 Unscrew the crankshaft end cap (A) and timing inspection cap (B)

19.6a Turn the engine anti-clockwise using the bolt...

19.6b ...until the line next to the F mark is central in the hole

19.7 Insert the feeler gauge between the base of the lobe and the top of the follower as shown

19.8 Turn the engine until the line next to the R mark is central in the hole

using the 17 mm socket on the alternator rotor bolt **(see illustration 19.6a)** until the line next to the 'R' mark on the rotor is in the centre of the inspection hole **(see illustration)**. The camshaft lobes will be pointing up and slightly towards each other. Check and adjust the valve clearance as described in Step 7.

9 When all clearances have been measured and charted, identify whether the clearance on any valve falls outside the specified range. If any do, the shim must be changed for one of a thickness that will restore the correct clearance.

10 Shim changing requires removal of the camshaft(s) (see Chapter 2). There is no need to remove both camshafts if shims from only one side of the cylinder need changing. Place rags over the spark plug holes and the cam chain tunnel to prevent a shim from dropping into the engine on removal. Work on one valve at a time to prevent the possibility of mixing up the followers, which must be returned to their original location. If you want to remove more than one shim and follower at a time, store them in a marked container or bag, denoting which cylinder and which valve the follower and shim are from, so that they do not get mixed up.

11 With the camshaft removed, remove the cam follower of the valve in question, then retrieve the shim from the inside of the follower **(see illustrations)**. The follower is best removed with a magnet or using the suction created by a valve grinding tool, but long nosed pliers can be used with care. If the shim is not in the follower, pick it out of the top of the valve spring retainer using either a magnet, a screwdriver with a dab of grease on it (the shim will stick to the grease), or a very small screwdriver and a pair of pliers **(see illustration)**. Do not allow the shim to fall into the engine.

12 A size mark should be stamped on one face of the shim – a shim marked 175 is 1.75 mm thick. If the mark is not visible measure the shim thickness using a micrometer **(see illustration)**. It is recommended that the shim be measured anyway to check whether it has worn. Shims are available in 0.05 mm increments from 1.20 to 2.20 mm. If the shim

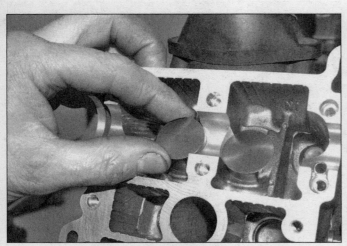

19.11a Lift the follower out...

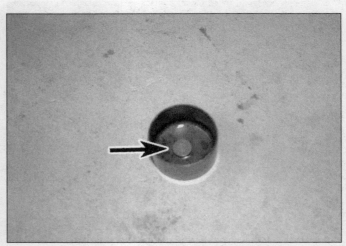

19.11b ...and retrieve the shim (arrowed) from inside it...

19.11c ...or from the top of the valve

19.12 Check the thickness of the shim using a micrometer

MEASURED TAPPET CLEARANCE (mm)	PRESENT SHIM SIZE (mm) 1.20	1.25	1.30	1.35	1.40	1.45	1.50	1.55	1.60	1.65	1.70	1.75	1.80	1.85	1.90	1.95	2.00	2.05	2.10	2.15	2.20
0.00-0.04	■	■	1.20	1.25	1.30	1.35	1.40	1.45	1.50	1.55	1.60	1.65	1.70	1.75	1.80	1.85	1.90	1.95	2.00	2.05	2.10
0.05-0.09	■	1.20	1.25	1.30	1.35	1.40	1.45	1.50	1.55	1.60	1.65	1.70	1.75	1.80	1.85	1.90	1.95	2.00	2.05	2.10	2.15
0.10-0.20	SPECIFIED CLEARANCE/NO ADJUSTMENT REQUIRED																				
0.21-0.25	1.30	1.35	1.40	1.45	1.50	1.55	1.60	1.65	1.70	1.75	1.80	1.85	1.90	1.95	2.00	2.05	2.10	2.15	2.20	2.20	
0.26-0.30	1.35	1.40	1.45	1.50	1.55	1.60	1.65	1.70	1.75	1.80	1.85	1.90	1.95	2.00	2.05	2.10	2.15	2.20			
0.31-0.35	1.40	1.45	1.50	1.55	1.60	1.65	1.70	1.75	1.80	1.85	1.90	1.95	2.00	2.05	2.10	2.15	2.20				
0.36-0.40	1.45	1.50	1.55	1.60	1.65	1.70	1.75	1.80	1.85	1.90	1.95	2.00	2.05	2.10	2.15	2.20					
0.41-0.45	1.50	1.55	1.60	1.65	1.70	1.75	1.80	1.85	1.90	1.95	2.00	2.05	2.10	2.15	2.20						
0.46-0.50	1.55	1.60	1.65	1.70	1.75	1.80	1.85	1.90	1.95	2.00	2.05	2.10	2.15	2.20							
0.51-0.55	1.60	1.65	1.70	1.75	1.80	1.85	1.90	1.95	2.00	2.05	2.10	2.15	2.20								
0.56-0.60	1.65	1.70	1.75	1.80	1.85	1.90	1.95	2.00	2.05	2.10	2.15	2.20									
0.61-0.65	1.70	1.75	1.80	1.85	1.90	1.95	2.00	2.05	2.10	2.15	2.20										
0.66-0.70	1.75	1.80	1.85	1.90	1.95	2.00	2.05	2.10	2.15	2.20											
0.71-0.75	1.80	1.85	1.90	1.95	2.00	2.05	2.10	2.15	2.20												
0.76-0.80	1.85	1.90	1.95	2.00	2.05	2.10	2.15	2.20													
0.81-0.85	1.90	1.95	2.00	2.05	2.10	2.15	2.20														
0.86-0.90	1.95	2.00	2.05	2.10	2.15	2.20															
0.91-0.95	2.00	2.05	2.10	2.15	2.20																
0.96-1.00	2.05	2.10	2.15	2.20																	
1.01-1.05	2.10	2.15	2.20																		
1.06-1.10	2.15	2.20																			
1.11-1.15	2.20																				

H31236

19.13a Shim selection chart – intake valves

MEASURED TAPPET CLEARANCE (mm)	PRESENT SHIM SIZE (mm) 1.20	1.25	1.30	1.35	1.40	1.45	1.50	1.55	1.60	1.65	1.70	1.75	1.80	1.85	1.90	1.95	2.00	2.05	2.10	2.15	2.20
0.05-0.09	■	■	■	1.20	1.25	1.30	1.35	1.40	1.45	1.50	1.55	1.60	1.65	1.70	1.75	1.80	1.85	1.90	1.95	2.00	2.05
0.10-0.14	■	■	1.20	1.25	1.30	1.35	1.40	1.45	1.50	1.55	1.60	1.65	1.70	1.75	1.80	1.85	1.90	1.95	2.00	2.05	2.10
0.15-0.19	■	1.20	1.25	1.30	1.35	1.40	1.45	1.50	1.55	1.60	1.65	1.70	1.75	1.80	1.85	1.90	1.95	2.00	2.05	2.10	2.15
0.20-0.30	SPECIFIED CLEARANCE/NO ADJUSTMENT REQUIRED																				
0.31-0.35	1.30	1.35	1.40	1.45	1.50	1.55	1.60	1.65	1.70	1.75	1.80	1.85	1.90	1.95	2.00	2.05	2.10	2.15	2.20	2.20	
0.36-0.40	1.35	1.40	1.45	1.50	1.55	1.60	1.65	1.70	1.75	1.80	1.85	1.90	1.95	2.00	2.05	2.10	2.15	2.20			
0.41-0.45	1.40	1.45	1.50	1.55	1.60	1.65	1.70	1.75	1.80	1.85	1.90	1.95	2.00	2.05	2.10	2.15	2.20				
0.46-0.50	1.45	1.50	1.55	1.60	1.65	1.70	1.75	1.80	1.85	1.90	1.95	2.00	2.05	2.10	2.15	2.20					
0.51-0.55	1.50	1.55	1.60	1.65	1.70	1.75	1.80	1.85	1.90	1.95	2.00	2.05	2.10	2.15	2.20						
0.56-0.60	1.55	1.60	1.65	1.70	1.75	1.80	1.85	1.90	1.95	2.00	2.05	2.10	2.15	2.20							
0.61-0.65	1.60	1.65	1.70	1.75	1.80	1.85	1.90	1.95	2.00	2.05	2.10	2.15	2.20								
0.66-0.70	1.65	1.70	1.75	1.80	1.85	1.90	1.95	2.00	2.05	2.10	2.15	2.20									
0.71-0.75	1.70	1.75	1.80	1.85	1.90	1.95	2.00	2.05	2.10	2.15	2.20										
0.76-0.80	1.75	1.80	1.85	1.90	1.95	2.00	2.05	2.10	2.15	2.20											
0.81-0.85	1.80	1.85	1.90	1.95	2.00	2.05	2.10	2.15	2.20												
0.86-0.90	1.85	1.90	1.95	2.00	2.05	2.10	2.15	2.20													
0.91-0.95	1.90	1.95	2.00	2.05	2.10	2.15	2.20														
0.96-1.00	1.95	2.00	2.05	2.10	2.15	2.20															
1.01-1.05	2.00	2.05	2.10	2.15	2.20																
1.06-1.10	2.05	2.10	2.15	2.20																	
1.11-1.15	2.10	2.15	2.20																		
1.16-1.20	2.15	2.20																			
1.21-1.25	2.20																				

H31237

19.13b Shim selection chart – exhaust valves

thickness is less than its denomination, this must be taken into account when selecting a new shim.

13 Using the appropriate shim selection chart, find where the measured valve clearance and existing shim thickness values intersect and read off the shim size required **(see illustrations). Note:** *If the existing shim is marked with a number not ending in 0 or 5, round it up or down as appropriate to the nearest number ending in 0 or 5 so that the chart can be used.* **Note:** *If the required replacement shim is greater than 2.20 mm (the largest available), the valve is probably not seating correctly due to a build-up of carbon deposits and should be checked and cleaned or resurfaced as required (see Chapter 2).*

14 Obtain the replacement shim, then lubricate it with molybdenum disulphide oil (a 50/50 mixture of molybdenum disulphide grease and engine oil) and fit it into the recess in the top of the valve spring retainer with the size mark facing up **(see illustration)**.

15 Check that the shim is correctly seated, then lubricate the follower with molybdenum disulphide oil and fit it onto the valve,

19.14 Fit the shim into its recess...

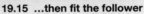

19.15 ...then fit the follower

19.17 Fit the caps using a new washer (A) and O-ring (B)

making sure it fits squarely in its bore **(see illustration)**. Repeat the process for any other valves until the clearances are correct, then install the camshafts (see Chapter 2).

16 Rotate the crankshaft anti-clockwise several turns to seat the new shim(s) **(see illustration 19.6a)**, then check the clearances again.

17 Install all disturbed components in a reverse of the removal sequence, referring to the relevant Chapters. Fit the timing inspection cap using a new sealing washer, and the crankshaft end cap using a new O-ring smeared with grease, and tighten them to the torque settings specified at the beginning of the Chapter **(see illustration)**.

18 Check and adjust the idle speed (see Section 8).

Chapter 2
Engine, clutch and transmission

Contents

Degrees of difficulty

Easy, suitable for novice with little experience	**Fairly easy,** suitable for beginner with some experience	**Fairly difficult,** suitable for competent DIY mechanic	**Difficult,** suitable for experienced DIY mechanic	**Very difficult,** suitable for expert DIY or professional

Specifications

General

Capacity	645 cc
Bore	81.0 mm
Stroke	62.6 mm
Compression ratio	
2004 to 2011 DL models	11.5 to 1
2012-on DL models and all SFV models	11.2 to 1
Cylinder identification	Front cyl No. 1, rear cyl No. 2
Cooling system	Liquid cooled
Clutch	Wet multi-plate
Transmission	Six-speed constant mesh
Final drive	Chain and sprockets

Camshafts

	Standard	Service limit
Intake camshaft lobe height		
2004 to 2011 DL models	35.480 to 35.530 mm	35.18 mm
2012-on DL models	35.480 to 35.550 mm	35.18 mm
SFV models	36.380 to 36.425 mm	36.08 mm
Exhaust camshaft lobe height		
2004 to 2011 models	33.480 to 33.530 mm	33.18 mm
2012-on DL models	33.480 to 33.550 mm	33.18 mm
SFV models	35.680 to 35.725 mm	35.38 mm
Camshaft bearing oil clearance		
2004 to 2011 DL models	0.032 to 0.066 mm	0.150 mm
2012-on DL models and all SFV models	0.027 to 0.069 mm	0.150 mm
Camshaft runout (max)	0.10 mm	
Journal diameter	21.959 to 21.980 mm	
Journal holder internal diameter		
2004 to 2011 DL models	22.012 to 22.025 mm	
2012-on DL models and all SFV models	22.007 to 22.028 mm	

Cylinder head

Warpage (max)	0.05 mm

Valves, guides and springs

Valve clearances	see Chapter 1
Intake valve	
Stem diameter	
2004 to 2011 DL models	4.465 to 4.480 mm
2012-on DL models and all SFV models	4.475 to 4.490 mm
Guide bore diameter	4.500 to 4.512 mm
Stem-to-guide clearance	
2004 to 2011 DL models	0.020 to 0.047 mm
2012-on DL models and all SFV models	0.010 to 0.037 mm
Stem deflection (max – see text)	0.35 mm
Seat width	0.9 to 1.1 mm
Head thickness (min)	0.5 mm
Radial runout at head (max)	0.03 mm
Stem runout (max)	0.05 mm
Spring free lengths (min)	
2004 to 2011 DL models	
Outer spring	39.8 mm
Inner spring	36.8 mm
2012-on DL models and all SFV models	37.1 mm
Exhaust valve	
Stem diameter	4.455 to 4.470 mm
Guide bore diameter	4.500 to 4.512 mm
Stem-to-guide clearance	0.030 to 0.057 mm
Stem deflection (max – see text)	0.35 mm
Seat width	0.9 to 1.1 mm
Head thickness (min)	0.5 mm
Radial runout at head (max)	0.03 mm
Stem runout (max)	0.05 mm
Spring free lengths (min)	
2004 to 2011 DL models	
Outer spring	39.8 mm
Inner spring	36.8 mm
2012-on DL models and all SFV models	37.1 mm

Cylinders

Bore diameter	81.000 to 81.015 mm
Taper (max)	0.05 mm
Ovality (max)	0.05 mm
Warpage (max)	0.05 mm
Cylinder compression	
Standard	185 to 242 psi (13 to 17 Bars)
Service limit	156 psi (11 Bars)
Max. difference between cylinders	28 psi (2 Bars)

Pistons

Piston diameter (measured 20 mm up from skirt, at 90° to piston pin axis)
  Standard
    2004 to 2006 DL models . . . . 80.950 to 80.955 mm
    2007 to 2011 DL models . . . . 80.940 to 80.955 mm
    2012-on DL models and all SFV models . . . . 80.970 to 80.985 mm
  Service limit . . . . 80.88 mm
  Oversize (2004 to 2011 DL models only) . . . . +0.50 mm

	Standard	**Service limit**
Piston-to-bore clearance		
2004 to 2011 DL models	0.055 to 0.065 mm	0.120 mm
2012-on DL models and all SFV models	0.025 to 0.035 mm	0.120 mm
Piston pin diameter	19.992 to 20.000 mm	19.980 mm
Piston pin bore diameter	20.002 to 20.008 mm	20.030 mm
Piston pin-to-bore clearance	0.002 to 0.016 mm	0.05 mm
Connecting rod small-end internal diameter	20.010 to 20.018 mm	20.040 mm
Piston pin-to-connecting rod small-end clearance	0.010 to 0.026 mm	0.06 mm

Piston rings

Ring thickness
  Top ring – 2004 to 2006 DL models . . . . 1.17 to 1.19 mm
  Top ring – 2007 to 2011 DL models . . . . 0.76 to 0.81 mm
  Top ring – 2012-on DL models and all SFV models . . . . 0.76 to 0.81 mm and 1.08 to 1.10 mm
  2nd ring. . . . . 0.97 to 0.99 mm
Groove thickness in piston
  Top ring – 2004 to 2006 DL models . . . . 1.21 to 1.23 mm
  Top ring – 2007 to 2011 DL models . . . . 0.83 to 0.85 mm
  Top ring – 2012-on DL models and all SFV models . . . . 0.83 to 0.85 mm and 1.30 to 1.32 mm
  2nd ring. . . . . 1.01 to 1.03 mm
  Oil ring . . . . 2.01 to 2.03 mm
Ring-to-groove clearance (max)
  Top ring. . . . . 0.180 mm
  2nd ring. . . . . 0.150 mm

End gap (free)	**Top ring**	**2nd ring**
2004 to 2006 DL models		
Standard.	9.5 mm (approx)	11.0 mm (approx)
Service limit	7.6 mm	8.8 mm
2007 DL models		
Standard.	7.0 mm (approx)	11.0 mm (approx)
Service limit	5.6 mm	8.8 mm
2008 to 2011 DL models		
Standard.	7.0 mm (approx)	11.5 mm (approx)
Service limit	5.6 mm	8.8 mm
2012-on DL models and all SFV models		
Standard.	6.5 mm (approx)	9.0 mm (approx)
Service limit	5.2 mm	7.2 mm

End gap (installed)
  2004 to 2007 DL models
    Standard . . . . 0.20 to 0.35 mm
    Service limit . . . . 0.70 mm
  2008 to 2011 DL models
    Standard
      Top ring . . . . 0.20 to 0.30 mm
      2nd ring. . . . . 0.30 to 0.45 mm
    Service limit . . . . 0.70 mm
  2012-on DL models and all SFV models
    Standard . . . . 0.06 to 0.18 mm
    Service limit . . . . 0.50 mm

Lubrication system

Oil type, viscosity and capacity . . . . see Chapter 1
Oil pressure (at main oil gallery plug, with engine warm)
  2004 to 2011 DL models . . . . 14 to 57 psi (1 to 4 Bars)
  2012-on DL models and all SFV models . . . . 28 to 85 psi (2 to 6 Bars)

Crankshaft and main bearings

Main journal diameter. . . . . 41.985 to 42.000 mm
Runout (max) . . . . 0.05 mm

Connecting rods and big-end bearings

Big-end side clearance
    Standard . . . . 0.170 to 0.320 mm
    Service limit . . . . 0.50 mm
Big-end width . . . . 20.95 to 21.00 mm
Crankpin width . . . . 42.17 to 42.22 mm
Big-end bearing oil clearance
    Standard . . . . 0.032 to 0.056 mm
    Service limit . . . . 0.08 mm
Crankpin diameter . . . . 37.976 to 38.000 mm
For connecting rod small-end specifications see under 'Pistons'.

Clutch

Friction plate
    Quantity 7
    Thickness
        Standard . . . . 2.92 to 3.08 mm
        Service limit . . . . 2.62 mm
    Tab width
        Standard . . . . 13.7 to 13.8 mm
        Service limit . . . . 12.9 mm
Plain plate (all models)
    Quantity 6
    Warpage (max) . . . . 0.10 mm
Springs
    Free length . . . . 53.1 mm
    Service limit . . . . 50.5 mm

Selector drum and forks

Selector fork end thickness . . . . 5.3 to 5.4 mm
Selector fork groove width in gear . . . . 5.5 to 5.6 mm
Fork-to-groove clearance
    Standard . . . . 0.1 to 0.3 mm
    Service limit . . . . 0.5 mm

Transmission

Primary reduction . . . . 2.088 to 1 (71/34)
Final reduction
    DL models . . . . 3.133 to 1 (47/15)
    SFV models . . . . 3.066 to 1 (46/15)
1st gear . . . . 2.461 to 1 (32/13)
2nd gear . . . . 1.777 to 1 (32/18)
3rd gear . . . . 1.380 to 1 (29/21)
4th gear . . . . 1.125 to 1 (27/24)
5th gear . . . . 0.961 to 1 (25/26)
6th gear . . . . 0.851 to 1 (23/27)

Torque settings

Alternator cover bolts . . . . 10 Nm
Alternator rotor bolt
    2004 to 2011 DL models . . . . 120 Nm
    2012-on DL models and all SFV models . . . . 140 Nm
Cam chain tensioner blade pivot bolts . . . . 10 Nm
Cam chain tensioner cap bolt . . . . 23 Nm
Cam chain tensioner mounting bolts . . . . 10 Nm
Camshaft holder bolts . . . . 10 Nm
Clutch nut . . . . 50 Nm
Clutch spring bolts . . . . 10 Nm
Connecting rod bolts
    Stage 1 torque . . . . 21 Nm
    Stage 2 angle . . . . 90° (1/4 turn)
Crankcase bolts
    8 mm bolts . . . . 26 Nm
    6 mm bolts . . . . 11 Nm
Crankshaft end cap . . . . 11 Nm
Cylinder block nuts . . . . 10 Nm

Torque settings (continued)

Cylinder head bolts
  10 mm bolts
    Initial setting . . . . 25 Nm
    Final setting . . . . 42 Nm
  6 mm bolts . . . . 10 Nm
Engine mounting bolts
  DL models
    Adjuster bolts . . . . 12 Nm
    Adjuster bolt locknuts. . . . . 45 Nm
    Engine bracket bolts. . . . . 35 Nm
    Front mounting bolt nut . . . . 93 Nm
    Upper and lower rear mounting bolt nuts. . . . . 55 Nm
    Spacer pinch bolt . . . . 25 Nm
  SFV models
    Front mounting bolts . . . . 55 Nm
    Middle mounting bolt nut . . . . 93 Nm
    Upper and lower rear mounting bolt nuts. . . . . 55 Nm
Gearchange mechanism centralising spring locating pin . . . . 19 Nm
Gearchange selector drum cam plate bolt. . . . . 13 Nm
Gearchange stopper arm bolt . . . . 10 Nm
Main oil gallery plug
  2004 to 2011 models . . . . 18 Nm
  2012-on DL models and all SFV models . . . . 21 Nm
Oil cooler
  2004 to 2011 DL models
    Cooler hose banjo bolts . . . . 23 Nm
    Cooler mounting bolts . . . . 10 Nm
  2012-on DL models and all SFV models
    Cooler mounting bolt . . . . 70 Nm
Oil gallery jet bolt . . . . 18 Nm
Oil pressure relief valve . . . . 27 Nm
Oil spray pipe screw. . . . . 8 Nm
Oil strainer plate bolts . . . . 10 Nm
Piston oil jet retainer bolts . . . . 10 Nm
Primary drive gear bolt. . . . . 70 Nm
Timing mark inspection cap. . . . . 23 Nm
Starter clutch bolts. . . . . 25 Nm
Valve cover bolts . . . . 14 Nm

1 General information

The engine/transmission unit is a liquid-cooled 90° V-twin, fitted parallel with the frame. The engine has four valves per cylinder, operated by double overhead camshafts. The camshafts are chain driven off the crankshaft.

The engine/transmission unit is constructed in aluminium alloy and the crankcase is divided vertically. The crankcase incorporates a wet sump, pressure fed lubrication system, and houses an oil pump that is gear driven off the clutch housing. The water pump is gear driven off the crankshaft. The one-piece forged crankshaft runs in two main bearings. The left-hand end of the crankshaft carries the alternator rotor. The ignition timing triggers are incorporated in the alternator rotor.

The clutch is of the wet multi-plate type and is gear driven off the crankshaft. The transmission is of the six-speed constant mesh type. Final drive to the rear wheel is via chain and sprockets.

2 Component access

Operations possible with the engine in the frame

The components and assemblies listed below can be removed without having to remove the engine/transmission assembly from the frame. If however, a number of areas require attention at the same time, removal of the engine is recommended.

Oil cooler
Valve covers
Cam chain tensioners
Camshafts, cam chains and blades
Throttle bodies
Cylinder heads
Cylinders
Pistons
Water pump
Clutch
Gearchange mechanism
Primary drive gear
Oil pump
Alternator
Starter clutch
Starter motor
Oil pressure switch
Gear position switch

Operations requiring engine removal

It is necessary to remove the engine/transmission assembly from the frame to gain access to the following components.

Oil strainer and oil pressure relief valve
Crankshaft and bearings
Connecting rods and bearings
Transmission shafts
Selector drum and forks

3 Engine wear assessment

Cylinder compression check

Special tool: *A compression gauge is needed. You are best off using the type with a threaded hose and adaptor to fit the spark plug holes – there are cheaper ones that have a coned rubber tip that is pressed onto the spark plug hole, but they are not as good, especially when access is restricted. Depending on the outcome of the initial test, a squirt-type oil can may also be needed.*

1 Poor engine performance can be caused by leaking valves, incorrect valve clearances, a leaking head gasket, or worn pistons, piston rings or cylinder walls. A cylinder compression check will highlight these conditions and can also indicate the presence of excessive carbon deposits in the cylinder heads, and a leakdown test (for which special equipment is needed – consult a Suzuki dealer) will pinpoint the actual cause(s) of the problem.

2 Start by making sure the valve clearances are correctly set (see Chapter 1). Also make sure the battery is well charged.

3 Run the engine until it is at normal operating temperature.

4 On 2004 to 2006 DL models remove both spark plugs (see Chapter 1). On all other models disconnect the plug caps from all four spark plugs, and remove the outer plug from each cylinder (see Chapter 1).

5 Make sure the gauge hose/adapter threads are the same as the spark plug – 10 mm diameter, 1.0 mm pitch. Fit the gauge into the vacant spark plug hole of the front cylinder **(see illustration)**.

6 With the ignition switch ON, the kill switch set to RUN, the clutch lever pulled in, and the throttle held fully open, turn the engine over on the starter motor until the gauge reading has built up and stabilised **(see illustration)**.

7 Compare the reading on the gauge to the cylinder compression figures specified at the beginning of the Chapter.

8 Repeat the test for the rear cylinder.

9 If a reading is low, it could be due to a worn cylinder bore, piston or rings, failure of the head gasket, or worn valve seats. To determine which is the cause, pour a small quantity of engine oil into the spark plug hole to seal the rings, then repeat the compression test. If the figures are noticeably higher the cause is worn cylinder, piston or rings. If there is no change the cause is a leaking head gasket or worn valve seats.

10 If the reading is high there could be a build-up of carbon deposits in the combustion chambers. Remove the cylinder heads and scrape all deposits off the pistons and the cylinder heads (Section 12).

Leak-down (cylinder leakage) test

11 A leak down or 'cylinder leakage' test is similar to a compression test in that it tells you how well a cylinder is sealing, but it does so by testing how much pressure is lost through leakage, as opposed to how much pressure is created through compression. Many professionals prefer a leak-down test to a compression test as it more accurately pin-points the cause of the problem before any disassembly is done, as it is easy to tell where the leakage is occurring. Generally however the required equipment is more expensive than for a compression test and a source of compressed air is essential. If you think a test is needed take the bike to a suitably equipped dealer or workshop. If you decide to purchase your own equipment follow the manufacturer's instructions.

12 A leak-down test can also be used in conjunction with a compression test to diagnose other kinds of problems, such as a faulty valve train component, incorrect valve timing, faulty ignition or fuel delivery problems.

Engine oil pressure check

Special tool: *An oil pressure gauge is required to perform this test, along with an adapter that threads into the main oil gallery.*

13 An oil pressure check can provide useful information about the condition of the engine's lubrication system, and can also be used as an indicator of excessive wear in the engine if no specific faults with the lubrication or pressure warning system are found.

14 The oil pressure warning light should come on when the ignition switch is turned ON and extinguish a few seconds after the engine is started. If the light stays on, or comes on whilst the engine is running, low oil pressure is indicated – stop the engine immediately and carry out an oil level check *(see Pre-ride checks)*. If the oil level is correct, drain the oil and remove the filter (see Chapter 1), and check the drained oil and the filter for sludge that reduces its ability to flow. In order to check the pick-up strainer for blockage the engine must be removed from the frame and the crankcase split, so it is obviously best to check the pressure first. Note that it is possible that the cause of the light staying on or coming on while the engine is running is an electrical fault, so make sure the oil pressure switch, warning light and circuit are all functioning correctly (see Chapter 8). If all appears good an oil pressure check must be carried out.

15 Support the bike upright and have some rags to catch and mop up any residual oil that gets lost in between removing the gallery plug and fitting the gauge.

16 Run the engine until it is at normal operating temperature.

17 Unscrew the main oil gallery plug, located on the left-hand side of the engine just behind the oil filter **(see illustration)**. Screw the gauge adapter in its place. Connect the oil pressure gauge to the adapter.

18 Check the oil level (see *Pre-ride checks*).

19 Start the engine and run it at 3000 rpm whilst watching the gauge reading. The oil pressure should be similar to that given in the Specifications at the start of this Chapter – note that if the engine is not at normal temperature the reading will be high.

20 If the pressure is significantly lower than the standard, either the pick-up strainer is blocked, the pressure relief valve is stuck open, the oil pump or its drive mechanism is faulty, or there is other engine damage. Also make sure the correct grade oil is being used.

3.5 Select the correct adapter and thread it into the plug hole

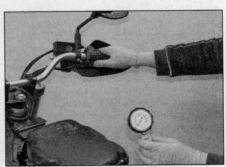

3.6 Checking cylinder compression

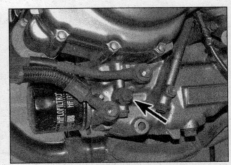

3.17 Main oil gallery plug (arrowed)

4.8a Pull the caps off the plugs

4.8b Move the heat shield out of the way

4.9 Detach the hose from each reed valve

Begin diagnosis by checking the oil strainer and relief valve, then check the oil pump (Section 21). If those items check out okay, and all passages are clear, chances are the bearing oil clearances are excessive and the engine needs to be overhauled.

21 If the pressure is too high, either an oil passage or the oil filter is clogged, the relief valve is stuck closed or the wrong grade of oil is being used.

22 If the pressure is as it should be, and if not already done, then check the oil pressure switch, warning light and circuit (see Chapter 8).

23 Stop the engine and let it cool, then remove the gauge and adapter and fit the main oil gallery plug using a new sealing washer, and tighten it to the torque setting specified at the beginning of the Chapter for your model.

 Warning: Be careful when removing the pressure gauge adapter as the exhaust, the engine and the oil itself can cause severe burns.

24 Check the oil level (see *Pre-ride checks*).

4 Engine removal and installation

Caution: The engine is very heavy. Engine removal and installation should be carried out with the aid of at least one assistant;

personal injury or damage could occur if the engine falls or is dropped.
Note: *As each mounting bolt is removed store it along with any related washer, nut and spacer to avoid parts getting mixed up, making installation easier. If you are removing the engine for an overhaul it is best to remove the alternator and clutch covers and slacken the alternator rotor bolt, primary drive gear bolt and clutch nut with the engine still in the frame – refer to the relevant Sections in this Chapter.*

Removal

1 Support the bike upright on level ground, and tie the front brake on. Work can be made easier by raising the machine to a suitable working height on an hydraulic ramp or a suitable platform. Make sure the bike is secure and will not topple over (also see *Tools and Workshop Tips* in the Reference section).

2 Remove the seat. On 2004 to 2011 DL models remove the fairing side panels, and on later DL models remove the complete fairing assembly; on all DL models remove the left-hand side cover, and where fitted the crashbars and belly pan (see Chapter). On SFV models remove the side covers and radiator covers (see Chapter 7).

3 Disconnect the negative (–ve) lead from the battery (see Chapter 8).

4 If the engine is dirty, particularly around its mountings, wash it thoroughly. This makes work much easier and rule out the possibility of caked on lumps of dirt falling into some vital component.

5 Drain the engine oil and the coolant (see Chapter 1). If required remove the oil filter (see Chapter 1). On 2004 to 2011 DL models remove the oil cooler with its hoses (Section 6).

6 Remove the fuel tank, air filter housing, throttle bodies and exhaust system (see Chapter 4). Plug the engine intake ducts with clean rag.

7 Remove the radiator along with its hoses, noting their routing (see Chapter 3). Remove the thermostat housing along with its hoses (see Chapter 3). Remove the coolant reservoir (see Chapter 3). Detach and remove any remaining coolant hoses as required according to what work is to be carried out, noting their positions and routing.

8 Pull the cap off each spark plug **(see illustration)**. Release any clamps securing the HT leads to the engine. On SFV models displace the heat shield from the rear cylinder valve cover **(see illustration)**.

9 On 2004 to 2011 DL models detach the PAIR hoses from the valve covers and remove the hoses **(see illustration)**.

10 Disconnect the alternator and CKP sensor wiring connectors **(see illustrations)**. Feed the wiring down to the alternator, noting its routing and releasing any ties.

4.10a Alternator and CKP sensor connectors (arrowed) – DL

4.10b Alternator connector (arrowed)...

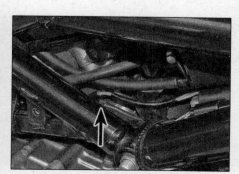

4.10c ...and CKP sensor connector (arrowed) – SFV

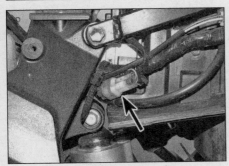

4.11a GP switch connector (arrowed) –
2004 to 2011 DL

4.11b GP switch connector (arrowed) –
2012-on DL

4.11c GP switch connector (arrowed) –
SFV

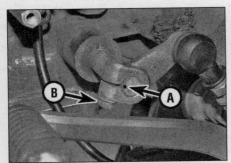

4.12a Alignment mark (A), gearchange arm
pinch bolt (B) – DL

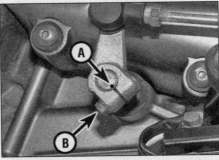

4.12b Alignment mark (A), gearchange
arm pinch bolt (B) – SFV

11 Disconnect the gear position switch wiring connector **(see illustrations)**.

12 Make an alignment mark between the slit in the gearchange linkage arm and the shaft, then unscrew the pinch bolt and slide the arm off **(see illustrations)**.

13 On 2004 to 2011 DL models remove the front sprocket cover (see Chapter 6). Disconnect the clutch cable from the release mechanism (Section 18). Remove the front sprocket (see Chapter 6) – after removing the sprocket fit the release mechanism back onto the engine to protect the seal and pushrod.

14 On 2012-on DL models and all SFV models remove the front sprocket outer cover (see Chapter 6). Remove the sidestand switch (see Chapter 8). Remove the speed sensor (see Chapter 4). Remove the front sprocket (see Chapter 6). Disconnect the clutch cable from the release mechanism (Section 18).

15 Disconnect the starter motor lead **(see illustrations)**. Remove the starter motor if required (see Chapter 8).

16 Disconnect the oil pressure switch wire **(see illustration)**.

17 Disconnect the engine earth wiring connector – locate it by tracing the black/white wire connected to the battery earth lead.

18 On DL models unscrew the footrest bracket bolts, displace the footrest bracket/brake pedal assembly and swivel it sideways so the master cylinder pushrod remains in line **(see illustrations)**.

4.15a Starter lead nut (arrowed) – 2004 to
2011 DL

4.15b Starter lead nut (arrowed) – 2012-on
DL and all SFV

4.16 Undo the screw and detach the wire

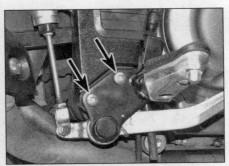

4.18a Unscrew the bolts (arrowed)...

4.18b ...and displace the assembly as
shown so the pedal is clear of the engine

4.20 Unscrew the nut (arrowed) then withdraw the bolt

4.21 Unscrew the locknut (arrowed) using a peg spanner

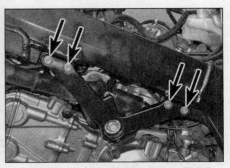

4.22 Unscrew the bolts (arrowed) and remove the bracket

19 Position a hydraulic or mechanical jack under the engine with a block of wood between them. Make sure the jack is centrally positioned so the engine will not topple in any direction when the last mounting bolt is removed. Raise the jack to take the weight of the engine, but make sure it is not lifting the bike and taking the weight of that as well. The idea is to support the engine so that there is no pressure on any of the mounting bolts once they have been slackened, so they can be easily withdrawn.

DL models

Special tool: *The Suzuki peg spanner (part No. 09940-14990) or a suitable equivalent (that can be made by cutting pegs into the rim of a 26 mm socket) is required to slacken and tighten the adjuster bolt locknuts.*
Note: *The engine mounting bolt nuts are self-locking and should only be used once – use new nuts when refitting the engine.*
20 Unscrew the nut on the right-hand end of the front mounting bolt **(see illustration)**. Withdraw the bolt.
21 Unscrew the locknut on the front mounting adjuster using the Suzuki peg spanner or equivalent **(see illustration)**. Now unscrew

4.23 Unscrew the nut (arrowed)

4.24 Unscrew the locknut (arrowed) using the peg spanner

the adjuster, leaving it flush with the inside of the bracket.
22 Remove the engine bracket from the left-hand side, disconnecting the coil wiring connector(s) and noting the HT lead routing **(see illustration)**.
23 Unscrew the nut on the right-hand end of the lower rear mounting bolt **(see illustration)**. Withdraw the bolt.
24 Unscrew the locknut on the lower rear mounting adjuster using the peg spanner

(see illustration). Now unscrew the adjuster, leaving it flush with the inside of the frame.
25 Check that the engine is properly supported by the jack. Release any hoses and wiring secured to the engine but not coming away with it.
26 Slacken the pinch bolt holding the upper rear mounting bolt spacer **(see illustration)**.
27 Hold the engine and unscrew and remove the upper rear mounting bolt **(see illustration)**.

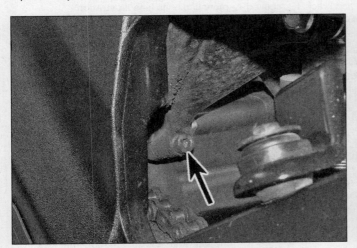

4.26 Slacken the pinch bolt (arrowed)

4.27 Unscrew the upper rear bolt (arrowed)

4.29 Unscrew the nuts (arrowed)

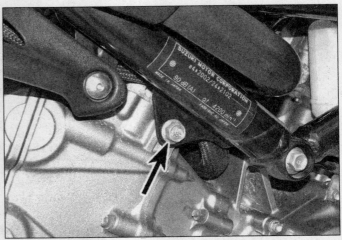

4.30a Front mounting bolt (arrowed), left-hand side

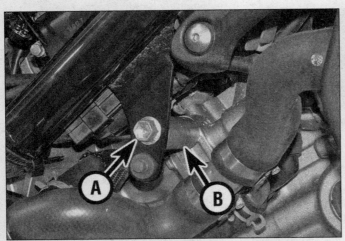

4.30b Front mounting bolt (A) and spacer (B), right-hand side

4.32a Withdraw the upper rear bolt (arrowed)...

28 The engine can now be removed from the frame (see *Caution* above). Check that all wiring, cables and hoses are free and clear, then carefully lower the jack a bit and manoeuvre the engine as required to clear the frame, slipping the drive chain off the output shaft as you do. Fully lower the jack, then with the aid of an assistant remove the jack from under the engine and remove the engine from the left-hand side. Remove the adjusters and spacer from the frame and bracket if required, noting which fits where and how they fit.

SFV models

Note: *The engine mounting bolt nuts are self-locking and should only be used once – use new nuts when refitting the engine.*

29 Unscrew the nuts on the right-hand ends of the upper and lower rear and middle mounting bolts **(see illustration)**.
30 Unscrew the front mounting bolt on each side and remove the spacer from between the engine and frame on the right **(see illustration)**.
31 Check that the engine is properly supported by the jack. Release any hoses and wiring secured to the engine but not coming away with it.
32 Hold the engine and withdraw the upper and lower rear and middle mounting bolts **(see illustrations)**.
33 The engine can now be removed from the frame (see *Caution* above). Check that all wiring, cables and hoses are free and clear, then carefully lower the jack a bit and manoeuvre the engine as required to clear the frame, slipping the drive chain off the output shaft as you do. Fully lower the jack, then with the aid of an assistant remove the jack from under the engine and remove the engine from the left-hand side.

4.32b ...the lower rear bolt (arrowed)...

4.32c ...and the middle bolt (arrowed)...

Installation

Note: *Smear grease onto the bolt shafts to prevent corrosion that could lead to them seizing in the engine.*

34 On DL models, if removed, fit the adjusters into the frame and bracket, threading them in from the outside until they are flush with the inside. Also fit the spacer for the upper rear mounting bolt into the lug on the left-hand side of the frame.

35 Manoeuvre the engine into position under the frame and lift it onto the jack. Raise the engine, taking care not to catch any part of the engine on the frame, and loop the drive chain around the output shaft as early as possible. Raise and move the engine as required to align all the mounting bolt holes. Note that it may be necessary to adjust the jack as the bolts are installed.

DL models

36 Seat one side of the spacer for the upper rear mounting bolt in the cut-out in the crankcase. Slide the bolt in from the right-hand side and thread it finger-tight into the spacer **(see illustration 4.27)**.

37 Clean the threads of the engine bracket bolts and apply some fresh threadlock. Fit the bracket and tighten the bolts to 35 Nm **(see illustration 4.22)**.

38 Slide the lower rear mounting bolt in from the left-hand side **(see illustration 4.24)**. Fit a new nut and tighten it finger-tight **(see illustration 4.23)**.

39 Slide the front mounting bolt in from the left-hand side **(see illustration 4.21)**. Fit a new nut and tighten it finger-tight **(see illustration 4.20)**.

40 Tighten the adjusters for the front and lower rear mounts to 12 Nm. Fit the locknuts and tighten them to 45 Nm using the peg spanner **(see illustration 4.21)**.

41 Tighten the upper rear mounting bolt to 55 Nm **(see illustration 4.27)**. Tighten the pinch bolt for the spacer to 25 Nm **(see illustration 4.26)**.

42 Tighten the nut on the front mounting bolt to 93 Nm **(see illustration 4.20)**.

43 Tighten the nut on the lower rear mounting bolt to 55 Nm **(see illustration 4.23)**.

SFV models

44 Slide the upper and lower rear and middle mounting bolts in from the left-hand side **(see illustrations 4.32a, b and c)**. Fit new nuts and tighten them finger-tight.

45 Fit the right-hand front bolt with its spacer and tighten it finger-tight **(see illustration 4.30b)**.

46 Clean the threads of the left-hand front bolt and apply some fresh threadlock. Fit the bolt and tighten it finger-tight **(see illustration 4.30a)**.

47 Tighten the front mounting bolts to 55 Nm.

48 Tighten the middle mounting bolt nut to 93 Nm **(see illustration 4.32c)**.

49 Tighten the upper and lower rear mounting bolt nuts to 55 Nm **(see illustrations 4.32a and b)**.

All models

50 The remainder of the installation procedure is the reverse of removal, noting the following points:

● Make sure all wires, cables and hoses are correctly routed and connected, and secured by any clips or ties.
● Use new gaskets on the exhaust pipe connections.
● When fitting the gearchange linkage arm onto the shaft, align the slit in the arm with the mark made on the shaft, and tighten the pinch bolt **(see illustration 4.12a or b)**.
● Refill the engine with the correct type and quantity of oil and coolant (see Chapter 1).
● Check throttle and clutch cable freeplay (see Chapter 1).
● Start the engine and check that there are no oil or coolant leaks.

5 Engine overhaul information

1 Before beginning the engine overhaul, read through the related procedures to familiarise yourself with the scope and requirements of the job. Overhauling an engine is not all that difficult, but it is time consuming. Check on the availability of parts and make sure that any necessary special tools are obtained in advance.

2 Most work can be done with a decent set of typical workshop hand tools, although a number of precision measuring tools are required for inspecting parts to determine if they are worn.

3 To ensure maximum life and minimum trouble from a rebuilt engine, everything must be assembled with care in a spotlessly clean environment.

Disassembly

4 Before disassembling the engine, thoroughly clean and degrease its external surfaces. This will prevent contamination of the engine internals, and will also make the job a lot easier and cleaner. A high flash-point solvent, such as paraffin (kerosene) can be used, or better still, a proprietary engine degreaser such as Gunk. Use old paintbrushes and toothbrushes to work the solvent into the various recesses of the casings. Take care to exclude solvent or water from the electrical components and intake and exhaust ports.

 Warning: The use of petrol (gasoline) as a cleaning agent should be avoided because of the risk of fire.

5 When clean and dry, position the engine on the workbench, leaving suitable clear area for working. Gather a selection of small containers, plastic bags and some labels so that parts can be grouped together in an easily identifiable manner. Also get some paper and a pen so that notes can be taken. You will also need a supply of clean rag, which should be as absorbent as possible.

6 Before commencing work, read through the appropriate section so that some idea of the necessary procedure can be gained. When removing components note that great force is seldom required, unless specified (checking the specified torque setting of the particular bolt being removed will indicate how tight it is, and therefore how much force should be needed). In many cases, a component's reluctance to be removed is indicative of an incorrect approach or removal method – if in any doubt, re-check with the text.

7 When disassembling the engine, keep 'mated' parts that have been in contact with each other during engine operation together (e.g. each piston with its piston rings and connecting rod, valves with their associated components). These 'mated' parts must be reinstalled together and in their original location.

8 A complete engine/transmission disassembly should be done in the following general order with reference to the appropriate Sections.

Remove the thermostat housing (see Chapter 3)
Remove the valve covers
Remove the cam chain tensioners
Remove the camshafts
Remove the cylinder heads
Remove the cylinder blocks
Remove the pistons
Remove the starter motor (see Chapter 8)
Remove the water pump (see Chapter 3)
Remove the clutch
Remove the gearchange mechanism
Remove primary drive gear
Remove the oil pump
Remove the alternator rotor and starter clutch
Remove the cam chain guide blades
Remove the cam chains
Separate the crankcase halves
Remove the crankshaft and connecting rods
Remove the transmission shafts and the selector drum and forks

Reassembly

9 Reassembly is accomplished by reversing the general disassembly sequence.

6 Oil cooler

2004 to 2011 DL models

Removal

1 The oil cooler is on the front of the engine. Drain the engine oil (see Chapter 1).

2 To remove the cooler with its feed and return hoses, position a drain tray below the engine on the left-hand side. Note the alignment of the hose banjo unions with the crankcase, then unscrew the banjo bolts and detach the

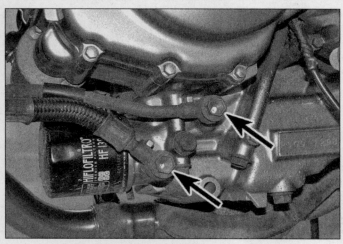

6.2 Oil hose banjo bolts (arrowed) – engine side

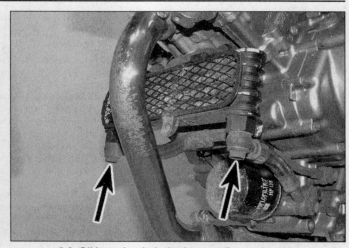

6.3 Oil hose banjo bolts (arrowed) – cooler side

hoses (see illustration). Note that new sealing washers must be used.

3 To remove the cooler without its feed and return hoses, position a drain tray below the cooler. Note the alignment of the hose banjo unions with the cooler, then unscrew the banjo bolts and detach the hoses (see illustration). Note that new sealing washers must be used.

4 Unscrew the cooler mounting bolts and remove the cooler (see illustration). Note the spacers in the mounting grommets.

Inspection

5 If required undo the screw securing the mesh guard and remove the guard, noting how it locates at the top – if the screw is corroded apply some penetrating fluid before trying to undo it.

6 Check for any signs of oil leakage from the hoses or cooler, and replace them with new ones if necessary.

7 Check the cooler fins for mud, dirt and insects that may impede the flow of air. If the fins are dirty, clean them using water or low pressure compressed air directed from the inner side. If the fins are bent or distorted, straighten them carefully with a small screwdriver. If the air flow is restricted over

more then 20% of the surface area, replace the cooler with a new one.

Installation

8 Installation is the reverse of removal, noting the following:
● Check the condition of the mounting grommets and replace them with new ones if they are damaged or deteriorated. Make sure the spacers are in the mounting grommets.
● Fit the mesh guard before installing the cooler.
● Use new sealing washers on each side of the banjo unions.
● Make sure the unions are butted against the lugs on the cooler and the crankcase.
● Tighten the banjo bolts and the mounting bolts to the torque settings specified at the beginning of this Chapter.
● Fill the engine with the correct type and quantity of oil (see Chapter 1).

2012-on DL models and all SFV models

Removal

9 The oil cooler is on the front of the engine.

10 Drain the engine oil and remove the filter (see Chapter 1). Drain the coolant (see Chapter 1).

11 Place the container with the drained coolant below the cooler to catch the residual fluid. Slacken the cooler hose clamps and detach the hoses (see illustration).

12 Unscrew the centre bolt with its washer and remove the cooler (see illustration). Remove the O-ring – a new one must be used (see illustration 6.14a).

13 Check the cooler body for cracks and dents and any evidence of coolant leakage and replace it with a new one if necessary. Also check the hoses for splits, cracks, hardening and deterioration and fit new ones if required.

Installation

14 Installation is the reverse of removal, noting the following:
● Make sure the mating surfaces of the crankcase and the cooler are clean and dry.
● Check the condition of the hoses and replace them with new ones if required.
● Use a new O-ring on the cooler body and

6.4 Oil cooler mounting bolts (arrowed)

6.11 Detach the hoses, being prepared for some more coolant

6.12 Unscrew the bolt and remove the cooler

6.14a Fit a new O-ring into the groove

6.14b Seat the tabs on each side of the lug

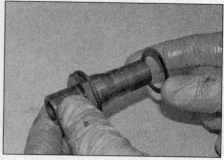

6.14c Make sure the washer is fitted

smear it with grease. Make sure it seats in its groove **(see illustration)**.
● Seat the tabs on the top of the cooler body on each side of the lug on the crankcase **(see illustration)**.
● Fit the washer onto the bolt and tighten the bolt to the torque setting specified at the beginning of the Chapter **(see illustration)**.
● Make sure the coolant hoses are pressed fully onto their unions and are secured by the clamps.
● Fit a new filter and fill the engine with the correct type and quantity of oil (see Chapter 1).
● Refill the cooling system (see Chapter 1).

7 Valve covers

Removal

1 To access the front cylinder valve cover, on SFV models remove the radiator covers (see Chapter 7), and on all models unscrew the radiator lower mount **(see illustration)**, or if preferred remove the radiator (see Chapter 3).
2 To access the rear cylinder valve cover, remove the fuel tank (see Chapter 4). On 2007-on DL models remove the coolant reservoir (see Chapter 3).
3 Pull the spark plug cap(s) off the plug(s) and secure it/them clear of the cover **(see illustration 4.8a)**. On 2004 to 2011 DL

models, disconnect the PAIR valve hose **(see illustration 4.9)**. On SFV models move the heat shield aside **(see illustration 4.8b)**.
4 Unscrew the valve cover bolts, noting which fits where and the difference in the washers **(see illustration)**. Remove the washers with the bolts if they are loose. Check their condition and replace them with new ones if required.
5 Lift the valve cover off the cylinder head **(see illustration)** If it is stuck, do not try to lever it off with a screwdriver. Tap it gently around the sides with a rubber hammer or block of wood to dislodge it. The rubber gasket is normally glued into the groove in the cover, and is best left there if it is reusable. If the gasket is in any way damaged, deformed or deteriorated, replace it with a new one.
6 On 2004 to 2011 DL models remove the air passage dowel and O-ring **(see illustration)**.

Installation

7 Clean the mating surface of the cylinder head with solvent, removing all traces of old sealant.
8 Check the valve cover gasket for any signs of damage or deterioration and replace it with new a one if necessary (it is best to use a new one whatever the apparent condition). If a new one is used, clean all traces of the old sealant from the groove in the cover and clean it with solvent. Apply a smear of a suitable sealant (such as Suzuki Bond no. 1215) into the groove, then fit the new gasket making sure it locates correctly **(see illustration)**. Also apply the sealant to the gasket half-circle seats. If the old gasket is being reused, clean off all of the old sealant from the half-circles.
9 Smear the washers with clean engine oil. If removed, fit them into the cover, making sure

7.1 Unscrew the bolt (arrowed) so you can move the radiator forwards

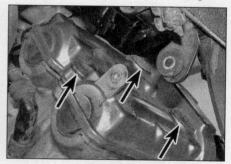

7.4 Valve cover bolts (arrowed)

7.5 Removing the front valve cover

7.6 Remove the dowel and O-ring (arrowed)

7.8 Make sure the gasket locates in the groove

7.9a Fit the lubricated washers, using new ones if necessary…

7.9b …and in the correct place and way round

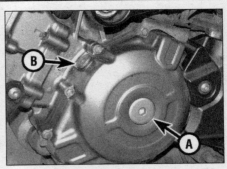

8.3 Remove the crankshaft end cap (A) and the timing inspection cap (B)

the metallic side of the thicker one faces out and is fitted with the long-shouldered bolt **(see illustrations)**.

10 On 2004 to 2011 DL models fit the air passage dowel and O-ring, using a new one if necessary **(see illustration 7.6)**.

11 Position the valve cover on the cylinder head, making sure the gasket stays in place, and that the correct cover is fitted on each head – the front cylinder cover has a threaded bore for the radiator mount in its right-hand end **(see illustration 7.4)**. Fit the bolts and tighten them to the torque setting specified at the beginning of the Chapter.

12 On SFV models replace the heat shield **(see illustration 4.8b)**. Fit the spark plug cap(s) **(see illustration 4.8a)**. On 2004 to 2011 DL models, connect the PAIR valve hose **(see illustration 4.9)**.

13 Install all other components (Steps 1 and 2).

8 Camshafts and followers

1 Remove the valve covers (see Section 7).
2 Remove the spark plugs (see Chapter 1).
3 Unscrew the crankshaft end cap and the timing mark inspection cap from the alternator cover **(see illustration)**. Note that a new O-ring and sealing washer should be used.
4 Start with the front cylinder. Turn the engine using a 17 mm socket on the alternator rotor bolt and turning it in an anti-clockwise direction only until the line next to the 'F' mark on the rotor aligns with the notch in the timing mark inspection hole **(see illustrations)**. At this point make sure that the cylinder is at TDC (top dead centre) on the compression stroke (and not the exhaust stroke) by checking the camshaft lobe positions and camshaft and sprocket markings – the camshaft lobes should be slightly raised from the head and pointing away from each other and the scribe lines on the end of each camshaft should be parallel with the cylinder head and the sprocket markings should be as shown **(see illustration)**. If the marks do not align as described, turn the engine anti-clockwise through one full turn (360°) until the 'F' mark

again aligns with the notch – the lobes and marks should now all align as described indicating the front cylinder is at TDC on compression.

5 Remove the cam chain top guide (see Section 10) and the cam chain tensioner (see Section 9).

6 Mark each camshaft holder according to its cylinder (i.e. front or rear), and its location (i.e. intake or exhaust) – there should already be IN and EX marks, but as the camshaft holders are interchangeable between the cylinders they

8.4a Turn the engine anti-clockwise using a socket on the timing rotor bolt…

must be marked F or R as well so they cannot be inadvertently interchanged. Working on one camshaft at a time and starting with the intake camshaft,

Caution: Make sure the holder lifts up squarely and is not sticking on a dowel or being distorted by some of the bolts being slackened more than the others as it could easily break.

7 Unscrew the bolts securing the intake camshaft holder, slackening them evenly and a little at a time in a criss-cross pattern,

8.4b …until the line next to the F mark aligns with the notch

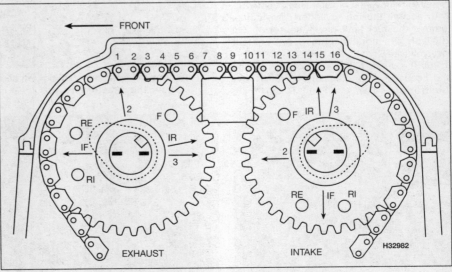

8.4c Front cylinder valve timing marks

8.7a Camshaft holder bolts (arrowed)

8.7b Lift the camshaft and disengage the chain

starting at the ends and working to the middle, then remove the holder (see illustration). Remove the two dowels if they are loose. Remove the intake camshaft, disengaging the cam chain from the sprocket as you do (see illustration).

8 Repeat Step 7 for the exhaust camshaft, then lay the cam chain over the front of the head and secure it with a piece of wire. On completion cover the top of the cylinder head with a rag to prevent anything falling into the engine. The camshafts are marked for identification – INF (intake camshaft, front cylinder), and EXF (exhaust camshaft, front cylinder) but if these marks are unclear make your own.

9 Now do the rear cylinder. Hold the front cylinder cam chain tight to prevent it getting trapped between the drive sprocket and the crankcase when turning the engine. Turn the engine anti-clockwise through one full turn (360°) from the TDC position for the front cylinder, until the 'F' mark again aligns with the notch (see illustrations 8.4a and b). At this point the rear cylinder is at 90° ATDC (after top dead centre) on the ignition stroke, and the camshaft lobes and camshaft and sprocket markings should be as shown (see illustration).

10 Repeat Steps 5 to 8 for the rear cylinder, removing the exhaust camshaft before the intake, noting the difference in markings (INR

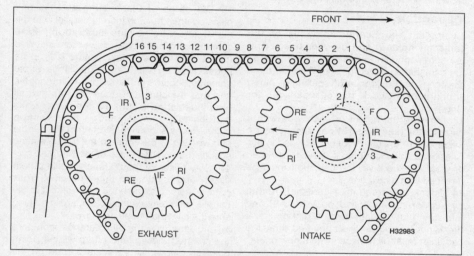

8.9 Rear cylinder valve timing marks

– intake camshaft, rear cylinder, and EXR – exhaust camshaft, rear cylinder) or making your own as required for the rear cylinder identity (see illustration).

11 If you are removing the followers and shims, obtain a container which is divided into eight compartments, and label each compartment with the identity of a valve location in the cylinder head, for example

the front cylinder, intake camshaft, left-hand valve could be marked F-I-L. If a container is not available, use labelled plastic bags. Lift each cam follower out of the cylinder head using either a magnet or a pair of pliers and store it in its corresponding compartment in the container (see illustration). Retrieve the shim from either the inside of the follower (see illustration) or pick it out of the top of

8.10 Lift the camshaft and disengage the chain

8.11a Lift out the follower...

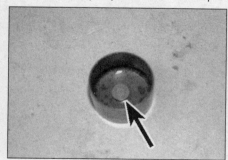

8.11b ...and remove the shim (arrowed) from inside it...

8.11c ...or from the top of the valve, using a magnet...

8.11d ...or a screwdriver with a dab of grease

8.13 Measure the height of each camshaft lobe with a micrometer

the valve, using either a magnet, a small screwdriver with a dab of grease on it (the shim will stick to the grease), or a screwdriver and a pair of pliers **(see illustrations)**. Do not allow the shim to fall into the engine.

Inspection

12 Inspect the bearing surfaces of the camshaft holders and cylinder heads and the corresponding journals and the lobes on the camshafts – look for score marks, deep scratches and evidence of spalling (a pitted appearance). Check the oil passages for clogging.

13 Measure the height of each lobe with a micrometer **(see illustration)** and compare the results to the minimum height listed in this Chapter's Specifications. If damage is noted or wear is excessive, the camshaft must be replaced with a new one.

14 Check the amount of camshaft runout by supporting each end on V-blocks, and measuring any runout using a dial gauge. If the runout exceeds the specified limit the camshaft must be replaced with a new one.

Refer to Tools and Workshop Tips in the Reference section for details of how to read a micrometer and dial gauge.

15 Next, check each camshaft journal oil clearance. Work on one camshaft at a time when doing this. Clean the camshaft and the bearing surfaces in the cylinder head and

camshaft holder with a clean lint-free cloth, then lay the camshaft in its correct location in the head (see Step 8 or 10), positioning it with the lobes facing away from the valves so there is no contact between them.

16 Cut strips of Plastigauge and lay one piece on each bearing journal parallel with the camshaft centreline **(see illustration)**. Make sure the camshaft holder dowels are installed then fit the holder, making sure it is in its correct location (see Step 6), the flange on the camshaft locates in the groove in the holder, and that the camshaft does not rotate at all **(see illustration 8.29b)**. Fit the holder bolts and tighten them evenly and a little at a time in a criss-cross sequence, starting in the middle and working to the ends, to the torque setting specified at the beginning of the Chapter.

17 Now unscrew the bolts, slackening them evenly and a little at a time in a criss-cross pattern starting at the ends and working to the middle, then remove the holder, again making sure the camshaft does not turn.

18 To determine the oil clearance, compare the crushed Plastigauge (at its widest point) on each journal to the scale printed on the Plastigauge container **(see illustration)**. Compare the results to this Chapter's Specifications. If the oil clearance is greater than specified, measure the diameter of the camshaft journal with a micrometer **(see illustration)**. If it is within specifications, replace the cylinder head and camshaft holders with new ones (they come as a matched set). If the journal diameter is less than the specified limit, replace the camshaft

with a new one and recheck the clearance. If the clearance is still too great, also replace the cylinder head and camshaft holders.

Before replacing the camshafts, cylinder head or holders because of damage, check with motorcycle cylinder head specialists to see whether worn components can be renovated. Due to the cost of new components it is recommended that all options be explored before condemning them as trash!

19 Except in cases of oil starvation, the cam chains should wear very little. If a chain has stretched excessively, which makes it difficult to maintain proper tension, or if it is stiff or the links are binding or kinking, replace it with a new one. Refer to Section 10 for replacement.

20 Check each sprocket for cracks and other damage, and replace the camshaft with a new one if necessary – the sprockets are not available separately. If the sprocket teeth are worn, the cam chain is also worn, as will be the drive sprocket on the crankshaft. If wear this severe is apparent, the entire engine should be disassembled for inspection.

21 Inspect the cam chain guides and tensioner blade (see Section 10).

22 Inspect the outer surface of each cam follower for evidence of scoring or other damage. If a follower is in poor condition, it is probable that the bore in the cylinder head

8.16 Plastigauge strip on journal

8.18a Measuring the crushed strip

8.18b Measure the diameter of the journal with a micrometer

8.24 Fit the follower onto the valve

8.26a Check the identification letters to make sure you have the correct camshaft

8.26b Lay the exhaust camshaft onto the head and engage the chain

in which it works is also damaged. Check the clearance between each follower and its bore. If the clearance is excessive or the bore is out-of-round or tapered, replace the follower or cylinder head with a new one as required.

Installation

23 Lubricate each shim with molybdenum disulphide oil (a 50/50 mixture of molybdenum disulphide grease and engine oil) and fit it into its recess in the top of the valve spring retainer with the size mark facing up **(see illustration 8.11d)**. Make sure each shim is returned to the valve from which it was removed.

24 Check that the shim is correctly seated, then lubricate each follower with molybdenum disulphide oil and fit it onto its valve, making sure it sits square in its bore **(see illustration)**. Make sure each follower is returned to the valve from which it was removed.

25 If only one cylinder has been worked on, the engine should be correctly positioned for installation unless it has been turned for some other reason. If the engine has been turned, align the engine so that the cylinder that has its camshafts installed is positioned with its timing marks correctly aligned as described in Step 4 (front cylinder) or Step 9 (rear cylinder), then turn the engine anti-clockwise one full turn (360°) until the 'F' mark again aligns with the notch, all the time holding the loose cam chain taut so it does not bind around its drive sprocket on the crankshaft. The engine will now be correctly positioned for installation. If both cylinder camshafts have been removed,

install the camshafts on the front cylinder first.

26 To install the front cylinder camshafts, check that the cam chain is engaged around the lower sprocket teeth on the crankshaft and that the crankshaft is positioned as described in Step 4. Apply a smear of molybdenum disulphide oil (a mixture of 50% molybdenum disulphide grease and 50% engine oil) to the camshaft journals. Keeping the front run of the cam chain taut, lay the exhaust camshaft (identified by EXF) **(see illustrations)** onto the cylinder head, positioning it so that the scribe lines on the end of the shaft are parallel with the cylinder head, the 1F arrow on the sprocket points forwards and is flush with the top of the cylinder head mating surface, and the 2 mark points directly away from the head **(see illustration 8.4c)**. Check that the chain is tight at the front so that there is no slack between the crankshaft sprocket and the exhaust camshaft sprocket – move the chain around the sprocket so that the slack is taken up if required, then check that all marks are still correctly aligned.

27 Starting with and including the cam chain pin that is directly above the 2 mark on the exhaust camshaft sprocket, count 16 pins along the chain towards the intake side and mark the pin. Lay the intake camshaft (identified by INF) **(see illustration 8.26a)** onto the cylinder head, positioning it so that the scribe lines on the end of the shaft are parallel with the cylinder head, then engage the chain with the sprocket so that the 3 mark on the

sprocket aligns with the marked 16th pin **(see illustrations 8.7b and 8.4c)**. Again check that the chain is tight at the front and between the sprockets – any slack in the chain must lie in the portion of the chain in the back of the cylinder so that it can be taken up by the tensioner.

28 Before proceeding further, check that everything aligns as described and shown in Steps 4, 26 and 27. If it doesn't, the valve timing will be inaccurate and the valves could contact the pistons when the engine is turned over. DO NOT turn the engine until the camshaft holders are installed as the camshafts could jump out of position.

29 If removed, fit the exhaust camshaft holder dowels into the cylinder head or holder (see Step 6 for holder identification), then fit the holder, making sure it is the right way round and seats correctly, with the flange on the camshaft locating in the groove in the holder **(see illustrations)**. Fit the holder bolts and tighten them evenly and a little at a time in a criss-cross pattern, starting in the middle and working to the ends, making sure the holder is drawn down evenly and does not bind on anything, to the torque setting specified at the beginning of the Chapter. Repeat for the intake camshaft holder **(see illustration)**.
Caution: Whilst tightening the bolts, make sure the holder is being pulled squarely down and is not binding on the dowels or tilting to one side – if it does, adjust the relevant bolts until the holder is again square to the head. The holder is likely to

8.29a Check the identification letters to make sure you have the correct camshaft holder

8.29b Make sure the dowels (arrowed) are fitted in either the head...

8.29c ...or the holder, then fit the holders

8.31a Check the identification letters to make sure you have the correct camshaft

8.31b Lay the intake camshaft onto the head and engage the chain

break if it's not tightened down evenly and squarely.

30 Install the front cylinder cam chain tensioner (see Section 9).

31 Before installing the rear cylinder camshafts, hold the cam chain to prevent it bunching around the crankshaft sprocket and rotate the crankshaft 360° to realign the F mark with the notch. Check that the cam chain is engaged around the lower sprocket teeth on the crankshaft. Apply a smear of molybdenum disulphide oil (a mixture of 50% molybdenum disulphide grease and 50% engine oil) to the camshaft journals. Keeping the front run of the cam chain taut, lay the intake camshaft (identified by INR) **(see illustrations)** onto the cylinder head, positioning it so that the scribe lines on the end of the shaft are parallel with the cylinder head, the 1R arrow on the sprocket points forwards and is flush with the top of the cylinder head mating surface, and the 2 mark points directly away from the head **(see illustration 8.9)**. Check that the chain

is tight at the front so that there is no slack between the crankshaft sprocket and the intake camshaft sprocket, and that all marks are still correctly aligned (see Step 9). If any slack is evident, move the chain around the sprocket so that the slack is taken up.

32 Starting with and including the cam chain pin that is directly above the 2 mark on the intake camshaft sprocket, count 16 pins along the chain towards the exhaust side and mark the pin. Lay the exhaust camshaft (identified by EXR) **(see illustration 8.31a)** onto the cylinder head, positioning it so that the scribe lines on the end of the shaft are parallel with the cylinder head, then engage the chain with the sprocket so that the 3 mark on the sprocket aligns with the marked 16th pin **(see illustrations 8.10 and 8.9)**. Again check that the chain is tight at the front and between the sprockets – any slack in the chain must lie in the portion of the chain in the back of the cylinder so that it can be taken up by the tensioner.

33 Before proceeding further, check that everything aligns as described in Steps 9, 31 and 32. If it doesn't, the valve timing will be inaccurate and the valves could contact the pistons when the engine is turned over. DO NOT turn the engine until the camshaft holders are installed as the camshafts could jump out of position.

34 If removed, fit the intake camshaft holder dowels into the cylinder head or holder (see Step 6 for holder identification) **(see illustration 8.29a)**, then fit the holder, making sure it is the right way round and seats correctly, with the flange on the camshaft locating in the groove in the holder **(see illustration)**. Fit the holder bolts and tighten them evenly and a little at a time in a criss-cross pattern, starting in the middle and working to the ends, making sure the holder is drawn down evenly and does not bind on anything, to the torque setting specified at the beginning of the Chapter. Repeat for the exhaust camshaft holder **(see illustration)**.

8.34a Fit the intake camshaft holder...

8.34b ...then the exhaust camshaft holder

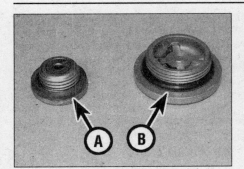

8.40 Fit the caps using a new washer (A) and O-ring (B) if required

Caution: Whilst tightening the bolts, make sure the holder is being pulled squarely down and is not binding on the dowels or tilting to one side – if it does, adjust the relevant bolts until the holder is again square to the head. The holder is likely to break if it's not tightened down evenly and squarely.

35 Install the rear cylinder cam chain tensioner (see Section 9).

36 Before proceeding further, again check that everything aligns as described in Step 4 for the front cylinder and Step 9 for the rear cylinder. If it doesn't, the valve timing will be inaccurate and the valves will contact the piston when the engine is turned over **(see illustrations 8.4c and 8.9)**.

37 Rotate the engine anti-clockwise through two full turns (720°) and re-check that the valve timing for both cylinders is correct (see

Steps 4 and 9). Also recheck the cam chain pin count between the sprockets (see Step 27 for the front cylinder and 32 for the rear cylinder) in case the chain jumped when the engine was being turned. If the chain has jumped, check that the tensioner for that chain has released correctly (see Section 9).

38 Check the valve clearances (Chapter 1) and adjust if necessary.

39 Install the cam chain top guides (see Section 10).

40 Fit the timing mark inspection cap using a new sealing washer, and the crankshaft end cap using a new O-ring smeared with grease **(see illustration)**. Tighten the caps to the torque settings specified at the beginning of the Chapter.

41 Install the valve covers (see Section 7).

42 Install the spark plugs (see Chapter 1).

43 Check the engine oil level and top up if necessary (see *Daily (pre-ride) checks*).

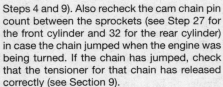

9 Cam chain tensioners

Removal

1 To access the front cylinder tensioner remove the air filter housing, and for best access the throttle bodies (see Chapter 4) **(see illustration)**.

2 To access the rear cylinder tensioner, on DL models remove the swingarm (see Chapter 5), and on SFV models remove the right-hand

side cover (see Chapter 7) **(see illustration)**.

3 It is advisable to set the valve timing marks before removing the tensioner – doing so means you can check that the chain does not jump a tooth on the camshaft sprocket with the tensioner removed – refer to Section 8, steps 1 to 4 for the front cylinder marks, then step 9 for the rear cylinder.

4 Unscrew the tensioner cap bolt carefully (it is under spring pressure), then remove the bolt and sealing washer and withdraw the spring from the tensioner body **(see illustration)**. Remove the tensioner mounting bolts, noting the wire clamp on the front tensioner, and lift the tensioner off **(see illustration)**. Remove the gasket. Pull the oil jet out **(see illustration)**. Remove the O-ring from the jet – a new one must be used.

5 Discard the gasket and cap bolt sealing washer – new ones must be used on installation. Lift the tensioner ratchet and check that the plunger moves smoothly in and out of the tensioner body **(see illustration)**. Make sure you cannot push the plunger in against the ratchet when it is locked.

Installation

6 Make sure the tensioner and cylinder block surfaces are clean and dry.

7 Clean the oil jet with solvent and blow it through with compressed air if available. Fit a new O-ring onto the jet and smear it with grease. Squirt some oil into the passage, then press the jet in with the slotted end facing out **(see illustration 9.4c)**.

9.1 Cam chain tensioner (arrowed) – front cylinder

9.2 Cam chain tensioner (arrowed) – rear cylinder, from behind on a DL

9.4a Unscrew the cap bolt and remove the spring

9.4b Unscrew the mounting bolts and remove the tensioner

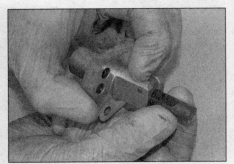

9.4c Remove the gasket then withdraw the oil jet

9.5 Check the plunger moves smoothly and freely with the ratchet lifted, and locks securely against it in place

9.9 Always use a new gasket

8 Lift the tensioner ratchet and push the plunger all the way into the body **(see illustration 9.5)**.

9 The tensioner for the front cylinder is marked F-UP, and the rear is marked R-UP. Fit a new gasket **(see illustration)**. Fit the tensioner with the UP mark at the top and tighten the bolts to the torque setting specified at the beginning of the Chapter, not forgetting the wire clamp with the upper bolt on the front tensioner **(see illustration 9.4b)**.

10 Fit the tensioner spring, then fit the cap bolt with a new sealing washer and tighten it to the specified torque setting **(see illustration 9.4a)** – you should hear the ratchet click as the

plunger extends. If the valve cover has been removed, check that the cam chain tension has been taken up.

11 Recheck the valve timing marks (see Step 3) and install the valve cover(s). Fit the timing mark inspection cap using a new sealing washer and the crankshaft end cap using a new O-ring smeared with grease **(see illustration 8.40)**. Tighten the caps to the torque settings specified at the beginning of the Chapter.

12 Install the components removed for access (see Chapters 4, 5 and/or 7 as required).

10 Cam chain guides and blades

Top guide

1 Remove the valve cover (see Section 7).

2 Unscrew the bolts and remove the top guide **(see illustration)**. Check the sliding surface and edges of the guide for excessive wear, deep grooves, cracking and other obvious damage, and replace it with a new one if necessary.

3 Installation is the reverse of removal.

Front guide blade

4 Remove the cylinder head (see Section 12).

5 Draw the blade out of the engine, noting how it locates **(see illustration)**. Check the sliding surface and edges of the blade for excessive wear, deep grooves, cracking and other obvious damage, and replace it with a new one if necessary.

6 When fitting the blade, locate the lugs on the blade in the cut-outs in the cylinder block **(see illustration)**. Install the cylinder head as described in Section 12.

Tensioner blade

7 For the front cylinder remove the intake camshaft (see Section 8) and the alternator rotor and starter clutch (see Section 22). If the cylinder head is being removed as well, proceed with that now and continue this procedure afterwards, as it makes removing the blade easier.

8 For the rear cylinder remove the exhaust camshaft (see Section 8) and the clutch (see Section 17). If the cylinder head is being removed as well, proceed with that now and continue this procedure afterwards, as it makes removing the blade easier.

9 Unscrew the pivot bolt and draw the blade out of the engine, noting the washer that fits between the blade and the crankcase **(see illustrations)**.

10 Check the sliding surface and edges of

10.2 Unscrew the three bolts and remove the top guide

10.5 Removing the front guide blade

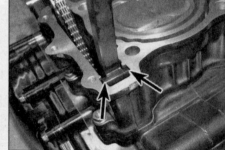

10.6 Make sure the lugs locate correctly in the cutouts

10.9a Front cylinder tensioner blade pivot bolt (arrowed)

10.9b Rear cylinder tensioner blade pivot bolt (arrowed)

10.11a Installing the front cylinder tensioner blade

10.11b Installing the rear cylinder tensioner blade

11.3 Removing the front cylinder cam chain

the blade for excessive wear, deep grooves, cracking and other obvious damage, and replace it with a new one if necessary.

11 When fitting the tensioner blade, do not omit the washer that fits between the blade and the crankcase **(see illustrations)**. Tighten the pivot bolt to the torque setting specified at the beginning of the Chapter. Install the remaining components in a reverse of the removal procedure.

11 Cam chains

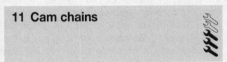

Front cylinder cam chain

Removal

1 Drain the engine oil (see Chapter 1).
2 Remove the cylinder head (see Section 12), and the cam chain guide blade and tensioner blade (see Section 10).
3 Drop the cam chain down its tunnel and remove it from the end of the crankshaft **(see illustration)**.

Inspection

4 Check the chain for binding, kinks and any obvious damage and replace it with a new one if necessary.

5 Check the sprocket teeth on the crankshaft for wear and damage. The teeth are integral with the crankshaft, so if any significant wear or damage is found, the crankshaft must be replaced with a new one. Also check the camshaft sprocket teeth for wear. If the sprockets are worn and new camshafts and/or crankshaft are being fitted, fit a new chain as a matter of course.

Installation

6 Hook the cam chain onto a piece of wire and draw the chain up through its tunnel, making sure its bottom end engages around the sprocket on the crankshaft **(see illustration 11.3)**. Secure the chain at the top to prevent it falling back down the tunnel.
7 Install the cam chain tensioner blade and guide blade (see Section 10). Install the cylinder head (see Section 12).
8 Replenish the engine oil (see Chapter 1).

Rear cylinder cam chain

Removal

9 Drain the engine oil (see Chapter 1).
10 Remove the cylinder head (see Section 12).
11 Remove the clutch (see Section 17), the primary drive gear (see Section 20), and the cam chain guide blade and tensioner blade (see Section 10).
12 Drop the cam chain down its tunnel and

remove it from the end of the crankshaft **(see illustration)**. Slide the cam chain sprocket off the end of the crankshaft **(see illustration)**.

Inspection

13 Check the chain for binding, kinks and any obvious damage and replace it with a new one if necessary.
14 Check the cam chain sprocket on the crankshaft for wear or damage to both the outer teeth and the inner splines. Also check the camshaft sprocket teeth for wear. If the sprockets are worn and new camshafts and crankshaft sprocket are being fitted, fit a new chain as a matter of course.

Installation

15 Slide the sprocket onto the crankshaft with the flanged end innermost, aligning the punch marks on the outer faces of the sprocket and shaft **(see illustration 11.12b)**. Hook the cam chain onto a piece of wire and draw the chain up through its tunnel, making sure its bottom end engages around the sprocket **(see illustration 11.12a)**. Secure the chain at the top to prevent it falling back down the tunnel.
16 Install the cam chain tensioner blade and guide blade (see Section 10), then the primary drive gear (see Section 20), then the clutch (see Section 17).
17 Install the cylinder head (see Section 12).
18 Replenish the engine oil (see Chapter 1).

11.12a Removing the rear cylinder cam chain

11.12b Slide the sprocket off the shaft

12.5 Slacken the clamp (arrowed) and detach the hose – front cylinder shown

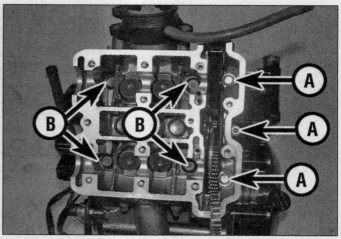

12.6 Cylinder head 6 mm bolts (A) and 10 mm bolts (B)

12 Cylinder heads

Removal

1 Remove the throttle bodies, and the exhaust system (see Chapter 4).
2 Remove the valve cover (see Section 7).
3 Remove the spark plug(s) (see Chapter 1).
4 Remove the camshafts (see Section 8). If you are overhauling the head, also remove the followers and shims.
5 Slacken the clamp securing the coolant hose to its union on the cylinder head and detach the hose (see illustration).
6 The cylinder head is secured by three 6 mm bolts and four 10 mm bolts (see illustration). First unscrew and remove the three 6 mm bolts. Now unscrew the four 10 mm bolts, slackening them evenly and a little at a time in a criss-cross pattern until they are all loose. Remove the bolts and their washers. Take

care not to drop any of the washers down the cam chain tunnel.
7 Hold the cam chain up and pull the cylinder head up off the block, then pass the cam chain down through the tunnel (see illustration). Do not let the chain fall into the crankcase – secure it with a piece of wire or metal bar to prevent it from doing so. If the head is stuck, tap around the base of it with a soft-faced mallet. Do not try to free it by inserting a screwdriver between the head and cylinder block – you'll damage the sealing surfaces. Note that the front head is marked 'F' and the rear 'R' (see illustration 12.16).
8 Remove the old gasket (see illustration 12.15).
9 Remove the two dowels from the cylinder block if loose (see illustration 12.15). If either appears to be missing it is probably stuck in the underside of the cylinder head.
10 If required, remove the cam chain guide blade from the front of the cam chain tunnel (see Section 10).
11 Check the cylinder head gasket and

the mating surfaces on the cylinder head and block for signs of leakage, which could indicate warpage. Refer to Section 13 and check the cylinder head.
12 Clean all traces of old gasket material from the cylinder head and block. If a scraper is used, take care not to scratch or gouge the soft aluminium. Be careful not to let any of the gasket material drop into the crankcase, the cylinder bore or the oil and coolant passages. Unless you are removing the cylinder block, cover it with a clean rag to prevent any debris falling in.

Installation

13 If removed, fit the cam chain guide blade into the front of the cam chain tunnel (see Section 10).
14 If removed, fit the two dowels into the cylinder block (see illustration 12.15).
15 Make sure both cylinder head and block mating surfaces are clean, then lay the new head gasket in place, locating it over the dowels (see illustration). The gasket can

12.7 Lift the head up off the block

12.15 Lay the gasket onto the head, locating it over the dowels (arrowed)

only fit one way, so if the holes do not line up properly it is upside down. Never re-use the old gasket.

16 Make sure you have the correct head for the cylinder being worked on – the front head is marked 'F' and the rear 'R' **(see illustration)**. Carefully lower the head onto the block, feeding the cam chain up the tunnel as you do **(see illustration 12.7)** – it is helpful to have an assistant to pass the chain up and slip a piece of wire through it to prevent it falling back into the engine. Keep the chain taut to prevent it becoming disengaged from the crankshaft sprocket.

17 Lubricate the threads of the 10 mm bolts and the washers with clean oil. Fit the bolts and washers, with the chamfered side of the washers facing up, and tighten the bolts finger-tight **(see illustration)**.

18 Now tighten the 10 mm bolts evenly and a little at a time in a criss-cross pattern first to the initial torque setting specified at the beginning of the Chapter, and then to the final setting **(see illustration)**.

19 Fit the 6 mm bolts and tighten them to the specified torque setting **(see illustration)**.

20 Install all other components that have been removed in a reverse of the removal procedure, referring to the relevant sections and Chapters where necessary.

12.16 Each cylinder head is marked – make sure you have the correct one

12.17 Fit the 10 mm bolts with their washers...

12.18 ...and tighten them as described to the specified torque setting

12.19 Install and tighten the 6 mm bolts

13 Cylinder heads and valves – overhaul

Special tool: *A valve spring compressor is needed.*

1 Because of the complex nature of this job and the special tools and equipment required, most owners leave servicing of the valves, valve seats and valve guides to a professional. However, you can make an initial assessment of whether the valves are seating correctly, and therefore sealing, by pouring a small amount of solvent into each of the valve ports. If the solvent leaks past any valve into the combustion chamber area the valve is not seating correctly and sealing.

2 With the correct tools (a valve spring compressor is essential – make sure it is suitable for motorcycle work), you can also remove the valves and associated components from the cylinder head, clean them and check them for wear to assess the extent of the work needed, and, unless seat cutting or guide replacement is required, grind in the valves and reassemble them in the head.

3 A dealer service department or specialist can replace the guides and re-cut the valve seats.

4 After the valve service has been performed, be sure to clean it very thoroughly before installation on the engine to remove any metal particles or abrasive grit that may still be present from the valve service operations. Use

compressed air, if available, to blow out all the holes and passages.

Disassembly

5 Before proceeding, arrange to label and store the valves along with their related components in such a way that they can be returned to their original locations without

getting mixed up **(see illustration)**. Note that 2004 to 2011 DL models have two springs per valve (one fits inside the other), and 2012-on DL models and all SFV models have one spring per valve.

6 Compress the valve spring(s) on the first valve with a spring compressor, making sure it is correctly located onto each end of the valve

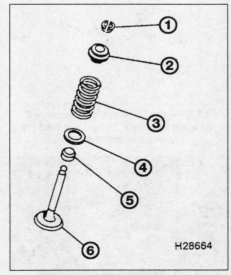
13.5 Valve components

1 Collets
2 Spring retainer
3 Spring(s)
4 Spring seat
5 Valve stem oil seal
6 Valve

There is a quick way of removing valve components that avoids having to use a spring compressor: select a socket that seats on the valve retainer and give it a sharp tap with a soft hammer – this compresses the spring without moving the valve itself and unseats the collets. Note that a valve spring compressor has to be used when refitting the valve assembly.

13.6a Compressing the valve springs using a valve spring compressor

13.6b Make sure the compressor locates correctly both on the top of the spring retainer...

13.6c ...and on the bottom of the valve

assembly **(see illustration)**. On the top of the valve the adaptor needs to be about the same size as the spring retainer – if it is too big it will contact the follower bore and mark it, and if it is too small it will be difficult to remove and install the collets **(see illustration)**. On the underside of the head make sure the plate (where present) on the compressor only contacts the valve and not the soft aluminium of the head **(see illustration)** – if the plate is too big for the valve, use a spacer between them. Do not compress the spring(s) any more than is absolutely necessary.

Caution: Take great care not to mark the cam follower bore with the spring compressor.

7 Remove the collets, using a magnet or a screwdriver with a dab of grease on it **(see illustration)**. Carefully release the valve spring compressor and remove the spring retainer, noting which way up it fits, the spring(s) and the valve **(see illustrations 13.31b and a, and 13.30)**. If the valve binds in the guide

and won't pull through, push it back into the head and deburr the area around the collet groove with a very fine file or whetstone **(see illustration)**.

8 Pull the valve stem seal off the top of the valve guide with pliers and discard it (the old seals should never be reused), then remove the spring seat noting which way up, it fits – using a magnet is the easiest way to remove the seat from the head **(see illustrations)**.

9 Repeat the procedure for the remaining valves. Remember to keep the parts for each valve together so they can be reinstalled in the same location.

10 Clean the cylinder head with solvent and dry it thoroughly. Compressed air will speed the drying process and ensure that all holes and recessed areas are clean. **Note:** *Do not use a wire brush mounted in a drill motor to clean the combustion chambers as the head material is soft and may be scratched or eroded away by the wire brush.*

11 Clean all of the valve springs, collets,

retainers and spring seats with solvent and dry them thoroughly. Do the parts from one valve at a time so that no mixing of parts between valves occurs.

12 Scrape off any deposits that may have formed on the valve, then use a motorised wire brush to remove deposits from the valve heads and stems. Again, make sure the valves do not get mixed up.

Inspection

13 Inspect the head very carefully for cracks and other damage. If cracks are found, a new head is required. Check the camshaft bearing surfaces for wear and evidence of seizure. Check the camshafts and holders for wear as well (see Section 8).

14 Using a precision straight-edge and a feeler gauge set to the warpage limit listed in the specifications at the beginning of the Chapter, check the head gasket mating surface for warpage. Refer to *Tools and Workshop Tips* in the Reference section for details of how to use the straight-edge. If the head is warped beyond the limit specified at the beginning of this Chapter, consult a Suzuki dealer or take it to a specialist repair shop for an opinion, though be prepared to have to buy a new one.

15 Examine the valve seats in the combustion chamber. If they are pitted, cracked or burned, the head will require work beyond the scope of the home mechanic. Measure the valve seat width and compare it to this Chapter's Specifications **(see illustration)**. If it is outside of the range, or if it varies around its circumference, overhaul is required.

13.7a Remove the collets as described

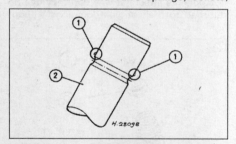

13.7b If the valve stem (2) won't pull through the guide, deburr the area (1) above the collet groove

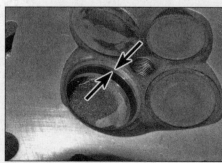

13.15 Measure the valve seat width with a ruler (or for greater precision use a Vernier caliper)

13.8a Pull the seal off the valve stem...

13.8b ...then remove the spring seat

13.16a Measure the amount of wobble as shown, relocating the gauge to measure in both directions

13.16b Measure the valve stem diameter with a micrometer...

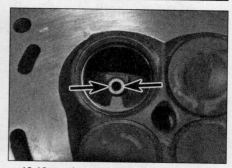

13.16c ...then measure the guide bore using a small hole gauge, and measure the small hole gauge with a micrometer

16 Clean the valve guides to remove any carbon build-up, then slide each valve into its guide in turn so that its face is 10 mm above the seat. Mount a dial gauge against the side of the valve face and measure the amount of stem deflection (wobble) between the valve stem and its guide – you need to measure in two perpendicular directions, so take the first measurement, then relocate the dial gauge and take a second measurement **(see illustration)**. If the deflection exceeds the limit specified, remove the valve and measure the valve stem diameter **(see illustration)**. Also measure the inside diameter of the guide with a small hole gauge and micrometer **(see illustration)**. Measure the guide at the ends and at the centre to determine if it is worn in a bell-mouth pattern (more wear at the ends). Subtract the stem diameter from the valve guide diameter to obtain the valve stem-to-guide clearance. If the stem-to-guide clearance is greater than listed in this Chapter's Specifications, replace whichever component is worn beyond its specifications with a new one. If the valve guide is within specifications, but is worn unevenly, it should be replaced with a new one.

17 Carefully inspect each valve face, stem and collet groove area for cracks, pits and burned spots **(see illustration)**. Measure the thickness of the valve head and compare it to the specifications **(see illustration)**. If it is worn below the service limit renew the valve.

18 Rotate the valve and check for any obvious indication that it is bent, in which case it must be renewed. Using V-blocks and a dial gauge, measure the valve stem runout

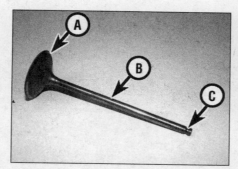

13.17a Check the valve face (A), stem (B) and collet groove (C) for signs of wear and damage

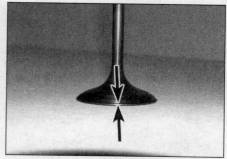

13.17b Measure the thickness of the valve head

and the valve head runout and compare the results to the specifications **(see illustration)**. If either measurement exceeds the service limit specified, the valve must be replaced with a new one.

19 Check the end of the stem for pitting and excessive wear.

20 Check the end of each valve spring for wear and pitting. Measure the spring free lengths and compare them to the specifications **(see illustration)**. If any spring is shorter than specified it has sagged and must be replaced with a new one. Also place the spring upright on a flat surface and check it for bend by placing a ruler against it, or alternatively lay it against a set-square **(see illustration)**. If the bend in any spring is excessive, it must be replaced with a new one.

21 Check the spring seats, retainers and

collets for obvious wear and cracks. Any questionable parts should not be reused, as extensive damage will occur in the event of failure during engine operation.

22 If the inspection indicates that no overhaul work is required, the valve components can be reinstalled in the head.

Reassembly

23 Unless a valve service has been performed, before installing the valves they should be ground in (lapped) to ensure a positive seal between the valves and seats. This procedure requires coarse and fine valve grinding compound and a valve grinding tool (either hand-held or drill driven – note that some drill-driven tools specify using only a fine grinding compound). If a grinding tool is not available, a piece of rubber or plastic hose

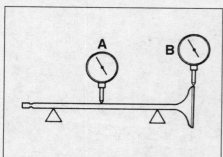

13.18 Measure the valve stem runout (A) and the valve head runout (B)

13.20a Measure the free length of the valve springs...

13.20b ...and check they are not bent

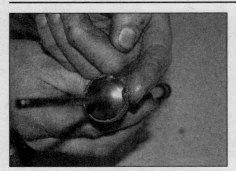

13.24 Apply the lapping compound very sparingly, in small dabs, to the valve face only

13.25 Rotate the valve grinding tool back and forth between the palms of your hands

13.28 Fit the spring seat, making sure it is the correct way up

13.29a Fit a new valve stem seal...

13.29b ...using either your finger...

13.29c ...or a deep socket, or seal installation tool to press it squarely into place

can be slipped over the valve stem (after the valve has been installed in the guide) and used to turn the valve.

24 Apply a small amount of coarse grinding compound to the valve face (see illustration). Smear some molybdenum disulphide oil (a 50/50 mixture of molybdenum disulphide grease and engine oil) to the valve stem, then slip the valve into the guide (see illustration 13.30). Note: *Make sure each valve is installed in its correct guide and be careful not to get any grinding compound on the valve stem.*

25 Attach the grinding tool to the valve and rotate the tool between the palms of your hands. Use a back-and-forth motion (as though rubbing your hands together) rather than a circular motion (i.e. so that the valve rotates alternately clockwise and anti-clockwise rather than in one direction only) (see illustration). If a motorised tool is being used, take note of the correct drive speed for it – if your drill runs too fast and is not variable, use a hand tool instead. Lift the valve off the seat and turn it at regular intervals to distribute the grinding compound properly. Continue the grinding procedure until the valve face and seat contact area is of uniform width, and unbroken around the entire circumference.

26 Carefully remove the valve and wipe off all traces of grinding compound, making sure none gets in the guide. Use solvent to clean the valve and wipe the seat area thoroughly with a solvent soaked cloth.

27 Repeat the procedure with fine valve grinding compound, then use solvent to clean the valve and flush the guide, and wipe the seat area thoroughly with a solvent soaked cloth. Repeat the entire procedure for the remaining valves. On completion thoroughly clean the entire head again, then blow through all passages with compressed air. Make sure all traces of the grinding compound have been removed before assembling the head.

28 Working on one valve at a time, lay the spring seat in place in the cylinder head with its shouldered side facing up (see illustration). As it is easy to cock the seat on the top of the valve guide, and then tricky to get it to sit properly, fit it using a rod (such as a screwdriver) as a guide for it to slide down.

29 Fit a new valve stem seal onto the guide, then use finger pressure, a stem seal fitting tool or an appropriate size deep socket to push the seal squarely onto the end of the valve guide until it is felt to clip into place (see illustrations). Make sure the seal does not get cocked sideways as it could be damaged.

30 Coat the valve stem with molybdenum disulphide oil (a 50/50 mixture of molybdenum disulphide grease and engine oil), then slide it into its guide, rotating it slowly to avoid damaging the seal (see illustration). Check that the valve moves up-and-down freely in the guide.

31 Next, fit the spring(s), with the closer-wound coils facing down into the cylinder head (see illustration). Fit the spring retainer, with its shouldered side facing down

13.30 Lubricate the stem and insert the valve in the guide

13.31a Fit the valve spring(s)...

so that it fits into the top of the spring(s) **(see illustration)**.

32 Apply a small amount of grease to the collets to help hold them in place. Compress the valve spring(s) with a spring compressor, making sure it is correctly located onto each end of the valve assembly (see Step 6) **(see illustrations 13.6a, b and c)**. Do not compress the spring(s) any more than is necessary to slip the collets into place. Locate each collet in turn into the groove in the valve stem using a screwdriver with a dab of grease on it **(see illustration 13.7a)**. Carefully release the compressor, making sure the collets seat and lock in the retaining groove.

33 Repeat the procedure for the remaining valves. Remember to keep the parts for each valve together and separate from the other valves so they can be reinstalled in the same location.

34 Support the cylinder head on blocks so the valves can't contact the work surface, then tap the end of each valve stem lightly to seat the collets in their grooves **(see illustration)**.

> **HAYNES HINT**
> *Check for proper sealing of the valves by pouring a small amount of solvent into each of the valve ports. If the solvent leaks past any valve into the combustion chamber the valve grinding operation on that valve should be repeated.*

35 After the cylinder head and camshafts have been installed, set the valve clearances (see Chapter 1).

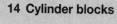
14 Cylinder blocks

Removal

1 Remove the cylinder head (see Section 12) and the cam chain guide blade (see Section 10). On 2004 to 2011 DL models detach the crankcase breather hose from the front cylinder.

2 Unscrew the two cylinder block nuts **(see illustration)** – note the wiring clamp secured by the front nut on the rear cylinder block on 2004 to 2011 DL models, and by the rear nut on later DL models and all SFV models.

3 Hold the cam chain up and pull the cylinder block up off the crankcase, taking care not to allow the connecting rod to knock against the crankcase once the piston is free, then pass the cam chain down through the tunnel and drape it over the tensioner blade **(see illustration)**. Do not let the chain fall into the crankcase – secure it with a piece of wire or metal bar to prevent it from doing so. If the block is stuck, tap around its base with a soft-faced mallet. Do not try to free it by inserting a screwdriver between the block and crankcase – you'll damage the surfaces. Note that each block is marked 'FRONT' or 'REAR' according to its location. After the block has

been removed, stuff clean rags around the piston to prevent anything falling into the crankcase.

4 Remove the old gasket **(see illustration 14.16)**. Pull the oil jet out, taking great care not to drop it into the crankcase – make sure the rag covers the holes completely **(see illustration 14.14b)**. Remove the O-ring and discard it **(see illustration 14.14a)**.

5 If they are loose, remove the two dowels from the cylinder block or crankcase **(see illustration 14.16)**.

6 Check the base gasket and the mating surfaces on the cylinder head and block for signs of leakage, which could indicate warpage. Refer below and check the block.

7 Clean all traces of old gasket material from the cylinder block and crankcase. If a scraper is used, take care not to scratch or gouge the soft aluminium. Be careful not to let any of the gasket material drop into the crankcase or the oil passages.

13.31b ...then fit the spring retainer

13.34 Tap the end of the valve stem to seat the collets

Inspection

8 Do not attempt to separate the liner from the cylinder block.

9 Check the bore walls carefully for scratches and score marks.

10 Using a precision straight-edge and a feeler gauge set to the warpage limit listed in the specifications at the beginning of the Chapter, check the top mating surface of the cylinder for warpage. Refer to *Tools and Workshop Tips* in the Reference section for details of how to use the straight-edge. If warpage is excessive the cylinder must be renewed.

11 Using a telescoping bore gauge and a micrometer (see *Tools and Workshop Tips*), check the dimensions of each bore to assess the amount of wear, taper and ovality. Measure near the top (but below the level of the top piston ring at TDC), centre and bottom (but above the level of the oil ring at BDC) of the bore, both parallel to and across the crankshaft axis **(see illustrations)**.

14.2 Slacken the two cylinder block nuts (arrowed)

14.3 Lift the block up off the crankcase and remove it

14.11a Use a bore gauge...

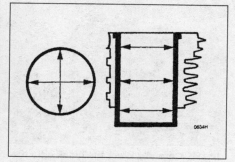
14.11b ...and measure at the points shown

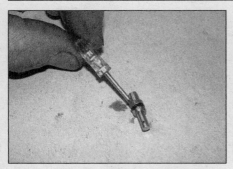

14.14a Fit a new O-ring onto the oil jet

14.14b Push the oil jet into its orifice

14.16 Fit the two dowels (arrowed) and seat the new gasket over them

Compare the results to the specifications at the beginning of the Chapter. If the bores are worn, oval or tapered beyond the service limit, on 2004 to 2011 DL models they can be re-bored, and an oversize (+0.5) set of pistons and rings are available from Suzuki. Note that the person carrying out the re-bore must be aware of the piston-to-bore clearance for the oversize piston (see Specifications). On later DL models and all SFV models the cylinder liners must not be re-bored as they have an electrochemical plating finish.

12 If the precision measuring tools are not available, take the cylinder to a Suzuki dealer or specialist motorcycle repair shop for assessment and advice.

Installation

13 Check that the mating surfaces of the cylinder and crankcase are free from oil, sealant and pieces of old gasket.

14 Clean the oil jet with solvent and blow it through with compressed air if available. Fit a new O-ring onto the jet and smear it with grease **(see illustration)**. Squirt some oil into the passage, then press the jet in with the slotted end facing out **(see illustration)**.

15 If removed, fit the dowels into the crankcase or into the block, and push them firmly home **(see illustration 14.16)**.

16 Remove the rag from around the piston, taking care not to let the connecting rod fall against the rim of the crankcase. Apply a smear of sealant (Suzuki Bond 1215 or equivalent) across each crankcase joint. Lay the new base gasket in place, locating it over the dowels (if they are in the crankcase) **(see illustration)**. The gasket can only fit one way, so if the holes do not line up properly it is upside down or it is the wrong gasket – the front and rear cylinder gaskets are different. Never re-use the old gasket.

17 Space the piston rings gaps as described in Section 16.

18 Lubricate the cylinder bore, piston and piston rings with clean engine oil **(see illustration)**. Turn the crankshaft so the piston is at its highest point (TDC). It is useful to place a support under the piston so that it remains level and at TDC while the block is fitted, otherwise the downward pressure will cock the piston and/or turn the crankshaft and the piston will drop.

19 Make sure you have the correct block for the cylinder being worked on – they are marked 'FRONT' and 'REAR' **(see illustration)**. Fit the cylinder squarely onto the piston crown, and carefully compress and feed each ring into the bore as you gently push the cylinder down **(see illustrations)**. If possible, have an assistant support the cylinder while this is done.

20 When the piston is correctly located in the bore, hook the cam chain up the tunnel and secure it to prevent it dropping back down. Remove the support if used, and press the cylinder down onto the base gasket, making sure the dowels locate.

21 Fit the two cylinder block nuts, along with the wiring clamp secured by the front nut on the rear cylinder block on 2004 to 2011 DL models, and by the rear nut on later DL models and all SFV models, and tighten them finger-tight only at this stage **(see illustration 14.2)**.

22 When both blocks are installed, hold them down, keep the cam chains taut, and turn the crankshaft a little way in each direction to check that everything moves as it should.

23 Install the cam chain guide blade (see Section 10) and the cylinder head (see Section 12).

14.18 Lubricate the pistons, rings and bore with new oil

14.19a Make sure you have the correct cylinder

15 Pistons

Removal

1 Remove the cylinder block (see Section 14).

2 If working on both cylinders, before removing the piston from the connecting rod, use paint or a sharp scriber to write the

14.19b Carefully lower the block onto the piston...

14.19c ...feeding the piston rings into the bore

15.2 Note the mark on the piston which faces the exhaust side

15.3a Prise the circlip out from one side of the piston

15.3b Push the piston pin out from the other side then withdraw it and remove the piston

cylinder identity and piston orientation on the crown of each piston (or on the inside of the skirt if the piston is dirty and going to be cleaned). Each piston crown has a circular indent that points to the exhaust side, though it may be invisible until the piston is cleaned **(see illustration)**.

3 Carefully prise out the circlip on each side of the piston using needle-nose pliers or a small flat-bladed screwdriver inserted into the notch **(see illustration)**. Push the piston pin out and remove the piston from the connecting rod **(see illustration)**. Once removed the circlips must not be reused. Slide the pin back into its piston so that related parts do not get mixed up.

> **HAYNES HiNT** *If a piston pin is a tight fit in the piston bosses, use a heat gun to heat the piston – this will expand the alloy piston sufficiently to release its grip on the pin. If the piston pin is particularly stubborn, extract it using a drawbolt tool, but be careful to protect the piston's working surfaces.*

4 Using your thumbs or a piston ring removal and installation tool, carefully remove the rings from the piston **(see illustrations 16.9, 16.8c, 16.6c, b and a)**. Do not nick or gouge the piston in the process. Carefully note which way up each ring fits and in which groove as they must be installed in their original positions if being reused.

5 Scrape all traces of carbon from the top of the piston. A hand-held wire brush or a piece of fine emery cloth can be used once most of the deposits have been scraped away. Do not, under any circumstances, use a wire brush mounted in a drill motor to remove deposits from the piston; the piston material is soft and will be eroded away by the wire brush.

6 Use a piston ring groove cleaning tool to remove any carbon deposits from the ring grooves. If a tool is not available, a piece broken off an old ring will do the job. Be very careful to remove only the carbon deposits. Do not remove any metal and do not nick or gouge the sides of the ring grooves.

7 Once the deposits have been removed, clean the piston with solvent and dry it thoroughly. If the identification mark previously made on the piston is cleaned off, be sure to re-mark it with the correct identity. Make sure the oil return holes below the oil ring groove are clear.

Inspection

8 Carefully inspect each piston for cracks around the skirt, at the pin bosses and at the ring lands. Normal piston wear appears as even, vertical wear on the thrust surfaces of the piston. If the skirt is scored or scuffed, the engine may have been suffering from overheating and/or abnormal combustion, which causes excessively high operating temperatures. Also check that the circlip grooves are not damaged.

9 A hole in the top of the piston, in one

extreme, or burned areas around the edge of the piston crown, indicate that pre-ignition or knocking under load have occurred. If you find evidence of any problems the cause must be corrected or the damage will occur again (see *Fault Finding* in the *Reference* section).

10 Measure the piston ring-to-groove clearance by laying each piston ring in its groove and slipping a feeler gauge in beside it **(see illustration)**. Make sure you have the correct ring for the groove. Check the clearance at three or four locations around the groove. If the clearance is greater than specified, replace both the piston and rings as a set. If new rings are being used, measure the clearance using the new rings. If the clearance is greater than that specified, the piston is worn and must be replaced with a new one. The 2012-on DL models and all SFV models use a stepped top ring, for which two dimensions are given in the Specifications for ring thickness and ring groove width **(see illustration)**.

11 Check the piston-to-bore clearance by measuring the bore (see Section 14), then measure the piston 20 mm up from the bottom of the skirt and at 90° to the piston pin axis **(see illustration)**. Make sure each piston is matched to its correct cylinder. Refer to the Specifications at the beginning of the Chapter and subtract the piston diameter from the bore diameter to obtain the clearance. If it is greater than the specified figure, the piston must be replaced with a new one (assuming the bore itself is within limits).

15.10a Fit the ring into the groove and measure clearance with a feeler gauge

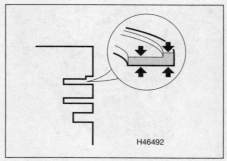

H46492

15.10b Note the stepped ring and groove profiles

15.11 Measure the piston diameter with a micrometer

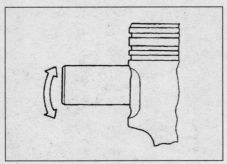

15.12a Slip the pin into the piston and check for freeplay between them

15.12b Measure the external diameter of the pin...

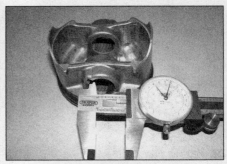

15.12c ...and the internal diameter of the bore in the piston

15.16a Slide the pin through the piston and connecting rod...

15.16b ...and secure it with the circlip, locating the open end away from the notch in the piston

16 Piston rings

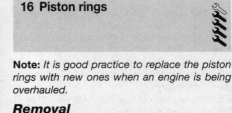

Note: *It is good practice to replace the piston rings with new ones when an engine is being overhauled.*

Removal

1 See Section 15, Step 4.

Inspection

2 Whether re-using the old rings or fitting new ones, check the end gaps of the top and 2nd rings, both with the rings free (i.e. flat on a work surface) and with them fitted in the bore, as follows. Lay out each piston with its ring set and keep them together so the rings will be matched with the same piston and bore during the measurement procedure and engine assembly.

3 With the ring flat on the work surface, measure its end gap using a Vernier caliper **(see illustration)**. Now insert the ring into the top of the bore and square it up with the bore walls by pushing it in with the top of the piston **(see illustration)**. The ring should be at least 20 mm below the top edge of the bore, so it is within its area of travel in the bore. Slip a feeler gauge between the ends of the ring and compare the measurement to the specifications at the beginning of the Chapter **(see illustration)**.

4 If the gap is larger or smaller than specified, double check to make sure that you have the

12 Apply clean engine oil to the piston pin, insert it into the piston and check for any freeplay between the two **(see illustration)**. Measure the pin external diameter near each end, and the pin bores in the piston **(see illustrations)**. Calculate the difference to obtain the piston pin-to-piston pin bore clearance. Compare the result to the specifications at the beginning of the Chapter. If the clearance is greater than specified, replace the components that are worn beyond their specified limits. Repeat the measurements between the middle of the pin and the connecting rod small-end.

Installation

13 Inspect and install the piston rings (see Section 16).
14 Lubricate the piston pin, the piston pin bore and the connecting rod small-end bore

with molybdenum disulphide oil (a 50/50 mixture of molybdenum disulphide grease and clean engine oil).
15 When fitting the pistons onto the connecting rods make sure that the circular indent on the piston crown points to the exhaust side i.e. to the front of the engine for the front cylinder piston, and to the rear for the rear piston) **(see illustration 15.2)**.
16 Fit a *new* circlip into one side of the piston (do not reuse old circlips). Line up the piston on its correct connecting rod, and insert the piston pin from the other side **(see illustration)**. Secure the pin with the other *new* circlip **(see illustration)**. When fitting the circlips, compress them only just enough to fit them in the piston, and make sure they are properly seated in their grooves with the open end away from the removal notch.
17 Install the cylinder block (see Section 14).

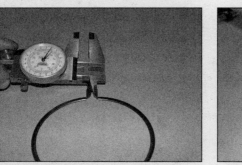

16.3a Measure the free end gap of the piston ring...

16.3b ...then fit the ring into the bore and square it up with the piston...

16.3c ...and measure the installed end gap

16.6a Fit the oil ring expander in its groove...

16.6b ...then fit the lower side rail...

16.6c ...and the upper side rail

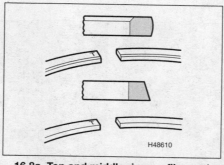

16.8a Top and middle ring profiles and marking – 2004 to 2011 DL

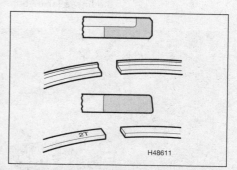

16.8b Top and middle ring profiles and marking – 2012-on DL and all SFV

correct rings before proceeding; excess end gap is not critical unless it exceeds the service limit.

5 If the service limit is exceeded with new rings, check the bore for wear (see Section 14). If the gap is too small, the ring ends may come in contact with each other during engine operation, which can cause serious damage.

Installation

6 Fit the oil control ring (lowest on the piston) first. It is composed of three separate components, namely the expander and the upper and lower side-rails. Slip the expander into the groove, making sure the ends don't overlap **(see illustration)**. Next fit the lower

side-rail **(see illustration)**. Do not use a piston ring installation tool on the side-rails as they may be damaged. Instead, place one end of the side-rail into the groove between the expander and the ring land. Hold it firmly in place and slide a finger around the piston while pushing the rail into the groove. Next, fit the upper side-rail in the same manner **(see illustration)**. Check that the ends of the expander have not overlapped.

7 After the three oil ring components have been installed, check to make sure that both the upper and lower side-rails can be turned smoothly in the ring groove.

8 Fit the second (middle) ring next – it can be identified by its cross-section profile **(see**

illustrations). Make sure that the ring is fitted with the letter(s) facing up. Fit the ring into the middle groove in the piston **(see illustration)**. Do not expand the ring any more than is necessary to slide it into place. To avoid breaking the ring, use a piston ring installation tool.

9 Finally, fit the top ring in the same manner into the top groove in the piston **(see illustration)**. On 2004 to 2011 DL models make sure the letter near the end gap is facing up, and on later DL models and all SFV models make sure the stepped side faces up.

10 Once the rings are correctly installed, check they move freely without snagging and stagger their end gaps as shown **(see illustration)**.

16.8c Fit the middle ring into its groove...

16.9 ...then fit the top ring

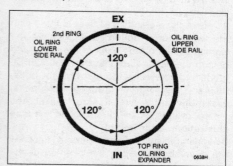

16.10 Arrange the ring end gaps as shown

17.2a On 2004 to 2011 DL models release the clamps and detach the hoses (arrowed)

17.2b On all other models release the clamps and detach the hoses (arrowed)

17.2c On all models pull the pump drain hose off its union

17.3 Clutch cover bolts (arrowed)

17 Clutch

Removal

1 Drain the engine oil and the cooling system (see Chapter 1).

2 A one-piece crankcase cover is fitted with the water pump bolted to it. Release the clamps securing the hoses to the cover and detach the hoses (see illustrations). On DL models unscrew the footrest bracket bolts, displace the footrest bracket/brake pedal assembly and swivel it sideways so the master cylinder pushrod remains in line (see illustrations 4.18a and b).

3 Working in a criss-cross pattern, unscrew the cover bolts, noting the position of the hose clip(s) and bracket (according to model), and lift the cover away from the engine

together with the water pump, being prepared to catch any residual oil (see illustration). Note the location of the two dowels and remove them for safekeeping if they are loose.

4 Hold the clutch to prevent it turning. Working

in a criss-cross pattern, gradually slacken the clutch pressure plate bolts until spring pressure is released, then remove the bolts, collars (2012-on DL models only), springs and the pressure plate (see illustrations). Withdraw the pressure plate lifter, noting the thrust washer and bearing (see

17.4a Unscrew the bolts (arrowed) and remove the collars (where fitted) and springs...

17.4b ...and the pressure plate

17.4c Withdraw the pressure plate lifter...

17.4d ...and if required the pushrod

17.5 Remove the clutch plates as a pack

17.6a Unstake the clutch nut...

17.6b ...then unscrew it as described – here a commercially available holding tool is being used

17.11 Measure the thickness of the friction plates...

illustration). If required withdraw the right-hand pushrod from the input shaft using a hooked piece of wire to draw it out (see illustration).

5 Grasp the complete set of clutch plates and remove them as a pack (see illustration). Alternatively, remove the plates one by one, keeping them in order, using a bent piece of wire to hook them out where necessary. Unless the plates are being replaced with new ones, keep them assembled in their original order. Note that the innermost friction plate has a wider internal diameter so that it will fit over the anti-judder spring assembly; remove the anti-judder spring, noting which way round it fits, and the spring seat.

6 Bend the lock washer tab off the clutch nut (see illustration). To remove the clutch nut the transmission input shaft must be locked. This can be done in several ways. If the engine is in the frame, engage top gear and have an assistant hold the rear brake on

hard with the rear tyre in firm contact with the ground. Alternatively, the Suzuki service tool (Pt. No. 09920-53740) or a commercially available equivalent can be used to hold the clutch centre whilst the nut is slackened (see illustration). Unscrew the nut and remove the lockwasher – a new washer must be used.

7 Slide the clutch centre off the shaft (see illustration 17.25).

8 Slide the thrust washer off the shaft (see illustration 17.24).

9 Slide the clutch housing off the shaft, noting that you may have to prevent the spacer in the centre of the housing from sliding with it by pressing on its rim using a very small screwdriver (see illustration 17.23a).

10 Slide the shouldered spacer off the shaft.

Inspection

11 After an extended period of service the clutch friction plates will wear and cause

clutch slip. Measure the thickness of each friction plate using a Vernier caliper (see illustration). If any plate has worn to or beyond the service limit given in the Specifications at the beginning of the Chapter, or if any of the plates smell burnt or are glazed, the friction plates must be replaced with a new set.

12 Also measure the width of the friction plate tabs (see illustration) and replace the plates with a new set if the tabs are worn to the service limit.

13 The plain plates should not show any signs of excess heating (bluing). Check for warpage using a flat surface and feeler gauges (see illustration). If any plate exceeds the maximum permissible amount of warpage, or shows signs of bluing, all plain plates must be replaced with a new set.

14 Measure the free length of each clutch spring using a Vernier caliper (see illustration). If any spring is below the service

17.12 ...and the width of the tabs

17.13 Check the plain plates for warpage

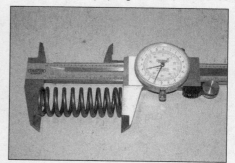

17.14a Measure the free length of the clutch springs...

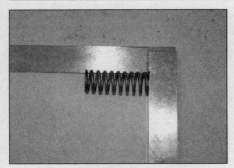

17.14b ...and check they are not bent

17.16a Check the friction plate tabs and housing slots...

17.16b ...and the plain plate teeth and centre slots as described

17.17 Check the bush (arrowed) for wear

17.18a Withdraw the left-hand pushrod

17.18b Remove the retainer plate...

limit specified, replace all the springs with new set. Also place each spring upright on a flat surface and check it for bend by placing a ruler against it, or alternatively lay it against a set square **(see illustration)**. If the bend in any spring is excessive, all springs must be replaced with new ones.

15 Check the anti-judder spring and seat for wear, damage and deformation. If any is found, or if the clutch has been juddering, replace them with new ones.

16 Inspect the friction plate tabs and the clutch housing slots for burrs and indentations **(see illustration)**. Similarly check for wear between the inner teeth of the plain plates and the slots in the clutch centre **(see illustration)**. Wear of this nature will cause clutch drag and slow disengagement during gear changes as the plates will snag when the pressure plate is lifted. With care a small amount of wear can be corrected by dressing with a fine file, but if

this is excessive the worn components should be replaced with new ones.

17 Check the bush in the clutch housing and the spacer it runs on for signs of wear, damage and scoring. The oil retention groove in the bush must be distinctly visible. Replace the housing and/or spacer with new ones if necessary **(see illustration)**.

18 Check the clutch pressure plate, the lifter, the bearing and the thrust washer for signs of roughness, wear or damage. If not already done, withdraw the right-hand pushrod from the input shaft (see Step 4) **(see illustration 17.4d)**. Check that the pushrod is straight. To access the left-hand pushrod, on 2004 to 2011 DL models remove the front sprocket cover (see Chapter 6), then displace the release mechanism (see Step 19), and on later DL models and all SFV models remove the alternator cover (see Section 22). Withdraw the pushrod **(see illustration)**. To access

the oil seal, remove the front sprocket (see Chapter 6). Unscrew the oil seal retainer plate bolts and remove the plate **(see illustration)**. Lever out the old seal using a screwdriver, then drive a new seal squarely into place **(see illustration)**. Fit the retainer plate, making sure the gear position switch switch wiring is correctly routed behind the tab, and tighten its bolts.

19 Check the clutch release mechanism for smooth operation and any signs of wear or damage. If the action is rough, on 2004 to 2011 DL models detach the clutch cable (see Section 18), then unscrew the two bolts securing the mechanism to the engine and remove it for cleaning and re-greasing **(see illustrations)**. Reassemble the mechanism and fit it back onto the crankcase (make sure you fit the left-hand pushrod and associated components first – Step 18), then attach the clutch cable (see Section 18). On 2012-on

17.18c ...to access the oil seal (arrowed)

17.19a Unscrew the bolts and remove the release mechanism...

17.19b ...then disassemble it, clean it and re-grease it – early DL

17.19c On later models, remove the push-piece and seal

17.19d You will have to carefully drive the shaft out to displace the bearing and seal

17.19e Correct fitting of return spring ends and washer

17.23a Fit the clutch housing...

17.23b ...making sure related gear teeth engage correctly

17.23c Insert a rod into one of the holes to align the offset gear teeth

DL models and all SFV models remove the alternator cover (Section 22), then remove the push-piece and the lower oil seal **(see illustration)**. Drive the shaft out – this will bring the upper oil seal and bearing with it **(see illustration)**. There is another bearing for the bottom end of the shaft that may require an internal expanding puller to remove it. Replace the oil seals and bearings with new ones. Fit the bearings with the marked end facing up and the oil seals with the marked side facing out, and grease all components before fitting them (make sure you fit the left-hand pushrod and associated components first – Step 18). Make sure the washer is fitted under the return spring, and the spring ends locate correctly **(see illustration)**.

20 Check the teeth of the primary driven gear on the back of the clutch housing and the corresponding teeth of the primary drive gear on the crankshaft. Replace the clutch housing and/or primary drive gear with new ones if worn or chipped teeth are discovered (refer to Section 20 for the primary drive gear). To remove the oil pump drive gear refer to Section 21.

Installation

Note: *If the primary drive gear has been removed and not yet installed, do so before installing the clutch (see Section 20).*

21 Remove all traces of old gasket from the crankcase and clutch cover surfaces.

22 Smear the outside of the shouldered spacer with engine oil. Slide the spacer onto the shaft with the shouldered end innermost.

23 Slide the clutch housing onto the spacer, engaging the teeth on the oil pump drive gear with those on the driven gear, and the teeth on the primary driven gear with those on the primary drive gear **(see illustrations)** – on 2012-on DL models and all SFV models the primary drive gear has a sprung offset gear, the teeth of which must be aligned with the main gear by inserting a suitable rod in the holes between them in order for the driven gear teeth to engage **(see illustration)**. Check the oil pump gears are engaged by trying to turn the driven gear.

24 Slide the thrust washer onto the shaft **(see illustration)**.

25 Slide the clutch centre onto the shaft **(see illustration)**.

26 Slide a *new* lock washer onto the shaft

17.24 Slide the thrust washer onto the shaft...

17.25 ...followed by the clutch centre

17.26a Fit a new lock washer...

17.26b ...then fit the clutch nut...

17.26c ...and tighten it to the specified torque

17.26d Bend up the lock washer tab to secure the clutch nut

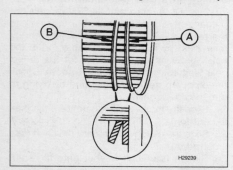

17.27 Fit the spring seat (A) and spring (B) as shown

then fit the clutch nut, with its chamfered side facing out **(see illustrations)**. Using the method employed on removal to lock the input shaft (see Step 6), tighten the nut to the torque setting specified at the beginning of the Chapter **(see illustration)**. **Note:** *Check that the clutch centre rotates freely after tightening the clutch nut.* Bend up one side of the lock washer against one of the flats on the clutch nut **(see illustration)**.

27 Fit the spring seat, then fit the anti-judder spring *with its outer edge raised off the spring seat* **(see illustration)**.

28 Coat each clutch plate with engine oil as you fit them, and build up the plates in the housing as follows: start with the friction plate with the wider internal diameter that fits over the anti-judder spring assembly. Next fit a plain plate, then alternate friction plates and plain plates until all are installed **(see illustrations)**.

29 If removed, smear molybdenum grease onto each end of the pushrod and slide it into the input shaft **(see illustration 17.4d)**. Lubricate the pressure plate lifter, the bearing and thrust washer with clean oil, then fit

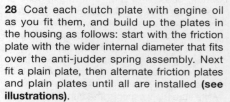

17.28a Fit the friction plate with the larger ID first...

17.28b ...then alternate plain plates...

17.28c ...and friction plates

17.29a Fit the bearing and washer onto the lifter...

17.29b ...then fit the assembly into the shaft

17.30a Fit the pressure plate, making sure it locates as described...

17.30b ...then fit the springs, collars and bolts

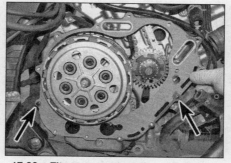

17.32a Fit a new gasket onto the dowels (arrowed)...

17.32b ...then install the cover

the bearing and washer onto the lifter (see illustration). Slide the lifter into the input shaft (see illustration).

30 Fit the pressure plate into the clutch centre, making sure it seats correctly with its inner rim castellations locating in the slots in the centre – if there is any clearance between the clutch plates as you push on the pressure plate then it has not located properly (see illustration). Fit the clutch springs, collars (where fitted) and bolts and tighten the bolts evenly in a criss-cross sequence to the specified torque setting (see illustration).

31 Check the clutch lever freeplay and adjust if necessary (see Chapter 1).

32 Make sure the dowels are in place in the crankcase, then fit a new cover gasket over the dowels (see illustration). Fit the crankcase cover, making sure the water pump driven gear engages correctly with its drive gear (turn the complete pump housing slightly as required to facilitate this), and the dowels locate correctly (see illustration). Tighten the cover bolts evenly in a criss-cross sequence (see illustration 17.3).

33 Fit the hoses and secure them with their clamps (see illustrations 17.2a, b and c). On DL models fit the footrest bracket/brake pedal assembly (see illustration 4.18a).

34 Add coolant and engine oil (see Chapter 1). Check that there are no leaks.

18 Clutch cable

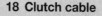

Removal

1 Where fitted on DL models remove the handguard (see Chapter 7). Pull the rubber cover off the adjuster in the clutch lever bracket (see illustration). Fully slacken the lockring, then screw the adjuster fully in. This resets it to the beginning of its adjustment range.

2 On 2004 to 2011 DL models remove the front sprocket cover (see Chapter 6). Fully slacken the adjuster top locknut (see

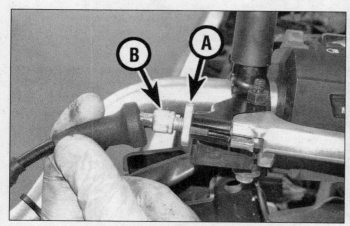

18.1 Pull the boot off, slacken the lockring (A) and turn the adjuster (B) fully in

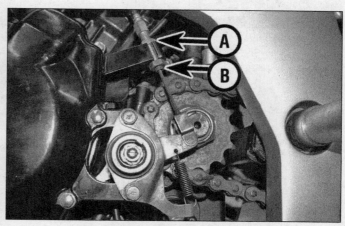

18.2a Top locknut (A), bottom locknut (B)

18.2b Bend down the tab (arrowed)...

18.2c ...and slip the cable end out of the arm

18.2d Remove the bottom locknut...

18.2e ...and withdraw the cable

in so that cable freeplay is at a maximum **(see illustration)**. Draw the lower end of the cable out of its holder, then detach the cable end from the arm **(see illustrations)**.

4 Align the slots in the top adjuster and lockring with that in the lever bracket, then pull the outer cable end from the socket in the adjuster and release the inner cable end from the lever **(see illustrations)**.

5 Take note of the exact routing of the cable and any guides that hold it – incorrect installation could result in poor steering movement and affect clutch action. Carefully withdraw the cable – if it gets stuck do not be tempted to pull it out using force as you will only damage something.

> **HAYNES HiNT** *Before removing the cable from the bike, tape the lower end of the new cable to the upper end of the old cable. Slowly pull the lower end of the old cable out, guiding the new cable down into position. Using this method will ensure the cable is routed correctly.*

Installation

6 Installation is the reverse of removal. Apply grease to the cable ends. Make sure the cable is correctly routed. On 2004 to 2011 DL models do not forget to bend up the tab in the release arm to secure the cable end **(see illustration)**. Adjust the amount of clutch lever freeplay (see Chapter 1).

illustration). Using a small flat-bladed screwdriver, bend down the tab securing the inner cable end in the release arm and slip the cable out of the arm **(see illustrations)**. Thread the bottom locknut off the adjuster

and draw the cable out of its bracket **(see illustrations)**.

3 On 2012-on DL models and all SFV models fully slacken the locknut on the cable adjuster near the top yoke, then turn the adjuster fully

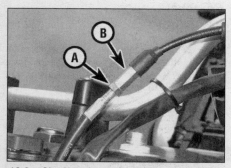

18.3a Slacken the locknut (A) and turn the adjuster (B) in

18.3b Draw the cable out of the holder...

18.3c ...and detach the end from the arm

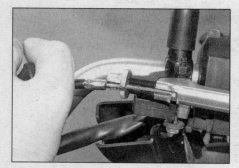

18.4a Align the slots and slip the cable out of the bracket...

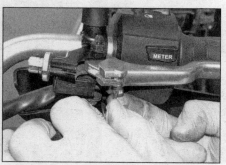

18.4b ...and detach it from the lever

18.6 Bend up the tab to secure the cable

19 Gearchange mechanism

Removal

1 Make sure the transmission is in neutral. Remove the clutch (see Section 17). Block the holes into the crankcase with clean rag to prevent anything falling in.

2 Note the alignment of the slit in the gearchange linkage arm with the punch mark on the shaft, or make your own mark if none is visible, then unscrew the pinch bolt and slide the arm off **(see illustration 4.12a or b)**.

3 Remove the circlip and washer from the shaft **(see illustrations)**.

4 Note how the gearchange selector arm locates onto the pins in the selector drum cam plate, and how the gearchange shaft centralising spring ends locate. Withdraw the gearchange shaft from the engine, making sure the inner washer comes with it and does

19.3a Remove the circlip...

19.3b ...and slide the washer off

not stick on the crankcase **(see illustration)**.

5 Note how the stopper arm spring ends locate and how the roller on the arm locates in the neutral detent on the selector drum cam, then unscrew the stopper arm bolt and remove the arm, the washer, and the spring, noting how they fit **(see illustration)**.

6 If necessary, unscrew the bolt securing the cam plate to the selector drum and remove

the plate – use a screwdriver located between a cam and the bearing retainer plate as shown to prevent the drum turning **(see illustration)**. Note that there are two locating pins that fit between the cam plate and the drum – it is advisable to place some rag in the bottom of the crankcase to catch the pins should they drop out. Otherwise remove the pins for safekeeping **(see illustration)**.

19.4 Note how the spring ends locate then withdraw the shaft

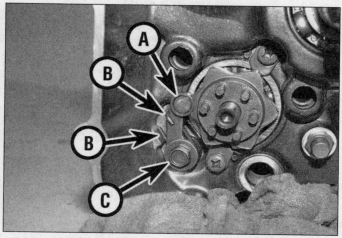

19.5 Note how the roller (A) and the spring ends (B) locate, then unscrew the bolt (C) and remove the arm

19.6a Use a screwdriver located as shown to prevent the drum turning while unscrewing the bolt

19.6b Note the locating pins (arrowed) that fit in the holes in the back of the plate and remove them for safekeeping

19.7 Lever out the seal

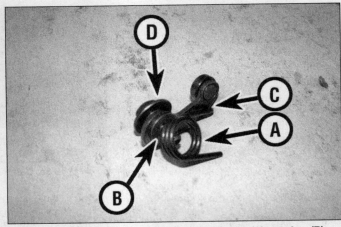

19.8a Stopper arm assembly – return spring (A), washer (B), stopper arm (C), bolt (D)

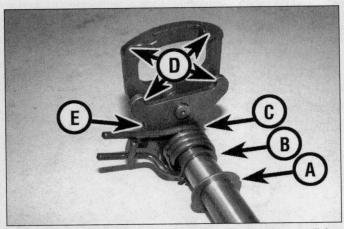

19.8b Selector arm assembly – washer (A), circlip (B), centralising spring (C), pawls (D), lower pawl plate (E)...

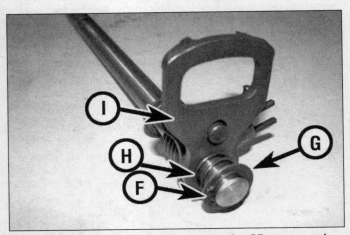

19.8c ...circlip (F), washer (G), thrust spring (H), upper pawl plate (I)

7 Whenever the shaft is removed a new oil seal should be fitted. Lever the old seal out with a screwdriver or seal hook **(see illustration)**.

Inspection

8 Inspect the stopper arm return spring and the shaft centralising spring and thrust spring **(see illustrations)**. If they are fatigued, worn or damaged they must be replaced with new ones – each is retained by a circlip. Also check that the centralising spring locating pin in the crankcase is tight **(see illustration 19.15b)**. If it is loose, remove it, clean the threads, and apply a non-permanent thread locking compound to its threads, then tighten it to the torque setting specified at the beginning of the Chapter.

9 Check the gearchange shaft is straight and look for any damage to the splines. If the shaft is bent you can attempt to straighten it, but if the splines are damaged the shaft must be replaced with a new one.

10 Inspect the selector arm pawls and the pins on the cam plate for wear and replace them with new ones if necessary **(see illustrations 19.8b and c)**. The selector arm upper pawl plate can be separated from the lower (which is integral with the shaft) after removing the washer, circlip and thrust spring – note how the hole in the upper plate locates over the pin on the lower one.

11 Check the stopper arm roller and the cam plate detents **(see illustration 19.8a)**. If they are worn or damaged they must be replaced with new ones. Check that the roller spins freely.

Installation

12 Press or drive a new shaft oil seal squarely into place, with its marked side facing out, using your fingers or a seal driver or suitable socket if necessary – the seal sits slightly deeper than the rim of its bore so make sure it is fully in place using a seal driver socket **(see illustrations)**.

19.12a Fit the new seal with the marked side facing out...

19.12b ...and press or drive it into place

19.13a Fit the threadlocked bolt...

19.13b ...and tighten it to the specified torque, locking the drum as before

19.14 Install the stopper arm assembly as described

19.15a Slide the shaft into the crankcase...

19.15b ...and locate the spring ends around the pin (arrowed)

ends locate correctly each side of the locating pin in the crankcase (see illustrations).

16 Slide the washer onto the left-hand end of the shaft and fit the circlip, making sure it locates in its groove (see illustrations 19.3b and a).

17 Slide the gearchange lever onto the shaft, aligning the punch mark on the shaft end with the slit in the clamp, or you own marks if made. Tighten the pinch bolt and check that the gearchange mechanism works correctly.

18 Remove the rag used to block the holes. Install the clutch (see Section 17).

20 Primary drive gear

Caution: The primary drive gear bolt has left-hand threads, meaning that it must be undone in a clockwise direction and tightened in an anti-clockwise direction.

Removal

1 Remove the clutch (see Section 17). Unscrew the crankshaft end cap from the alternator cover (see illustration).

2 To unscrew the primary drive gear bolt the crankshaft must be prevented from turning. To do this, counter-hold the crankshaft using a 17 mm socket on the alternator rotor bolt (see illustration). Due to the left-hand threads

13 Clean the threads of the cam plate bolt. If removed, fit the locating pins into the end of the selector drum (see illustration 19.6b). Fit the cam plate, making sure the holes in the back locate correctly on the pins – they are offset slightly so the cam can only fit one way. Apply a suitable thread locking compound to the threads of the bolt and tighten it to the torque setting specified at the beginning of the Chapter, locking the plate to prevent it turning as on removal (see illustrations).

14 Clean the threads of the stopper arm bolt. Fit the stopper arm bolt through the stopper arm, then fit the washer and return spring (see illustration 19.8a). Apply a threadlock to the threads of the bolt. Fit the assembly onto the crankcase, making sure the spring ends

locate correctly over the stopper arm and against the crankcase, and partially tighten the bolt (see illustration). Lift the stopper arm using a screwdriver as a lever or a pair of pliers, then fully tighten the bolt, locating the roller onto the neutral detent in the cam as they become aligned (see illustration 19.5). Tighten the bolt to the specified torque setting. Afterwards make sure the arm is free to move and is returned by the pressure of the spring.

15 Make sure the inner washer is on the gearchange shaft and the centralising spring ends are correctly located on each side of the tab on the lower pawl plate (see illustration 19.8b). Slide the shaft into its hole in the engine, making sure the centralising spring

20.1 Unscrew the end cap (arrowed)

20.2 Counter-hold the rotor bolt

20.3a Unscrew the bolt (arrowed)...

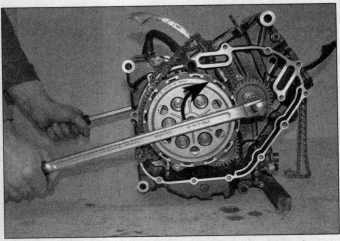

20.3b ...turning it clockwise as it has left-hand threads

of the primary drive gear bolt the alternator rotor bolt is effectively being tightened by this action, but as it is set to a higher torque setting there is no danger of it tightening more and stripping out.

3 With the crankshaft locked, unscrew the primary drive gear bolt, remembering that it has left-hand threads and so must be slackened by turning it clockwise instead of anti-clockwise (see illustrations).

4 Mark the outer faces of the water pump drive gear and the primary drive gear so they can be installed the correct way round on refitting. Slide the water pump gear and the primary drive gear off the end of the crankshaft (see illustrations).

Inspection

5 Check the teeth of the primary drive gear and the corresponding teeth of the primary driven gear on the back of the clutch housing. Replace the clutch housing and/or primary drive gear with new ones if worn or chipped teeth are discovered.

Installation

6 Slide the primary drive gear onto the crankshaft with the marking made previously

facing outwards (see illustration 20.4b). Slide the water pump drive gear onto the shaft with the marking made previously facing outwards (see illustration 20.4a).

7 Fit the bolt and tighten it finger-tight, remembering that it has left-hand threads and so must be tightened in an anti-clockwise direction (see illustration). Lock the crankshaft by counter-holding the alternator bolt as on removal – there is no danger of the bolt coming undone as it is set to a higher torque setting than the primary drive gear bolt is being tightened to. With the crankshaft locked, tighten the primary drive gear bolt to the torque setting specified at the beginning of the Chapter (see illustration), but first check that your torque wrench can be set to tighten left-hand threaded bolts – some of them can't, which means you will keep on tightening, expecting the wrench to click at the correct setting, whereas you will actually be tightening the bolt too much which could strip the threads, or the alternator rotor bolt will begin to unscrew!

8 Fit the crankshaft end cap using a new O-ring smeared with grease. Tighten the cap to the torque setting specified at the beginning of the Chapter.

9 Install the clutch (see Section 17).

20.4a Slide the pump drive gear off the shaft...

20.4b ...followed by the primary drive gear

20.7a Fit the bolt...

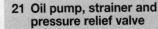

20.7b ... and tighten it in an anti-clockwise direction to the specified torque

21 Oil pump, strainer and pressure relief valve

Oil pump

Pressure check

1 See Section 3. If the pressure is as specified at the beginning of the Chapter then the pump is good. If the pressure is lower than it should be, and all other possible causes (as listed in Section 3) have been eliminated, then the pump is worn or faulty and must be replaced with a new one. No individual components are available.

21.3a Remove the circlip...

21.3b ...and slide the gear off

21.3c Withdraw the drive pin...

Removal

2 Remove the clutch (see Section 17). Block the holes into the crankcase with clean rag to prevent anything falling in.

3 Remove the circlip securing the driven gear and slide the gear off the shaft, noting how it locates onto the drive pin **(see illustrations)**. Withdraw the pin from the shaft and slide off the washer **(see illustrations)**.

4 Undo the three screws or bolts (according to model) and remove the pump **(see illustrations)**.

Inspection

5 Check the pump body for cracks and other damage. Rotate the shaft and check that it turns smoothly and freely.

6 Check the driven gear teeth for wear and damage and replace it with a new one if necessary. Similarly check the drive gear on the back of the clutch housing **(see illustration)**. The drive gear is secured by a circlip – mark the outer face of the gear, remove the circlip and lift the gear off, then remove the pin that locates between the cut-outs in the gear and clutch housing hub to lock them together. Fit the gear in reverse order, making sure the pin locates correctly, the gear is the correct way round and the circlip seats in its groove.

Installation

7 Before fitting the pump, prime it by pouring oil into the outlet and turning the shaft by hand **(see illustration)**. This ensures that oil is being pumped as soon as the engine is turned over.

8 Fit the pump, making sure it locates

21.3d ...and remove the washer

21.4a Undo the screws (arrowed)...

21.4b ...and remove the pump

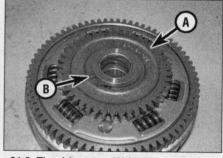

21.6 The drive gear (A) is secured on the back of the clutch housing by a circlip (B)

correctly into the crankcase **(see illustration)**. Apply a suitable non-permanent thread locking compound to the pump screws or bolts and tighten them **(see illustration)**.

9 Slide the washer onto the shaft, then fit the

drive pin through the hole **(see illustrations 21.3d and c)**. Locate the cut-outs in the driven gear over the drive pin ends and secure the gear with the circlip, making sure it locates in its groove **(see illustrations 21.3b and a)**.

21.7 Prime the pump with new oil

21.8a Locate the pump on the crankcase...

21.8b ...then threadlock the screws and tighten them

21.12 Unscrew the bolts (arrowed), then remove the plate...

21.13 ...and withdraw the strainer

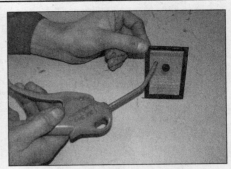

21.14 Clean the strainer as described

10 Remove the rag used to block the holes. Install the clutch (see Section 17).

Oil strainer

Removal

11 Remove the engine from the frame (see Section 4) and separate the crankcase halves (see Section 23).
12 Unscrew the strainer plate bolts and remove the plate (see illustration).
13 Withdraw the strainer from its housing, noting which way round it fits and how it locates in the slots (see illustration).

Inspection

14 Clean the strainer in solvent and blow it through with compressed air (see illustration). Check the mesh for holes or splits at the edges and replace it with a new one if necessary.

Installation

15 Fit the strainer back into its housing thin end first, locating the edges in the slots and making sure the protrusion faces down and out (see illustration).
16 Clean the strainer plate bolts, then apply a suitable non-permanent thread locking compound. Fit the plate and tighten the bolts to the specified torque setting (see illustration).
17 Reassemble the crankcase halves (see Section 23).

Pressure relief valve

Removal

18 Remove the engine from the frame (see Section 5) and separate the crankcase halves (see Section 23).
19 Unscrew and remove the relief valve (see illustration).

Inspection

20 Press down on the plunger and check that it moves freely in the body and returns under spring pressure (see illustration). If it doesn't, replace the valve with a new one – it cannot be disassembled and no individual components are available.

Installation

21 Fit the valve into the crankcase and tighten it to the torque setting specified at the beginning of the Chapter (see illustration).
22 Reassemble the crankcase halves (see Section 23).

22 Alternator rotor and starter clutch

Note: *The alternator stator and charging system testing are covered in Chapter 8.*

Check

1 The operation of the starter clutch can be checked while it is in situ. Remove the starter motor (see Chapter 8). Check that the starter idle/reduction gear is able to rotate freely clockwise as you look at it via the starter motor aperture, but locks when rotated anti-clockwise. If not, the starter clutch is faulty and should be removed for inspection.

Removal

2 Support the bike upright. Either drain the engine oil (see Chapter 1), or place a container under the engine to catch the oil that will come

21.15 Fit the strainer, making sure the protrusion (arrowed) is as shown...

21.16 ...then fit the plate

21.19 Unscrew the relief valve (arrowed)...

21.20 ...and check it as described

21.21 Fit the valve and tighten it to the specified torque

22.3a Displace the speed sensor

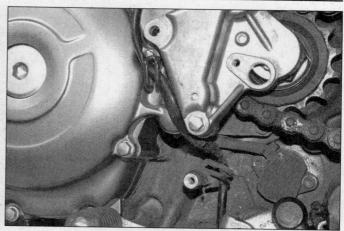

22.3b Release the wiring

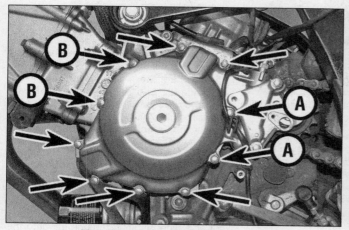

22.5 Alternator cover bolts (arrowed)

A = 65 mm bolts (all others 35 mm), B = bolts with sealing washers

22.6 Using a rotor strap to hold the rotor while unscrewing the bolt

out when the cover is removed. Disconnect the clutch cable from the release mechanism (Section 18).

3 On 2012-on DL models and all SFV models remove the front sprocket outer cover (see Chapter 6), then unscrew the speed sensor bolt and displace the sensor **(see illustration)**. Release the sidestand switch wiring **(see illustration)**. On DL models remove the belly pan if fitted (see Chapter 7).

4 If you want to remove the alternator cover or stator completely, disconnect the alternator and CKP sensor wiring connectors **(see illustration 4.10a or b and c)** – to access them on DL models remove the air filter housing (see Chapter 4), and on SFV models remove the right-hand side cover (see Chapter 7). Feed the wiring to the alternator cover, releasing it from any guides and noting its routing.

5 Working in a criss-cross pattern, evenly slacken the alternator cover bolts, noting the positions of the longer bolts and the bolts with sealing washers, and on 2012-on DL models and all SFV models the clutch cable bracket

and the clamp **(see illustration)**. Draw the cover off the engine, noting that it will be restrained by the force of the rotor magnets – if the wiring is still connected support or tie the cover to one side. Remove the gasket – a new one must be used on installation. Remove the dowels from either the cover or the crankcase if they are loose.

6 To remove the rotor bolt it is necessary to stop the rotor from turning. The best way is to use a commercially available rotor strap, but take care to avoid the ignition triggers around the rotor **(see illustration)**. If one is not available, try placing the transmission in gear and having an assistant sit on the seat and apply the rear brake whilst you unscrew the bolt. Note that the bolt will be very tight. Alternatively, Suzuki produce a service tool (Pt. No. 09930-44530) which fits around the inner boss of the rotor and can be held to prevent rotation. Note the washer fitted with the bolt when it is removed.

7 To remove the rotor from the shaft it is necessary to use a rotor puller, either the Suzuki service tool (Pt. No. 09930-30450)

or a commercial available equivalent from a motorcycle dealer – do not use a legged puller to remove the rotor. Thread the rotor puller into the centre of the rotor and turn it until the rotor is displaced from the shaft, holding the rotor as described above to prevent the engine turning. If the rotor doesn't come off easily tap the end of the tool when it is tight, and if necessary heat the rotor hub using a hot air gun. Remove the Woodruff key from its slot in the crankshaft if loose **(see illustration)**.

22.7a Remove the Woodruff key...

22.7b ...and slide the driven gear off

22.8 Withdraw the shaft and remove the gear

22.9 Check that the starter driven gear rotates freely anti-clockwise

22.11a Check the condition of the sprags (A) and gear hub (B) as described

22.11b Sprag assembly bolts (arrowed)

Remove the starter driven gear from the crankshaft (see illustration).
8 Withdraw the idle/reduction gear shaft from the crankcase and remove the gear, noting which way round it fits (see illustration).

Inspection and disassembly

9 With the alternator rotor face down on a workbench, check that the starter driven gear rotates freely when turned anti-clockwise and locks against the rotor clockwise (see illustration). If it doesn't, the starter clutch should be dismantled for further investigation.
10 Withdraw the starter driven gear from the starter clutch. If the gear appears stuck, turn it anti-clockwise as you withdraw it to free it from the starter clutch.
11 Check the condition of the sprags inside the clutch body and the corresponding surface on the driven gear hub (see illustration). If they are

damaged, marked or flattened at any point, they should be replaced with new ones. To remove the sprag assembly, hold the rotor using a strap and unscrew the bolts inside it (see illustration). Remove the sprag assembly from the rotor, noting how it fits. Install the sprag assembly in a reverse sequence – make sure the arrow on the housing faces out. Apply clean engine oil to the sprags. Clean the bolts and apply a suitable non-permanent thread locking compound and tighten them to the torque setting specified at the beginning of the Chapter.
12 Check the bush in the starter driven gear and its corresponding surface on the crankshaft. If the bush has worn so the oil retention grooves are very shallow or no longer distinguishable replace the driven gear with a new one.
13 Check the teeth of the starter motor drive shaft, idle/reduction gear and starter driven

gear. Replace the gears and/or starter motor if worn or chipped teeth are discovered on related gears. Also check the idle/reduction gear shaft for damage, and check that the gear is not a loose fit on the shaft.

Installation

14 Clean all traces of old gasket off the cover and crankcase mating surfaces and wipe them with a suitable solvent.
15 Lubricate the starter driven gear bush and slide the gear onto the crankshaft with the raised section of the hub facing out (see illustration 22.7b).
16 Clean the tapered end of the crankshaft and the corresponding mating surface on the inside of the rotor with a suitable solvent. Fit the Woodruff key into its slot in the crankshaft if removed (see illustration).
17 Lubricate the idle/reduction gear shaft with clean engine oil. Locate the gear against the crankcase with the smaller pinion facing out and slide the shaft through and into the crankcase (see illustration 22.8).
18 If separated, fit the starter clutch onto the back of the rotor (Step 11).
19 Make sure that no metal objects have attached themselves to the magnet on the inside of the rotor. Slide the rotor onto the shaft, making sure the groove on the inside is aligned with and fits over the Woodruff key, and the key does not dislodge, and the driven gear teeth mesh with those on the idle/reduction gear (see illustration).

22.16 Fit the key into its slot

22.19 Slide the rotor over the key

22.20a Fit the lubricated bolt...

22.20b ...and tighten to the specified torque

22.21a Fit a new gasket onto the dowels (arrowed)...

22.21b ...then fit the cover

20 Fit the bolt with its washer and tighten it to the torque setting specified at the beginning of the Chapter, holding the rotor as on removal **(see illustrations)**.

21 Fit the dowels into the cover or crankcase if removed. Lay a new gasket over the dowels **(see illustration)**. Fit the cover, noting that the rotor magnets will forcibly draw the cover/stator on, making sure the dowels locate **(see illustration)**. Fit the cover bolts using new sealing washers with the two bolts at the front, and making sure the longer bolts are in the correct place, and

not forgetting the cable bracket and clamp on 2012-on DL models and all SFV models, and tighten them evenly in a criss-cross sequence to the specified torque **(see illustration 22.5)**.

22 On 2012-on DL models and all SFV models route and secure the sidestand switch wiring and fit the speed sensor **(see illustrations 22.3b and a)**. Fit the front sprocket cover. On all models refer to Section 18 and connect the lower end of the clutch cable.

23 If disconnected reconnect the wiring connectors, making sure the wiring is correctly

routed and secured **(see illustration 4.10a or b and c)**.

24 Fill the engine with oil, or top it up to the correct level, as required according to your removal method (see Chapter 1).

23 Crankcase separation and reassembly

Separation

1 To access the crankshaft and connecting rods, transmission components and the main and big-end bearings, the engine must be removed from the frame (Section 4), and the crankcases must be separated.

2 Before the crankcases can be separated the following components must be removed:

Starter motor (Chapter 8)
Oil cooler (2012-on DL models and all SFV models – Section 6)
Cylinder heads (Section 12)
Cylinder blocks (Section 14)
Pistons (Section 15)
Clutch (Section 17)
Gearchange mechanism and selector drum cam plate (Section 19)
Primary drive gear (Section 20)
Oil pump (Section 21)
Alternator rotor and starter clutch (Section 22)
Cam chains and blades (Sections 10 and 11)

3 Undo the oil spray pipe retainer plate screw and remove the plate, noting how it locates against the end of the pipe **(see illustration)**. Withdraw the pipe from the crankcase **(see illustration)**.

4 If the transmission shafts are being removed, unscrew the oil seal retainer plate bolts and remove the plate, noting how it fits **(see illustration 17.18b)**. Remove the spacer from the end of the output shaft **(see**

23.3a Undo the screw (A) and remove the retainer plate (B)

23.3b Withdraw the oil pipe from the crankcase

23.4a Slide the spacer out of the seal and off the shaft...

23.4b ...and remove the O-ring from its inside

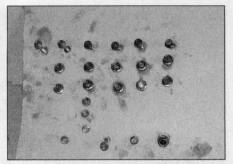

23.6 Example of a cardboard template for bolt storage

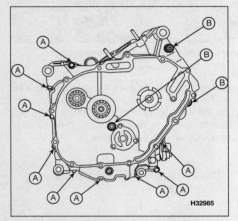

23.7 Right-hand crankcase 6 mm bolts (A) and 8 mm bolts (B)

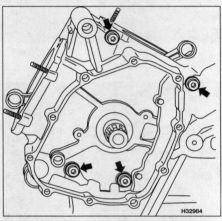

23.8 Left-hand crankcase 8 mm bolts (arrowed)

illustration). Note the O-ring that fits inside the spacer **(see illustration)** – a new one must be used.

5 If the selector drum is being removed, remove the gear position switch (see Chapter 8).

6 As there are different sizes of bolt used to join the crankcases, draw an outline of each crankcase half on a piece of cardboard, then punch a hole for each bolt – as each one is removed, store it in its relative position in the card, along with any wiring/hose clamp where present **(see illustration)**. This will ensure all bolts and washers are installed in the correct location on reassembly.

7 Unscrew the nine 6 mm bolts in the right-hand side of the crankcase. *As each bolt is removed, store it in its relative position in the cardboard template* **(see illustration)**.

8 Next unscrew the four 8 mm bolts in the left-hand side of the crankcase, slackening them evenly and a little at a time in a criss-cross pattern until they are all loose, then remove the bolts **(see illustration)**.

9 Carefully turn the engine over onto its left-hand side and support it on wooden blocks so the end of the transmission output shaft is off the work surface. Unscrew the three 8 mm bolts in the right-hand side of the crankcase, slackening them evenly and a little at a time in a criss-cross pattern until they are all loose, then remove the bolts **(see illustration 23.7)**.

10 Carefully lift the right-hand crankcase half off the left-hand half, if necessary using a soft hammer to tap around the joint and gently on the shaft ends to separate the halves **(see illustration)**. *If the halves do not separate easily, make sure all fasteners have been removed. Do not try and separate the halves by levering between the crankcase mating surfaces as they are easily scored and will leak oil afterwards. If the transmission input shaft sticks in its bearing and is lifting with the crankcase, tap the end of it with a soft-faced hammer. If necessary, obtain an expanding clamp (brake piston expanders work very well) and some wood to protect the crankcase, then place the clamp in the cylinder opening and carefully expand the clamp to force the halves apart* **(see illustration)**. The right-hand side crankcase half will come away by itself,

23.10a Carefully separate the crankcase halves

23.10b An expanding clamp can be used as shown if required

23.17 Make sure the lower rod is positioned for the front cylinder, and the higher one for the rear

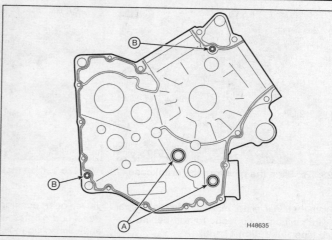

23.18 Make sure the O-rings (A) and dowels (B) are installed, and apply sealant to the shaded areas of the mating surface

leaving the crankshaft, transmission shafts, and selector drum and forks in the left-hand half.

11 Remove the two locating dowels from the crankcase if they are loose (they could be in either crankcase half), noting their locations **(see illustration 23.18)**. Remove the oil passage O-rings. Check that the thrust washer is on the right-hand end of the transmission output shaft – if not, it is probably stuck to the bearings in the right-hand crankcase half.

12 Refer to Sections 24 onwards for the removal, inspection and installation of the components housed within the crankcases.

Reassembly

13 Remove all traces of sealant from the crankcase mating surfaces. If not already done, clean the oil strainer before the cases are assembled (see Section 21).

14 Support the left-hand half on wooden blocks so the end of the transmission output shaft is off the work surface. Check that all components and their bearings are in place in the right and left-hand crankcase halves. Fit new O-rings smeared with grease into the grooves around the oil passages. Check that the transmission output shaft thrust washer is in place on the right-hand end of the shaft.

15 Generously lubricate the transmission shafts, selector drum and forks, and the crankshaft, particularly around the bearings, with molybdenum disulphide oil (a mixture of 50% molybdenum disulphide grease and 50% engine oil), then use a rag soaked in high flash-point solvent to wipe over the mating surfaces of both halves to remove all traces of oil.

16 Fit the two locating dowels in the left-hand crankcase half **(see illustration 23.18)**.

17 Make sure that each connecting rod is positioned correctly for its cylinder **(see illustration)**.

18 Apply a small amount of suitable sealant (such as Suzuki Bond 1207B or equivalent) to the mating surface of the crankcase half **(see illustration)**.

Caution: Apply the sealant only to the tinted areas shown in the illustration. Do not apply an excessive amount as it will ooze out when the case halves are assembled and may obstruct oil passages. Do not apply sealant near bearings or oil passages.

19 Carefully fit the right-hand crankcase half onto the left-hand half **(see illustration 23.10a)**. Make sure the dowels and shaft ends all locate correctly into the right-hand crankcase half.

Caution: The crankcase halves should fit together without being forced. If the casings are not correctly seated, separate them and investigate the problem. Do not attempt to pull them together using the crankcase bolts as the casing will crack and be ruined.

20 Check that the right-hand crankcase half is correctly seated. **Note:** *The crankcase halves should fit together without being forced. If the casings are not correctly seated, remove the right-hand half and investigate the problem. Do not attempt to pull them together using the bolts as the casing could crack and be ruined.*

21 Clean the threads of the right-hand crankcase bolts and insert them in their original locations **(see illustration 23.7)**. Secure all bolts finger-tight. Stand the engine

upright. Clean and fit the left-hand crankcase bolts and tighten them finger-tight **(see illustration 23.8)**.

22 Now tighten the 8 mm bolts evenly and a little at a time in a criss-cross pattern to the torque setting specified at the beginning of the Chapter. Now tighten the 6 mm bolts in the same way.

23 Go round all the 8 mm bolts on each side again and check that they are all at the correct torque setting. Now do the 6 mm bolts.

24 With all crankcase bolts tightened, check that the crankshaft and transmission shafts rotate smoothly and easily. Select each gear in turn (you will have to fit the cam plate onto the selector drum and turn it by hand to do this) and check the operation of the transmission in each gear, then select neutral and check that the shafts can turn freely and independently of each other. If there are any signs of undue stiffness, tight or rough spots, or of any other problem, the fault must be rectified before proceeding further.

25 If removed, install the gear position switch (see Chapter 8).

26 If removed, fit a new O-ring inside the transmission output shaft spacer **(see illustration)**. Smear the inside and outside of the spacer with grease. Slide the spacer onto the shaft and into the seal, making sure the grooved end fits innermost **(see illustration)**.

23.26a Fit a new O-ring into the groove, then grease the spacer...

23.26b ...and slide it onto the shaft and into the seal

23.27a Slide the pipe into the crankcase...

23.27b ...then locate the retainer plate...

23.27c ...and secure them with the threadlocked screw

Fit the retainer plate, making sure the neutral switch wiring is correctly routed behind the tab **(see illustration 17.18b)**.

27 Slide the oil spray pipe into the crankcase, making sure the protruding section of the end is at the top **(see illustration)**. Fit the retainer plate, making sure it locates correctly, and tighten the screw to the specified torque setting **(see illustrations)**.

28 Install all other removed assemblies in the reverse of the sequence given in Step 2.

24 Crankcases

1 After the crankcases have been separated, remove the oil strainer and pressure relief

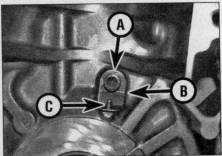

24.2 Unscrew the bolt (A), remove the retainer (B) and withdraw the oil jet (C) – there is one in each crankcase half

valve, gear position switch (if not already done) and oil pressure switch, the crankshaft and connecting rods, transmission shafts, and selector drum and forks, referring to the relevant Sections of this Chapter, and to Chapter 8 for the gear position and oil pressure switches. Refer to Sections 28 and 29 and to *Tools and Workshop Tips* in the Reference Section for checks and information on the selector drum and transmission shaft bearings. Refer to Sections 25 and 26 and to *Tools and Workshop Tips* in the Reference Section for checks and information on the crankshaft main bearings.

2 Undo the piston oil jet retainer bolts, then pull the oil jets out of the crankcases **(see illustration)**. Remove the O-rings and discard them. Also remove the bolt from the bottom of the angled oil gallery on the outside of the left-hand crankcase half and withdraw the transmission oil jet; remove the plug from the side of the oil gallery and the plug from the top – then use a length of wire inserted in the top of the gallery to push out the jet. Discard its O-ring. Clean the jets with solvent and blow them through with compressed air if available.

3 Remove the oil baffle-plate from the outside of the left-hand crankcase half if required **(see illustration)**.

4 If not already done, remove the oil seal retainer plate **(see illustration 17.18b)**. Lever out the transmission output shaft oil seal, clutch pushrod oil seal, and gearchange shaft oil seal with a flat-bladed screwdriver **(see illustrations)**.

5 Remove all traces of old gasket sealant from the mating surfaces. Clean up minor damage

to the surfaces with a fine sharpening stone or grindstone.

6 Clean the crankcases thoroughly with new solvent and dry them with compressed air. Blow out all oil passages with compressed air. *Caution: Be very careful not to nick or gouge the crankcase mating surfaces or oil leaks will result. Check both crankcase halves very carefully for cracks and other damage.*

7 Check that the cylinder block nut studs are tight in each crankcase half. If any are loose, remove them, then clean their threads and apply a suitable non-permanent thread locking compound and tighten them securely. Refer *Tools and Workshop Tips* in the Reference section at the end of this manual for details of how to slacken and tighten studs using two nuts locked together.

8 Small cracks or holes in aluminium castings can be repaired with an epoxy resin adhesive as a temporary measure. Permanent repairs can only be done by argon-arc welding, and only a specialist in this process is in a position to advise on the economy or practical aspect of such a repair. If any damage is found that can't be repaired, replace the crankcase halves with a new set.

9 Damaged threads can be economically reclaimed using a diamond section wire insert, for example of the Heli-Coil type (though there are other makes), which is easily fitted after drilling and re-tapping the affected thread.

10 Sheared studs or screws can usually be removed with extractors, which consist of a tapered, left-hand thread screw of very hard

24.3 The external baffle is secured by two bolts (arrowed)

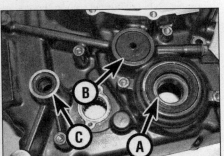

24.4a Lever out the transmission shaft seal (A), the pushrod seal (B) and the gearchange shaft seal (C)...

24.4b ...using a screwdriver

24.11a Lubricate the seal lips with grease...

24.11b ...and drive them in if necessary using a suitable socket

24.12a Fit a new O-ring onto each piston jet...

24.12b ...then fit it into its passage...

24.12c ...and secure it with the retainer and the threadlocked bolt

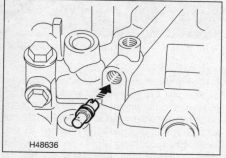

24.12d Transmission oil gallery jet installation

steel. These are inserted into a pre-drilled hole in the stud, and usually succeed in dislodging the most stubborn stud or screw. If a stud has sheared above its bore line, it can be removed using a conventional stud extractor that avoids the need for drilling.

 Refer to Tools and Workshop Tips for details of installing a thread insert and using screw extractors.

11 Fit new transmission output shaft, clutch pushrod and gearchange shaft oil seals (see illustration 24.4a), lubricating their lips with grease and using a suitable socket to drive them into place if required (see illustrations). Do not fit the seal retainer plate until the gear position switch is installed.
12 Fit new O-rings smeared with oil onto the piston oil jets and fit them into their passages with the tapered ends pointing out (see illustrations). Apply a suitable non-permanent thread locking compound to the retainer bolts, then fit the retainers and tighten the bolts to the specified torque setting (see illustration). Fit a new O-ring smeared with oil onto the transmission oil gallery jet and fit it into the gallery, making sure the slotted end goes in first, and using a suitable rod to push it onto its seat (see illustration). Fit a new sealing washer onto the gallery bolt and tighten it to the specified torque setting.
13 Install all other components and assemblies, referring to the Steps above and

the relevant Sections of this and the other Chapters, before reassembling the crankcase halves. Clean the threads of the oil baffle-plate bolts and apply thread-lock (see illustration 24.3).

25 Connecting rod and main bearing information

1 Even though main and connecting rod bearings are generally replaced with new ones during the engine overhaul, the old bearings should be retained for close examination as they may reveal valuable information about the condition of the engine.
2 Bearing failure occurs mainly because of lack of lubrication, the presence of dirt or other foreign particles, overloading the engine and/or corrosion. Regardless of the cause of bearing failure, it must be corrected before the engine is reassembled to prevent it from happening again.
3 When examining the connecting rod bearings, remove them from the connecting rods and caps and lay them out on a clean surface in the same general position as their location on the crankshaft journals. This will enable you to match any noted bearing problems with the corresponding crankshaft journal.
4 Dirt and other foreign particles get into the engine in a variety of ways. It may be left in the engine during assembly or it may pass through filters or breathers. It may get into the oil and

from there into the bearings. Metal chips from machining operations and normal engine wear are often present. Abrasives are sometimes left in engine components after reconditioning operations, especially when parts are not thoroughly cleaned using the proper cleaning methods. Whatever the source, these foreign objects often end up imbedded in the soft bearing material and are easily recognised. Large particles will not imbed in the bearing and will score or gouge the bearing and journal. The best prevention for this cause of bearing failure is to clean all parts thoroughly and keep everything spotlessly clean during engine reassembly. Frequent and regular oil and filter changes are also recommended.
5 Lack of lubrication or lubrication breakdown has a number of interrelated causes. Excessive heat (which thins the oil), overloading (which squeezes the oil from the bearing face) and oil leakage or throw off (from excessive bearing clearances, worn oil pump or high engine speeds) all contribute to lubrication breakdown. Blocked oil passages will also starve a bearing and destroy it. When lack of lubrication is the cause of bearing failure, the bearing material is wiped or extruded from the steel backing of the bearing. Temperatures may increase to the point where the steel backing and the journal turn blue from overheating.

 Refer to Tools and Workshop Tips for bearing fault finding.

26.2 Lift the crankshaft out

26.8 Measure the journal diameter

6 Riding habits can have a definite effect on bearing life. Full throttle low speed operation, or labouring the engine, puts very high loads on bearings, which tend to squeeze out the oil film. These loads cause the bearings to flex, which produces fine cracks in the bearing face (fatigue failure). Eventually the bearing material will loosen in pieces and tear away from the steel backing. Short trip riding leads to corrosion of bearings, as insufficient engine heat is produced to drive off the condensed water and corrosive gases produced. These products collect in the engine oil, forming acid and sludge. As the oil is carried to the engine bearings, the acid attacks and corrodes the bearing material.

7 Incorrect bearing installation during engine assembly will lead to bearing failure as well. Tight fitting bearings that leave insufficient bearing oil clearances result in oil starvation. Dirt or foreign particles trapped behind a bearing shell result in high spots on the bearing that lead to failure.

8 To avoid bearing problems, clean all parts thoroughly before reassembly, double check all bearing clearance measurements and lubricate the new bearings with clean engine oil during installation.

26 Crankshaft and main bearings

Removal

1 Separate the crankcase halves (refer to Section 23).

2 Lift the crankshaft out of the left-hand crankcase half (see illustration). If it appears stuck, tap it gently using a soft-faced mallet.

3 If required, remove the connecting rods (see Section 27).

Inspection

4 Clean the crankshaft with solvent, using a rifle-cleaning brush to scrub out the oil passages. If available, blow the crank dry with compressed air, and also blow through the oil passages. Check the cam chain sprocket on the left-hand end for wear or damage. If any of the sprocket teeth are excessively worn, chipped or broken, the crankshaft must be replaced with a new one.

5 Refer to Section 25 and examine the main bearings. If they are scored, badly scuffed or appear to have been seized, new bearing shells must be installed (see below). Always replace the shells as a set, never on one side only. If they are badly damaged, check the corresponding crankshaft journal. Evidence of extreme heat, such as discoloration, indicates that lubrication failure has occurred. Be sure to thoroughly check the oil pump and pressure relief valve as well as all oil holes and passages before reassembling the engine.

6 Inspect the crankshaft journals, paying particular attention where damaged bearings have been discovered. If the journals are scored or pitted in any way a new crankshaft will be required. Note that undersizes are not available, precluding the option of re-grinding the crankshaft.

7 Place the crankshaft on V-blocks and check the runout at the main bearing journals using a dial gauge. Compare the reading to the maximum specified at the beginning of the Chapter. If the runout exceeds the limit, the crankshaft must be renewed.

8 Using a micrometer, measure the diameter of the crankshaft main bearing journals (see illustration). If a journal is below the range specified, it is worn and the crankshaft must be replaced with a new one. Always fit new main bearings if a new crankshaft is fitted.

Main bearing selection

9 New main bearings are supplied on a selected fit basis according to the code letter stamped into each crankcase half adjacent to the bearing housing (see illustration). If the crankcase code letter is A, the bearing shell colour-code is GREEN; if the letter is B, the colour-code is BLACK; if the letter is C, the colour-code is BROWN. The colour code is marked on the side of each bearing shell.

Main bearing removal and installation

10 Removing and installing of the main bearings requires the use of a hydraulic press and a two-piece Suzuki special tool (Pt. No. 09913-60221) in order to avoid damaging either the crankcase or the new bearings, though it is possible to use a drawbolt arrangement in conjunction with the special tool if a press is not available. It is therefore advised that this procedure is undertaken by a Suzuki dealer or a suitably equipped specialist.

11 Remove the old bearings by pressing them out from the inside of the crankcase using the driver piece of the tool. Do not reuse the bearings after removal even if they appear to be in good condition.

12 Before fitting the new shells chamfer off the sharp edge of the bearing housing on the inner side of the crankcase using a fine oilstone, then thoroughly clean the housing.

13 Apply molybdenum disulphide oil (a mixture of 50% molybdenum disulphide

26.9 Main bearing code letter (arrowed)

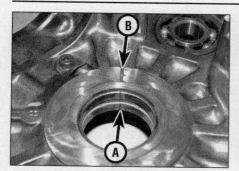

26.13 Align the mating edges (A) with the index line (B)

27.2 Measure the connecting rod big-end side clearance

27.3 Note the rod size code numbers

grease and 50% engine oil) to the outside of each new shell. Assemble the new shells in the holder, aligning the colour-code edge with the index line, then fit the tool halves together and tighten the bolts to 23 Nm. Seat the shell holder on the inner side of the crankcase with the colour-code (recessed) side of the shells facing up, and aligning the tool joints with the lines on the crankcase (see illustration). Fit the driver into the recessed side of the holder so it sits on the rim of each shell. Press the new shells in until the driver piece of the tool comes up against the shell holder.

Installation

14 If removed, fit the connecting rods onto the crankshaft (see Section 27).
15 Apply molybdenum disulphide oil (a mixture of 50% molybdenum disulphide grease and 50% engine oil) to the main bearings. Carefully lower the tapered (alternator) end of the crankshaft into position in the left-hand crankcase (see illustration 26.2).
16 Reassemble the crankcase halves (see Section 23).

27 Connecting rods and bearings

Note: *The connecting rod bolts are of the stretch type and can only be used in a running engine once, though they can be used when performing the oil clearance check to prevent having to buy two sets of new bolts.*
Special tool: *A degree disc is required for tightening the connecting rod bolts, although the angle can easily be established without it.*

Removal

1 Remove the crankshaft (see Section 26).
2 Before removing the rods from the crankshaft, measure the big-end side clearance between the rods and the crank web with a feeler gauge (see illustration). If the clearance is greater than the service limit listed in this Chapter's Specifications, refer to Step 6.
3 Using paint or a felt marker pen, mark the relevant cylinder identity on each connecting rod (i.e. FRONT or REAR). The left-hand side

(alternator end) of the crankpin holds the front cylinder rod, and the right-hand side (primary drive gear end) of the crankpin holds the rear cylinder rod. Mark across the cap-to-connecting rod join to ensure that the cap is fitted the correct way around on reassembly. Do not obscure the existing marking on the intake side of each connecting rod (mark the cylinder ID on the other side – in this way the FRONT marking for the front cylinder rod will in fact be facing the front of the engine, and the REAR marking will be facing the rear). The number already marked is the connecting rod big-end size code (see illustration).
4 Partially unscrew the big-end cap bolts, then tap the bolt heads with a soft-faced hammer to separate the connecting rod and cap, then remove the bolts and detach the rods and caps from the crankpin (see illustrations). Keep the rod, cap, bolts and (if they are to be re-used) the bearing shells

together in their correct positions to ensure correct installation.

Inspection

5 Check the connecting rods for cracks and other obvious damage.
6 If the side clearance measured in Step 1 exceeds the service limit, measure the width of each rod's big-end and the width of the crankpin (see illustrations). If either big-end is narrower than specified replace the rod with a new one. If the width of the crankpin is greater than specified replace the crankshaft with a new one.
7 If not already done (see Section 15), apply clean engine oil to the piston pin, insert it into the connecting rod small-end and check for any freeplay between the two. Measure the pin OD in the middle and the small-end bore ID and compare the measurements to the specifications at the beginning of the

27.4a Unscrew the connecting rod big-end cap bolts (arrowed)...

27.4b ...and separate the rods from the crankpin

27.6a Measure the width of each rod's big-end...

27.6b ...and the width of the crankpin

27.11 Remove the shells from the rod and cap

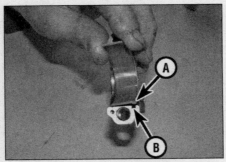

27.12 Fit the shell into its housing making sure the tab (A) locates in the notch (B)

27.19 Crankpin journal size numbers

Chapter. Calculate the difference between the measurements taken to obtain the piston pin-to-small end clearance and compare the result to the specifications. Replace components that are worn beyond the specified limits with new ones.

8 Refer to Section 25 and examine the connecting rod bearing shells. If they are scored, badly scuffed or appear to have seized, new shells must be installed. Always replace the shells in the connecting rods as a set. If they are badly damaged, check the corresponding crankpin. Evidence of extreme heat, such as discoloration, indicates that lubrication failure has occurred. Be sure to thoroughly check the oil pump and pressure relief valve as well as all oil holes and passages before reassembling the engine.

9 Have the rods checked for twist and bend by a Suzuki dealer if you are in doubt they are straight.

Oil clearance check

10 Whether new bearing shells are being fitted or the original ones are being re-used, the connecting rod bearing oil clearance should be checked prior to reassembly.

11 Remove the bearing shells from the connecting rod and cap (see illustration). Clean the backs of the shells and the bearing locations in both the rod and cap.

12 Press the bearing shells into their locations, ensuring that the tab on each shell engages the notch in the connecting rod/cap (see illustration). Make sure the bearings are fitted in the correct locations and take care not to touch any shell's bearing surface with your fingers.

13 Cut a length of the Plastigauge (it should be slightly shorter than the width of the crankpin) and place it on the (cleaned) crankpin journal. Lubricate the connecting rod bolts with clean engine oil. Fit the (clean) connecting rod assemblies, shells and caps (see illustration 27.4b). Make sure the rods and caps are fitted the correct way around so the previously made markings align (see Step 3). Using the old bearing cap bolts, tighten them in two stages as described in Step 23 – it is highly advisable to have an assistant to hold the crankshaft and rods down on the bench to prevent any movement between them

which will smear the Plastigauge and ruin the measurement. Now slacken the cap bolts and remove the connecting rod assemblies, again taking great care not to rotate the connecting rod.

14 Compare the width of the crushed Plastigauge at its widest point to the scale printed on the Plastigauge envelope to obtain the connecting rod bearing oil clearance.

15 If the clearance is within the range listed in this Chapter's Specifications and the bearings are in perfect condition, they can be reused.

16 If the clearance is beyond the service limit, replace the bearing shells with new ones (see Steps 19 and 20) and check the oil clearance once again. Always replace all of the shells as a set.

17 If the clearance is still greater than the service limit listed in this Chapter's Specifications, the crankpin journal is worn and the crankshaft should be replaced with a new one.

18 On completion carefully scrape away all traces of the Plastigauge material from the crankpin and bearing shells using a fingernail or other object which is unlikely to score the shells.

Bearing shell selection

19 New bearing shells for the big-end bearings are supplied on a selected fit basis. Size numbers stamped on the crankshaft and rods are used to identify the correct replacement bearings. The crankpin journal size number is stamped on one crankshaft web and will be either 1, 2 or 3 – the left-hand

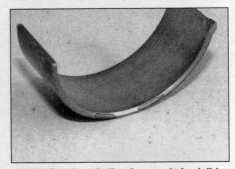

27.20 Bearing shell colour code is visible on edge of shell

number with the L before it corresponds to the left-hand side (alternator end) of the crankpin which holds the front cylinder rod, and the right-hand number with the R after it corresponds to the right-hand side (primary drive gear end) of the crankpin which holds the rear cylinder rod (see illustration). The connecting rod size number is marked across the flat face of the connecting rod and cap and will be either 1 or a 2 (see illustration 27.3).

20 A range of bearing shells is available. Select the correct bearing shells for each connecting rod in accordance with the table below. The bearings themselves are identified by a colour (see table) – the colour is marked on one edge of the shell (see illustration).

Connecting rod code	Crankpin journal size		
	1	2	3
1	Green	Black	Brown
2	Black	Brown	Yellow

Installation

21 Work on one rod at a time, and make sure it is installed on the correct side of the crankpin, and the correct way round (see Step 3). Clean the backs of the bearing shells and the bearing housings in both cap and rod. If new shells are being fitted, ensure that all traces of the protective grease are cleaned off using paraffin (kerosene). Wipe the shells, cap and rod dry with a clean lint free cloth. Fit the bearing shells in the connecting rod and cap, making sure the tab on each shell engages the notch in the rod/cap (see illustrations 27.11 and 12).

22 Lubricate each shell's bearing surface with molybdenum disulphide oil (a 50/50 mixture of molybdenum disulphide grease and clean engine oil). Fit the connecting rod onto the crankpin and fit the cap onto the rod (see illustration 27.4b). Make sure the cap is fitted the correct way around so the previously made markings align (see Step 3). Check to make sure that all components have been returned to their original locations using the marks made on disassembly.

23 Apply engine oil to the threads and under the heads of the new connecting rod

bolts. Fit the bolts and tighten them in two stages as follows: first, tighten them to the torque setting specified at the beginning of the Chapter. Second, using a degree disc if available, tighten the bolts in one go through 90° or a quarter-turn **(see illustrations)**. If you inadvertently tighten through more than the specified angle do not loosen the bolt off and retighten it – replace the bolt with a new one and repeat the tightening sequence.

24 Check that the rod rotates smoothly and freely on the crankpin. If there are any signs of roughness or tightness, remove the rod and re-check the bearing clearance.

25 Install the crankshaft (see Section 26).

27.23a Lubricate and install the bolts...

27.23b ...and tighten them to the specified torque setting and angle as described

28 Selector drum and forks

Removal

1 Separate the crankcase halves (Section 23).
2 The selector forks are not marked for identification, so it is best to mark them yourself using a felt pen according to where and which way up each fits.
3 Withdraw the selector fork shafts from the crankcase **(see illustration)**. Pivot each fork out of its track in the selector drum and remove it noting how it locates in the groove in its pinion **(see illustration)**. Withdraw the selector drum from the crankcase **(see illustration)**. Once removed, slide the forks back onto the shafts in their correct order and way round **(see illustration)**.

Inspection

4 Inspect the selector forks for any signs of wear or damage, especially around the fork ends where they engage with the groove in the gear pinion. Check that each fork fits correctly in its pinion groove. Check closely to see if the forks are bent. If the forks are in any way damaged they must be replaced with new ones.
5 Slip each fork in turn into the groove in its gear pinion on the transmission shaft and measure the fork-to-groove clearance using a feeler gauge **(see illustration)**. Compare the

results to the specifications at the beginning of the Chapter. If the clearance exceeds the service limit specified, measure the thickness of the fork ends and the width of

the groove and compare the readings to the specifications **(see illustrations)**. Replace whichever components are worn beyond their specifications with new ones.

28.3a Withdraw the shafts (arrowed)...

28.3b ...then remove the forks...

28.3c ...and the drum

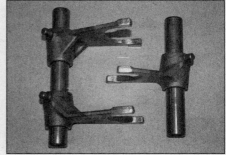

28.3d Slide the forks back on the shafts

28.5a Measure the fork-to-groove side clearance using a feeler gauge

28.5b Measure the thickness of the fork end...

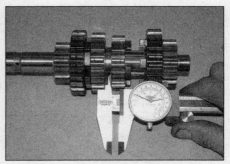

28.5c ...and the width of the groove

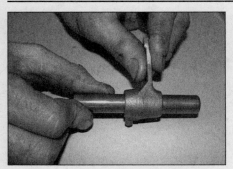

28.6 Check the fit of the fork on the shaft as described

28.8 Check the drum grooves and fork guide pins

28.9a Check the needle bearing (arrowed) in the left half...

6 Check that the forks fit correctly on their shaft **(see illustration)**. They should move freely with a light fit but no appreciable freeplay. Replace the forks and/or shafts with new ones if they are worn. Check that the fork shaft holes in the casing are neither worn nor damaged.

7 Check the selector fork shafts are straight by rolling them along a flat surface. A bent shaft will cause difficulty in selecting gears and make the gearchange action heavy. Replace the shafts with new ones if they are bent.

8 Inspect the selector drum grooves and selector fork guide pins for signs of wear or damage **(see illustration)**. If either component shows signs of wear or damage the fork(s) and drum must be replaced with new ones.

9 Check that the selector drum bearings in each crankcase half rotate freely and smoothly and are tight in the casing **(see illustrations)**. Remove the old bearings and fit new ones if necessary (see *Tools and Workshop Tips* in the Reference Section). The bearing in the right crankcase half is held by two retainers, secured by screws **(see illustration 29.9b)**. On installation apply a suitable non-permanent thread locking compound to the screws.

Installation

10 Apply clean oil to the journal on the left-hand end of the selector drum. Slide the drum into position in the crankcase **(see illustration 28.3c)**.

11 Apply molybdenum disulphide oil (a 50/50 mixture of molybdenum disulphide grease and clean engine oil) to the selector fork ends. Slide each fork into the groove of its gear pinion on the correct transmission shaft according to the identification marks made on removal, and locate the guide pin on the end of each fork into its groove in the selector drum – you may have to move the forks and their pinions up to achieve this **(see illustrations)**.

12 Lubricate the selector fork shafts with molybdenum disulphide oil (a 50/50 mixture

28.9b ...and the ball bearing (A) in the right half, which is secured by two retainers (B)

28.11a Locate the input shaft fork in its pinion and then in the drum

28.11b Locate the lower output shaft fork in its pinion groove...

28.11c ...then locate the guide pin in the selector drum

28.11d Locate the upper output shaft fork in its pinion groove...

28.11e ...then locate the guide pin in the selector drum

28.12a Lubricate each shaft...

28.12b ...then fit them through the fork(s) and into the crankcase

29.3 Grasp the shafts and lift them out of the crankcase

29.7 Position the shafts side by side so the relative pinions mesh

of molybdenum disulphide grease and clean engine oil) and slide each through its fork(s) and into its bore in the crankcase (see illustrations).
13 Reassemble the crankcase halves (see Section 23).

29 Transmission shaft removal and installation

Removal

1 Separate the crankcase halves (Section 23).
2 Remove the selector drum and forks (see Section 28).
3 Grasp the input shaft and output shaft and withdraw them from the crankcase as an assembly, noting their relative positions and how they fit together (see illustration). If the output shaft is tight in the crankcase, gently tap the bottom of the shaft using a soft-faced hammer or drift. Separate the shafts. Note the thrust washer on the right-hand end of the output shaft. On 2004 to 2011 DL models,

note the O-ring and wave washer on the left-hand end of the input shaft.
4 Lever the output shaft oil seal out of the crankcase and discard it as a new one must be used (see illustration 24.4b). If necessary, the transmission shafts can be disassembled and inspected for wear or damage (see Section 30).

Installation

5 Smear the lips of a new output shaft oil seal with grease and fit it into the crankcase, using a suitable socket to drive it into place if necessary (see illustrations 24.11a and b).
6 Support the left-hand half of the crankcase on wooden blocks so the end of the transmission output shaft does not contact the work surface as it is installed. On 2004 to 2011 DL models make sure that the wave washer and O-ring are installed on the left-hand end of the input shaft.
7 Lay the input shaft and output shaft side by side on the bench so that the pinions for each gear mesh together (see illustration). Make sure that the shafts are the correct way round,

in which case the smallest pinion on the input shaft meshes with the largest pinion on the output shaft. Lubricate the left-hand end of each shaft with clean engine oil.
8 Grasp the input shaft and output shaft and fit them into the left-hand crankcase (see illustration 29.3), making sure that both ends engage in their bearings (see illustration). If the output shaft is tight in the bearing, gently

29.8a Make sure the shaft ends locate in their bearings

29.8b Tap the end of the output shaft if it is tight

30.2a Release the circlip from its groove and slide it along the shaft...

30.2b ...then slide the pinions along and remove the snap-ring

tap on the end of the shaft to ease it in **(see illustration)**. Make sure that the thrust washer is on the right-hand end of the output shaft **(see illustration 30.35c)**.

9 Install the selector drum and forks (see Section 28).

10 Reassemble the crankcase halves (Section 23).

30 Transmission shaft overhaul

Note: *References to the right- and left-hand ends of the transmission shafts are made as though they are installed in the engine and the engine is the correct way up.*

1 Remove the transmission shafts from the crankcase (see Section 29). Always disassemble the transmission shafts separately to avoid mixing up the components.

Input shaft disassembly

2 On 2004 to 2011 DL models, remove the O-ring and wave washer on the left-hand end of the shaft. On all models, reach behind the 6th gear pinion with circlip pliers, spread the circlip and slide it toward the 3rd/4th gear pinion **(see illustration)**. Slide the 6th and 2nd gear pinions back to expose the snap-ring on the end of the shaft, then remove it **(see illustration)**. Slide the 2nd gear pinion off the shaft having marked its outer face as a guide to refitting, then slide the 6th gear pinion off

the shaft, followed by the bush and the thrust washer **(see illustrations 30.18a and 30.17c, b and a)**.

3 Remove the circlip, then slide the combined 3rd/4th gear pinion off the shaft **(see illustrations 30.16b and a)**.

4 Remove the circlip securing the 5th gear pinion, then slide the thrust washer, the 5th gear pinion and its bush off the shaft **(see illustrations 30.15d, c, b and a)**.

5 The 1st gear pinion is integral with the shaft **(see illustration)**.

Input shaft inspection

6 Wash all of the components in clean solvent and dry them off.

7 Check the gear teeth for cracking, chipping, pitting and other obvious wear or damage. Any pinion that is damaged must be replaced with a new one.

8 Inspect the dogs and the dog holes in the gears for cracks, chips, and excessive wear especially in the form of rounded edges. Make sure mating gears engage properly. Replace the paired gears as a set if necessary.

9 Check for signs of scoring or bluing on the pinions, bushes and shaft. This could be caused by overheating due to inadequate lubrication. Check all the oil holes and passages are clear. Replace any damaged pinions or bushes.

10 Check that each pinion moves freely on the shaft or its bush but without undue freeplay. Check that each bush moves freely on the shaft but without undue freeplay.

11 The shaft is unlikely to sustain damage

unless the engine has seized, placing an unusually high loading on the transmission, or the machine has covered a very high mileage. Check the surface of the shaft, especially where a pinion turns on it, and replace the shaft if it has scored or picked up, or if there are any cracks. Damage of any kind can only be cured by replacement.

12 Check the washers and replace any that are bent or appear weakened or worn. Use new ones if in any doubt. Note that you must use new circlips when overhauling gearshafts.

13 Check that the transmission shaft bearings in each crankcase half rotate freely and smoothly and are tight in the casing **(see illustration)**. Remove the old bearings and fit new ones if necessary (see *Tools and Workshop Tips* in the Reference Section).

Input shaft reassembly

14 During reassembly, apply molybdenum disulphide oil (a 50/50 mixture of molybdenum disulphide paste or grease and clean engine oil) to the mating surfaces of the shaft, pinions and bushes. When fitting the circlips, do not expand the ends any further than is necessary. Fit the stamped circlips so that their chamfered side faces the pinion it secures, i.e. so that its sharp edge faces the direction of thrust load (see Tools and Workshop Tips in the *Reference* section).

15 Slide the 5th gear pinion bush onto the left-hand end of the shaft, followed by the 5th gear pinion with its dogs facing away from the integral 1st gear **(see illustrations)**.

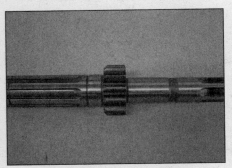

30.5 The 1st gear pinion is integral with the shaft

30.13 Check the transmission shaft bearings in each half

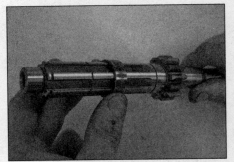

30.15a Slide the 5th gear pinion bush...

30.15b ...the 5th gear pinion...

30.15c ...and the thrust washer onto the shaft...

30.15d ...then fit the circlip...

30.15e ...making sure it locates correctly

30.16a Slide the 3rd/4th gear pinion onto the shaft...

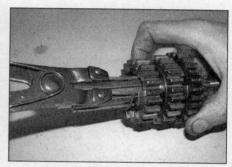

30.16b ...then fit the circlip, positioning it as described

Slide the thrust washer onto the shaft (see illustration). Fit the circlip, making sure that it locates correctly in the groove in the shaft (see illustrations).

16 Slide the combined 3rd/4th gear pinion onto the shaft, so that the larger (4th gear) pinion faces the 5th gear pinion dogs (see illustration). Fit the circlip onto the shaft but do not locate it in its groove – slide it past the groove and as far towards the 3rd/4th gear pinion as possible (see illustration).

17 Slide the splined thrust washer onto the shaft, followed by the 6th gear pinion splined bush, aligning the oil hole in the bush with that in the shaft (see illustrations). Slide the 6th gear pinion onto the bush, with its dog holes facing the dogs on the 3rd gear pinion (see illustration).

18 Slide the 2nd gear pinion onto the shaft (using the mark made on removal to identify its outer face) and secure it with the snap-ring, making sure it is properly seated in its groove

30.17a Slide the splined thrust washer...

30.17b ...the 6th gear pinion splined bush...

30.17c ...and the 6th gear pinion onto the shaft

30.18a Slide the 2nd gear pinion onto the shaft...

30.18b ...then fit the snap-ring...

30.18c ...making sure it locates correctly

30.18d Slide the pinions towards the end of the shaft and fit the circlip into its groove...

(see illustrations); note that the pinion should have a recess in its outer face to accommodate the snap-ring and the gear teeth on the inner face should have a slight chamfer. Now slide the 6th and 2nd gear pinions along to expose the groove for the 3rd/4th gear pinion circlip, then move the circlip along the shaft and fit it into the groove **(see illustrations)**. On 2004 to 2011 DL models, fit the wave washer and O-ring on the left-hand end of the input shaft.

19 Check that all components have been correctly installed **(see illustration)**.

Output shaft disassembly

20 Remove the thrust washer from the right-hand end of the shaft **(see illustration 30.35c)**.
21 Slide the 1st gear pinion and its bush or bearing (according to model) off the shaft, followed by the thrust washer and the 5th

gear pinion **(see illustrations 30.35b and a, and 30.34b and a)**.
22 Remove the circlip securing the 4th gear pinion, then slide the thrust washer, the pinion and its splined bush off the shaft **(see illustration 30.33d, c, b and a)**.
23 Slide the tabbed lockwasher off the shaft, then turn the slotted splined washer to offset the splines and slide it off the shaft, noting how they fit together **(see illustrations 30.32c and a)**.
24 Slide the 3rd gear pinion, its bush and the thrust washer off the shaft **(see illustrations 30.31c, b and a)**.
25 Remove the circlip securing the 6th gear pinion, then slide the pinion off the shaft **(see illustrations 30.30b and a)**.
26 Remove the circlip securing the 2nd gear pinion, then draw the collared bush out of the pinion and slide it off the shaft, followed by the pinion **(see illustrations 30.29c, b and a)**.

Output shaft inspection
27 Refer to Steps 6 to 13 above.

Output shaft reassembly
28 During reassembly, apply molybdenum disulphide oil (a 50/50 mixture of molybdenum disulphide paste or grease and clean engine oil) to the mating surfaces of the shaft, pinions and bushes. When fitting the circlips, do not expand the ends any further than is necessary. Fit the stamped circlips so that their chamfered side faces the pinion it secures, i.e. so that its sharp edge faces the direction of thrust load (see Tools and Workshop Tips of the *Reference* section).
29 Slide the 2nd gear pinion onto the shaft with its dog holes facing away from the shaft shoulder, then slide its bush into

30.18e ...making sure it locates correctly

30.19 The assembled input shaft should be as shown

30.29a Slide the 2nd gear pinion onto the shaft...

30.29b ...and fit the bush into its centre

30.29c Fit the circlip...

30.29d ...making sure it locates correctly

30.30a Slide the 6th gear pinion onto the shaft...

30.30b ...then fit the circlip...

30.30c ...making sure it locates correctly

30.31a Slide the splined thrust washer...

30.31b ...the 3rd gear pinion splined bush...

the centre of it (see illustrations). Secure them in place with the circlip, making sure it is properly seated in its groove (see illustrations).

30 Slide the 6th gear pinion onto the shaft with its selector fork groove facing away from the 2nd gear pinion, and secure it in place with

the circlip, making sure it is properly seated in its groove (see illustrations).

31 Slide the splined thrust washer onto the shaft, followed by the 3rd gear pinion splined bush, aligning the oil hole in the bush with that in the shaft (see illustrations). Slide the 3rd gear pinion onto the bush with its

dog holes facing the 6th gear pinion (see illustration).

32 Slide the slotted splined washer onto the shaft and locate it in its groove, then turn it in the groove so that the splines on the washer align with the splines on the shaft and secure the washer in the groove (see illustrations).

30.31c ...and the 3rd gear pinion onto the shaft

30.32a Slide the slotted splined washer onto the shaft...

30.32b ...and turn it so that it is positioned as shown

30.32c Slide the lock washer onto the shaft with its tabs facing in...

30.32d ...and locate the tabs in the slots

30.33a Slide the 4th gear pinion splined bush...

30.33b ...the 4th gear pinion...

30.33c ...and the splined thrust washer onto the shaft...

30.33d ...then fit the circlip...

30.33e ...making sure it locates correctly

30.34a Slide the 5th gear pinion...

30.34b ...and the thrust washer onto the shaft

30.35a Slide the 1st gear pinion bush (shown) or bearing...

30.35b ...and the 1st gear pinion onto the shaft...

30.35c ...then fit the thrust washer

30.36 The assembled output shaft should be a shown

Slide the lockwasher onto the shaft, and locate the tabs on the lockwasher into the slots in the outer rim of the splined washer **(see illustrations)**.
33 Slide the 4th gear pinion bush onto the shaft, aligning the oil hole in the bush with that in the shaft, then slide the 4th gear pinion onto the bush with the dog holes facing away from the 3rd gear pinion **(see illustrations)**. Slide the splined washer onto the shaft, then secure them in place with the circlip, making sure it is properly seated in its groove **(see illustrations)**.
34 Slide the 5th gear pinion onto the shaft with its selector fork groove facing the 4th gear pinion, followed by the thrust washer **(see illustrations)**.
35 Slide the 1st gear pinion bush or bearing onto the shaft, then fit the pinion onto the bush or bearing with the dog holes facing the 5th gear pinion, followed by the thrust washer **(see illustrations)**.
36 Check that all components have been correctly installed **(see illustration)**.

31 Running-in procedure

1 Make sure the engine oil and coolant levels are correct (see *Pre-ride checks*).

2 Make sure there is fuel in the tank.
3 Turn the ignition 'ON'. Check the transmission is in neutral.
4 Start the engine, then allow it to idle until it reaches normal operating temperature.
5 Make sure the oil pressure warning light goes out after starting the engine.
6 If a lubrication failure is suspected, stop the engine immediately and try to find the cause. If an engine is run without oil, even for a short period of time, severe damage will occur. Check carefully that there are no oil or coolant leaks and make sure the transmission and controls, especially the brakes and clutch, work properly before road testing the machine.
7 Treat the machine gently for the first few miles to allow the oil to circulate throughout the engine and any new parts installed to seat.
8 Great care is necessary if the engine has been extensively overhauled. – the bike will have to be run in as when new. This means more use of the transmission and a restraining hand on the throttle until at least 500 miles (800 km) have been covered. There is no point in keeping to any set road speed – the main idea is to keep from labouring the engine and to gradually increase performance up to the 1000 mile (1600 km) mark. These recommendations apply less when only a

partial overhaul has been done, though it does depend to an extent on the nature of the work carried out and which components have been renewed. Experience is the best guide, since it is easy to tell when an engine is running freely. If in any doubt, consult a Suzuki dealer. The following maximum engine speed limitations, which Suzuki provide for new motorcycles, can be used as a guide.

Up to 500 miles (800 km)
Do not exceed 5000 rpm

500 to 1000 miles (1000 to 1600 km)
Vary throttle position/speed.
Do not exceed 7500 rpm

Over 1000 miles (1600 km)
Normal riding.
Do not exceed tachometer red line

9 Upon completion of the road test, and after the engine has cooled down completely, recheck the valve clearances (see Chapter 1) and check the engine oil and coolant levels (see *Pre-ride checks*).
10 After running the rebuilt engine for 1000 miles (1600 km), change the engine oil and filter (see Chapter 1).

2•64

Notes

Chapter 3
Cooling system

Contents

Degrees of difficulty

Easy, suitable for novice with little experience	**Fairly easy,** suitable for beginner with some experience	**Fairly difficult,** suitable for competent DIY mechanic	**Difficult,** suitable for experienced DIY mechanic	**Very difficult,** suitable for expert DIY or professional

Specifications

Coolant
Mixture type and capacity . . . . see Chapter 1

Cooling fan switch
2004 to 2011 DL models and all SFV models
   Switch closes (fan ON) . . . . approx. 98°C
   Switch opens (fan OFF) . . . . approx. 92°C
2012-on DL models
   Switch closes (fan ON) . . . . approx. 105°C
   Switch opens (fan OFF) . . . . approx. 99°C

ECT sensor
2004 to 2011 DL models
   Resistance at 20°C . . . . approx. 2.450 K-ohms
   Resistance at 40°C . . . . approx. 1.148 K-ohms
   Resistance at 60°C . . . . approx. 0.587 K-ohms
   Resistance at 80°C . . . . approx. 0.322 K-ohms
2012-on DL models and all SFV models
   Resistance at 20°C . . . . approx. 2.450 K-ohms
   Resistance at 40°C . . . . approx. 0.811 K-ohms
   Resistance at 60°C . . . . approx. 0.318 K-ohms
   Resistance at 80°C . . . . approx. 0.142 K-ohms

Thermostat
2004 to 2011 DL models
   Opening temperature . . . . approx. 88°C
   Valve lift . . . . 8 mm (min) @ 100°C
2012-on DL models
   Opening temperature . . . . approx. 82°C
   Valve lift . . . . 8 mm (min) @ 95°C
SFV models
   Opening temperature . . . . approx. 76.5°C
   Valve lift . . . . 8 mm (min) @ 100°C

Radiator
Cap valve opening pressure . . . . 13 to 18 psi (0.9 to 1.25 Bar)

Torque settings
Cooling fan switch (2004 to 2011 DL models) . . . . 17 Nm
ECT sensor
   2004 to 2011 DL models . . . . 19 Nm
   2012-on DL models and all SFV models . . . . 18 Nm

1 General information

The cooling system uses a water/anti-freeze coolant to carry away excess heat from the engine and maintain as constant a temperature as possible. The cylinders are surrounded by a water jacket from which the heated coolant is circulated by thermo-syphonic action in conjunction with a water pump, which is driven by a gear on the right-hand end of the crankshaft. The hot coolant passes upwards to the thermostat and through to the radiator. The coolant flows across the core of the radiator, then to the water pump and back to the engine. On 2012-on DL models and all SFV models coolant also circulates through the oil cooler on the front of the engine.

A thermostat is fitted in the system to prevent the coolant flowing through the radiator when the engine is cold, therefore accelerating the speed at which the engine reaches normal operating temperature. An engine coolant temperature (ECT) sensor mounted in the thermostat housing provides information to the ECM (engine control module), and to the temperature gauge on the instrument panel. A cooling fan fitted to the back of the radiator aids cooling in extreme conditions by drawing extra air through. The fan motor is controlled by a thermostatic switch mounted in it on 2004 to 2011 DL models, and by a relay that receives a signal from the ECM, itself acting on information from the ECT sensor, on later DL models and all SFV models.

The complete cooling system is partially sealed and pressurised, the pressure being controlled by a valve contained in the spring-loaded filler cap. By pressurising the coolant the boiling point is raised, preventing premature boiling in adverse conditions. The overflow pipe from the system is connected to a reservoir into which excess coolant is expelled under pressure. The discharged coolant automatically returns to the radiator by the vacuum created when the engine cools.

⚠ *Warning: Do not remove the pressure cap from the filler neck when the engine is hot. Scalding hot coolant and steam may be blown out under pressure, which could cause serious injury. When the engine has cooled, place a thick rag, like a towel, over the pressure cap; slowly rotate the cap anti-clockwise to the first stop. This procedure allows any residual pressure to escape. When the steam has stopped escaping, press down on the cap while turning it anti-clockwise and remove it. Caution: Do not allow anti-freeze to come in contact with your skin or painted surfaces of the motorcycle. Rinse off any spills immediately with plenty of water. Anti-freeze is highly toxic if ingested. Never leave anti-freeze lying around in an open container or in puddles on the floor;*

children and pets are attracted by its sweet smell and may drink it. Check with the local authorities about disposing of used anti-freeze. Many communities will have collection centres which will see that anti-freeze is disposed of safely. Caution: At all times use the specified type of anti-freeze, and always mix it with distilled water in the correct proportion, or use pre-mixed coolant. The anti-freeze contains corrosion inhibitors that are essential to avoid damage to the cooling system. A lack of these inhibitors could lead to a build-up of corrosion that would block the coolant passages, resulting in overheating and severe engine damage. Distilled water must be used as opposed to tap water to avoid a build-up of scale that would also block the passages.

2 Cooling fan and fan switch or relay

1 If the engine is overheating and the cooling fan does not come on, first check the cooling fan fuse (see Chapter 8), then check the switch or relay (according to model), then check the fan motor (see below).

Cooling fan switch (2004 to 2011 DL models)

Check

2 Remove the fairing right-hand side panel (see Chapter 7).
3 If the engine is overheating and the cooling fan isn't coming on, disconnect the wiring connector from the switch on the right-hand side of the radiator **(see illustration)**. Using a jumper wire, connect between the terminals in the loom side of the connector. Turn the ignition switch ON. The fan should come on. If it does, the fan switch is faulty and must be replaced with a new one. If it does not come on check for battery voltage at the black/red wire terminal in the connector with the ignition ON. If no voltage is present, check the wire for continuity to the fusebox (see Chapter 8). If voltage is present test the fan motor itself (see below).

4 If the fan is on the whole time, disconnect the switch wiring connector **(see illustration 2.3)**. The fan should stop. If it does, the switch is faulty and must be replaced with a new one. If it doesn't, check the wiring between the fan and the switch for a short to earth, and the fan itself.
5 If the fan works but is suspected of cutting in and out at the wrong temperatures, fit a new switch.

Removal and installation

⚠ *Warning: The engine must be completely cool before carrying out this procedure.*
6 Remove the fairing right-hand side panel (see Chapter 7).
7 Drain the cooling system (see Chapter 1).
8 Disconnect the wiring connector from the switch on the right-hand side of the radiator **(see illustration 2.3)**. Unscrew the switch. Discard the O-ring – a new one must be used.
9 Fit the switch using a new O-ring smeared with coolant and tighten it to the torque setting specified at the beginning of the Chapter. Take care not to overtighten the switch as the radiator could be damaged.
10 Reconnect the wiring and refill the cooling system (see Chapter 1).

Cooling fan relay (2012-on DL models and all SFV models)

Check

11 Remove the relay (Steps 16 and 17).
12 Set a multimeter to test continuity and connect it across terminals 1 and 2 on the relay **(see illustration)**. There should be no continuity (infinite resistance). Using a fully-charged 12 volt battery and two insulated jumper wires, connect the positive (+) terminal of the battery to terminal 3 on the relay, and the negative (–) terminal to terminal 4. At this point the relay should be heard to click and the multimeter read 0 ohms (continuity). If so, the relay is good. If not replace the relay with a new one.
13 If the relay is good, check the connector for loose or broken wires and terminals.
14 If the fan is on the whole time, refer to Steps 16 and 17 and remove the relay – the

2.3 Cooling fan switch wiring connector (arrowed)

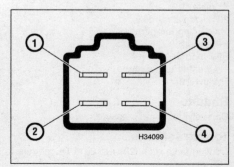

2.12 Fan relay terminal identification

2.17a Cooling fan relay (arrowed) – DL

2.17b Cooling fan relay (arrowed) – SFV

2.19a Cooling fan wiring connector (arrowed) – 2004 to 2011 DL

2.19b Cooling fan wiring connector (arrowed) – 2012-on DL

2.19c Cooling fan wiring connector (arrowed) – SFV

2.24 Cooling fan bolts (arrowed)

fan should stop. If it does, the relay is defective and must be replaced with a new one.

15 If the fan works but is suspected of cutting in at the wrong temperature, check the ECT sensor (see Section 3).

Removal and installation

16 Remove the seat, and on SFV models the right-hand side cover (see Chapter 7).
17 Displace the relay and disconnect the wiring **(see illustrations)**.
18 Installation is the reverse of removal.

Cooling fan

Check

19 The cooling fan is on the back of the radiator. On DL models remove the right-hand fairing side panel (see Chapter 7). On SFV models remove the right-hand radiator cover (see Chapter 7). Disconnect the fan wiring connector **(see illustrations)**.
20 On 2004 to 2011 DL models disconnect the fan switch wiring connector **(see illustration 2.3)**. Now you need to identify which of the two terminals in the switch connector goes to the fan – you can do this by continuity testing the black/red wire from the fan connector to the switch connector to identify the terminal that wire goes to, which means the terminal to the fan is the other one (refer to the wiring diagram at the end of Chapter 8 and all should be clear – basically what you have to do in this test is by-pass the switch). Using a 12 volt battery and two jumper

wires with suitable connectors, connect the battery positive (+) lead to the wire terminal in the switch connector that goes to the fan, and the battery negative (–) lead to the blue wire terminal in the fan connector. Once connected the fan should operate. If it does not, and the connectors and the wiring are good, then the fan motor is faulty. Individual components are not available for the fan assembly.
21 On 2012-on DL models and all SFV models, using a 12 volt battery and two jumper wires with suitable connectors, connect the battery positive (+) lead to the blue wire terminal on the fan side of the wiring connector, and the battery negative (-) lead to the black wire terminal. Once connected the fan should operate. If it does not, and the connector and the wiring between it and the motor are good, then the fan motor is faulty.
22 If the fan works, check the black/white wire from the loom side of the fan connector for continuity to earth, and check all wiring and connectors in the circuit for a fault or break.

Removal and installation

⚠️ *Warning: The engine must be completely cool before carrying out this procedure.*

23 Remove the radiator (see Section 5). On 2004 to 2011 DL models disconnect the fan switch wiring connector **(see illustration 2.3)**.
24 Unscrew the bolts and remove the fan **(see illustration)**.
25 Installation is the reverse of removal.

3 Temperature display and ECT sensor

Temperature display

1 The circuit consists of the ECT sensor mounted in the thermostat housing, and the temperature display and warning light in the instrument cluster.
2 If the display/warning light do not work, check the ECT sensor and its connector (see below). If that is good check the wiring connector on the back of the instrument cluster, then check the wiring between the connectors (see Chapter 8). If no faults are found but there is still a problem the instrument cluster could be faulty. Special equipment is needed to test the instruments – the best action is to take the bike to a Suzuki dealer for assessment.

ECT sensor

Check

3 The sensor is mounted in the thermostat housing. The resistance of the sensor changes with temperature – see the Specifications at the beginning of the chapter. While in theory it is possible to bench-test the sensor at those temperatures, in practice the test is difficult to set up and perform. However you can test the resistance of the sensor in the bike with the engine cold, warm and hot.
4 On SFV models remove the throttle bodies (see Chapter 4).

3.5 ECT sensor wiring connector (arrowed) – DL shown from right-hand side

4.3a Thermostat housing (arrowed)

4.3b Detach the cover and remove the thermostat (arrowed)

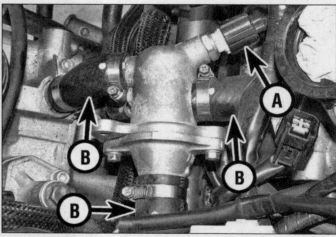

4.4 Disconnect the ECT sensor connector (A) then detach the hoses (B)

5 Disconnect the ECT sensor wiring connector **(see illustration 3.5 for DL models or 4.4 for SFV models)**.
6 Connect the probes of a multimeter set to read resistance to the terminals on the sensor and take several readings as the engine warms up. Resistance should decrease as temperature increases – if the sensor fails it is most likely to give a zero, constant, or infinite resistance reading at all temperatures.

Removal and installation

 Warning: The engine must be completely cool before carrying out this procedure.

7 The sensor is mounted in the thermostat housing. Drain the cooling system (see Chapter 1).
8 On SFV models remove the throttle bodies (see Chapter 4).
9 Disconnect the ECT sensor wiring connector **(see illustration 3.5 for DL models or 4.4 for SFV models)**.
10 Unscrew and remove the sensor, and discard the sealing washer.

11 Fit a new sealing washer onto the sensor. Fit the sensor and tighten it to the torque setting specified at the beginning of the Chapter. Connect the wiring.
12 Refill the cooling system (see Chapter 1).

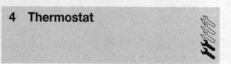

4 Thermostat

1 The thermostat is automatic in operation and should give many years service without requiring attention. In the event of a failure, the valve will probably jam open, in which case the engine will take much longer than normal to warm up. Conversely, if the valve jams shut, the coolant will be unable to circulate and the engine will overheat. Neither condition is acceptable – the fault must be investigated promptly.

Removal

2 Drain the cooling system (see Chapter 1).

3 Access to the thermostat is from the left-hand side of the bike **(see illustration)**, but if preferred remove the throttle bodies (see Chapter 4) and access it from the top. Unscrew the cover bolts and detach it from the housing **(see illustration)**. Withdraw the thermostat, noting how it fits.
4 To remove the thermostat housing remove the throttle bodies (see Chapter 4). Disconnect the ECT sensor wiring connector **(see illustration)**. Slacken the hose clamps and detach the hoses either from the housing or from the engine and radiator as required, and remove the housing, either with or without its hoses.

Thermostat check

5 Examine the thermostat visually before carrying out the test. If it remains in the open position at room temperature, it should be replaced with a new one. Also check the condition of the seal.
6 Suspend the thermostat by a piece of wire in a container of cold water. Place a

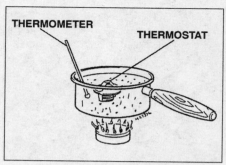

4.6 Thermostat testing set-up

5.3a Horn wiring connectors (arrowed) – 2004 to 2011 DL

5.3b Horn wiring connectors (arrowed) – 2012-on DL

thermometer capable of reading temperatures up to 110°C in the water so that the bulb is close to the thermostat **(see illustration)**. Heat the water, noting the temperature when the thermostat opens, and compare the result with the specifications given at the beginning of the Chapter. Also check the amount the valve opens after it has been heated for a few minutes and compare the measurement to the specifications. If the readings obtained differ from those given, the thermostat is faulty and must be replaced with a new one.

7 In the event of thermostat failure, if the thermostat is permanently closed, as an emergency measure only it can be removed and the machine used without it (this is better than leaving it in as the engine will overheat). If it is permanently open you are better to leave it in. In both cases take care when starting the engine from cold as it will take much longer than usual to warm up. Ensure that a new unit is installed as soon as possible.

Installation

8 Installation is the reverse of removal, noting the following:

● Check the thermostat seal for signs of damage or deterioration and fit a new thermostat if necessary.
● Fit the thermostat into the housing with the hole at the top **(see illustration 4.3b)**.
● If the housing was removed make sure all hoses are fully pushed on to the unions and are secured by the clamps.
● On completion refill the cooling system (see Chapter 1).

5.4a Detach the hoses (arrowed) from the right-hand side of the radiator...

5.4b ...and from the left-hand side

5 Radiator

Note: *If the radiator is being removed as part of the engine removal procedure, detach the hoses from their unions on the engine rather than on the radiator and remove the radiator complete with its hoses. Note the routing of the hoses.*

Removal

⚠️ **Warning: The engine must be completely cool before carrying out this procedure.**

1 On 2004 to 2011 DL models remove the fairing side panels, and on 2012-on DL models remove the complete fairing assembly (see Chapter 7). On SFV models remove the radiator covers (see Chapter 7).

2 Drain the cooling system (see Chapter 1).
3 Disconnect the fan wiring connector **(see illustration 2.19a, b or c)**. On DL models disconnect the horn wiring connectors **(see illustrations)**.
4 Slacken the clamps securing the hoses to the radiator and detach them **(see illustrations)**.
5 On 2004 to 2011 DL models release the fan wiring connector from the shroud and the speed sensor wire from its clamp **(see illustration)**. Unscrew the radiator mounting bolts and displace the radiator from the lug on the left-hand side **(see illustrations 5.6b and c)**, then release the shroud clips on the top and the peg on each side, and remove the radiator, taking care not to catch the fins on anything **(see illustrations)**. If required remove the horn (see Chapter 8).
6 On 2012-on DL models release the two

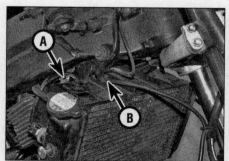

5.5a Release the connector (A) and the wire (B)

5.5b Release the shroud clips (arrowed)...

5.5c ...and the shroud pegs

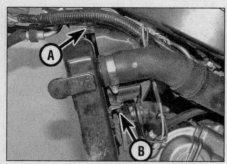

5.6a Release the trim clip (A) on each side and the peg (B)

5.6b Unscrew the bolts (arrowed)...

5.6c ...and displace the radiator from the lug (arrowed)

5.7 Unscrew the bolt (arrowed)

5.9 Note the collars and check the condition of the grommets

● Make sure that the fan wiring is correctly connected (see illustration 2.19a, b or c).
● On completion refill the cooling system (see Chapter 1).

Pressure cap check

12 If problems such as overheating or loss of coolant occur, check the entire system as described in Chapter 1. If there are no obvious problems and leaks the pressure cap should be checked by a Honda dealer with the special tester required to do the job. If the cap is defective, replace it with a new one.

trim clips and the peg on the left-hand side securing the radiator shroud **(see illustration)**. Unscrew the radiator mounting bolts and displace the radiator from the shroud on the right-hand side and the lug on the left and remove the radiator, taking care not to catch the fins on anything **(see illustrations)**. If required remove the horn (see Chapter 8).
7 On SFV models unscrew the radiator mounting bolts on the right-hand side **(see illustration 5.6b)**. Unscrew the bolt on the left-hand side and remove the radiator, taking care not to catch the fins on anything **(see illustration)**.
8 If required remove the cooling fan (see Section 2).
9 Note the arrangement of the collars and rubber grommets in the radiator mounts **(see illustration)**. Replace the grommets with

new ones if they are damaged, deformed or deteriorated.
10 Check the radiator for signs of damage and clear any dirt or debris that might obstruct air flow and inhibit cooling. If the radiator fins are badly damaged or broken the radiator must be replaced with a new one.

Installation

11 Installation is the reverse of removal, noting the following.
● Make sure the rubber grommets are in place and the collars are fitted in them **(see illustration 5.9)**.
● Make sure the coolant hoses are in good condition (see Chapter 1), are pushed fully onto their unions and are securely retained by their clamps, using new ones if necessary **(see illustrations 5.4a and b)**.

6 Water pump

Check

1 Refer to Chapter 1, Section 10.

Removal

2 Refer to Chapter 2, Section 17, Steps 1 to 3, and remove the clutch cover – the water pump is mounted inside it.
3 Remove the circlip securing the pump driven gear and draw the gear off the shaft **(see illustration)**. Withdraw the drive pin from the shaft and remove the washer **(see illustrations)**.
4 Separate the pump assembly from the

6.3a Release the circlip and remove the gear...

6.3b ...the drive pin...

6.3c ...and the washer

6.4a Remove the pump from the cover

6.4b Remove the O-rings (arrowed)

6.5a Undo the screws (arrowed) and remove the cover...

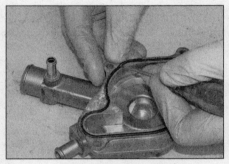

6.5b ...and its O-ring

6.7a Remove the E-clip...

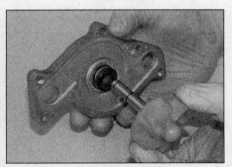

6.7b ...and withdraw the impeller

clutch cover (see illustration). Remove the pump body and coolant passage O-rings – new ones must be used (see illustration).

Inspection

5 Undo the two screws on the back of the assembly and separate the pump body from the cover (see illustration). Discard the cover O-ring as a new one must be used (see illustration).

6 To check the pump impeller bearings, wiggle the impeller back-and-forth and spin it by hand. If there is excessive movement, or the bearings are noisy or rough when turned, they must be replaced with new ones.

7 Remove the E-clip and withdraw the impeller from the pump body (see illustrations). Check that the shaft is at right-angles to the impeller.

8 Check the condition of the rubber damper and its holder on the rear face of the impeller. Do not remove them from the shaft unnecessarily, as they cannot be reused. If they are damaged or deteriorated, lever off the old ones with a flat-bladed screwdriver

(see illustration). Apply coolant to the new ones and press them squarely down the shaft and into the back of the impeller, setting them flush with the face (see illustration).

9 Inspect the pump body for corrosion or a build-up of scale and clean with de-scaler and/or steel wool as necessary, then rinse the pump body in running clean water.

Seal and bearing removal and installation

10 Follow Steps 2 to 7 to remove the impeller from the pump body.

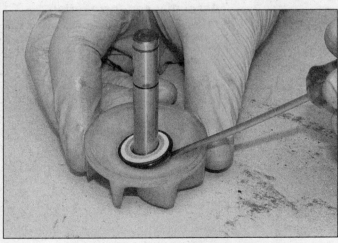

6.8a Lever out the damper assembly...

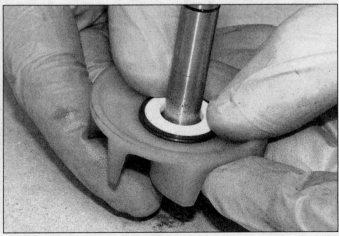

6.8b ...and press a new one in

6.11a First remove the inner part of the seal...

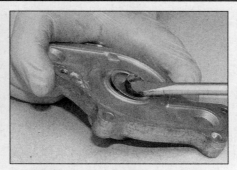

6.11b ...then dig the seat out...

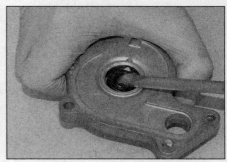

6.11c ...and lever the oil seal out

6.12 Drive the bearings out using a socket

6.14 Drive the bearings in using a socket that bears only on the outer race

11 Remove the mechanical seal by digging it out using a screwdriver, then lever the oil seal out **(see illustrations)**.

12 Place the pump on wooden blocks and drive the bearings out from the inside using a socket **(see illustration)** – heat the outside of the bearing housing using a hot air gun to ease removal if necessary.

13 Clean any traces of sealant from around the mechanical seal seat with a suitable solvent.

14 Drive each bearing into the pump body with its marked side facing out using a suitable socket on the outer race until it is seated **(see illustration)**.

15 Use a socket to press or drive the oil seal into the body with the marked side facing out until it is flush with the drain hole lip as shown **(see illustrations)** – do not set it any deeper. Smear some grease onto the seal lip.

16 Press or carefully drive the new mechanical seal into the pump body using a suitable sized socket or driver that bears only on the outer rim of the seal seat and not on the centre **(see illustrations)**. Make sure the seal rim is correctly seated **(see illustration)**.

17 Assemble the pump.

Assembly and installation

18 Wrap a single layer of insulating tape around the inner end of the driveshaft to protect the seal lips. Smear the tape and shaft

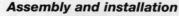

6.15a Press the new oil seal in...

6.15b ...setting it as shown

6.16a Fit the new mechanical seal...

6.16b ...and drive it in as described...

6.16c ...until the rim is seated

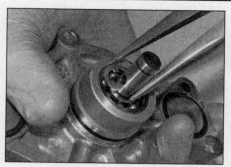

6.18 Secure the shaft with the E-clip

6.19a Fit a new O-ring...

6.19b ...then fit the cover

with grease. Slide the shaft into the pump body and push the impeller against the seal to expose the clip groove **(see illustration 6.7b)**. Fit the E-clip, making sure it locates correctly in the groove **(see illustration)**.

19 Smear the new cover O-ring with coolant and fit it into its groove **(see illustration)**. Fit the cover onto the pump and tighten the two screws **(see illustration)**.

20 Smear the new coolant passage O-rings with grease and fit them into the grooves in the back of the pump **(see illustration)**. Smear the new pump body O-ring with grease and fit it into its groove in the body.

21 Push the pump into the clutch cover, aligning the bolt holes **(see illustration 6.4)**.

22 Fit the washer onto the shaft, then slide the drive pin into its hole **(see illustrations 6.3c and b)**. Fit the driven gear onto the shaft, locating the cut-outs over the drive pin ends **(see illustration)**. Secure the gear with the circlip, making sure it locates correctly in its groove **(see illustration 6.3a)**.

23 Refer to Chapter 2, Section 17, Steps 32 to 34, and install the clutch cover

6.20 Lubricate and fit the new O-rings

6.22 Fit the gear as shown, seating the cut-outs over the pin

7 Coolant reservoir

7.2a Detach the hose

7.2b Unscrew the bolt (arrowed)...

Removal

2004 to 2006 DL models

1 Remove the fuel tank (see Chapter 4). Get a suitable container to hold the coolant.

2 Detach the breather hose from the top of the reservoir **(see illustration)**. Unscrew the bolt, lift the reservoir out, remove the cap and tip the coolant into the container **(see illustrations)**.

3 Detach the hose from the bottom of the reservoir.

2007-on DL models

4 Remove the fuel tank (see Chapter 4). Get a suitable container to hold the coolant.

5 Detach the breather hose from the top of the reservoir **(see illustration)**. Unscrew the

7.2c ...then lift and empty the reservoir

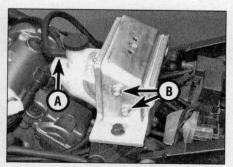

7.5a Detach the hose (A), then unscrew the bolts (B)...

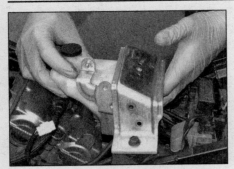

7.5b ...draw the reservoir out and empty it...

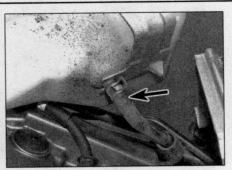

7.6 ...then detach the hose (arrowed)

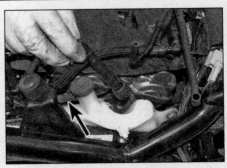

7.8a Pull the plug cap off, then detach the hose (arrowed)

bolts, draw the reservoir out, remove the cap and tip the coolant into the container (**see illustration**).

6 Detach the hose from the bottom of the reservoir (**see illustration**).

SFV models

7 Raise the fuel tank (see Chapter 4). Get a suitable container to hold the coolant.

8 Pull the outer plug cap off the rear cylinder and detach the breather hose from the top of the reservoir (**see illustration**). Unscrew the bolt, lift the reservoir out, remove the cap and tip the coolant into the container (**see illustration**).

9 Detach the hose from the bottom of the reservoir.

Installation

10 Installation is the reverse of removal. Refill the reservoir to the FULL level line with the specified coolant mixture (see *Pre-ride checks*).

7.8b Unscrew the bolt (arrowed) then lift and empty the reservoir

8.4 Outlet union bolt (arrowed)

8 Coolant hoses and unions

Removal

1 Before removing a hose, drain the coolant (see Chapter 1).

2 Use a screwdriver to slacken the larger-bore hose clamps, then slide them back along the hose and clear of the union spigot. The smaller-bore hoses are secured by spring clamps which can be expanded by squeezing their ears together with pliers.

Caution: The radiator unions are fragile. Do not use excessive force when attempting to remove the hoses.

3 If a hose proves stubborn, release it by rotating it on its union before working it off. If all else fails, cut the hose with a sharp knife. Whilst this means replacing the hose with a new one – it is preferable to buying a new radiator.

4 The outlet union on each cylinder head can be removed by unscrewing its bolt (**see illustration**). Remove the O-ring – a new one must be used.

Installation

5 Slide the clamps onto the hose and then work the hose on to its union as far as the spigot where present.

HAYNES HiNT *If the hose is difficult to push on its union, soften it by soaking it in very hot water, or alternatively a little soapy water on the union can be used as a lubricant.*

6 Rotate the hose on its unions to settle it in position before sliding the clamps into place and tightening them securely.

7 To fit each outlet union, smear a new O-ring with coolant and fit it onto the end of the union. Fit the union and tighten the bolt.

8 Refill the cooling system (see Chapter 1).

Chapter 4
Engine management system

Contents

Degrees of difficulty

Easy, suitable for novice with little experience	Fairly easy, suitable for beginner with some experience	Fairly difficult, suitable for competent DIY mechanic	Difficult, suitable for experienced DIY mechanic	Very difficult, suitable for expert DIY or professional

Specifications

General information

Cylinder numbering . . . . Front – No. 1, rear – No. 2
Spark plugs . . . . see Chapter 1
Engine idle speed. . . . . 1200 to 1400 rpm

Fuel

Grade
  European models . . . . Regular unleaded, minimum 91 RON (Research Octane Number)
  US and Canada models . . . . Unleaded, minimum 87 (R/2+M/2 method)
Fuel tank capacity (including reserve)
  2004 to 2011 DL models . . . . 22 litres
  2012-on DL models . . . . 20 litres
  SFV models . . . . 14.5 litres

Fuel pump

Operating pressure. . . . . 43 psi (3.0 Bar)
Pump flow rate
  2004 to 2006 DL models . . . . min. 168 ml per 10 seconds at operating pressure
  2007 to 2011 DL models . . . . min. 75 ml per 6 seconds at operating pressure
  2012-on DL models . . . . min. 167 ml per 10 seconds at operating pressure
  SFV models . . . . min. 166 ml per 10 seconds at operating pressure

Fuel injection system test data

Crankshaft position (CKP) sensor
    Resistance . . . .   130 to 240 ohms
    Peak voltage. . . . .   above 3.7 V
Engine coolant temperature (ECT) sensor
    Input voltage. . . . .   4.5 to 5.5 V
    Resistance . . . .   2.45 K-ohms @ 20°C approx.
Gear position (GP) switch voltage
    2004 to 2011 DL models . . . .   above 1.0 V
    2012-on DL models and all SFV models . . . .   above 0.6 V
Idle speed control valve resistance . . . .   29 to 31 ohms @ 20°C approx.
Injector resistance . . . .   11 to 13 ohms
Injector voltage. . . . .   Battery voltage (12 V approx.)
Intake air pressure (IAP) sensor
    Input voltage. . . . .   4.5 to 5.5 V
    Output voltage
        2004 to 2006 DL models . . . .   2.7 V approx. at idle speed
        2007 to 2011 DL models . . . .   1.6 V approx. at idle speed
        2012-on DL models and all SFV models . . . .   2.5 V approx. at idle speed
Intake air temperature (IAT) sensor
    Input voltage. . . . .   4.5 to 5.5 V
    Resistance . . . .   2.45 to 2.6 K-ohms @ 20°C
Oxygen sensor
    Resistance
        2004 to 2006 DL models . . . .   4 to 5 ohms @ 23°C
        2007 to 2011 DL models . . . .   11 to 15 ohms @ 23°C
        2012-on DL models and all SFV models . . . .   8 ohms @ 23°C
    Output voltage
        2004 to 2011 DL models
            At idle speed. . . . .   max. 0.4 V
            At 5000 rpm . . . .   min. 0.6 V
        2012-on DL models and all SFV models
            At idle speed. . . . .   max. 0.45 V
            At 6000 rpm . . . .   min. 0.6 V
PAIR solenoid valve
    Resistance . . . .   20 to 24 ohms @ 20°C
    Input voltage. . . . .   Battery voltage (12 V approx.)
Secondary throttle position (STP) sensor – 2004 to 2006 DL models
    Input voltage. . . . .   4.5 to 5.5 V
    Output voltage
        Valves closed . . . .   0.58 V approx.
        Valves open. . . . .   4.40 V approx.
    Resistance
        Valves closed . . . .   0.58 K-ohms approx.
        Valves open. . . . .   4.38 K-ohms approx.
Secondary throttle position (STP) sensor – 2007-on DL models and all SFV models
    Input voltage. . . . .   4.5 to 5.5 V
    Output voltage
        Valves closed . . . .   0.6 V approx.
        Valves open. . . . .   4.5 V approx.
Secondary throttle valve (STV) servo
    2004 to 2006 DL models . . . .   7.0 to 14.0 ohms approx.
    2007-on DL models and all SFV models . . . .   7.0 ohms approx.
Throttle position (TP) sensor
    Input voltage. . . . .   4.5 to 5.5 V
    Output voltage
        Closed. . . . .   1.1 V approx.
        Open. . . . .   4.3 V approx.
    Resistance
        Closed. . . . .   1.12 K-ohms approx.
        Open. . . . .   4.26 K-ohms approx.
Tip-over (TO) sensor
    Resistance
        2004 to 2006 DL models . . . .   19.1 to 19.7 K-ohms
        2007-on DL models and all SFV models . . . .   16.5 to 22.3 K-ohms
    Voltage
        Sensor horizontal . . . .   0.4 to 1.4 V approx.
        Sensor tilted (see text) . . . .   3.7 to 4.4 V approx.

Fuel level sensor

Resistance
  2004 to 2006 DL models
    Full position . . . . 4 ohms approx.
    Empty position . . . . 182 ohms approx.
  2007 to 2011 DL models
    Full position . . . . max. 9 ohms
    Empty position . . . . min. 167 ohms
  2012-on DL models
    Full position . . . . 9 to 11 ohms
    Empty position . . . . 213 to 219 ohms
  SFV models
    Full position . . . . 10 to 20 ohms
    Empty position . . . . 84 to 90 ohms

Ignition coils

2004 to 2006 DL models
  Primary winding resistance . . . . 2 to 5 ohms
  Secondary winding resistance . . . . 24 to 37 K-ohms
2007-on DL models
  Primary winding resistance . . . . 1 to 5 ohms
  Secondary winding resistance . . . . 25 to 40 K-ohms
SFV models
  Primary winding resistance . . . . 1 to 3 ohms
  Secondary winding resistance . . . . 25 to 45 K-ohms

Torque settings

Exhaust system
  2004 to 2011 DL models and all SFV models
    Downpipe flange bolts . . . . 23 Nm
    Mounting bolts . . . . 23 Nm
    Clamp bolts . . . . 23 Nm
  2012-on DL models
    Downpipe flange bolts . . . . 23 Nm
    Mounting bolts . . . . 23 Nm
    Clamp bolts . . . . 18 Nm
Fuel pump bolts . . . . 10 Nm
Oxygen sensor
  2004 to 2011 DL models . . . . 48 Nm
  2012-on DL models and all SFV models . . . . 25 Nm

---

1   General information and precautions

General information

All models are fitted with a fully electronic engine management system that controls both the fuelling and ignition from one engine control module, or ECM.

Fuel system

The fuel system consists of the fuel tank, incorporating the fuel pump, filter and pressure regulator, the fuel hose to the fuel rail on the throttle bodies, and the injectors that are located in each throttle body – two for each cylinder. The fuel pump is activated initially by the ignition switch and then by a relay. Fuel pressure is controlled within the pump by a pressure regulator. In the event of the machine falling over, a tip-over sensor cuts power to the fuel pump, injectors and ignition coils.

The entire fuel injection system is controlled by the engine control module (ECM), which monitors data sent from the various system sensors and adjusts fuel delivery to the engine accordingly. If a fault develops in the injection system, the FI warning LED illuminates on the instrument cluster, either on continuously or blinking depending on the severity of the fault, and FI is displayed on the LCD, either alternating with the temperature readout or continuously, depending on the severity of the fault, and a fault code is registered in the ECM. In the case of a minor fault (FI light on and LCD alternating between FI and the clock or odometer, according to model) the engine will continue to run enabling the machine to be ridden, although performance will be significantly reduced. For comprehensive fault diagnosis and certain service procedures, a Suzuki mode select switch (Pt. No. 09930-82720) is required.

All models have dual valve throttle bodies. The main valve on the front cylinder throttle body is actuated by the throttle cables from the handlebar twistgrip, the secondary valve is actuated by the secondary throttle valve (STV) servo controlled by the ECM. The corresponding valves on the rear cylinder throttle body are actuated by link rods from the front cylinder throttle body. The secondary valves smooth air flow into the throttle body. Throttle position sensors for both valves are located on the rear cylinder throttle body.

On 2004 to 2011 DL models a pulse secondary air (PAIR) system introduces filtered air into the exhaust ports in the cylinder heads to promote the burning of excess fuel in the exhaust gases. The PAIR solenoid valve, located on the underside of the air filter housing, is controlled by the ECM. California models feature an EVAP emission control system that prevents fuel vapour escaping into the atmosphere from the fuel tank.

Ignition system

The transistorised electronic ignition system is combined with the fuel injection system, both being controlled by the ECM (engine control module). The ignition system comprises timing triggers around the alternator rotor, a crankshaft position sensor (CKP sensor), the engine control module (ECM), the ignition coils and the spark plugs.

The triggers on the alternator rotor, which is on the left-hand end of the crankshaft, generate a signal in the CKP sensor as the crankshaft rotates. The ECM calculates the ignition timing and supplies the ignition coils with the signals to produce a spark at the plugs. There is no provision for adjusting the ignition timing.

The system incorporates a starter safety circuit (see Section 12 in Chapter 1 for more information).

Note: *Individual engine management system components can be checked but not repaired. If system troubles occur, and the faulty component can be isolated, the only cure for the problem in most cases is to replace the part with a new one. Keep in mind that most electronic parts, once purchased, cannot be returned. To avoid unnecessary expense, make very sure the faulty component has been positively identified before buying a new part.*

Precautions

⚠️ *Warning: Petrol (gasoline) is extremely flammable, so take extra precautions when you work on any part of the fuel system. Always remove the battery (see Chapter 8). Don't smoke or allow open flames or bare light bulbs near the work area, and don't work in a garage where a natural gas-type appliance is present. If you spill any fuel on your skin, rinse it off immediately with soap and water. When you perform any kind of work on the fuel system, wear safety glasses and have a fire extinguisher suitable for a class B type fire (flammable liquids) on hand.*

It is vital that no dirt or debris is allowed to enter the fuel tank or the fuel rail assembly whilst the fuel hose is disconnected. Any foreign matter in the fuel system components could result in injector damage or malfunction. Ensure the ignition is switched OFF before disconnecting or reconnecting any fuel injection system wiring connector. If a connector is disconnected or reconnected with the ignition switched ON, the ECM could be damaged.

Always perform service procedures in a well-ventilated area to prevent a build-up of fumes.

Never work in a building containing a gas appliance with a pilot light, or any other form of naked flame. Ensure that there are no naked light bulbs or any sources of flame or sparks nearby.

Do not smoke (or allow anyone else to smoke) while in the vicinity of petrol (gasoline) or of components containing it. Remember the possible presence of vapour from these sources and move well clear before smoking.

Check all electrical equipment belonging to the house, garage or workshop where work is being undertaken (see the Safety first! section of this manual). Remember that certain electrical appliances such as drills, cutters etc, create sparks in the normal course of operation and must not be used near petrol (gasoline) or any component containing it. Again, remember the possible presence of fumes before using electrical equipment.

Always mop up any spilt fuel and safely dispose of the rag used.

Any stored fuel that is drained off during servicing work must be kept in sealed containers that are suitable for holding petrol (gasoline), and clearly marked as such; the containers themselves should be kept in a safe place. Note that this last point applies equally to the fuel tank if it is removed from the machine; also remember to keep its filler cap closed at all times.

Read the *Safety first!* section of this manual carefully before starting work.

2 Fuel tank

⚠️ **Warning: Refer to the precautions given in Section 1 before starting work.**

Note: *Removing the tank involves a small amount of unavoidable fuel spillage, which is obviously dangerous. Refer to the precautions given in Section 1 before starting work, and have plenty of rag to hand. Once the tank has been removed, rest it on some soft rag to prevent damaging the paintwork or hose*

unions. Try to time the removal procedure with a near empty tank, which makes it much easier to lift.

2004 to 2011 DL models

Raise

1 Make sure the fuel cap is secure.
2 Remove the seat, the fairing side panels, and the fuel tank trim panels (see Chapter 7).
3 Unscrew the rear mounting bolt and remove the tank prop with the upper rubber **(see illustrations 2.16)**.
4 Raise the rear of the tank, remove the lower rubber, and fit the prop between the tank and the bracket, making sure it is secure **(see illustrations 2.17a and b)**.

Removal

5 Raise the rear of the tank (see above).
6 Disconnect the fuel pump wiring connector **(see illustration 2.19)**.
7 Disconnect the fuel tank drain hose **(see illustration)**.
8 Place a wad of rag for catching any residual fuel in the hose under the connector. Release the clip on the hose connector and disconnect it from its union on the bottom of the tank **(see illustrations 2.21a and b)**.
9 Remove the support and lower the tank.
10 Remove the front pivot bolt **(see illustration)**. Carefully lift the tank off the frame and remove it.
11 Note the pivot bolt sleeve in the front mount and remove it if required **(see illustration)**. Check all the tank rubbers and hoses for signs of damage or deterioration and replace them with new ones if necessary.

Installation

12 Installation is the reverse of removal, noting the following.
● Check that the tank mounting rubbers and pivot bolt sleeve are fitted.
● Make sure the tank seats correctly around the front rubbers.
● Align the fuel supply hose connector with its union on the tank and push it on fully so that the clip engages, then check it is secure by trying to pull it off. Make sure the drain hose is pushed fully onto its union.

2.7 Disconnect the hose (arrowed)

2.10 Unscrew the nut and withdraw the bolt

2.11 Remove the sleeve if required

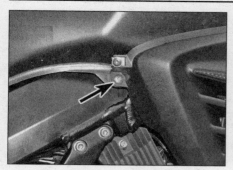

2.14 Undo the screw (arrowed)

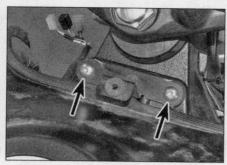

2.15 Unscrew the bolts (arrowed)

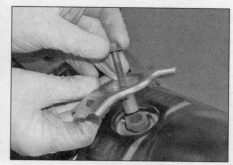

2.16 Unscrew the bolt and remove the prop

● Start the engine and check that there is no sign of fuel leakage.

2012-on DL models

Raise

13 Make sure the fuel cap is secure.
14 Remove the seat, the side covers, and the fuel tank trim panels (see Chapter 7). Undo the fairing side panel screw **(see illustration)**.
15 Unscrew the front bolts and remove the bracket **(see illustration)**.
16 Unscrew the rear mounting bolt and remove the tank prop with the upper rubber **(see illustration)**.
17 Raise the rear of the tank, remove the lower rubber, and fit the prop between the tank and the bracket, making sure it is secure **(see illustrations)**.

Removal

18 Raise the rear of the tank (see above).
19 Disconnect the fuel pump wiring connector **(see illustration)**.
20 Disconnect the fuel tank drain and breather hoses **(see illustration)**.
21 Place a wad of rag for catching any residual fuel in the hose under the connector. Release the clip on the hose connector and disconnect it from its union on the bottom of the tank **(see illustrations)**.
22 Remove the support and lower the tank. Carefully lift the tank off the frame and remove it **(see illustration)**.

2.17a Raise the tank, remove the rubber...

2.17b ...and fit the prop

2.19 Disconnect the wiring connector

2.20 Disconnect the hoses (arrowed)

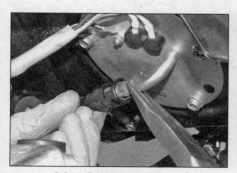

2.21a Release the clips...

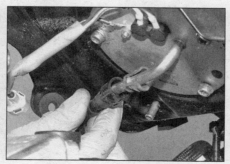

2.21b ...and pull the hose off

2.22 Carefully lift the tank off

2.23 Check all the mounting rubbers

2.24a Make sure the collars are fitted from the underside

2.24b Make sure the tank seats around the front rubbers (arrowed)

2.26 Remove the prop (arrowed)

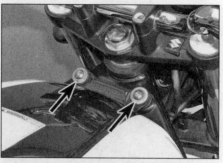

2.27 Unscrew the bolts (arrowed)

2.28 Raise the tank and fit the prop as described

23 Check all the tank rubbers and hoses for signs of damage or deterioration and replace them with new ones if necessary **(see illustration).**

Installation

24 Installation is the reverse of removal, noting the following.
● Check that the tank mounting rubbers are fitted **(see illustration 2.23)**. Make sure the collars are in the front mounts **(see illustration 2.24a)**.
● Make sure the tank seats correctly around the front rubbers **(see illustration 2.24b)**.

● Align the fuel supply hose connector with its union on the tank and push it on fully so that the clip engages, then check it is secure by trying to pull it off. Make sure the drain and breather hoses are pushed fully onto their unions.
● Start the engine and check that there is no sign of fuel leakage.

SFV models

Raise

25 Make sure the fuel cap is secure.
26 Remove the seat (see Chapter 7). Remove the fuel tank prop **(see illustration)**.

27 Unscrew the front bolts **(see illustration)**.
28 Raise the front of the tank and fit the prop, locating the ringed end over the steering stem nut and the other end in one of the front mounting holes, making sure it is secure **(see illustration)**.

Removal

29 Raise the front of the tank (see above).
30 Disconnect the fuel pump wiring connector **(see illustration)**.
31 Disconnect the fuel tank drain and breather hoses **(see illustration)**.
32 Place a wad of rag for catching any

2.30 Disconnect the wiring connector (arrowed)

2.31 Disconnect the hoses (arrowed)

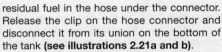
2.34a Unscrew the nut and withdraw the bolt

2.34b Carefully lift the tank off

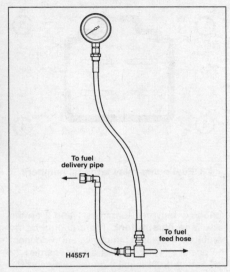
3.2 Fuel pressure check set-up

residual fuel in the hose under the connector. Release the clip on the hose connector and disconnect it from its union on the bottom of the tank (see illustrations 2.21a and b).

33 Remove the support and lower the tank.

34 Remove the rear pivot bolt (see illustration). Carefully lift the tank off the frame and remove it (see illustration).

35 Check all the tank rubbers and hoses for signs of damage or deterioration and replace them with new ones if necessary.

Installation

36 Installation is the reverse of removal, noting the following.
● Check that the tank mounting rubbers are fitted. Make sure the collars are in the front mounts.
● Align the fuel supply hose connector with its union on the tank and push it on fully so that the clip engages, then check it is secure by trying to pull it off. Make sure the breather hose is pushed fully onto its union.
● Start the engine and check that there is no sign of fuel leakage.

Repair

37 Repairs to the fuel tank should be carried out by a professional who has experience in this critical and potentially dangerous work. Even after cleaning and flushing of the fuel system, explosive fumes can remain and ignite during repair of the tank.

38 If the fuel tank is removed from the bike, it should not be placed in an area where sparks or open flames could ignite the fumes coming

out of the tank. Be especially careful inside garages where a natural gas-type appliance is located – the pilot light could cause an explosion.

3 Fuel pressure check

  Warning: Refer to the precautions given in Section 1 before starting work.

Special Tool: *A fuel pressure gauge is required for this procedure.*

1 To check the fuel pressure, a suitable gauge, gauge hose and adapters are needed. Suzuki provides service tools (Pt. Nos. 09915-77331, 09915-74521, 09940-40211 and 09940-40220) for this purpose.

2 Raise the fuel tank, then disconnect the fuel hose from the fuel pump (see Section 2). Use the adapters to connect the gauge between the fuel pump and the fuel hose as shown (see illustration).

3 Turn the ignition switch ON and check the pressure reading on the gauge. The pressure should be as specified at the beginning of this Chapter.

4 Turn the ignition OFF and disconnect the gauge and adapters. Use a rag to catch any residual fuel as before. Reconnect the fuel hose to the pump (see Section 2).

5 If the pressure is too low, check for a leak in the fuel supply system, a blocked fuel filter

(see Section 6), a faulty pressure regulator or a faulty fuel pump.

6 If the pressure is too high, either the pressure regulator or the fuel pump check valve is faulty.

7 Suzuki provides no test procedure for the pressure regulator. A new regulator is available as an integral part of the pump filter cartridge. Remove the pump and make sure the filter cartridge/regulator has not come loose from the pump assembly (this is unlikely), then if necessary disassemble the pump and replace the cartridge/regulator with a new one (see Section 6). The fuel check valve is an integral part of the pump and is not available separately.

4 Fuel pump relay

1 Remove the seat, and on SFV models the right-hand side cover (see Chapter 7).

2 Displace the relay and disconnect the wiring connector (see illustrations).

3 Using a multimeter or test light, check for

4.2a Fuel pump relay (arrowed) – 2004 to 2011 DL

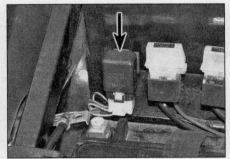
4.2b Fuel pump relay (arrowed) – 2012-on DL

4.2c Fuel pump relay (arrowed) – SFV

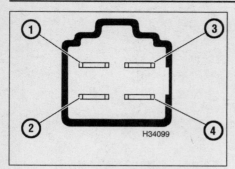

4.3 Fuel pump relay terminal numbers

5.3a Unscrew the bolts (arrowed)...

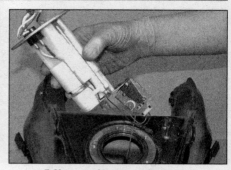

5.3b ...and remove the pump

continuity between terminals 1 and 2 on the relay (see illustration). There should be no continuity. Now use jumper wires to connect the positive (+) terminal of a fully charged 12 volt battery to terminal 3 on the relay and the negative (-) battery terminal to relay terminal 4. There should now be continuity shown across terminals 1 and 2. If the relay fails either of the checks, renew it.

5 Fuel pump

⚠️ **Warning: Refer to the precautions given in Section 1 before starting work.**

1 The fuel pump assembly, incorporating the pump, strainer, level sensor and filter cartridge/pressure regulator, is located inside the fuel tank. When the ignition is switched ON, it should be possible to hear the pump run for a few seconds until the system is up to pressure. If you can't hear anything, first check the fuse (see Chapter 8), then check the relay (see Section 4). If they are good, check the wiring and terminals for physical damage or loose or corroded connections and rectify as necessary (see the *Wiring Diagrams* at the end of Chapter 8). If the pump still will not run, check the tip-over (TO) sensor (see Section 14). If that is good, and assuming the ECM is OK, fit a new pump assembly – the pump

motor itself is not available separately, though the strainer, level sensor and filter cartridge/pressure regulator all are. Note that if the pump has failed and you are buying a complete new pump assembly, before discarding the old assembly remove the strainer components, the level sensor, and the filter cartridge/pressure regulator and keep them as spares, just in case (see Section 6).

Removal

2 The fuel pump is located inside the fuel tank. Remove the tank and pump the fuel out into a suitable container using a hand pump (see Section 2).
3 Turn the tank upside down and rest it on some clean rag. Undo the pump bolts evenly in a criss-cross pattern and carefully lift out the pump, taking care not to snag the level sensor arm (see illustrations). Remove the O-ring – a new one must be fitted.
4 If required, disassemble the pump to clean the strainer, replace the filter cartridge/pressure regulator, and check the operation of the level sensor (see Section 6).

Installation

5 Check that all the wiring terminals for the fuel pump and the level sensor are secure.
6 Smear the new O-ring lightly with grease and fit it into the recess around the aperture on the underside of the fuel tank (see illustration).
7 Fit the pump and align the holes in the base with the threaded holes in the tank – the fuel

hose union points to the left-hand side of the bike (or to the right-hand side of the tank as you look at it upside down on the bench) (see illustration). Clean the threads of the bolts and apply a suitable thread locking compound to the bolts. Tighten the bolts finger-tight at first, then tighten them evenly and a little at a time in the sequence shown to the torque setting specified at the beginning of the Chapter (see illustration). Now go round the bolts again in the same sequence and to the same torque.
8 Install the fuel tank (see Section 2). Make sure there is no fuel leakage around the pump base.

6 Fuel strainer, filter cartridge/ pressure regulator, and fuel level sensor

⚠️ **Warning: Refer to the precautions given in Section 1 before starting work.**

2004 to 2006 DL models

Fuel strainer

1 Remove the fuel pump (see Section 5).
2 Undo the nuts and remove the washers securing the pump and level sensor feed wires to the terminals on the base and detach the wires, noting their position. Undo the screws on the holding arms coming off the pump base and detach the pump and level sensor

5.6 Fit a new O-ring into the groove

5.7a Make sure the pump is the correct way round

5.7b Tighten the bolts evenly in the numbered sequence

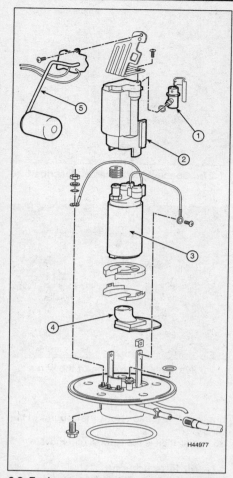

6.2 Fuel pump assembly – 2004 to 2006 DL

1 *Pressure regulator*   4 *Strainer*
2 *Filter cartridge*   5 *Level sensor*
3 *Pump*

earth wires, then remove the clip nuts (see illustration).

3 Remove the fuel level sensor (Step 14) – although not actually necessary it is easy to damage the sensor arm so removal is advised as a precaution.

4 Pull the pump assembly out of the base. Discard the O-ring on the base fuel union as a new one must be fitted on reassembly. Clean any sediment out of the pump base.

5 Clean any sediment off the strainer gauze with a soft brush or low pressure compressed air. If the strainer is damaged, or if there is sediment inside it, a new one should be fitted – release the clips and remove the fuel pump seat and rubber cushion, then remove the strainer from the bottom of the pump.

6 Install the components in the reverse order of disassembly, noting the following:
● Fit a new O-ring to the pump base fuel union and smear it with engine oil.
● Make sure the clip nuts are in place on both holding arms for the wire terminal retaining screws.

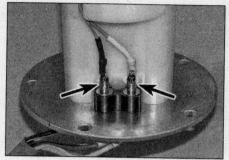

6.17 Detach the wires (arrowed)

● Do not forget the washers with the wiring terminal nuts – the spring washer goes between the plain washer and the nut.

Fuel filter cartridge/pressure regulator

7 Remove the fuel pump (see Section 5).
8 Remove the fuel level sensor (Step 14).
9 Carefully separate the fuel filter cartridge/pressure regulator from the pump. Discard the rubber bush and the O-ring on the base fuel union as new ones must be used. There is no need to detach the fuel pressure regulator as it is an integral part of the filter cartridge and the new cartridge will come with one fitted.
10 Install the components in the reverse order of disassembly, noting the following:
● Fit a new rubber bush between the filter cartridge and the pump and a new O-ring smeared with engine oil onto the pump base fuel union.

Fuel level sensor

11 Remove the fuel pump (see Section 5).
12 To check the sensor trace the wires from it and detach them from their terminals as in Step 2. Connect the probes of an ohmmeter to the wire terminals and measure the resistance of the sensor with the float in the raised (tank full) and lowered (tank empty) positions and compare the readings to the specifications at the beginning of the Chapter. Replace the sensor with a new one if necessary.
13 If the tests show the level sensor to be good, check the wiring circuit to the instrument cluster (see Chapter 8).

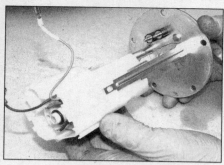

6.19 Pull the pump assembly off

14 To remove the sensor detach the wires as in Step 2, then undo the screws and remove the sensor. Note the routing of the wiring.
15 Installation is the reverse of removal.

2007-on DL models and all SFV models

Fuel strainer

16 Remove the fuel pump (see Section 5).
17 Detach the pump and level sensor feed wires from the terminals on the base, noting their position (see illustration).
18 Remove the fuel level sensor (Step 29). Remove the fuel filter cartridge/pressure regulator (Step 24).
19 Pull the pump assembly off the base (see illustration).
20 Remove the strainer from the bottom of the pump (see illustration). Clean any sediment off the strainer gauze with a soft brush or low pressure compressed air. If the strainer is damaged, or if there is sediment inside it, a new one should be fitted.
21 Install the components in the reverse order of disassembly.

Fuel filter cartridge/pressure regulator

22 Remove the fuel pump (see Section 5).
23 Remove the fuel level sensor (Step 29).
24 Carefully draw the fuel filter cartridge/pressure regulator squarely up off the pump (see illustration). Remove the O-rings from the top of the pump and the base union and

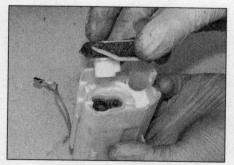

6.20 Remove the strainer

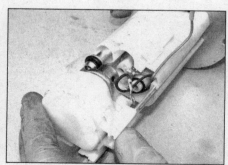

6.24a Remove the filter/regulator assembly...

6.24b ...and its O-rings...

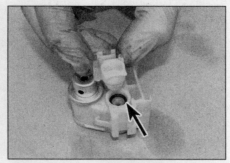

6.24c ...then remove the joint piece and its O-ring (arrowed)

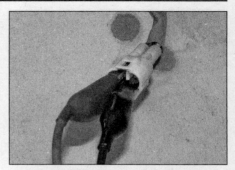

6.27a Connect the meter as described...

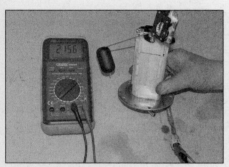

6.27b ...and test the sensor with the float lowered...

6.27c ...and raised

6.29a Note the routing of the wires

discard them as new ones must be used **(see illustration)**. Remove the joint piece from the bottom of the filter cartridge and discard its O-ring **(see illustration)**. Do not detach the fuel pressure regulator as it is an integral part of the filter cartridge and the new cartridge will come with one fitted.

25 Install the components in the reverse order of disassembly, noting the following:

● Fit new O-rings smeared with engine oil onto the joint piece, the pump and the base fuel union **(see illustrations 6.24c and b)**.

Fuel level sensor

26 Remove the fuel pump (see Section 5).

27 To check the sensor connect the positive probe of an ohmmeter to the red/black wire terminal in the connector and the negative probe to the black/white wire terminal and measure the resistance of the sensor with the float in the lowered (tank empty) and raised (tank full) positions **(see illustrations)**. Compare the readings to the specifications at the beginning of the Chapter. Replace the sensor with a new one if necessary.

28 If the tests show the level sensor to be good, check the wiring circuit to the instrument cluster (see Chapter 8).

29 To remove the sensor detach the level sensor feed wire from its terminal on the base **(see illustration 6.17)** and free it from its guide, noting its routing **(see illustration)**. Undo the screws securing the sensor and detach the pump and level sensor earth wires, noting which connects where **(see illustrations)**. Separate the sensor from its

bracket if required. Note the routing of the wiring.

30 Installation is the reverse of removal.

7 Air filter housing

⚠️ *Warning: Refer to the precautions given in Section 1 before starting work.*

2004 to 2006 DL models
Removal

1 Remove the fuel tank (see Section 2).

2 Disconnect the wiring connector from the intake air temperature (IAT) sensor **(see illustration)**.

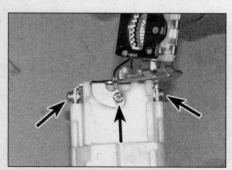

6.29b Undo the screws (arrowed) and detach the wires...

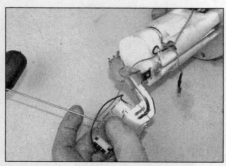

6.29c ...and remove the sensor

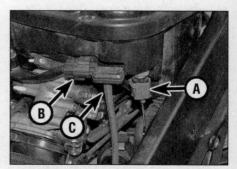

7.2 IAT sensor connector (A), IAP sensor connector (B) and vacuum hose (C)

7.4a Front clamp screw (arrowed)

7.4b Rear clamp screw (arrowed)

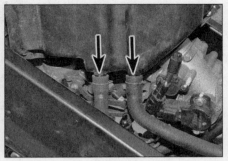

7.5a Crankcase breather hoses (arrowed)

3 Disconnect the wiring connector and the vacuum hose from the intake air pressure (IAP) sensor **(see illustration 7.2)**.

4 Loosen the clamp screws securing the housing to the throttle bodies **(see illustrations)**.

5 Displace the housing, then disconnect the crankcase breather hoses from the left-hand side of the housing and the PAIR solenoid valve wiring connector and hose from the right, then remove the housing **(see illustrations)**.

Installation

6 Installation is the reverse of removal, noting the following.

● Connect the PAIR system wiring connector and hose and the breather hoses before fitting the housing onto the throttle bodies **(see illustrations 7.5b and a)**.

● Make sure all hoses are fully pushed on to their unions and secured with their clips where fitted.

● Make sure the housing locates correctly on the throttle bodies and tighten the clamp screws securely.

● Make sure all wiring connectors are securely connected.

2007 to 2011 DL models

Removal

7 Remove the fuel tank (see Section 2).

8 Disconnect the wiring connector and the vacuum hose from each intake air pressure (IAP) sensor **(see illustration 7.13)**.

9 Loosen the clamp screws securing the housing to the throttle bodies **(see illustrations 7.4a and b)**.

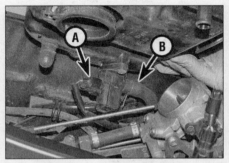

7.5b PAIR valve connector (A) and hose (B)

10 Displace the housing, then disconnect the idle speed control (ISC) hose and the PAIR solenoid valve wiring connector and hose from the right-hand side of the housing and the crankcase breather hoses and the intake air temperature (IAT) sensor wiring connector from the left, then remove the housing.

Installation

11 Installation is the reverse of removal, noting the following:

● Connect the PAIR valve wiring connector and hose, the ISC hose, the IAT sensor wiring connector and the breather hoses before fitting the housing onto the throttle bodies.

● Make sure all hoses are fully pushed on to their unions and secured with their clips where fitted.

● Make sure the housing locates correctly on

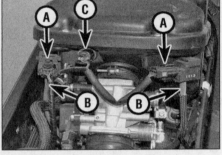

7.13 IAP sensor connectors (A) and vacuum hoses (B), IAT sensor connector (C)

the throttle bodies and tighten the clamp screws securely.

● Make sure all wiring connectors are securely connected.

2012-on DL models and all SFV models

Removal

12 Remove the fuel tank (see Section 2).

13 Disconnect the wiring connector and the vacuum hose from each intake air pressure (IAP) sensor **(see illustration)**.

14 Disconnect the IAT sensor wiring connector **(see illustration 7.13)**.

15 Loosen the clamp screws securing the housing to the throttle bodies **(see illustrations)**.

16 Displace the housing, then disconnect the crankcase breather hose and remove the housing **(see illustration)**.

7.15a Front clamp screw (arrowed)

7.15b Rear clamp screw (arrowed)

7.16 Displace the housing and disconnect the crankcase breather hose

8.2 Release the idle speed adjuster (arrowed)

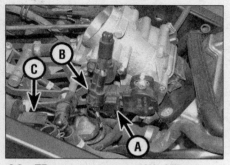

8.3a TP sensor connector (A), STP sensor connector (B), STV servo connector (C) – 2004 to 2006 DL

8.3b Disconnect the STP sensor connector...

Installation

17 Installation is the reverse of removal, noting the following:
- Connect the breather hose before fitting the housing onto the throttle bodies.
- Make sure all hoses are fully pushed on to their unions and secured with their clips where fitted.
- Make sure the housing locates correctly on the throttle bodies and tighten the clamp screws securely.
- Make sure all wiring connectors are securely connected.

8.3c ...TP sensor connector...

8.3d ...and STV servo connector – all other models

8 Throttle bodies

 Warning: Refer to the precautions given in Section 1 before starting work.

Removal

1 Remove the fuel tank (see Section 2) and the air filter housing (see Section 7).
2 On 2004 to 2006 DL models release the idle speed adjuster from its holder **(see illustration)**.
3 Disconnect the throttle position (TP) sensor, secondary throttle position (STP) sensor, and secondary throttle valve (STV) servo wiring connectors, noting which connects to what **(see illustrations)**.

4 Disconnect the fuel injector wiring connectors, noting which connects to what **(see illustration)** – you can do this after displacing the throttle bodies for easier access from the underside if necessary.
5 On 2007 to 2011 DL models disconnect the two idle speed control (ISC) valve hoses.
6 On California models, disconnect the EVAP system purge hose(s) and wiring connector as required according to model.
7 Disconnect the throttle cables (see Section 9).
8 Slacken the clamp screws securing the throttle bodies to the intake stubs, then ease the assembly up off the stubs **(see illustrations)**.
9 If required disconnect the fuel supply hose(s).
Caution: Tape over or stuff clean rag into each cylinder head intake after removing

the throttle body assembly to prevent anything getting in.
Caution: Do not snap the throttle cam/valves from fully open to fully closed once the cables have been disconnected because this can lead to engine idle speed problems. Do not attempt to disassemble the throttle bodies any further than removal of the fuel rail and injectors (Section 10) and the sensors (Section 14).

Inspection

10 Check over the entire assembly, looking for damaged or distorted components. Make sure the throttle valve linkage opens smoothly and returns under spring pressure (but do not let it snap forcibly closed).
11 Check the condition of all hoses and

8.4 Fuel injector connectors (arrowed)

8.8a Front clamp screw (arrowed)

8.8b Rear clamp screw (arrowed) – 2012 DL shown

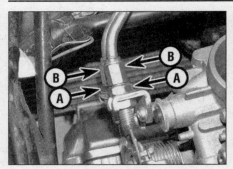

9.2a Loosen the nuts (A), unscrew the adjusters (B)...

9.2b ...slip the cables out of the bracket...

9.2c ...and detach the ends from the pulley

replace them with new ones if they are in any way damaged or deteriorated.

Installation

12 Installation is the reverse of removal, noting the following.

● Do not forget to remove the covers or plugs from the intakes on the cylinder heads.
● Lubricate the inside of the rubbers with a light smear of engine oil to aid installation. Make sure the throttle bodies are fully engaged with the intake stubs before tightening the clamps.
● Make sure the terminals in the wiring connectors are clean.
● Check the operation of the throttle cables and adjust freeplay as necessary (see Chapter 1).
● Check the operation of the STV servo (see Section 14).
● Check the engine idle speed on 2004 to

2006 DL models and adjust if necessary (see Chapter 1).

9 Throttle cables

> **Warning: Refer to the precautions given in Section 1 before proceeding.**

Removal

1 Remove the air filter housing (see Section 7).
2 Mark each cable according to its position in the bracket on the front throttle body. Loosen the upper locknuts securing the cable adjusters, then unscrew the adjusters and slip the cables out of the bracket, noting how the lower nuts are captive on the underside **(see illustrations)**. Detach the inner cable ends

from the throttle pulley, noting how they fit – the upper cable is the throttle opening cable, the lower cable is the throttle closing cable **(see illustration)**.
3 On 2004 to 2006 DL models, pull the rubber boot off the throttle pulley housing on the handlebars **(see illustration)**. Where fitted and if required for improved access remove the handguard (see Chapter 7). Undo the housing screws and separate the halves, noting how the elbows locate **(see illustrations)**. Detach the cable ends from the twistgrip pulley, noting how they fit **(see illustration)**. Note that the opening cable elbow is colour-coded gold and the closing cable is colour-coded silver.
4 On 2007-on DL models and all SFV models mark each cable according to its position in the switch housing on the handlebar. Undo the cable retainer screw **(see illustration)**. Undo the housing screws and separate the halves **(see illustration)**. Detach the cable

9.3a Pull the boot off

9.3b Undo the screws (arrowed)...

9.3c ...detach the housing...

9.3d ...and the cable ends

9.4a Undo the screw (arrowed)

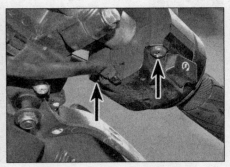

9.4b Undo the screws (arrowed)...

9.4c ...detach the cable ends...

9.4d ...and draw the cables out

9.7 Align the mating surfaces with the punch mark (arrowed)

ends from the twistgrip pulley, noting how they fit, then pull the cables out of the housing **(see illustrations)**.
5 Remove the cables from the machine, noting their correct routing.

Installation

6 Thread the cables through to the throttle bodies and up to the handlebars, making sure they are correctly routed – they must not interfere with any other component and should not be kinked or bent sharply.
7 On 2004 to 2006 DL models lubricate the cable ends with multi-purpose grease and attach them to the twistgrip, making sure the gold-elbowed cable is on the top **(see illustration 9.3d)**. Fit the cable elbows in the housing halves **(see illustration 9.3c)**, then join the halves around the handlebar, aligning the mating surfaces with the punch mark on the handlebar, and fit the screws **(see illustration)**. Fit the rubber boot **(see illustration 9.3a)**.
8 On 2007-on DL models and all SFV models fit the throttle opening cable elbow into the upper socket in the switch housing and the closing cable elbow into the lower, then locate the open end of the retainer plate around the shoulder on the opening cable elbow and secure the plate with its screw **(see illustrations 9.4d**

and a). Lubricate the end of each cable with multi-purpose grease. Connect the cable ends to the pulley **(see illustration 9.4c)**. Ensure the cables are correctly aligned on the pulley, then fit the housing halves – make sure the peg on the bottom half locates in the hole in the underside of the handlebar **(see illustration)**. Fit the screws and tighten them.
9 Check that the twistgrip pulley turns freely.
10 Fit the lower end of each cable onto the throttle pulley; the throttle opening cable goes around the top of the pulley, the closing cable goes around the bottom **(see illustration 9.2c)**.
11 Fit the cables adjusters into the bracket so the nuts are located on each side **(see illustration 9.2b)**. Pull the adjusters up so the bottom nuts are captive in the bracket then thread the adjusters into the bracket so there is 1 mm clearance between the adjusters and the locknuts with the locknuts tightened onto the bracket **(see illustration 9.2a)**.
12 Adjust the cables as described in Chapter 1.
13 Install the air filter housing (see Section 7). Fit the handguard if removed on DL models.
14 Start the engine and check the action of the throttle, and that the idle speed does not rise as the handlebars are turned. If it does, check the routing of the cables and correct the problem before riding the motorcycle.

10 Fuel rail(s) and injectors

⚠️ *Warning: Refer to the precautions given in Section 1 before starting work.*

Check

1 Make sure the ignition is OFF. Remove the air filter housing (see Section 7). Identify the faulty injector by the fault code and disconnect the injector wiring connector **(see illustration 8.4)**. Using an ohmmeter or multimeter set to the ohms scale, measure the resistance between the terminals on the injector **(see illustration)**. If the result is as specified, check that there is no continuity between each terminal and earth (ground). If there is continuity the injector is faulty and a new one must be installed (see below).
2 Connect the positive (+) probe of a voltmeter to the yellow/red wire terminal on the loom side of the wiring connector and the negative (-) probe to earth (ground) to check the input voltage. Turn the ignition ON and note the voltage. **Note:** *Injector voltage can only be detected for 3 seconds after the ignition has been turned ON.* Turn the ignition

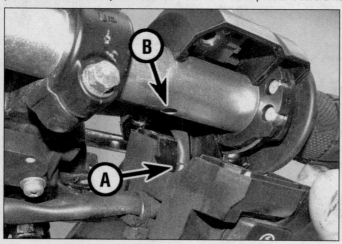

9.8 Locate the peg (A) in the hole (B)

10.1 Checking the resistance of an injector

10.7 Fuel rail screws (arrowed) – 2004 to 2011 DL

10.8a Fuel rail screws (arrowed) – 2012-on DL and all SFV

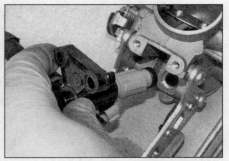

10.8b Remove the rail and injector...

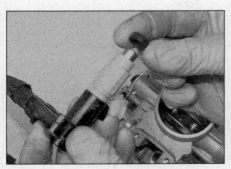

10.8c ...and remove the seal

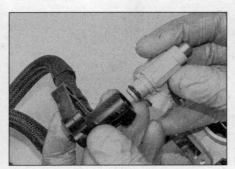

10.9a Remove the injector...

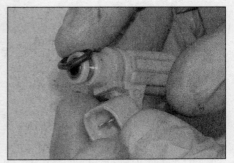

10.9b ...and remove the O-ring

OFF. If the input voltage is not as specified at the beginning of the Chapter, refer to the Wiring Diagrams at the end of Chapter 8 and check for a fault in the yellow/red wire to the fuel pump relay.

3 If the input voltage is as specified, check the grey/white wire (front cyl) and/or the grey/black wire (rear cyl) for continuity to the ECM connector.

Removal

4 Remove the air filter housing (see Section 7). Clean around the base of each injector using an air gun and/or a soft brush.

5 If you want to detach the fuel hose place a rag underneath the union on the fuel rail to catch any residual fuel, then release the clips on the hose connector and pull the hose off.

6 Mark each injector connector according to its location (i.e. front or rear).

7 On 2004 to 2011 DL models disconnect both injector connectors **(see illustration 8.4)**. Undo the fuel rail assembly screws and remove the rail along with both injectors **(see illustration)**. Remove the seals, either from the injector seats in the throttle bodies, or from the injector nozzles **(see illustration 10.8c)**. Inspect the hose and replace the fuel rail assembly with a new one if there are any signs of cracking or deformation.

8 On 2012-on DL models and all SFV models disconnect the relevant injector connector **(see illustration 8.4)**. Undo the fuel rail screws and remove the rail along with the injector **(see illustrations)**. Remove the seal, either

from the injector seat in the throttle body, or from the injector nozzle **(see illustration)**.

9 Pull the injector(s) out of the rail(s) **(see illustration)**. Remove the O-ring from the top of each removed injector **(see illustration)**. New seals and O-rings must be used.

10 Modern fuels contain detergents that should keep the injectors clean and free of gum or varnish from fuel residue. If an injector is suspected of being blocked, clean it through with injector cleaner. If the injector is clean but its performance is suspect, and the checks in Steps 1 to 3 are inconclusive, replace it with a new one.

Installation

11 Fit a new O-ring lubricated with clean engine oil into the groove in the top of each removed injector **(see illustration 10.9b)**.

12 Fit the injector(s) into the rail(s), aligning the connector socket with the shaped side of the injector housing **(see illustration 10.9a)**.

13 Fit a new seal lubricated with clean engine oil onto the injector nozzle(s) **(see illustration 10.8c)**.

14 Seat the injector nozzle(s) in the throttle bodies making sure the seal(s) stay(s) in place and locate correctly **(see illustration 10.8b)**. Fit and tighten the screws **(see illustration 10.7 or 10.8a)**.

15 Connect the wiring to the injector(s) **(see illustration 8.4)** – the connector with the grey/white wire is for the front injector, the connector with the grey/black is for the rear.

16 If disconnected, align the fuel supply hose connector with its union on the rail and push it on fully so that the clip engages, then check it is secure by trying to pull it off.

17 Install the air filter housing and fuel tank. Run the engine and check the fuel system for leaks and correct function before taking the bike out on the road.

11 Fast idle system

2004 to 2006 DL models

1 The fast idle mechanism is actuated by the STV servo when the engine is cold and should cancel automatically after a period determined by ambient and engine temperatures and lapsed time.

2 To check the system the engine should be cold. Start the engine and check the fast idle speed on the tachometer – it should be 1500 to 2000 rpm.

3 Leave the engine running and check that the fast idle speed reduces automatically as the engine warms, and falls to the normal idle speed for a warm engine. If necessary, adjust the idle speed (see Chapter 1).

4 If the fast idle speed is not within the specifications, remove the air filter housing (see Section 7).

5 Disconnect the STV servo wiring connector

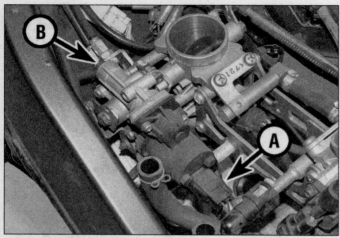

11.5 STV servo wiring connector (A). STV servo shaft (B)

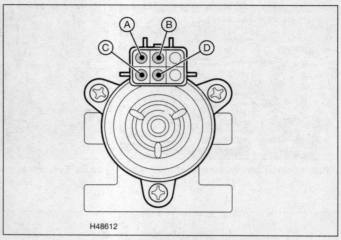

11.9 ISC valve terminal identification

(see illustration). Turn the ignition ON. Fully open the secondary throttle valves by turning the valve servo shaft by hand – do not try to turn the valves themselves.

6 Connect the positive (+) probe of a voltmeter to the red wire terminal in the throttle position (TP) sensor wiring connector and the negative (-) probe to the black/brown wire terminal to check the output voltage (see illustration 8.3a). If the result is not as specified (TP sensor closed), turn the fast idle adjuster on the front edge of the throttle cable pulley below the STV servo until the voltage is within specification. Turn the ignition OFF.

7 Connect the STV servo wiring connector and install the air filter housing (see Section 7). When the engine is cold, start it, leave it running and check that the fast idle speed is correct and cancels automatically when the engine coolant temperature reaches 40 to 50°C. At that point the idle speed should fall to the normal (warm engine) specification. If necessary, adjust the engine idle speed (see Chapter 1).

2007 to 2011 DL models

8 Idle speed is controlled by the idle speed control (ISC) valve – there is no manual means of adjustment. If a C40 fault code is indicated, the idle speed will have deviated from its pre-set value or there may be a problem with the power supply to the ISC motor. Use of the Suzuki SDS tester (available to a dealer) will enable full diagnosis of the ISC valve and also erase the fault code from the ECM memory – refer to a dealer for this service. Before doing this check the valve as follows.

9 Make sure that the ignition is OFF, then remove the air filter housing (see Section 7). Disconnect the ISC valve wiring connector. Check the internal circuitry of the valve using a multimeter set to the continuity function. There should be no continuity between terminal pins A and C in the valve socket, and also no continuity between terminal pins B and D (see illustration). Now test the resistance between terminal pins A

and B, then between terminal pins C and D – a reading of approx. 30 ohms should be indicated. If the readings are wildly different, the ISC valve should be considered faulty.

10 Check the wiring between the ISC valve wire connector and the ECM connector for continuity – use the relevant wiring diagram at the end of this manual to identify the six wires.

11 To remove the valve, disconnect the wiring connector, followed by the three hoses – take note of their positions as an aid to refitting. Unscrew the two bolts and remove the valve.

12 The valve can only be purchased as a complete part, although there is nothing lost by undoing the screws and separating the valve from the body to examine the valve unit for damage or a build up of carbon deposits and to check that its sealing O-ring is in good condition.

13 Fit the valve and reconnect the three hoses, securing them with their wire clips. Reconnect the wiring connector. The valve position must now be restored to its pre-set mode.

14 With the ignition OFF, connect the mode select switch (see Section 13) and turn it ON. Now turn the ignition switch ON, then OFF. Wait at least five seconds then turn the mode select switch OFF and disconnect it from the wiring plug.

2012-on DL models and all SFV models

15 Fast idle speed is controlled automatically by the idle speed control valve. It is pre-set at the factory using the SDS software and cannot be adjusted without it. If the fast idle speed is incorrect take the bike to a dealer.

12 Engine management system description

1 The system consists of two main component groups, the fuel supply circuit and the electronic control circuit.

2 The fuel supply circuit consists of the tank, pump and filter, pressure regulator and injectors. Fuel is pumped under pressure from the tank to the fuel rails, from which the individual injectors are fed. When the engine is off, fuel pressure is maintained in the system by a check valve in the pump. When the pump is running, operating pressure is maintained by the pump's pressure regulator which incorporates a pressure relief valve, releasing fuel back into the tank should the system become over-pressurised. The injectors spray pressurised fuel into the throttle bodies where it mixes with air and vaporises, before entering the cylinder where it is compressed and ignited.

3 The electronic control circuit consists of the engine control module (ECM), which operates and co-ordinates both the fuel injection and ignition systems, and the various sensors that provide the ECM with information on engine operating conditions.

4 The ECM monitors signals from the following sensors:
- Intake air temperature (IAT) sensor
- Intake air pressure (IAP) sensor(s)
- Throttle position (TP) sensor
- Secondary throttle position (STP) sensor
- Crankshaft position (CKP) sensor
- Engine coolant temperature (ECT) sensor
- Gear position (GP) sensor
- Tip over (TO) sensor
- Oxygen sensor – K7 models onward

5 Based on the information it receives, the ECM calculates the appropriate ignition and fuel requirements of the engine. By varying the length of the electronic pulse it sends to each injector, the ECM controls the length of time the injectors are held open and thereby the amount of fuel that is supplied to the engine. Fuel supply varies according to the engine's needs for starting, warming-up, idling, cruising and acceleration.

6 In the event of an abnormality in any of the sensor signals, the ECM will determine whether the engine can still be run safely. If it can, a back-up mode replaces the sensor signal

13.2a Mode select switch connector (arrowed) – 2004 to 2011 DL

13.2b Mode select switch connector – 2012-on DL

13.2c Mode select switch connector (arrowed) – SFV

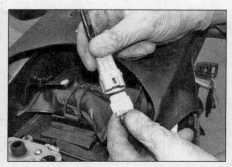

13.2d Remove the cover and connect the switch...

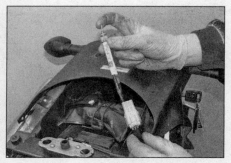

13.2e ...and use it as described

with a fixed signal, restricting performance but allowing the bike to be ridden home or to a dealer. When this occurs, the LCD display in the instrument cluster will indicate the letters FI every two seconds, alternating with the clock or odometer, according to model, the FI symbol will illuminate and the panel warning light will come on. If the fault is too serious, the appropriate system will be shut down and the engine will not run. When this occurs, the LCD display in the instrument cluster will indicate the letters FI continuously and the FI symbol and panel warning light will flash. See Section 13 for fault finding.

7 In the event of no signal being received from the ECM within 3 seconds of the ignition being switched ON, the LCD panel will display the letters CHEC. This is not a fault code in itself, but will occur if the ignition is ON for the stated time but if the kill switch is in the OFF position, or if the starter safety circuit has a fault (see Chapter 1), or if the ignition fuse has blown (see Chapter 8). It will also occur if a wiring connector between the ECM and instrument cluster has become disconnected. Do not disconnect the wiring connectors from the ECM or disconnect the battery before

accessing the fault codes as they will be erased.

8 The system incorporates three safety circuits. When the ignition is switched ON, the fuel pump runs for three seconds and pressurises the system. Thereafter the pump automatically switches off until the engine is started. The second circuit incorporates a tip-over sensor that automatically switches off the fuel pump and cuts the ignition and injection circuits if the motorcycle falls over. The third circuit incorporates a rev limiter signal that cuts the fuel injector circuit when engine rpm reaches the designated safety limit.

13 Engine management system fault diagnosis

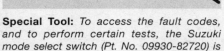

Special Tool: *To access the fault codes, and to perform certain tests, the Suzuki mode select switch (Pt. No. 09930-82720) is required.*

1 The system incorporates a self-diagnostic function whereby any faults are stored in the ECM memory.

2 On DL models remove the seat (see Chapter 7). On SFV models remove the right-hand side cover (see Chapter 7). Locate the mode select switch wiring connector **(see illustrations)**. Remove the connector cover. Check the ignition switch and the select switch are OFF, then connect the select switch **(see illustrations)**.

3 Start the engine, or if it will not start, crank the engine on the electric starter for at least four seconds. Turn the mode select switch ON. The fault code(s) will be displayed on the LCD panel on the instrument cluster, at two-second intervals and in ascending order if there is more than one. Note the codes, then turn the ignition OFF. Identify the faults from the table. **Note:** *Do not disconnect the ECM wiring connectors, battery leads or main fuse before recording the fault codes. The ECM memory is erased when the connectors are disconnected.*

4 To check the engine management system components see Section 14.

5 Once the fault has been corrected, turn the ignition switch ON. If the fault has been cleared, the instrument display will indicate the code C00. Turn the mode select switch OFF and ignition switch OFF and disconnect the mode select switch. Refit the wiring connector cover and install the seat or side cover.

Fault code	Faulty component – symptoms	Possible causes
CHEC	No ECM signal – engine will not run	Kill switch OFF
		Faulty wiring or wiring connector
		Faulty ignition safety interlock system (clutch switch, sidestand switch, diode or gear position switch)
		Damaged ignition fuse
C00	No fault	System clear
C12	Crankshaft position sensor – engine will not run	Faulty wiring or wiring connector
		Damaged sensor or timing trigger
C13	Intake air pressure sensor (for rear cylinder on 2007-on DL models and all SFV models) – engine will run, air pressure signal fixed	Faulty wiring or wiring connector
		Damaged sensor
C14	Throttle position sensor – engine will run, throttle position and ignition timing fixed	Faulty wiring or wiring connector
		Damaged sensor
C15	Engine coolant temperature sensor – engine will run, coolant temperature signal fixed	Faulty wiring or wiring connector
		Damaged sensor
C17	Intake air pressure sensor for front cylinder on 2007-on DL models and SFV models – engine will run, air pressure signal fixed	Faulty wiring or wiring connector
		Damaged sensor
C21	Intake air temperature sensor – engine will run, air temperature signal fixed	Faulty wiring or wiring connector
		Damaged sensor
C23	Tip-over sensor – engine will not run	Faulty wiring or wiring connector
		Damaged sensor
C24	No. 1 (front) cylinder ignition coil – engine will run on other cylinder, fuel supply to No. 1 cylinder cut	Faulty wiring or wiring connector
		Damaged ignition coil
		Faulty power supply for the ignition system
C25	No. 2 (rear) cylinder ignition coil – engine will run on other cylinder, fuel supply to No. 2 cylinder cut	Faulty wiring or wiring connector
		Damaged ignition coil
		Faulty power supply for the ignition system
C28	Secondary throttle valve servo – engine will run, valve fixed in closed position	Faulty wiring or wiring connector
		Damaged servo motor
C29	Secondary throttle position sensor – engine will run, throttle valve fixed in closed position	Damaged sensor
C31	Gear position sensor – engine will run, signal fixed in 6th gear	Faulty wiring or wiring connector
		Damaged sensor
		Faulty gearchange mechanism
C32	No. 1 fuel injector – engine will run on other cylinder	Faulty wiring or wiring connector
		Damaged fuel injector
C33	No. 2 fuel injector – engine will run on other cylinder	Faulty wiring or wiring connector
		Damaged fuel injector
C40	Idle speed control valve – idle speed too low or high, engine will run	Faulty wiring or wiring connector
		Faulty valve
C41	Fuel pump control system – engine will not run	Faulty wiring or wiring connector to pump and/or pump relay
		Faulty pump relay (see Section 4)
		Damaged fuel pump (see Section 5)
C42	Ignition switch or immobiliser (where fitted) – engine will not run	Faulty wiring or wiring connector
		Damaged switch or immobiliser (see Chapter 8 for switch and see your dealer for immobiliser)
C44	Heated oxygen sensor – signal fixed to normal, engine will run	Faulty wiring or wiring connector
		Faulty sensor
C49	PAIR system control valve – valve inactive, engine will run	Faulty wiring or wiring connector
		Faulty control valve
C60	Cooling fan relay	Faulty wiring or wiring connector
		Faulty relay
C62	EVAP system purge control solenoid valve – engine will run	Faulty wiring or wiring connector
		Faulty valve
C65	Idle speed control system – idle speed too low or high, engine will run	Faulty wiring or wiring connector
		Faulty valve

14 Engine management system sensors

Caution: *Ensure the ignition is switched OFF before disconnecting/reconnecting any fuel injection system wiring connector. If a connector is disturbed with the ignition switched ON the engine control module (ECM) could be damaged.*

1 If a fault is indicated on any of the system components, first check the wiring and connectors between the appropriate component and the engine control module (ECM); see *Wiring Diagrams* at the end of Chapter 8. A continuity test of all wires will locate a break or short in any circuit. Inspect the terminals inside the wiring connectors and ensure they are not loose or corroded. Spray the inside of the connectors with an electrical terminal cleaner before reconnection.

2 It is possible to undertake some checks on system components using a multimeter and comparing the results with the specifications at the beginning of this Chapter. **Note:** *Different meters may give slightly different results to those specified even though the component being tested is not faulty – do not consign a component to the bin before having it double-checked.* However, some faults will only become evident when a component is tested with a peak voltage tester, in which case the checks should be undertaken by a Suzuki dealer.

3 If after a thorough check the source of a fault has not been identified, it is possible that the ECM itself is faulty. Suzuki provides no test specifications for the ECM. In order to determine conclusively that the unit is defective, it should be substituted with a known good one. If the problem is then rectified, the original unit is proven faulty. Note that Suzuki have their own (dealer only) SDS fault diagnosis software which provides a more in depth analysis and diagnosis of the system – if you cannot locate or rectify a fault take the bike to a dealer equipped with the system.

Crankshaft position (CKP) sensor

4 Make sure the ignition is OFF. On 2012-on DL models remove the air filter housing (Section 7). On SFV models remove the right-hand side cover (see Chapter 7). Disconnect CKP sensor wiring connector **(see illustrations)**.

5 Using an ohmmeter or multimeter set to the ohms scale, measure the resistance between the terminals on the sensor side of the connector. If the result is as specified, check that there is no continuity between each terminal and earth (ground).

6 If the results are not as specified, first check the wiring between the connector and the alternator cover for damage, then follow the procedure in Chapter 2, remove the cover and inspect the sensor. If required, clean the

14.4a CKP sensor connector (arrowed) – DL

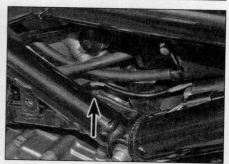

14.4b CKP sensor connector (arrowed) – SFV

sensor head – a build-up of dirt and/or debris can affect the signal sent to the ECM – then check the resistance again. Also check the triggers on the alternator rotor for damage. If all is good check the wires between the connector and the ECM.

7 If the results are good, have the sensor peak voltage tested by a Suzuki dealer.

8 To remove the sensor, see Chapter 8 – it is part of the alternator stator assembly and is not available separately.

Intake air pressure (IAP) sensor

9 Make sure the ignition is OFF. Raise the fuel tank (see Section 2). On 2004 to 2006 DL models, the IAP sensor is on the rear of the air filter housing **(see illustration 7.2)**. All other models have a sensor on each rear corner of the housing **(see illustration 7.13)**. Check the condition of the vacuum hose from the sensor(s) and make sure the hose is a tight fit at each end with no air leaks.

10 To check the input voltage, disconnect the sensor wiring connector and turn the ignition ON. Connect the positive (+) probe of a voltmeter to the red wire terminal on the loom side of the wiring connector and the negative (-) probe first to earth (ground), then to the black/brown wire terminal. Turn the ignition OFF. If the input voltage is not as specified in both cases, check the wiring to the ECM and the ECM connector terminals.

11 If the input voltage is good, reconnect the wiring to the sensor(s), then start the engine and allow it idle. Insert the positive (+) probe of a voltmeter into the green/black or green/yellow (according to sensor being tested on models with two) wire terminal in the connector and the negative (-) probe into the black/brown wire terminal to check the output voltage. If the result is as specified, take the sensor to a Suzuki dealer for vacuum testing, otherwise fit a new sensor.

12 To remove the sensor disconnect the wire connector and the vacuum hose, then either undo the screw securing the sensor to the housing or ease the sensor sleeve off its tab, according to model. On installation make sure the wiring connector terminals are clean and that the vacuum hose is a tight fit on the sensor union.

Throttle position (TP) sensor

Note: *The TP sensor is secured by Torx security screws (single screw on K7 models onward) that have a raised pip in their centres and will require the appropriate security Torx bit to turn them.*

13 Make sure the ignition is OFF. Raise the fuel tank (see Section 2) – the TP sensor is the lower of the two sensors located on the left-hand side of the rear throttle body **(see illustration 14.37)**. Disconnect the sensor wiring connector **(see illustration 8.3a or c)**. Turn the ignition ON and connect the positive (+) probe of a voltmeter to the red wire terminal on the loom side of the wiring connector and the negative (-) probe first to earth (ground), and then to the black/brown wire terminal to check the input voltage. Turn the ignition OFF. If the input voltage is not as specified in both cases, check the wiring to the ECM and the connector terminals.

14 If the input voltage is good check for continuity between the pink/white wire terminal on the sensor and earth (ground). There should be no continuity.

15 Using an ohmmeter set to the K-ohms scale, measure the resistance between the pink/white and black/brown wire terminals on the sensor, first with the throttle closed, then with the throttle fully open. If the results are as specified, reconnect the wiring connector.

16 Turn the ignition ON and connect the positive (+) probe of a voltmeter to the pink/white wire terminal and the negative (-) probe to the black/brown wire terminal in the connector to check the output voltage, first with the throttle closed, then with the throttle fully open. Turn the ignition OFF. If the results are not as specified, the sensor is faulty.

17 To remove the TP sensor, first disconnect its wiring connector. Mark the position of the sensor to aid installation, then undo the Torx screws (see **Note** above) securing the sensor and remove it (access to the Torx screws is made easier by displacing the throttle bodies – see Section 8). Note how the end of the throttle shaft engages the slot in the sensor.

18 Installation is the reverse of removal. Apply some grease to the seal in the sensor socket in the throttle body. Ensure that the throttle shaft engages correctly in the slot in

14.22a ECT sensor connector (arrowed) – DL

14.22b ECT sensor connector (arrowed) – SFV

the sensor and align any register marks before lightly tightening the Torx screws. Ensure the wiring connector terminals are clean.

19 To check and adjust the position of the TP sensor, first warm up the engine and check the idle speed, on 2004 to 2006 DL models adjusting it if necessary (see Chapter 1). Turn the engine OFF and connect the mode select switch to the wiring connector (see Section 13).

20 Turn the select switch ON. A code C00 will be displayed on the LCD panel on the instrument cluster with a line in front of it. If the line is in the mid-way position i.e. -C00, the TP sensor is adjusted correctly. If the line is above or below the mid-way position (_C00 or ¯C00), loosen the Torx screws and carefully rotate the sensor until the line is in the mid-way position, then tighten the screws.

Engine coolant temperature (ECT) sensor

21 The engine coolant temperature (ECT) sensor is mounted in the thermostat housing between the engine cylinders. On SFV models remove the throttle bodies (Section 8).

22 Disconnect the sensor wiring connector and turn the ignition ON **(see illustrations)**. Connect the positive (+) probe of a voltmeter to the black/blue wire terminal on the loom side of the connector and the negative (-) probe first to earth (ground), then to the black/brown wire terminal to check the input voltage. Turn the ignition OFF. If the input voltage is not as specified in both cases, check the wiring to the ECM and the ECM connector terminals.

23 Using an ohmmeter or multimeter set to the K-ohms scale, measure the resistance between the terminals on the sensor itself with the engine cold. If the result is not as specified, the sensor is faulty.

24 If the sensor is working correctly, the resistance should drop as the engine warms up. A check for sensor performance is described in Chapter 3. Also refer to Chapter 3 for the removal and installation procedure.

Intake air temperature (IAT) sensor

25 Make sure the ignition is OFF. Raise the fuel tank (see Section 2). The IAT sensor is on the rear of the air filter housing **(see illustration 7.2 or 7.13)**. Disconnect the sensor wiring connector and turn the ignition ON. Connect the positive (+) probe of a voltmeter to the dark green wire terminal on the loom side of the wiring connector and the negative (-) probe first to earth (ground), then to the black/brown wire terminal to check the input voltage. Turn the ignition OFF. If the input voltage is not as specified in both cases, check the wiring to the ECM and the ECM connector terminals.

26 Using an ohmmeter or multimeter set to the K-ohms scale, measure the resistance between the terminals on the sensor itself – on 2007 to 2011 DL models you will need to remove the air filter housing to do this (Section 7). If the result is not as specified, the sensor is faulty. **Note:** *The sensor resistance should drop as the engine warms up – the sensor performance can be checked in the same way as the ECT sensor (see Chapter 3).*

27 To remove the sensor on 2004 to 2006 DL models, disconnect the wiring connector, then unscrew the sensor – note the sealing ring on the sensor body and replace it with a new one on installation if it is damaged. On 2007 to 2011 DL models remove the air filter housing (Section 7). On 2007-on DL models and all SFV models, undo the screw and pull the sensor out of the air filter housing **(see illustration)** – note the O-ring and replace it with a new one on installation if it is damaged.

Tip-over (TO) sensor

28 Make sure the ignition is OFF. Remove the seat (see Chapter 7) to access the TO sensor **(see illustrations)**. Detach the sensor and its holder from its bracket.

29 Disconnect the wiring connector from the sensor. Using an ohmmeter or multimeter set to the K-ohms scale, measure the resistance between the red and black/brown wire terminals on the sensor. Compare the result to that given in the Specifications at the beginning of this Chapter; if the result is good, reconnect the wiring connector.

30 With the connector reconnected, turn the ignition ON and insert the positive (+) probe of a voltmeter into the pink/white wire terminal on the loom side of the wiring connector and the negative (-) probe into the black/brown wire terminal and check the voltage with the sensor held horizontally. Now tilt the sensor 65° or more from the horizontal, first one way and then the other, and note the voltage reading. If the results are not as specified the sensor is faulty and must be replaced with a new one.

31 Fit the sensor with the UP mark at the top and make sure the connector is secure.

Secondary throttle valve (STV) servo – 2004 to 2006 models

32 Remove the air filter housing (see Section 7). The STV servo is on the left-hand side of the front throttle body **(see illustration 11.5)**.

33 Turn the ignition ON and check the operation of the secondary throttle valves (in the top of each throttle body) in start-up mode. From part-open the valves should open fully and then return to the part-open position. Turn the ignition OFF. If the valves do not move as described, check the wiring from the servo to

14.27 IAT sensor screw (arrowed)

14.28a TO sensor (arrowed) – DL

14.28b TO sensor (arrowed) – SFV

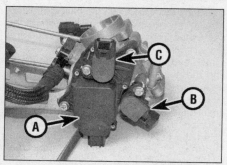

14.37 STV servo (A), TP sensor (B), STP sensor (C)

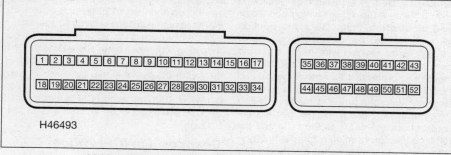

H46493

14.38 ECM connector terminal identification (loom side)

the ECM and check the connector terminals.
Note: *The valves should open and close together by the same amount – if not, follow the procedure in Section 16 and synchronise them.*

34 Disconnect the wiring connector from the servo. Check that there is no continuity between the left-hand terminal on the servo and earth (ground).

35 Using an ohmmeter or multimeter set to the ohms scale, measure the resistance between the two servo terminals. If the result is not as specified, the servo is faulty. If the result is as specified, have the ECM checked by a Suzuki dealer.

36 The servo is not available separately from the throttle bodies – if the servo is faulty a new throttle body assembly must be installed (Section 8).

Secondary throttle valve (STV) servo – 2007-on DL models and all SFV models

37 Remove the air filter housing (see Section 7). The STV servo is on the left-hand side of the rear throttle body **(see illustration)**.

38 Turn the ignition ON and check the operation of the secondary throttle valves (in the top of each throttle body) in start-up mode. The valves should go from the fully open position to 10° open. Turn the ignition OFF. If the valves do not move as described, check the wiring for continuity from the servo connector to the ECM connector – black/light green wire to terminal 35, pink/white wire to terminal 37, green wire to terminal 44 and white/black wire to terminal 46 **(see illustration)**.

39 Remove the throttle bodies (see Section 12). Using a multimeter set to the ohms function, check for continuity between each pin in the servo connector and earth, making four tests in total – no continuity should be indicated.

40 Now connect the meter probes between terminals 1 and 2, then 3 and 4 – in each case a reading of 7 ohms should be obtained **(see illustration)**.

41 If the results are not as specified the STV servo is most likely faulty, although have your findings confirmed by a Suzuki dealer before fitting a new throttle body assembly.

Secondary throttle position (STP) sensor – 2004 to 2006 DL models

Note: *The STP sensor is secured by Torx security screws (with a raised pip in their centres) that will require the appropriate security Torx bit to turn them.*

42 Remove the air filter housing (see Section 7). The STP sensor is the upper of the two sensors located on the left-hand side of the rear throttle body – disconnect the sensor wiring connector **(see illustration 8.3a)**. Turn the ignition ON and connect the positive (+) probe of a voltmeter to the red wire terminal on the loom side of the wiring connector and the negative (-) probe first to earth (ground), and then to the black/brown wire terminal to check the input voltage. Turn the ignition OFF. If the input voltage is not as specified in both cases, check the wiring to the ECM and the connector terminals.

43 If the input voltage is good, check for continuity between the yellow wire terminal and earth (ground) on the sensor side of the connector. There should be no continuity.

44 Close the secondary throttle valves by turning the valve servo shaft by hand – do not try to turn the valves themselves **(see illustration 11.5)**. Using an ohmmeter or multimeter set to the K-ohms scale, measure the sensor resistance between the yellow and black wire terminals. Now open the secondary throttle valves by turning the valve servo shaft and measure the resistance.

45 If the results are not as specified, check the sensor adjustment as follows. Ensure

14.40 STV terminal identification

the secondary throttle valves are still fully open and loosen the sensor Torx screws. Connect the ohmmeter or multimeter set to the K-ohms scale between the yellow and black wire terminals as before and note the sensor resistance, then carefully rotate the sensor until the resistance reading is within specification. Tighten the sensor screws. Check the resistance with the valves fully closed.

46 If the specified resistance cannot be obtained, the STP sensor is faulty.

47 If the results are as specified, reconnect the sensor wiring connector and disconnect the STP servo wiring connector, then turn the ignition ON. Insert the positive (+) probe of a voltmeter into the yellow wire terminal and the negative (-) probe into the black/brown wire terminal on the loom side of the STP sensor connector to check the output voltage with the secondary throttle valves fully open and then fully closed. Turn the ignition OFF and reconnect the STV servo wiring connector. If the output voltage is not as specified the STP sensor is faulty. If the output voltage is good, have the ECM checked by a Suzuki dealer.

48 To remove the sensor, first disconnect the wiring connector. Mark the position of the sensor to aid installation, then undo the Torx screws (see **Note** above) and remove the sensor – note how the end of the throttle shaft engages the slot in the sensor.

49 Installation is the reverse of removal. Apply some grease to the seal in the sensor socket in the throttle body. Make sure that the throttle shaft engages correctly in the slot in the sensor and align any marks before lightly tightening the Torx screws. Make sure the wiring connector terminals are clean. After installation adjust the sensor as described in Step 20.

Secondary throttle position (STP) sensor – 2007-on DL models and all SFV models

Note: *The STP sensor is secured by a Torx security screw (with a raised pip in its centre) that will require the appropriate security Torx bit to turn it.*

50 The STP sensor is the upper of the two sensors located on the left-hand side of the rear throttle body **(see illustration 14.37)**.

Remove the air filter housing (see Section 7) and disconnect the sensor wiring connector **(see illustration 8.3b)**. Turn the ignition ON and connect the positive (+) probe of a voltmeter to the red wire terminal on the loom side of the wiring connector and the negative (-) probe first to earth (ground), and then to the black/brown wire terminal to check the input voltage. Turn the ignition OFF. If the input voltage is not as specified in both cases, check the wiring to the ECM and the ECM connector terminals for continuity – yellow wire to terminal 4, red wire to terminal 5 and black/brown wire to terminal 12 **(see illustration 14.38)**.

51 Reconnect the STP sensor wire connector. Connect the voltmeter positive probe to the yellow wire terminal and the negative probe to the black/brown wire terminal. Disconnect the wiring connector from the STP servo, then turn the ignition ON. Use finger pressure only to operate the secondary butterfly valve in the top of the throttle body, noting the output voltage shown on the meter – compare this

with the value given in the Specifications with valve open and then with the valve closed.

52 If the output voltage is incorrect, adjust the STP sensor position by slackening the sensor mounting screw (see **Note** above) and rotating the sensor body until the voltage reading is 0.6V with the butterfly valve closed. Tighten the screw once the correct setting has been achieved. Turn the ignition OFF and reconnect the STP servo connector and refit the air filter housing.

Gear position (GP) switch

53 Support the bike on an auxiliary stand and raise the sidestand. The GP switch is located in the left-hand side of the crankcase below the front sprocket **(see illustration)**. On 2004 to 2011 DL models remove the left-hand side cover (see Chapter 7). On 2012-on DL models and all SFV models raise the fuel tank (see Section 2). Trace the wiring from the switch and disconnect it at the 3-pin connector with blue, pink and black/white wires **(see illustrations)**.

54 Connect the probes of an ohmmeter or

continuity tester between the blue and black/white wire terminals on the switch side of the connector. With the transmission in neutral there should be continuity. If not, remove the switch and check the contacts on its inside and the plungers in the end of the selector drum (see Chapter 8).

55 Reconnect the wiring connector and ensure the engine kill switch is in the RUN position. Turn the ignition switch ON and insert the positive (+) probe of a voltmeter into the pink wire terminal in the connector and connect the negative (-) probe to earth (ground) to check the output voltage. Select each gear in turn and check that the voltage is above the specified minimum in each gear. Turn the ignition OFF.

56 If the output voltage is not as specified, either the pink wire to the GP switch or the GP switch itself is faulty (see Chapter 8).

57 If the output voltage is as specified, first check the voltage following the procedure in Chapter 8, then check the wiring and connectors from the switch to the ECM.

14.53a GP switch (arrowed)

14.53b GP switch connector (arrowed) – 2004 to 2011 DL

14.53c GP switch connector (arrowed) – 2012-on DL

14.53d GP switch connector (arrowed) – SFV

14.64a Oxygen sensor connector
(arrowed) – 2004 to 2011 DL

14.64b Oxygen sensor connector – 2012-on
DL

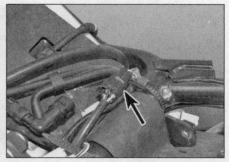

14.64c Oxygen sensor connector (arrowed)
– SFV

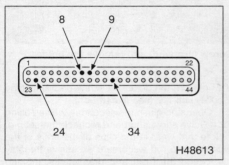

14.66 ECM connector terminal
identification (loom side)

14.68a Oxygen sensor (arrowed) – DL

14.68b Oxygen sensor (arrowed) – SFV

Fuel injectors

58 Refer to Section 10.

Fuel pump control system

59 Refer to Section 4 for fuel pump relay checks.
60 Refer to Section 5 for fuel pump and wiring checks.
Note: *A fault with both fuel injectors is also indicated by fault code C41.*

PAIR solenoid valve (2004 to 2011 DL models)

61 The solenoid valve is mounted on the underside of the air filter housing. Displace the air filter housing (see Section 7), then disconnect the wiring connector **(see illustration 7.5b)**.
62 Using an ohmmeter or multimeter set to the ohms scale, measure the resistance between the terminals on the valve. If the result is not as specified, refer to Section 19 and test the operation of the valve.
63 If the resistance is as specified, connect the wiring connector and turn the ignition ON. Connect the positive (+) probe of a voltmeter to the brown wire terminal on the loom side of the wiring connector and the negative (-) probe to earth (ground) to check the input voltage. Turn the ignition OFF. If the input voltage is not as specified, check the wiring to the ECM and the ECM connector terminals (Section 15).

Oxygen sensor

64 The heated oxygen sensor is threaded into the exhaust system between the downpipes

and the silencer **(see illustration 14.68a or b)**. To access the wiring connector, on 2004 to 2011 DL models and all SFV models raise the fuel tank (Section 2), and on 2012-on DL models remove the right-hand side cover (see Chapter 7). Trace the wiring up to the connector and disconnect it **(see illustrations)**. To check the sensor's heater element resistance, connect a multimeter set to the ohms function between the two white wire connectors. Compare the reading with the value given in the Specifications.
65 Check the heater element input voltage with the connector halves joined. Connect the white/black wire terminal on the wire harness side of the connector with the meter positive probe and earth the meter negative probe. Turn the ignition ON – battery voltage should be shown on the meter.
66 On 2004 to 2006 DL models check the white/green wire between the oxygen sensor wiring connector (harness side) and terminal 24 of the ECM connector (see Section 15) for continuity **(see illustration)**. Similarly check the black/brown wire between the sensor connector and terminal 34, the white/black wire between the sensor connector and terminal 8, and the orange/green wire between the sensor connector and terminal 9.
67 On 2007-on DL models and all SFV models check the white/green wire between the oxygen sensor wiring connector (harness side) and terminal 6 of the ECM connector (see Section 15) for continuity **(see illustration 14.38)**. Similarly check the black/ brown wire between the sensor connector and

terminal 12, and the white/black wire between the sensor connector and terminal 37.
68 To remove the sensor, use an open-end spanner or a dedicated socket that has a cut-out for the wiring to unscrew it from the exhaust pipe **(see illustrations)**. Take care not to damage the sensor tip when refitting and tighten the sensor to the specified torque setting if possible.

15 Engine control module (ECM)

Check

1 If the tests shown in the preceding Sections have failed to isolate the cause of a fault, and the engine management system fuses and fuel pump relay and all wiring connectors are good, it is possible that the ECM itself is faulty. No details are available with which the unit can be tested. The best way to determine whether it is faulty or not is to substitute it with a known good one, having first checked all other components in the ignition system. Otherwise, take the unit to a Suzuki dealer for assessment.

Removal and installation

2 Make sure the ignition is OFF.
3 Remove the seat (see Chapter 7). Disconnect the battery negative (-ve) lead.
4 On DL models release the battery strap **(see illustration)**. On SFV models remove

15.4a Release the strap

15.4b Undo the screw (arrowed) and remove the holder

15.4c Lift the ECM out and disconnect the wiring

the tank prop **(see illustration 2.26)** and the battery holder **(see illustration)**. Lift the ECM out and disconnect the wiring connector(s) **(see illustration)**.

5 Installation is the reverse of removal. Make sure the wiring connectors are clean and secure.

16 Secondary throttle valve synchronisation (2004 to 2006 DL models)

⚠️ *Warning: Refer to the precautions given in Section 1 before proceeding.*

1 Make sure the ignition is OFF. Remove the air filter housing (see Section 7).

2 Work on the front throttle body first. Turn the valve servo shaft by hand until the secondary butterfly valve is parallel with the top rim of the throttle body – use a Vernier gauge to check the distance between the front and back edges of the valve and the rim is identical **(see illustration)**. Note: *Do not try to turn the valve itself.*

3 Now make the same measurements on the rear throttle body valve – do this carefully to avoid disturbing the position of the front throttle body valve. The valve should be parallel with the top edge of the throttle body;

if not, turn the adjusting screw on the linkage pulley until it is **(see illustration)**.

4 Open and close the secondary valves using the valve servo shaft and recheck the setting. Note that wear in the clips at the ends of the connecting rod will create excessive freeplay between the front and rear valves, making synchronisation difficult.

5 It is recommended that a dynamic check of throttle body synchronisation is carried out before the air filter housing is installed (see Chapter 1).

17 Exhaust system

⚠️ *Warning: If the engine has been running the exhaust system will be very hot. Allow the system to cool before carrying out any work.*

16.2 Turn the servo shaft to set the front throttle body valve parallel

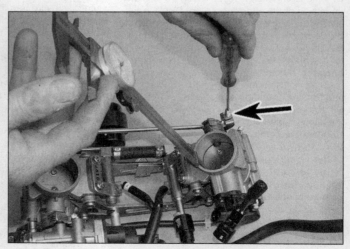

16.3 Turn the linkage adjusting screw (arrowed) to set the rear throttle body valve parallel

17.1a Unscrew the bolts (arrowed) and remove the belly pan bracket

17.1b Unscrew the bolts (arrowed) and remove the footrest bracket

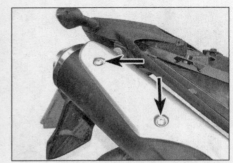

17.1c Undo the screws (arrowed) and remove the shield

 HAYNES HiNT *Exhaust system clamp bolts tend to become corroded and seized. It is advisable to spray them with WD40 or a similar product before attempting to slacken them.*

DL models

Removal

1 Remove the belly pan if fitted (see Chapter 7). Remove the belly pan bracket **(see illustration)**. Remove the passenger footrest bracket **(see illustration)**. Remove the silencer heat shield **(see illustration)**.

2 Slacken the clamp bolt securing the rear cylinder downpipe **(see illustration)**.

3 Refer to Section 14, Step 64 and disconnect the oxygen sensor wiring connector. Feed the connector down to the sensor, releasing it from any ties and noting its routing.

4 Unscrew the front cylinder downpipe flange bolts **(see illustration)**.

5 Support the exhaust system and unscrew the middle mounting bolts, counter-holding the nuts on the silencer mounts, then lower the system and remove it **(see illustrations)**. Remove the gasket from the front cylinder head exhaust port and discard it – a new one must be used **(see illustration)**.

6 If required slacken the clamp bolt securing the front cylinder downpipe and remove the pipe from the rest of the system **(see illustration)**.

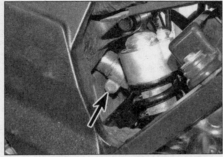

17.2 Slacken the clamp (arrowed)

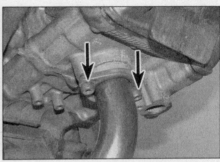

17.4 Unscrew the flange bolts (arrowed)

17.5a Unscrew the bolts at the rear (arrowed)…

17.5b …and the middle bolt (arrowed)…

17.5c …and remove the system

17.5d Lever the gasket out

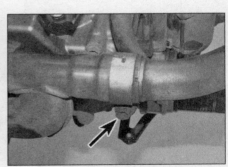

17.6 Slacken the clamp (arrowed)

17.7 Rear downpipe bolts (arrowed)

17.13 Fit a new gasket into the port

7 If required remove the rear cylinder downpipe **(see illustration)** – to do this remove the shock absorber and swingarm (see Chapter 5). Remove the gasket from the exhaust port and discard it – a new one must be used **(see illustration 17.5d)**.

8 Sealing rings are fitted in the exhaust system where the downpipes fit in. Check their condition and replace with new ones if damaged or deformed or no longer sealing correctly.

9 Remove the collars from the mounts and check the condition of the rubber bushes – if they are worn or deteriorated replace them with new ones. Replace any badly rusted bolts and clamps with new ones.

Installation

10 Clean all corrosion off the mounting bolts and apply a smear of copper grease to the threads to prevent them seizing in the future.

11 Fit the rear cylinder downpipe if removed – apply a smear of grease to the new exhaust

port gasket to keep it in place, then fit the gasket in the port **(see illustration 17.13)**. Fit the downpipe and tighten the flange bolts to the torque setting specified at the beginning of the Chapter **(see illustration 17.7)**. Install the shock absorber and swingarm (see Chapter 5).

12 Fit new sealing rings into the downpipe sockets as required – remove the clamps and expand the slotted housing rim sections if necessary to ease fitment and avoid damage to the rings, which are fragile. Apply a suitable exhaust sealant (such as Permatex 1372) to the sealing rings. If removed fit the front cylinder downpipe but do not yet tighten the clamp bolt so the pipe can be correctly aligned as you fit it.

13 Apply a smear of grease to the new front cylinder exhaust port gasket to keep it in place, then fit the gasket in the port **(see illustration)**. Check the front and rear clamps are correctly fitted, then manoeuvre the system into position so that it locates over

the rear cylinder downpipe **(see illustration 17.5c)**. Align the mounts and loosely fit the bolts **(see illustration 17.5b and a)**.

14 Once the system is installed and correctly aligned, tighten all the fixings to the torque settings specified at the beginning of the Chapter for your model, tightening the downpipe bolts first, then the mounting bolts, then the clamp bolts.

15 Do not forget to reconnect the oxygen sensor wiring connector, and make sure the wiring is correctly routed. Run the engine and check that there are no exhaust gas leaks. Install all remaining components (see Step 1).

SFV models

Removal

16 To remove the silencer slacken the clamp bolt **(see illustration)**. Unscrew the mounting bolt nut, then support the silencer, withdraw the bolt, collect the washer, and draw the silencer off **(see illustrations)**.

17 Slacken the clamp bolt securing the rear cylinder downpipe **(see illustration)**.

18 Remove the front heat shield from the right-hand side.

19 Refer to Step 64 in Section 14 and disconnect the oxygen sensor wiring connector. Feed the connector down to the sensor, releasing it from any ties and noting its routing.

20 Unscrew the front cylinder downpipe flange bolts **(see illustration 17.4)**.

21 Support the exhaust system and unscrew the mounting bolts, then lower the system and remove it **(see illustrations)**. Remove the gasket from the front cylinder head exhaust

17.16a Slacken the clamp (arrowed)

17.16b Counter-hold the bolt on the inside and unscrew the nut

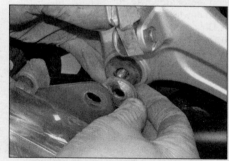

17.16c Note the washer between the silencer bracket and the footrest bracket

17.17 Slacken the clamp (arrowed)

17.21a Unscrew the bolts (arrowed) on the left...

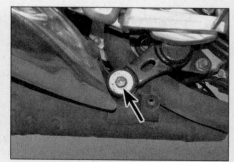

17.21b ...and the bolt (arrowed) on the right, and remove the system

port and discard it – a new one must be used **(see illustration 17.5d)**.

22 If required slacken the clamp bolt securing the front cylinder downpipe and remove the pipe from the rest of the system.

23 Remove the rear cylinder downpipe if required **(see illustration 17.7***)* – to do this remove the right-hand side cover (see Chapter 7). Remove the gasket from the exhaust port and discard it – a new one must be used **(see illustration 17.5d)**.

24 Sealing rings are fitted in the exhaust system where the downpipes fit in. Check their condition and replace with new ones if damaged or deformed or no longer sealing correctly.

25 Remove the collars and check the condition of the rubber bushes – if they are worn or deteriorated replace them with new ones. Replace any badly rusted bolts and clamps with new ones.

Installation

26 Clean all corrosion off the mounting bolts and apply a smear of copper grease to the threads to prevent them seizing in the future.

27 Fit the rear cylinder downpipe if removed – apply a smear of grease to the new exhaust port gasket to keep it in place, then fit the gasket in the port **(see illustration 17.13)**. Fit the downpipe and tighten the flange bolts to the torque setting specified at the beginning of the Chapter. Install the right-hand side cover (see Chapter 7).

28 Fit new sealing rings into the downpipe sockets and silencer socket if necessary – remove the clamps and expand the slotted housing rim sections if necessary to ease fitment and avoid damage to the rings, which are fragile. Apply a suitable exhaust sealant (such as Permatex 1372) to the sealing rings.

29 If removed fit the front cylinder downpipe but do not yet tighten the clamp bolt so the pipe can be correctly aligned as you fit it.

30 Apply a smear of grease to the new front cylinder exhaust port gasket to keep it in place, then fit the gasket in the port **(see illustration 17.13)**.

31 Ensure the front and rear clamps are correctly fitted, then manoeuvre the system into position so that it locates over the rear cylinder downpipe, and locate the front downpipe in the port. Align the mounts and the downpipe flange and loosely fit the bolts **(see illustrations 17.21a and b)**.

32 Fit the silencer, not forgetting the washer between it and the footrest bracket, then loosely fit the nut and bolt **(see illustrations 17.16c and b)**.

33 Once the system is installed and correctly aligned, tighten all the fixings to the torque settings specified at the beginning of the Chapter for your model, tightening the downpipe bolts first, then the mounting bolts, then the clamp bolts. Fit the heat shield.

34 Do not forget to reconnect the oxygen sensor wiring connector, and make sure the wiring is correctly routed. Run the engine and check that there are no exhaust gas leaks.

18 Catalytic converter

General information

1 There is a catalytic converter incorporated in the exhaust system to minimise the level of exhaust pollutants released into the atmosphere.

2 A catalytic converter consists of a canister containing a fine mesh impregnated with a catalyst material, over which the hot exhaust gases pass. The catalyst speeds up the oxidation of harmful carbon monoxide, unburned hydrocarbons and soot, effectively reducing the quantity of harmful products released into the atmosphere via the exhaust gases.

3 The catalytic converter is of the closed-loop type with exhaust gas oxygen content information being fed back to the engine control module (ECM) by the oxygen sensor.

5 Refer to Section 17 for exhaust system removal and installation, and Section 14 for oxygen sensor removal and installation information.

Precautions

6 The catalytic converter is a reliable and simple device which needs no maintenance in itself, but there are some facts of which an owner should be aware if the converter is to function properly for its full service life.

● DO NOT use leaded or lead replacement petrol (gasoline) – the additives will coat the precious metals, reducing their converting efficiency and will eventually destroy the catalytic converter.

● Always keep the ignition and fuel systems well-maintained in accordance with the manufacturer's schedule – if the fuel/air mixture is suspected of being incorrect have it checked on an exhaust gas analyser.

● If the engine develops a misfire, do not ride the bike at all (or at least as little as possible) until the fault is rectified.

● DO NOT use fuel or engine oil additives – these may contain substances harmful to the catalytic converter.

● DO NOT continue to use the bike if the

19.7 PAIR control valve screws (arrowed)

engine burns oil to the extent of leaving a visible trail of blue smoke.

● Remember that the catalytic converter and oxygen sensor are FRAGILE – do not strike them with tools during servicing work.

19 PAIR system (2004 to 2011 DL models)

General information

1 To reduce the amount of unburned hydrocarbons released in the exhaust gases, a pulse secondary air supply (PAIR) system is fitted. The system consists of the control valve (mounted on the underside of the air filter housing), the reed valves (one in each valve cover) and the hoses linking them. The control valve is actuated electronically by the ECM.

2 When the valve is open it allows filtered air to be drawn through the reed valves and cylinder head passages and into the exhaust ports. The air mixes with the exhaust gases, causing any unburned particles of the fuel in the mixture to be burnt in the exhaust port/pipes. This process changes a considerable amount of hydrocarbons and carbon monoxide into relatively harmless carbon dioxide and water. The reed valves in the valve cover are fitted to prevent the flow of exhaust gases back up the cylinder head passages and into the air filter housing.

Testing

3 Raise the fuel tank (see Section 2).

4 To test the solenoid valve remove it from the air filter housing (Step 7). Check that the hose ports are clean – the presence or carbon deposits indicates a faulty system.

5 Check the operation of the valve by blowing through the air intake port – air should flow through the control valve and out of the output port. Using a pair of auxiliary wires now apply battery voltage (12 volts) across the terminals in the control valve connector and repeat the check – no air should flow through the control valve. Disconnect the battery. If the valve does not behave as described check its resistance by connecting an ohmmeter between the terminals and compare the reading obtained to that given in the Specifications. Replace the valve with a new one if faulty.

6 Check the operation of each reed valve by blowing through its hose (disconnect them at the 3-way junction) – air should flow through the valve. Now suck on the hose – you should not be able to suck air back up, indicating the reed valve is closing and sealing correctly. If you can suck air through, remove the valve for cleaning (see below), then test again.

Component renewal

Control valve

7 Remove the air filter housing (Section 7). Undo the screws and remove the valve **(see illustration)**.

8 Installation is the reverse of removal.

19.9 Unscrew the bolt (arrowed)

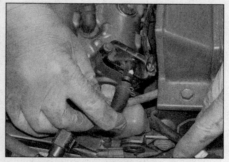

19.10 Detach the hose

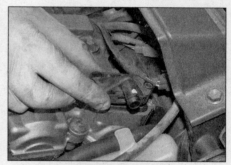

19.11a Remove the cover...

19.11b ...and lift the valve out

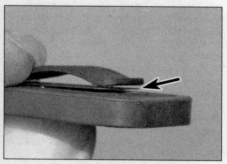

19.12a Check the reed (arrowed) is not stuck to its seat

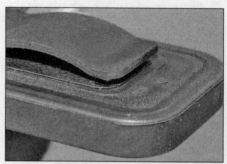

19.12b Make sure there is no gap between the reed and its seat

Reed valves

9 To access the front cylinder valve unscrew the radiator lower mounting bolt and pivot the bottom of the radiator forward (see illustration). To access the rear cylinder valve raise the fuel tank (see Section 2).

10 Release the clamp and detach the hose (see illustration).

11 Unscrew the bolts and remove the cover (see illustration). Remove the reed valve, noting which way around it fits (see illustration).

12 Gently push the reed off its seat from the underside to check it is not stuck (see illustration). Release it and make sure there is no gap between it and its seat (see illustration). Check the condition of the rubber around the valve. Replace the valve with a new one if necessary.

13 Installation is the reverse of removal. Make sure the valves and housings are clean and free of carbon deposits, and that the valves seat correctly. Clean the threads of the cover bolts and apply some fresh threadlock.

20 Ignition system check

⚠ **Warning: The energy levels in electronic systems can be very high. On no account should the ignition be switched on whilst the plugs or caps are being held. Shocks from the HT circuit can be most unpleasant. Secondly,**

it is vital that the engine is not turned over or run with any of the plug caps removed, and that the plugs are soundly earthed (grounded) when the system is checked for sparking. The ignition system components can be seriously damaged if the HT circuit becomes isolated.

1 As no means of adjustment is available, any failure of the system can be traced to failure of a system component or a simple wiring fault. Of the two possibilities, the latter is by far the most likely. In the event of failure, check the system in a logical fashion, as described below.

2 To access the front cylinder spark plug cap(s) unscrew the radiator lower mounting bolt and pivot the bottom of the radiator forward (see illustration 19.9). To access the rear cylinder spark plug cap(s) raise the fuel tank (see Section 2).

3 Make sure the ignition is OFF. Work on one cylinder at a time – on twin plug models test one plug at a time (even though each plug in a twin plug head is fired by the same coil, you need to test both in case a cap or lead has developed a fault and only one plug is sparking).

4 Pull the cap off the plug (see illustration). Connect the cap to a spare spark plug (preferably use a new plug).

5 Earth the plug against the cylinder head – do not earth the plug against the valve cover itself. If necessary, hold the spark plug with an insulated tool.

⚠ **Warning: Do not remove any of the spark plugs from the engine to perform this check – atomised**

fuel being pumped out of the open spark plug hole could ignite, causing severe injury! Make sure the plugs are securely held against the engine – if they are not earthed when the engine is turned over, the ECM could be damaged.

6 Check that the kill switch is in the RUN position and the transmission is in neutral, then turn the ignition switch ON and turn the engine over on the starter motor. If the system is in good condition a regular, fat blue spark should be evident at the plug electrodes. If the spark appears thin or yellowish, or is non-existent, further investigation is necessary. Turn the ignition OFF and repeat the check for each plug cap or coil.

7 The ignition system must be able to produce a spark that is capable of jumping at least a 6 mm gap. Simple ignition spark gap testing tools are commercially available (see illustration) – follow the manufacturer's instructions, and set the gap at 6 mm.

20.4 Pull the relevant cap off the plug

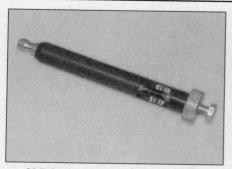
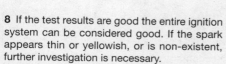

20.7 Ignition spark gap testing tool

21.1a Front cylinder ignition coil (arrowed) – DL

21.1b Rear cylinder ignition coil (arrowed) – DL

8 If the test results are good the entire ignition system can be considered good. If the spark appears thin or yellowish, or is non-existent, further investigation is necessary.

9 Ignition faults can be divided into two categories, namely those where the ignition system has failed completely, and those that are due to a partial failure. The likely faults are listed below, starting with the most probable source of failure. Work through the list systematically, referring to the subsequent sections for full details of the necessary checks and tests. **Note:** *Before checking the following items ensure that the battery is fully charged and that all fuses are in good condition.*

● Loose spark plug cap or lead connection, faulty spark plug cap or HT lead, faulty spark plug, dirty, worn or corroded plug electrodes.
● Loose, corroded or damaged wiring connections, broken or shorted wiring between any of the component parts of the ignition system.
● Faulty gear position switch, clutch switch or sidestand switch (see Chapter 8).
● Faulty ignition coil(s) (Section 21).
● Faulty ignition switch or engine kill switch (see Chapter 8).
● Faulty crankshaft position (CKP) sensor

(Section 14) or damaged triggers on alternator rotor (Chapter 2).
● Faulty engine control module (Section 15).
10 If the above checks don't reveal the cause of the problem, have the ignition system tested by a Suzuki dealer.

21 Ignition coils

1 On DL models the front cylinder coil is on the inside of the left-hand engine mounting bracket, and the rear cylinder coil is on the inside of the right-hand bracket **(see illustrations)**.
2 On SFV models both coils are on the inside of the frame on the right-hand side of the engine – the top coil is for the rear cylinder **(see illustration)**.

Check

3 Check each coil visually for loose or damaged connectors and terminals, cracks and other damage.
4 On 2004 to 2006 DL models disconnect the primary circuit wiring connectors from the coil, noting which fits where **(see illustration)**.

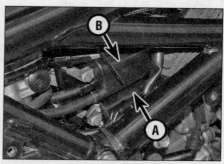

21.2 Front cylinder ignition coil (A), rear cylinder ignition coil (B) – SFV

On 2007-on DL models and all SFV models trace the primary wiring from the coil and disconnect the connector **(see illustration)**.
5 Pull the cap(s) off the relevant spark plugs **(see illustration 20.4)** – to access the front cylinder spark plug cap(s) unscrew the radiator lower mounting bolt and pivot the bottom of the radiator forward **(see illustration 19.9)**. To access the rear cylinder spark plug cap(s) raise the fuel tank (see Section 2).

2004 to 2006 DL models

6 To check the condition of the primary

21.4a Primary wiring connectors (arrowed) – 2004 to 2006 DL, rear cylinder coil

21.4b Primary wiring connector (arrowed) – rear cylinder coil 2007-on DL shown

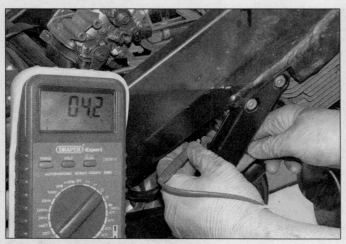

21.6 To test the coil primary resistance, connect the multimeter leads to the primary wiring terminals – 2004 to 2006 DL shown

21.7 Testing the coil secondary resistance – 2004 to 2006 DL

windings, set a multimeter to the ohms x 1 scale. Connect the meter probes to the primary terminals and measure the resistance (see illustration).

7 To check the resistance of the secondary windings, set the meter to the K-ohm scale. Connect one meter probe to the orange/white (front coil) or black/orange (rear coil) wire terminal on the coil and the other probe to the contact in the plug cap and measure the resistance (see illustration).

2007-on DL models and all SFV models

8 To check the condition of the primary windings, set a multimeter to the ohms x 1 scale. Connect the meter probes to the primary terminals in the coil side of the wiring connector and measure the resistance. If the reading obtained is not as given in the Specifications, it is likely that the coil is defective.

9 To check the resistance of the secondary windings, set the meter to the K-ohm scale. Connect one meter probe to the contact in one of the spark plug caps and the other probe to

the other cap and measure the resistance (see illustration).

All models

10 If the primary and secondary winding readings obtained are not as given in the Specifications, it is likely that the coil is defective. Have the system peak voltage tested by a dealer.

11 Note that in the case of the secondary winding test the problem could be due to a faulty plug cap. Unscrew the plug cap(s) and test the coil again, allowing a reduction for the cap (see illustrations).

Removal and installation

12 Pull the cap(s) off the relevant spark plugs (see illustration 20.4) – to access the front cylinder spark plug cap(s) unscrew the radiator lower mounting bolt (see illustration 19.9). To access the rear cylinder spark plug cap(s) raise the fuel tank (see Section 2).

13 On 2004 to 2006 DL models disconnect the primary circuit wiring connectors from the coil, noting which fits where (see illustration 21.4a). On 2007-on DL models and all SFV

models trace the primary wiring from the coil and disconnect the connector (see illustration 21.4b).

14 Unscrew the bolts and remove the coil, noting the routing of the lead(s) – on SFV models remove the top (rear cylinder) coil first.

15 Installation is the reverse of removal.

22 Ignition timing

1 There is no means of adjusting the ignition timing, and since no component is subject to mechanical wear, there is no provision for any checks (i.e. there are no timing marks).

2 Before assuming the ignition timing is not right, check all other aspects of the system as described in the Sections 20 and 21.

3 If there is still a fault the ECM could be faulty, so it is best to take the bike to a Suzuki dealer for assessment – they may have a spare ECM that can be plugged in to see if it cures the fault.

21.9 Testing the coil secondary resistance – 2007-on DL and SFV

21.11a Unscrew the cap from the lead...

21.11b ... and check the resistance of the cap

Chapter 5
Frame and suspension

Contents

Degrees of difficulty

| **Easy,** suitable for novice with little experience | 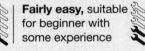 | **Fairly easy,** suitable for beginner with some experience | | **Fairly difficult,** suitable for competent DIY mechanic | | **Difficult,** suitable for experienced DIY mechanic | | **Very difficult,** suitable for expert DIY or professional | |

Specifications

Front forks

Fork oil type . . . . Suzuki SS-08 fork oil or 10W fork oil
Fork oil capacity (per fork)
  2004 to 2006 DL models . . . . 524 cc
  2007 to 2011 DL models . . . . 528 cc
  2012-on DL models . . . . 530 cc
  SFV models . . . . 517 cc
Fork oil level*
  2004 to 2006 DL models . . . . 143 mm
  2007 to 2011 DL models . . . . 139 mm
  2012-on DL models . . . . 139 mm
  SFV models . . . . 96 mm
Fork spring free length (min)
  2004 to 2011 DL models
    Standard . . . . 444.1 mm
    Service limit . . . . 435 mm
  2012-on DL models
    Standard . . . . 451.1 mm
    Service limit . . . . 442 mm
  SFV models
    Standard . . . . 446.5 mm
    Service limit . . . . 437 mm
Fork tube runout limit . . . . 0.2 mm
*Oil level is measured from the top of the tube with the fork spring removed and the leg fully compressed.

Rear suspension

Swingarm pivot bolt runout (max) . . . . 0.3 mm

Torque settings

Fork damper rod bolt . . . .   20 Nm
Fork top bolt . . . .   23 Nm
Fork clamp bolts
   Top yoke . . . .   23 Nm
   Bottom yoke . . . .   23 Nm
Front brake master cylinder clamp bolts . . . .   10 Nm
Handlebar clamp bolts . . . .   23 Nm
Shock absorber bolts/nuts . . . .   50 Nm
Sidestand pivot bolt
   DL models . . . .   50 Nm
   SFV models . . . .   10 Nm
Sidestand pivot bolt nut . . . .   40 Nm
Steering head bearing adjuster nut . . . .   45 Nm
Steering head bearing locknut (DL models) . . . .   80 Nm
Steering stem nut . . . .   90 Nm
Suspension linkage bolts/nuts . . . .   78 Nm
Swingarm pivot
   DL models
      Pivot bolt . . . .   15 Nm
      Pivot bolt locknut . . . .   90 Nm
      Pivot bolt nut . . . .   100 Nm
   SFV models
      Pivot bolt nut . . . .   100 Nm

1 General information

DL models have an aluminium twin-spar diamond frame using the engine as a stressed member. SFV models have a steel trellis frame using the engine as a stressed member.

Front suspension is by a pair of oil-damped telescopic forks, 43 mm on DL models and 41 mm on SFV models, with adjustable spring pre-load.

Rear suspension is by aluminium swingarm and a single shock absorber, via a rising rate linkage. The rear shock has adjustable spring pre-load and rebound damping on DL models and adjustable spring pre-load on SFV models.

The swingarm pivots through the frame.

2 Frame inspection and repair

1 The frame should not require attention unless accident damage has occurred. In most cases, fitting a new frame is the only satisfactory remedy for such damage. A few frame specialists have the jigs and other equipment necessary for straightening frames to the required standard of accuracy, but even then there is no simple way of assessing to what extent the frame may have been over stressed.

2 After a high mileage, the frame should be examined closely for signs of cracking or splitting at the welded joints. Loose engine mounting bolts can cause ovaling or fracturing of the mounting points. Minor damage can often be repaired by welding, depending on the extent and nature of the damage.

3 Remember that a frame that is out of alignment will cause handling problems. If, as the result of an accident, misalignment is suspected, it will be necessary to strip the machine completely so the frame can be thoroughly checked.

3 Footrests, brake pedal and gearchange lever

Footrests

1 To remove a footrest remove the E-clip from the bottom of the pivot pin, then withdraw the

3.1 Remove the E-clip (arrowed), then draw the pivot pin out the top

pin and remove the footrest (see illustration). On the front footrests note how the return spring ends locate. On the rear footrests note the shaped retaining washer on DL models or how the detent plate, ball and spring fit on SFV models.

2 If necessary you can replace the footrest rubbers with new ones – on the front footrests undo the screws on the underside to release the rubber, noting which screw fits where and the fitting of the setting plate on DL models (see illustration). On the rear footrests on DL models remove the retaining washer then slide the rubber off, noting how it locates around the end plate.

3 Installation is the reverse of removal. Apply a small amount of grease to the pivot pin.

Brake pedal

DL models

4 Remove the split pin and washer from the clevis pin securing the brake pedal to the

3.2 Undo the screws (arrowed) to release the rubber

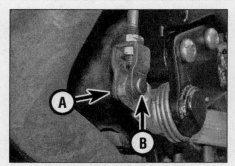

3.4 Remove the split pin and washer (A) and withdraw the clevis pin (B)

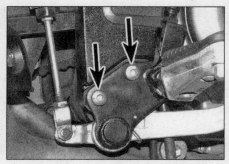

3.5 Footrest bracket bolts (arrowed)

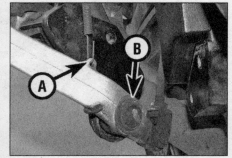

3.6 Unhook the spring (A), then release the circlip (B)

master cylinder pushrod (see illustration). Withdraw the clevis pin and separate the pushrod from the pedal.

5 Unscrew the footrest bracket bolts and displace the bracket (see illustration).

6 Unhook the brake light switch spring (see illustration). Release the circlip and remove the washer, then slide the pedal off its pivot, unhooking the return spring.

7 Installation is the reverse of removal. Clean all old grease and dirt off the pedal and pivot, and apply some fresh grease.

SFV models

8 Remove the split pin and washer from the clevis pin securing the brake pedal to the master cylinder pushrod (see illustration). Withdraw the clevis pin and separate the pushrod from the pedal.

9 Unscrew the silencer mounting bolt and the footrest bracket bolts and displace the bracket, noting the washer (see illustrations).

10 Unhook the brake light switch spring and the brake pedal return spring (see illustration). Release the circlip and remove the washer, then slide the pedal off its pivot.

11 Installation is the reverse of removal. Clean all old grease and dirt off the pedal and pivot, and apply some fresh grease.

Gearchange lever and linkage
Removal

12 Make an alignment mark between the slit in the gearchange linkage arm and the shaft, then unscrew the pinch bolt and slide the arm off (see illustrations).

3.8 Remove the split pin and washer (A) and withdraw the clevis pin (B)

3.9b ...then unscrew the footrest bracket bolts (arrowed)...

3.9a Counter-hold the bolt and unscrew the nut...

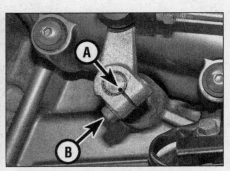

3.9c ...and collect the washer from between it and the silencer

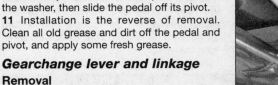

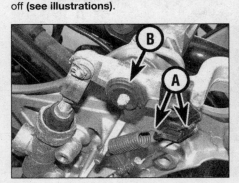

3.10 Unhook the springs (A), then release the circlip (B)

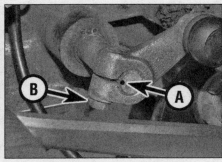

3.12a Alignment mark (A), gearchange arm pinch bolt (B) – DL

3.12b Alignment mark (A), gearchange arm pinch bolt (B) – SFV

3.13a Release the circlip...

3.13b ...remove the washer...

3.13c ...and the lever

13 Release the circlip and remove the washer, then slide the lever off its pivot **(see illustrations)**.

14 Prior to disassembling the linkage note how far the rod is threaded into the lever and arm as this determines the height of the lever relative to the footrest. Slacken the locknut on each end of the linkage rod – the rod has left-hand threads on one end (mark that end of the rod as a guide for refitting it) then thread the lever and arm off the rod. Replace the rubber boots with new ones if required.

15 Check all components for wear and damage – all are available separately.

Installation

16 Installation is the reverse of removal, noting the following:

● Clean off all old grease from the pivot components and apply fresh grease.

● If the linkage was disassembled leave the locknuts loose for the time being so the height of the lever can be adjusted.

● Align the slit in the arm with the mark made on the shaft, and tighten the pinch bolt **(see illustration 3.12a or b)**.

● Adjust the gear lever height as required by screwing the linkage rod in or out of

the lever and arm. Tighten the locknuts on completion.

4 Sidestand

Removal

1 Support the bike on an auxiliary stand. Retract the sidestand.

2 Unhook the stand springs **(see illustration)**. Unscrew the nut from the pivot bolt, then unscrew the bolt and remove the stand **(see illustration)**.

Installation

3 Clean off all old grease and dirt from the pivot bolt and stand and apply fresh grease to the pivot surfaces. Tighten the pivot bolt to the torque setting specified at the beginning of the Chapter for your model, then counter-hold the bolt and tighten the nut to the specified torque **(see illustration 4.2b)**.

4 Reconnect the springs and check that they hold the stand securely up when not in use – an accident is almost certain to occur if the

stand extends while the machine is in motion **(see illustration 4.2a)**.

5 Handlebars and levers

Handlebars

Removal

Note: *The handlebars can be displaced from the top yoke without having to remove the individual assemblies from them – follow Step 8 only. If you do this, cover the instrument cluster with some rag and lay the handlebar assembly on it.*

1 Remove the mirrors, and if fitted on DL models remove the hand guards (see Chapter 7).

2 Refer to Chapter 4 and detach the throttle cables – on 2007-on DL models and all SFV models create slack in the throttle cables using the adjuster (see Chapter 1), or if necessary detach the cable ends from the throttle cam on the throttle body before detaching them from the twistgrip.

4.2a Sidestand springs (arrowed)

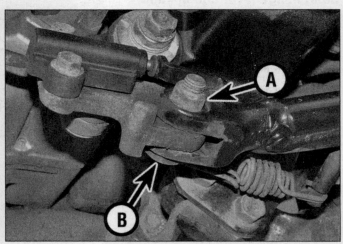

4.2b Sidestand pivot nut (A) and bolt (B)

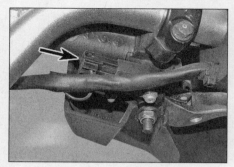

5.3a Disconnect the wiring connector (arrowed)

5.3b Unscrew the bolts (arrowed) and displace the master cylinder assembly

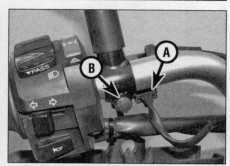

5.4 Clutch switch wiring connector (A), lever bracket clamp bolt (B)

5.5 Switch housing screws (arrowed)

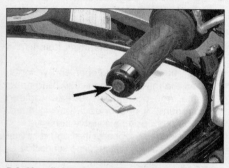

5.6 Handlebar end-weight screw (arrowed)

3 Disconnect the wires from the brake light switch **(see illustration)**. Unscrew the two front brake master cylinder assembly clamp bolts and position the assembly clear of the handlebar, making sure no strain is placed on the hydraulic hose **(see illustration)**. Keep the master cylinder reservoir upright to prevent possible fluid leakage.

4 Disconnect the wires from the clutch switch and slacken the clutch lever bracket clamp bolt **(see illustration)**. Refer to Chapter 2 and detach the clutch cable from the lever and bracket.

5 Where present releasing any wiring ties from the handlebars. Displace the switch housing(s) by undoing the screws **(see illustration)**.

6 Unscrew the right handlebar end-weight retaining screw, then remove the weight from the end of the handlebar and slide the throttle twistgrip off the end **(see illustration)**.

7 Unscrew the left handlebar end-weight retaining screw, then remove the weight from the end of the handlebar and slide off the grip. If the grip has been glued on, you will probably have to slit it with a knife to remove it. Slide the clutch lever assembly off the handlebar.

8 Carefully prise the blanking caps out of the handlebar clamp bolts **(see illustration)**. Support the handlebars, then unscrew the bolts, noting the washers, and remove the clamps and the handlebars **(see illustrations)** – if you are just displacing the handlebars with everything attached free the cables and wiring from any guides on the top yoke, as required according to model.

5.8a Prise the blanking caps out...

Installation

9 Installation is the reverse of removal, noting the following.
● Align the punch mark on the front of the handlebar with the mating surfaces of

5.8b ...unscrew the bolts (arrowed)...

the left handlebar holder and clamp **(see illustration 5.9a)**.
● Fit the handlebar clamps with the punch mark at the front **(see illustration 5.9b)**. Make sure the washers are fitted with the

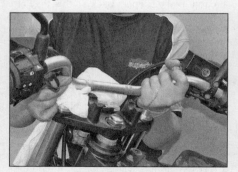

5.8c ...and displace or remove the handlebars

5.9a Align the clamp mating surfaces with the punch mark (arrowed)

5.9b Fit the clamps with the punch marks (arrowed) to the front

clamp bolts. Tighten the front bolts first to the specified torque setting, then tighten the rear bolts to the specified torque.

● Apply some grease to the throttle twistgrip section of the handlebar. Refer to Chapter 4 for installation of the throttle cables.

● Make sure the front brake master cylinder assembly clamp is installed with the mirror mounting facing up and the clamp mating surfaces aligned with the punch mark on the bottom of the handlebar **(see illustration 5.9c)**. Tighten the clamp bolts to the specified torque setting, tightening the top bolt first.

● Align the clutch lever bracket clamp mating surfaces with the punch mark on the bottom of the handlebar **(see illustration 5.9d)**.

● Make sure the pin in one half of each switch housing locates in its hole in the handlebar.

● When fitting the handlebar end-weights, clean the threads of the screws and apply some non-permanent thread locking compound. If new grips are being fitted, secure them using a suitable adhesive.

● Do not forget to reconnect the front brake light switch and clutch switch wiring connectors.

Levers

10 On DL models if fitted remove the hand guard (see Chapter 7).

11 To remove the brake lever undo the pivot bolt locknut, then undo the bolt and remove the lever **(see illustration)**.

12 To free the clutch lever, refer to Chapter 1 and create some freeplay in the cable. Unscrew the

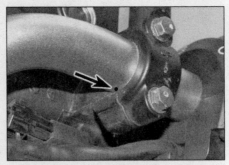

5.9c Align the clamp mating surfaces with the punch mark (arrowed)

5.11 Note the washer fitted with the pivot arrangement on DL fitted with hand guards

nut on the underside of the lever bracket **(see illustration)**. Unscrew the pivot bolt and remove the lever, detaching the cable end as you do so.

13 Installation is the reverse of removal. Apply

5.9d Align the clamp mating surfaces with the punch mark (arrowed)

5.12 Note the spacer (arrowed) fitted with the pivot arrangement on DL fitted with hand guards

silicone grease to the contact area between the master cylinder pushrod tip and the lever. Apply grease to the pivot bolt shafts and the contact areas between the lever and its bracket. Tighten the pivot screw fairly lightly, then hold it and tighten the locknut.

6 Fork removal and installation

Removal

1 On 2004 to 2011 DL models remove the fairing side panels, and on 2012-on DL models remove the complete fairing assembly (see Chapter 7).

2 Remove the front wheel (see Chapter 6). Tie the front brake calipers back so that they are out of the way.

3 Remove the front mudguard (see Chapter 7).

4 Release the speed sensor wiring from the fork as required according to model. Note the routing of all cables, hoses and wiring around the forks.

5 Working on one fork at a time, slacken the fork clamp bolt in the top yoke **(see illustration)**. If the fork oil is being changed, or if the fork is to be disassembled, slacken the fork top bolt **(see illustration)**.

6 Slacken the fork clamp bolts in the bottom yoke, and remove the fork by twisting it and pulling it downwards **(see illustrations)**.

6.5a Top yoke fork clamp bolt (arrowed)

6.6a Bottom yoke fork clamp bolts (arrowed)

6.5b Slacken the top bolt if required

6.6b Draw the fork down and out of the yokes

HAYNES HINT *If the fork legs are seized in the yokes, spray the area with penetrating oil and allow time for it to soak in before trying again.*

Installation

7 Remove any traces of corrosion from the fork tube and the yokes. Make sure you fit the forks on the correct side – the fork with the axle clamp bolt goes on the right-hand side on 2004 to 2011 DL models and SFV models, and on the left on 2012-on DL models. As you fit each fork make sure all cables, hoses and wiring are routed on the correct side of the fork.

8 Slide the fork up through the bottom yoke and into the top yoke and set the top of the fork tube (not the top bolt) flush with the upper surface of the yoke on DL models, and 1.5 mm above it on SFV models **(see illustration)**, then tighten the fork clamp bolts in the bottom yoke to the torque setting specified at the beginning of the Chapter **(see illustrations 6.6a)**.

9 If the fork oil was changed or if the fork has been dismantled, tighten the fork top bolt to the specified torque setting **(see illustration 6.5b)**.

10 Now tighten the fork clamp bolts in the top yoke to the specified torque **(see illustration 6.5a)**.

11 Install the front mudguard (see Chapter 7) and the front wheel (see Chapter 6). Make sure all cables, hoses and wiring are correctly routed and secured.

12 On DL model install the fairing side panels (see Chapter 7). Check the operation of the front forks and brakes before taking the machine out on the road.

6.8 Set the top of the fork tube as described for your model – this shows a DL fork tube flush with the top of the yoke so just the top bolt rim protrudes

7 Fork oil change

1 After a high mileage the fork oil will deteriorate and its damping and lubrication qualities will be impaired. Always change the oil in both fork legs.

2 Remove the fork – make sure you loosen the top bolt while the leg is still clamped in the bottom yoke (see Section 6).

3 Unscrew the fork top bolt from the top of the inner tube – the bolt is under pressure from the fork spring, so use a ratchet tool so it does not need to be removed from the bolt as you unscrew it, and maintain some downward pressure on it, particularly as you come to the end of the threads, or alternatively hold the

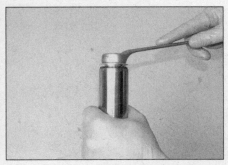

7.3 Thread the top bolt out of the tube

tool still and twist the fork tube to unthread it from the bolt **(see illustration)**.

4 Slide the inner tube down and remove the spacer, washer and spring **(see illustrations)**.

5 Invert the fork leg over a suitable container and pump it several times to expel as much oil as possible **(see illustration)**. Support the fork upside down in the container for a while to allow it to drain, then pump the fork again. If the fork oil contains metal particles inspect the fork bushes for wear (see Section 8). Wipe any excess oil off the spring and the spacer with a clean rag.

6 Stand the fork upright. Slowly pour in the specified quantity and grade of fork oil **(see illustration)**. Now pump the fork slowly at least ten times to distribute the oil evenly and expel all air from the damper. Leave the fork to stand for ten minutes to allow the oil to settle and any air to rise.

7 Slide the inner tube down gently until it seats on the bottom. Measure the oil level from the top of the tube **(see illustration)**. Add

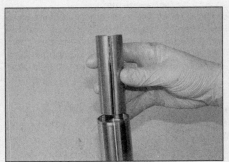

7.4a Remove the spacer...

7.4b ...the washer...

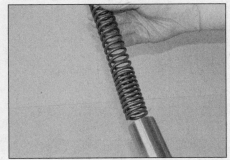

7.4c ...and the spring

7.5 Drain the oil as described

7.6 Fill the fork slowly to prevent air bubbles and overfilling

7.7 Measure the distance from the top of the tube to the oil

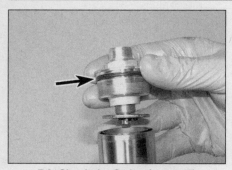

7.9 Check the O-ring (arrowed)

8.2 Remove the axle clamp bolt

8.3 Slacken the damper rod bolt

or subtract oil until it is at the level specified at the beginning of this Chapter.

8 Pull the inner tube out, then fit the spring with the closer wound coils or tapered end at the bottom, then fit the washer and the spacer **(see illustrations 7.4c, b and a)**.

9 If the top bolt O-ring is damaged or deteriorated fit a new one **(see illustration)**. Smear some fork oil onto the O-ring. Extend the inner tube and fit the top bolt into it, compressing the spring as you do, and thread it in, making sure it does not cross-thread, keeping downward pressure on the spring,

8.6 Tip the damper rod out

using a ratchet tool or by turning the tube while holding the bolt still, and tighten it as much as possible holding the inner tube by hand. **Note:** *Tighten the top bolt to the specified torque setting when the fork has been installed in the bike and is held in the bottom yoke, but before the top yoke clamp bolt is tightened.*

10 Install the fork (see Section 6).

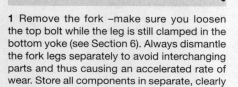

8 Fork overhaul

1 Remove the fork –make sure you loosen the top bolt while the leg is still clamped in the bottom yoke (see Section 6). Always dismantle the fork legs separately to avoid interchanging parts and thus causing an accelerated rate of wear. Store all components in separate, clearly marked containers.

Disassembly

2 When doing the right-hand fork on 2004 to 2011 DL models and SFV models, and the left-hand fork on 2012-on DL models, remove the axle clamp bolt **(see illustration)**. On SFV models, if required remove the fork protector.

3 Lay the fork flat on the bench with the caliper mounting lugs to the left. Hold the fork down and slacken then lightly retighten the damper rod bolt in the base of the fork **(see illustration)**. If the damper rod rotates inside the fork whilst attempting to unscrew the bolt, compress the fork so that the spring exerts pressure on the rod whilst the bolt is unscrewed. Alternatively, if available use an air wrench.

4 Refer to the Section 7, Steps 3 to 5 and drain the oil from the fork.

5 Remove the damper rod bolt and its sealing washer from the bottom of the fork **(see illustration 8.20b)**. A new sealing washer must be used on reassembly.

6 Tip the damper rod and its spring out **(see illustration)**.

7 Carefully prise out the dust seal from the top of the outer tube **(see illustration)**.

8 Carefully prise out the oil seal retaining clip, taking care not to scratch the surface of the inner tube **(see illustration)**.

9 To separate the inner and outer tubes it is necessary to displace the top bush and the oil seal from the outer tube. To do this grasp the inner tube in one hand and the outer tube in the other and compress them slightly, then pull them apart repeatedly until the bush and

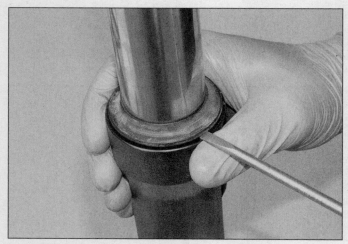

8.7 Prise out the dust seal using a flat-bladed screwdriver

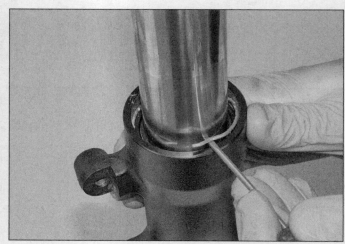

8.8 Prise out the retaining clip using a flat-bladed screwdriver

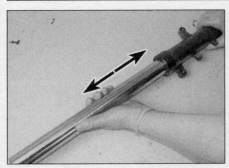

8.9a To separate the tubes pull them apart firmly several times...

8.9b ...the slide-hammer effect will displace the oil seal, washer and top bush

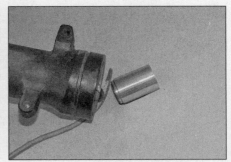

8.9c Tip the oil lock piece out

seal are tapped out **(see illustrations)**. Tip the oil lock piece out of the outer tube **(see illustration)**.

10 Slide the oil seal, the washer, and the top bush off the top of the inner tube, noting which way up they fit **(see illustration 8.9b)**. Discard the oil seal and the dust seal as new ones must be used. Do not remove the bottom bush from the inner tube unless it is being replaced with a new one – to remove it carefully lever its ends apart using a screwdriver and slide it out of its recess **(see illustration)**.

Inspection

11 Clean all parts in solvent and blow them dry with compressed air, if available.

12 Check the fork inner tube for score marks, dents, pitting, scratches, flaking of its surface and excessive or abnormal wear. If corrosion damage is excessive the inner tubes can be re-chromed using hard chrome. Otherwise fit a new tube. Check the tube for runout using V-blocks and a dial gauge. If the amount of runout exceeds the service limit specified, a new tube should be fitted.

 Warning: If the inner tube is bent or exceeds the runout limit, it should not be straightened; replace it with a new one.

8.10 Carefully lever the ends apart to expand it

13 Check the fork outer tube for cracks. Check the fork seal seat and housing for nicks, gouges and scratches. If damage is evident, leaks will occur. Also check the oil seal washer for damage or distortion and fit a new one if necessary.

14 Check the spring for cracks and other damage. Measure the spring free length and compare the measurement to the specifications at the beginning of the Chapter **(see illustration)**. If it is defective or sagged below the service limit, replace the springs in both forks with new ones. Never renew only one spring. Also check the rebound spring on the damper rod.

15 Examine the working surfaces of the bushes

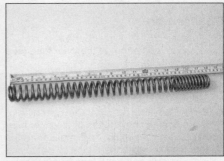

8.14 Check the free length of the spring

(i.e. the outer surface of the bottom bush and the inner surface of the top bush) **(see illustration)**; if the grey Teflon outer surface has been worn away to reveal the copper inner surface over more than 75% of the surface area, or if the bushes are scored or badly scuffed (which can easily occur during the tube separation process), they must be replaced with new ones. Note that it is a good idea to replace the bushes with new ones as a matter of course as part of a fork overhaul, and Suzuki specify to do this.

16 Check the damper rod, the piston ring in its head, and the rebound spring fitted on it, for damage and wear **(see illustration)**.

8.15 Check the working surface (arrowed) of each bush for wear

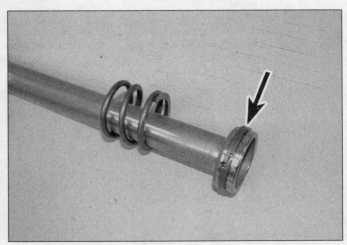

8.16 Check the damper, rebound spring and piston ring (arrowed)

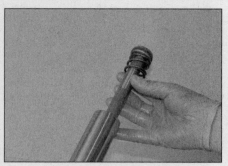

8.18a Fit the damper rod into the tube…

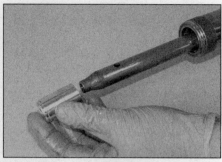

8.18b …then fit the oil lock piece onto the protruding end

8.19 Slide the inner tube into the outer tube

Reassembly

17 If necessary, fit a new bottom bush into its recess in the bottom of the inner tube **(see illustration 8.10)**.

18 If removed fit the piston ring into the groove in the head of the damper rod, and slide the rebound spring on **(see illustration 8.16)**. Smear fork oil onto the piston ring. Slide the damper into the top of the inner tube and all the way down so it protrudes from the bottom **(see illustration)**. Fit the oil lock piece onto the bottom of the rod **(see illustration)**.

19 Apply a smear of the specified clean fork oil to the surface of the bottom bush. Slide the inner tube fully into the outer tube **(see illustration)**.

20 Clean the threads of the damper rod bolt.

Lay the fork flat on the bench with the caliper mounting lugs to the right. Fit a new sealing washer onto the bolt and apply a few drops of a suitable non-permanent thread locking compound **(see illustration)**. Fit the bolt into the bottom of the outer tube and thread it into the damper rod, tightening it to the torque setting specified at the beginning of the Chapter **(see illustrations)**. If the rod rotates inside the tube as you tighten the bolt, wait until the fork is fully reassembled and tighten it then (the pressure of the spring on the rod will prevent it from turning).

21 Apply a smear of the specified clean fork oil to the inner surface of the top bush. Slide the bush down the inner tube and seat it in the top of the outer tube **(see illustration)**.

Slide the oil seal washer onto the bush **(see illustration)**.

22 Support the fork upright. Slide the inner tube to its full extent from the outer tube and have an assistant hold it – this is so that any accidental scratching while fitting the top bush and oil seal is confined to the area that does not affect the oil seal. Using either the Suzuki service tool (Pt. No. 09940-52861) or a suitable drift, carefully drive the top bush fully into its recess – the oil seal washer prevents damaging the edges of the bush **(see illustration)**. If using a drift, wrap tape around it to prevent scratching the inner tube. Make sure the bush enters the recess squarely.

23 Lift the washer to check the bush is seated fully and squarely in its recess in the

8.20a Fit a new sealing washer and apply threadlock…

8.20b …install the bolt with a new sealing washer…

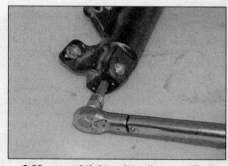

8.20c …and tighten it to the specified torque

8.21a Slide the top bush down and into the outer tube…

8.21b …then seat the washer on the bush…

8.22 …and drive the bush in and onto its seat

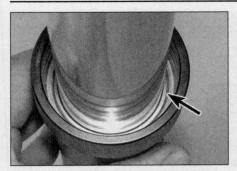

8.23 Make sure the bush (arrowed) has been fully driven in

8.24a Slide the seal down and into the outer tube...

8.24b ...then fit the old seal halves on top and drive the new seal in and onto its seat using the old seal as an interface

outer tube, then wipe the recess clean and re-seat the washer (see illustration).

24 Apply a smear of the clean fork oil to the lips of the new oil seal. Slide the seal onto the tube with its marked side facing up (see illustration). Remove the springs from the old oil seal and cut the seal in half using a hacksaw. Fit the old seal halves above the new seal to act as an interface to avoid damaging the new seal and drive the seal squarely into place (see illustrations). The new seal is seated when the old seal is flush with the rim of the outer tube – at this point remove the old seal and check that the retaining clip groove is fully exposed (see illustrations). If not drive the new seal in some more until it is.

25 Fit the retaining clip, making sure it is correctly located in its groove (see illustration).

26 Press the dust seal into the top of the outer tube (see illustration).

27 Refer to Section 7, Steps 6 to 9 and fill the fork with oil and finish reassembly.

28 If the damper rod bolt requires tightening (see Step 20), place the fork upside down on the floor between two pieces of wood (so the pre-load adjuster is off the floor), then have an assistant compress the fork so that the spring

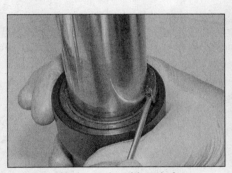

8.24c Hook out the old seal pieces...

presses on the damper rod head and tighten the bolt to the specified torque setting.

29 On SFV models fit the fork protector if removed, using a new one if necessary, and aligning the tab with the cut-out.

30 Fit the axle clamp bolt loosely into the bottom of the right-hand fork on 2004 to 2011 DL models and all SFV models, and the left-hand fork on 2012-on DL models (see illustration 8.2). Install the fork (see Section 6).

8.24d ...and make sure the retaining clip groove (arrowed) is fully exposed

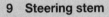 9 Steering stem

Special tool: Either the Suzuki special tool (Pt. Nos. 09940-14911, and also 09940-14960 on DL models), equivalent peg spanner, or a suitably sized C-spanner are useful for this procedure – see Step 7.

8.25 Fit the retaining clip in its groove...

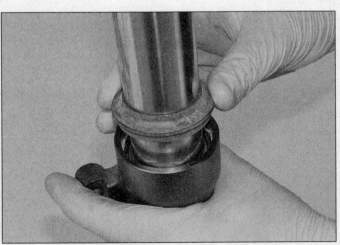

8.26 ...then press the dust seal in

9.2a Disconnect the turn signal wiring connectors (arrowed)

9.2b Headlight bracket bolts (arrowed)

9.2c Unscrew the bolt (arrowed) on each side

9.5a Release the wiring, cables and hose from the guides (arrowed)

Removal

1 On 2004 to 2011 DL models remove the fairing side panels, and on 2012-on DL models remove the complete fairing assembly (see Chapter 7).

2 On SFV models remove the headlight and instrument cluster (see Chapter 8). Disconnect the turn signal wiring connectors (see illustration). Unscrew the headlight bracket bolts and remove the bracket, noting the rubber hats on the top prongs and how they locate in the underside of the top yoke (see illustration). Unscrew the instrument bracket bolts and remove the bracket (see illustration).

3 As a precaution, remove the fuel tank (see Chapter 4) – though not actually essential, this will prevent the possibility of damage should a tool slip.

4 Remove the front forks (see Section 6).

5 Displace the handlebars from the top yoke (see Section 5) – on DL models release the wiring, cables and hose from their guides (see illustration). Displace the brake hose from the bottom yoke (see illustrations).

6 Wrap a layer of masking tape around the steering stem nut to prevent marking it. Unscrew the nut and remove the washer (see illustration). Gently ease the top yoke up off the steering stem and position it clear, using rag to protect other components (see illustration).

7 On DL models, unscrew and remove the locknut, using either a C-spanner, a peg

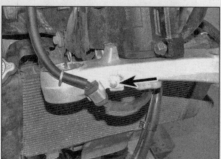

9.5b Brake hose holder bolt (arrowed) – DL

9.5c Brake hose holder bolt (arrowed) – SFV

9.6a Unscrew the steering stem nut and remove the washer...

9.6b ...and lift the top yoke off

9.7a Unscrew the locknut...

spanner or a drift located in one of the notches **(see illustration)**. Remove the lockwasher, noting how it fits **(see illustration)**.

8 If the Suzuki tool is not available, make an alignment mark between the adjuster nut and the frame – this can serve as a rough guide for the tightness of the adjuster nut on installation. As you unscrew the nut count the number of turns.

9 Support the bottom yoke and unscrew the adjuster nut using a peg-spanner, a C-spanner, or a drift located in one of the notches **(see illustration)**. Remove the grease seal, inner race and bearing from the top of the steering head **(see illustration)**. Gently lower the bottom yoke and steering stem out of the frame **(see illustration)**.

10 Remove the bearing from the base of the steering stem **(see illustration)**.

11 Remove all traces of old grease from the bearings and races and check them for wear or damage as described in Section 10. **Note:** *Do not attempt to remove the races from the steering head or the steering stem unless they are to be replaced with new ones (see Section 10).*

Installation

12 Check the condition of the grease seals and replace them with new ones if necessary – to fit a new lower bearing seal you have to remove the inner race first (see Section 10). Smear a liberal quantity of lithium-based multi-purpose grease onto the bearing races,

and work some grease well into both the upper and lower bearings, and smear the seals. Fit the lower bearing onto the steering stem **(see illustration 9.10)**.

13 Carefully lift the steering stem/bottom yoke up through the steering head and support it there **(see illustration 9.9d)**. Fit the upper bearing, the inner race and the grease seal **(see illustrations 9.9c and b)**. Thread the adjuster nut onto the steering stem and tighten it finger-tight **(see illustration 9.9a)**.

14 If the Suzuki service tool is available, tighten the adjuster nut to the torque setting specified at the beginning of the Chapter, then turn the steering stem through its full lock at least five times. Now slacken the adjuster nut by 1/4 to 1/2 a turn.

9.7b ...and remove the lockwasher

9.9a Unscrew the adjuster nut...

9.9b ...and remove the grease seal...

9.9c ...the inner race and upper bearing...

9.9d ...then remove the bottom yoke/ steering stem

9.10 Remove the lower bearing from the stem

9.15 Tightening the adjuster nut using a C-spanner

9.17 Fit one of the forks to align the yokes

15 If the Suzuki tool is not available, tighten the nut the number of turns recorded on removal using a C-spanner until the marks align, then turn it by 1/4 to 1/2 a turn more to pre-load the bearings **(see illustration)**. Turn the steering from lock-to-lock five times, then slacken the nut by 1/4 to 1/2 a turn until the marks align.

Caution: Take great care not to apply excessive pressure because this will cause premature failure of the bearings.

16 On DL models fit the washer, locating the inner tab in the groove **(see illustration 9.7b)**. Fit the locknut and tighten to the specified torque **(see illustration 9.7a)**.

17 Fit the top yoke onto the steering stem and forks **(see illustration 9.6b)**. Fit the washer and the steering stem nut finger-tight **(see illustration 9.6a)**. Fit one fork up into the yokes to align them and tighten the bottom

yoke clamp bolts to secure the fork **(see illustration)**. Tighten the steering stem nut to the torque setting specified at the beginning of the Chapter.

18 Install the remaining components in a reverse of the removal procedure, referring to the relevant Sections or Chapters, and to the torque settings specified at the beginning of the Chapter.

19 Carry out a final check of the steering head bearing freeplay as described in Chapter 1, and if necessary re-adjust.

10 Steering head bearings

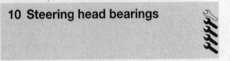

Inspection

1 Remove the steering stem (see Section 9).

2 Remove all traces of old grease from the bearings and races.

3 Inspect the races – they should be polished and free from indentations **(see illustrations)**. Inspect the bearing balls for signs of wear, damage or discoloration, and examine the ball retainer cage for signs of cracks or splits. If there are any signs of wear on any of the above components both upper and lower bearing assemblies must be renewed as a set. Only remove the outer races in the steering head and the lower bearing inner race on the steering stem if they need to be replaced with new ones – do not re-use them once they have been removed.

Replacement

4 The outer races are an interference fit in the steering head – tap them from position using a suitable drift, locating it in the notches that expose the inner rim of the race, and moving from notch to notch so the race is driven out square **(see illustrations)**. Tap firmly and evenly between the recesses to ensure the race is driven out squarely.

5 Press the new outer races into the head using a drawbolt arrangement **(see illustration)**, or drive them in using a large diameter tubular drift. Ensure that the drawbolt washer or drift (as applicable) bears only on the outer edge of the race and does not contact the working surface. Alternatively, have the races installed by a Suzuki dealer equipped with the bearing race installation tools.

> **HAYNES HINT** *Installation of new bearing outer races is made much easier if the races are left overnight in the freezer. This causes them to contract slightly making them a looser fit. Alternatively, use a freeze spray.*

10.3a Check the outer races (top arrowed) in the top and bottom of the steering head

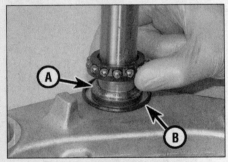

10.3b The lower bearing inner race (A) is on the steering stem, with a grease seal (B) underneath

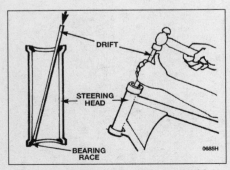

10.4a Drive the bearing races out with a brass drift...

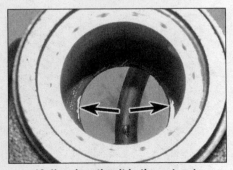

10.4b ...locating it in the cut-outs (arrowed)

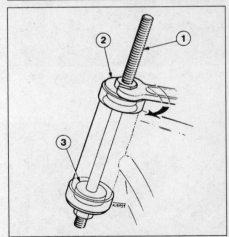

10.5 Drawbolt arrangement for fitting steering stem bearing races

1 Long bolt or threaded bar
2 Thick washer
3 Guide for lower race

6 Only remove the lower bearing inner race from the steering stem if a new one is being fitted. To remove the race, position the yoke on its front with the stem resting on a piece of wood so the threads are clear to prevent damage. Tap under the race using a cold chisel to displace it, and if required use two screwdrivers placed on opposite sides to work it free, using blocks of wood to improve leverage and protect the yoke (see illustrations). If the race is firmly in place it will be necessary to use a puller (see illustration). Take the steering stem to a Suzuki dealer if required. Remove the seal – a new one must be used.

7 Fit the new seal with its dished side facing up. Fit the new lower race onto the steering stem. Drive the race into position using a length of tubing with an internal diameter slightly larger than the steering stem, and make sure that it bears only on the inner rim of the race and does not contact the working surface (see illustration) – heating the race and cooling the steering stem will make installation easier, or use an hydraulic press if necessary.

8 Install the steering stem (see Section 9).

11 Rear shock absorber

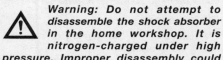

⚠️ **Warning: Do not attempt to disassemble the shock absorber in the home workshop. It is nitrogen-charged under high pressure. Improper disassembly could result in serious injury.**

Removal

1 Support the motorcycle on an auxiliary stand that does not take the weight through any part of the rear suspension, or by using a

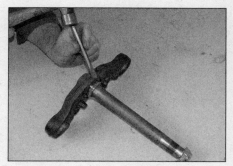

10.6a Remove the lower bearing race using a cold chisel...

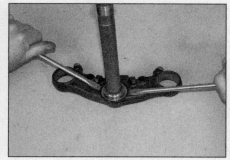

10.6b ...and/or screwdrivers...

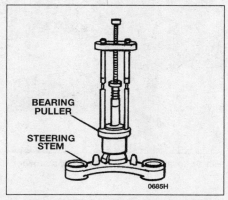

BEARING PULLER

STEERING STEM

0685H

10.6c ...or using a puller if necessary

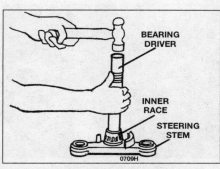

BEARING DRIVER

INNER RACE

STEERING STEM

0709H

10.7 Drive the new inner race on using a suitable bearing driver or a length of pipe that bears only against the inner rim and not the bearing surface

hoist – we placed the bike on its sidestand and positioned an axle stand under the frame on the right-hand side (see illustration). Tie the front brake lever to the handlebar to ensure the bike can't roll forward. Position a support under the rear wheel or swingarm so that it does not drop when the shock absorber is removed, but also making sure that the weight of the machine is off the rear suspension so that the shock is not compressed. Make a

note of which side the bolts go in from, and which way round the shock absorber fits.

2 On SFV models remove the side covers (see Chapter 7).

3 On all DL models unscrew the remote pre-load adjuster bolts, displace the adjuster and release the hose from its clamp, and on 2012-on DL650A models also unscrew the brake pipe guide bolt (see illustration).

4 Unscrew the nut and withdraw the bolt

11.1 One way of supporting the bike

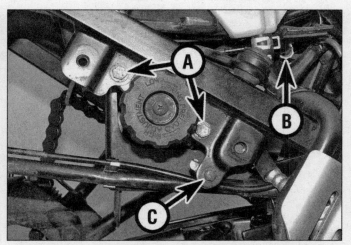

11.3 Pre-load adjuster bolts (A), clamp (B) and guide bolt (C)

11.4 Unscrew the nut, withdraw the bolt and displace the rods

11.5 Unscrew the nut, withdraw the bolt and displace the arm

11.6a Unscrew the top bolt nut (arrowed)…

11.6b …withdraw the bolt…

11.6c …and remove the shock absorber

11.7 Check for corrosion and oil leakage on the rod (arrowed)

securing the linkage rods to the swingarm and move the rods down (see illustration).

5 Unscrew the nut and withdraw the bolt securing the bottom of the shock absorber and move the linkage arm down (see illustration).

6 Unscrew the nut on the bolt securing the top of the shock absorber (see illustration). Support the shock and withdraw the bolt, then remove the shock absorber, on DL models feeding the adjuster down and noting the routing of the hose (see illustrations).

Inspection

7 Check the shock absorber for obvious physical damage and oil leakage, and the spring for looseness, cracks or signs of fatigue (see illustration).

8 Check the bush in the top of the shock absorber for wear or damage (see illustration).

9 On DL models check the adjuster hose for damage.

10 Parts are not available for the original equipment shock absorber. If it is worn or damaged, it must be replaced with a new one. Before disposing of the old shock absorber, you should release the nitrogen gas from the top. To do this, make a drill point where shown (see illustrations). Mount the shock in a vice. Drill a hole using a sharp 2 or 3 mm drill bit to release the gas – it is best to cover the shock and drill and avert your face to prevent the possibility of injury, making sure the material used does not get caught in the chuck as it spins.

 Warning: Wear protective eyewear and be very careful when releasing the gas pressure – it is possible for fine debris particles to be released

with it, and as the pressure is high these could damage your eyes if done carelessly.

Installation

11 Installation is the reverse of removal, noting the following:

● Smear grease onto the shock absorber bolt shafts. Fit the bolts in from the left side.
● On DL models fit the shock absorber with the remote pre-load adjuster hose facing back.
● Fit all nuts/bolts loosely at first, and when all components are in place tighten them to the torque settings specified at the beginning of the Chapter.
● On DL models do not forget to secure the adjuster hose in its clamp, and where relevant to refit the brake hose guide (see illustration 11.3).

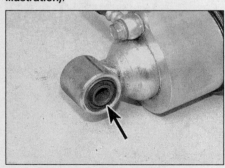

11.8 Check the bush (arrowed)

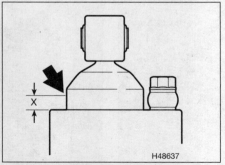

11.10a Shock absorber gas dispersal drill point (arrowed) – DL

X = 7 mm

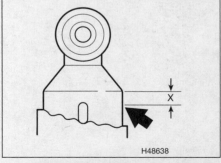

11.10b Shock absorber gas dispersal drill point (arrowed) – SFV

X = 7 mm

12.4 Unscrew the nut, withdraw the bolt and remove the rods

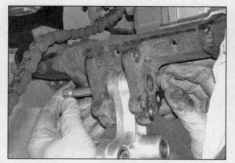

12.5a Unscrew the nut, withdraw the bolt and remove the arm…

12.5b …along with the washers on DL

12.6a Withdraw the sleeves and check the bearings

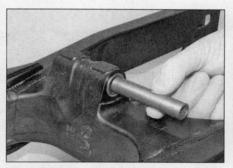

12.6b Withdraw the sleeve and check the bearings in the swingarm

12.12 Each rod has a marked side, though corrosion may make it difficult to see

12 Rear suspension linkage

Removal

1 Support the motorcycle on an auxiliary stand that does not take the weight through any part of the rear suspension, or by using a hoist. Tie the front brake lever to the handlebar to ensure the bike can't roll forward. Position a support under the rear wheel or swingarm so that it does not drop when the shock absorber is removed, but also making sure that the weight of the machine is off the rear suspension so that the shock is not compressed. Make a note of which side the bolts go in from, and which way round the shock absorber fits.
2 Unscrew the nut and withdraw the bolt securing the linkage rods to the swingarm **(see illustration 11.4)**.
3 Unscrew the nut and withdraw the bolt securing the bottom of the shock absorber to the linkage arm **(see illustration 11.5)**.
4 Unscrew the nut and withdraw the bolt securing the linkage rods to the linkage arm and remove the rods **(see illustration)**.
5 Unscrew the nut and withdraw bolt securing the linkage arm to the frame, remove the linkage arm, and on DL models collect the washers that fit between it and the bracket on each side **(see illustrations)**.

Inspection

6 Withdraw the sleeves from the linkage arm

and from the rod's pivot in the swingarm **(see illustrations)**.
7 Thoroughly clean all components, removing all traces of dirt, corrosion and grease.
8 Check the linkage rods and arm closely, looking for obvious signs of wear such as heavy scoring, or for damage such as cracks or distortion. Replace worn or damaged components with new ones as required.
9 Check the condition of the bearings. Fit the sleeves back in and check for play between them and the bearings. Refer to *Tools and Workshop Tips* in the Reference section for more information on bearings. Inspect all components closely, looking for obvious signs of wear such as heavy scoring, or for damage such as cracks or distortion. Replace worn or damaged components with new ones as required.
10 Worn bearings can be driven or drawn out

13.2 Withdraw the adjuster from each side of the swingarm

of their bores, but note that removal will destroy them; new bearings should be obtained before work commences. Pack the new bearings with lithium-based multi-purpose grease and press or draw them into their bores – do not drive them in. In the absence of a press, a suitable drawbolt tool can be made up as described in *Tools and Workshop Tips* in the Reference section. When fitting the new bearings set their marked outer facing rim flush with the surface of the housing in the linkage arm or swingarm.
11 Lubricate the bearings and sleeves with grease and slide them into the bearings **(see illustrations 12.6a and b)**.

Installation

12 Installation is the reverse of removal, noting the following:
● Make sure the marked side of each linkage rod faces out **(see illustration)**.
● Fit all nuts/bolts loosely at first, and when all components are in place tighten them to the torque settings specified at the beginning of the Chapter.

13 Swingarm

Removal

1 Remove the exhaust system (see Chapter 4).
2 Remove the rear wheel (see Chapter 6). Remove the chain adjusters, noting how they fit **(see illustration)**.

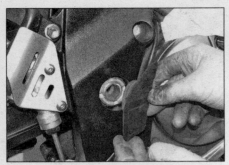

13.5 Remove the pivot caps

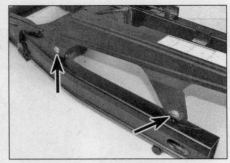

13.6a Chainguard screws (arrowed)

13.6b Use a peg spanner to unscrew the locknut (arrowed)

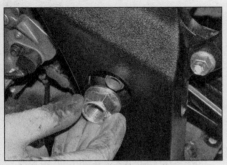

13.6c Unscrew the nut...

13.6d ...withdraw the pivot bolt and remove the swingarm

3 Either remove the rear shock absorber, or if preferred just detach the linkage rods from the swingarm and the linkage arm from the shock absorber (Section 11).

4 Release the brake hose and where fitted the speed sensor wire from the swingarm.

5 On DL models remove the swingarm pivot cap from each side (see illustration).

6 On DL models, if required remove the chainguard (see illustration). Unscrew the swingarm pivot locknut using the Suzuki tool (Part No. 09940-14940) or equivalent peg spanner (that can be made by cutting sections out of the rim of a 28 or 30 mm socket) (see illustration). Hold the pivot bolt using a 19 mm hex bit and unscrew the nut (see illustration). Unscrew the pivot bolt. Withdraw the bolt and manoeuvre the swingarm back out of the frame (see illustration).

7 On SFV models remove the chainguard (see illustrations). Unscrew the pivot bolt nut and remove the washer (see illustration). Withdraw the bolt and manoeuvre the swingarm back out of the frame.

8 If required remove the chain slider (see illustration).

Inspection

9 Remove the collar (DL models) or sleeve (SFV models) from each side of the pivot (see illustrations).

10 Thoroughly clean all pivot components,

13.7a Undo the screws (arrowed)...

13.7b ...and the screws (arrowed) and remove the chainguard

13.7c Pivot bolt nut (arrowed)

13.8 Chain slider (arrowed) – DL shown

13.9 Remove the collar (shown) or sleeve from each side

13.12 Check the bearing (arrowed) in each side

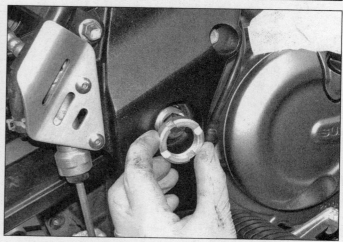

13.18 Fit the locknut and tighten it using the peg spanner

removing all traces of dirt, corrosion and old grease.

11 Check the swingarm closely, looking for obvious signs of wear such as heavy scoring, or for damage such as cracks or distortion.

12 Check the condition of the bearings – there is a needle bearing in each side **(see illustration)**. Fit the collar or sleeve back in each needle bearing and check for play between them. Refer to *Tools and Workshop Tips* in the Reference section for more information on bearings. Inspect all components closely, looking for obvious signs of wear such as heavy scoring, or for damage such as cracks or distortion. Replace worn or damaged components with new ones as required.

13 Worn bearings can be pulled out of their bores using an expanding internal puller, but note that removal will damage them. Heat around the bearing housing with a hot air gun to ease removal. Remove the inner sleeve that sits between the bearings, and clean it. Fit it back in before fitting the second bearing. Pack the new bearings with the lithium-based multi purpose grease, and press or draw them in with the marked side facing out, setting them flush with the rim of the housing – do not drive them in. In the absence of a press, a suitable

drawbolt tool can be made up as described in *Tools and Workshop Tips* in the Reference section.

14 Lubricate the collars or sleeves with grease. Fit them into the bearings **(see illustration 13.9)**.

15 Check the chain slider for wear and damage and fit a new one if necessary.

Installation

16 Fit the chain slider if removed **(see illustration 13.8)**.

17 Clean the swingarm pivot bolt and smear it with grease. Offer up the swingarm and slide the pivot bolt through from the right-hand side on DL models **(see illustration 13.6d)**, and from the left on SFV models.

18 On DL models tighten the pivot bolt to the torque setting specified at the beginning of the Chapter using the 19 mm hex bit. Now hold the bolt, fit the nut and tighten to the specified torque. Fit the locknut and tighten to the specified torque **(see illustration)**. Check the swingarm moves up and down smoothly and freely. Fit the chainguard if removed **(see illustration 13.6a)**. Fit the swingarm pivot caps **(see illustration 13.5)**.

19 On SFV models fit the washer and nut onto the pivot bolt, then hold the bolt and tighten

the nut to the torque setting specified at the beginning of the Chapter **(see illustration 13.7c)**. Check the swingarm moves up and down smoothly and freely. Fit the chainguard **(see illustrations 13.7b and a)**.

20 Secure the brake hose and where fitted the speed sensor wire to the swingarm.

21 Install the remaining components in reverse order. Check the operation of the rear suspension and brake before taking the bike on the road.

14 Suspension adjustment

Front forks

1 The forks have adjustable spring pre-load.

2 Pre-load is adjusted by turning the adjuster in the fork top bolt **(see illustration)**. To increase the pre-load, turn the adjuster clockwise. To decrease the pre-load, turn the adjuster anti-clockwise. The settings are identified by lines on the adjuster. The standard position is with the third line from the top level with the top bolt hex on 2004 to 2011 DL models and all SFV models, and the second line from the top on 2012-on DL models. The maximum position is with the adjuster flush with the top bolt hex, and the minimum is with the fifth line level on 2004 to 2011 DL models and SFV models, and the fourth line just level on 2012-on DL models.

Rear shock absorber

DL models

3 The shock absorber has adjustable spring pre-load and rebound damping.

4 Pre-load is adjusted by turning the knob on the right-hand side of the bike **(see illustration)**. Turning it clockwise increases pre-load, and anti-clockwise decreases it. Visible lines on the adjuster body indicate the

14.2 Fork pre-load adjuster (arrowed) shown with third line above top bolt hex

14.4 Spring pre-load adjuster (arrowed) – DL

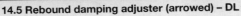

14.5 Rebound damping adjuster (arrowed) – DL

14.7a Spring pre-load adjuster (arrowed)...

amount of pre-load – the standard position is with two lines visible, the softest position with no lines visible, and the hardest with five lines visible.

5 Rebound damping is adjusted by turning the screw on the bottom of the shock absorber on the left-hand side **(see illustration)**. To increase damping, turn the screw clockwise. To decrease damping, turn the screw anti-clockwise. To set the standard position, turn the screw clockwise until it lightly seats, then turn it anti-clockwise 1 turn on 2004 to 2011 Europe and Australia models, 1 1/2 turns on 2004 to 2011 US and Canada models, and 2 turns on all 2012-on models, so that the punch marks align.

SFV models

6 The shock absorber has adjustable spring pre-load.

7 Pre-load is adjusted using a suitable C-spanner (one is provided in the toolkit) on the adjuster ring on the top of the shock absorber **(see illustrations)**. Turn it clockwise to decrease pre-load and anti-clockwise to increase it. The amount of pre-load is indicated by the position of the adjuster relative to its stop. There are seven positions – the standard setting is number 3.

14.7b ...turn it using the tool provided – SFV

Chapter 6
Brakes, wheels and final drive

Contents

Degrees of difficulty

Easy, suitable for novice with little experience 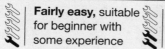 | **Fairly easy,** suitable for beginner with some experience | **Fairly difficult,** suitable for competent DIY mechanic | **Difficult,** suitable for experienced DIY mechanic | **Very difficult,** suitable for expert DIY or professional

Specifications

Brake fluid
Brake fluid type . . . .   DOT 4

Brake pads
Friction material minimum thickness . . . .   1.0 mm

Front brake discs
Thickness
  DL models
    Standard . . . .   5.0 mm
    Service limit . . . .   4.5 mm
  SFV models
    Standard . . . .   4.5 mm
    Service limit . . . .   4.0 mm
Maximum runout . . . .   0.3 mm

Rear brake disc
Thickness
  Standard . . . .   5.0 mm
  Service limit . . . .   4.5 mm
Maximum runout . . . .   0.3 mm

ABS system
Wheel speed sensor air gap
  2007 to 2011 DL models . . . .   0.3 to 1.5 mm
  2012-on DL models . . . .   0.25 to 1.65 mm
  SFV models
    Front sensor . . . .   0.20 to 1.86 mm
    Rear sensor . . . .   0.21 to 1.57 mm

Wheels

Maximum wheel runout (front and rear)	
Axial (side-to-side)	2.0 mm
Radial (out-of-round)	2.0 mm
Maximum axle runout (front and rear)	0.25 mm
Rim size	
DL models	
Front	19 x MT2.50
Rear	17 x MT4.00
SFV models	
Front	17 x MT3.50
Rear	17 x MT5.00

Tyres

Tyre pressures	see *Pre-ride* checks
Tyres	
DL models	
Front	110/80-R19M/C (59H) tubeless
Rear	150/70-R17M/C (69H) tubeless
SFV models	
Front	120/70-ZR17M/C (58W) tubeless
Rear	160/60-ZR17M/C (69W) tubeless

Refer to the owners handbook or the tyre information label on the swingarm for approved tyre brands.

Final drive

Drive chain slack and lubricant	see Chapter 1
Drive chain size, no. of links (original equipment type)	
2004 to 2006 DL models	525, 116 links (DID525V8)
2007 to 2011 DL models	525, 118 links (DID525V8)
2012-on DL models	525, 118 links (RK525SMOZ8)
SFV models	520, 112 links (DID520VM2)
Joining link sideplate distance (outside to outside)	
2004 to 2011 DL models	18.7 to 18.9 mm
2012-on DL models	18.6 to 18.9 mm
SFV models	17.1 to 17.3 mm
Joining link staked ends diameter	
DID	5.50 to 5.80 mm
RK	5.45 to 5.85 mm
Sprocket sizes (No. of teeth)	
DL models	
Front (engine) sprocket	15
Rear (wheel) sprocket	47
SFV models	
Front (engine) sprocket	15
Rear (wheel) sprocket	46

Torque settings

ABS wheel speed rotor bolts	6 Nm
Brake caliper bleed valves	
Front calipers	7.5 Nm
Rear caliper	6 Nm
Brake disc bolts (front and rear)	23 Nm
Brake hose banjo bolts	23 Nm
Brake pipe flare nuts	16 Nm
Front axle	65 Nm
Front axle clamp bolt	23 Nm
Front brake caliper mounting bolts	39 Nm
Front brake master cylinder clamp bolts	10 Nm
Front sprocket nut	145 Nm
Rear axle nut	100 Nm
Rear brake pad pin	17 Nm
Rear brake caliper mounting bolt	23 Nm
Rear brake caliper slider pin	27 Nm
Rear brake master cylinder mounting bolts	10 Nm
Rear sprocket nuts	60 Nm
Speed sensor rotor bolt (speedometer)	
2012-on DL models	28 Nm
SFV models	25 Nm

1 General information

All models covered in this manual are fitted with cast alloy wheels designed for tubeless tyres only. Both front and rear brakes are hydraulically operated disc brakes.

The hydraulic braking system has two twin piston sliding calipers at the front, and a single piston sliding caliper at the rear.

An ABS system is fitted on DL650A and SFV650A models.

Caution: Disc brake components rarely require disassembly. Do not disassemble components unless absolutely necessary. If an hydraulic brake hose is loosened or disconnected, the banjo union sealing washers must be replaced with new

ones and the system must be bled upon reassembly. Do not use solvents on internal brake components. Solvents will cause the seals to swell and distort. Use only clean DOT 4 brake fluid for cleaning. Use care when working with brake fluid as it can injure your eyes and it will damage painted surfaces and plastic parts.

2 Front brake pads

Caution: Do not operate the brakes while a caliper is off the disc.

1 Displace the brake hose holder from the mudguard (**see illustrations**). Lay some rag over the mudguard to prevent the loose guides scratching it.

2 Unscrew the caliper mounting bolts and

slide the caliper off the disc (**see illustration**).
3 Pull the retaining clip out of the pad pin, then withdraw the pin (**see illustrations**). Pivot the inner pad out of the caliper until it clears the bracket then slide it sideways off its post (**see illustration**). Remove the outer pad, noting how it locates against the guide (**see illustration**).
4 If required remove the shim from the back of each pad, noting how it fits (**see illustration**) – note that new pads should come with new shims where applicable, but make sure they do, especially if fitting after-market pads, before discarding the old ones (the shims are also available separately if required).
5 Slide the caliper and bracket apart (**see illustration**). Clean all old grease off the slider pins. Check the condition of the rubber boots and replace them with new ones if necessary.
6 Inspect the surface of each pad for contamination and check that the friction

2.1a Brake hose holder bolt (arrowed) – DL, right-hand side

2.1b Brake hose holder bolt (arrowed) – DL, left-hand side

2.2 Unscrew the bolts (arrowed) and slide the caliper off

2.3a Remove the clip...

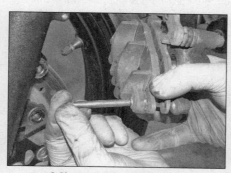

2.3b ...withdraw the pin...

2.3c ...then remove the inner pad...

2.3d ...and the outer pad

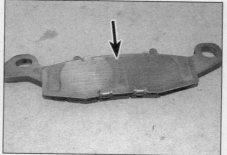

2.4 Brake pad shim (arrowed)

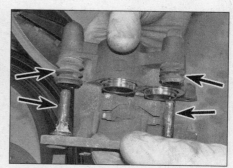

2.5 Slide the caliper and bracket apart. Clean and check the pins and the boots (arrowed)

2.8a Press the pistons in using hand pressure…

2.8b …some grips and a piece of wood…

2.8c …or a purpose-made tool

material has not worn to or beyond its service limit (see Chapter 1, Section 2). If any pad is worn, fouled with oil or grease, or heavily scored or damaged, fit a complete set of new pads. Also check that wear is even across each pad – uneven wear is indicative of a sticking or seized piston (see Steps 8 and 9). **Note:** *It is not possible to degrease the friction material; if the pads are contaminated in any way they must be replaced with new ones.*

7 If the pads are in good condition clean them carefully, using a fine wire brush that is completely free of oil and grease to remove all traces of road dirt and corrosion. Using a pointed instrument, dig out any embedded particles of foreign matter. Spray with a dedicated brake cleaner.

8 Remove the pad spring from the caliper if required, noting which way round it fits **(see illustration 2.12a)**. Clean around the exposed section of each piston to remove any dirt or debris that could cause the seals to be damaged. If new pads are being fitted check the fluid level in the reservoir before pushing the pistons in to create room for them (see *Pre-ride checks*) – if the fluid level is not near the LOWER level line it may be necessary to remove the master cylinder reservoir cap, plate and diaphragm and remove some fluid. If new pads are being fitted, now push the pistons all the way back into the caliper to create room for them; if the old pads are still serviceable push the pistons in a little way. To push the pistons back use finger pressure or a piece of wood or metal as leverage, or

place the old pads back in the caliper and use a metal bar or a screwdriver inserted between them (but take care not to damage the friction surface if the pads are being re-used), or use grips or a G-clamp and a piece of wood, with rag or card to protect the caliper body **(see illustrations)**. Alternatively obtain a proper piston-pushing tool from a good tool supplier **(see illustration)**. If the pistons are difficult to push back, remove the bleed valve cap, then attach a length of clear hose to the bleed valve and place the open end in a suitable container, then open the valve and try again (see Section 11). Take great care not to draw any air into the system. If in doubt, bleed the brakes afterwards.

9 If a piston appears seized, first block or hold the other piston using wood or cable-ties, then apply the brake lever and check whether the piston in question moves at all. If it moves out but can't be pushed back in the chances are there is some hidden corrosion stopping it. If it doesn't move at all, or to fully clean and inspect the pistons, disassemble the caliper and overhaul it (see Section 3).

10 Remove all traces of corrosion from the pad pin and check for wear and damage.

11 Check the condition of the brake disc (see Section 4).

12 Clean the pad spring and fit it into the caliper if removed, making sure it locates correctly **(see illustration)**. Clean the pad guide on the bracket and check it is correctly fitted **(see illustration)**.

13 Smear the slider pins and inside the rubber

boots with silicone grease **(see illustration 2.5)**. Slide the caliper and bracket together, making sure each boot lip locates correctly in the groove in the pin.

14 Where fitted and if removed fit the shim onto the back of each pad, making sure it locates correctly **(see illustration 2.4)**. Clean the outer face of each shim so it is shiny.

15 Fit the outer pad into the caliper so that the shim on the back is against the pistons, making sure the inner end locates correctly against the guide on the bracket **(see illustration 2.3d)**. Fit the inner pad over its post, then slide it across and pivot it down **(see illustration 2.3c)**. Press the pads up against the pad spring to align the holes and insert the pad pin **(see illustration 2.3b)**. Secure the pin with the retaining clip, making sure it fits through the hole in the pin – if necessary rotate the pad pin to align the hole correctly **(see illustration 2.3a)**. Use a new clip if the old one is corroded or deformed in any way.

16 Slide the caliper onto the disc making sure the pads locate correctly on each side **(see illustration)**. Fit the caliper mounting bolts and tighten them to the torque setting specified at the beginning of the Chapter.

17 Fit the brake hose holder onto the fork **(see illustration 2.1a or b)**.

18 Operate the brake lever until the pads contact the discs. Check the level of fluid in each reservoir and top-up if necessary (see *Pre-ride checks*).

19 Check the operation of the brakes before riding the motorcycle.

2.12a Make sure the pad spring (arrowed)…

2.12b …and guide (arrowed) are clean and correctly fitted

2.16 Slide the caliper onto the disc and fit the bolts

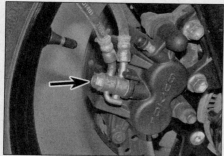

3.2a Brake hose banjo bolt (arrowed) and hose arrangement – right-hand caliper

3.2b Brake hose banjo bolt (arrowed) – left-hand caliper

3.2c Seal the banjo using a nut and bolt and the sealing washers

3 Front brake calipers

⚠️ **Warning: Overhaul of the brake calipers must be done in a spotlessly clean work area to avoid contamination and possible failure of the brake hydraulic system components. Do not, under any circumstances, use petroleum-based solvents to clean brake parts. Use clean DOT 4 brake fluid, dedicated brake cleaner or denatured alcohol only, as described. To prevent damage from spilled brake fluid, always cover paintwork when working on the braking system, and have plenty of absorbent rag to hand to catch and wipe off any spilled fluid.**

Removal

Note: *If the caliper is being overhauled (usually due to sticking pistons or fluid leaks) read through the entire procedure first and make sure that you have obtained all the new parts required, including some new DOT 4 brake fluid.*

Caution: Do not operate the brakes while a caliper is off the disc.

1 If you just want to displace the calipers for front wheel or fork removal, displace the brake hose holders from the forks (see illustrations 2.1a and b). Lay some rag over the mudguard to prevent the loose guides scratching it. Unscrew the caliper mounting bolts and slide the caliper assembly off the disc (see illustration 2.2). Tie the front brake calipers and hoses back so that they are out of the way.

2 If the caliper is being completely removed or overhauled, stuff some rag around the brake hose banjo union. Note the alignment of the brake hose(s) (see illustrations). Unscrew the hose banjo bolt and detach the union(s), catching the brake fluid. Seal the union(s) – one way of doing this is to fit a suitable bolt and nut with the old sealing washers (see illustration). Note that new sealing washers will be required later.

3 If the caliper is being overhauled, follow the procedure in Section 2, Steps 1 to 5,

and remove the brake pads – this involves removing the caliper from the disc and sliding the caliper and bracket apart.

Overhaul

4 Clean the exterior of the caliper with denatured alcohol or brake system cleaner. Have some clean rag ready to catch any spilled brake fluid.

5 To remove the pistons you need either a supply of compressed air, or a piston removal tool, or if neither are available a good pair of external circlip removal pliers (see illustration).

6 If you use compressed air wedge some rag or a piece of wood between the piston and the inner side of the caliper (see illustration 7.6a). Gradually and progressively apply the compressed air, starting with a fairly low pressure, to the fluid passage and allow the

piston to ease out of the bore (see illustration 7.6b). Make sure the pistons are displaced evenly, using a piece of wood to block one while another moves if necessary.

7 If you are using a dedicated tool or the circlip pliers, grip the inner wall then twist and pull the piston out, keeping it square to the bore wall. Do not try to remove a piston by levering it out or by using pliers or other grips that may scratch the outer wall, unless you are prepared to fit a new piston, and possibly a new caliper.

8 If a piston is stuck in its bore due to corrosion the caliper should be replaced with a new one.

9 Mark each piston and the caliper body to ensure that the pistons can be matched to their original bores on reassembly.

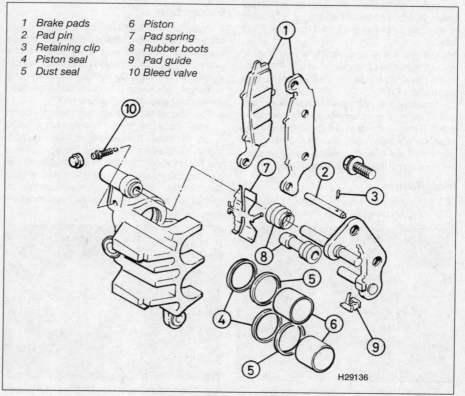

1 Brake pads
2 Pad pin
3 Retaining clip
4 Piston seal
5 Dust seal
6 Piston
7 Pad spring
8 Rubber boots
9 Pad guide
10 Bleed valve

H29136

3.5 Front brake caliper components

3.18 Use a new sealing washer on each side of the banjo union

10 Remove the dust seals and the piston seals from the bores using a plastic tool to avoid scratching the bores **(see illustration 7.9)**. Discard the seals – new ones must be fitted on reassembly.

11 Clean the pistons and bores with clean brake fluid. If compressed air is available, blow it through the fluid passages to ensure they are clear (make sure it is filtered and unlubricated).
Caution: Do not, under any circumstances, use a petroleum-based solvent to clean brake parts.

12 Inspect the caliper bores and pistons for signs of corrosion, nicks and burrs and loss of plating. If surface defects are present, the pistons and/or the caliper assembly must be replaced with new ones.

13 Lubricate the new piston seals with clean brake fluid and fit them into the inner grooves in the caliper bores **(see illustrations 7.12a and b)**.

14 Lubricate the new dust seals with clean brake fluid or silicone grease and fit them into the outer grooves in the caliper bores **(see illustration 7.13)**.

15 Lubricate the pistons with clean brake fluid and fit them, closed-end first, into the caliper bores, taking care not to displace the seals **(see illustration 7.14a)**. Using your thumbs, push the pistons all the way in, making sure they enter the bore square **(see illustration 7.14b)**.

Installation

16 If the caliper was overhauled refer to Section 2 and if not already done clean and check the pads, pad pin, slider pins, rubber boots, guide and spring. Fit the brake pads into the caliper and the caliper onto the disc.

17 If the caliper was just displaced slide it onto the disc making sure the pads locate correctly on each side **(see illustration 2.16)**. Fit the caliper mounting bolts and tighten them to the torque setting specified at the beginning of the Chapter.

18 If detached, connect the brake hose(s) to the caliper, using new sealing washers on each side of the banjo union(s), and align it/them as noted on removal **(see illustration)** – where two hoses are fitted with one banjo bolt on the front caliper three washers are needed, one on the outer side of each union and one between the unions **(see illustration 3.2a and b)**. Tighten the banjo bolt to the specified torque setting.

19 Fit the brake hose holder onto the fork **(see illustration 2.1a or b)**.

20 Refer to Section 11 and bleed the system.

21 Operate the brake lever until the pads contact the discs. Check the level of fluid in each reservoir and top-up if necessary (see *Pre-ride checks*).

22 Check that there are no fluid leaks and test the operation of the brakes before riding the motorcycle.

4 Front brake discs

Inspection

1 Inspect the surface of the disc for score marks and other damage. Light scratches are normal after use and won't affect brake operation, but deep grooves and heavy score marks will reduce braking efficiency and accelerate pad wear. If a disc is badly grooved it must be replaced with a new one.

2 The disc must not be allowed to wear down to a thickness less than the service limit listed in this Chapter's Specifications. The minimum thickness is also stamped on the disc. Check the thickness of the disc in the middle of the pad contact area using a micrometer **(see illustration)** – do not measure across the rim of the disc with a ruler. Replace the disc with a new one if necessary.

3 To check if the disc is warped, position the bike on the centrestand and support it so the front wheel is off the ground. Mount a dial gauge to the fork leg, with the gauge plunger touching the surface of the disc about 2 mm from its outer edge **(see illustration)**. Rotate the wheel and watch the gauge needle, comparing the reading with the limit listed in the Specifications at the beginning of this Chapter. If the runout is greater than the service limit, check the wheel bearings for play (see Chapter 1). If the bearings are worn, install new ones (see Section 19) and repeat this check. If the disc runout is still excessive, remove the disc (Steps 4 and 5) and check for corrosion where it seats on the hub and clean it up if necessary. You can also try moving the disc around the wheel one bolt hole at a time and after each movement rechecking for runout. In most cases a new disc will have to be fitted.

Removal

4 Remove the wheel (see Section 17).
Caution: Don't lay the wheel down and allow it to rest on either disc – the disc could become warped. Set the wheel on wood blocks so the wheel rim supports the weight of the wheel.

5 If you are not replacing the disc with a new one, mark the relationship of the disc to the wheel, so it can be installed in the same position and on the same side as originally fitted. Unscrew the disc bolts, loosening them evenly and a little at a time in a criss-cross pattern to avoid distorting the disc, then remove the disc **(see illustration)**.

Installation

6 Before fitting the disc, make sure there is no dirt or corrosion where the disc seats on the hub. If the disc does not sit flat when it is bolted down, it will appear to be warped when checked or when the front brake is used.

7 Fit the disc on the wheel with its marked side facing out, aligning the previously applied matchmarks (if you're reinstalling the original disc), and making sure the arrow points in the direction of normal rotation.

8 Clean the threads of the bolts and apply fresh thread locking compound, and tighten them evenly and a little at a time in a criss-cross

4.2 Check disc thickness using a micrometer

4.3 Checking disc runout with a dial gauge

4.5 Brake disc bolts (arrowed)

pattern to the torque setting specified at the beginning of this Chapter. Clean the disc using acetone or brake system cleaner. If a new disc has been installed, remove any protective coating from its working surfaces and fit new brake pads.

9 Install the front wheel (see Section 17).

10 Operate the brake lever until the pads contact the discs. Check the level of fluid in each reservoir and top-up if necessary (see *Pre-ride checks*).

11 Check the operation of the brakes before riding the motorcycle.

5.1 Disconnect the brake light switch connector (arrowed)

5.3 Slacken the cover screws

5 Front brake master cylinder

⚠️ *Warning: Overhaul must be done in a spotlessly clean work area to avoid contamination and possible failure of the brake hydraulic system components. Do not, under any circumstances, use petroleum-based solvents to clean brake parts. Use clean DOT 4 brake fluid, dedicated brake cleaner or denatured alcohol only, as described. To prevent damage from spilled brake fluid, always cover paintwork when working on the braking system, and have plenty of absorbent rag to hand to catch and wipe off any spilled fluid.*

Note: *If the master cylinder is being overhauled (usually due to sticking or poor action, or fluid leaks), a rebuild kit is available*

that includes the boot, circlip, piston, seal, cup and spring. Some DOT 4 brake/clutch fluid is also required.

Removal

1 Disconnect the brake light switch wiring connector **(see illustration)**.

2 Remove the brake lever (see Chapter 5). Remove the mirror (see Chapter 7).

3 Slacken the reservoir cover screws **(see illustration)**.

4 Stuff some rag under the master cylinder. Note the alignment of the brake hose. Unscrew the hose banjo bolt and detach the banjo union, catching the brake fluid **(see illustration)**. Seal the union – one way of doing this is to fit a suitable bolt and nut with the old sealing washers **(see illustration 3.2c)**. Note that new sealing washers will be required later.

5 Unscrew the master cylinder clamp bolts then lift the master cylinder away from the handlebar **(see illustration)**.

6 Remove the reservoir cover, diaphragm plate and the diaphragm and tip the fluid from the master cylinder and reservoir into a suitable container for disposal (do not re-use the fluid or mix it with new fluid). Wipe any remaining fluid out of the reservoir with a clean rag.

Overhaul

7 Remove the rubber boot from the master cylinder **(see illustration)**.

8 Push the piston in and use circlip pliers to remove the circlip, then slide out the piston assembly and spring, noting how they fit **(see illustrations)**.

9 Clean the master cylinder and reservoir with clean brake fluid.

5.4 Brake hose banjo bolt (arrowed)

5.5 Unscrew the clamp bolts (arrowed) and remove the master cylinder

5.7 Remove the boot from the end of the master cylinder piston...

5.8a ...then depress the piston, remove the circlip...

5.8b ...and draw out the piston...

5.8c ...and spring

5.12a Make sure the seal is correctly installed on the piston

5.12b Fit the cup onto the end of the spring

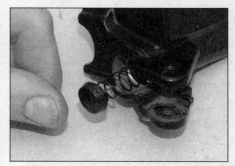

5.13a Fit the spring into the master cylinder

5.13b Push the piston into the bore...

5.13c ...then fit the circlip...

5.13d ...and push the piston in and locate the circlip in the groove

Caution: Do not, under any circumstances, use a petroleum-based solvent to clean brake parts.

10 Check the master cylinder bore for corrosion, scratches, nicks and score marks. If damage or wear is evident, the master cylinder must be replaced with a new one.

11 The dust boot, circlip, piston and its cup and seal, and the spring are all included in a master cylinder rebuild kit, and all other components are available individually. Use all of the new parts, regardless of the apparent condition of the old ones.

12 Lubricate the piston, cup, seal and master cylinder bore with clean brake fluid. If not already done fit the seal onto the piston with the lipped side facing the inner end, and fit the cup onto the spring, locating the peg in the hole **(see illustrations)**.

13 Fit the spring into the master cylinder,

making sure the lips on the cup do not turn inside out **(see illustration)**. Slide the piston into the master cylinder, making sure the lips on the seal do not turn inside out **(see illustration)**. Push the piston in to compress the spring and fit the new circlip, making sure it locates in the groove **(see illustrations)**.

14 Smear the outer end of the piston and the inside of the boot with silicone grease. Carefully push the wide rim of the boot onto its seat in the master cylinder **(see illustration)**. Locate the narrow end lips in the groove in the piston **(see illustration)**.

15 Inspect the reservoir diaphragm and fit a new one it if it is damaged or deteriorated.

Installation

16 Attach the master cylinder to the handlebar and fit the back of the clamp with the mirror mount facing up, aligning the clamp

mating surfaces with the punch mark on the underside of the handlebar **(see illustration)**. Tighten the upper bolt to the torque setting specified at the beginning of this Chapter, followed by the lower bolt.

17 Connect the brake hose to the master cylinder, using new sealing washers on each side of the banjo fitting **(see illustration 3.18)**. Align the hose as noted on removal **(see illustration 5.4)**. Tighten the banjo bolt to the torque setting specified at the beginning of this Chapter.

18 Install the brake lever (see Chapter 5) and the mirror (see Chapter 7).

19 Connect the brake light switch wiring **(see illustration 5.1)**.

20 Refer to Section 11 and bleed the system. Check that there are no fluid leaks and test the operation of the brakes before riding the motorcycle.

5.14a Fit the boot onto the pushrod...

5.14b ...and locate its rim in the groove

5.16 Align the mating surface with the punch mark (arrowed)

6 Rear brake pads

6.1 Remove the plug then slacken the pin bolt behind it

6.2a Unscrew the bolt...

Caution: *Do not operate the brake pedal with the pads removed or the caliper off the disc.*

1 Remove the pad retaining pin plug **(see illustration)**. Slacken the pad pin.

2 Unscrew the caliper rear mounting bolt **(see illustration)**. Withdraw the pad pin then pivot the back of the caliper up and remove the pads, noting how they fit **(see illustrations)**.

3 If required remove the shim and insulator from the back of each pad, noting how they fit **(see illustration)** – note that new pads should come with new shims and insulators, but make sure they do, especially if fitting after-market pads, before discarding the old ones (the shims and insulators are also available separately if required).

4 Inspect the surface of each pad for contamination and check that the friction material has not worn to or beyond its service limit (see Chapter 1, Section 2). If any pad is worn, fouled with oil or grease, or heavily scored or damaged, fit a complete set of new pads. Also check that wear is even across each pad – uneven wear is indicative of a sticking or seized piston (see Steps 6 and 7). **Note:** *It is not possible to degrease the friction material; if the pads are contaminated in any way they must be replaced with new ones.*

5 If the pads are in good condition clean them carefully, using a fine wire brush that is completely free of oil and grease to remove all traces of road dirt and corrosion. Using a pointed instrument, dig out any embedded particles of foreign matter. Spray with a dedicated brake cleaner.

6 Remove the pad spring from the caliper if required, noting which way round it fits **(see illustration 6.10a)**. Clean around the exposed section of the piston to remove any dirt or debris that could cause the seals to be damaged. If

6.2b ...withdraw the pin...

6.2c ...and remove the pads

new pads are being fitted check the fluid level in the reservoir before pushing the piston in to create room for them (see *Pre-ride checks*) – if the fluid level is not near the LOWER level line it may be necessary to remove the master cylinder reservoir cover, plate (SFV models) and diaphragm and remove some fluid. If new pads are being fitted, now push the piston all the way back into the caliper to create room for them; if the old pads are still serviceable push the piston in a little way. To push the piston back use finger pressure or a piece of wood or metal as leverage, or place the old pads back in the caliper and use a metal bar or a screwdriver inserted between them (but take care not to

damage the friction surface if the pads are being re-used), or use grips or a G-clamp and a piece of wood, with rag or card to protect the caliper body **(see illustration)**. Alternatively obtain a proper piston-pushing tool from a good tool supplier **(see illustration 2.8c)**. If the piston is difficult to push back, remove the bleed valve cap, then attach a length of clear hose to the bleed valve and place the open end in a suitable container, then open the valve and try again (see Section 11). Take great care not to draw any air into the system. If in doubt, bleed the brakes afterwards.

7 If the piston appears seized, disassemble the caliper and overhaul it (see Section 7). If

6.3 Remove the shim (arrowed) from the back if required

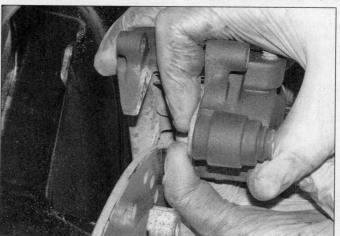

6.6 Push the piston back into the caliper

6.10a Make sure the pad spring (arrowed)...

6.10b ...and guide (arrowed) are clean and correctly fitted

it moves out but can't be pushed back in the chances are there is some hidden corrosion stopping it.

8 Remove all traces of corrosion from the pad pin and check for wear and damage.

9 Check the condition of the brake disc (see Section 8).

10 Clean the pad spring and fit it into the caliper if removed, making sure it locates correctly (see illustration). Clean the pad guide on the bracket and check it is correctly fitted (see illustration).

11 Clean all old grease off the bolt shank, and remove the sleeve from its boot and clean that too. Check the condition of the rubber boots and replace them with new ones if necessary (you need to remove the caliper to do the front boot in the bracket – see Section 7). Smear the inside of the rubber boot and the sleeve with silicone grease.

12 If removed fit the insulator and shim onto the back of each pad, making sure they locate correctly (see illustration 6.3). Clean the outer face of each shim so it is shiny.

13 Fit the pads into the caliper with the friction material facing the disc – make sure that the inner ends locate correctly against the guide on the bracket (see illustration). Secure the pads with the pad pin (see illustration 6.2b).

14 Pivot the caliper down and fit the mounting bolt (see illustration 6.2a). Tighten the bolt and the pad pin to the specified torque setting, then fit the plug (see illustration 6.1).

15 Operate the brake pedal until the pads contact the disc. Check the level of fluid in each reservoir and top-up if necessary (see Pre-ride checks).

16 Check the operation of the brakes before riding the motorcycle.

7 Rear brake caliper

⚠ **Warning: Overhaul must be done in a spotlessly clean work area to avoid contamination and possible failure of the brake hydraulic system components. Do not, under any circumstances, use petroleum-based solvents to clean brake parts. Use clean DOT 4 brake fluid, dedicated brake cleaner or denatured alcohol only, as described. To prevent damage from spilled brake fluid, always cover paintwork when working on the braking system, and have plenty of absorbent rag to hand to catch and wipe off any spilled fluid.**

Removal

Note: *If the caliper is being overhauled (usually due to a sticking piston or fluid leak) read through the entire procedure first and make sure that you have obtained all the new parts required, including some new DOT 4 brake fluid.*

Caution: Do not operate the brake pedal while the caliper is off the disc.

1 If the caliper is being completely removed or overhauled, stuff some rag around the brake hose banjo union. Note the alignment of the brake hose. Unscrew the hose banjo bolt and detach the union, catching the brake fluid (see illustration). Seal the union – one way of doing this is to fit a suitable bolt and nut with the old sealing washers (see illustration 3.2c). Note that new sealing washers will be required later.

2 Follow Steps 1 and 2 in Section 6 and remove the brake pads.

3 If the brake hose has been detached, pivot the caliper all the way up then slide it out of the bracket. If the hose is still connected loosely refit the rear mounting bolt then unscrew and remove the front slider pin, remove the rear bolt and lift the caliper off (see illustration).

6.13 Make sure the pads seat correctly against the guide

7.1 Brake hose banjo bolt (arrowed)

7.3 Front slider pin (arrowed)

7.6a Use compressed air to force the piston out...

7.6b ...and remove it

7.9 Remove the seals

Overhaul

4 Clean the exterior of the caliper with denatured alcohol or brake system cleaner. Have some clean rag ready to catch any spilled brake fluid.

5 To remove the piston you need either a supply of compressed air, or a piston removal tool, or if neither are available a good pair of external circlip removal pliers.

6 If you use compressed air wedge some rag or a piece of wood between the piston and the inner side of the caliper **(see illustration)**. Gradually and progressively apply the compressed air, starting with a fairly low pressure, to the fluid passage and allow the piston to ease out of the bore **(see illustration)**.

7 If you are using a dedicated tool or the circlip pliers grip the inner wall, then twist and pull the piston out, keeping it square to the bore wall. Do not try to remove the piston by levering it out or by using pliers or other grips that may scratch the outer wall, unless you are prepared to fit a new piston, and possibly a new caliper.

8 If the piston is stuck in its bore due to corrosion the caliper should be replaced with a new one.

9 Remove the dust seal and the piston seal from the bore using a plastic tool to avoid scratching **(see illustration)**. Discard the seals – new ones must be fitted on reassembly.

10 Clean the piston and bore with clean brake fluid. If compressed air is available, blow it through the fluid passages to ensure they are clear (make sure it is filtered and unlubricated).

Caution: Do not, under any circumstances, use a petroleum-based solvent to clean brake parts.

11 Inspect the caliper bore and piston for signs of corrosion, nicks and burrs and loss of plating. If surface defects are present, the piston and/or the caliper assembly must be replaced with new ones.

12 Lubricate the new piston seal with clean brake fluid and fit it into the inner groove in the caliper bore **(see illustrations)**.

13 Lubricate the new dust seal with silicone grease and fit it into the outer groove in the caliper bore **(see illustration)**.

14 Lubricate the piston with clean brake fluid and fit it, closed-end first, into the caliper bore, taking care not to displace the seals **(see illustration)**. Using your thumbs, push the piston all the way in, making sure it enters the bore square **(see illustration)**.

Installation

15 Refer to Section 6 and clean and check the pads, pad guide and spring, caliper mounting bolt and slider pin, and rubber boots.

16 If the brake hose has been detached, slide the caliper into the bracket then fit the pads (see Section 6). If the hose is still connected position the caliper and fit the front slider pin, tightening it finger-tight, then fit the pads (see Section 6), then tighten the front slider pin to the specified torque.

17 If detached connect the brake hose to the caliper, using new sealing washers on each side of the banjo fitting **(see illustration 3.18)**. Align the fitting as noted on removal **(see illustration 7.1)**. Tighten the banjo bolt to the specified torque setting.

18 Refer to Section 11 and bleed the system. Check that there are no fluid leaks and test the operation of the brakes before riding the bike.

7.12a Lubricate the new piston seal with brake fluid...

7.12b ...then fit it into the lower groove

7.13 Lubricate the new dust seal with silicone grease and fit it into the upper groove

7.14a Fit the piston...

7.14b ...and push it all the way in

8.3 Rear brake disc bolts (arrowed)

8 Rear brake disc

Inspection

1 Refer to Section 4 of this Chapter, noting that the dial gauge should be attached to the swingarm.

Removal

2 Remove the rear wheel (see Section 18).
3 If you are not replacing the disc with a new one, mark the relationship of the disc to the wheel so it can be installed in the same position. Unscrew the disc bolts, loosening them evenly and a little at a time in a criss-cross pattern to avoid distorting the disc, then remove the disc **(see illustration)**.

Installation

4 Before fitting the disc, make sure there is no dirt or corrosion where the disc seats on the hub. If the disc does not sit flat when it is bolted down, it will appear to be warped when checked or when the rear brake is used.
5 Fit the disc on the wheel with its marked side facing out, aligning the previously applied matchmarks (if you're reinstalling the original disc).
6 Either fit the new bolts, or clean the threads of the original bolts and apply fresh thread locking compound. Tighten the bolts evenly and a little at a time in a criss-cross pattern to the torque setting specified at the beginning of this Chapter. Clean the disc using acetone or brake system cleaner. If a new disc has been installed, remove any protective coating from its working surfaces and fit new brake pads.
7 Install the rear wheel (see Section 18).
8 Operate the brake pedal several times to bring the pads into contact with the disc. Check the operation of the brakes before riding the motorcycle.

9 Rear brake master cylinder

> ⚠ **Warning: Overhaul must be done in a spotlessly clean work area to avoid contamination and possible failure of the brake hydraulic system components. Do not, under any circumstances, use petroleum-based** solvents to clean brake parts. Use clean DOT 4 brake fluid, dedicated brake cleaner or denatured alcohol only, as described. To prevent damage from spilled brake fluid, always cover paintwork when working on the braking system, and have plenty of absorbent rag to hand to catch and wipe off any spilled fluid.

Removal

Note: If the master cylinder is being overhauled (usually due to sticking or poor action, or fluid leaks) a rebuild kit is available that includes the boot, circlip, piston, seal, cup and spring. Some DOT 4 brake/clutch fluid is also required.

1 Remove the right-hand side cover (see Chapter 7). On SFV models release the reservoir hose clamp **(see illustration)**.
2 Place some rag around the master cylinder. Note the alignment of the brake hose **(see illustrations)**. Unscrew the banjo bolt and detach the union, catching the brake fluid. Seal the union – one way of doing this is to fit a suitable bolt and nut with the old sealing washers **(see illustration 3.2c)**. Note that new sealing washers will be required later.
3 Straighten the ends of the split pin and withdraw it from the master cylinder pushrod pin, then remove the washer **(see illustration)**. Withdraw the pin.
4 Unscrew the reservoir mounting bolt and displace the reservoir **(see illustrations)**.
5 Unscrew the master cylinder bolts, remove the heel guard on DL models, and remove

9.1 Release the clamp (arrowed)

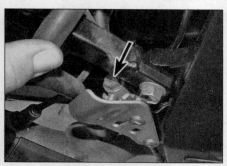

9.2a Brake hose banjo bolt (arrowed) – DL

9.2b Brake hose banjo bolt (arrowed) – SFV

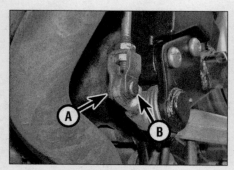

9.3 Remove the split pin and washer (A) and withdraw the clevis pin (B)

9.4a Reservoir bolt (arrowed) – DL

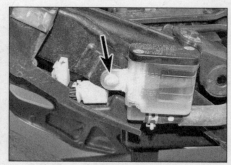

9.4b Reservoir bolt (arrowed) – SFV

9.5a Master cylinder bolts (arrowed) – DL

9.5b Master cylinder bolts (arrowed) – SFV

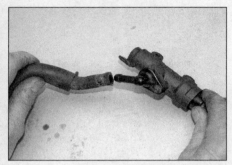

9.6 Release the clip and pull the hose off its union

the master cylinder and reservoir **(see illustrations)**.

Overhaul

6 Undo the reservoir cover screws and remove the plate (SFV models) and diaphragm, then tip the fluid from the reservoir into a suitable container for disposal (do not re-use the fluid or mix it with new fluid). Wipe any remaining fluid out of the reservoir with a clean rag. Detach the reservoir hose from its union on the master cylinder **(see illustration)**. If required, release the reservoir hose union circlip and detach it from the master cylinder. Remove the O-ring – a new one must be used. Check the condition of the reservoir hose and replace it with a new one if there are any cracks or other damage.

7 Mark the position of the clevis locknut on

the pushrod, then loosen the locknut and thread the clevis nut, clevis and locknut off the pushrod.

8 Carefully remove the dust boot from the master cylinder **(see illustration)**. Depress the pushrod and use circlip pliers to remove the circlip **(see illustration)**. Slide out the pushrod assembly, piston and spring, noting how they fit **(see illustration)**. Lay the parts out in the proper order to prevent confusion during reassembly.

9 Clean the master cylinder and reservoir with clean DOT 4 brake fluid. If compressed air is available, blow it through the fluid galleries to ensure they are clear (make sure the air is filtered and unlubricated).

Caution: Do not, under any circumstances, use a petroleum-based solvent to clean brake parts.

10 Check the master cylinder bore for corrosion, scratches, nicks and score marks. If damage or wear is evident, the master cylinder must be replaced with a new one. If the master cylinder is in poor condition, then the caliper should be checked as well.

11 The dust boot, circlip, piston, seal, cup and spring are all included in the master cylinder rebuild kit. Use all of the new parts, regardless of the apparent condition of the old ones.

12 Smear the cup and seal with new brake fluid. If the seal is not already on the piston, fit it into its groove so the wider end will fit into the master cylinder first **(see illustrations)**. Fit the cup onto the narrow end of the spring **(see illustration)**. Lubricate the master cylinder bore with new brake fluid.

13 Fit the spring wide-end first into the master

9.8a Remove the rubber boot...

9.8b ...then release the circlip...

9.8c ...and remove the pushrod, piston and spring

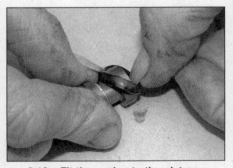

9.12a Fit the seal onto the piston...

9.12b ...as shown

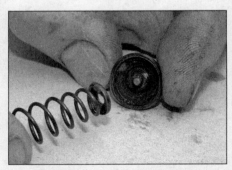

9.12c Fit the cup onto the end of the spring, locating the peg in the hole

9.13 Fit the spring making sure the cup locates correctly in the bore...

9.14 ...then push the piston in

cylinder and push the cup in, making sure its lips do not turn inside out **(see illustration)**.

14 Lubricate the piston with clean brake fluid and slide it into the master cylinder and up against the cup and spring **(see illustration)**. Make sure the lips on the seal do not turn inside out.

15 Smear some silicone grease onto the rounded end of the pushrod and locate it against the end of the piston **(see illustration)**. Push the piston in using the pushrod until the washer is beyond the circlip groove, then fit the new circlip, making sure it locates properly **(see illustration)**.

16 Smear some silicone grease onto the rubber boot lips. Fit the rubber boot, making sure the lips are seated correctly in the master cylinder and around the pushrod **(see illustrations)**.

17 Fit the clevis locknut, the clevis and the clevis nut onto the master cylinder pushrod end. Position the clevis as noted on removal and tighten the locknut.

18 If removed fit a new fluid reservoir hose union O-ring smeared with brake fluid, then press the union into the master cylinder and secure it with the circlip. Fit the hose onto the union and secure it with the clamp **(see illustration 9.6)**. Check that the hose is secured with a clip at the reservoir end as well.

Installation

19 Fit the master cylinder onto the bracket, along with the heel guard on DL models, and tighten the bolts to the torque setting specified at the beginning of the Chapter **(see illustration 9.5a or b)**.

20 Secure the reservoir with its bolt, and on SFV models fit the hose clamp.

21 Align the pushrod with the brake pedal, then insert the pin **(see illustration 9.3)**. Fit the washer and a new split pin, bending the ends round to lock it.

22 Connect the brake hose to the master cylinder, using new sealing washers on each side of the banjo fitting **(see illustration 3.18)**. Align the fitting as noted on removal **(see illustration 9.2a or b)**. Tighten the banjo bolt to the specified torque setting.

23 Refer to Section 11 and bleed the system. Check that there are no fluid leaks and test the operation of the brakes before riding the motorcycle.

24 On SFV models reconnect the hose clamp. On all models, install the right-hand side cover (see Chapter 7).

10 Brake hoses and fittings

Inspection

1 Check brake hose condition according to the brake system check interval in the service schedule (see Chapter 1). Twist and flex the hoses while looking for cracks, bulges and seeping hydraulic fluid. Check extra carefully around the areas where the hoses connect with the banjo fittings, as these are common areas for hose failure.

9.15a Position the circlip on the washer...

9.15b ...then depress the pushrod and fit the circlip into the groove

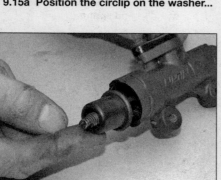

9.16a Fit the new boot...

9.16b ...then press it into the cylinder...

9.16c ...and make sure it is correctly located around the pushrod

2 On ABS models also check the brake pipes and the hose and pipe joints, for signs of fluid leakage and for any dents or cracks in the pipes.

Removal and installation

3 Drain all old brake fluid from the system (see Section 11).

4 The brake hoses have banjo fittings on each end. Cover the surrounding area with plenty of rags and unscrew the banjo bolt at each end of the hose, noting the alignment of the fitting with the master cylinder or brake caliper (see illustrations 3.2a and b, 5.4, 7.1, and 9.2a or b). Free the hose from any clips or guides and remove it, noting its routing. Discard the sealing washers. **Note:** *Do not operate the brake lever or pedal while a brake hose is disconnected.*

5 Position the new hose, making sure it isn't twisted or otherwise strained, and ensure that it is correctly routed through any clips or guides and is clear of all moving components.

6 Check that the fittings align correctly, then fit the banjo bolts, using new sealing washers on both sides of the fittings (see illustration 3.18) – where two hoses are fitted with one banjo bolt on the front caliper three washers are needed, one on the outer side of each union and one between the unions. Tighten the banjo bolts to the torque setting specified at the beginning of this Chapter.

7 The brake pipes on models with ABS are held by flare nuts. There are no sealing washers. Unscrew the nuts and detach the pipes. Make sure the pipe is correctly positioned, fitted into any clips, and with any joint blocks secured, before tightening the nuts. If the correct tools are available tighten

the nuts to the torque setting specified at the beginning of this Chapter for your model.

8 Refill the system with new DOT 4 brake fluid (see *Pre-ride checks*) and bleed the air from it (see Section 11).

9 Check the operation of the brakes before riding the motorcycle.

---

11 Brake system bleeding and fluid change

Bleeding

1 Bleeding a brake is the process of removing aerated brake fluid from the master cylinder, the hose(s)/pipe(s) and the brake caliper(s). Bleeding is necessary whenever a brake system hydraulic connection is loosened, after a component or hose is replaced with a new one, when a master cylinder or caliper is overhauled, or when there is a spongy feel to the lever and it travels all the way back to the handlebar, and where braking force is less than it should be, and it is not due to any mechanical fault in the system (i.e. a sticking piston in the caliper, or a pad that is not moving as it should due to corrosion, for example on the pad pin). Leaks in the system may also allow air to enter, but leaking brake fluid will reveal their presence and warn you of the need for repair.

2 Brake bleeding is considered by some as a bit of a black art – seasoned professionals sometimes have trouble getting a good firm feel in the brake lever, while a first timer may

have no trouble at all. One of the problems, particularly with the front brakes, is that you are working against natural principles – science dictates that air bubbles in a liquid will rise to the top, but the process entails pumping the brake fluid and any air bubbles it contains down from the master cylinder at the top to the bleed valve in the caliper at the bottom, so while the fluid is moving down the air bubbles will want to rise. Air bubbles can also get trapped, particularly where there are high points in its path, and when there are extra components and pipes such as on ABS models.

3 To bleed the brakes using the conventional method, you will need some new DOT 4 brake fluid, a length of clear flexible hose, a small container partially filled with clean brake fluid, some rags, and a spanner to fit the brake caliper bleed valve. Bleeding kits that include the hose, a one-way valve and a container are available relatively cheaply from a good auto store, and simplify the task. You also need a block of wood as a support for the fluid container.

4 Cover painted components to prevent damage in the event that brake fluid is spilled. *Caution: Brake fluid attacks painted finishes and plastics – to prevent damage from spilled fluid, always cover paintwork when working on the braking system, and clean up any spills immediately using brake cleaner.*

Front brake system

5 Turn the handlebars so the reservoir is level. Undo the reservoir cover screws and remove the cover, diaphragm plate and diaphragm (see illustration 5.3). Slowly pump the brake lever a few times to dislodge any fine air bubbles from the small hole in the bottom of the reservoir (see illustrations). Now hold the lever in to force any large air bubbles out of the large hole (see illustration).

6 Pull the dust cap off the bleed valve on the left-hand caliper (see illustration). If using a ring spanner (which is preferable to an open-ended one) fit it onto the valve (see illustration 11.10b). Attach one end of the bleeding hose to the bleed valve and, if not using a kit, submerge the other end in the clean brake fluid in the container.

7 Check the fluid level in the reservoir – keep it topped up and do not allow the level to drop below the bottom of the window during the procedure (see illustration).

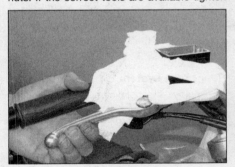

11.5a Pump the lever...

11.5b ...and check for fine air bubbles from the small hole (A). Large hole (B)

11.5c Air bubble rising from the large hole

11.6 Left-hand caliper bleed valve (arrowed)

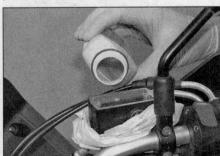

11.7 Keep the reservoir topped up

11.8 Bleeding the front brake system (right-hand caliper shown)

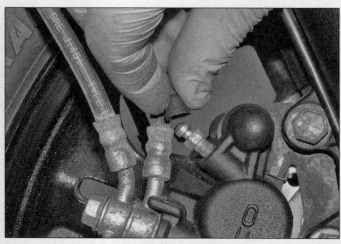

11.10a Remove the cap...

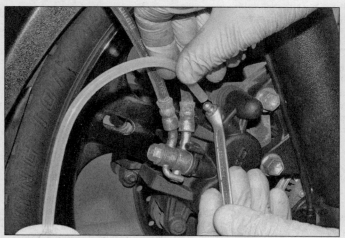

11.10b ...fit a ring spanner onto the valve hex then connect the bleed hose

11.12 Undo the screws and remove the cover, diaphragm plate and diaphragm

8 Slowly squeeze the brake lever a few times, then hold it on and open the bleed valve a quarter turn (see illustration). When the valve is opened, brake fluid will flow out of the master cylinder into the clear tubing, and the lever will move to the handlebar. If there is air in the system there will be air bubbles in the brake fluid coming out of the caliper.

9 Tighten the bleed valve, then release the

brake lever. Repeat the process, topping the reservoir up when necessary, until no air bubbles are visible in the brake fluid leaving the caliper, and the lever is firm when applied with the bleed valve closed. On completion tighten the bleed valve.

10 Now transfer the equipment to the bleed valve on the right-hand caliper (see illustrations). Repeat the bleeding procedure.

Rear brake system

11 Remove the right-hand side cover (see Chapter 7).

12 Undo the reservoir cover screws and remove the cover, diaphragm plate (SFV models) and diaphragm (see illustration). Slowly pump the brake pedal a few times to dislodge any air bubbles from the holes in the bottom of the reservoir.

13 Pull the dust cap off the caliper bleed valve (see illustration). If using a ring spanner (which is preferable to an open-ended one) fit it onto the valve (see illustration 11.10b). Attach one end of the bleeding hose to the bleed valve and, if not using a kit, submerge the other end in the clean brake fluid in the container.

14 Check the fluid level in the reservoir – keep it topped up and do not allow the level to drop below the lower level line during the procedure (see illustration).

15 Slowly press the brake pedal a few times then hold it down and open the bleed valve

11.13 Removing the cap from the rear caliper bleed valve

11.14 Keep the reservoir topped up

11.15 Bleeding the rear brake system

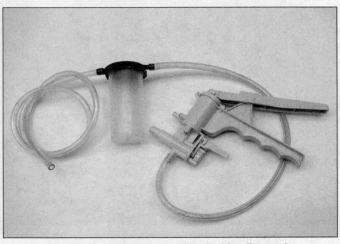

11.19 A vacuum-operated brake bleeding tool

a quarter turn **(see illustration)**. When the valve is opened, brake fluid will flow out of the master cylinder into the clear tubing, and the pedal will move down. If there is air in the system there will be air bubbles in the brake fluid coming out of the caliper.

16 Tighten the bleed valve, then release the brake pedal. Repeat the process, topping the reservoir up when necessary, until no air bubbles are visible in the brake fluid leaving the caliper, and the pedal is firm when applied with the bleed valve closed. On completion tighten the bleed valve.

Both systems

17 If it is not possible to produce a firm feel to the lever or pedal, the fluid may be full of many tiny air bubbles rather than a few big ones. To remedy this apply some pressure to the system, for the front brake by tying the front brake lever lightly back to the handlebar, and for the rear by tying a weight to the brake pedal – do not apply too much pressure or the cup and seals in the master cylinder and caliper may fail. Let the fluid stabilise for a few hours, after which the tiny bubbles should either have risen to the top in the reservoir, or have formed into one or more big bubbles that can be more easily bled out by repeating the bleeding procedure.

18 If you are still having trouble look for any high point in the system in which a pocket of air may become trapped. Displace and agitate the hose or pipe so the bubble can be dislodged (but take care not to bend a pipe) – tapping it may help. If necessary displace the master cylinder and/or the caliper(s), and free the brake hose(s) from guides and move the parts around to dislodge the air and encourage it towards a bleed valve – refer to the relevant Sections as required to displace components. On models with ABS it is not practical to disturb the modulator as the pipes have to be detached, allowing more air to enter the system – if you cannot get the system to bleed correctly take the bike to a Suzuki dealer.

19 If bleeding the system using the conventional tools and methods stated does not give satisfactory results, or if otherwise preferred, you can use a commercially available vacuum-type brake bleeding tool, such as the Mity-vac, following the manufacturer's instructions **(see illustration)**. This type of tool literally sucks the fluid out by creating a vacuum at the bleed valve. Users of such tools often get confused by the amount of air that appears to be in the brake fluid – more often than not this is caused by the vacuum sucking air past the bleed valve threads (air provides less resistance to the vacuum than the brake fluid) where it mixes with the fluid being drawn out. If this is the case the vacuum applied may be too great, or the bleed valve may have been loosened too much. One way to get round this is to remove the bleed valve and wrap some PTFE tape around its threads, but note that doing so will be a bit messy, so have some rag to hand.

20 When the system has been successfully bled there should be a good and progressively firm feel as the lever or pedal is applied, and the lever or pedal should not be able to travel all the way back to the handlebar or down to its stop.

21 On completion remove the equipment used and make sure the bleed valve is tight (to the torque setting specified at the beginning of the Chapter if you have a suitable torque wrench), then fit the dust cap. Top-up the reservoir, then fit the diaphragm, diaphragm plate, and cover or cap. Check for spilled brake fluid and clean up as required. Check the entire system for fluid leaks.

22 Check the operation of the brake before riding the motorcycle.

Fluid change

23 Changing the brake fluid is a similar process to bleeding the brakes and requires the same materials plus a suitable tool (such as a syringe, or alternatively lots of absorbent rag or paper) for removing the fluid from the reservoir.

24 Cover painted components and fit the

equipment to the relevant caliper following the appropriate Steps in the bleeding procedure given above. Remove the reservoir cover, diaphragm plate (where fitted) and diaphragm **(see illustrations 5.3 and 11.12)**. Remove the fluid from the reservoir into a suitable container, either by sucking it up using a tool as shown, drawing it out into a syringe, or soaking it up in some paper towel **(see illustration)**. Wipe the reservoir clean. Fill the reservoir with new brake fluid **(see illustration 11.7 or 11.14)**. Squeeze or press the brake lever or pedal and open the bleed valve **(see illustrations 11.8 and 11.15)**. When the valve is opened, brake fluid will flow out of the caliper into the clear tubing, and the lever will move toward the handlebar, or the pedal will move down.

25 Tighten the bleed valve, then slowly release the brake lever or pedal. Keep the reservoir topped-up with new fluid at all times or air may enter the system and greatly increase the length of the task. Repeat the process until new fluid can be seen emerging from the caliper bleed valve.

 HAYNES HiNT *Old brake fluid is invariably much darker in colour than new fluid, making it easy to see when all old fluid has been expelled from the system.*

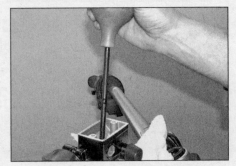

11.24 Sucking the brake fluid out

12.6a Mode select switch connector (arrowed) – 2012-on

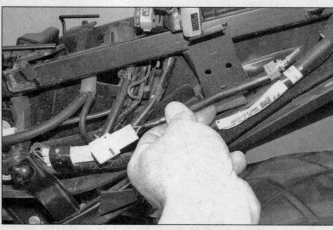

12.6b Connect the switch and turn it ON

26 On completion remove the equipment used and make sure the bleed valve is tight (to the torque setting specified at the beginning of the Chapter if you have a suitable torque wrench), then fit the dust cap. Top-up the reservoir, then fit the diaphragm, diaphragm plate, and cover or cap. Check for spilled brake fluid and clean up as required. Check the entire system for fluid leaks.

27 Check the operation of the brakes before riding the motorcycle.

Draining the system for overhaul

28 Draining the brake fluid is again a similar process to bleeding the brakes. The quickest and easiest way is to use a commercially available vacuum-type brake bleeding tool (see Step 19) – follow the manufacturer's instructions. Otherwise follow the procedure described above for changing the fluid, but quite simply do not put any new fluid into the reservoir – the system fills itself with air instead.

29 When it comes to refilling the system start by adding new fluid from a sealed container to the reservoir, then perform the bleeding procedure as described above until the fluid comes out of the bleed valve, and keep at it until you are certain there is no more air left in the system.

12 ABS operation

1 The ABS prevents the wheels from locking up under hard braking or on uneven road surfaces. A sensor on each wheel transmits information about the speed of rotation to the ABS control unit; if the unit senses that a wheel is about to lock, it releases brake pressure to that wheel momentarily, preventing skidding.

2 The ABS is self-checking and is activated when the ignition switch is turned on – the ABS indicator light in the instrument cluster will come on and will remain on until road speed increases above 3 mph (5 kmh) at which point, if the ABS is normal, the light will go off. Note: If the ABS indicator light does not come on initially there is a fault in the indicator light system.

Fault code retrieval

Special tool: To access the fault code, and to perform certain tests, the Suzuki mode select switch (Pt. No. 09930-82710) is required – it is not expensive.

Note: The ABS indicator may diagnose a fault if tyre sizes other than those specified by Suzuki are fitted, if the tyre pressures are incorrect, if the machine has been run continuously over bumpy roads, if the front wheel comes off the ground whilst riding (wheelie) or if the machine is on an auxiliary stand with the engine running and the rear wheel turning.

3 If the indicator light remains on, or starts flashing while the machine is being ridden, there is a fault in the system and the ABS function will be switched off – the brakes will still operate but without the ABS function.

4 If a fault is indicated, details will be stored in the ABS control unit memory in the form of a fault code – up to six codes can be stored. Note: Don't disconnect the battery or the ABS control unit connector until the fault code has been confirmed – disconnection will erase the control unit memory.

5 Before reading out the fault code, carry out a general check of the tyres (see Note above) and the braking system – check that the fluid level in the front and rear master cylinders is correct, that the pads are not worn down to the wear indicators and that there is no air in the brake system. Also check that the battery is in good condition and fully charged and that both ABS fuses are in good condition and not blown.

6 To access the fault code, and to perform certain tests, the Suzuki mode select switch (Pt. No. 09930-82710) is required. Remove the seat on 2007 to 2011 DL models, and the left-hand side cover on 2012-on models (see Chapter 7); on SFV models remove the right-hand side cover (see Chapter 7). Make sure the ignition switch is OFF. Identify the mode select switch connector with the orange and black/white wires and remove its cap **(see illustration)**. Plug the mode select switch into the connector and set it to the ON position **(see illustration)**. Turn the ignition switch ON.

7 The fault code will be represented as a series of flashes of the ABS indicator light – all the two digit fault codes given in the accompanying table are displayed as 0.4 second flashes, with a 1.6 pause between the tens and units. Thus the example shown indicates fault code 42 as four 0.4 second flashes, followed by a 1.6 second pause, then two 0.4 second flashes **(see illustration)**. If a

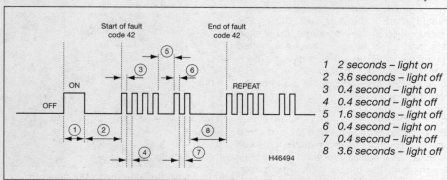

1	2 seconds – light on
2	3.6 seconds – light off
3	0.4 second – light on
4	0.4 second – light off
5	1.6 seconds – light off
6	0.4 second – light on
7	0.4 second – light off
8	3.6 seconds – light off

H46494

12.7 Example of ABS fault code readout – code 42 represented second fault code has been recorded, a 3.6 second pause will separate the two codes. If there is more than one stored code they are given in numerical order. The cycle will repeat until the mode select switch is turned OFF or five minutes have lapsed. The system can store up to six fault codes (if a seventh occurs, the oldest will be erased). Record the code and identify the fault from the table in Section 13. Turn the ignition switch OFF.

Fault code erasing

8 Once the fault has been corrected, reset the control unit memory as follows. Ensure the ignition switch is OFF. Connect the mode select switch and turn it ON. Turn the ignition switch ON. While the fault codes are being displayed, turn the mode select switch OFF, then after 12.5 seconds, turn it ON then OFF three times, each time leaving it ON for more than one second. After erasing the fault codes, the system will resume its normal self-diagnosis mode.

9 Repeat the fault code retrieval procedure (see Steps 6 and 7) to check that the codes have been erased. Note that if no faults are recorded the indicator light will flash for 3.6 seconds at every 3.6 second interval **(see illustration 12.7)**.

13 ABS fault diagnosis

1 If a fault is indicated in the ABS, first check that the battery is fully charged, then check the ABS fuses (see Chapter 8).

2 If a fault appears, identify the cause using the fault code table.

3 Refer to the relevant Steps below for the faulty component being checked and first make sure that the relevant system wiring connectors are securely connected and free of corrosion – poor connections are the cause of the majority of problems, then make any specific checks detailed. Also check the wiring itself for any obvious faults or breaks, referring to the wiring diagrams at the end of Chapter 8. Refer to Chapter 8, Section 2, for general electrical fault finding procedures and equipment. In the case of a wheel speed sensor related problem also check the sensor tip and rotor are not dirty or damaged (Section 14).

4 If after a thorough check, the source of a fault has not been identified, have the system tested by a Suzuki dealer.

ABS indicator light does not come on

5 First check the signal fuse, then check the orange/green wire between the fusebox and the instrument cluster (see Chapter 8).

6 Make sure the ignition is off. Refer to Section 14, Steps 16 to 18, and disconnect the ABS control unit wiring connector.

7 Turn the ignition ON. Using a multimeter

Fault code/flashes	Faulty component or symptoms	Possible causes
ABS light does not come on with ignition	No voltage at instrument cluster No voltage at ABS control unit	Damaged signal fuse Faulty wiring or wiring connector Faulty LED
ABS light stays on continuously	No voltage at ABS control unit ABS control unit Mode select switch connector	Faulty wiring or wiring connector Internal fault
13 – SFV only	Front wheel sensor rotor	Damaged rotor or debris caught between rotor and sensor head Deformed wheel
14 – SFV only	Rear wheel sensor rotor	Damaged rotor or debris caught between rotor and sensor head Deformed wheel
22 – SFV only	Front wheel sensor actuator circuit	Front wheel locking or brake dragging Incorrect sensor installation or air gap
23 – SFV only	Rear wheel sensor actuator circuit	Rear wheel locking or brake dragging Incorrect sensor installation or air gap
25	Front wheel speed sensor circuit Front wheel speed sensor Front wheel sensor rotor	Wrong tyre size or pressure Deformed wheel Faulty wiring or wiring connector Faulty sensor Damaged sensor rotor
35	ABS motor fuse No voltage at ABS control unit ABS control unit	Fuse blown Faulty wiring or wiring connector Internal fault
41	Front wheel speed sensor	Incorrect sensor installation Faulty wiring or wiring connector Damaged sensor rotor Faulty ABS control unit
42	Front wheel speed sensor open circuit	Faulty wiring or wiring connector Dirty or damaged sensor Faulty ABS control unit
43 – SFV only	Front wheel speed sensor short circuit	Faulty sensor or wiring
44	Rear wheel speed sensor	Incorrect sensor installation Faulty wiring or wiring connector Damaged sensor rotor Faulty ABS control unit
45	Rear wheel speed sensor open circuit	Faulty wiring or wiring connector Dirty or damaged sensor Faulty ABS control unit
46 – SFV only	Rear wheel speed sensor short circuit	Faulty sensor or wiring
47	Supply voltage increased*	Faulty battery Faulty regulator/rectifier Faulty wiring
48	Supply voltage decreased*	Discharged or faulty battery Faulty alternator or regulator/rectifier Faulty wiring
55	ABS control unit	Internal fault
61	ABS valve fuse ABS solenoid	Fuse blown Faulty ABS control unit

*ABS light goes out when voltage returns to normal

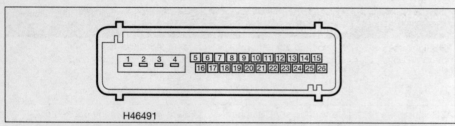

13.7a ABS control unit wiring connector terminal identification (loom side) – 2007 to 2011 DL

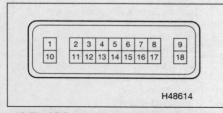

13.7b ABS control unit wiring connector terminal identification (loom side) – 2012-on DL

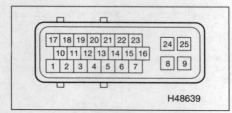

13.7c ABS control unit wiring connector terminal identification (loom side) – SFV

set to the dc volts function, measure the voltage between the following terminal pins on the wire harness side of the connector (see illustrations).

2007 to 2011 DL – pin 12 (positive probe) and pin 4 (negative probe)
2012-on DL – pin 11 (positive probe) and pin 9 (negative probe)
SFV – pin 21 positive probe) and pin 24 (negative probe)

Between 7.5 and 9.5 V should be shown on DL models and 7 V or more on SFV models. If no voltage is shown check the wiring to the instrument cluster and the terminals of the instrument cluster connector. If the wiring is good, the ABS indicator light may be faulty. **Note:** *If the indicator light LED has failed a new instrument cluster will have to be fitted (see Chapter 8).* Turn the ignition OFF when the check is complete.
8 If there is voltage in Step 7, using a continuity tester or multimeter set to the resistance function, test for continuity between the following terminal pin on the wire harness side (positive probe) of the connector and earth (negative probe). Continuity shown exist if the earth circuit is good, indication that the ABS control unit is faulty – have it tested by a Suzuki dealer.

2007 to 2011 DL – pin 4
2012-on DL – pin 9
SFV – pin 24, then pin 25

ABS indicator light stays on continuously

9 First check the ignition fuse (see Chapter 8).
10 If the fuse is good, refer to Section 14, Steps 16 to 18, and disconnect the ABS control unit wiring connector.
11 Turn the ignition ON. Using a multimeter set to the dc volts function, measure the

voltage between the following terminal pins on the wire harness side of the connector (see illustration 13.7a, b or c). Battery voltage should be shown. If there is no voltage, inspect the wiring for damage.

2007 to 2011 DL – pin 18 (positive probe) and pin 4 (negative probe)
2012-on DL – pin 6 (positive probe) and pin 9 (negative probe)
SFV – pin 16 positive probe) and pin 24 (negative probe)

12 If there is voltage in Step 11, measure the voltage as described in Step 7. Between 7.5 and 9.5 V should be shown on DL models and 7 V or more on SFV models. If there is no voltage, check the wiring to the instrument cluster and the terminals of the instrument cluster connector. Turn the ignition OFF.
13 If there is voltage check the orange and black/white wires between the control unit wiring connector and the mode select switch connector (see Section 12) for continuity, and make sure there is no short to earth. Otherwise it is likely the ABS control unit is faulty – have it tested by a Suzuki dealer.

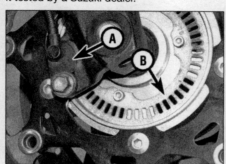

13.22 Check the front sensor (A) and rotor (B)

Code 25 – Speed sensor malfunction

14 Ensure that the tyre size and pressure are correct (see Specifications at the beginning of the Chapter).
15 Check the speed sensor rotor condition, particularly that nothing has become trapped between the segments (see illustration 13.22 and 13.30a).
16 Follow the procedure in Step 23 (front) or Step 30 (rear) and check the speed sensor air gap.
17 If the checks fail to identify the fault, have the ABS control unit checked by a Suzuki dealer.

Code 35 – ABS motor fuse

18 Turn the ignition ON and listen for any operating noise from the ABS control unit. If there is any noise with the machine at a standstill the fault is likely to be in the ABS control unit – have it checked by a Suzuki dealer.
19 Check the ABS motor fuse (see Chapter 8).
20 If the fuse is good, follow the procedure in Section 14, Steps 16 to 18, and check the ABS control unit wiring connector is secure, then disconnect it and check that the terminals are clean and undamaged.
21 Turn the ignition ON. Test for battery voltage between the following terminal pins on the wire harness side of the connector (see illustration 13.7a,b or c). If there is no voltage, inspect the wiring for damage. If there is voltage replace the control unit with a new one.

2007 to 2011 DL – pin 2 (positive probe) and pin 1 (negative probe)
2012-on DL – pin 10 (positive probe) and pin 18 (negative probe)
SFV – pin 9 positive probe) and pin 25 (negative probe)

Code 41 – Front wheel speed sensor signal malfunction

22 Check that the sensor is mounted securely and the rotor is clean and in good condition without anything trapped between its segments (see illustration).
23 Use feeler gauge blades to measure the air gap between the sensor tip and the rotor segments and compare it with the value given in the Specifications (see illustration). If the

13.23 Measuring front wheel sensor air gap

gap is outside of this figure, there may be a problem with the rotor not seating correctly on the wheel hub, or the sensor or its bracket being out of line. Note that there are no shims available to adjust the air gap setting. Refer to Section 14 for sensor removal details.

Code 42 – Front wheel speed sensor open circuit

24 Remove the air filter housing to access the sensor wiring connector on DL models (see Chapter 4); on SFV models the connector is on the left-hand side of the frame headstock. Check the wiring for damage and make sure that the connector is secure, then disconnect it and check that the terminals are clean and undamaged **(see illustrations)**. Reconnect the connector.
25 Follow the procedure in Section 14, Steps 16 to 18, and check the ABS control unit wiring connector is secure, then disconnect it and check that the terminals are clean and undamaged.
26 Test for continuity between the following terminal pins in the loom side of the connector **(see illustration 13.7a, b or c)**. If continuity is shown, check the wiring between the connector and the sensor for a fault.

> 2007 to 2011 DL – pin 16 and pin 5
> 2012-on DL – pin 16 and pin 7
> SFV – pin 12 and pin 3

27 If no continuity is indicated, test between pin 16 and earth on DL models, and pin 12 and earth on SFV models – no continuity

should be shown. If it is, disconnect the wheel speed sensor connector and test for continuity between the white wire terminal and earth on the sensor side of the connector. No continuity should be shown. If continuity is shown, the speed sensor is faulty.
28 Test for continuity between the following terminal pin and earth in the loom side of the ABS control unit connector.

> 2007 to 2011 DL – pin 5
> 2012-on DL – pin 7
> SFV – pin 3

No continuity should be shown. If it is, disconnect the wheel speed sensor connector and test for continuity between the black wire terminal and earth on the sensor side of the connector. No continuity should be shown. If continuity is shown, the speed sensor is faulty.
29 Finally, check the white/red wire between the ABS control unit connector harness side and the wheel speed sensor connector – continuity should be shown. Similarly check the black/red wire.

Code 43 – Front wheel speed sensor short circuit – SFV

30 Follow the procedure in Section 14, Steps 16 to 18, and check the ABS control unit wiring connector is secure, then disconnect it and check that the terminals are clean and undamaged.
31 Test for continuity between pin 3 and pin 12 on the loom side of the connector

(see illustration 13.7c). If there is continuity, inspect the wiring to the front wheel sensor for damage. If the wiring is good, it is likely the speed sensor is faulty – have it checked by a Suzuki dealer.
32 Using a multimeter set to the volts scale, connect the positive (+) probe to pin 3 and the negative probe to pin 24 on the loom side of the connector. Turn the ignition ON and check for voltage. Turn the ignition OFF. There should be no voltage. If voltage is indicated, inspect the sensor circuit and power supply wiring for damage. If no voltage is indicated, it is likely the ABS control unit is faulty – have it checked by a Suzuki dealer.

Code 44 – Rear wheel speed sensor signal malfunction

33 Follow the procedure in Steps 22 and 23 and check the rear wheel speed sensor and rotor **(see illustrations)**. Note that the sensor locates directly in the rear caliper bracket.

Code 45 – Rear wheel speed sensor open circuit

34 Follow the procedure in Section 14, Steps 16 to 18, and check the ABS control unit wiring connector is secure, then disconnect it and check that the terminals are clean and undamaged.
35 Remove the seat and if required the left-hand side cover to access the sensor wiring connector on DL models (see Chapter 7); on SFV models remove the ABS control unit cover to access the connector **(see illustrations)**. Check the wiring for damage and make sure that the connector is secure, then disconnect

13.24a Front wheel sensor connector (arrowed) – DL

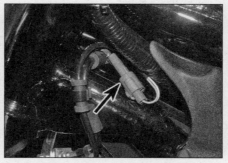
13.24b Front wheel sensor connector (arrowed) – SFV

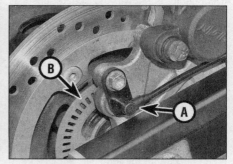
13.33a Check the rear sensor (A) and rotor (B)

13.33b Measuring rear wheel sensor air gap

13.35a Rear wheel sensor connector (arrowed) – DL

13.35b Rear wheel sensor connector (arrowed) – SFV

it and check that the terminals are clean and undamaged. Reconnect the connector.

36 Test for continuity between the following terminals on the loom side of the connector **(see illustration 13.7a, b or c)**. If continuity is shown, check the wiring between the connector and the sensor for a fault.

    2007 to 2011 DL – pin 19 and pin 7
    2012-on DL – pin 15 and pin 14
    SFV – pin 2 and pin 18

37 If no continuity is indicated, test between pin 7 and earth on 2007 to 2011 DL models, or between pin 15 and earth on 2012-on DL models, and between pin 18 and earth on SFV models. No continuity should be shown. If it is, disconnect the wheel speed sensor connector and test for continuity between the white wire terminal and earth on the sensor side of the connector. No continuity should be shown. If continuity is shown, the speed sensor is faulty.

38 Test for continuity between the following terminal pin and earth in the loom side of the ABS control unit connector.

    2007 to 2011 DL – pin 19
    2012-on DL – pin 14
    SFV – pin 2

No continuity should be shown. If it is, disconnect the wheel speed sensor connector and test for continuity between the black wire terminal and earth on the sensor side of the connector. No continuity should be shown. If continuity is shown, the speed sensor is faulty.

39 Finally, check the white/yellow wire between the ABS control unit connector harness side and the wheel speed sensor connector – continuity should be shown. Similarly check the black/yellow wire.

Code 46 – Rear wheel speed sensor short circuit – SFV

40 Follow the procedure in Section 14, Steps 16 to 18, and check the ABS control unit wiring connector is secure, then disconnect it and check that the terminals are clean and undamaged.
41 Test for continuity between pin 2 and

pin 18 on the loom side of the connector **(see illustration 13.7c)**. If there is continuity, inspect the wiring to the rear wheel sensor for damage. If the wiring is good, it is likely the speed sensor is faulty – have it checked by a Suzuki dealer.
42 Using a multimeter set to the volts scale, connect the positive (+) probe to pin 2 and the negative probe to pin 24 on the loom side of the connector. Turn the ignition ON and check for voltage. Turn the ignition OFF. There should be no voltage. If voltage is indicated, inspect the sensor circuit and power supply wiring for damage. If no voltage is indicated, it is likely the ABS control unit is faulty – have it checked by a Suzuki dealer.

Code 47, 48 – Supply voltage

43 Check the battery voltage (see Chapter 8). If the voltage is good, check the output of the charging system (see Chapter 8).
44 If the charging system is good, follow the procedure in Section 14, Steps 16 to 18, and check the ABS control unit wiring connector is secure, then disconnect it and check that the terminals are clean and undamaged.
45 With the control unit wiring connector disconnected, connect a voltmeter between the following terminal pins on the loom side of the connector **(see illustration 13.7a, b or c)**.

    2007 to 2011 DL – pin 18 (positive probe)
        and pin 4 (negative probe)
    2012-on DL – pin 6 (positive probe) and
        pin 9 (negative probe)
    SFV – pin 16 (positive probe) and pin 24
        (negative probe)

Start the engine and warm it up to normal operating temperature. Switch the headlight main (HI) beam ON and briefly increase the engine speed to 5000 rpm. Measure the voltage. If the correct supply voltage (14 to 15V) is shown, it is likely the ABS control unit is faulty – have it checked by a Suzuki dealer. If the voltage is outside the specifications, inspect the ABS wiring loom for damage.

Code 55 – Control unit malfunction

46 Follow the procedure in Step 23 to check that the front and rear speed sensor air gaps

are correct, that the components are not damaged and that the speed sensor and rotor fixings are tight.
47 If the checks fail to identify the fault, follow the procedure in Section 12 to erase the fault code, then activate the self-checking procedure. If the fault code remains it is likely the ABS control unit is faulty – have it checked by a Suzuki dealer.

Code 61 – ABS solenoid malfunction

48 Check the ABS valve fuse (see Chapter 8). If the fuse is good, follow the procedure in Section 14, Steps 16 to 18, and check the ABS control unit wiring connector is secure, then disconnect it and check that the terminals are clean and undamaged.
49 Check for battery voltage between the following terminal pins on the loom side of the connector **(see illustration 13.7a, b or c)**. If there is no voltage, inspect the wiring for damage.

    2007 to 2011 DL – pin 3 (positive probe)
        and pin 4 (negative probe)
    2012-on DL – pin 1 (positive probe) and
        pin 9 (negative probe)
    SFV – pin 8 (positive probe) and pin 24
        (negative probe)

50 If there is voltage, it is likely the ABS control unit is faulty – have it tested by a Suzuki dealer.

14 ABS components

Front wheel sensor

1 On DL models remove the air filter housing to access the sensor wiring connector (see Chapter 4); on SFV models the connector is located alongside the steering head on the left-hand side. Trace the wheel sensor wiring to the connector and disconnect it **(see illustration 13.24a or b)**.
2 Release the sensor wiring guides and feed the wire down to the sensor, noting its routing. Unscrew the sensor bolt and remove the sensor **(see illustrations)**.

14.2a Removing the front wheel sensor – DL

14.2b Front wheel sensor wiring guide (arrowed)...

14.2c ...and sensor bolts – SFV

Brakes, wheels and final drive 6•23

3 Make sure the tip of the sensor, its mounting surfaces, and the sensor rotor are clean and show no signs of damage. Fit the sensor and tighten the bolt. Check the air gap (Section 13, Step 23). Feed the wiring up to the connector, routing and securing it as noted on removal. Install the air filter housing (see Chapter 4).

Front sensor rotor

4 Remove the front wheel (see Section 17). On 2007 to 2011 DL models remove the sensor bracket.

5 Undo the screws securing the rotor and lift it off **(see illustration)**.

6 Make sure there is no dirt or corrosion where the ring seats on the hub – if the ring does not sit flat the signals from the sensor could be distorted. Fit the rotor with the 50T (DL) or 44H (SFV) mark facing out.

7 Install the front wheel (see Section 17). Check the sensor air gap (Section 13, Step 23).

Rear wheel sensor

8 On DL models remove the seat and if required the left-hand side cover to access the sensor wiring connector (see Chapter 7). On SFV models remove the ABS unit cover to access the sensor wiring connector. Disconnect the wheel sensor wiring connector **(see illustration 13.35a or b)**.

9 Release the sensor wiring guides and feed the wire down to the sensor, noting its routing.

14.5 Front wheel sensor rotor screws (arrowed)

14.9b Wiring guide (arrowed)...

Unscrew the sensor bolt and remove the sensor **(see illustrations)**.

10 Make sure the tip of the sensor, its mounting surfaces, and the sensor rotor are clean. Fit the sensor and tighten the bolt.

14.9a Removing the rear wheel sensor – DL

14.9c ...and rear wheel sensor – SFV

Check the air gap (Section 13, Step 33). Feed the wiring up to the connector, routing and securing it as noted on removal.

11 Install the seat or side cover according to model.

Rear sensor rotor

12 Remove the rear wheel (see Section 18).

13 Undo the screws securing the rotor and lift it off **(see illustration 14.5)**.

14 Make sure there is no dirt or corrosion where the ring seats on the hub – if the ring does not sit flat the signals from the sensor could be distorted. Fit the rotor with the 50T mark facing out.

15 Install the rear wheel (see Section 18). Check the air gap (Section 13, Step 33).

ABS control unit/modulator

Note: *Before removing the modulator drain all old brake fluid from the brake system, then fill with new fluid on installation (see Section 11). The modulator cannot be dismantled for overhaul, and no component parts are available. If it fails, it must be replaced with a new one.*

DL models

16 On 2007 to 2011DL models, and for best access on 2012-on DL models (though you can do it without), remove the battery (see Chapter 8), then displace or remove all the electrical components around the battery and remove the battery tray.

17 Remove the control unit cover **(see illustrations)**.

18 Release and disconnect the modulator wiring connector **(see illustration)**.

14.17a Unscrew the bolt (arrowed)...

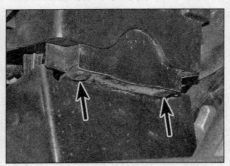

14.17b ...release the trim clips (arrowed)...

14.17c ...and remove the cover – 2012-on DL shown

14.18 Use a screwdriver to release the connector

19 Cover the area around the modulator with clean rag to prevent damage to paintwork in the event that brake fluid is spilled.

20 Unscrew the brake pipe nuts and detach the pipes **(see illustration)**. Plug the holes in the modulator and seal the pipes to prevent dirt entering the system.

21 Unscrew the bolts and remove the control unit **(see illustration)**.

22 Installation is the reverse of removal, noting the following:

● Do not tighten any of the pipe nuts until all pipes are loosely connected to ensure correct alignment.

● Make sure the wiring connector is secure.

● Follow the procedure in Section 11 to refill and bleed the brake system. Check that there are no fluid leaks and test the operation of the brakes before riding the motorcycle.

Caution: Brake fluid attacks painted finishes and plastics – to prevent damage from spilled fluid, always cover paintwork when working on the braking system, and clean up any spills immediately using brake cleaner.

SFV models

23 Remove the battery (see Chapter 8). Displace the fuse/relay block and starter relay from their mounting tabs **(see illustration)**. Ease the ECM out of its location in front of the battery housing; there is no need to disconnect the wiring **(see illustration)**.

24 Remove the control unit cover from the right-hand side; it is retained by two trim clips and a screw **(see illustrations)**.

14.20 Brake pipe nuts (arrowed) – 2012-on DL shown

14.23a Displace the fusebox/relay unit (A) and starter relay (B)

14.21 Control unit bolts (arrowed) – 2012-on DL shown

14.23b Ease the ECM out

25 Remove the right-hand side cover (see Chapter 7).

26 Remove the two bolts and three screws which retain the battery housing to the frame and rear mudguard **(see illustrations)**.

Manoeuvre the housing free being careful not to pull on the surrounding wiring. Take note of the heat shield's position on the front of the housing.

27 Release its orange catch and disconnect

14.24a Remove the trim clip (arrowed) at the rear...

14.24b ...and front of the control unit right-hand cover

14.24c Remove the screw...

14.24d ...and manoeuvre the cover out

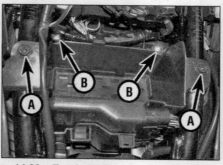

14.26a Two bolts (A), two screws (B)...

14.26b ...and single screw (C) retain the battery housing

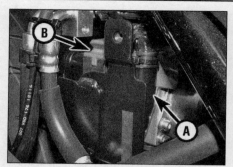

14.27 Control unit connector (A) and catch (B)

14.28 Trim clip (arrowed) at top of left-hand cover

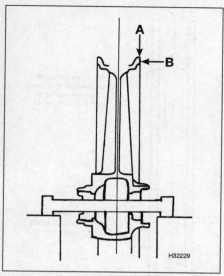

15.3 Check the wheel for radial (out-of-round) runout (A) and axial (side-to-side) runout (B)

the modulator wiring connector **(see illustration)**.

28 Remove the control unit cover from the left-hand side; it is retained by a trim clip on the top edge and a bolt on the underside **(see illustration)**.

29 Cover the area around the modulator with clean rag to prevent damage to paintwork in the event that brake fluid is spilled. Unscrew the brake pipe nuts and detach the pipes. Plug the holes in the modulator and seal the pipes to prevent dirt entering the system.

30 Unscrew the bolts and remove the control unit.

31 Installation is the reverse of removal, noting the following:
● Do not tighten any of the pipe nuts until all pipes are loosely connected to ensure correct alignment.
● Make sure the wiring connector is secure.
● Follow the procedure in Section 11 to refill and bleed the brake system. Check that there are no fluid leaks and test the operation of the brakes before riding the motorcycle.

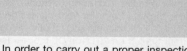

15 Wheel inspection and repair

1 In order to carry out a proper inspection of the wheels, support the bike on an auxiliary stand. Clean the wheels thoroughly to remove mud and dirt that may interfere with the inspection procedure or mask defects. Make a general check of the wheels (see Chapter 1) and tyres (see *Pre-ride checks*).

2 Inspect the wheels for cracks, flat spots on the rim and other damage. Look very closely for dents in the area where the tyre bead contacts the rim. Dents in this area may prevent complete sealing of the tyre against the rim, which leads to deflation of the tyre over a period of time. If damage is evident, or if runout in either direction is excessive, the wheel will have to be replaced with a new one. Never attempt to repair a damaged alloy wheel.

3 To check axial (side-to-side) runout of the wheel rim attach a dial gauge to the fork or the

swingarm and position its tip against the side of the wheel rim. Spin the wheel slowly and check the amount of run-out, comparing it to the specification listed at the beginning of the Chapter **(see illustration)**.

4 In order to accurately check radial (out of round) runout with the dial gauge, remove the wheel from the machine, and the tyre from the wheel. With the axle clamped in a vice and the dial gauge positioned on the top of the rim, the wheel can be rotated to check the runout **(see illustration 15.3)**.

5 An easier, though slightly less accurate, method is to attach a stiff wire pointer to the fork or the swingarm and position the end a fraction of an inch from the wheel rim where the wheel and tyre join. If the wheel is true, the distance from the pointer to the rim will be constant as the wheel is rotated. **Note:** *If wheel runout is excessive, check the wheel bearings very carefully before renewing the wheel.*

16 Wheel alignment check

1 Misalignment of the wheels due to a bent frame or forks can cause strange and possibly serious handling problems. If the frame or forks are at fault, repair by a frame specialist or renewal are the only options.

2 To check wheel alignment you will need an assistant, a length of string or a perfectly

straight piece of wood and a ruler. A plumb bob or spirit level for checking that the wheels are vertical will also be required.

3 Support the bike upright. Measure the width of both tyres at their widest points. Subtract the smaller measurement from the larger measurement, then divide the difference by two. The result is the amount of offset that should exist between the front and rear tyres on both sides of the machine.

4 If the string method is used, have your assistant hold one end of it about halfway between the floor and the rear axle, with the string touching the back edge of the rear tyre sidewall.

5 Run the other end of the string forward and pull it tight so that it is roughly parallel to the floor **(see illustration)**. Slowly bring the string into contact with the front edge of the rear tyre sidewall, then turn the front wheel until it is parallel with the string. Measure the distance from the front tyre sidewall to the string.

6 Repeat the procedure on the other side of the motorcycle. The distance from the front tyre sidewall to the string should be equal on both sides.

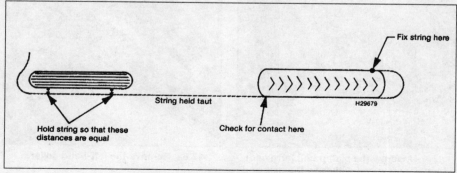

16.5 Wheel alignment check using string

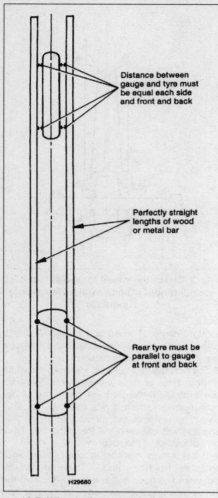

16.7 Wheel alignment check using a straight-edge

Distance between gauge and tyre must be equal each side and front and back

Perfectly straight lengths of wood or metal bar

Rear tyre must be parallel to gauge at front and back

H29680

7 As previously mentioned, a perfectly straight length of wood or metal bar may be substituted for the string **(see illustration)**.

8 If the distance between the string and tyre is greater on one side, or if the rear wheel appears to be out of alignment, have your machine checked by a Suzuki dealer or frame specialist.

9 If the front-to-back alignment is correct, the wheels still may be out of alignment vertically.

10 Using a plumb bob or spirit level, check the rear wheel to make sure it is vertical. To do this, hold the string of the plumb bob against the tyre upper sidewall and allow the weight to settle just off the floor. If the string touches both the upper and lower tyre sidewalls and is perfectly straight, the wheel is vertical. If it is not, adjust the stand until it is.

11 Once the rear wheel is vertical, check the front wheel in the same manner. If both wheels are not perfectly vertical, the frame and/or major suspension components are bent.

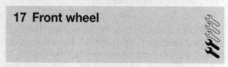

17 Front wheel

Removal

1 Support the bike on an auxiliary stand so that the front wheel is just off the ground. Always make sure the motorcycle is properly supported.

2 Displace the front brake calipers (see Section 3). Support the calipers with a cable-tie or a bungee cord so that no strain is placed on the hydraulic hoses. There is no need to disconnect the hoses from the calipers. **Note:** *Do not operate the front brake lever with the calipers removed.*

3 On models with ABS displace the speed sensor **(see illustration 14.9)** – there is no need to disconnect the wiring.

4 Slacken the axle clamp bolt in the bottom of the right-hand fork on 2004 to 2011 DL models and all SFV models, and in the left-hand fork on 2012-on DL models **(see illustration)**. Unscrew the axle using a 12 mm hex bit. Take the weight of the wheel, then withdraw the axle **(see illustration 17.4)**. Carefully lower the wheel.

5 On 2004 to 2011 DL models displace the speed sensor from the left-hand side. On 2007 to 2011 DL models with ABS models remove the wheel sensor bracket. Remove the wheel from between the forks.

6 On 2012-on DL models remove the flanged collar from the left-hand side of the wheel, and the collar from the right-hand side **(see illustrations)**. On SFV models remove the collar from the left-hand side of the wheel. Remove the wheel from between the forks.

Caution: Don't lay the wheel down and allow it to rest on a disc – the disc could become warped. Set the wheel on wood blocks so the disc doesn't support the weight of the wheel.

7 Clean all old grease off the collars, axle and seals. Check the axle is straight by rolling it on a flat surface such as a piece of plate glass (first remove any corrosion using steel wool). If the equipment is available, place the axle in V-blocks and check for runout using a dial gauge. If the axle is bent replace it with a new one.

8 Check the condition of the grease seals and wheel bearings (see Section 19).

Installation

9 Apply a smear of grease to the inside of the speed sensor or wheel collars(s) according to model, and also to the outside where they fit into a seal. On 2012-on DL models fit the collar onto the right-hand side of the wheel **(see illustration 17.6b)**. On SFV models fit the collar onto the left-hand side of the wheel.

10 Each side of the wheel can be identified using the directional arrow (denoting the normal direction of wheel rotation) on the tyre and on the brake disc. Manoeuvre the wheel into position between the forks – check it is the correct way round using the directional arrows. On 2004 to 2011 DL models fit the speed sensor. On 2007 to 2011 DL models with ABS models locate the wheel sensor bracket. On 2012-on DL models fit the flanged collar onto the left-hand side of the wheel **(see illustration 17.6a)**.

11 Apply a thin coat of grease to the axle. Lift the wheel into place, making sure the collar(s)/sensor/bracket remain in position, and seating the lug on the fork in the cut-out in the sensor or sensor bracket according to model. Slide the axle through from the right-hand side on 2004 to 2011 DL models and all SFV models, and from the left on 2012-on DL models **(see illustration 17.4)**.

12 Tighten the axle to the torque setting specified at the beginning of the Chapter.

17.4 Unscrew the clamp bolt (arrowed) then unscrew and withdraw the axle and lower the wheel

17.6a Remove the left-hand collar...

17.6b ...and the right-hand collar

13 Lower the front wheel to the ground. Install the brake calipers (see Section 3).

14 Apply the brake lever a few times to bring the pads back into contact with the discs, then with the front brake applied pump the front forks a few times to settle all components in position.

15 Tighten the axle clamp bolt to the specified torque.

16 On ABS models, fit the sensor, then check the air gap (Section 13, Step 23).

17 Clean the discs using brake system cleaner. Check for correct operation of the brakes before riding the motorcycle.

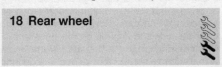

18 Rear wheel

Removal

1 Support the bike on an auxiliary stand so that the rear wheel is off the ground. Tie the front brake lever to the handlebar. Always make sure the motorcycle is properly supported.

2 On models with ABS displace the speed sensor **(see illustration 14.9)** – there is no need to disconnect the wiring.

3 Create some slack in the chain (see Chapter 1).

4 If required remove the brake pads (see Section 6) – this will making installation of the wheel easier.

5 Unscrew the axle nut, on DL models remove the adjustment marker and on SFV models remove the washer **(see illustrations)**.

6 Take the weight of the wheel, then withdraw the axle, on DL models along with the adjustment marker, and lower the wheel to the ground **(see illustration)**. If the axle is difficult to withdraw, drive it out using a soft-faced mallet to prevent damage to the threads. Remove the chain adjuster from each side of the swingarm if required **(see illustration)**.

7 Disengage the chain from the sprocket **(see illustration)**. Draw the wheel back until the caliper bracket can be slid back off its guide on the swingarm, then lift it out from between the swingarm and the wheel and support it clear **(see illustration)**. Remove the wheel. Fit the caliper bracket back onto the swingarm if required, and secure it using a cable-tie.

Caution: Do not lay the wheel down and

18.5a Rear axle nut and adjustment marker (arrowed) – DL

18.5b Rear axle nut and washer (arrowed) – SFV

18.6a Withdraw the axle and lower the wheel

18.6b Remove the adjusters if required

allow it to rest on the disc or the sprocket – they could become warped. Set the wheel on wood blocks so the disc or the sprocket doesn't support the weight of the wheel. Do not operate the brakes with the wheel removed.

8 Remove the spacer from each side of the wheel, noting which fits where **(see illustration)**. Clean all old grease off the spacers, axle and seals.

9 Check the axle is straight by rolling it on a flat surface such as a piece of plate glass (if the axle is corroded, first remove the corrosion with steel wool). If the equipment is available, place the axle in V-blocks and check for runout using a dial gauge. If the axle is bent replace it with a new one.

10 Check the condition of the grease seals and wheel bearings (see Section 19). Check the condition of the sprocket coupling (see Section 23).

Installation

11 Apply a smear of grease to the inside of the wheel spacers, and also to the outside where they fit into the wheel. On DL models fit the thin-walled spacer into the right-hand side and the thick-walled one into the left **(see illustration 18.8)**. On SFV models fit the shouldered spacer into the right-hand side of the wheel and the plain spacer into the left. Apply a thin coat of grease to the axle. If the caliper bracket is located on the swingarm displace it and support it clear.

12 On DL models fit the adjustment marker onto the axle.

13 Manoeuvre the wheel into position between the ends of the swingarm. Slide the brake caliper bracket between the wheel and the swingarm **(see illustration 18.7b)** and locate it on its guide. Engage the drive chain with the sprocket **(see illustration 18.7a)**.

18.7a Slip the chain off the sprocket

18.7b Draw the wheel back and displace the caliper bracket when clear

18.8 Remove the spacers

Slide the chain adjusters into the swingarm if removed **(see illustration 18.6b)**.

14 Lift the wheel into position and slide the axle in from the left on DL models and from the right on SFV models **(see illustration 18.6a)**, making sure the spacers and caliper bracket remain correctly installed. On DL models locate the adjustment marker in the channel in the swingarm. Check that everything is correctly aligned. Fit the adjustment marker or washer onto the end of the axle, then fit the axle nut but leave it loose **(see illustration 18.5a or b)**.

15 Install the brake pads if removed (Section 6).

16 Check and adjust the drive chain slack (see Chapter 1). On completion tighten the axle nut to the torque setting specified at the beginning of the Chapter.

17 On ABS models, fit the sensor, then check the air gap (Section 13, Step 23).

18 Clean the disc using brake system cleaner. Check the operation of the brakes carefully before riding the bike.

19.3 Lever out the bearing seal(s)

19.4a Move the spacer to expose the inner race (arrowed)...

19.4d ...then fit the slide-hammer and jar the bearing out

19 Wheel bearings

Note: *Always replace the wheel bearings in sets, never individually. Applying some heat to the bearing housing using a hot air gun will make removal and installation easier, and chilling the new bearings in a fridge or freezer before fitting them also helps.*

Front wheel bearings

1 Remove the wheel (see Section 17). Support the wheel on wood blocks so that the wheel rim supports the weight of the wheel.

2 Inspect the seals and bearings – check that the bearing inner race turns smoothly and that the outer race is a tight fit in the hub (see *Tools and Workshop Tips* in the Reference Section). **Note:** *Do not remove the bearings unless they are going to be replaced with new ones.* If new components are needed, it is best to remove the discs (Section 4), and on ABS models the sensor rotor (Section 14), to prevent them being damaged or distorted during bearing removal.

3 Lever the seal out from the right-hand side of the hub on DL models, and from each side on SFV models, using a flat-bladed screwdriver or a seal hook **(see illustration)**. Take care not to damage the hub. New seals must be fitted on reassembly.

4 Move the left-hand end of the centre spacer to one side to expose the inner race of the left-hand bearing, then locate a drift on it and drive the bearing out **(see illustrations)**.

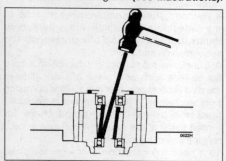

19.4b ...then drive the bearing out using a drift locating it as shown

19.7 Using a socket to drive the bearing in

If you can't move the spacer, or if you can't get sufficient purchase with the drift, remove the bearings using an internal expanding puller with slide-hammer attachment – select the correct attachment and locate it between the inner race of the upper bearing and the spacer, then tighten the inner bolt to expand and lock the puller **(see illustration)**. Attach the slide-hammer, hold the wheel firmly down and jar the bearing out **(see illustration)**. Having removed the first bearing remove the spacer which fits between the bearings.

5 Remove the other bearing in the same way, or drive it out using a suitable drift (such as a socket on an extension) inserted from the opposite side and located on the inner race.

6 Thoroughly clean the hub area of the wheel with a suitable solvent and inspect the bearing housing for scoring and wear.

7 If the new bearing has an open side pack grease into it. Fit the new bearings with the marked and sealed side facing outwards. On DL models fit the left-hand bearing first, and on SFV models fit the right-hand bearing first. Drive it into the hub using a bearing driver or suitable socket that seats on the outer race **(see illustration)**. Make sure the bearing fits squarely and all the way onto its seat.

8 Turn the wheel over and fit the bearing spacer. Fit the second bearing in the same way until the inner race seats on the spacer.

9 Fit the new seal(s) into the hub using finger pressure or a suitable driver that bears on the outer rim, setting it/them flush with the hub **(see illustration)**. Smear the seal lips with grease.

10 Install the brake discs and sensor rotor if

19.4c Fit the attachment under the bearing...

19.9 Fit the seal, setting it flush with the rim

19.12 Lift the sprocket coupling off the wheel

19.23 Remove the spacer

19.25 Lever out the bearing seal

removed (see Sections 4 and 14). Clean the discs using brake system cleaner, then install the wheel (see Section 17).

Rear wheel bearings

11 Remove the wheel (see Section 18). If required remove the disc (see Section 8) to prevent it being damaged or distorted during bearing removal – if you do leave it in place, take care to support the wheel on wood blocks so that the wheel rim supports the weight of the wheel.

12 Lift the sprocket coupling out of the hub **(see illustration)**.

13 Inspect the seal and bearings in both sides of the hub – check that the bearing inner race turns smoothly and that the outer race is a tight fit in the hub (see *Tools and Workshop Tips* in the Reference section). **Note:** *Do not remove the bearings unless they are going to be replaced with new ones.*

14 If new components are needed lever out the bearing seal from the right-hand side of the hub using a flat-bladed screwdriver or a seal hook **(see illustration 19.3)**. Take care not to damage the hub. Discard the seal as a new one should be fitted on reassembly.

15 Move the left-hand end of the centre spacer to one side to expose the inner race of the left-hand bearing, then locate a drift on it and drive the bearing out **(see illustrations 19.4a and b)**. If you can't move the spacer, or if you can't get sufficient purchase with the drift, remove the bearings using an internal expanding puller, either of the screw-type or with slide-hammer attachment – select the correct attachment and locate it between the inner race of the upper bearing and the spacer, then tighten the inner bolt to expand and lock the puller **(see illustration 19.4c)**.

Either tighten the puller bolt to draw the bearing out, or attach the slide-hammer, hold the wheel firmly down and jar the bearing out **(see illustration 19.4d)**. Having removed the first bearing remove the spacer which fits between the bearings.

16 Remove the other bearing in the same way, or drive it out using a suitable drift (such as a socket on an extension) inserted from the opposite side and located on the inner race.

17 Thoroughly clean the hub area of the wheel with a suitable solvent and inspect the bearing housing for scoring and wear.

18 If the new bearing has an open side pack grease into it. Fit the new bearings with the marked and sealed side facing outwards. Fit the right-hand bearing first. Drive it into the hub using a bearing driver or suitable socket that seats on the outer race **(see illustration 19.7)**. Make sure the bearing fits squarely and all the way onto its seat.

19 Turn the wheel over and fit the bearing spacer. Fit the second bearing in the same way until the inner race seats on the spacer.

20 Fit the new seal into the right-hand side of the hub using finger pressure or a suitable driver that bears on the outer rim, setting it flush with the hub **(see illustration 19.9)**. Smear the seal lips with grease.

21 Check the sprocket coupling/rubber dampers (see Section 23). Fit the coupling **(see illustration 19.12)**. Clean the brake disc using acetone or brake system cleaner. Install the wheel (see Section 18).

Sprocket coupling bearing

22 Remove the wheel (see Section 18). Lift the sprocket coupling out of the hub **(see illustration 19.12)**.

23 Remove the bearing spacer from inside the coupling **(see illustration)**.

24 Inspect the seal and bearing – check that the bearing inner races turn smoothly and that the outer race is a tight fit in the coupling (see *Tools and Workshop Tips* in the Reference Section). **Note:** *Do not remove the bearing unless it is being replaced with a new one.*

25 If new components are needed lever out the bearing seal using a flat-bladed screwdriver or a seal hook **(see illustration)**. Take care not to damage the rim of the coupling. Discard the seal – a new one must be fitted.

26 Support the coupling on blocks of wood, sprocket side down, and drive the bearing out from the inside using a bearing driver or socket **(see illustration)**.

27 Thoroughly clean the coupling with a suitable solvent and inspect the bearing housing for scoring and wear.

28 If the new bearing has an open side pack grease into it. Fit the new bearing with the marked side facing outwards. Drive it into the coupling using a driver or suitable socket on the outer race of the bearing (see *Tools and Workshop Tips*) **(see illustration)**. Make sure the bearing fits squarely and all the way onto its seat.

29 Fit the bearing spacer **(see illustration 19.23)**.

30 Fit the new seal into the coupling **(see illustration)**. Level the seal with the rim of the coupling with a small block of wood. Smear the seal lip with grease.

31 Check the sprocket coupling/rubber dampers (see Section 23). Fit the coupling **(see illustration 19.12)**. Install the wheel (see Section 18).

19.26 Drive the bearing out from the inside

19.28 Drive the bearing in from the outside

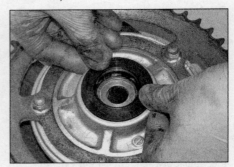
19.30 Press the new seal into the hub

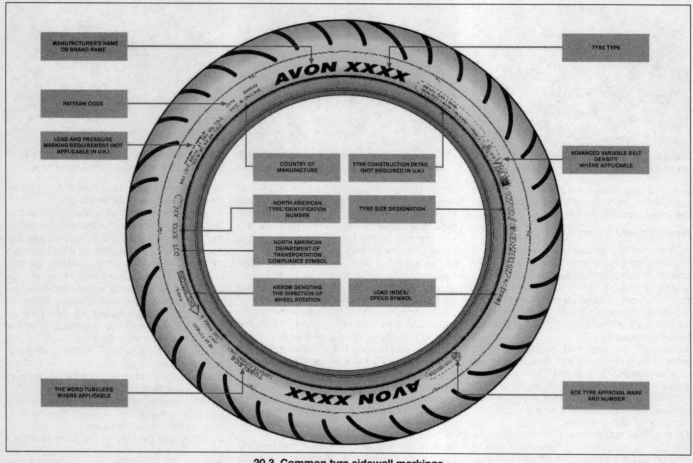

MANUFACTURER'S NAME
OR BRAND NAME

TYRE TYPE

PATTERN CODE

LOAD AND PRESSURE
MARKING REQUIREMENT (NOT
APPLICABLE IN U.K.)

ADVANCED VARIABLE BELT
DENSITY
WHERE APPLICABLE

COUNTRY OF
MANUFACTURE

TYRE CONSTRUCTION DETAIL
(NOT REQUIRED IN U.K.)

NORTH AMERICAN
TYRE IDENTIFICATION
NUMBER

TYRE SIZE DESIGNATION

NORTH AMERICAN
DEPARTMENT OF
TRANSPORTATION
COMPLIANCE SYMBOL

ARROW DENOTING
THE DIRECTION OF
WHEEL ROTATION

LOAD INDEX/
SPEED SYMBOL

THE WORD TUBELESS
WHERE APPLICABLE

ECE TYPE APPROVAL MARK
AND NUMBER

20.3 Common tyre sidewall markings

20 Tyres

General information

1 The wheels on all models are designed to take tubeless tyres only. Tyre sizes are given in the Specifications at the beginning of this chapter.
2 Refer to the *Pre-ride checks* listed at the beginning of this manual for tyre maintenance.

Fitting new tyres

3 When selecting new tyres, refer to the tyre information in the Owner's Handbook. Ensure that front and rear tyre types are compatible, the correct size and correct speed rating; if necessary seek advice from a Suzuki dealer or tyre fitting specialist **(see illustration)**.
4 It is recommended that tyres are fitted by a motorcycle tyre specialist rather than attempted in the home workshop. This is particularly relevant in the case of tubeless tyres because the force required to break the seal between the wheel rim and tyre bead is substantial, and is usually beyond

the capabilities of an individual working with normal tyre levers. Additionally, the specialist will be able to balance the wheels after tyre fitting.
5 Note that punctured tubeless tyres can in some cases be repaired. External repairs made using a repair kit should only ever be considered as a temporary measure to get you to a dealer for a new tyre, and riding at speed or with any extra load should be avoided. Internal repairs carried out by a motorcycle tyre fitting specialist are better. Make sure a wheel with a repaired tyre is balanced before it is fitted back on the bike. Seek advice from the repairer regarding the speed and load capabilities of a repaired tyre.

21 Drive chain

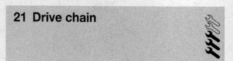

Note: *The original equipment drive chain fitted to these models has a staked-type master (joining) link which can be disassembled using either the Suzuki service tool, Pt. No. 09922-22711, or one of several commercially-available drive chain cutting/staking tools. Such chains can be recognised by the master*

joining link side plate's identification marks (and usually its different colour), as well as by the staked ends of the link's two pins which look as if they have been deeply centre-punched, instead of peened over as with all the other pins.

Removal

1 If possible support the bike on an auxiliary stand so that the rear wheel is off the ground. Locate the joining link in a suitable position to work on by rotating the back wheel **(see illustration)**. Slacken the drive chain as described in Chapter 1.

21.1 The joining link has different pin ends

2 Remove the chainguard (see Chapter 5, Section 13).
3 Remove the front sprocket cover(s) (see Section 22).
4 Split the chain at the joining link using the chain tool, following carefully the manufacturer's operating instructions (see also *Tools and Workshop Tips* in the Reference Section). Remove the chain from the bike, noting its routing around the swingarm.

Check and cleaning

5 Refer to Chapter 1, Section 1, for details of routine checks, and cleaning with the chain installed on the sprockets. Whenever the drive chain is inspected, the sprockets should be inspected also (see Section 22). You should always renew the chain and sprockets as a set – worn sprockets can ruin a new drive chain and *vice versa*.
6 If the chain is extremely dirty remove it from the motorcycle and soak it in paraffin (kerosene) for approximately five or six minutes, then clean it using a soft brush.
Caution: Don't use gasoline (petrol), solvent or other cleaning fluids which might damage its internal sealing properties. Don't use high-pressure water. Remove the chain, wipe it off, then blow dry it with compressed air immediately. The entire process shouldn't take longer than ten minutes – if it does, the O-rings in the chain rollers could be damaged.

Installation

⚠️ *Warning: NEVER install a drive chain which uses a clip-type master (split) link. Use ONLY the correct service tools to secure the staked-type of master link – if you do not have access to such tools, have the chain replaced by a Suzuki dealer.*
Caution: Before fitting a new chain check the sprockets and fit new ones if necessary – worn sprockets can ruin a new drive chain.

Note: *The specifications referred to in Steps 8 and 9 only apply to the drive chain types fitted as original equipment (see Specifications).*

7 Route the drive chain around the sprockets leaving the two ends mid-way between the sprockets along the bottom run.
8 Follow carefully the instructions of both the chain manufacturer and the tool manufacturer. DO NOT re-use old joining link components. Referring to *Tools and Workshop Tips* in the Reference Section, install the new joining link from the inside using new O-rings. Fit the new sideplate using new O-rings and with its identification marks facing out, and press it on until the distance between the outer sides of the sideplates is within the measurements specified at the beginning of the Chapter.
9 Stake the new link pins using the chain tool. Check the joining link and staking for any signs of cracking. If there is any evidence of cracking, the joining link, O-rings and sideplate must be removed and new ones fitted. Measure the diameter of the staked ends in two directions and check that it is evenly staked and within the measurements specified at the beginning

of the Chapter. Check that the link pivots freely.
10 Install the sprocket cover(s) (see Section 22).
11 Install the chainguard.
12 On completion, adjust and lubricate the chain following the procedures described in Chapter 1.

22 Sprockets

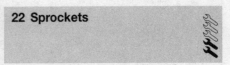

Front sprocket cover removal and installation

1 On 2004 to 2011 DL models unscrew the bolts and remove the cover (**see illustration**).
2 On SFV models mark the alignment of the slit in the gearchange linkage arm with the shaft, then unscrew the pinch bolt and slide the arm off (**see illustration**).
3 On 2012-on DL models and all SFV models unscrew the bolts and remove the outer cover (**see illustration**). Displace the speed sensor (**see illustration**). Unscrew the bolts

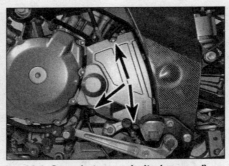

22.1 Sprocket cover bolts (arrowed)

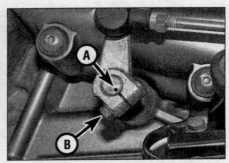

22.2 Alignment mark (A), gearchange arm pinch bolt (B)

22.3a Outer sprocket cover bolts (arrowed)

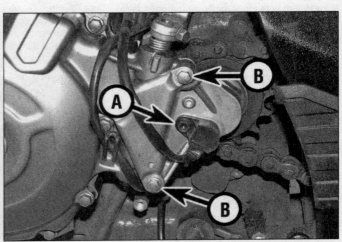

22.3b Speed sensor bolt (A), inner sprocket cover bolts (B)

22.3c Inner sprocket cover dowels (arrowed)

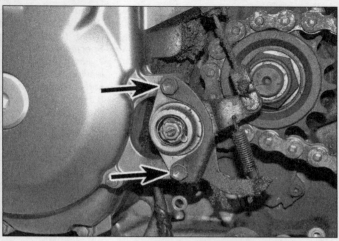

22.8 Release mechanism bolts (arrowed)

22.9 Speed sensor rotor bolt (arrowed)

22.10 Bend the tabs down...

and remove the inner cover. Remove the two dowels if loose (see illustration).

4 Installation is the reverse of removal. On SFV models align the slit in the gearchange linkage arm with mark made on the shaft (see illustration 22.2).

Sprocket check

5 Check the wear pattern on both sprockets (see Chapter 1, Section 1). If the sprocket teeth are worn excessively, replace both sprockets as a set. Whenever the sprockets are inspected, the drive chain should be inspected also (see Chapter 1). Always renew the chain and sprockets as a set – a worn drive chain can ruin new sprockets and vice versa.

6 Adjust and lubricate the chain following the procedures described in Chapter 1.

Caution: Before fitting new sprockets check the chain and fit a new one if necessary – a worn drive chain can ruin new sprockets.

Sprocket removal and installation

Front sprocket

7 Remove the front sprocket cover(s) (see Steps 1 to 3).

8 On 2004 to 2011 DL models unscrew the two bolts securing the clutch release mechanism and displace it – there is no need to detach the cable (see illustration).

9 On 2012-on DL models and all SFV models hold the rear brake on, unscrew the speed sensor rotor bolt and remove the rotor (see illustration).

10 Bend the lockwasher tab(s) back off the side of the sprocket nut (see illustration).

11 Have an assistant apply the rear brake, then unscrew and remove the nut (see illustration). Remove the lockwasher, and on SFV models the inner washer – a new lockwasher must be used (see illustration).

22.11a ...unscrew the nut...

22.11b ...and remove the washer(s)

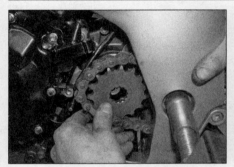

22.13 Remove the sprocket

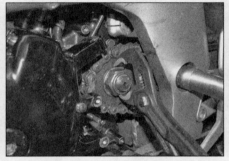

22.17 Bend the rim of the washer up against the nut

22.22 Rear sprocket nuts (arrowed)

12 Fully slacken the drive chain as described in Chapter 1. If the rear sprocket is being removed as well, remove the rear wheel now to give full slack (see Section 18). Otherwise disengage the chain from the rear sprocket if required to provide more slack.
13 Slide the chain and sprocket off the shaft, then slip the sprocket out of the chain (see illustration).
14 Clean the threads on the end of the output shaft.
15 Engage the new sprocket with the chain, making sure the marked side is facing out, and slide it on the shaft (see illustration 22.13).
16 If removed, fit the rear sprocket now, and install the wheel (see Section 18). If the chain was merely disengaged, fit it back onto the rear sprocket. Take up the slack in the chain (see Chapter 1).
17 On SFV models fit the inner washer. On all models fit a new lockwasher (see illustration 22.11b). Apply some thread locking compound to the shaft threads. Fit the nut and tighten it to the torque setting specified at the beginning of the Chapter, holding the rear brake on to prevent the sprocket turning (see illustration 22.11a). Bend the lockwasher tab(s) up against the side of the nut (see illustration).
18 On 2012-on DL models and all SFV models fit the speed sensor rotor, then hold the rear brake on and tighten the bolt to the specified torque setting (see illustration 22.9).
19 On 2004 to 2011 DL models fit the clutch release mechanism (see illustration 22.8). Check the clutch cable freeplay and adjust if necessary (see Chapter 1).
20 Fit the sprocket cover(s) (see above). Adjust and lubricate the chain following the procedures described in Chapter 1.

Rear sprocket

21 Remove the rear wheel (see Section 18).

Rest it sprocket side up on some blocks of wood.
22 Unscrew the sprocket nuts and lift the sprocket off, noting which way round it fits (see illustration).
23 Fit the sprocket onto the hub with the marked side facing out. On SFV models make sure the sprocket bolts are all correctly secured by trying to turn the threaded ends – if necessary lift the sprocket coupling out and seat the bolt heads in their sockets on the inner side of the coupling. Fit the nuts, hold the wheel and tighten the nuts evenly and in a criss-cross sequence to the torque setting specified at the beginning of the Chapter.
24 Install the rear wheel (see Section 18).

23 Rear sprocket coupling/ rubber dampers

1 Remove the rear wheel (see Section 18). Check for play between the sprocket coupling and the wheel hub by turning the sprocket

23.1 Check for any rotational play between the coupling and wheel

(see illustration). Any play indicates worn rubber damper segments.
Caution: Do not lay the wheel down on the disc as it could become warped. Lay the wheel on wooden blocks so that the disc is off the ground.
2 Lift the sprocket coupling off the wheel leaving the rubber dampers in position (see illustration 19.12). Note the spacer inside the coupling. Check the coupling for cracks or any obvious signs of damage.
3 Lift the rubber damper segments from the wheel and check them for cracks, hardening and general deterioration (see illustration). Replace them with a new set if necessary.
4 Smear the mating surface of the hub and coupling with grease.
5 Checking and replacement procedures for the sprocket coupling bearing are in Section 19.
6 Installation is the reverse of removal. Make sure the spacer is correctly installed in the coupling (see illustration 19.23). Align the coupling correctly with the rubber dampers and press it fully into the hub.
7 Install the rear wheel (see Section 18).

23.3 Check the rubber dampers as described

Notes

Chapter 7
Bodywork

Contents

Degrees of difficulty

| **Easy,** suitable for novice with little experience | | **Fairly easy,** suitable for beginner with some experience | | **Fairly difficult,** suitable for competent DIY mechanic | | **Difficult,** suitable for experienced DIY mechanic | | **Very difficult,** suitable for expert DIY or professional | |

1 General information

This Chapter covers the procedures necessary to remove and install the bodywork. Since many service and repair operations on these motorcycles require the removal of the body panels, the procedures are grouped here and referred to from other Chapters.

In the case of damage to the bodywork, it is usually necessary to remove the broken component and replace it with a new (or used) one. Note that there are however some companies that specialise in 'plastic welding'

and there are a number of bodywork repair kits now available for motorcycles.

When attempting to remove any body panel, first study it closely, noting any fasteners and associated fittings, to be sure of returning everything to its correct place on installation. Refer to Section 2 for more information on the types of trim clip used and how to release and refit them. In some cases the aid of an assistant will be required when removing panels, to help avoid the risk of damage to paintwork. Once the evident fasteners have been removed, try to withdraw the panel as described but DO NOT FORCE IT – if it will not release, check that all fasteners have been removed and try again.

When installing a body panel, first study it closely, noting any fasteners and associated fittings removed with it, to be sure of returning everything to its correct place. Check that all fasteners are in good condition, including the trim clips and damping/rubber mounts; replace any faulty fasteners with new ones before the panel is reassembled. Check also that all mounting brackets are straight and repair them or replace them with new ones if necessary before attempting to install the panel.

Tighten the fasteners securely, but be careful not to overtighten any of them or the panel may break (not always immediately) due to the uneven stress.

2.2a Push the centre pin (arrowed)...

2.2b ...into the body to release the clip

2.2c Push the centre pin out before installing the clip, then push it in when installed to lock it

2.3 Pull the centre pin (arrowed) out to release the clip, and push it back in to lock it

2.4a Undo the centre screw then pull the clip out

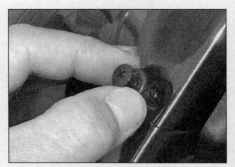

2.4b Fit the clip in the hole then push the centre in to lock it

2 Trim clips

1 Three types of plastic trim clip may be used, so carefully note which fits where when removing the body panels.

2 The first and most widely used type has a centre pin that you push into the body of the clip to allow the clip to be drawn out of the panel **(see illustrations)**. To install the clip, first expand the pawls of the clip body and push the centre pin back out **(see illustration)**. Now fit the clip body into its hole, then push the centre pin in so that it is flush with the clip head. The clip should now be locked in place.

3 The second type has a protruding centre pin that you pull out of the body of the clip to allow the clip to be drawn out of the panel **(see illustration)**. To install the clip, fit the clip body into its hole, then push the centre pin in. The clip should now be locked in place.

4 The third type of trim clip has a Phillips screw head in the centre that you unscrew, then pull the body of the clip out of the panel **(see illustration)**. When installing them, insert it in the panel then push the centre fully into the body **(see illustration)**. As they are made of plastic, the threads easily become worn in which case the centres may not unscrew. If this happens, lever the centre out of the body using a small screwdriver and replace the trim clip with a new one.

3 2004 to 2011 DL models

Seat

1 Unlock the seat using the ignition key, turning it clockwise, then lift the rear of the seat and draw it back and off, noting how the tabs locate **(see illustration)**.

2 Installation is the reverse of removal. Make sure the seat locates correctly. Push down on the back of the seat to engage the latch.

Fuel tank trim panels

3 Remove the seat.

4 To remove the side panels undo the screw at the front, then carefully pull the rear edge away to release the pegs top and bottom from the grommets **(see illustrations)**.

3.1 Unlock and remove the seat

3.4a Undo the screw (arrowed)...

3.4b ...then release the pegs (arrowed) from the grommets

3.5a Release the trim clips (arrowed)...

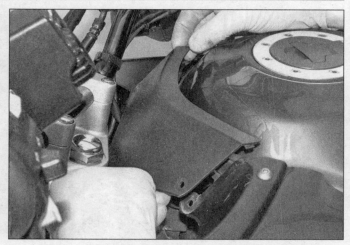

3.5b ...then release the tabs and remove the panel

5 To remove the top panel release the two trim clips, and remove the panel (see illustrations).
6 Installation is the reverse of removal. Make sure the grommets are in good condition, and smear them with oil or grease.

Grab-rack

7 Remove the seat.

8 Unscrew the four bolts and lift the grab-rack off (see illustration).
9 If required remove the carrier pad from the rack by carefully levering up each corner to release the pegs.
10 Installation is the reverse of removal.

Side covers

11 Remove the seat and the grab-rack.
12 Release the trim clip(s) on the underside,

then undo the screw at the front (see illustrations). Carefully pull the cover away to release the peg from the grommet, then release the tabs at the back (see illustrations).
13 Installation is the reverse of removal. Make sure the grommets are in good condition, and smear them with oil or grease.

Fairing side panels

14 Release the seven trim clips and undo

3.8 Grab-rack bolts (arrowed)

3.12a Side cover trim clips (arrowed) – left-hand cover

3.12b Side cover trim clip (arrowed) – right-hand cover

3.12c On both side covers, undo the screw (arrowed)...

3.12d ...then release the peg (arrowed) from the grommet...

3.12e ...and the tabs at the back

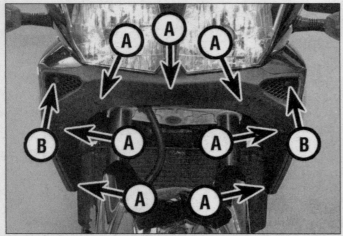

3.14a Release the trim clips (A) and undo the screws (B)...

3.14b ...and remove the inner panel

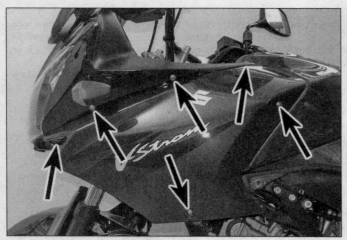

3.15a Undo the screws (arrowed)...

3.15b ...then lift the instrument surround panel to release the peg (arrowed)

the two screws securing the inner panel and remove it from between the side panels **(see illustrations)**.

15 Undo the screws, noting which fits where, then lift the side section of the instrument surround panel to release its peg from the grommet in the side panel and remove the panel **(see illustrations)**.

16 Installation is the reverse of removal.

Instrument surround panel

17 Remove the fuel tank top trim panel (Step 5).

18 Undo the two screws, then release the two trim clips **(see illustrations)**. Carefully pull the panel back to release the pegs from the grommets **(see illustration)**. Disconnect the instrument cluster wiring connector and remove the panel **(see**

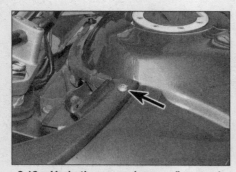

3.18a Undo the screw (arrowed) on each side...

3.18b ...then release the trim clips (arrowed)

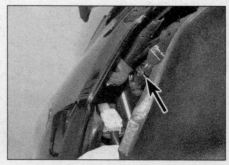

3.18c Release the peg (arrowed) on each side...

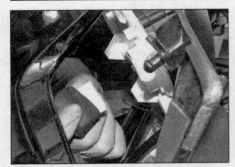

3.18d ...disconnect the wiring and remove the panel

3.21 Windshield screws (arrowed)

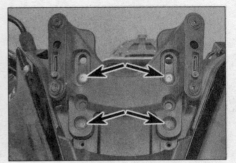

3.22 Windshield bracket bolts (arrowed)

illustration). Remove the instrument cluster from the panel if required (see Chapter 8).
19 Installation is the reverse of removal. Make sure the grommets are in good condition, and smear them with oil or grease.

Windshield and bracket

20 Undo the screws and remove the covers.
21 Undo the screws, noting the washers, and remove the windshield **(see illustration)**.
22 If required unscrew the four bolts, noting which fits where, and remove the windshield bracket **(see illustration)**.

23 Installation is the reverse of removal. The windshield bracket can be set in two positions, high or low, by selecting the appropriate bolt holes **(see illustration)**.

Fairing

24 Remove the fairing side panels.
25 Remove the instrument surround panel.
26 Remove the windshield and its bracket.
27 Disconnect the front turn signal wiring connectors **(see illustration)**.

28 Undo the screws and carefully pull the fairing forwards to release the pegs from the grommets **(see illustrations)**.
29 If required remove the turn signals (see Chapter 8).
30 Installation is the reverse of removal. Make sure the grommets are in good condition, and smear them with oil or grease.

Front mudguard

31 Unscrew the bolts on each side, noting which fits where and how the rear bolt secures

3.23 Set the windshield at the desired height by aligning the appropriate bolt holes

3.27 Disconnect the turn signal connector (arrowed) on each side

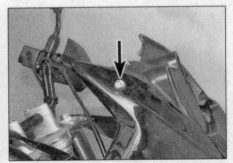

3.28a Undo the screw (arrowed) on each side...

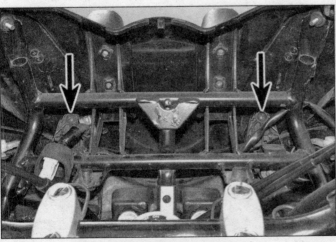

3.28b ...and the screws on the back...

3.28c ...then release the peg (arrowed) on each side

3.31a Mudguard bolts (arrowed)

3.31b Release the brake hose guide from the underside

the brake hose **(see illustration)**. Lift the mudguard and release the brake hose guide from the underside, taking care not to scratch it on the brake hose holders, and remove it forwards **(see illustration)**.

32 Installation is the reverse of removal.

Mirrors

33 Refer to Section 4, Steps 37 and 38.

Hand guards

34 Refer to Section 4, Steps 39 to 41.

Belly pan

35 Refer to Section 4, Step 42.

4 2012-on DL models

Seat

1 Unlock the seat using the ignition key, turning it clockwise, then lift the rear of the seat and draw it back and off, noting how the tabs locate **(see illustration)**.

2 Installation is the reverse of removal. Make sure the seat locates correctly. Push down on the back of the seat to engage the latch.

Grab-rack

3 Remove the seat.

4 Remove the carrier pad from the rack by carefully levering it up to release the pegs **(see illustration)**.

5 Unscrew the four bolts and lift the grab-rack off **(see illustration)**.

6 Installation is the reverse of removal.

Side covers

7 Remove the seat and the grab-rack.

8 Undo the screws and release the trim clips **(see illustration)**. Carefully pull the cover away to release the peg from the grommet **(see illustration)**.

9 If required separate the front and rear sections by releasing the trim clip and undoing the screw **(see illustration)**.

10 Installation is the reverse of removal. Make sure the grommets are in good condition, and smear them with oil or grease.

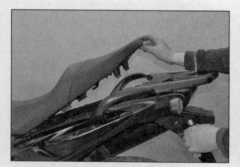

4.1 Unlock and remove the seat

4.4 Release and remove the pad

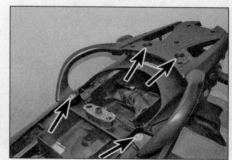

4.5 Grab-rack bolts (arrowed)

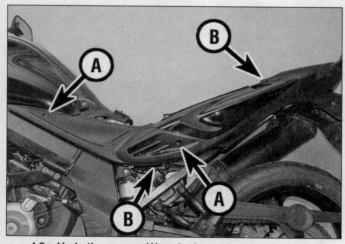

4.8a Undo the screws (A) and release the trim clips (B)...

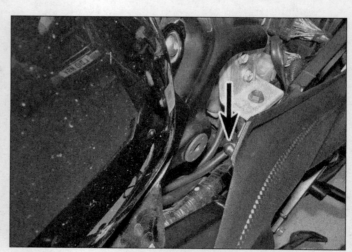

4.8b ...then release the peg (arrowed) and remove the cover

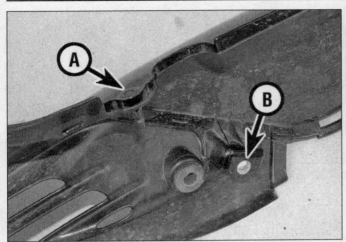

4.9 Release the trim clip (A) and undo the screw (B)

4.12a Undo the screws (arrowed)…

Fuel tank trim panels

11 Remove the seat.
12 To remove the side panels undo the screws, then carefully pull the panel away to release the Velcro patches and the tabs **(see illustrations)**.
13 To remove the front panel undo the two screws and release the two trim clips, and remove the panel **(see illustrations)**.

14 Installation is the reverse of removal. Make sure the grommets are in good condition, and smear them with oil or grease.

Windshield

15 Undo the screws and remove the windshield **(see illustration)**.
16 Installation is the reverse of removal. The windshield can be set in different positions by selecting the appropriate bolt holes – remove the blanking caps and reposition the rubber well-nuts and caps as required **(see illustration)**.

Instrument surround panels

17 To remove the rear panel release the trim clips, then undo the screws and carefully displace

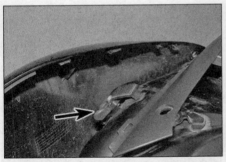

4.12b …release the Velcro and the tab (arrowed)…

4.12c …and the tabs from the slots

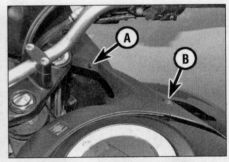

4.13a Release the trim clip (A) and undo the screw (B) on each side…

4.13b …and remove the panel

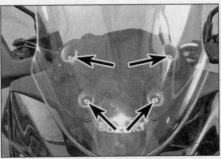

4.15 Windshield screws (arrowed)

4.16 Remove the caps and position the well-nuts (arrowed) as required

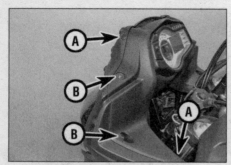

4.17a Release the trim clips (A) and undo the screws (B)...

4.17b ...noting which fits where...

4.17c ...then release the peg (arrowed) on each side...

4.17d ...and disconnect the wiring

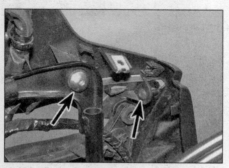

4.18a Undo the screws (arrowed) on each side...

the panel **(see illustrations)**. Disconnect the instrument cluster wiring connector and remove the panel **(see illustration)**. Remove the instrument cluster from the panel if required (see Chapter 8).

18 To remove the front panel remove the windshield, the rear panel and the fairing. Undo the screws, release the tabs, the peg and the wiring and remove the panel **(see illustrations)**.

19 Installation is the reverse of removal.

Fairing assembly (complete)

20 Remove the fuel tank trim panels.

21 Pull the rubber boot off the front loom wiring connectors and disconnect them, then release the wiring clamp **(see illustrations)**.

22 Undo the screw on each side **(see illustration)**.

4.18b ...release the tabs...

4.18c ...and the peg (arrowed)...

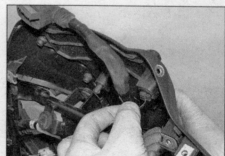

4.18d ...and release the wiring

4.21a Pull the boot (arrowed) off...

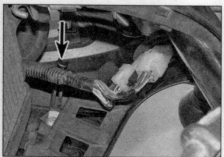

4.21b ...disconnect the connectors and release the clamp (arrowed)

4.22 Undo the screw (arrowed) on each side

4.23a Unscrew the bolts (arrowed)

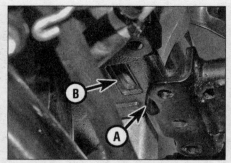

4.23b Move the assembly to the right so the tab (A) clears the slot (B)…

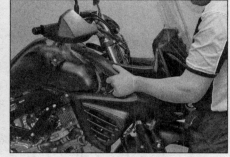

4.23c …then draw it forwards off the bike…

23 Unscrew the two fairing stay bolts (see illustration). Displace the tab on the rear of the bracket from the slot in the steering head, then draw it forwards to release it from the locating tongues on each side of the radiator and remove it (see illustrations).

24 Installation is the reverse of removal. Make sure the rubber caps are fitted on the locating tongues (see illustration 4.23d).

Fairing front panels

25 Remove the windshield and rear instrument surround panel.

26 Undo the screws, release the clips and carefully pull the upper section of the fairing forwards to release the Velcro patches (see illustrations).

4.23d …noting how the tongues (arrowed) locate in the slots on each side

4.26a Undo the screw (arrowed) on each side…

4.26b …and the four along the back

4.26c Release the clips along the back…

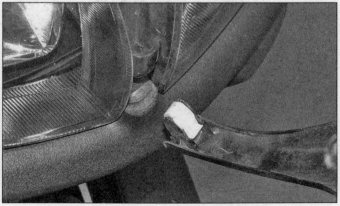

4.26d …and the bottom clip at the front…

4.26e …and the Velcro patches (arrowed)

4.27a Release the trim clip (arrowed) on each side...

4.27b ...then undo the screws (arrowed)...

4.27c ...and remove the panel

4.30a Turn signal connector (arrowed)

27 Release the trim clips, then undo the screws and remove the lower section **(see illustrations)**.

28 Installation is the reverse of removal. Make sure the grommets are in good condition, and smear them with oil or grease.

Fairing side panels

29 Remove the fuel tank trim panels and fairing front panels.

30 When removing the left-hand panel disconnect the front turn signal wiring connector and the air temperature sensor connector **(see illustrations)**. Release the wiring clamp, the connector boot and any cable-ties **(see illustration)**.

31 When removing the right-hand panel disconnect the front turn signal wiring connector and release the tie.

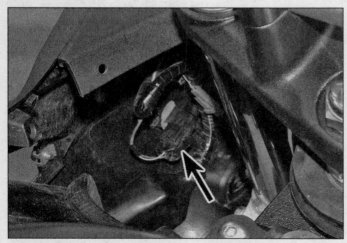

4.30b Ambient air temperature sensor connector (arrowed)

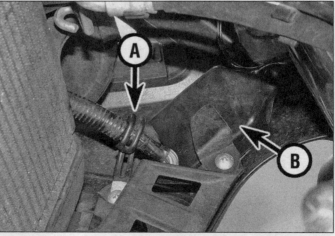

4.30c Release the clamp (A) and free the connector boot from its holder (B)

4.37 Bottom hex (A), stem nut (B)

4.39 Slacken the screw (arrowed)

4.40a Slacken the nut (arrowed) enough to release the guard...

4.40b ...then undo the screw (arrowed) and remove the guard

4.41a Slacken the nut (arrowed) enough to release the guard...

4.41b ...then undo the nut and remove the washer...

32 Unscrew the bolt, release the panel and draw it forwards to release it from the locating tongues on the side of the radiator and remove it **(see illustrations 4.22 and 4.23d)**.
33 If required remove the turn signals and air temperature sensor (see Chapter 8).
34 Installation is the reverse of removal. Make sure the rubber caps are fitted on the locating tongues

Front mudguard

35 Unscrew the bolts on each side, noting which fits where and how the rear bolt secures the brake hose **(see illustration 3.31a)**. Lift the mudguard and release the brake hose guide

from the underside, taking care not to scratch it on the brake hose holders, and remove it forwards **(see illustration 3.31b)**.
36 Installation is the reverse of removal.

Mirrors

37 Pull the boot up off the base. Unscrew the mirror using the bottom hex **(see illustration)**.
38 Installation is the reverse of removal. To adjust the position of the mirror stem, counter-hold the base hex, slacken the stem nut, adjust the position, and tighten the stem nut.

Hand guards

39 Slacken the handlebar end-weight screw on the relevant side **(see illustration)**.

40 To remove the right-hand guard, slacken the nut on the underside, noting how the washer sits between it and the guard **(see illustration)**. Undo the screw on the top and remove the guard **(see illustration)**.
41 To remove the left-hand guard, slacken the nut on the underside, noting how the washers sit on each side of the guard **(see illustration)**. Undo the nut on the top and remove the washer **(see illustration)**. Lift the guard off the stud and remove it **(see illustration)**.

Belly pan

42 Undo the two screws on each side **(see illustration)**.

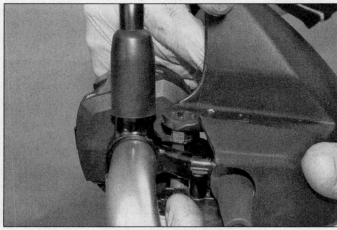

4.41c ...and lift the guard off

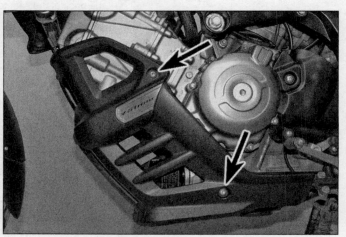

4.42 Belly-pan screws (arrowed)

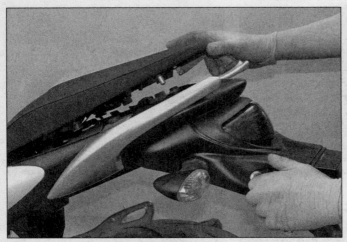

5.1 Unlock and remove the seat

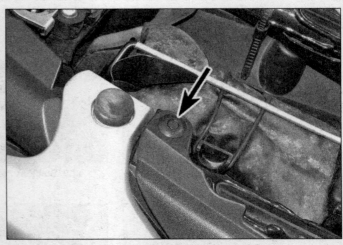

5.4a Release the trim clip (arrowed)…

5.4b …then unscrew the bolts

5.4c Release the pegs (arrowed) on the side…

5 SFV models

Seat

1 Unlock the seat using the ignition key, turning it clockwise, then lift the rear of the seat and draw it back and off, noting how the tabs locate **(see illustration)**.
2 Installation is the reverse of removal. Make sure the seat locates correctly. Push down on the back of the seat to engage the latch.

Side covers

3 Remove the seat.
4 Release the trim clip, then unscrew bolts (see illustrations). Carefully pull the cover away and then back to release the pegs from the grommets **(see illustrations)**.
5 If required separate the sections by undoing the screws and releasing the clips **(see illustrations)**.
6 Installation is the reverse of removal. Make sure the grommets are in good condition, and smear them with oil or grease.

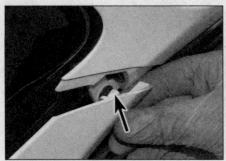

5.4d …and at the front

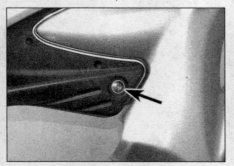

5.5a Undo the screw (arrowed)…

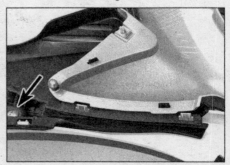

5.5b …and the screw (arrowed), then release the clips

Radiator covers

7 Undo the screws **(see illustration)**. Carefully pull the cover forwards to release it from the tongues on the side of the radiator **(see illustration)**.

8 Installation is the reverse of removal. Make sure the rubber caps are fitted on the locating tongues

Grab-rail and rear cover

9 Remove the seat and side covers.
10 Remove the blanking caps, then unscrew the bolts and remove the rails **(see illustrations)**.
11 Remove the rear cover **(see illustration)**.
12 Installation is the reverse of removal.

Front mudguard

13 Unscrew the bolts on each side, noting which fits where and how the rear bolt secures the brake hose **(see illustration 3.31a)**. Lift the mudguard and release the brake hose guide from the underside, taking care not to scratch it on the brake hose holders, and remove it forwards **(see illustration 3.31b)**.
14 Installation is the reverse of removal.

Mirrors

15 Unscrew the mirror using the bottom hex **(see illustration)**.
16 Installation is the reverse of removal.

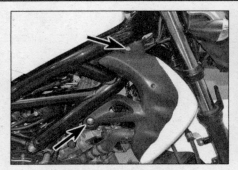

5.7a Undo the screws (arrowed)...

5.7b ...then pull the cover forwards

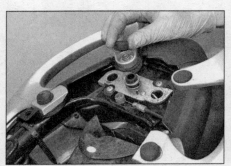

5.10a Remove the caps...

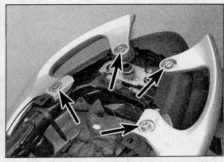

5.10b ...and unscrew the bolts (arrowed)...

5.10c ...noting the collars

5.11 Lift the rear cover off

5.15 Mirror hex (arrowed)

Chapter 8
Electrical system

Contents

Degrees of difficulty

Easy, suitable for novice with little experience	**Fairly easy,** suitable for beginner with some experience	**Fairly difficult,** suitable for competent DIY mechanic	**Difficult,** suitable for experienced DIY mechanic	**Very difficult,** suitable for expert DIY or professional

Specifications

Battery

Type
2004 to 2011 DL models	YTX12-BS
2012-on DL models	FTX12-BS
SFV models	YT12A-BS
Capacity	12 V, 10 Ah

Voltage
Fully-charged	12.8 V
Discharged	12.0 V

Charging rate
Normal rate	1.2 A for 5 to 10 hrs
Quick rate	5 A for 1 hr

Charging system

Alternator stator coil resistance
DL models	0.2 to 0.7 ohms
SFV models	0.3 to 1.2 ohms
Nominal output	375 W @ 5000 rpm
Regulated voltage (no load)	14.0 to 15.5 V (DC) @ 5000 rpm
Un-regulated voltage (no load)	60 V (AC) @ 5000 rpm
Current leakage	around 2 mA (max)

Starter relay

Resistance	3 to 6 ohms

Fuses

See Section 5 and fusebox lid for fuse identification

DL models
Main	30A
Headlight	
High beam	15A
Low beam	15A
Ignition	10A
Fuel injection system	10A
Radiator fan	15A
Signal system	15A
ABS system (A models)	
2007 to 2011 models	
Valve	25A
Motor	40A
2012-on models	
Valve	15A
Motor	25A

SFV models
Main	30A
Headlight	
High beam	10A
Low beam	10A
Ignition	15A
Fuel injection system	10A
Radiator fan	15A
Signal system	10A
ABS system (A models)	
Valve	15A
Motor	20A

Bulbs
Headlight(s)	60/55 W
Sidelight(s)	5 W
Brake/tail lights	21/5 W
Licence plate light	5 W
Turn signal lights	21 W
Instrument illumination	LED
Instrument warning lights	LED

Torque settings
Oil pressure switch	14 Nm

1 General information

All models have a 12 volt electrical system charged by a three-phase alternator with a separate regulator/rectifier.

The regulator maintains the charging system output within the specified range to prevent overcharging, and the rectifier converts the ac (alternating current) output of the alternator to dc (direct current) to power the lights and other components and to charge the battery. The alternator rotor is mounted on the left-hand end of the crankshaft with the stator in the cover.

The starter motor is mounted on the front of the engine. The starting system includes the motor, the battery, the relay and the various wires and switches. Some of the switches are part of a starter safety circuit that prevents the engine from being started under certain conditions (see Chapter 1).

Note: *Keep in mind that electrical parts, once purchased, often cannot be returned. To avoid unnecessary expense, make very sure the faulty component has been positively identified before buying a replacement part.*

2 Electrical system fault finding

1 A typical electrical circuit consists of an electrical component, the switches, relays, etc, related to that component and the wiring and connectors that link the component to the battery and the frame.

2 Before tackling any troublesome electrical circuit, first study the wiring diagram thoroughly to get a complete picture of what makes up that individual circuit. Trouble spots, for instance, can often be narrowed down by noting if other components related to that circuit are operating properly or not. If several components or circuits fail at one time, chances are the fault lies either in the fuse or in a common earth (ground) connection, as several circuits are often routed through the same fuse and earth (ground) connections.

3 Electrical problems often stem from simple causes, such as loose or corroded connections or a blown fuse. Prior to any electrical fault finding, always visually check the condition of the fuse, wires and connections in the problem circuit. Intermittent failures can be especially frustrating, since you can't always duplicate the failure when it's convenient to test. In such situations, a good practice is to clean all connections in the affected circuit, whether or not they appear to be good – where possible use a dedicated electrical cleaning spray along with sandpaper, wire wool or other abrasive material to remove corrosion, and a dedicated electrical protection spray to prevent further problems. All of the connections and wires should also be wiggled to check for looseness which can cause intermittent failure.

4 If you don't have a multimeter it is highly advisable to obtain one – they are not

2.4a A digital multimeter can be used for all electrical tests

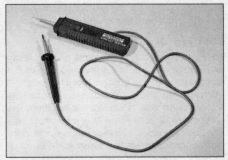

2.4b A battery-powered continuity tester

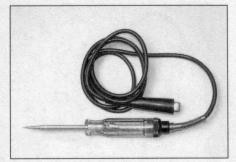

2.4c A simple test light is useful for voltage tests

expensive and will enable a full range of electrical tests to be made **(see illustration)**. Go for a modern digital one with LCD display as they are easier to use. A continuity tester and/or test light are useful for certain electrical checks as an alternative, though are limited in their usefulness compared to a multimeter **(see illustrations)**.

Continuity checks

5 The term continuity describes the uninterrupted flow of electricity through an electrical circuit. Continuity can be checked with a multimeter set either to its continuity function (a beep is emitted when continuity is found), or to the resistance (ohms / Ω) function, or with a dedicated continuity tester. Both instruments are powered by an internal battery, therefore the checks are made with the ignition OFF. As a safety precaution, always disconnect the battery negative (-) lead before making continuity checks, particularly if ignition switch checks are being made.

6 If using a multimeter, select the continuity function if it has one, or the resistance (ohms) function. Touch the meter probes together and check that a beep is emitted or the meter reads zero, which indicates continuity. If there is no continuity there will be no beep or the meter will show infinite resistance. After using the meter, always switch it OFF to conserve its battery.

7 A continuity tester can be used in the same way – its light should come on or it should beep to indicate continuity in the switch ON

position, but should be off or silent in the OFF position.

8 Note that the polarity of the test probes doesn't matter for continuity checks, although care should be taken to follow specific test procedures if a diode or solid-state component is being checked.

Switch continuity checks

9 If a switch is at fault, trace its wiring to the wiring connectors. Separate the connectors and inspect them for security and condition. A build-up of dirt or corrosion here will most likely be the cause of the problem – clean up and apply a water dispersant such as WD40, or alternatively use a dedicated contact cleaner and protection spray.

10 If using a multimeter, select the continuity function if it has one, or the resistance (ohms) function, and connect its probes to the terminals in the connector **(see illustration)**. Simple ON/OFF type switches, such as brake light switches, only have two wires whereas combination switches, like the handlebar switches, have many wires. Study the wiring diagram to ensure that you are connecting to the correct pair of wires. Continuity should be indicated with the switch ON and no continuity with it OFF.

Wiring continuity checks

11 Many electrical faults are caused by damaged wiring, often due to incorrect routing or chaffing on frame components. Loose, wet or corroded wire connectors can also be the cause of electrical problems.

12 A continuity check can be made on a single length of wire by disconnecting it at each end and connecting the meter or continuity tester probes to each end of the wire **(see illustration)**. Continuity (low or no resistance – 0 ohms) should be indicated if the wire is good. If no continuity (high resistance) is shown, suspect a broken wire.

13 To check for continuity to earth in any earth wire connect one probe of your meter or tester to the earth wire terminal in the connector and the other to the frame, engine, or battery earth (-) terminal. Continuity (low or no resistance – 0 ohms) should be indicated if the wire is good. If no continuity (high resistance) is shown, suspect a broken wire or corroded or loose earth point (see below).

Voltage checks

14 A voltage check can determine whether power is reaching a component. Use a multimeter set to the dc voltage scale, or a test light. The test light is the cheaper component, but the meter has the advantage of being able to give a voltage reading.

15 Connect the meter or test light in parallel, i.e. across the load **(see illustration)**.

16 First identify the relevant wiring circuit by referring to the wiring diagram at the end of this manual. If other electrical components share the same power supply (i.e. are fed from the same fuse), take note whether they are working correctly – this is useful information in deciding where to start checking the circuit.

17 If using a meter, check first that the meter

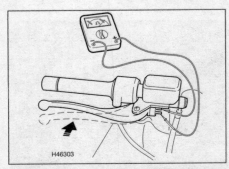

2.10 Continuity should be indicated across switch terminals when lever is operated

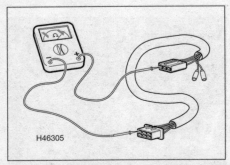

2.12 Wiring continuity check. Connect the meter probes across each end of the same wire

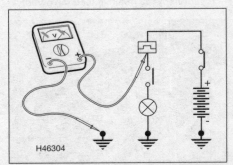

2.15 Voltage check. Connect the meter positive probe to the component and the negative probe to earth

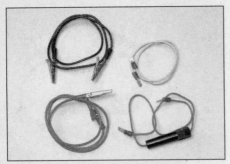

2.23 A selection of insulated jumper wires

leads are plugged into the correct terminals on the meter (red to positive (+), black to negative (-). Set the meter to the dc volts function, where necessary at a range suitable for the battery voltage – 0 to 20 vdc. Connect the meter red probe (+) to the power supply wire and the black probe to a good metal earth (ground) on the bike's frame or directly to the battery negative terminal. Battery voltage should be shown on the meter with the ignition switch, and if necessary any other relevant switch, ON.

18 If using a test light, connect its positive (+) probe to the power supply terminal and its negative (-) probe to a good earth (ground) on the bike's frame. With the switch, and if necessary any other relevant switch, ON, the test light should illuminate.

19 If no voltage is indicated, work back towards the fuse continuing to check for voltage. When you reach a point where there

is voltage, you know the problem lies between that point and your last check point.

Earth (ground) checks

20 Earth connections are made either directly to the engine or frame via the mounting of the component, or by a separate wire into the earth circuit of the wiring harness. Alternatively a short earth wire is sometimes run from the component directly to the bike's frame.

21 Corrosion is a common cause of a poor earth connection, as is a loose earth terminal fastener.

22 If total or multiple component failure is experienced, check the security of the main earth lead from the negative (-) terminal of the battery, the earth lead bolted to the engine, and the main earth point(s) on the frame. If corroded, dismantle the connection and clean all surfaces back to bare metal. Remake the connection and prevent further corrosion from forming by smearing battery terminal grease over the connection.

23 To check the earth of a component, use an insulated jumper wire to temporarily bypass its earth connection **(see illustration)** – connect one end of the jumper wire to the earth terminal or metal body of the component and the other end to the bike's frame. If the circuit works with the jumper wire installed, the earth circuit is faulty.

24 To check an earth wire first check for corroded or loose connections, then check the wiring for continuity (Step 13) between each connector in the circuit in turn, and then to its earth point, to locate the break.

Caution: Be extremely careful when handling or working around the battery. The electrolyte is very caustic and an explosive gas (hydrogen) is given off when the battery is charging.

Removal and installation

1 Make sure the ignition is switched OFF.
2 Remove the seat (see Chapter 7).
3 Unscrew the negative (–) terminal bolt first and disconnect the lead from the battery **(see illustration)**. Lift up the red insulating cover to access the positive (+) terminal, then unscrew the bolt and disconnect the lead.
4 On DL models release the battery strap **(see illustration)**. Lift the battery out **(see illustration)**.
5 On SFV models release the tank prop from its clips **(see illustration)**. Remove the single screw and press the clip alongside it in to free the battery holder from the battery housing **(see illustration)**. Lift the battery out. Note that the holder can be rested on the frame leaving the tip-over sensor attached **(see illustration)**.
6 Installation is the reverse of removal. Clean the battery terminals and lead ends with a wire brush, emery paper or steel wool. Reconnect the leads, connecting the positive (+) terminal first.

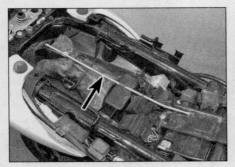

3.3 Disconnect the negative lead first then disconnect the positive lead (arrowed)

3.4a Unhook the strap...

3.4b ...then remove the battery

3.5a Remove the prop (arrowed)...

3.5b ...then undo the screw (arrowed) and remove the holder

3.5c Rest the holder and tip-over sensor on the frame tube

HAYNES HiNT *Battery corrosion can be kept to a minimum by applying a layer of battery terminal grease or petroleum jelly (Vaseline) to the terminals after the leads have been connected. DO NOT use a mineral-based grease.*

3.8 Checking battery voltage

4.2 Battery connected to a charger

Inspection and maintenance

7 The battery on all models is of the maintenance free (sealed) type, therefore requiring no regular maintenance. However, the following checks should still be performed. **Note:** *Do not attempt to remove the battery caps to check the electrolyte level or battery specific gravity. Removal will damage the caps, resulting in electrolyte leakage and battery damage.*

8 Check the state of charge by measuring the voltage at the battery terminals **(see illustration)**. Connect the voltmeter positive (+) probe to the battery positive (+) terminal, and the negative (–) probe to the battery negative (–) terminal. When fully-charged there should be 12.8 volts (or more) present. If the voltage falls below 12 volts remove the battery (see above), and recharge it as described below in Section 4.

9 Check the battery terminals and leads are tight and free of corrosion. If corrosion is evident, clean the terminals as described above, then protect them from further corrosion (see *Haynes Hint*).

10 Keep the battery case clean to prevent current leakage, which can discharge the battery over a period of time (especially when it sits unused). Wash the outside of the case with a solution of baking soda and water. Rinse the battery thoroughly, then dry it.

11 Look for cracks in the case and replace the battery with a new one if any are found. If acid has been spilled on the frame or battery box, neutralise it with a baking soda and water solution, dry it thoroughly, then touch up any damaged paint.

12 If the motorcycle sits unused for long periods of time, disconnect the leads from the battery terminals, negative (–) terminal

first. Refer to Section 4 and charge the battery once every month to six weeks.

4 Battery charging

Caution: Be extremely careful when handling or working around the battery. The electrolyte is very caustic and an explosive gas (hydrogen) is given off when the battery is charging.

1 Remove the battery (see Section 3). Connect the charger to the battery, making sure that the positive (+) lead on the charger is connected to the positive (+) terminal on the battery, and the negative (–) lead is connected to the negative (–) terminal.

2 Suzuki recommend that the battery is charged at the normal rate specified at the beginning of the Chapter. A higher 'quick charge' rate can be used if absolutely necessary for a short time only (see Specifications) – excess use could cause damage to the battery. If a normal domestic charger is used check that after a possible initial peak, the charge rate falls to a safe level **(see illustration)**. If the battery becomes hot during charging **stop**. Further charging will cause damage. Note that there are many bike-specific chargers available from good suppliers that are designed for the maintenance and recovery of motorcycle batteries, in particular catering for the

requirements of heavily discharged MF batteries. They are not expensive, and are a worthwhile investment, especially if the bike is not used over winter. Follow the manufacturer's instructions.

3 If the recharged battery discharges rapidly if left disconnected it is likely that an internal short caused by physical damage or sulphation has occurred. A new battery will be required. A sound item will tend to lose its charge at about 1% per day.

4 Install the battery (see Section 3).

5 If the motorcycle sits unused for long periods of time, charge the battery once every month to six weeks and leave it disconnected.

5 Fuses

1 The electrical system as a whole is protected by the main fuse, and individual circuits are protected by other fuses of different ratings.

2 To access all fuses remove the seat (see Chapter 7).

3 The main fuse and a spare are fitted with the starter relay **(see illustration)**.

4 All other fuses (except the ABS fuses on A models) are housed in the fusebox **(see illustration)**. Unclip the lid to access the fuses **(see illustration)**. The location, identity and rating of each fuse is marked on the underside of the lid.

5.3 Remove the relay cover to access the main fuse and its spare (arrowed)

5.4a Fusebox (arrowed)

5.4b Unclip the lid to access the fuses

5.5a ABS system fuseholders (arrowed) – DL

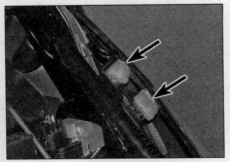

5.5b ABS system fuseholders (arrowed) – SFV

5.5c Unclip the lid to access the fuse

5 The ABS motor and valve fuses are each fitted in a separate holder (see illustrations). Unclip the lid to access the fuse (see illustration).

6 A spare fuse of each rating is provided in the fusebox. Spare ABS fuses are housed in each holder (see illustration 5.5a).

7 The fuses can be removed and checked visually – use the tool provided in the toolkit, your fingers, or a suitable pair of pliers (see illustration).

8 A blown fuse is easily identified by a break in the element (see illustration), but if there is any doubt check the fuse for continuity (see Section 2). Each fuse is clearly marked with its rating and must only be replaced by a fuse of the correct rating. If a spare fuse is used, always replace it with a new one so that a spare of each rating is carried on the bike at all times.

 Warning: Never put in a fuse of a higher rating or bridge the terminals with any other substitute, however temporary it may be. Serious damage may be done to the circuit, or a fire may start.

9 If the new fuse blows immediately check the wiring circuit very carefully for evidence of a short-circuit. Look for bare wires and chafed, melted or burned insulation.

10 Occasionally a fuse will blow or cause an open-circuit for no obvious reason. Corrosion of the fuse ends and fusebox terminals may occur and cause poor fuse contact. If this happens, remove the corrosion with a wire brush or emery paper, then spray the fuse end and terminals with electrical contact cleaner.

5.7 Pull the fuse out

6 Lighting system check

Note: Refer to electrical system fault finding in Section 2 and to the wiring diagram for your model at the end of this Chapter.

1 If a light fails first check the bulb (see relevant Section), and the bulb terminals in the holder. If none of the lights work, check the battery (see Section 3). Low battery voltage indicates either a faulty battery or a defective charging system. Refer to Section 3 for battery checks and Section 27 for charging system tests. Also check the relevant fuse (Section 5) – if there is more than one problem at the same time, it is likely to be a fault relating to a multi-function component, such as one of the fuses governing more than one circuit, or the ignition switch. When checking for a blown filament in a bulb, it is advisable to back up a visual check with a continuity test of the filament as it is not always apparent that a bulb has blown.

Headlight

2 DL models have two twin filament bulbs. If a headlight beam in one bulb fails to work, first check the bulb (see Section 7). If the same headlight beam in each bulb fails to work, first check the fuse (see Section 5).

3 SFV models have one twin filament bulb. If a headlight beam fails to work, first check the bulb (see Section 7), then check the fuse (see Section 5).

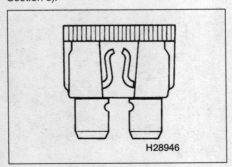

5.8 A blown fuse can be identified by a break in its element

4 If the low beam does not work, check for battery voltage at the black/blue (DL models) or white (SFV models) wire terminal in the headlight wiring connector with the ignition ON and the dimmer switch set to LO. If there is voltage, check for continuity to earth (ground) in the black/white wire from the wiring connector.

5 If the high beam does not work, check for battery voltage at the yellow wire terminal in the headlight wiring connector with the ignition ON and the dimmer switch set to HI. If there is voltage, check for continuity to earth (ground) in the black/white wire from the wiring connector.

6 If there was no voltage at the connector, the problem lies in the wiring or connectors, or the dimmer switch. Refer to Section 19 for the switch testing procedures, and to Section 2 and the wiring diagrams at the end of this Chapter for your model, and check the complete circuit.

Tail light

7 2004 to 2011 DL models have two tail light bulbs. 2012-on DL models and all SFV models have one tail light bulb.

8 If the tail light fails to work, check the bulb (see Section 9). If it is good, check there is battery voltage at the relevant wire terminal in the bulb holder with the ignition switch ON (refer to the wiring diagram for your model for wire colour). If voltage is present, check there is continuity to earth (ground) in the black/white wire from the bulbholder. If no voltage is indicated, check the wiring and connectors between the tail light and the fusebox.

Brake light

9 2004 to 2011 DL models have two brake light bulbs. 2012-on DL models and all SFV models have one brake light bulb.

10 If a/the brake light fails to work, check the bulb (see Section 9). If it is good, check there is battery voltage at the relevant wire terminal (refer to the wiring diagram for your model for wire colour) in the bulbholder with the ignition ON, and first with the front brake lever on, then with the rear brake pedal on. If voltage is present with one brake on but not the other, then the switch or its wiring is faulty. If voltage is present in both cases, check there is continuity to earth (ground) in the black/white wire from the bulbholder. If no voltage is indicated, check the signal fuse (Section 5), then check the wiring and connectors between the brake light and the brake switches, and the fusebox, then check the brake light switches themselves. Refer to Section 14 for the switch testing procedures.

Sidelight

11 DL models have two sidelights, SFV models have one.

12 If the sidelight fails to work, check the bulb (see Section 7). If it is good, check there is battery voltage at the brown wire terminal in the sidelight wiring connector with the ignition switch ON. If voltage is present, check there is continuity to earth (ground) in the black/white wire from the wiring connector. If no voltage is indicated, check the wiring and connectors between the sidelight and the fusebox.

Licence plate light

13 If the light fails to work, check the bulb (see Section 9). If the bulb is good, check there is battery voltage at the wire terminal (refer to the wiring diagram for your model for wire colour) on the loom side of the wiring connector with the ignition switch ON. If voltage is present, check there is continuity to earth (ground) in the black/white wire from the wiring connector. If no voltage is indicated, check the wiring and connectors between the light and the fusebox.

Turn signals

14 See Section 11.

Instrument and warning lights

15 See Section 16.

7 Headlight and sidelight bulbs

Note: The headlight bulbs are H4 halogen type. Do not touch the bulb glass as skin acids will shorten the bulb's service life. If the bulb is accidentally touched, it should be wiped carefully when cold with a rag soaked in methylated spirit and dried before fitting. Always use a paper towel or dry cloth when

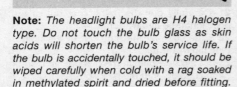

7.10 Release the bulbholder...

7.2 Disconnect the wiring connector...

7.4a Release the clip...

handling new bulbs to prevent injury if the bulb should break and to increase bulb life.

DL models

Headlight bulb

1 On 2004 to 2011 models remove the fairing side panel from the relevant side (see Chapter 7). Turn the handlebars as required to aid access.
2 Disconnect the wiring connector from the bulb **(see illustration)**.
3 Remove the rubber cover **(see illustration)**.
4 Release the retaining clip and remove the bulb **(see illustrations)**.
5 Fit the new bulb bearing in mind the information in the **Note** above. Make sure the bulb locates correctly and secure it with the retaining clip **(see illustrations 7.4b and a)**.
6 Fit the rubber cover **(see illustration 7.3)**.
7 Connect the wiring connector **(see illustration 7.2)**.

7.11 ...then pull the bulb out

7.3 ...then remove the cover

7.4b ...and remove the bulb

8 Check the headlight works.

Sidelight bulb

9 Remove the instrument surround panel (rear only on 2012-on models) (see Chapter 7).
10 Turn the bulbholder a quarter turn anti-clockwise and draw it out of the headlight **(see illustration)**.
11 Carefully pull the bulb out of the holder **(see illustration)**.
12 Fit the new bulb in the bulbholder, then fit the bulbholder into the headlight – make sure it locates and locks correctly.
13 Check the sidelight works then install the instrument surround panel.

SFV models

Headlight bulb

14 Remove the headlight (Section 8).
15 Remove the rubber cover **(see illustration)**.

7.15 Remove the cover

7.16a Release the clip...

7.16b ...and remove the bulb

7.21 Release the bulbholder...

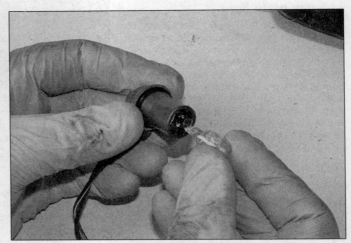

7.22 ...then pull the bulb out

16 Release the retaining clip and remove the bulb **(see illustrations)**.
17 Fit the new bulb bearing in mind the information in the **Note** above. Make sure the bulb locates correctly and secure it with the retaining clip **(see illustrations 7.16b and a)**.

18 Fit the rubber cover **(see illustration 7.15)**.
19 Install the headlight. Check it works.

Sidelight bulb

20 Remove the headlight (Section 8).

21 Carefully pull the bulbholder out of the headlight **(see illustration)**.
22 Carefully pull the bulb out of the holder **(see illustration)**.
23 Fit the new bulb in the bulbholder, then fit the bulbholder into the headlight.
24 Install the headlight. Check the sidelight works.

| 8 | Headlight | |

Removal

2004 to 2011 DL models

1 Remove the fairing (see Chapter 7).
2 Disconnect the headlight and sidelight wiring connectors and release the wiring from any ties **(see illustrations)**.
3 Undo the nuts and remove the washers, then draw the headlight off the bracket **(see illustration)**. Make sure the grommets are in

8.2a Disconnect the headlight connectors...

8.2b ...and the sidelight connectors

8.3 Unscrew the nuts (arrowed) on each side

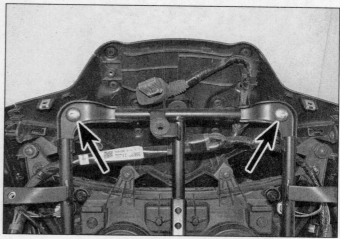

8.6a Unscrew the bolts (arrowed)…

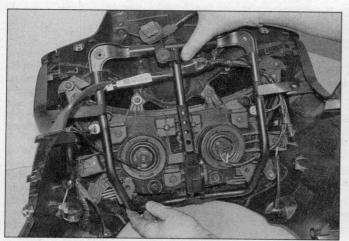

8.6b …and remove the bracket

8.7 Headlight screws (arrowed)

good condition – replace then with new ones if necessary.

4 If required remove the headlight bulbs and sidelight bulbholders (see Section 7).

2012-on DL models

5 Remove the complete fairing assembly (see Chapter 7).

6 Unscrew the bracket bolts, then pull the

bracket off to release the grommets from the pegs **(see illustrations)**.

7 Release the headlight wiring, then undo the screws, release the pegs from the fairing side panels, and pull the headlight off the Velcro patches **(see illustration)**.

8 If required remove the headlight bulbs and sidelight bulbholders (see Section 7).

SFV models

9 Undo the screw on each side and remove the headlight trim panels, noting how they locate **(see illustrations)**.

10 Unscrew the bolt on each side, then pivot the headlight down on its bottom mounts **(see illustrations)**. Disconnect the sidelight and headlight wiring connectors, then release the

8.9a Undo the screw (arrowed)…

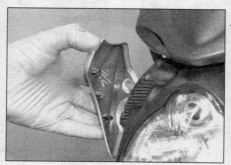

8.9b …and remove the panel

8.10a Unscrew the bolt (arrowed) on each side…

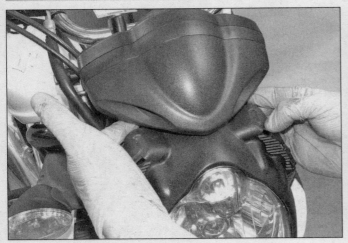

8.10b ...pivot the headlight down...

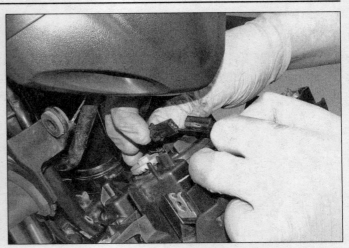

8.10c ...disconnect the sidelight connector...

8.10d ...and the headlight connector...

8.10e ...then release and remove the headlight

bottom mounts and remove the headlight **(see illustrations)**.

11 If required remove the headlight bulbs and sidelight bulbholders (see Section 7).

Installation

12 Installation is the reverse of removal. Make sure are the collars are fitted in the grommets.

Check the operation of the headlights and sidelights. Check the headlight aim.

Headlight aim

Note: *An improperly adjusted headlight may cause problems for oncoming traffic or provide poor, unsafe illumination of the road ahead. Before adjusting the headlight aim, be sure to consult with local traffic laws and regulations*

– for UK models refer to MOT Test Checks in the Reference section.

13 Before making any adjustment, check that the tyre pressures are correct and the suspension is adjusted as required. Make any adjustments to the headlight aim with the machine off its stand and on level ground, with the fuel tank half full and with an assistant sitting on the seat. If the bike is usually ridden with a passenger on the back, have a second assistant to do this. Make any adjustments horizontally first if required, then vertically.

14 On 2004 to 2011 DL models remove the fairing side panel from the relevant side (see Chapter 7). The horizontal alignment adjusters are on the top inner corner of each headlight, and the vertical alignment adjusters are on the bottom outer corner **(see illustration)**.

15 On 2012-on DL models remove the rear instrument surround panel (see Chapter 7) and turn the handlebars as required for best access. The horizontal alignment adjusters are on the top outer corner of each headlight, and the vertical alignment adjusters are on the bottom inner corner **(see illustration)**.

8.14 Horizontal adjuster (A), vertical adjuster (B) – right-hand headlight

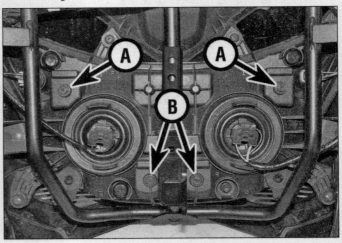

8.15 Horizontal adjusters (A), vertical adjusters (B)

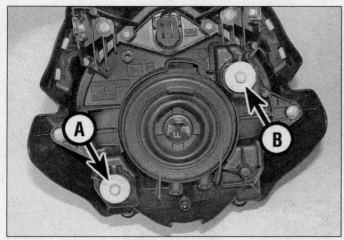

8.16 Horizontal adjuster (A), vertical adjuster (B)

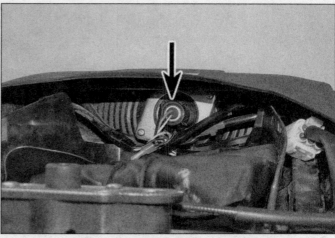

9.2 Release the bulbholder (arrowed)...

16 On SFV models the horizontal alignment adjuster is on the bottom left corner of the headlight, and the vertical alignment adjuster is on the top right corner (see illustration) – turn the handlebars as required for best access.

9 Brake/tail/licence plate light bulbs

Note: *It is a good idea to use a paper towel or dry cloth when handling bulbs to prevent injury if it breaks, and to increase bulb life.*

Brake/tail lights

DL models

1 Remove the seat (see Chapter 7).
2 Turn the bulbholder anti-clockwise to release it (see illustration).
3 Carefully push the bulb in and turn it anti-clockwise to release it (see illustration).
4 Check the socket terminals for corrosion and clean them if necessary.
5 Line up the pins of the new bulb with the slots in the socket, then push the bulb in and turn it clockwise until it locks into place.
6 Fit the bulbholder and turn it clockwise.

SFV models

7 Remove the cover from the underside of the rear mudguard (see illustrations).
8 Turn the bulbholder anti-clockwise to release it (see illustration).
9 Carefully push the bulb in and turn it anti-clockwise to release it (see illustration).
10 Check the socket terminals for corrosion and clean them if necessary.
11 Line up the pins of the new bulb with the slots in the socket, then push the bulb in and turn it clockwise until it locks into place.
12 Fit the bulbholder and turn it clockwise.

9.3 ...then remove the bulb from it

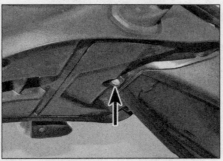

9.7a Undo the screw (arrowed)...

9.7b ...then release each side...

9.7c ...and remove the cover

9.8 Release the bulbholder...

9.9 ...then remove the bulb from it

9.14 Detach the cable

9.15a Undo the screw (arrowed) on each side…

9.15b …draw the assembly back and disconnect the wiring

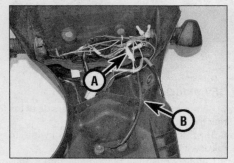

9.16a Disconnect the connector (A) and release the wire from the slot (B)

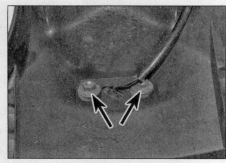

9.16b Undo the nuts (arrowed)…

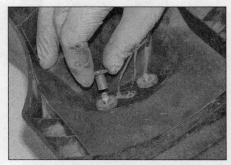

9.16c …and remove the collars

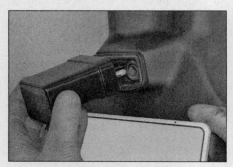

9.16d Displace the light…

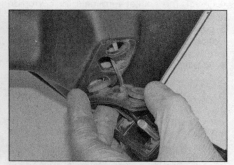

9.16e …and release the rubber base

Licence plate light

2004 to 2011 DL models

13 Remove the side covers (see Chapter 7).
14 Detach the seat lock cable **(see illustration)**.
15 Undo the screw on each side of the rear mudguard, then draw it back and disconnect the tail loom wiring connector **(see illustrations)**.
16 Disconnect the licence plate light connector and release the wire **(see illustration)**. Undo the nuts, remove the collars and detach the light unit and its rubber base **(see illustrations)**.
17 Pull the bulbholder out, then carefully pull the bulb out of the holder **(see illustrations)**.

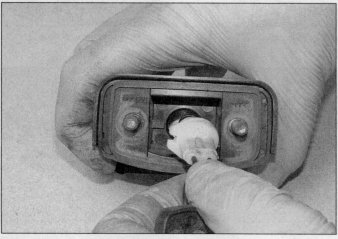

9.17a Release the bulbholder…

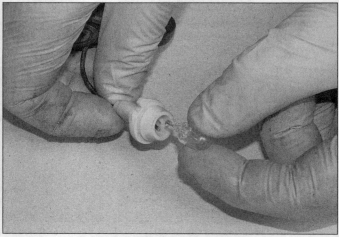

9.17b …and remove the bulb

9.20 Detach the cable

9.21 Disconnect the wiring

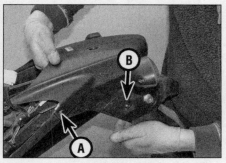

9.22a Release the trim clip (A) and undo the screw (B) on each side...

9.22b ...then draw the assembly back off the bike

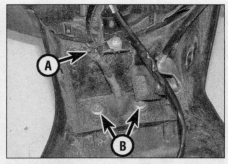

9.23a Release the clamp (A) then undo the nuts (B) and remove the washers

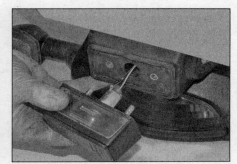

9.23b Draw the light off...

18 Fit the new bulb and all components in reverse order – seat the cut-out in the bulbholder over the rib on the light unit **(see illustration 9.17a)**.

2012-on DL models
19 Remove the side covers (see Chapter 7).
20 Detach the seat lock cable **(see illustration)**.
21 Disconnect the tail light/turn signal and licence plate light wiring connectors **(see illustration)**.
22 Release the trim clip and unscrew the bolt on each side of the rear mudguard assembly, then draw it back off the bike **(see illustrations)**.
23 Release the licence plate light wire from the clamp, then undo the nuts and remove the washers **(see illustration)**. Detach the light unit, remove the collars from the rubber base and release the base **(see illustrations)**.

9.23c ...remove the collars...

9.23d ...and the rubber base

24 Undo the screws and detach the lens, then carefully push the bulb in and turn it anti-clockwise to release it **(see illustrations)**.
25 Fit the new bulb and all components in reverse order.

SFV models
26 Remove the grab-rail and rear cover (see Chapter 7). Remove the cover from the underside of the rear mudguard **(see illustrations 9.7a, b and c)**.

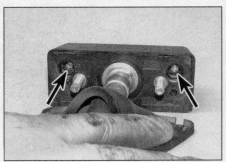

9.24a Undo the screws (arrowed)...

9.24b ...detach the lens...

9.24c ...and remove the bulb

9.27 Detach the cable

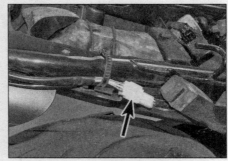

9.28a Tail light connector (arrowed)

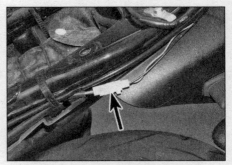

9.28b Licence plate light connector (arrowed)

27 Detach the seat lock cable **(see illustration)**.
28 Disconnect the tail light and licence plate light wiring connectors **(see illustrations)**.

Disconnect the turn signal wiring connectors **(see illustrations 13.7a and b)**. Release the wiring ties.
29 Unscrew the bolts on the underside side

of the rear mudguard assembly, then draw it back off the bike **(see illustrations)**.
30 Undo the two screws **(see illustration)**. Detach the turn signals **(see illustrations)**. Remove the bracket **(see illustration)**.
31 Draw the licence plate light wire down **(see illustration)**. Undo the nuts and remove the washers **(see illustration)**. Detach the light unit, remove the collars from the rubber base and release the base **(see illustrations 9.23b, c and d)**.
32 Undo the screws and detach the lens, then carefully push the bulb in and turn it anti-clockwise to release it **(see illustrations 9.24a, b and c)**.
33 Fit the new bulb and all components in reverse order.

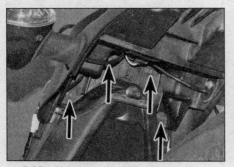

9.29a Unscrew the bolts (arrowed)…

9.29b …and remove the mudguard assembly

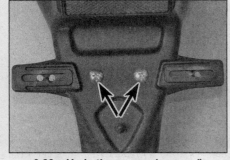

9.30a Undo the screws (arrowed)

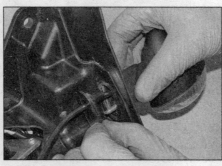

9.30b Detach each turn signal and its set plate…

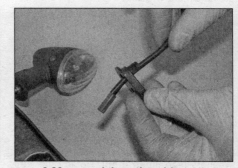

9.30c …and draw the wiring out

9.30d Lift the bracket out of the mudguard

9.31a Draw the wire (arrowed) down…

9.31b …then undo the nuts (arrowed) and remove the washers

10 Tail light

Removal

1 On 2004 to 2011 DL models refer to Section 13 and remove the rear turn signals. Lift the tail light assembly out of the rear mudguard. Turn the bulbholders anti-clockwise to release them. Undo the screws and detach the tail light from the bracket **(see illustration)**.

2 On 2012-on DL models refer to Section 13 and remove the rear turn signals. Turn the bulbholder anti-clockwise to release it **(see illustration)**. Undo the screw and remove the tail light.

3 On SFV models refer to Section 9, Steps 26 to 30 and remove the remove the rear mudguard and bracket. Turn the bulbholder anti-clockwise to release it. Unscrew the bolts and remove the tail light **(see illustration)**.

Installation

4 Installation is the reverse of removal. Make sure any grommets are in good condition – replace them with new ones if necessary. Check the operation of the tail and brake lights.

11 Turn signal circuit check

Note: *Refer to electrical system fault finding in Section 2 and to the wiring diagram for your model at the end of this Chapter.*

1 Most turn signal problems are the result of a burned out bulb or corroded socket. This is especially true when the turn signals function properly in one direction (although possibly too quickly), but fail to flash in the other direction. If this is the case, first check the bulbs, the sockets and the wiring connectors (see Sections 12 and 13). If all the turn signals

10.1 Tail light screws (arrowed) on 2004 to 2011 DL – note the wiring clamps

fail to work, check the fuse (see Section 5), and then check the relay (see Steps 2 to 4).

2 The turn signal relay is integrated in one component with the sidestand relay and diode circuit. To access the relay/diode unit remove the seat (see Chapter 7). The unit is next to the fusebox and plugs into a socket in the tray **(see illustration 21.11a or b)**. Pull the relay/diode unit out of its socket **(see illustration 21.11c)**.

3 Check for battery voltage at terminal G (the brown wire terminal) in the socket with the ignition ON **(see illustration 21.12)**. Turn the ignition OFF when the check is complete. If no voltage was present, check the wiring from the socket to the ignition switch (via the fusebox) for voltage and continuity. If voltage was present, check the light blue wire from the socket to the switch for continuity, and check the switch (refer to Section 19). Continue to check the wiring right through to the bulbs, referring to the appropriate wiring diagram at the end of this Chapter. Repair or renew the wiring or connectors as necessary.

4 If all is good so far, replace the relay with a new one.

12 Turn signal bulbs

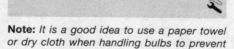

Note: *It is a good idea to use a paper towel or dry cloth when handling bulbs to prevent*

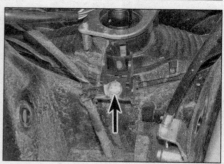

10.2 Tail light screw (arrowed) on 2012-on DL – note the wiring clamp

10.3 Tail light bolts (arrowed) on SFV – note the routing of the wiring and lock cable

injury if the bulb should break and to increase bulb life.

2004 to 2011 DL models

1 Undo the screw securing the lens and detach it from the housing **(see illustration)**.

2 Push the bulb in and twist it anti-clockwise to release it **(see illustration)**. Check the socket terminals for corrosion and clean them if necessary.

3 Line up the pins of the new bulb with the slots in the socket, then push the bulb in and turn it clockwise until it locks into place.

4 Fit the lens onto the housing and fit the screw **(see illustration)** – do not overtighten it as it is easy to strip the threads or crack the lens. Check the turn signal works.

12.1 Undo the screw and remove the lens

12.2 Push the bulb in and turn it anti-clockwise to release it

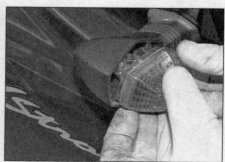

12.4 Make sure the lens locates correctly

12.5 Undo the screw and remove the lens

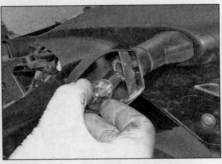

12.6 Push the bulb in and turn it anti-clockwise to release it

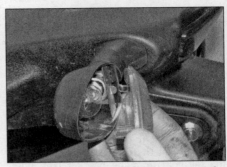

12.8 Make sure the lens locates correctly

12.9 Undo the screw and remove the turn signal from the shell

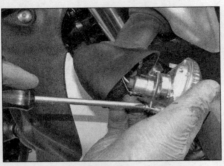

12.10 Undo the screw and remove the bulbholder from the lens

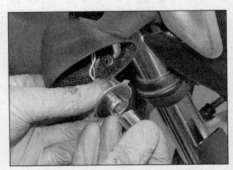

12.11 Push the bulb in and turn it anti-clockwise to release it

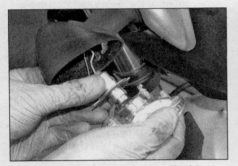

12.13a Fit the bulbholder into the lens...

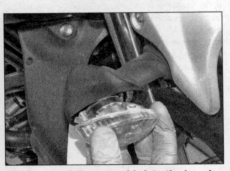

12.13b ...and the assembly into the housing

2012-on DL models

5 Undo the screw securing the lens and detach it from the housing (see illustration).
6 Push the bulb in and twist it anti-clockwise to release it (see illustration). Check the

socket terminals for corrosion and clean them if necessary.
7 Line up the pins of the new bulb with the slots in the socket, then push the bulb in and turn it clockwise until it locks into place.
8 Fit the lens onto the housing and fit the

screw (see illustration) – do not overtighten it as it is easy to strip the threads or crack the lens. Check the turn signal works.

SFV models

9 Undo the screw securing the turn signal and detach it from the housing (see illustration).
10 Undo the screw securing the bulbholder and detach it from the lens (see illustration).
11 Push the bulb in and twist it anti-clockwise to release it (see illustration). Check the socket terminals for corrosion and clean them if necessary.
12 Line up the pins of the new bulb with the slots in the socket, then push the bulb in and turn it clockwise until it locks into place.
13 Fit the bulbholder into the lens and the turn signal into the housing (see illustrations) – do not overtighten the screws as it is easy to strip the threads or crack the lens. Check the turn signal works.

13 Turn signal assemblies

Front turn signals

1 On 2004 to 2011 DL models remove the instrument surround panel (see Chapter 7). Disconnect the turn signal wiring connector (see illustration). Unscrew the nut and remove the turn signal, taking care as you draw the wire through.
2 On 2012-on DL models disconnect the turn signal wiring connector (see illustration).

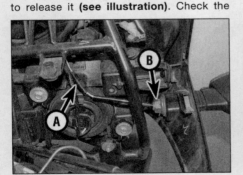

13.1 Front turn signal wiring connector (A), turn signal nut (B) – 2004 to 2011 DL

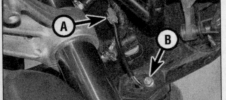

13.2 Front turn signal wiring connector (A), turn signal nut (B) – 2012-on DL

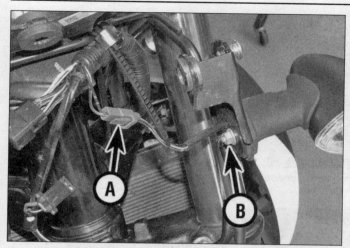

13.3 Front turn signal wiring connector (A), turn signal
nut (B) – SFV

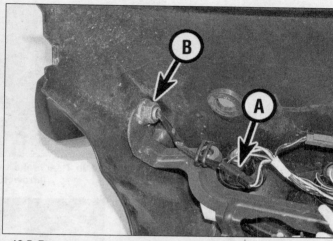

13.5 Rear turn signal wiring connector (A), turn signal nut (B) –
2004 to 2011 DL

Unscrew the nut and remove the turn signal, taking care as you draw the wire through.

3 On SFV models remove the headlight. Disconnect the turn signal wiring connector **(see illustration)**. Unscrew the nut and remove the turn signal, taking care as you draw the wire through.

4 Installation is the reverse of removal. Check the operation of the turn signal.

Rear turn signals

5 On 2004 to 2011 DL models refer to Section 9, Steps 13 to 15 and remove the rear mudguard assembly Disconnect the turn

signal wiring connector and release the wire from the clamp **(see illustration)**. Unscrew the nut and remove the turn signal, taking care as you draw the wire through.

6 On 2012-on DL models refer to Section 9, Steps 19 to 22 and remove the rear mudguard assembly. Disconnect the turn signal wiring connector. Unscrew the nut and remove the turn signal, taking care as you draw the wire through **(see illustration)**.

7 On SFV models remove the grab-rail and rear cover (see Chapter 7). Disconnect the turn signal wiring connector and release the cable-tie **(see illustrations)**. Remove the

cover from the underside of the rear mudguard **(see illustrations 9.7a, b and c)**. Unscrew the nut and remove the turn signal, taking care as you draw the wire through **(see illustration)**.

8 Installation is the reverse of removal. Check the operation of the turn signal.

14 Brake light switches

Circuit check

Note: *Refer to electrical system fault finding in Section 2 and to the wiring diagram for your model at the end of this Chapter.*

1 Before checking the switches, and if not already done, check the brake light circuit (see Section 6).

2 The front brake light switch is mounted on the underside of the brake master cylinder. Disconnect the wiring connector from the switch **(see illustration)**. Using a continuity tester, connect the probes to the terminals of the switch. With the brake lever at rest, there should be no continuity. With the brake lever applied, there should be continuity. If the switch does not behave as described, replace it with a new one.

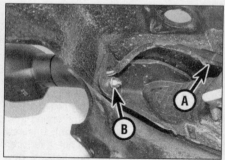

13.6 Rear turn signal wiring connector (A),
turn signal nut (B) – 2012-on DL

13.7a Right-hand turn signal connector
(arrowed) – SFV

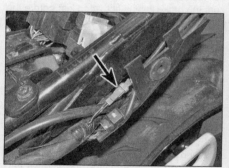

13.7b Left-hand turn signal connector
(arrowed) – SFV

13.7c Turn signal nut (arrowed) – SFV

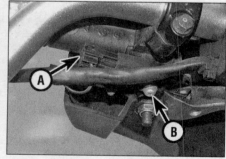

14.2 Front brake switch wiring connector
(A) and screw (B)

14.3a Rear brake switch wiring connector (arrowed) – 2004 to 2011 DL

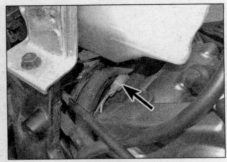

14.3b Rear brake switch wiring connector (arrowed) – 2012-on

14.3c Rear brake switch wiring connector (arrowed) – SFV

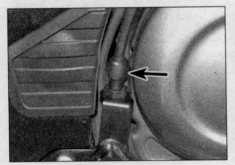

14.8a Rear brake light switch (arrowed) – DL

14.8b Rear brake light switch (arrowed) – SFV

14.9 Unhook the spring (arrowed) – DL shown

3 The rear brake light switch is mounted above the brake pedal between the clutch cover and the frame on DL models, and behind the footrest bracket on SFV models (see illustration 14.8a or b). On 2004 to 2011 DL models remove the right-hand fuel tank trim panel (see Chapter 7). On 2012-on DL models and all SFV models raise the fuel tank (see Chapter 4). Disconnect the switch wiring connector (see illustrations). Using a continuity tester, connect the probes to the terminals on the switch side of the wiring connector. With the brake pedal at rest, there should be no continuity. With the brake pedal applied, there should be continuity. If the switch does not behave as described, replace it with a new one, although check first that the spring has not become detached or broken, and the switch is adjusted correctly (see Chapter 1).
4 If the switches are good, check for voltage at the black/red (front switch – DL models), black/green (front switch – SFV models), or

orange/green (rear – all models) wire terminal in the loom side of the connector with the ignition switched ON – there should be battery voltage. If there's no voltage present, check the wiring between the switch and the fusebox (see the *Wiring Diagrams* at the end of this Chapter). If voltage is present, check the other wire for continuity from the connector to the brake light bulb wiring connector. Repair or renew the wiring as necessary. **Note:** *Front brake light switch wire colours change at the handlebar switch wiring connector.*

Switch replacement

Front brake lever switch

5 The switch is mounted on the underside of the brake master cylinder. Disconnect the wiring connector from the switch (see illustration 14.2).
6 Undo the single screw and remove the switch.

7 Installation is the reverse of removal. Make sure the peg on the switch is correctly located in its hole before tightening the screw. The switch isn't adjustable.

Rear brake pedal switch

8 The rear brake light switch is mounted above the brake pedal between the clutch cover and the frame on DL models, and behind the footrest bracket on SFV models (see illustrations). Raise the fuel tank (see Chapter 4). Disconnect the switch wiring connector (see illustration 14.3a, b or c). Feed the wiring down to the switch, noting its routing and releasing it from any ties.
9 Detach the end of the switch spring from the brake pedal (see illustration). Unscrew the switch from its adjustment nut. If required release the nut from the bracket – a new switch will come fitted with a new nut.
10 Installation is the reverse of removal. Make sure the brake light is activated just before the rear brake pedal takes effect. If adjustment is necessary, refer to Chapter 1, Section 2.

15 Instrument removal and installation

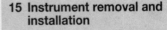

Removal

1 On DL models remove the instrument surround panel (see Chapter 7 – rear panel only on 2012-on models). Undo the screws and remove the instruments from the panel (see illustrations).

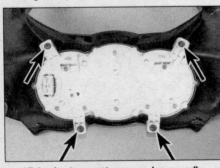

15.1a Instrument screws (arrowed) – 2004 to 2011 DL

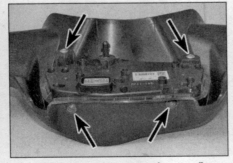

15.1b Instrument screws (arrowed) – 2012-on DL

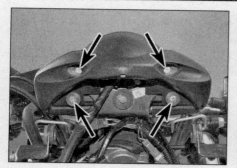

15.2a Undo the screws (arrowed)…

15.2b …and remove the cover – SFV

15.2c Undo the screw (arrowed)…

15.2d …and disconnect the wiring – SFV

15.2e Undo the nuts and screw (arrowed)…

15.2f …and remove the instruments – SFV

2 On SFV models undo the screws and remove the cover **(see illustrations)**. Undo the wiring clamp screw and disconnect the wiring connector **(see illustration)**. Undo the screw and nuts and remove the instruments **(see illustrations)**.

Installation

3 Installation is the reverse of removal. On SFV models check the rubber grommets in the bracket and replace them with new ones if necessary **(see illustration 15.2f)**.

16 Instrument check and disassembly

Note: *Refer to electrical system fault finding in Section 2 and to the wiring diagram for your model at the end of this Chapter.*
Note: *The tachometer, LCD display and LEDs are integral with the instrument panel printed circuit board (PCB) – separate components for the PCB are not available, but the PCB is available separately from the covers.*

Check

1 If all instrument and display functions fail at the same time, check the signal fuse (Section 5), then check the instrument wiring connector (Section 15).

Speedometer and speed sensor

2 If the speedometer, odometer or trip meter fail to work, take the motorcycle to a Suzuki

dealer for assessment. Special equipment is needed to check the operation of the speedometer and the speed sensor.

Tachometer

3 Suzuki provides no data for testing the tachometer. If the tachometer fails to work, take the motorcycle to a Suzuki dealer for assessment.
4 In normal operation, when the ignition is first turned ON, the tachometer needle will swing to full scale and then return to zero. This is part of the instrument's self checking procedure. If the tachometer pointer fails to return to zero (which may occur in very low temperatures), and switching the ignition OFF then ON again does not return it, it can be reset as follows. Make sure the ignition is OFF.
5 On DL models hold the ADJ button ON and turn the ignition ON. Release the ADJ button three to five seconds after turning the ignition ON, then press the ADJ button twice within four seconds. If the tachometer is working correctly, the tachometer needle should now be at zero. The whole reset procedure should be completed with ten seconds. Turn the ignition OFF.
6 On SFV models hold the ADJ button ON and turn the ignition ON. After five seconds and before ten seconds the tachometer needle should reset to zero. Turn the ignition OFF.

Coolant temperature display

7 The coolant temperature display is controlled by the coolant temperature sensor – refer to Chapter 3 for test details.

Ambient temperature display and freeze warning light – 2012-on DL models

8 The ambient temperature sensor is located inside the fairing on the left-hand side **(see illustration)**. Remove the fuel tank trim panels to access the sensor (see Chapter 7). Testing of the display, warning light and sensor is possible but requires equipment unlikely to be available in the home workshop.

Fuel level display

9 The fuel level display is controlled by the fuel level sensor – refer to Chapter 4 for test details.

Oil pressure warning

10 When the ignition is first turned ON and before the engine is started, the oil warning light and symbol should come on. When the engine is started they should extinguish.

16.8 Ambient air temperature sensor (arrowed)

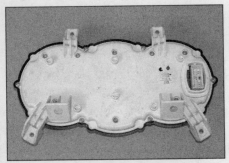

16.15a On 2004 to 2011 DL models undo the screws...

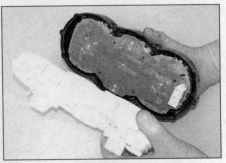

16.15b ...remove the rear cover...

16.15c ...and the front cover

16.15d On 2012-on DL models undo the screws...

16.15e ...remove the rear cover...

16.15f ...and the front cover

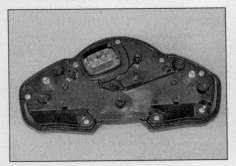

16.15g On SFV models undo the screws...

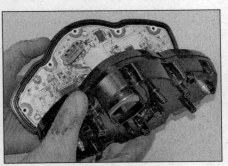

16.15h ...remove the rear cover...

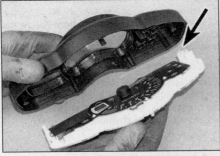

16.15i ...and the front cover, and remove the push rods (arrowed)

This is part of the instrument's self checking procedure.

11 If the display and light do not come on, turn the ignition OFF. Disconnect the wiring connector from the oil pressure switch (see Section 17). Turn the ignition ON and earth (ground) the wiring connector on the crankcase – the warning light and symbol should come on. If they don't check the wire between the oil pressure switch and instruments for continuity. If the wire is good the instrument board is faulty.

12 If the warning symbol and warning LED come on when the engine is running, and this is not due to low oil level or low oil pressure, disconnect the oil pressure switch wiring connector (see Section 17), then turn the ignition ON; the display and

light should be out. If they are on, the wire between the switch and instrument cluster must be earthed (grounded) at some point.

13 If all is good, replace the switch with a new one (Section 17).

Instrument board removal and installation

14 Remove the instrument cluster (see Section 15).

15 Undo the screws on the back of the instrument cluster and separate the front cover, instrument panel and rear cover **(see illustrations)**. Further dismantling is not possible.

16 Installation is the reverse of removal – on

2004 to 2011 DL models make sure the pegs locate correctly **(see illustration)**; on 2012-on DL models make sure the push rods locate

16.16a Make sure the board locates correctly on the pegs – 2004 to 2011 DL

16.16b Guide the push rod (arrowed) into its housing – 2012-on DL

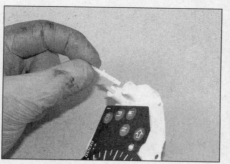

16.16c Fit the two push rods as shown – SFV

16.16d Check the seal is in good condition and correctly seated

correctly **(see illustration)**; on SFV models make sure the push rods are fitted **(see illustration)**. Where fitted make sure the seal is correctly seated **(see illustration)**.

Speed sensor removal and installation

17 On 2004 to 2011 DL models trace the wiring from the sensor, mounted in the left-hand side of the front wheel, and disconnect it at the connector. Free the wiring from any clips and feed it down to the sensor, noting its routing. Remove the front wheel (see Chapter 6). Remove the rotor and ring from the sensor housing and check them and the seal around the rim of the housing for wear and damage, replacing them with new ones if necessary **(see illustrations)**. Otherwise clean off all old grease and apply some new, then fit the ring and rotor back into the housing.

18 On 2012-on DL models and all SFV models remove the front sprocket outer cover (see Chapter 6). Raise the fuel tank (see Chapter 4). Unscrew the bolt and withdraw the sensor **(see illustration)**. Trace the wiring from the sensor and free it from any clips and ties. Disconnect the connector – with the sensor displaced there is ample slack in the wiring to pull the connector out for access. Feed the wiring down to the sensor, noting its routing. If required, remove the inner cover and check the condition of the speed sensor rotor (see Chapter 6) **(see illustration)**.

Instrument illumination and warning lights

19 All instrument illumination and warning

16.17a Remove the rotor and ring...

16.17b ...and check the seal (arrowed)

lights are LEDs that cannot be replaced with new ones – if one fails a new instrument cluster must be fitted.

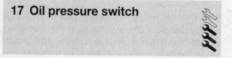

17 Oil pressure switch

Note: *Refer to electrical system fault finding in Section 2 and to the wiring diagram for your model at the end of this Chapter.*

Check

1 The oil pressure warning light and symbol should come on when the ignition switch is turned ON and extinguish a few seconds after the engine is started (if they don't come on with the ignition refer to Section 16). If they come on whilst the engine is running, stop the engine immediately and check the oil level (see *Pre-ride checks*). If the level is correct,

check the switch as described below, then if necessary carry out an oil pressure check (see Chapter 2).

2 The oil pressure switch is screwed into the front of the engine on the right-hand side. Pull the rubber cover off the switch and undo the wiring connector screw **(see illustration)**. With the ignition switched ON, earth (ground) the wire on the crankcase and check that the warning light and symbol come on. If they do, the switch is faulty and must be replaced with a new one. If they don't come on, refer to Section 16.

Removal

3 The oil pressure switch is screwed into the front of the engine on the right-hand side. Drain the engine oil (see Chapter 1).

4 Pull the rubber cover off the switch, then undo the screw securing the wiring connector **(see illustration 17.2)**.

5 Unscrew the switch.

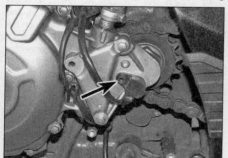

16.18a Speed sensor bolt (arrowed)

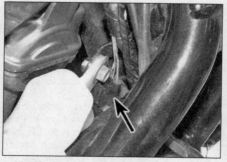

16.18b Speed sensor wiring connector (arrowed) – SFV

17.2 Pull back the rubber cover then undo the terminal screw and detach the wire

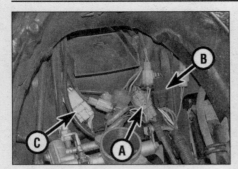

18.2a Front loom wiring connectors – 2004 to 2011 DL (A = ignition switch, B = right handlebar, C = left handlebar)

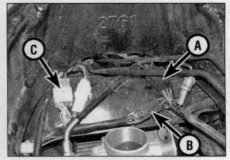

18.2b Front loom wiring connectors – 2012-on DL (A = ignition switch, B = right handlebar, C = left handlebar)

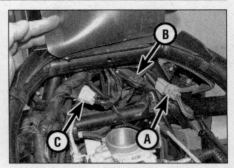

18.2c Front loom wiring connectors – SFV (A = ignition switch, B = right handlebar, C = left handlebar)

Installation

6 Apply a suitable sealant (such as Suzuki Bond 1207B or equivalent) to the upper portion of the switch threads near the body, leaving the bottom half of thread clean. Fit the switch and tighten it to the torque setting specified at the beginning of the Chapter.

7 Attach the wiring connector and secure it with the screw, then fit the rubber cover **(see illustration 17.2)**.

8 Replenish the engine with oil (see Chapter 1). Run the engine and check that the switch operates correctly without leakage.

18 Ignition switch

> ⚠ **Warning: To prevent the risk of short circuits, disconnect the battery negative (–) lead before making any ignition switch checks.**

Note: *Refer to electrical system fault finding in Section 2 and to the wiring diagram for your model at the end of this Chapter.*

Check

1 The switch can be checked for continuity using an ohmmeter or a continuity test light. Always disconnect the battery negative (–) lead, which will prevent the possibility of a short circuit, before making the checks (see Section 3). Before checking the switch check the main fuse (Section 5).

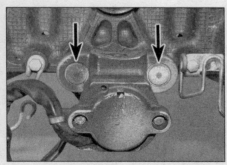

18.9 Ignition switch bolts (arrowed)

2 To access the connector, remove the air filter housing (see Chapter 4). Trace the wiring from the switch to the connector and disconnect it **(see illustrations)**. Check for loose or broken connections.

3 Using an ohmmeter or a continuity tester connected to the switch side of the connector, check the continuity of the connector terminal pairs shown with linked circles in the table for the ignition switch shown in the wiring diagram for your model at the end of this Chapter. Continuity should exist between those terminals when the switch is in the ON position.

4 If continuity is not shown check the wiring between the connector and the switch for a break. If the wiring is good replace the switch with a new one.

5 If the switch is good, reconnect the battery. Check there is battery voltage at the black/red wire terminal in the loom side of the connector. If not, there is a break in the wire between the connector and the main fuse terminal in the starter relay. If there is voltage check all other wires for continuity to the fusebox.

Removal

Note: *On some models the ignition switch is secured by shear-head bolts that can only be used once. To remove the bolts drive them around using a small cold chisel or punch, or drill the heads off after centre-punching them.*

6 Disconnect the battery negative (–) lead (see Section 3).

7 Refer to Step 2 to access the switch wiring connector, and disconnect it. Feed the wiring back to the switch, freeing it from any clips and ties and noting the routing.

8 If the switch is secured by Torx bolts, unscrew them and remove the switch from the yoke. Note that Torx screws with a raised pip in their centres will require a special security Torx bit.

9 If the switch is secured by shear-head bolts displace the handlebars from the top yoke, then remove the yoke (see Chapter 5, Sections 5 and 9). Protect and secure the yoke sufficiently, then undo the security bolts (see **Note**), and remove the switch **(see illustration)**.

Installation

10 Installation is the reverse of removal. Where Torx bolts are used clean the threads and apply some fresh threadlock. Where shear-head bolts are used fit new bolts (they come with a new switch and are also available separately) and tighten them until the heads shear off. Refer to Chapter 5 to install the top yoke and handlebars. Make sure the wiring is correctly routed and securely connected.

19 Handlebar switches

1 Generally speaking, the switches are reliable and trouble-free. Most troubles, when they do occur, are caused by dirty or corroded contacts, but wear and breakage of internal parts is a possibility that should not be overlooked. If breakage does occur, the entire switch and related wiring harness will have to be replaced with a new one, as individual parts are not available.

Check

Note: *Refer to electrical system fault finding in Section 2 and to the wiring diagram for your model at the end of this Chapter.*

2 The switches can be checked for continuity using an ohmmeter or a continuity test light. Always disconnect the battery negative (–) lead, which will prevent the possibility of a short circuit, before making the checks (see Section 3).

3 To access the connectors, on DL models remove the air filter housing (see Chapter 4), and on SFV models remove the front side cover on the side of the switch being tested (see Chapter 7). Trace the wiring from the switch to the connector and disconnect it **(see illustration 18.2a, b or c)**. Check for loose or broken connections.

4 Using an ohmmeter or a continuity tester connected to the switch side of the connector, check the continuity of the connector terminal pairs shown with linked circles in the table for the ignition switch shown in the wiring diagram for your model at the end of this Chapter. Continuity should exist between the terminals connected by a solid line on the diagram when the switch is in the indicated position.

5 If the continuity check indicates a problem exists, displace the switch housing (Steps 7 and 8), and spray the switch contacts with electrical contact cleaner (there is no need to remove the switch completely). If they are accessible, the contacts can be scraped clean with a knife or polished with crocus cloth. If switch components are damaged or broken, it should be obvious when the switch is disassembled.

Removal and installation

6 Refer to Step 3 to access the switch wiring connector, and disconnect it. Feed the wiring back to the switch, freeing it from any clips and ties and noting the routing.
7 If removing the right-hand switch disconnect the wiring connector from the brake light switch (see illustration 14.2). If removing the left-hand switch disconnect the wiring connector from the clutch switch (see illustration 22.2).
8 To remove the left-hand switch housing on all models and the right-hand switch housing on 2004 to 2006 DL models undo the screws and free the switch from the handlebar by separating the halves (see illustration).
9 To remove the right-hand switch housing on 2007-on DL models and all SFV models refer to Chapter 4 and detach the throttle cables.
10 Installation is the reverse of removal. Locate the pin in the switch housing in the hole in the handlebar (see illustration). Do not over-tighten the screws.

20 Gear position switch

Note: *Refer to electrical system fault finding in Section 2 and to the wiring diagram for your model at the end of this Chapter.*
1 The gear position switch is located in the left-hand side of the crankcase below the front sprocket. The neutral light should come on whenever the ignition switch is ON and the transmission is in neutral. The switch is part of the starter safety circuit that prevents the engine starting unless the clutch lever is pulled in.

Check

2 On 2004 to 2011 DL models remove the left-hand side cover (see Chapter 7). On 2012-on DL models and all SFV models raise the fuel tank (see Chapter 4). Trace the wiring from the switch and disconnect it at the connector (see illustrations). Make sure the transmission is in neutral.
3 With the connector disconnected and the ignition switch ON, the neutral light should be out. If not, the wire between the connector and instrument cluster must be earthed (grounded) at some point.
4 Check for continuity between the blue wire terminal on the switch side of the connector and the black/white (earth/ground) wire terminal. With the transmission in neutral, there

19.8 Switch housing screws (arrowed)

should be continuity. With the transmission in gear, there should be no continuity. If the tests prove otherwise, then the switch is faulty – remove it and check it as described below, and if necessary replace it with a new one.
5 Check the gear position function of the switch as follows. Support the machine upright on an auxiliary stand with the sidestand up. Make sure the wiring connector is securely connected. Using a multimeter set to the volts scale, insert probes into the pink and black/white wire terminals on the loom side of the connector and turn the ignition switch ON. Select 1st gear and note the voltage between the wire terminals, then select 2nd to 6th gear in sequence, noting the voltage in each gear. On 2004 to 2011 DL models compare the readings with those shown below. On 2012-on DL models and all SFV models there should be more than 0.6 volts in each gear. If the results are not as described it is likely that the

20.2a GP switch wiring connector – 2004 to 2011 DL

20.2c GP switch wiring connector – SFV

19.10 Locate the pin (A) in the hole (B)

gear position switch is faulty – remove it and check it as described below, and if necessary replace it with a new one.

Gear	Voltage (approx)
1st	1.36V
2nd	1.77V
3rd	2.49V
4th	3.23V
5th	4.10V
6th	4.55V

Removal

6 The switch is located in the left-hand side of the crankcase below the front sprocket. Drain the engine oil (see Chapter 1). Remove the front sprocket cover (outer on 2012-on DL models and all SFV models).
7 Refer to Step 3 to access the switch wiring connector, and disconnect it. Feed the wiring back to the switch, freeing it from any clips and ties and noting the routing (see illustration).

20.2b GP switch wiring connector – 2012-on DL

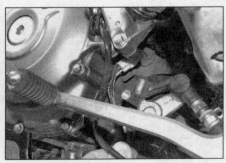

20.7 Note the routing of the wiring as you draw the connector down

20.8 GP switch screws (arrowed)

20.9 Remove the plungers and springs for safekeeping

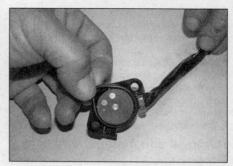

20.11 Fit a new O-ring onto the switch

8 Clean the chain grease and road dirt from the switch area. Undo the screws and remove the switch **(see illustration)**. Discard the O-ring – a new one should be used.

9 On 2004 to 2011 DL models remove the contact plungers and springs from the end of the selector drum **(see illustration)**. Check the condition of the plungers and springs and of the contacts on the inner face of the switch and replace worn or damaged parts with new ones.

10 On 2012-on DL models and all SFV models check the pin for wear and damage and make sure the switch body turns freely in the housing. Replace the switch with a new one if necessary.

Installation

11 On 2004 to 2011 DL models fit the springs and contact plungers into their bores in the end

21.2a Sidestand switch wiring connector – 2004 to 2011 DL

21.2b Sidestand switch wiring connector – 2012-on DL

of the selector drum **(see illustration 20.9)**. Fit the switch using a new O-ring smeared with grease **(see illustration)**. Clean the threads of the screws and apply some threadlock.

12 On 2012-on DL models and all SFV models fit the switch using a new O-ring smeared with grease, locating the pin in the offset hole in the drum. Clean the threads of the screws and apply some threadlock.

13 Route the wiring as noted on removal and connect the wiring connector. Check the operation of the neutral light.

14 Replenish the engine oil (see Chapter 1). Lower the fuel tank and/or install the covers.

21 Sidestand switch, relay and diodes

Note: *Refer to electrical system fault finding in Section 2 and to the wiring diagram for your model at the end of this Chapter.*

Sidestand switch

Check

1 The sidestand switch is mounted in front of the stand pivot. The switch is part of the safety circuit that prevents the engine starting or stops it running if the transmission is in gear and the sidestand is down. The sidestand switch relay and starter safety circuit diodes are integrated into one component with the turn signal relay **(see illustration 21.11a or b)**.

2 On DL models remove the left-hand side cover (see Chapter 7), and on SFV models

21.2c Sidestand switch wiring connector – SFV

raise the fuel tank (see Chapter 4). Trace the wiring from the switch and disconnect it at the connector **(see illustrations)**.

3 Check the operation of the switch using an ohmmeter or continuity test light. Connect the meter between the terminals on the switch side of the connector – meter positive (+) probe to the green wire terminal and negative (-) probe to the black/white wire terminal. With the sidestand up there should be continuity (zero resistance), with the stand down there should be no continuity (infinite resistance). If you have a meter with a diode testing function, set it accordingly and connect it as before – with the sidestand up there should be 0.4 to 0.6 volts, with the stand down there should be the voltage of the meter battery.

4 If the switch does not perform as expected, check that the fault is not caused by a sticking switch plunger due to the ingress of road dirt; spray the switch with a water dispersant aerosol **(see illustration)**. If the switch still does not work it is defective and must be replaced with a new one.

5 If the switch is good, check the sidestand relay (Steps 11 to 13) and diodes (Step 14). Also check the wiring between the various components (see *Wiring Diagrams* at the end of this Chapter).

Removal and installation

6 Disconnect the switch wiring (see Step 2). Feed the wiring back to the switch noting its routing and freeing it from any clips or ties.

7 Unscrew the bolts and remove the switch **(see illustration 21.4)**.

8 Clean the threads of the bolts and apply

21.4 Check the plunger moves smoothly and freely. Switch bolts (arrowed)

21.11a Relay/diode unit (arrowed) – DL

21.11b Relay/diode unit (arrowed) – SFV

21.11c Pull the unit off its socket

a suitable non-permanent thread locking compound, then fit the switch and tighten the bolts.

9 Make sure the wiring is correctly routed up to the connector and retained by clips and ties. Reconnect the wiring connector.

10 Install the side cover or fuel tank.

Sidestand relay

11 The sidestand relay is integrated in one component with the turn signal relay and diode circuit. To access the relay/diode unit remove the seat (see Chapter 7). The unit is next to the fusebox and plugs into a socket in the tray (see illustration). Pull the relay/diode unit out of its socket (see illustration).

12 Using an ohmmeter or continuity tester, check for continuity between the D and E terminals on the relay (see illustration). There should be no continuity (infinite resistance).

13 Now use jumper wires to connect the positive (+) terminal of a 12V battery to the D terminal on the relay and the negative (-) battery terminal to the C relay terminal, and again check for continuity between the D and E terminals. There should be continuity (zero resistance). If there is no continuity, fit a new relay.

Diodes

14 The diodes are integrated in one component with the turn signal relay and sidestand relay. Access the relay (see Step 11) and pull it off its connector.

15 Using a diode tester, connect the positive (+) probe to terminal C of the diode and the negative (-) probe to terminal A (see illustration 21.12). The tester should show 0.4 to 0.6 volts. Now reverse the probes. The tester should show its own battery voltage. Repeat the tests between terminal B and terminal A. The same results should be achieved. If it doesn't behave as stated, fit a new diode/turn signal relay/sidestand relay.

16 If the diodes are good, check the other components in the starter safety circuit (clutch switch, gear position switch, sidestand switch and relay) as described in the relevant sections of this Chapter. If all components are good, check the wiring between the various components (see the wiring diagrams at the end of this book).

22 Clutch switch

Note: Refer to electrical system fault finding in Section 2 and to the wiring diagram for your model at the end of this Chapter.

1 The clutch switch is on the underside of the clutch lever bracket. The switch is part of the starter safety circuit and the lever must be pulled in (switch on) to allow the engine to be started.

Check

2 To check the switch, disconnect the wiring connector (see illustration). Connect the probes of an ohmmeter or a continuity test light to the two switch terminals. With the clutch lever pulled in, there should be continuity (zero resistance). With the clutch lever out, there should be no continuity (infinite resistance).

3 If the switch is good, check the other components in the starter circuit as described in the relevant sections of this Chapter. If all components are good, check the wiring between the various components (see the Wiring Diagrams at the end of this Chapter).

Removal and installation

4 Disconnect the wiring connector from the clutch switch (see illustration 22.2). Undo the screw(s) and remove the switch (see illustration).

5 Installation is the reverse of removal. The switch isn't adjustable.

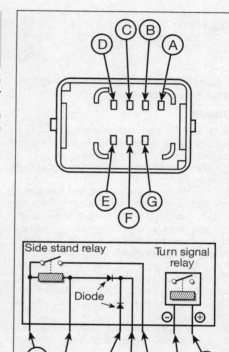

21.12 Relay/diode unit terminal identification and circuit diagram

22.2 Clutch switch wiring connector (arrowed)

22.4 Clutch switch screw (arrowed) – 2012 DL shown

23.1a Horn (arrowed) – 2004 to 2011 DL

23.1b Horn (arrowed) – 2012-on DL

23.1c Horn (arrowed) – SFV

23 Horn

1 There is a single horn mounted behind the radiator **(see illustrations)**.

Check

Note: *Refer to electrical system fault finding in Section 2 and to the wiring diagram for your model at the end of this Chapter.*

2 If the horn fails first check the signal fuse (Section 5).

3 If the fuse is good disconnect the wiring connectors from the horn. Check them for loose wires. Using two jumper wires, apply voltage from a fully-charged 12V battery directly to the terminals on the horn. If the horn doesn't sound, replace it with a new one.

4 If the horn sounds, refer to the wiring diagram for your model and check the wiring between the horn, the horn button and fusebox, and check the black/white wire for continuity to earth.

5 If all is good check the button contacts in the switch housing (see Section 19).

Replacement

6 Disconnect the wiring connectors from the horn. Unscrew the nut/bolt securing the horn.

7 Fit the horn and tighten the nut/bolt. Connect the wiring to the horn. Check that it works.

24 Starter relay

Note: *Refer to electrical system fault finding in Section 2 and to the wiring diagram for your model at the end of this Chapter.*

Check

1 If the starter circuit is faulty, first check the main and ignition fuses (see Section 5).

2 To access the starter relay, remove the seat (see Chapter 7) **(see illustration)**. Disconnect the battery negative (-ve) lead (see Section 3). Remove the plastic cover **(see illustration 24.9b)**.

3 Undo the bolt securing the starter motor lead to its terminal on the relay and disconnect the lead, then position it away from the terminal **(see illustration 24.9c)**. Reconnect the battery negative (-) lead. With the ignition ON, the engine kill switch in the RUN position, the transmission in neutral and the clutch pulled in, press the starter switch. The relay should be heard to click. Turn the ignition OFF.

4 If the relay doesn't click, disconnect the

relay wiring connector **(see illustration 24.9a)**. Connect the positive (+) probe of a voltmeter into the yellow/green wire terminal in the connector and the negative (-ve) probe into the black/yellow wire terminal. Check for battery voltage with the ignition ON, kill switch in the RUN position, clutch lever pulled in and starter switch pressed. If no voltage is present, check the terminals in the wiring connector, the wiring (see *Wiring Diagrams* at the end of this Chapter) and the other components in the starter circuit as described in the relevant sections of this Chapter.

5 If there is voltage present, remove the relay (Step 9).

6 Set a multimeter to the ohms scale and connect it across the relay's starter motor and battery lead terminals (A and B) **(see illustration)**. Use jumper wires to connect the positive (+) terminal of a 12V battery to the C terminal on the relay and the negative (-) battery terminal to the D relay terminal. The relay should be heard to click and there should be continuity (zero resistance) shown on the meter. Disconnect the battery. **Note:** *Do not apply battery voltage to the relay for more than 5 seconds to avoid damaging the relay coil.*

7 Now use the multimeter set to the ohms scale to measure the resistance between the relay's C and D terminals and compare the

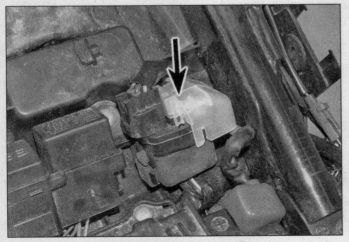

24.2 Starter relay (arrowed)

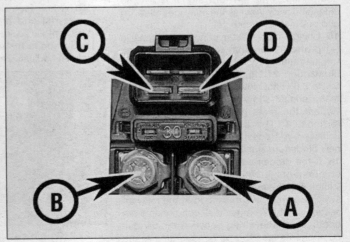

24.6 Starter relay terminal identification

24.9a Disconnect the wiring connector

24.9b Remove the cover

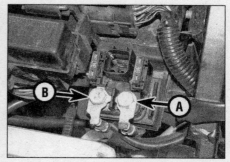

24.9c Starter motor lead terminal (A) and battery lead terminal (B)

result with the Specifications at the beginning of this Chapter. If the result of either test is not as specified, the relay is faulty and must be replaced with a new one.

Removal and installation

8 To access the starter relay, remove the seat (see Chapter 7). Disconnect the battery negative (-ve) lead.
9 Disconnect the relay wiring connector **(see illustration)**. Remove the plastic cover **(see illustration)**. Undo the bolts securing the starter motor and battery leads and remove the relay **(see illustration)**.
10 Installation is the reverse of removal. Make sure the terminal bolts are tight.

25 Starter motor removal and installation

Removal

1 The starter motor is mounted on the front of the crankcase. Disconnect the battery negative (–ve) lead (see Section 3).
2 Peel back the rubber terminal cover on the starter motor **(see illustrations)**. Unscrew the nut and detach the lead.
3 Unscrew the two bolts securing the starter motor to the crankcase, noting the wiring clamp secured by the bottom bolt **(see illustration)**. Slide the starter motor out, using

a screwdriver as leverage if required **(see illustration)**.
4 Remove the O-ring on the end of the starter motor – a new one must be used **(see illustration 25.5)**.

Installation

5 Fit a new O-ring smeared with grease onto the end of the starter motor, making sure it is seated in its groove **(see illustration)**.
6 Manoeuvre the motor into position, meshing starter motor teeth with those of the starter idle/reduction gear **(see illustration 25.3b)**. Fit and tighten the bolts, not forgetting the wiring clamp with the bottom bolt where fitted **(see illustration 25.3a)**.
7 Connect the starter lead **(see illustration 25.2a or b)**. Fit the rubber cover over the terminal.
8 Connect the battery.

25.2a Starter lead nut (arrowed) – 2004 to 2009 DL

26 Starter motor overhaul

Check

1 Remove the starter motor (see Section 25). Cover the body in some rag and clamp the motor mounting lugs in a soft-jawed vice – do not overtighten it.
2 Using a fully-charged 12 volt battery and two insulated jumper wires, connect the positive (+) terminal of the battery to the protruding terminal on the starter motor, and the negative (–) terminal to one of the motor's mounting lugs. At this point the starter motor should spin. If this is the case the motor is proved good, though it is worth disassembling it and checking it if you suspect it of not

25.2b Starter lead nut (arrowed) – 2010-on DL and 2011-on SFV

25.3a Unscrew the two bolts, noting the wire clamp...

25.3b ...and remove the motor

25.5 Fit a new O-ring

26.4 Note the alignment marks (arrowed), or make your own

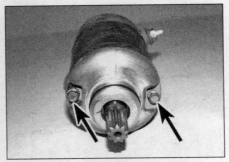

26.5a Unscrew and remove the two bolts (arrowed)...

26.5b ...then remove the front cover and sealing ring (arrowed)

working properly under load. If the motor does not spin, disassemble it for inspection.

2004 to 2009 DL models, and 2009 and 2010 SFV models

Disassembly

3 Remove the starter motor (see Section 25).
4 Note any alignment marks between the main housing and the front and rear covers, or make your own if they aren't clear **(see illustration)**.
5 Unscrew the two long bolts, noting the O-rings, then remove the front cover from the motor along with its sealing ring **(see illustrations)**. Remove the tabbed washer from the cover and slide the insulating washer and shim from the front end of the

armature, noting their correct fitted order **(see illustrations)**.
6 Remove the rear cover from the motor along with its sealing ring. Remove the shims from the rear end of the armature **(see illustration 26.21a)**.
7 Withdraw the armature from the main housing – it is held in by the attraction of the magnets, so take care not to lose your grip on the armature before the magnets lose theirs.
8 At this stage check for continuity between the terminal bolt and the brush on the insulated base – there should be continuity (zero resistance). Check for continuity between the terminal bolt and the cover – there should be no continuity (infinite resistance). Also check for continuity between the uninsulated

brush and the brushplate – there should be continuity (zero resistance). If there is no continuity when there should be or *vice versa*, identify the faulty component and replace it with a new one.
9 Noting the correct fitted location of each component, unscrew the nut from the terminal bolt and remove the plain washer, the one large and two small insulating washers **(see illustration)**. Remove the brushplate assembly and terminal bolt from the rear cover, noting how it locates **(see illustration)**. Remove the O-ring and the insulator from the bolt **(see illustration)**.
10 Move each brush spring end aside and slide the brushes out **(see illustration)**.

26.5c Remove the tabbed washer...

26.5d ...and the washer and shim (arrowed)

26.9a Unscrew the nut (arrowed) and remove the large and small insulating washers and the O-ring

26.9b Remove the brushplate assembly...

26.9c ...and the insulator

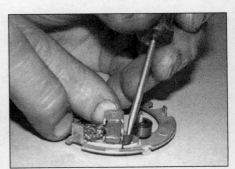

26.10 Move the spring end aside and withdraw the brush

26.11 Check each brush as described

26.12a Check the commutator bars

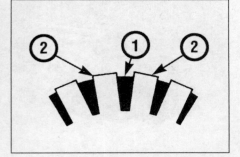

26.12b Check the depth of the Mica (1) between the bars (2)

Inspection

11 The parts of the starter motor that are most likely to require attention are the brushes (see illustration). Suzuki provides no measurements but if they are below 6 mm in length or otherwise obviously worn replace the brushplate assembly with a new one. If the brushes are not worn excessively, nor cracked, chipped, or otherwise damaged, they can be reused.

12 Inspect the commutator bars on the armature for scoring, scratches and discoloration (see illustration). The commutator can be cleaned and polished with crocus cloth or 400 grit (or finer) sandpaper, but do not use anything coarser. After cleaning, blow and wipe away any residue with a cloth soaked in electrical system cleaner or denatured alcohol. Check the

depth of the insulating Mica between each bar – it should be at least 1 mm below the surface (see illustration). As the bars wear, the Mica should be gently scratched away using a hacksaw blade to maintain the correct depth.

13 Using an ohmmeter or a continuity test light, check for continuity between the commutator bars (see illustration). Continuity should exist between each bar and all of the others. Also, check for continuity between the commutator bars and the armature shaft (see illustration). There should be no continuity (infinite resistance) between the commutator and the shaft. If the checks indicate otherwise, the armature is defective and a new starter motor must be obtained – the armature is not available separately.

14 Check the front end of the armature shaft for worn, cracked, chipped and broken teeth.

If the shaft is damaged or worn, a new starter motor must be obtained – the armature is not available separately.

15 Inspect the front and rear covers for signs of cracks or wear. Check the oil seal and the needle bearing in the front cover and the bush in the rear cover for wear and damage – the seal, bearing, bush and covers are not listed as being available separately so if necessary a new starter motor must be fitted (see illustrations).

16 Inspect the magnets in the main housing and the housing itself for cracks.

17 Inspect the insulating washers, O-ring, and sealing rings for signs of damage, deformation and deterioration and replace them with new ones if necessary.

Reassembly

18 Slide the brushes back into position in their housings and locate the brush spring ends onto the outer ends of the brushes (see illustration 26.10).

19 Fit the insulator (see illustration 26.9c). Insert the terminal bolt through its hole in the rear cover then fit the brushplate into the cover, making sure its tab is correctly located in the groove in the cover (see illustration 26.9b). Fit the O-ring down over the bolt and press it into place between the bolt and the cover (see illustration). Slide the small insulating washers onto the terminal bolt, followed by the large insulating washer and the plain washer. Fit the nut onto the terminal bolt and tighten it.

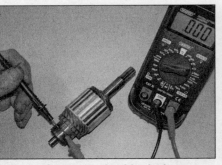

26.13a Continuity should exist between the commutator bars

26.13b There should be no continuity between the bars and the shaft

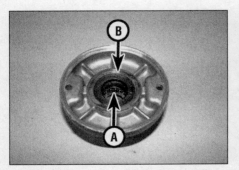

26.15a Check the seal (A) and needle bearing (B) in the front cover...

26.15b ...and the bush (arrowed) in the rear cover

26.19 Fit the O-ring and small insulating washers onto the terminal bolt, followed by the large insulating washer, the plain washer and the nut

26.21a Fit the shims...

26.21b ...then smear grease onto the shaft end

26.21c Locate the commutator bars against the brushes...

20 At this stage check again for continuity between the terminal bolt and the brush on the insulated base – there should be continuity (zero resistance). Check for continuity between the terminal bolt and the cover – there should be no continuity (infinite resistance). Also check for continuity between the uninsulated brush and the brushplate – there should be continuity (zero resistance). If there is no continuity when there should be or *vice versa*, identify the faulty component and replace it with a new one.

21 Fit the shims onto the rear of the armature shaft **(see illustration)**. Apply a smear of grease to the end of the shaft **(see illustration)**. Insert the armature into the brushplate at an angle so that the brushes locate against the commutator, then straighten the armature, pushing the brushes back into their housings against the springs, and slide it into the rear cover so that the shaft end locates in its bush **(see illustrations)**.

22 Fit the sealing ring onto the rear of the main housing **(see illustration)**. Grasp both the armature and the rear cover in one hand and hold them together – this will prevent the armature being drawn out by the magnets in the housing. Note however that you should take care not to let the housing be drawn forcibly onto the armature by the magnets. Carefully allow the housing to be drawn onto the armature, making sure the end with the cut-out faces the rear cover and aligns with the brushplate outer tab **(see illustration)** – aligning the marks between the cover and housing (Step 4) will help.

23 Apply a smear of grease to the front cover oil seal lip. Fit the tabbed washer into the cover so that its teeth are correctly located between the cover ribs **(see illustration 26.5c)**.

24 Fit the sealing ring onto the front of the housing **(see illustration)**. Slide the shim onto the front end of the armature shaft then fit the

washer **(see illustration 26.5d)**. Slide the front cover into position, aligning the marks made on removal **(see illustration 26.5b)**.

25 Check the marks made on removal are correctly aligned then fit the long bolts, not forgetting the O-rings (using new ones if necessary) and tighten them **(see illustration)**.

26 Install the starter motor (see Section 25).

2010-on DL models, and 2011-on SFV models

Disassembly

27 Remove the starter motor (see Section 25).

28 Note any alignment marks between the main housing and the front and rear covers, or make your own if they aren't clear **(see illustration)**.

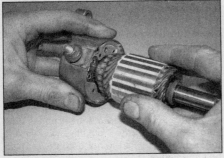

26.21d ...and slide the armature into the cover

26.22a Fit the sealing ring...

26.22b ...then carefully slide the housing over the armature

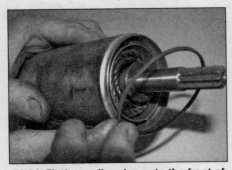

26.24 Fit the sealing ring onto the front of the housing

26.25 Fit the long bolts with their O-rings

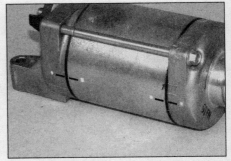

26.28 Note the alignment marks (highlighted) between the housing and the covers

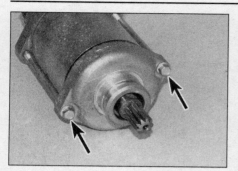

26.29a Unscrew the bolts (arrowed)...

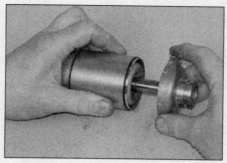

26.29b ...and remove the front cover...

26.30 ...and the rear cover

29 Unscrew the two long bolts and remove the front cover from the motor (see illustrations).
30 Remove the rear cover (see illustration).
31 Withdraw the armature from the main housing (see illustration) – it is held in by the attraction of the magnets, so take care not to lose your grip on the armature before the magnets lose theirs.
32 At this stage check for continuity between the terminal bolt and the positive brushes (see illustration) – there should be continuity (zero resistance). Check for continuity between the terminal bolt and the cover – there should be no continuity (infinite resistance). Also check for continuity between the negative and positive brushes – there should be no continuity (infinite resistance). If there is no continuity when there should be or *vice versa*, identify the faulty component and replace it with a new one.

33 Noting the correct fitted location of each component, unscrew the nut from the terminal bolt and remove the plain washer, the insulator, the terminal shield and the O-ring

26.31 Withdraw the armature

(see illustrations). Remove the positive brush and terminal bolt assembly, then remove the positive brush springs (see illustrations).
34 Undo the screw and remove the negative

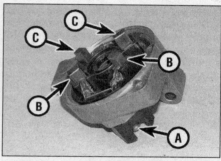

26.32 Terminal bolt (A), positive brushes (B), negative brushes (C)

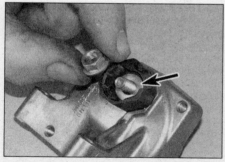

26.33a Undo the nut and remove the plain washer (arrowed)...

26.33b ...the insulator...

26.33c ...the shield...

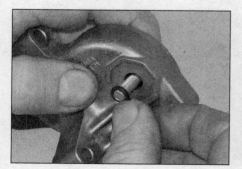

26.33d ...and the O-ring

26.33e Withdraw the terminal bolt and brush assembly (arrowed)...

26.33f ...and remove the brush springs

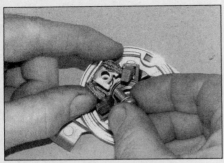

26.34a Undo the screw and remove the negative brush assembly...

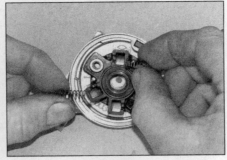

26.34b ...and springs...

26.34c ...then remove the brushholder

brush assembly **(see illustration)**. Remove the brush springs, then remove the holder **(see illustrations)**.

Inspection

35 The parts of the starter motor that are most likely to require attention are the brushes. Measure their length – if they are below 6.5 mm or otherwise obviously worn replace the brush assembly with a new one **(see illustration)**. If the brushes are not worn excessively, nor cracked, chipped, or otherwise damaged, they can be reused.

36 Inspect the commutator bars on

the armature for scoring, scratches and discoloration. The commutator can be cleaned and polished with crocus cloth or 400 grit (or finer) sandpaper, but do not use anything coarser. After cleaning, blow and wipe away any residue with a cloth soaked in electrical system cleaner or denatured alcohol. Check the depth of the insulating Mica between each bar – it should be at least 1 mm below the surface **(see illustration 26.12b)**. As the bars wear, the Mica should be gently scratched away using a hacksaw blade to maintain the correct depth.

37 Using an ohmmeter or a continuity

test light, check for continuity between the commutator bars **(see illustration)**. Continuity should exist between each bar and all of the others. Also, check for continuity between the commutator bars and the armature shaft **(see illustration)**. There should be no continuity (infinite resistance) between the commutator and the shaft. If the checks indicate otherwise, the armature is defective and a new starter motor bust be obtained – the armature is not available separately.

38 Check the front end of the armature shaft for worn, cracked, chipped and broken teeth. If the shaft is damaged or worn, a new starter motor must be obtained – the armature is not available separately.

39 Inspect the front and rear covers for signs of cracks or wear. Check the oil seal and the bearing in the front cover and the bush in the rear cover for wear and damage **(see illustration)** – the seal, bearing, bush and covers are not listed as being available separately so if necessary a new starter motor must be fitted.

40 Inspect the magnets in the main housing and the housing itself for cracks.

41 Inspect the terminal bolt shield, insulator, and O-ring, and the sealing rings on the housing, for signs of damage, deformation

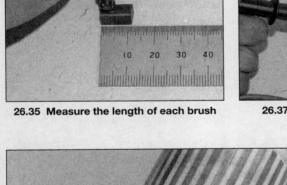

26.35 Measure the length of each brush

26.37a There should be continuity between the bars...

26.37b ...and no continuity between the bars and the shaft

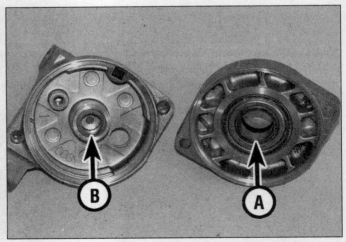

26.39 Check the bearing and seal (A) and the bush (B)

26.43 Fit the O-ring between the bolt and the cover

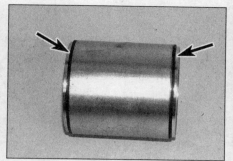

26.45 Main housing sealing rings (arrowed)

26.47 Align the marks when fitting the cover

and deterioration – only the O-ring and sealing rings are available separately.

Reassembly

42 Locate the brushholder on the rear cover (see illustration 26.34c). Fit the negative brush springs and brush assembly and secure it and the holder with the screw (see illustrations 26.34b and a).

43 Fit the positive brush springs into their housings (see illustration 26.33f). Fit the brushes and terminal bolt onto and through the holder and rear cover (see illustration 26.33e). Roll the O-ring down the bolt and press it into the gap between the bolt and the cover (see illustration). Fit the shield, aligning it as shown (see illustration 26.33c). Fit the insulator and the washer, then tighten the nut (see illustrations 26.33b and a). Locate the brushes in their housings against the springs, with the wires in the slots (see illustration 26.32).

44 To check for correct installation do the continuity checks described in Step 32.

45 If removed fit the sealing rings onto the main housing (see illustration).

46 Grasp the housing and carefully allow the armature to be drawn in, making sure the cut-out in the housing is at the same end as the commutator bars (see illustration 26.31).

47 Apply a smear of grease to the short end of the shaft. Fit the rear cover, aligning the marks, and making sure the brushes remain square and seat against the commutator (see illustration).

48 Apply a smear of grease to the front cover

oil seal lip. Slide the front cover on, aligning the marks (see illustration 26.29b).

49 Check the marks made on removal are correctly aligned then fit the long bolts and tighten them (see illustration 26.29a).

50 Install the starter motor (see Section 25).

27 Charging system testing

1 If the performance of the charging system is suspect, the system as a whole should be checked first, followed by testing of the individual components. Note: Before beginning the checks, make sure the battery is fully charged and that all system connections are clean and tight.

2 Checking the output of the charging system and the performance of the various components within the charging system requires the use of a multimeter (with voltage, current, resistance checking facilities).

3 When making the checks, follow the procedures carefully to prevent incorrect connections or short circuits resulting in irreparable damage to electrical system components.

Output test

4 Remove the seat (see Chapter 7). Start the engine and warm it up.

5 To check the regulated (DC) voltage output, allow the engine to idle with. Connect a multimeter set to the 0-20 volts DC scale to the

battery terminals, with the positive (+) meter probe to battery positive (+) terminal and the negative (-) meter probe to battery negative (-) terminal (see Section 3) (see illustration).

6 Slowly increase the engine speed to 5000 rpm and note the reading obtained. Compare the result with the Specification at the beginning of this Chapter. If the regulated voltage output is outside the specification, check the alternator and the regulator/rectifier (see Sections 28 and 29).

 HAYNES HiNT *Clues to a faulty regulator are constantly blowing bulbs, with brightness varying considerably with engine speed, and battery overheating.*

Leakage test

Caution: Always connect an ammeter in series, never in parallel with the battery, otherwise it will be damaged. Do not turn the ignition ON or operate the starter motor when the ammeter is connected – a sudden surge in current will blow the meter's fuse.

7 Remove the seat (see Chapter 7). Disconnect the battery negative (-) lead (see Section 3).

8 Set the multimeter to the Amps function and connect its negative (-) probe to the battery negative (-) terminal, and positive (+) probe to the disconnected negative (-) lead (see illustration). Always set the meter to a high amps range initially and then bring it down to the mA (milli Amps) range; if there is a high current flow in the circuit it may blow the meter's fuse.

9 Battery current leakage should not exceed the maximum limit (see Specifications). If a higher leakage rate is shown there is a short circuit in the wiring, although if an after-market immobiliser or alarm is fitted, its current draw should be taken into account. Disconnect the meter and reconnect the battery negative (-) lead.

10 If leakage is indicated, refer to Wiring Diagrams at the end of this Chapter to systematically disconnect individual electrical components and repeat the test until the source is identified.

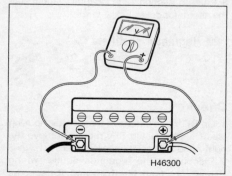

27.5 Checking the charging rate - connect the meter as shown

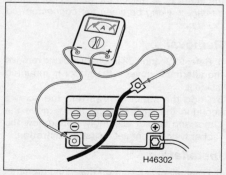

27.8 Checking the charging system leakage rate - connect the meter as shown

28.5 Alternator stator and CKP sensor screws (arrowed)

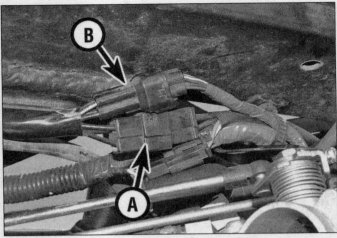

29.2a Alternator (A) and regulator/rectifier (B) wiring connectors (arrowed) – DL

29.2b Alternator wiring connector (arrowed)...

29.2c ...and regulator/rectifier wiring connector (arrowed) – SFV

28 Alternator stator

Check

1 On DL models remove the air filter housing (see Chapter 4). On SFV models remove the right-hand side cover (see Chapter 7).
2 Trace the wiring from the alternator cover and disconnect the wiring connector with the three wires (see illustration 29.2a, b or c). Check the connector terminals for corrosion and security.
3 Using a multimeter set to the ohms x 1 (ohmmeter) scale measure the resistance between each of the three wire terminals in the connector, taking a total of three readings, then check for continuity between each terminal and ground (earth). If the stator coil windings are in good condition the three readings should be within the range shown in

the Specifications at the start of this Chapter, and there should be no continuity (infinite resistance) between any of the terminals and ground (earth). If not, the alternator stator coil assembly is at fault and should be replaced with a new one. Note: *Before condemning the stator coils, check the fault is not due to damaged wiring between the connector and the stator.*

Removal

4 Refer to Section 22 in Chapter 2 and remove the alternator cover – the stator is mounted inside it.
5 Undo the stator screws and the screws securing the CKP sensor, then remove the stator and sensor assembly, noting how the rubber wiring grommet fits (see illustration).

Installation

6 Clean all old sealant off the wiring grommet and its cut-out in the cover.
7 Fit the stator and sensor into the cover,

aligning the rubber wiring grommet with the groove (see illustration 28.5). Fit and tighten the screws. Apply a suitable sealant to the wiring grommet, then press it into the cut-out in the cover. Secure the wiring with its clamp and tighten the screw.
8 Refer to Section 22 in Chapter 2 and install the alternator cover.

29 Regulator/rectifier

Check

1 On DL models remove the air filter housing (see Chapter 4). On SFV models remove the right-hand side cover (see Chapter 7).
2 Disconnect the regulator/rectifier wiring connectors (see illustrations). Check the connectors for loose wires and terminals and corrosion.

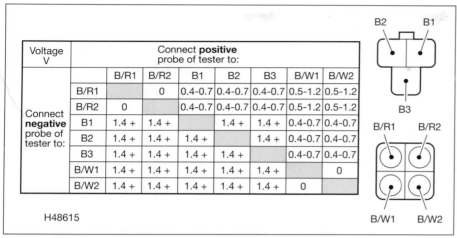

Voltage V	Connect positive probe of tester to:						
Connect negative probe of tester to:	B/R1	B/R2	B1	B2	B3	B/W1	B/W2
B/R1		0	0.4-0.7	0.4-0.7	0.4-0.7	0.5-1.2	0.5-1.2
B/R2	0		0.4-0.7	0.4-0.7	0.4-0.7	0.5-1.2	0.5-1.2
B1	1.4 +	1.4 +		1.4 +	1.4 +	0.4-0.7	0.4-0.7
B2	1.4 +	1.4 +	1.4 +		1.4 +	0.4-0.7	0.4-0.7
B3	1.4 +	1.4 +	1.4 +	1.4 +		0.4-0.7	0.4-0.7
B/W1	1.4 +	1.4 +	1.4 +	1.4 +	1.4 +		0
B/W2	1.4 +	1.4 +	1.4 +	1.4 +	1.4 +	0	

H48615

29.4a Regulator/rectifier test data and terminal identification – 2004 to 2011 DL

Voltage V	Connect positive probe of tester to:						
Connect negative probe of tester to:	B/R1	B/R2	B1	B2	B3	B/W1	B/W2
B/R1		0	0.4-0.7	0.4-0.7	0.4-0.7	0.5-1.2	0.5-1.2
B/R2	0		0.4-0.7	0.4-0.7	0.4-0.7	0.5-1.2	0.5-1.2
B1	1.4 +	1.4 +		1.4 +	1.4 +	0.4-0.7	0.4-0.7
B2	1.4 +	1.4 +	1.4 +		1.4 +	0.4-0.7	0.4-0.7
B3	1.4 +	1.4 +	1.4 +	1.4 +		0.4-0.7	0.4-0.7
B/W1	1.4 +	1.4 +	1.4 +	1.4 +	1.4 +		0
B/W2	1.4 +	1.4 +	1.4 +	1.4 +	1.4 +	0	

H48616

29.4b Regulator/rectifier test data and terminal identification – 2012-on DL

Voltage V	Connect positive probe of tester to:						
Connect negative probe of tester to:	B/R1	B/R2	B1	B2	B3	B/W1	B/W2
B/R1		0	0.1-0.8	0.1-0.8	0.1-0.8	0.3-1.0	0.3-1.0
B/R2	0		0.1-0.8	0.1-0.8	0.1-0.8	0.3-1.0	0.3-1.0
B1	1.4 +	1.4 +		1.4 +	1.4 +	0.1-0.8	0.1-0.8
B2	1.4 +	1.4 +	1.4 +		0.4-0.7	0.1-0.8	0.1-0.8
B3	1.4 +	1.4 +	1.4 +	1.4 +		0.1-0.8	0.1-0.8
B/W1	1.4 +	1.4 +	1.4 +	1.4 +	1.4 +		0
B/W2	1.4 +	1.4 +	1.4 +	1.4 +	1.4 +	0	

H48617

29.4c Regulator/rectifier test data and terminal identification – SFV

3 Check the wiring and connectors between the battery, regulator/rectifier and alternator for shorts, breaks, and loose or corroded terminals (see the wiring diagrams at the end of this chapter).

4 Using a multimeter set to diode test, measure the voltage between the various terminals on the regulator/rectifier side of the wiring connector as shown in the table for your model **(see illustrations)**. Note: *Depending on the multimeter used for the test, the results may vary from the specified figures. However, as long as the variance is constant, the test will give an indication of the condition of the regulator/rectifier. If the readings do not compare closely with those shown in the table, have the regulator/rectifier tested by a Suzuki dealer.*

5 If the regulator/rectifier appears to be good, check the wiring between the battery, regulator/rectifier and alternator, and the wiring connectors (see *Wiring Diagrams* at the end of this Chapter).

HAYNES HiNT *Clues to a faulty regulator are constantly blowing bulbs, with brightness varying considerably with engine speed, and battery overheating.*

Removal and installation

6 On DL models remove the air filter housing (see Chapter 4). On SFV models remove the right-hand side cover (see Chapter 7).

7 Make sure the ignition is off. Disconnect the wiring connectors **(see illustration 29.2a or b and c)**.

8 Unscrew the bolts and remove the regulator/rectifier **(see illustration)**.

9 Installation is the reverse of removal.

29.8 Regulator/rectifier mounting bolts (arrowed) – DL shown

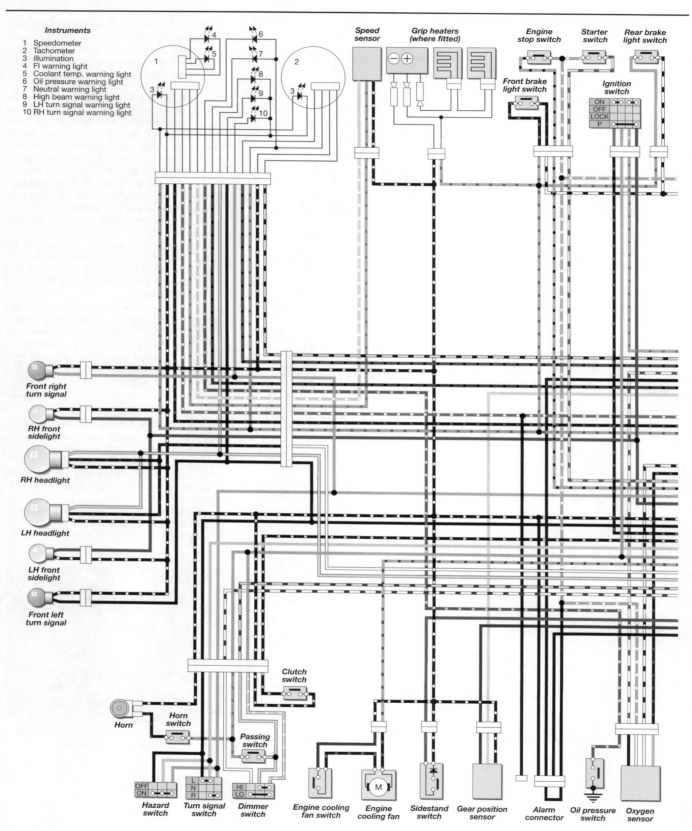

Instruments

1 Speedometer
2 Tachometer
3 Illumination
4 FI warning light
5 Coolant temp. warning light
6 Oil pressure warning light
7 Neutral warning light
8 High beam warning light
9 LH turn signal warning light
10 RH turn signal warning light

Speed sensor

Grip heaters (where fitted)

Engine stop switch

Starter switch

Rear brake light switch

Front brake light switch

Ignition switch

| ON | OFF | LOCK | P |

Front right turn signal

RH front sidelight

RH headlight

LH headlight

LH front sidelight

Front left turn signal

Clutch switch

Horn

Horn switch

Passing switch

Hazard switch

| OFF | ON |

Turn signal switch

| L | N | R |

Dimmer switch

| HI | LO |

Engine cooling fan switch

Engine cooling fan

Sidestand switch

Gear position sensor

Alarm connector

Oil pressure switch

Oxygen sensor

H47595

DL650K4 (2004) - Europe

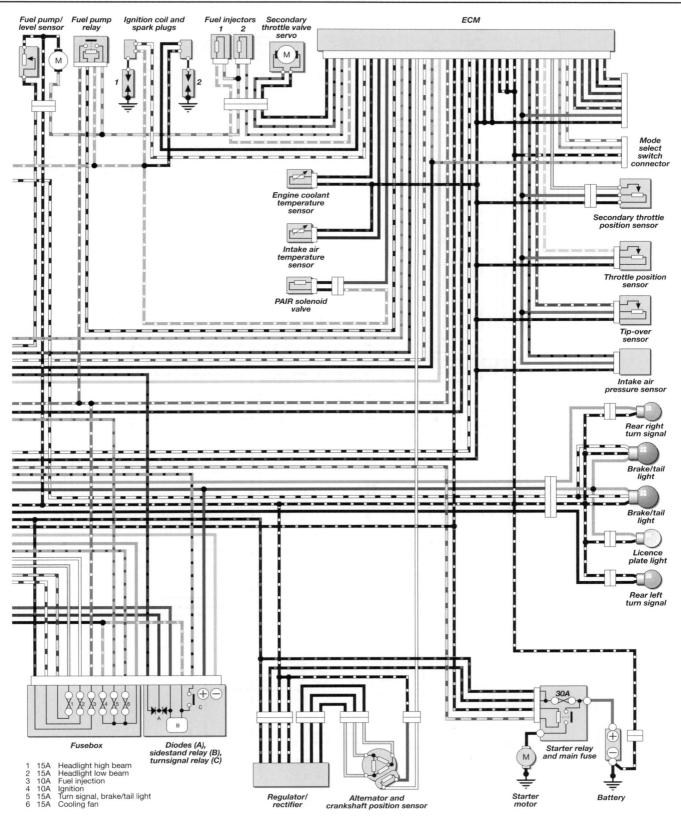

Fuel pump/ level sensor

Fuel pump relay

Ignition coil and spark plugs

Fuel injectors
1   2

Secondary throttle valve servo

ECM

Mode select switch connector

Engine coolant temperature sensor

Intake air temperature sensor

PAIR solenoid valve

Secondary throttle position sensor

Throttle position sensor

Tip-over sensor

Intake air pressure sensor

Rear right turn signal

Brake/tail light

Brake/tail light

Licence plate light

Rear left turn signal

Fusebox

Diodes (A), sidestand relay (B), turnsignal relay (C)

30A

Starter relay and main fuse

Regulator/ rectifier

Alternator and crankshaft position sensor

Starter motor

Battery

1 15A Headlight high beam
2 15A Headlight low beam
3 10A Fuel injection
4 10A Ignition
5 15A Turn signal, brake/tail light
6 15A Cooling fan

H47596

DL650K4 (2004) - Europe

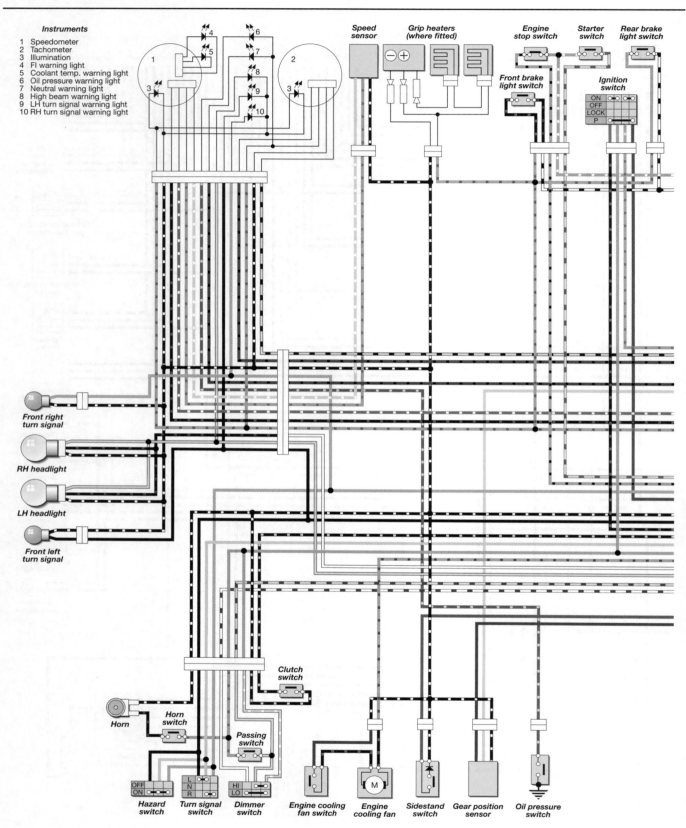

Instruments

1 Speedometer
2 Tachometer
3 Illumination
4 FI warning light
5 Coolant temp. warning light
6 Oil pressure warning light
7 Neutral warning light
8 High beam warning light
9 LH turn signal warning light
10 RH turn signal warning light

Speed sensor

Grip heaters (where fitted)

Engine stop switch

Starter switch

Rear brake light switch

Front brake light switch

Ignition switch

ON
OFF
LOCK
P

Front right turn signal

RH headlight

LH headlight

Front left turn signal

Clutch switch

Horn

Horn switch

Passing switch

OFF
ON

Hazard switch

L
N
R

Turn signal switch

HI
LO

Dimmer switch

Engine cooling fan switch

Engine cooling fan

Sidestand switch

Gear position sensor

Oil pressure switch

H47597

DL650K4 (2004) - US

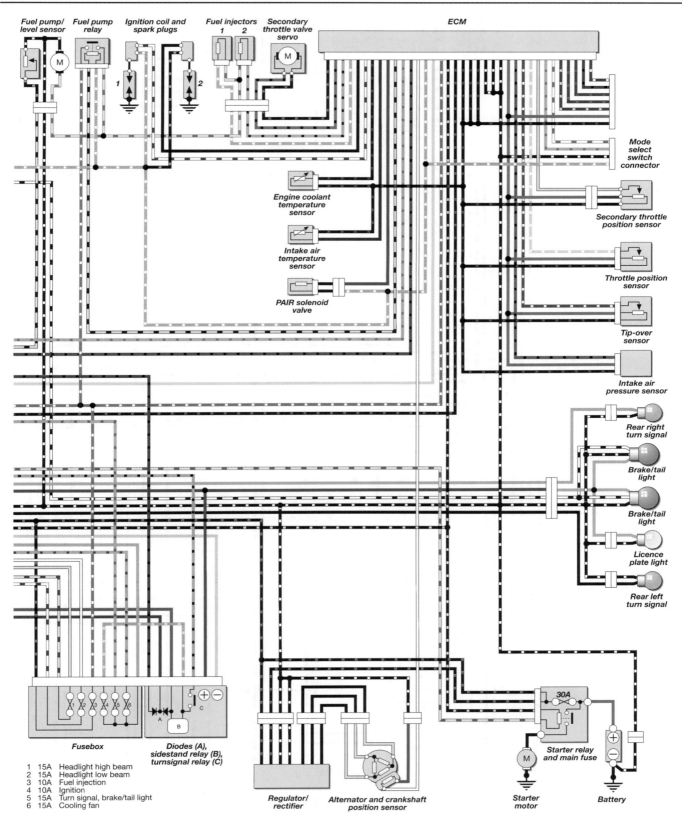

Fuel pump/ level sensor

Fuel pump relay

Ignition coil and spark plugs

Fuel injectors
1   2

Secondary throttle valve servo

ECM

Mode select switch connector

Engine coolant temperature sensor

Intake air temperature sensor

PAIR solenoid valve

Secondary throttle position sensor

Throttle position sensor

Tip-over sensor

Intake air pressure sensor

Rear right turn signal

Brake/tail light

Brake/tail light

Licence plate light

Rear left turn signal

Fusebox

Diodes (A), sidestand relay (B), turnsignal relay (C)

Regulator/ rectifier

Alternator and crankshaft position sensor

Starter motor

Starter relay and main fuse

Battery

30A

1   15A   Headlight high beam
2   15A   Headlight low beam
3   10A   Fuel injection
4   10A   Ignition
5   15A   Turn signal, brake/tail light
6   15A   Cooling fan

H47598

DL650K4 (2004) - US

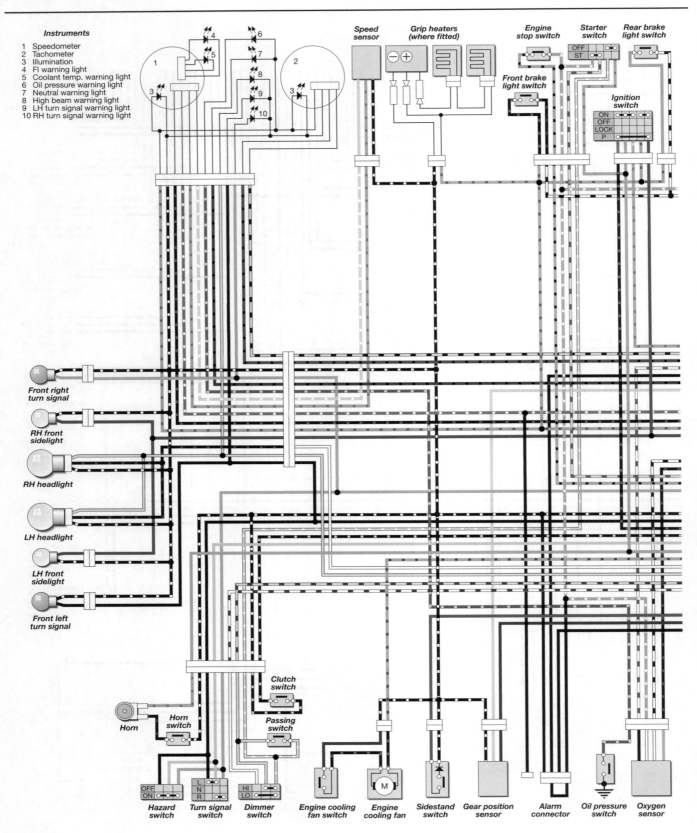

Instruments

1 Speedometer
2 Tachometer
3 Illumination
4 FI warning light
5 Coolant temp. warning light
6 Oil pressure warning light
7 Neutral warning light
8 High beam warning light
9 LH turn signal warning light
10 RH turn signal warning light

Speed sensor

Grip heaters (where fitted)

Engine stop switch

Starter switch

Rear brake light switch

Front brake light switch

Ignition switch

ON
OFF
LOCK
P

Front right turn signal

RH front sidelight

RH headlight

LH headlight

LH front sidelight

Front left turn signal

Clutch switch

Passing switch

Horn

Horn switch

Hazard switch

OFF
ON

Turn signal switch

L
N
R

Dimmer switch

HI
LO

Engine cooling fan switch

Engine cooling fan

Sidestand switch

Gear position sensor

Alarm connector

Oil pressure switch

Oxygen sensor

H47599

DL650K5 and K6 (2005 and 2006) - Europe

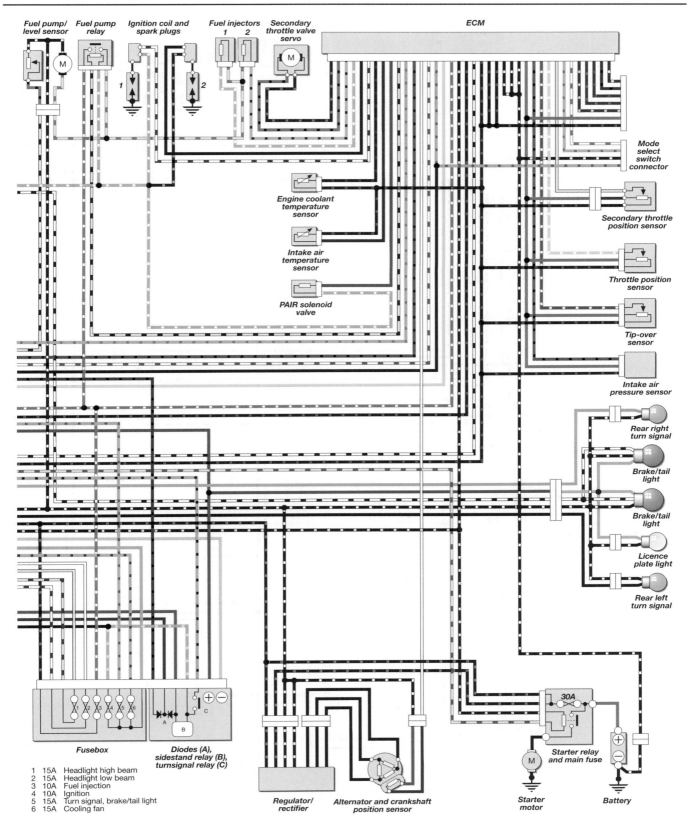

Fuel pump/ level sensor · Fuel pump relay · Ignition coil and spark plugs · Fuel injectors 1 2 · Secondary throttle valve servo · ECM

Engine coolant temperature sensor

Intake air temperature sensor

PAIR solenoid valve

Mode select switch connector

Secondary throttle position sensor

Throttle position sensor

Tip-over sensor

Intake air pressure sensor

Rear right turn signal

Brake/tail light

Brake/tail light

Licence plate light

Rear left turn signal

30A

Fusebox

Diodes (A), sidestand relay (B), turnsignal relay (C)

1 15A Headlight high beam
2 15A Headlight low beam
3 10A Fuel injection
4 10A Ignition
5 15A Turn signal, brake/tail light
6 15A Cooling fan

Regulator/ rectifier · Alternator and crankshaft position sensor · Starter motor · Starter relay and main fuse · Battery

H47600

DL650K5 and K6 (2005 and 2006) - Europe

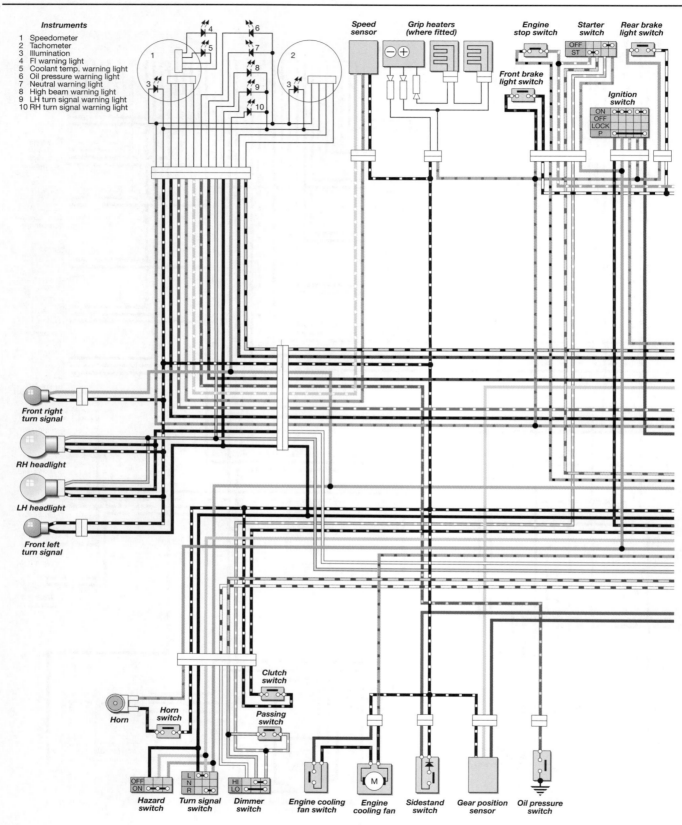

Instruments
1 Speedometer
2 Tachometer
3 Illumination
4 FI warning light
5 Coolant temp. warning light
6 Oil pressure warning light
7 Neutral warning light
8 High beam warning light
9 LH turn signal warning light
10 RH turn signal warning light

Speed sensor

Grip heaters (where fitted)

Engine stop switch

Starter switch

Rear brake light switch

Front brake light switch

Ignition switch

Front right turn signal

RH headlight

LH headlight

Front left turn signal

Horn

Horn switch

Clutch switch

Passing switch

Hazard switch

Turn signal switch

Dimmer switch

Engine cooling fan switch

Engine cooling fan

Sidestand switch

Gear position sensor

Oil pressure switch

H47601

DL650K5 and K6 (2005 and 2006) - US

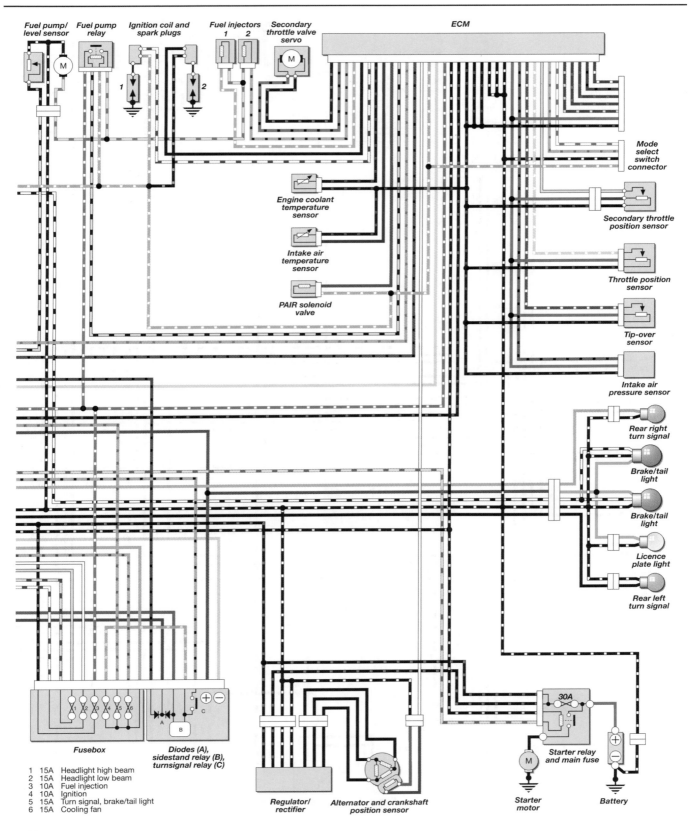

Fuel pump/level sensor

Fuel pump relay

Ignition coil and spark plugs

Fuel injectors
1 2

Secondary throttle valve servo

ECM

Mode select switch connector

Engine coolant temperature sensor

Intake air temperature sensor

PAIR solenoid valve

Secondary throttle position sensor

Throttle position sensor

Tip-over sensor

Intake air pressure sensor

Rear right turn signal

Brake/tail light

Brake/tail light

Licence plate light

Rear left turn signal

Fusebox

Diodes (A),
sidestand relay (B),
turnsignal relay (C)

Regulator/rectifier

Alternator and crankshaft position sensor

30A

Starter relay and main fuse

Starter motor

Battery

1 15A Headlight high beam
2 15A Headlight low beam
3 10A Fuel injection
4 10A Ignition
5 15A Turn signal, brake/tail light
6 15A Cooling fan

H47602

DL650K5 and K6 (2005 and 2006) - US

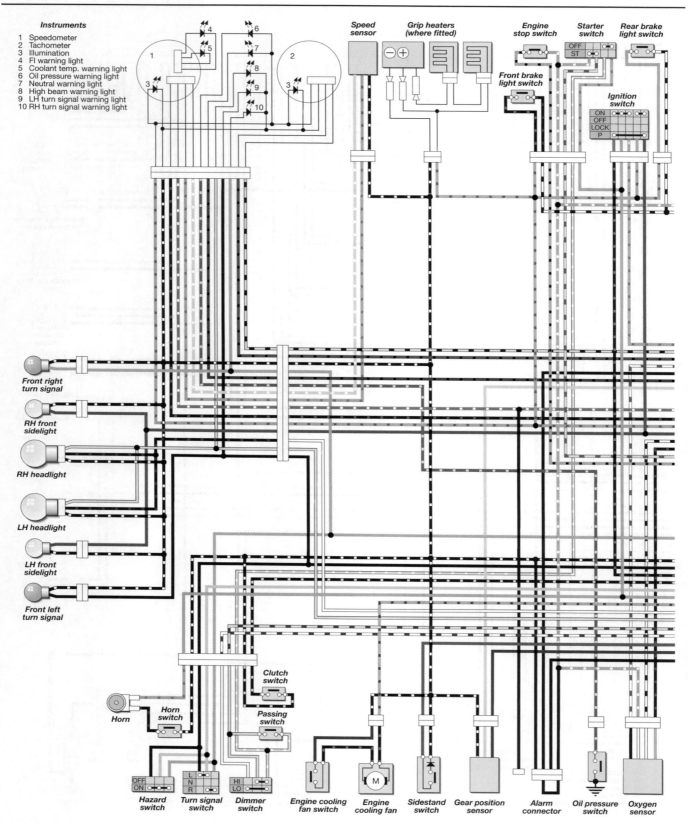

Instruments

1 Speedometer
2 Tachometer
3 Illumination
4 FI warning light
5 Coolant temp. warning light
6 Oil pressure warning light
7 Neutral warning light
8 High beam warning light
9 LH turn signal warning light
10 RH turn signal warning light

Speed sensor

Grip heaters (where fitted)

Engine stop switch

Starter switch

Rear brake light switch

Front brake light switch

Ignition switch

Front right turn signal

RH front sidelight

RH headlight

LH headlight

LH front sidelight

Front left turn signal

Horn

Horn switch

Clutch switch

Passing switch

Hazard switch

Turn signal switch

Dimmer switch

Engine cooling fan switch

Engine cooling fan

Sidestand switch

Gear position sensor

Alarm connector

Oil pressure switch

Oxygen sensor

H47603

DL650K7 to L1 (2007 to 2011) - Europe

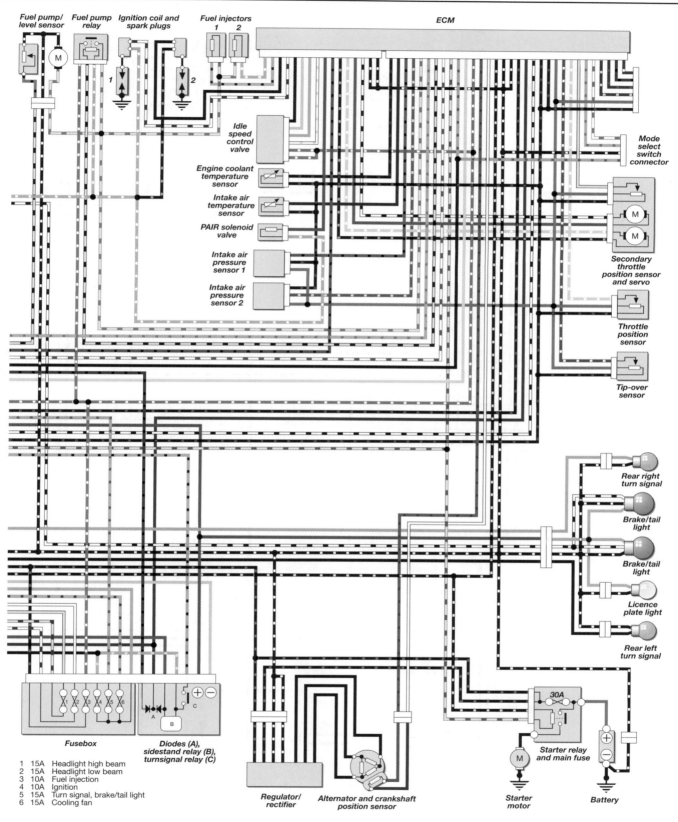

Fuel pump/ level sensor
Fuel pump relay
Ignition coil and spark plugs
Fuel injectors
ECM

Idle speed control valve

Engine coolant temperature sensor

Intake air temperature sensor

PAIR solenoid valve

Intake air pressure sensor 1

Intake air pressure sensor 2

Mode select switch connector

Secondary throttle position sensor and servo

Throttle position sensor

Tip-over sensor

Rear right turn signal

Brake/tail light

Brake/tail light

Licence plate light

Rear left turn signal

Fusebox

Diodes (A), sidestand relay (B), turnsignal relay (C)

30A

Starter relay and main fuse

Regulator/ rectifier

Alternator and crankshaft position sensor

Starter motor

Battery

1 15A Headlight high beam
2 15A Headlight low beam
3 10A Fuel injection
4 10A Ignition
5 15A Turn signal, brake/tail light
6 15A Cooling fan

H47560

DL650K7 to L1 (2007 to 2011) - Europe

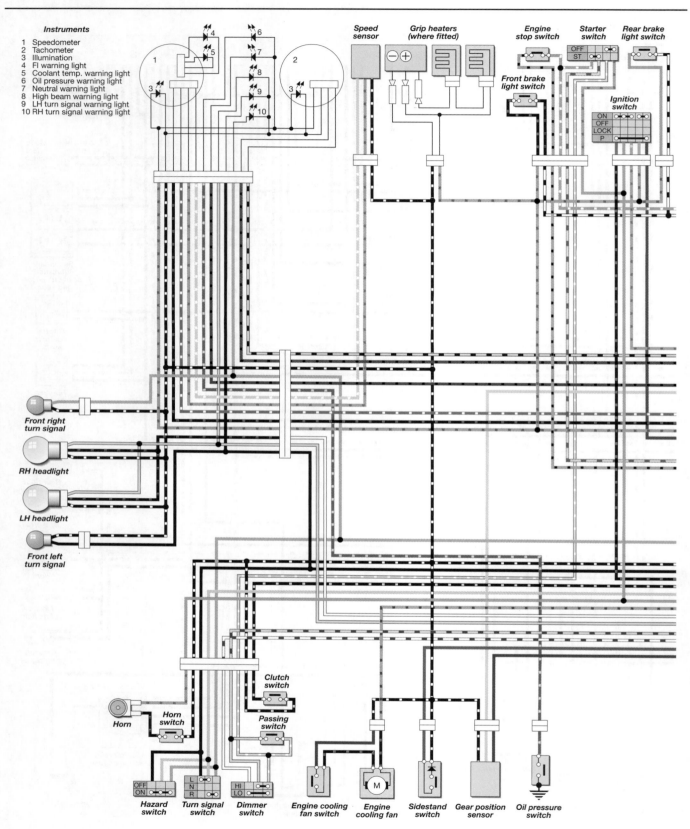

Instruments

1 Speedometer
2 Tachometer
3 Illumination
4 FI warning light
5 Coolant temp. warning light
6 Oil pressure warning light
7 Neutral warning light
8 High beam warning light
9 LH turn signal warning light
10 RH turn signal warning light

Speed sensor

Grip heaters (where fitted)

Engine stop switch

Starter switch

Rear brake light switch

Front brake light switch

Ignition switch

Front right turn signal

RH headlight

LH headlight

Front left turn signal

Horn

Horn switch

Clutch switch

Passing switch

Hazard switch

Turn signal switch

Dimmer switch

Engine cooling fan switch

Engine cooling fan

Sidestand switch

Gear position sensor

Oil pressure switch

H47605

DL650K7 to L1 (2007 to 2011) - US

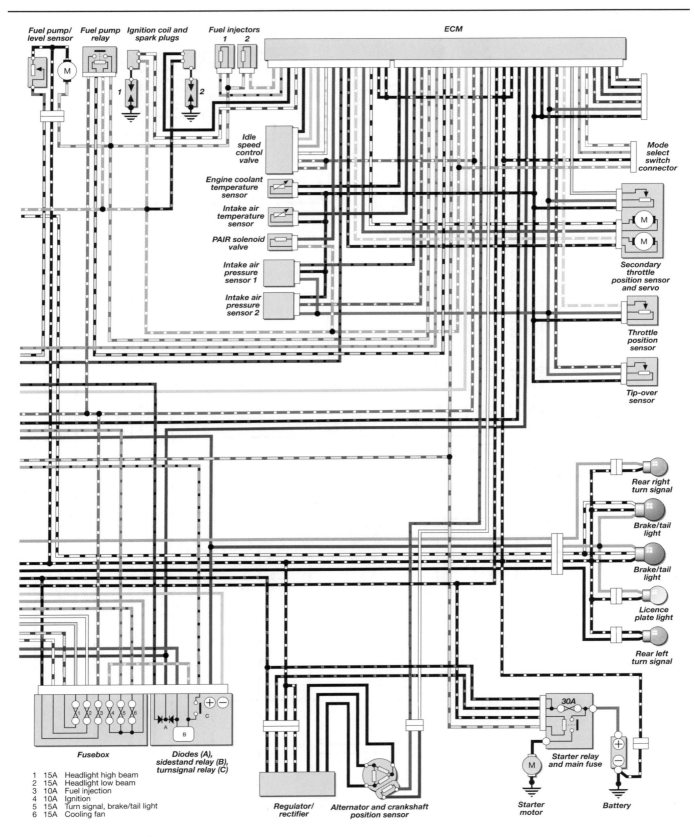

1 15A Headlight high beam
2 15A Headlight low beam
3 10A Fuel injection
4 10A Ignition
5 15A Turn signal, brake/tail light
6 15A Cooling fan

H47606

DL650K7 to L1 (2007 to 2011) - US

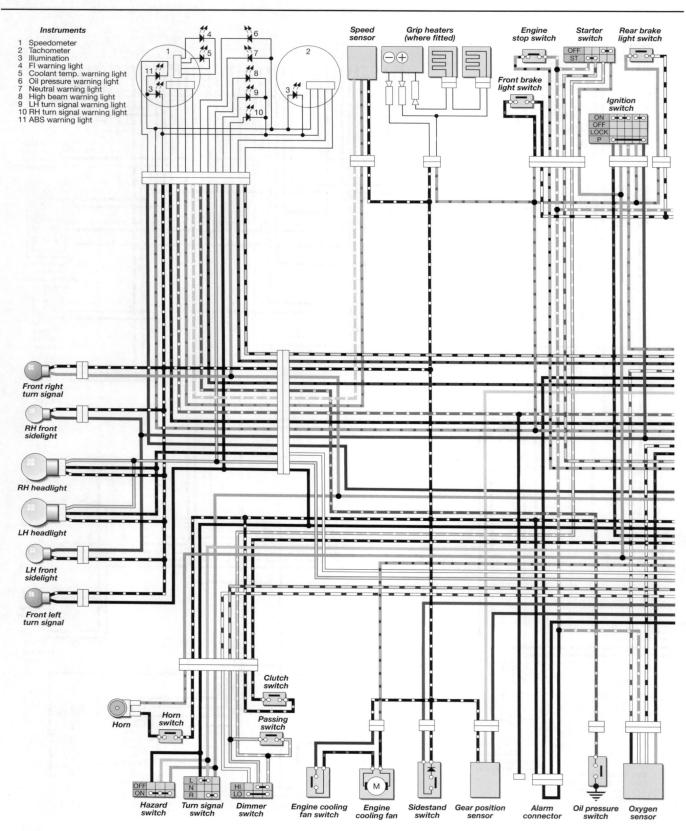

Instruments

1 Speedometer
2 Tachometer
3 Illumination
4 FI warning light
5 Coolant temp. warning light
6 Oil pressure warning light
7 Neutral warning light
8 High beam warning light
9 LH turn signal warning light
10 RH turn signal warning light
11 ABS warning light

Speed sensor

Grip heaters (where fitted)

Engine stop switch

Starter switch

Rear brake light switch

Front brake light switch

Ignition switch

ON
OFF
LOCK
P

Front right turn signal

RH front sidelight

RH headlight

LH headlight

LH front sidelight

Front left turn signal

Horn

Horn switch

Clutch switch

Passing switch

OFF
ON

Hazard switch

L
N
R

Turn signal switch

HI
LO

Dimmer switch

Engine cooling fan switch

M

Engine cooling fan

Sidestand switch

Gear position sensor

Alarm connector

Oil pressure switch

Oxygen sensor

H47607

DL650AK7 to AL1 (2007 to 2011) - Europe

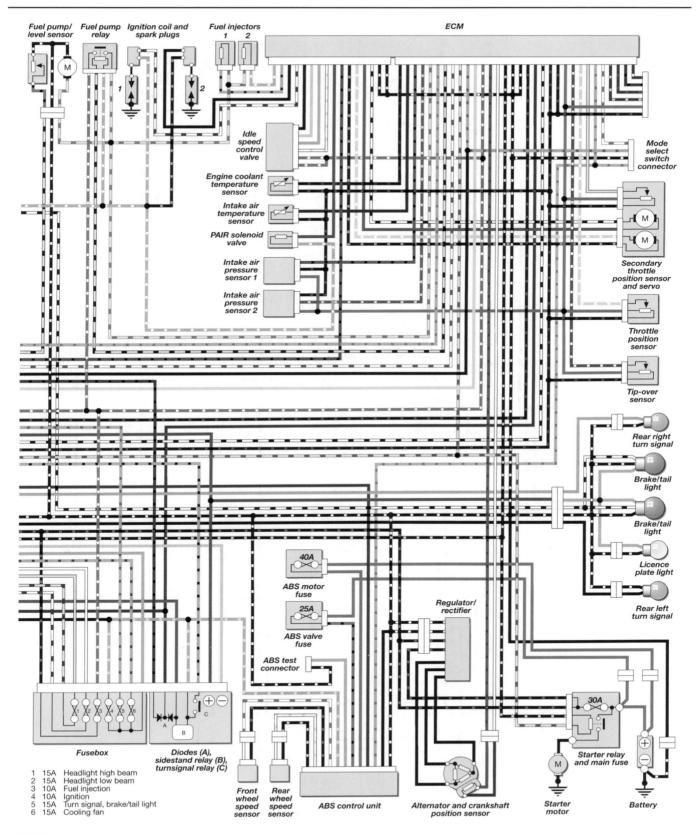

Fuel pump/level sensor

Fuel pump relay

Ignition coil and spark plugs

Fuel injectors
1 2

ECM

Idle speed control valve

Engine coolant temperature sensor

Intake air temperature sensor

PAIR solenoid valve

Intake air pressure sensor 1

Intake air pressure sensor 2

Mode select switch connector

Secondary throttle position sensor and servo

Throttle position sensor

Tip-over sensor

Rear right turn signal

Brake/tail light

Brake/tail light

Licence plate light

Rear left turn signal

40A
ABS motor fuse

25A
ABS valve fuse

ABS test connector

Regulator/rectifier

30A

Fusebox

Diodes (A), sidestand relay (B), turnsignal relay (C)

Front wheel speed sensor

Rear wheel speed sensor

ABS control unit

Alternator and crankshaft position sensor

Starter motor

Starter relay and main fuse

Battery

1 15A Headlight high beam
2 15A Headlight low beam
3 10A Fuel injection
4 10A Ignition
5 15A Turn signal, brake/tail light
6 15A Cooling fan

H47608

DL650AK7 to AL1 (2007 to 2011) - Europe

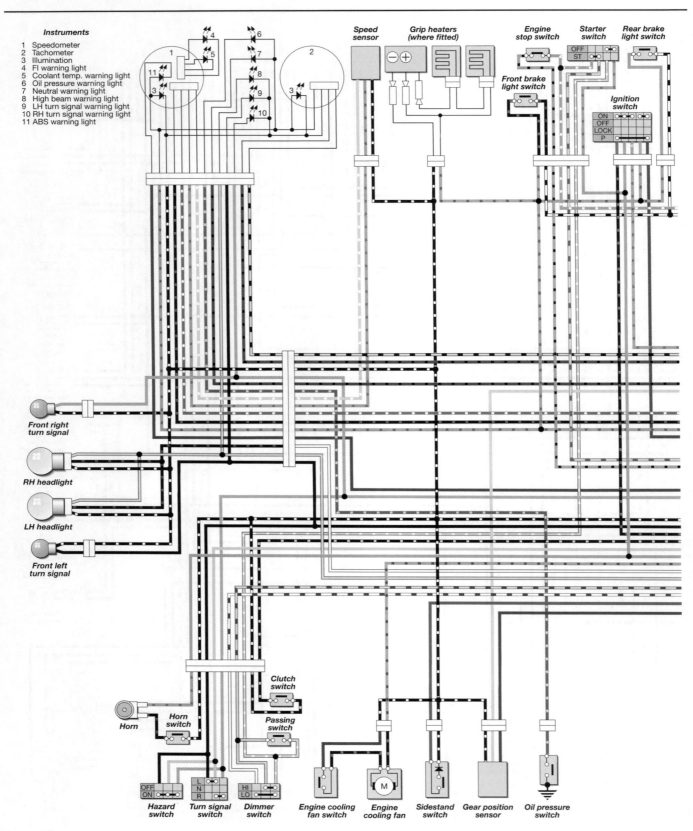

Instruments

1 Speedometer
2 Tachometer
3 Illumination
4 FI warning light
5 Coolant temp. warning light
6 Oil pressure warning light
7 Neutral warning light
8 High beam warning light
9 LH turn signal warning light
10 RH turn signal warning light
11 ABS warning light

Speed sensor

Grip heaters (where fitted)

Engine stop switch

Starter switch

Rear brake light switch

Front brake light switch

Ignition switch

Front right turn signal

RH headlight

LH headlight

Front left turn signal

Clutch switch

Horn

Horn switch

Passing switch

Hazard switch

Turn signal switch

Dimmer switch

Engine cooling fan switch

Engine cooling fan

Sidestand switch

Gear position sensor

Oil pressure switch

H47609

DL650AK7 to AL1 (2007 to 2011) - US

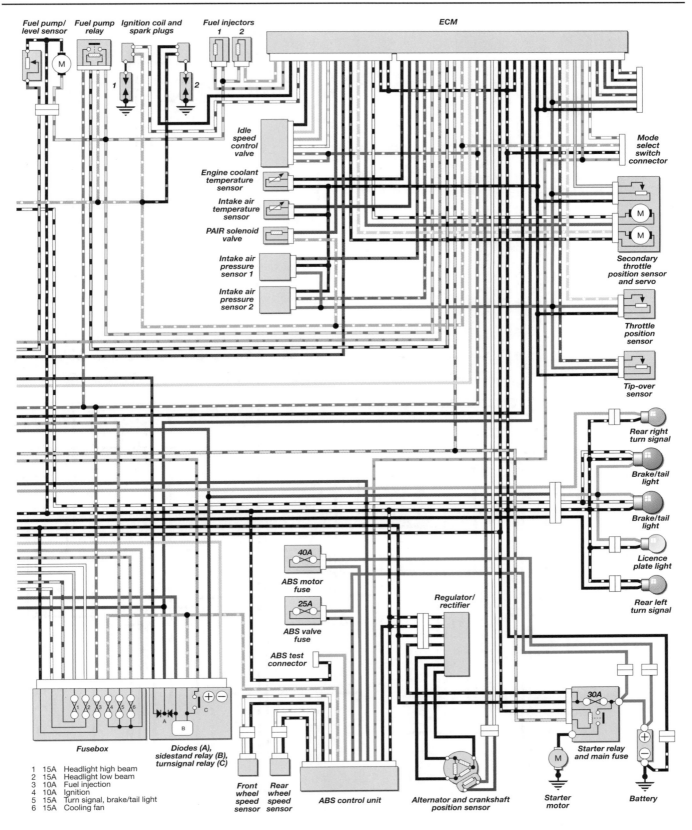

Fuel pump/level sensor
Fuel pump relay
Ignition coil and spark plugs
Fuel injectors
1 2
ECM

Idle speed control valve
Engine coolant temperature sensor
Intake air temperature sensor
PAIR solenoid valve
Intake air pressure sensor 1
Intake air pressure sensor 2

Mode select switch connector
Secondary throttle position sensor and servo
Throttle position sensor
Tip-over sensor

Rear right turn signal
Brake/tail light
Brake/tail light
Licence plate light
Rear left turn signal

40A
ABS motor fuse
25A
ABS valve fuse
ABS test connector

Regulator/rectifier

30A
Starter relay and main fuse

Fusebox

Diodes (A), sidestand relay (B), turnsignal relay (C)

Front wheel speed sensor
Rear wheel speed sensor
ABS control unit
Alternator and crankshaft position sensor
Starter motor
Battery

1 15A Headlight high beam
2 15A Headlight low beam
3 10A Fuel injection
4 10A Ignition
5 15A Turn signal, brake/tail light
6 15A Cooling fan

H47610

DL650AK7 to AL1 (2007 to 2011) - US

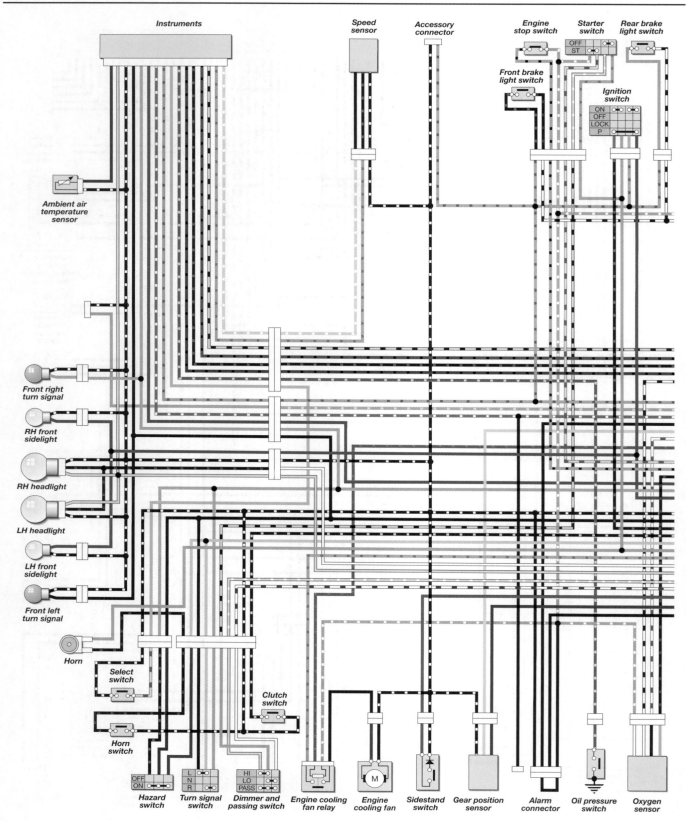

Instruments

Speed sensor

Accessory connector

Engine stop switch

Starter switch

Rear brake light switch

Front brake light switch

Ignition switch

Ambient air temperature sensor

Front right turn signal

RH front sidelight

RH headlight

LH headlight

LH front sidelight

Front left turn signal

Horn

Select switch

Horn switch

Clutch switch

Hazard switch

Turn signal switch

Dimmer and passing switch

Engine cooling fan relay

Engine cooling fan

Sidestand switch

Gear position sensor

Alarm connector

Oil pressure switch

Oxygen sensor

DL650LA2 and LA3 (2012-on) - Europe

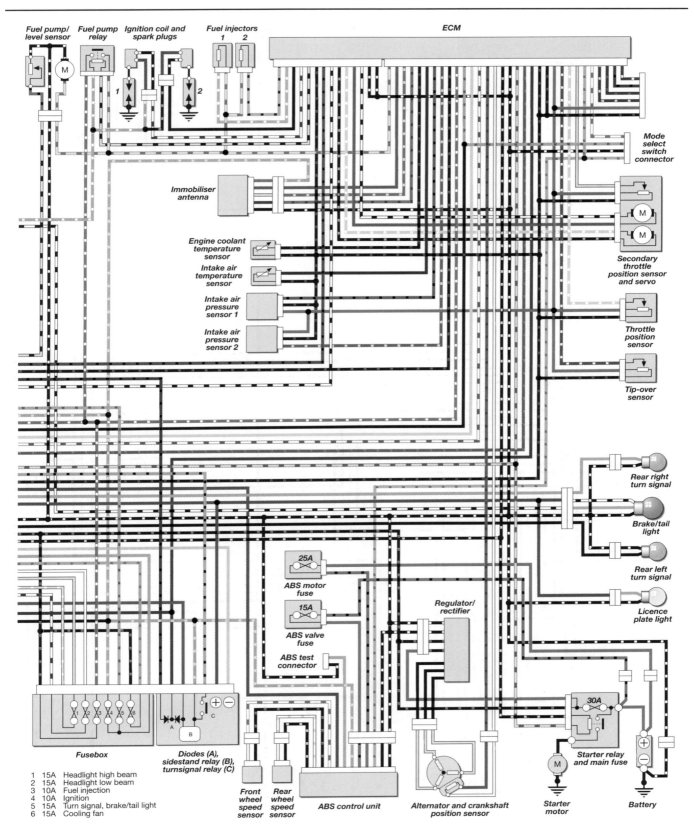

Fuel pump/ level sensor

Fuel pump relay

Ignition coil and spark plugs

Fuel injectors
1   2

ECM

Mode select switch connector

Immobiliser antenna

Secondary throttle position sensor and servo

Engine coolant temperature sensor

Intake air temperature sensor

Intake air pressure sensor 1

Throttle position sensor

Intake air pressure sensor 2

Tip-over sensor

Rear right turn signal

Brake/tail light

25A
ABS motor fuse

15A
ABS valve fuse

ABS test connector

Regulator/ rectifier

Rear left turn signal

Licence plate light

30A

Fusebox

Diodes (A), sidestand relay (B), turnsignal relay (C)

Front wheel speed sensor

Rear wheel speed sensor

ABS control unit

Alternator and crankshaft position sensor

Starter relay and main fuse

Starter motor

Battery

1   15A   Headlight high beam
2   15A   Headlight low beam
3   10A   Fuel injection
4   10A   Ignition
5   15A   Turn signal, brake/tail light
6   15A   Cooling fan

DL650LA2 and LA3 (2012-on) - Europe

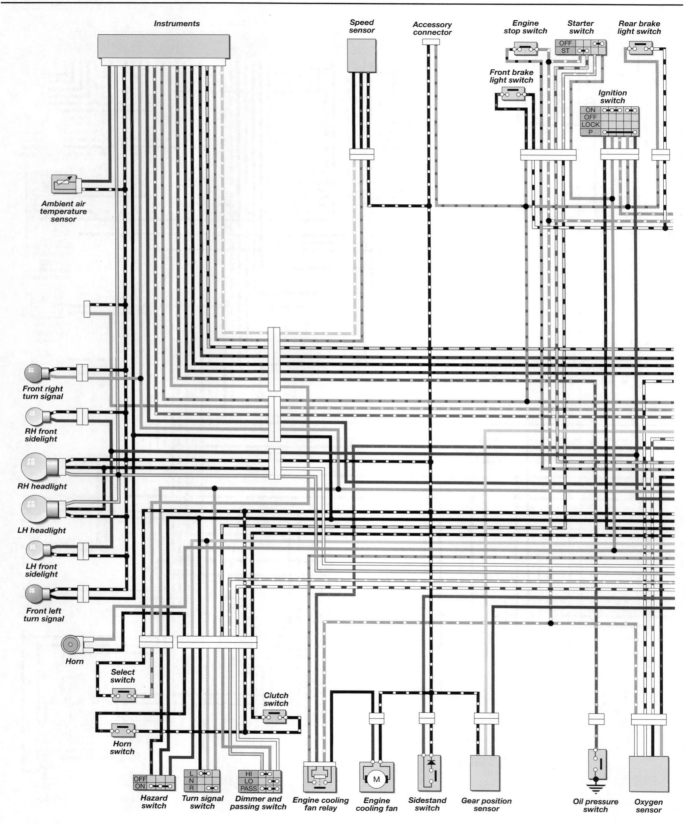

H47613

DL650LA2 and LA3 (2012-on) - US

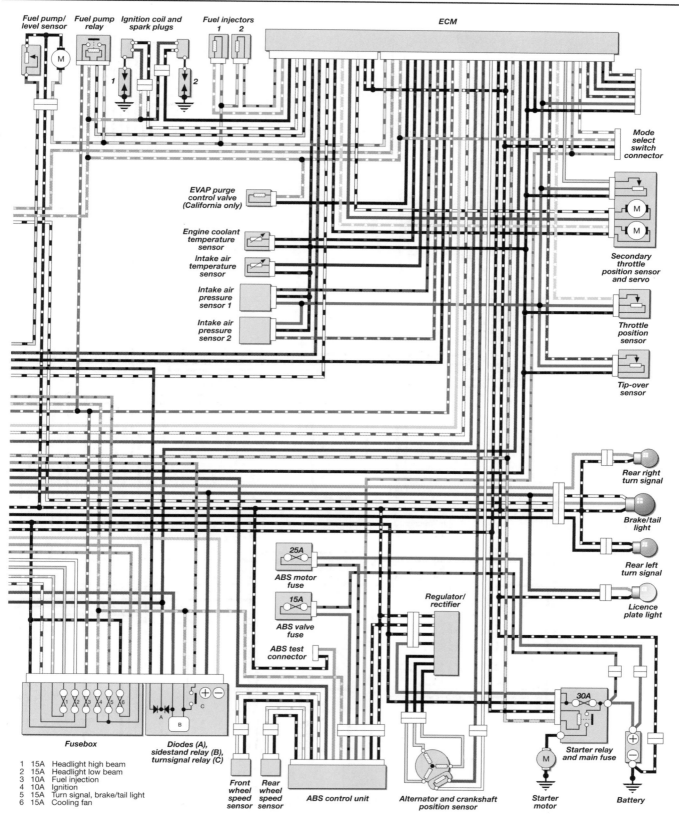

Fuel pump/ level sensor

Fuel pump relay

Ignition coil and spark plugs

Fuel injectors
1 2

ECM

Mode select switch connector

EVAP purge control valve (California only)

Engine coolant temperature sensor

Intake air temperature sensor

Intake air pressure sensor 1

Intake air pressure sensor 2

Secondary throttle position sensor and servo

Throttle position sensor

Tip-over sensor

Rear right turn signal

Brake/tail light

Rear left turn signal

Licence plate light

25A
ABS motor fuse

15A
ABS valve fuse

ABS test connector

Regulator/ rectifier

30A

Starter relay and main fuse

Fusebox

Diodes (A), sidestand relay (B), turnsignal relay (C)

Front wheel speed sensor

Rear wheel speed sensor

ABS control unit

Alternator and crankshaft position sensor

Starter motor

Battery

1 15A Headlight high beam
2 15A Headlight low beam
3 10A Fuel injection
4 10A Ignition
5 15A Turn signal, brake/tail light
6 15A Cooling fan

H47614

DL650LA2 and LA3 (2012-on) - US

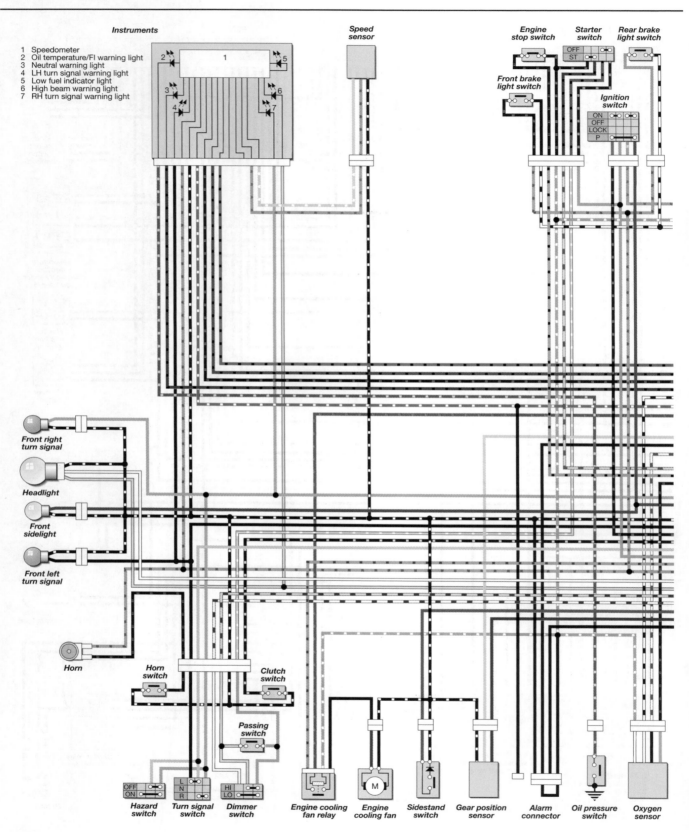

Instruments

1 Speedometer
2 Oil temperature/FI warning light
3 Neutral warning light
4 LH turn signal warning light
5 Low fuel indicator light
6 High beam warning light
7 RH turn signal warning light

Speed sensor

Engine stop switch

Starter switch

Rear brake light switch

Front brake light switch

Ignition switch

Front right turn signal

Headlight

Front sidelight

Front left turn signal

Horn

Horn switch

Clutch switch

Passing switch

Hazard switch

Turn signal switch

Dimmer switch

Engine cooling fan relay

Engine cooling fan

Sidestand switch

Gear position sensor

Alarm connector

Oil pressure switch

Oxygen sensor

H47615

SFV650

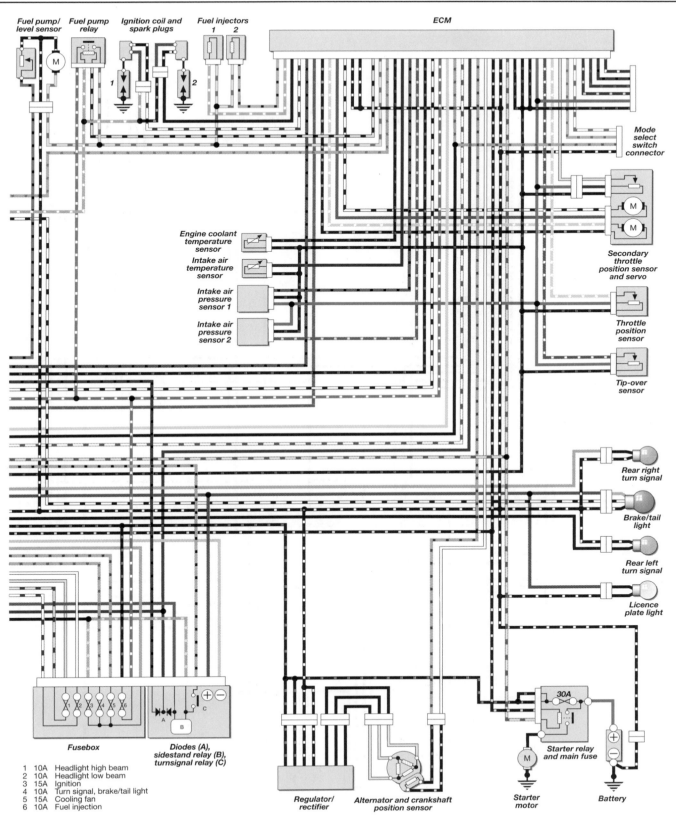

Fuel pump/
level sensor

Fuel pump
relay

Ignition coil and
spark plugs

Fuel injectors
1   2

ECM

Mode
select
switch
connector

Secondary
throttle
position sensor
and servo

Engine coolant
temperature
sensor

Intake air
temperature
sensor

Intake air
pressure
sensor 1

Intake air
pressure
sensor 2

Throttle
position
sensor

Tip-over
sensor

Rear right
turn signal

Brake/tail
light

Rear left
turn signal

Licence
plate light

30A

Fusebox

Diodes (A),
sidestand relay (B),
turnsignal relay (C)

Starter relay
and main fuse

Regulator/
rectifier

Alternator and crankshaft
position sensor

Starter
motor

Battery

1   10A   Headlight high beam
2   10A   Headlight low beam
3   15A   Ignition
4   10A   Turn signal, brake/tail light
5   15A   Cooling fan
6   10A   Fuel injection

H47616

SFV650

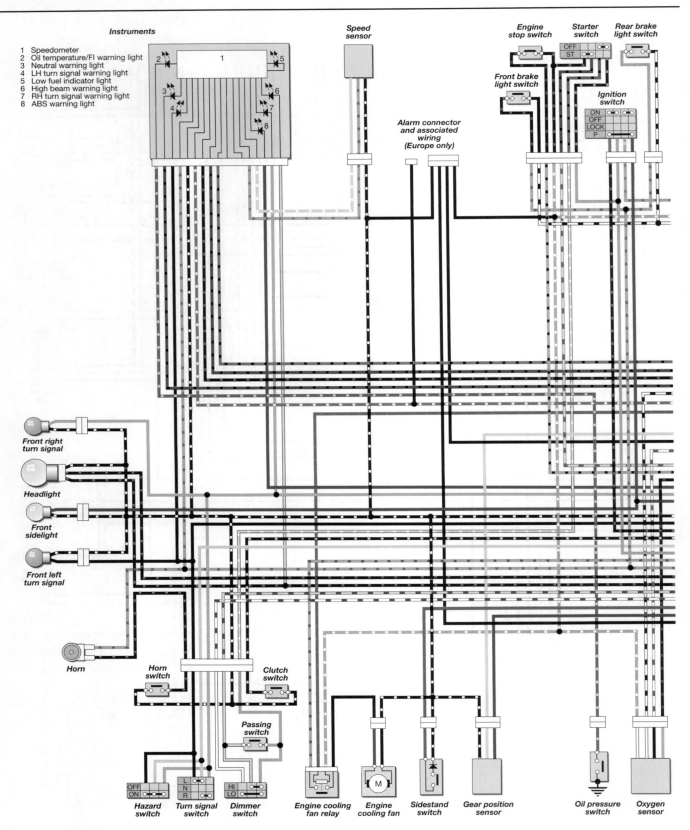

Instruments

1 Speedometer
2 Oil temperature/FI warning light
3 Neutral warning light
4 LH turn signal warning light
5 Low fuel indicator light
6 High beam warning light
7 RH turn signal warning light
8 ABS warning light

Speed sensor

Engine stop switch
Starter switch
Rear brake light switch
Front brake light switch
Ignition switch

Alarm connector and associated wiring (Europe only)

Front right turn signal

Headlight

Front sidelight

Front left turn signal

Horn

Horn switch
Clutch switch

Passing switch

Hazard switch
Turn signal switch
Dimmer switch
Engine cooling fan relay
Engine cooling fan
Sidestand switch
Gear position sensor
Oil pressure switch
Oxygen sensor

H47617

SFV650A

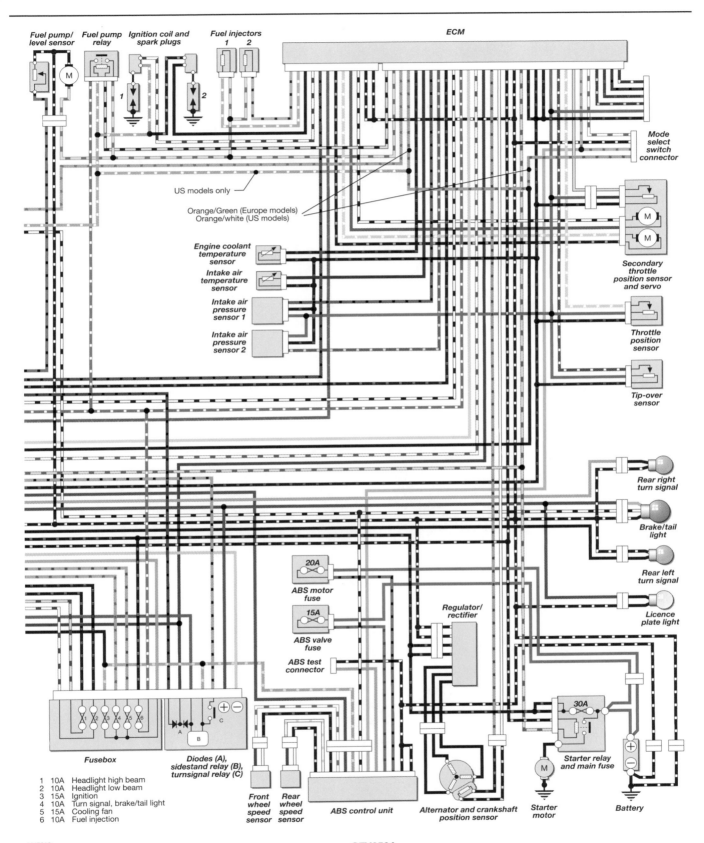

Fuel pump/ level sensor

Fuel pump relay

Ignition coil and spark plugs

Fuel injectors
1 2

ECM

Mode select switch connector

US models only

Orange/Green (Europe models)
Orange/white (US models)

Secondary throttle position sensor and servo

Engine coolant temperature sensor

Intake air temperature sensor

Intake air pressure sensor 1

Intake air pressure sensor 2

Throttle position sensor

Tip-over sensor

Rear right turn signal

Brake/tail light

Rear left turn signal

Licence plate light

20A
ABS motor fuse

15A
ABS valve fuse

ABS test connector

Regulator/ rectifier

30A

Fusebox

Diodes (A), sidestand relay (B), turnsignal relay (C)

Front wheel speed sensor

Rear wheel speed sensor

ABS control unit

Alternator and crankshaft position sensor

Starter motor

Starter relay and main fuse

Battery

1 10A Headlight high beam
2 10A Headlight low beam
3 15A Ignition
4 10A Turn signal, brake/tail light
5 15A Cooling fan
6 10A Fuel injection

H47618

SFV650A

Notes

Reference

Tools and Workshop Tips REF•2

● Building up a tool kit and equipping your workshop ● Using tools ● Understanding bearing, seal, fastener and chain sizes and markings ● Repair techniques

Security REF•20

● Locks and chains ● U-locks ● Disc locks ● Alarms and immobilisers ● Security marking systems ● Tips on how to prevent bike theft

Lubricants and fluids REF•23

● Engine oils ● Transmission (gear) oils ● Coolant/anti-freeze ● Fork oils and suspension fluids ● Brake/clutch fluids ● Spray lubes, degreasers and solvents

Conversion Factors REF•26

34 Nm × 0.738

= 25 lbf ft

● Formulae for conversion of the metric (SI) units used throughout the manual into Imperial measures

MOT Test Checks REF•27

● A guide to the UK MOT test ● Which items are tested ● How to prepare your motorcycle for the test and perform a pre-test check

Storage REF•32

● How to prepare your motorcycle for going into storage and protect essential systems ● How to get the motorcycle back on the road

Fault Finding REF•35

● Common faults and their likely causes ● Links to main chapters for testing and repair procedures

Technical Terms Explained REF•45

● Component names, technical terms and common abbreviations explained

Index REF•50

Buying tools

A toolkit is a fundamental requirement for servicing and repairing a motorcycle. Although there will be an initial expense in building up enough tools for servicing, this will soon be offset by the savings made by doing the job yourself. As experience and confidence grow, additional tools can be added to enable the repair and overhaul of the motorcycle. Many of the specialist tools are expensive and not often used so it may be preferable to hire them, or for a group of friends or motorcycle club to join in the purchase.

As a rule, it is better to buy more expensive, good quality tools. Cheaper tools are likely to wear out faster and need to be renewed more often, nullifying the original saving.

Warning: To avoid the risk of a poor quality tool breaking in use, causing injury or damage to the component being worked on, always aim to purchase tools which meet the relevant national safety standards.

The following lists of tools do not represent the manufacturer's service tools, but serve as a guide to help the owner decide which tools are needed for this level of work. In addition, items such as an electric drill, hacksaw, files, soldering iron and a workbench equipped with a vice, may be needed. Although not classed as tools, a selection of bolts, screws, nuts, washers and pieces of tubing always come in useful.

For more information about tools, refer to the Haynes *Motorcycle Workshop Practice Techbook* (Bk. No. 3470).

Manufacturer's service tools

Inevitably certain tasks require the use of a service tool. Where possible an alternative tool or method of approach is recommended, but sometimes there is no option if personal injury or damage to the component is to be avoided. Where required, service tools are referred to in the relevant procedure.

Service tools can usually only be purchased from a motorcycle dealer and are identified by a part number. Some of the commonly-used tools, such as rotor pullers, are available in aftermarket form from mail-order motorcycle tool and accessory suppliers.

Maintenance and minor repair tools

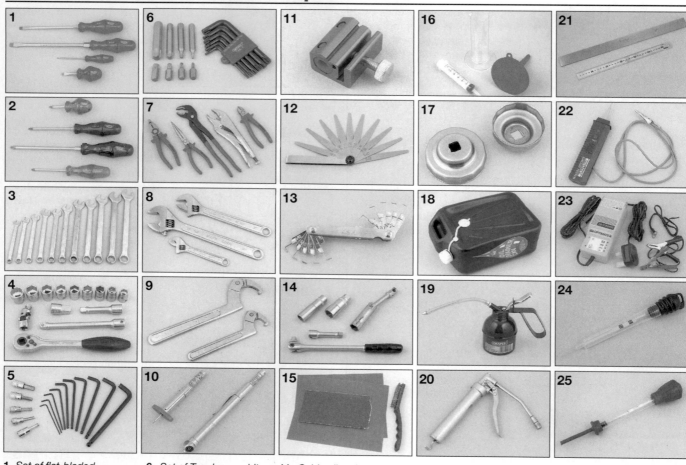

1 Set of flat-bladed screwdrivers
2 Set of Phillips head screwdrivers
3 Combination open-end and ring spanners
4 Socket set (3/8 inch or 1/2 inch drive)
5 Set of Allen keys or bits
6 Set of Torx keys or bits
7 Pliers, cutters and self-locking grips (Mole grips)
8 Adjustable spanners
9 C-spanners
10 Tread depth gauge and tyre pressure gauge
11 Cable oiler clamp
12 Feeler gauges
13 Spark plug gap measuring tool
14 Spark plug spanner or deep plug sockets
15 Wire brush and emery paper
16 Calibrated syringe, measuring vessel and funnel
17 Oil filter adapters
18 Oil drainer can or tray
19 Pump type oil can
20 Grease gun
21 Straight-edge and steel rule
22 Continuity tester
23 Battery charger
24 Hydrometer (for battery specific gravity check)
25 Anti-freeze tester (for liquid-cooled engines)

Repair and overhaul tools

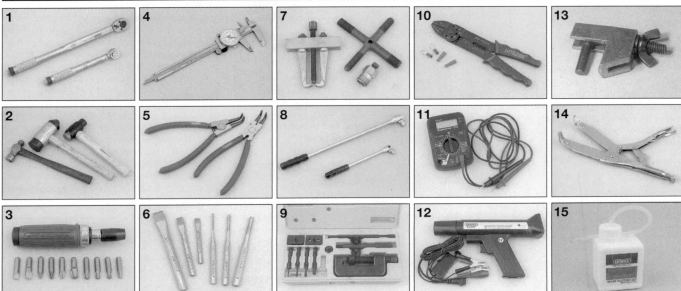

1 Torque wrench (small and mid-ranges)
2 Conventional, plastic or soft-faced hammers
3 Impact driver set
4 Vernier gauge
5 Circlip pliers (internal and external, or combination)
6 Set of cold chisels and punches
7 Selection of pullers
8 Breaker bars
9 Chain breaking/riveting tool set
10 Wire stripper and crimper tool
11 Multimeter (measures amps, volts and ohms)
12 Stroboscope (for dynamic timing checks)
13 Hose clamp (wingnut type shown)
14 Clutch holding tool
15 One-man brake/clutch bleeder kit

Specialist tools

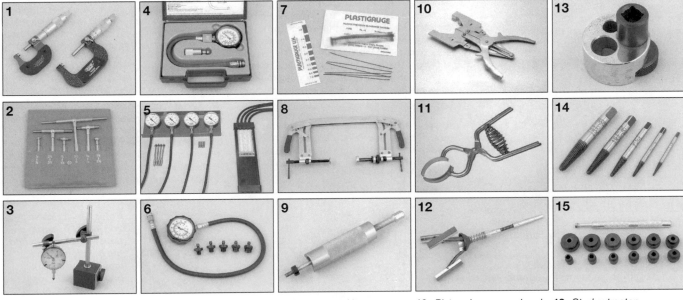

1 Micrometers (external type)
2 Telescoping gauges
3 Dial gauge
4 Cylinder compression gauge
5 Vacuum gauges (left) or manometer (right)
6 Oil pressure gauge
7 Plastigauge kit
8 Valve spring compressor (4-stroke engines)
9 Piston pin drawbolt tool
10 Piston ring removal and installation tool
11 Piston ring clamp
12 Cylinder bore hone (stone type shown)
13 Stud extractor
14 Screw extractor set
15 Bearing driver set

1 Workshop equipment and facilities

The workbench

● Work is made much easier by raising the bike up on a ramp - components are much more accessible if raised to waist level. The hydraulic or pneumatic types seen in the dealer's workshop are a sound investment if you undertake a lot of repairs or overhauls (see illustration 1.1).

1.1 Hydraulic motorcycle ramp

● If raised off ground level, the bike must be supported on the ramp to avoid it falling. Most ramps incorporate a front wheel locating clamp which can be adjusted to suit different diameter wheels. When tightening the clamp, take care not to mark the wheel rim or damage the tyre - use wood blocks on each side to prevent this.

● Secure the bike to the ramp using tie-downs (see illustration 1.2). If the bike has only a sidestand, and hence leans at a dangerous angle when raised, support the bike on an auxiliary stand.

1.2 Tie-downs are used around the passenger footrests to secure the bike

● Auxiliary (paddock) stands are widely available from mail order companies or motorcycle dealers and attach either to the wheel axle or swingarm pivot (see illustration 1.3). If the motorcycle has a centrestand, you can support it under the crankcase to prevent it toppling whilst either wheel is removed (see illustration 1.4).

1.3 This auxiliary stand attaches to the swingarm pivot

1.4 Always use a block of wood between the engine and jack head when supporting the engine in this way

Fumes and fire

● Refer to the Safety first! page at the beginning of the manual for full details. Make sure your workshop is equipped with a fire extinguisher suitable for fuel-related fires (Class B fire - flammable liquids) - it is not sufficient to have a water-filled extinguisher.

● Always ensure adequate ventilation is available. Unless an exhaust gas extraction system is available for use, ensure that the engine is run outside of the workshop.

● If working on the fuel system, make sure the workshop is ventilated to avoid a build-up of fumes. This applies equally to fume build-up when charging a battery. Do not smoke or allow anyone else to smoke in the workshop.

Fluids

● If you need to drain fuel from the tank, store it in an approved container marked as suitable for the storage of petrol (gasoline) (see illustration 1.5). Do not store fuel in glass jars or bottles.

1.5 Use an approved can only for storing petrol (gasoline)

● Use proprietary engine degreasers or solvents which have a high flash-point, such as paraffin (kerosene), for cleaning off oil, grease and dirt - never use petrol (gasoline) for cleaning. Wear rubber gloves when handling solvent and engine degreaser. The fumes from certain solvents can be dangerous - always work in a well-ventilated area.

Dust, eye and hand protection

● Protect your lungs from inhalation of dust particles by wearing a filtering mask over the nose and mouth. Many frictional materials still contain asbestos which is dangerous to your health. Protect your eyes from spouts of liquid and sprung components by wearing a pair of protective goggles (see illustration 1.6).

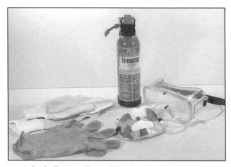

1.6 A fire extinguisher, goggles, mask and protective gloves should be at hand in the workshop

● Protect your hands from contact with solvents, fuel and oils by wearing rubber gloves. Alternatively apply a barrier cream to your hands before starting work. If handling hot components or fluids, wear suitable gloves to protect your hands from scalding and burns.

What to do with old fluids

● Old cleaning solvent, fuel, coolant and oils should not be poured down domestic drains or onto the ground. Package the fluid up in old oil containers, label it accordingly, and take it to a garage or disposal facility. Contact your local authority for location of such sites or ring the oil care hotline.

OIL CARE

Note: It is antisocial and illegal to dump oil down the drain. To find the location of your local oil recycling bank in the UK, call 03708 506 506 or visit www.oilbankline.org.uk

In the USA, note that any oil supplier must accept used oil for recycling.

Tools and Workshop Tips REF•5

2 Fasteners -
screws, bolts and nuts

Fastener types and applications

Bolts and screws

● Fastener head types are either of hexagonal, Torx or splined design, with internal and external versions of each type **(see illustrations 2.1 and 2.2)**; splined head fasteners are not in common use on motorcycles. The conventional slotted or Phillips head design is used for certain screws. Bolt or screw length is always measured from the underside of the head to the end of the item **(see illustration 2.11)**.

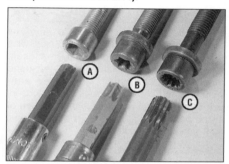

2.1 Internal hexagon/Allen (A), Torx (B) and splined (C) fasteners, with corresponding bits

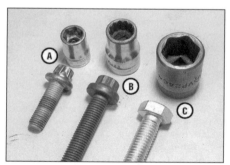

2.2 External Torx (A), splined (B) and hexagon (C) fasteners, with corresponding sockets

● Certain fasteners on the motorcycle have a tensile marking on their heads, the higher the marking the stronger the fastener. High tensile fasteners generally carry a 10 or higher marking. Never replace a high tensile fastener with one of a lower tensile strength.

Washers **(see illustration 2.3)**

● Plain washers are used between a fastener head and a component to prevent damage to the component or to spread the load when torque is applied. Plain washers can also be used as spacers or shims in certain assemblies. Copper or aluminium plain washers are often used as sealing washers on drain plugs.

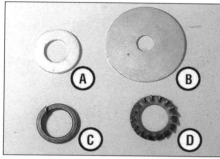

2.3 Plain washer (A), penny washer (B), spring washer (C) and serrated washer (D)

● The split-ring spring washer works by applying axial tension between the fastener head and component. If flattened, it is fatigued and must be renewed. If a plain (flat) washer is used on the fastener, position the spring washer between the fastener and the plain washer.

● Serrated star type washers dig into the fastener and component faces, preventing loosening. They are often used on electrical earth (ground) connections to the frame.

● Cone type washers (sometimes called Belleville) are conical and when tightened apply axial tension between the fastener head and component. They must be installed with the dished side against the component and often carry an OUTSIDE marking on their outer face. If flattened, they are fatigued and must be renewed.

● Tab washers are used to lock plain nuts or bolts on a shaft. A portion of the tab washer is bent up hard against one flat of the nut or bolt to prevent it loosening. Due to the tab washer being deformed in use, a new tab washer should be used every time it is disturbed.

● Wave washers are used to take up endfloat on a shaft. They provide light springing and prevent excessive side-to-side play of a component. Can be found on rocker arm shafts.

Nuts and split pins

● Conventional plain nuts are usually six-sided **(see illustration 2.4)**. They are sized by thread diameter and pitch. High tensile nuts carry a number on one end to denote their tensile strength.

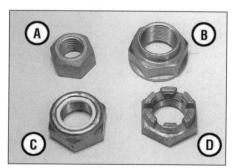

2.4 Plain nut (A), shouldered locknut (B), nylon insert nut (C) and castellated nut (D)

● Self-locking nuts either have a nylon insert, or two spring metal tabs, or a shoulder which is staked into a groove in the shaft - their advantage over conventional plain nuts is a resistance to loosening due to vibration. The nylon insert type can be used a number of times, but must be renewed when the friction of the nylon insert is reduced, ie when the nut spins freely on the shaft. The spring tab type can be reused unless the tabs are damaged. The shouldered type must be renewed every time it is disturbed.

● Split pins (cotter pins) are used to lock a castellated nut to a shaft or to prevent slackening of a plain nut. Common applications are wheel axles and brake torque arms. Because the split pin arms are deformed to lock around the nut a new split pin must always be used on installation - always fit the correct size split pin which will fit snugly in the shaft hole. Make sure the split pin arms are correctly located around the nut **(see illustrations 2.5 and 2.6)**.

2.5 Bend split pin (cotter pin) arms as shown (arrows) to secure a castellated nut

2.6 Bend split pin (cotter pin) arms as shown to secure a plain nut

Caution: If the castellated nut slots do not align with the shaft hole after tightening to the torque setting, tighten the nut until the next slot aligns with the hole - never slacken the nut to align its slot.

● R-pins (shaped like the letter R), or slip pins as they are sometimes called, are sprung and can be reused if they are otherwise in good condition. Always install R-pins with their closed end facing forwards **(see illustration 2.7)**.

2.7 Correct fitting of R-pin. Arrow indicates forward direction

Circlips (see illustration 2.8)

● Circlips (sometimes called snap-rings) are used to retain components on a shaft or in a housing and have corresponding external or internal ears to permit removal. Parallel-sided (machined) circlips can be installed either way round in their groove, whereas stamped circlips (which have a chamfered edge on one face) must be installed with the chamfer facing away from the direction of thrust load **(see illustration 2.9)**.

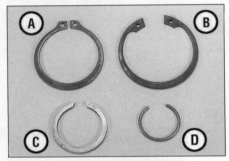

2.8 External stamped circlip (A), internal stamped circlip (B), machined circlip (C) and wire circlip (D)

● Always use circlip pliers to remove and install circlips; expand or compress them just enough to remove them. After installation, rotate the circlip in its groove to ensure it is securely seated. If installing a circlip on a splined shaft, always align its opening with a shaft channel to ensure the circlip ends are well supported and unlikely to catch **(see illustration 2.10)**.

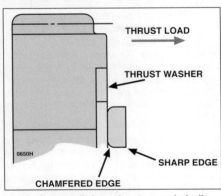

2.9 Correct fitting of a stamped circlip

THRUST LOAD
THRUST WASHER
SHARP EDGE
CHAMFERED EDGE
0650H

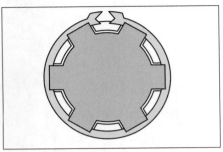

2.10 Align circlip opening with shaft channel

● Circlips can wear due to the thrust of components and become loose in their grooves, with the subsequent danger of becoming dislodged in operation. For this reason, renewal is advised every time a circlip is disturbed.

● Wire circlips are commonly used as piston pin retaining clips. If a removal tang is provided, long-nosed pliers can be used to dislodge them, otherwise careful use of a small flat-bladed screwdriver is necessary. Wire circlips should be renewed every time they are disturbed.

Thread diameter and pitch

● Diameter of a male thread (screw, bolt or stud) is the outside diameter of the threaded portion **(see illustration 2.11)**. Most motorcycle manufacturers use the ISO (International Standards Organisation) metric system expressed in millimetres, eg M6 refers to a 6 mm diameter thread. Sizing is the same for nuts, except that the thread diameter is measured across the valleys of the nut.

● Pitch is the distance between the peaks of the thread **(see illustration 2.11)**. It is expressed in millimetres, thus a common bolt size may be expressed as 6.0 x 1.0 mm (6 mm thread diameter and 1 mm pitch). Generally pitch increases in proportion to thread diameter, although there are always exceptions.

● Thread diameter and pitch are related for conventional fastener applications and the accompanying table can be used as a guide. Additionally, the AF (Across Flats), spanner or socket size dimension of the bolt or nut **(see illustration 2.11)** is linked to thread and pitch specification. Thread pitch can be measured with a thread gauge **(see illustration 2.12)**.

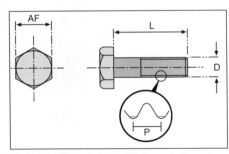

2.11 Fastener length (L), thread diameter (D), thread pitch (P) and head size (AF)

AF
L
D
P

2.12 Using a thread gauge to measure pitch

AF size	Thread diameter x pitch (mm)
8 mm	M5 x 0.8
8 mm	M6 x 1.0
10 mm	M6 x 1.0
12 mm	M8 x 1.25
14 mm	M10 x 1.25
17 mm	M12 x 1.25

● The threads of most fasteners are of the right-hand type, ie they are turned clockwise to tighten and anti-clockwise to loosen. The reverse situation applies to left-hand thread fasteners, which are turned anti-clockwise to tighten and clockwise to loosen. Left-hand threads are used where rotation of a component might loosen a conventional right-hand thread fastener.

Seized fasteners

● Corrosion of external fasteners due to water or reaction between two dissimilar metals can occur over a period of time. It will build up sooner in wet conditions or in countries where salt is used on the roads during the winter. If a fastener is severely corroded it is likely that normal methods of removal will fail and result in its head being ruined. When you attempt removal, the fastener thread should be heard to crack free and unscrew easily - if it doesn't, stop there before damaging something.

● A smart tap on the head of the fastener will often succeed in breaking free corrosion which has occurred in the threads **(see illustration 2.13)**.

● An aerosol penetrating fluid (such as WD-40) applied the night beforehand may work its way down into the thread and ease removal. Depending on the location, you may be able to make up a Plasticine well around the fastener head and fill it with penetrating fluid.

2.13 A sharp tap on the head of a fastener will often break free a corroded thread

● If you are working on an engine internal component, corrosion will most likely not be a problem due to the well lubricated environment. However, components can be very tight and an impact driver is a useful tool in freeing them (see illustration 2.14).

2.14 Using an impact driver to free a fastener

● Where corrosion has occurred between dissimilar metals (eg steel and aluminium alloy), the application of heat to the fastener head will create a disproportionate expansion rate between the two metals and break the seizure caused by the corrosion. Whether heat can be applied depends on the location of the fastener - any surrounding components likely to be damaged must first be removed (see illustration 2.15). Heat can be applied using a paint stripper heat gun or clothes iron, or by immersing the component in boiling water - wear protective gloves to prevent scalding or burns to the hands.

2.15 Using heat to free a seized fastener

● As a last resort, it is possible to use a hammer and cold chisel to work the fastener head unscrewed (see illustration 2.16). This will damage the fastener, but more importantly extreme care must be taken not to damage the surrounding component.

Caution: Remember that the component being secured is generally of more value than the bolt, nut or screw - when the fastener is freed, do not unscrew it with force, instead work the fastener back and forth when resistance is felt to prevent thread damage.

2.16 Using a hammer and chisel to free a seized fastener

Broken fasteners and damaged heads

● If the shank of a broken bolt or screw is accessible you can grip it with self-locking grips. The knurled wheel type stud extractor tool or self-gripping stud puller tool is particularly useful for removing the long studs which screw into the cylinder mouth surface of the crankcase or bolts and screws from which the head has broken off (see illustration 2.17). Studs can also be removed by locking two nuts together on the threaded end of the stud and using a spanner on the lower nut (see illustration 2.18).

2.17 Using a stud extractor tool to remove a broken crankcase stud

2.18 Two nuts can be locked together to unscrew a stud from a component

● A bolt or screw which has broken off below or level with the casing must be extracted using a screw extractor set. Centre punch the fastener to centralise the drill bit, then drill a hole in the fastener (see illustration 2.19). Select a drill bit which is approximately half to three-quarters the diameter of the fastener

2.19 When using a screw extractor, first drill a hole in the fastener . . .

and drill to a depth which will accommodate the extractor. Use the largest size extractor possible, but avoid leaving too small a wall thickness otherwise the extractor will merely force the fastener walls outwards wedging it in the casing thread.

● If a spiral type extractor is used, thread it anti-clockwise into the fastener. As it is screwed in, it will grip the fastener and unscrew it from the casing (see illustration 2.20).

2.20 . . . then thread the extractor anti-clockwise into the fastener

● If a taper type extractor is used, tap it into the fastener so that it is firmly wedged in place. Unscrew the extractor (anti-clockwise) to draw the fastener out.

Warning: Stud extractors are very hard and may break off in the fastener if care is not taken - ask an engineer about spark erosion if this happens.

● Alternatively, the broken bolt/screw can be drilled out and the hole retapped for an oversize bolt/screw or a diamond-section thread insert. It is essential that the drilling is carried out squarely and to the correct depth, otherwise the casing may be ruined - if in doubt, entrust the work to an engineer.

● Bolts and nuts with rounded corners cause the correct size spanner or socket to slip when force is applied. Of the types of spanner/socket available always use a six-point type rather than an eight or twelve-point type - better grip

2.21 Comparison of surface drive ring spanner (left) with 12-point type (right)

is obtained. Surface drive spanners grip the middle of the hex flats, rather than the corners, and are thus good in cases of damaged heads **(see illustration 2.21)**.

● Slotted-head or Phillips-head screws are often damaged by the use of the wrong size screwdriver. Allen-head and Torx-head screws are much less likely to sustain damage. If enough of the screw head is exposed you can use a hacksaw to cut a slot in its head and then use a conventional flat-bladed screwdriver to remove it. Alternatively use a hammer and cold chisel to tap the head of the fastener around to slacken it. Always replace damaged fasteners with new ones, preferably Torx or Allen-head type.

HAYNES HINT

A dab of valve grinding compound between the screw head and screw-driver tip will often give a good grip.

Thread repair

● Threads (particularly those in aluminium alloy components) can be damaged by overtightening, being assembled with dirt in the threads, or from a component working loose and vibrating. Eventually the thread will fail completely, and it will be impossible to tighten the fastener.

● If a thread is damaged or clogged with old locking compound it can be renovated with a thread repair tool (thread chaser) **(see illustrations 2.22 and 2.23)**; special thread

2.22 A thread repair tool being used to correct an internal thread

2.23 A thread repair tool being used to correct an external thread

chasers are available for spark plug hole threads. The tool will not cut a new thread, but clean and true the original thread. Make sure that you use the correct diameter and pitch tool. Similarly, external threads can be cleaned up with a die or a thread restorer file **(see illustration 2.24)**.

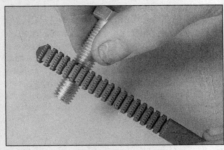

2.24 Using a thread restorer file

● It is possible to drill out the old thread and retap the component to the next thread size. This will work where there is enough surrounding material and a new bolt or screw can be obtained. Sometimes, however, this is not possible - such as where the bolt/screw passes through another component which must also be suitably modified, also in cases where a spark plug or oil drain plug cannot be obtained in a larger diameter thread size.

● The diamond-section thread insert (often known by its popular trade name of Heli-Coil) is a simple and effective method of renewing the thread and retaining the original size. A kit can be purchased which contains the tap, insert and installing tool **(see illustration 2.25)**. Drill out the damaged thread with the size drill specified **(see illustration 2.26)**. Carefully retap the thread **(see illustration 2.27)**. Install the

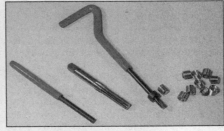

2.25 Obtain a thread insert kit to suit the thread diameter and pitch required

2.26 To install a thread insert, first drill out the original thread . . .

2.27 . . . tap a new thread . . .

2.28 . . . fit insert on the installing tool . . .

2.29 . . . and thread into the component . . .

2.30 . . . break off the tang when complete

insert on the installing tool and thread it slowly into place using a light downward pressure **(see illustrations 2.28 and 2.29)**. When positioned between a 1/4 and 1/2 turn below the surface withdraw the installing tool and use the break-off tool to press down on the tang, breaking it off **(see illustration 2.30)**.

● There are epoxy thread repair kits on the market which can rebuild stripped internal threads, although this repair should not be used on high load-bearing components.

Thread locking and sealing compounds

● Locking compounds are used in locations where the fastener is prone to loosening due to vibration or on important safety-related items which might cause loss of control of the motorcycle if they fail. It is also used where important fasteners cannot be secured by other means such as lockwashers or split pins.

● Before applying locking compound, make sure that the threads (internal and external) are clean and dry with all old compound removed. Select a compound to suit the component being secured - a non-permanent general locking and sealing type is suitable for most applications, but a high strength type is needed for permanent fixing of studs in castings. Apply a drop or two of the compound to the first few threads of the fastener, then thread it into place and tighten to the specified torque. Do not apply excessive thread locking compound otherwise the thread may be damaged on subsequent removal.

● Certain fasteners are impregnated with a dry film type coating of locking compound on their threads. Always renew this type of fastener if disturbed.

● Anti-seize compounds, such as copper-based greases, can be applied to protect threads from seizure due to extreme heat and corrosion. A common instance is spark plug threads and exhaust system fasteners.

3 Measuring tools and gauges

Feeler gauges

● Feeler gauges (or blades) are used for measuring small gaps and clearances (see illustration 3.1). They can also be used to measure endfloat (sideplay) of a component on a shaft where access is not possible with a dial gauge.

● Feeler gauge sets should be treated with care and not bent or damaged. They are etched with their size on one face. Keep them clean and very lightly oiled to prevent corrosion build-up.

3.1 Feeler gauges are used for measuring small gaps and clearances - thickness is marked on one face of gauge

● When measuring a clearance, select a gauge which is a light sliding fit between the two components. You may need to use two gauges together to measure the clearance accurately.

Micrometers

● A micrometer is a precision tool capable of measuring to 0.01 or 0.001 of a millimetre. It should always be stored in its case and not in the general toolbox. It must be kept clean and never dropped, otherwise its frame or measuring anvils could be distorted resulting in inaccurate readings.

● External micrometers are used for measuring outside diameters of components and have many more applications than internal micrometers. Micrometers are available in different size ranges, eg 0 to 25 mm, 25 to 50 mm, and upwards in 25 mm steps; some large micrometers have interchangeable anvils to allow a range of measurements to be taken. Generally the largest precision measurement you are likely to take on a motorcycle is the piston diameter.

● Internal micrometers (or bore micrometers) are used for measuring inside diameters, such as valve guides and cylinder bores. Telescoping gauges and small hole gauges are used in conjunction with an external micrometer, whereas the more expensive internal micrometers have their own measuring device.

External micrometer

Note: *The conventional analogue type instrument is described. Although much easier to read, digital micrometers are considerably more expensive.*

● Always check the calibration of the micrometer before use. With the anvils closed (0 to 25 mm type) or set over a test gauge

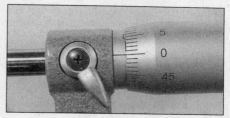

3.2 Check micrometer calibration before use

(for the larger types) the scale should read zero (see illustration 3.2); make sure that the anvils (and test piece) are clean first. Any discrepancy can be adjusted by referring to the instructions supplied with the tool. Remember that the micrometer is a precision measuring tool - don't force the anvils closed, use the ratchet (4) on the end of the micrometer to close it. In this way, a measured force is always applied.

● To use, first make sure that the item being measured is clean. Place the anvil of the micrometer (1) against the item and use the thimble (2) to bring the spindle (3) lightly into contact with the other side of the item (see illustration 3.3). Don't tighten the thimble down because this will damage the micrometer - instead use the ratchet (4) on the end of the micrometer. The ratchet mechanism applies a measured force preventing damage to the instrument.

● The micrometer is read by referring to the linear scale on the sleeve and the annular scale on the thimble. Read off the sleeve first to obtain the base measurement, then add the fine measurement from the thimble to obtain the overall reading. The linear scale on the sleeve represents the measuring range of the micrometer (eg 0 to 25 mm). The annular scale

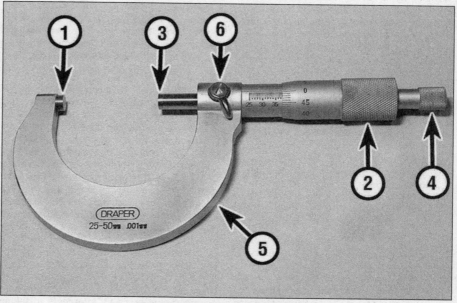

3.3 Micrometer component parts

1 Anvil	3 Spindle	5 Frame
2 Thimble	4 Ratchet	6 Locking lever

on the thimble will be in graduations of 0.01 mm (or as marked on the frame) - one full revolution of the thimble will move 0.5 mm on the linear scale. Take the reading where the datum line on the sleeve intersects the thimble's scale. Always position the eye directly above the scale otherwise an inaccurate reading will result.

In the example shown the item measures 2.95 mm **(see illustration 3.4)**:

Linear scale	2.00 mm
Linear scale	0.50 mm
Annular scale	0.45 mm
Total figure	2.95 mm

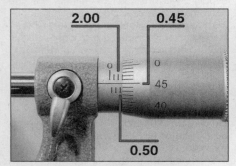

3.4 Micrometer reading of 2.95 mm

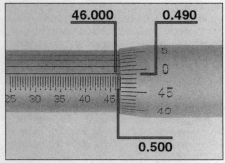

3.5 Micrometer reading of 46.99 mm on linear and annular scales . . .

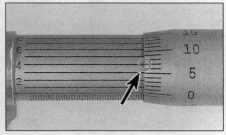

3.6 . . . and 0.004 mm on vernier scale

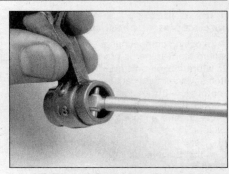

3.7 Expand the telescoping gauge in the bore, lock its position . . .

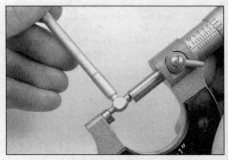

3.8 . . . then measure the gauge with a micrometer

3.9 Expand the small hole gauge in the bore, lock its position . . .

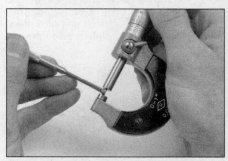

3.10 . . . then measure the gauge with a micrometer

Most micrometers have a locking lever (6) on the frame to hold the setting in place, allowing the item to be removed from the micrometer.
● Some micrometers have a vernier scale on their sleeve, providing an even finer measurement to be taken, in 0.001 increments of a millimetre. Take the sleeve and thimble measurement as described above, then check which graduation on the vernier scale aligns with that of the annular scale on the thimble **Note:** *The eye must be perpendicular to the scale when taking the vernier reading - if necessary rotate the body of the micrometer to ensure this.* Multiply the vernier scale figure by 0.001 and add it to the base and fine measurement figures.

In the example shown the item measures 46.994 mm **(see illustrations 3.5 and 3.6)**:

Linear scale (base)	46.000 mm
Linear scale (base)	00.500 mm
Annular scale (fine)	00.490 mm
Vernier scale	00.004 mm
Total figure	46.994 mm

Internal micrometer

● Internal micrometers are available for measuring bore diameters, but are expensive and unlikely to be available for home use. It is suggested that a set of telescoping gauges and small hole gauges, both of which must be used with an external micrometer, will suffice for taking internal measurements on a motorcycle.
● Telescoping gauges can be used to measure internal diameters of components. Select a gauge with the correct size range, make sure its ends are clean and insert it into the bore. Expand the gauge, then lock its position and withdraw it from the bore **(see illustration 3.7)**. Measure across the gauge ends with a micrometer **(see illustration 3.8)**.
● Very small diameter bores (such as valve guides) are measured with a small hole gauge. Once adjusted to a slip-fit inside the component, its position is locked and the gauge withdrawn for measurement with a micrometer **(see illustrations 3.9 and 3.10)**.

Vernier caliper

Note: *The conventional linear and dial gauge type instruments are described. Digital types are easier to read, but are far more expensive.*
● The vernier caliper does not provide the precision of a micrometer, but is versatile in being able to measure internal and external diameters. Some types also incorporate a depth gauge. It is ideal for measuring clutch plate friction material and spring free lengths.
● To use the conventional linear scale vernier, slacken off the vernier clamp screws (1) and set its jaws over (2), or inside (3), the item to be measured **(see illustration 3.11)**. Slide the jaw into contact, using the thumb-wheel (4) for fine movement of the sliding scale (5) then tighten the clamp screws (1). Read off the main scale (6) where the zero on the sliding scale (5) intersects it, taking the whole number to the left of the zero; this provides the base measurement. View along the sliding scale and select the division which lines up exactly with any of the divisions on the main scale, noting that the divisions usually represents 0.02 of a millimetre. Add this fine measurement to the base measurement to obtain the total reading.

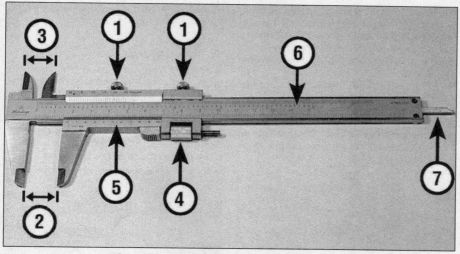

3.11 Vernier component parts (linear gauge)

1	Clamp screws	3	Internal jaws	5	Sliding scale	7	Depth gauge
2	External jaws	4	Thumbwheel	6	Main scale		

In the example shown the item measures 55.92 mm **(see illustration 3.12)**:

Base measurement	55.00 mm
Fine measurement	00.92 mm
Total figure	55.92 mm

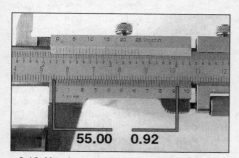

3.12 Vernier gauge reading of 55.92 mm

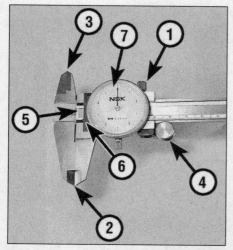

3.13 Vernier component parts (dial gauge)

1	Clamp screw	5	Main scale
2	External jaws	6	Sliding scale
3	Internal jaws	7	Dial gauge
4	Thumbwheel		

● Some vernier calipers are equipped with a dial gauge for fine measurement. Before use, check that the jaws are clean, then close them fully and check that the dial gauge reads zero. If necessary adjust the gauge ring accordingly. Slacken the vernier clamp screw (1) and set its jaws over (2), or inside (3), the item to be measured **(see illustration 3.13)**. Slide the jaws into contact, using the thumbwheel (4) for fine movement. Read off the main scale (5) where the edge of the sliding scale (6) intersects it, taking the whole number to the left of the zero; this provides the base measurement. Read off the needle position on the dial gauge (7) scale to provide the fine measurement; each division represents 0.05 of a millimetre. Add this fine measurement to the base measurement to obtain the total reading.

In the example shown the item measures 55.95 mm **(see illustration 3.14)**:

Base measurement	55.00 mm
Fine measurement	00.95 mm
Total figure	55.95 mm

3.14 Vernier gauge reading of 55.95 mm

Plastigauge

● Plastigauge is a plastic material which can be compressed between two surfaces to measure the oil clearance between them. The width of the compressed Plastigauge is measured against a calibrated scale to determine the clearance.

● Common uses of Plastigauge are for measuring the clearance between crankshaft journal and main bearing inserts, between crankshaft journal and big-end bearing inserts, and between camshaft and bearing surfaces. The following example describes big-end oil clearance measurement.

● Handle the Plastigauge material carefully to prevent distortion. Using a sharp knife, cut a length which corresponds with the width of the bearing being measured and place it carefully across the journal so that it is parallel with the shaft **(see illustration 3.15)**. Carefully install both bearing shells and the connecting rod. Without rotating the rod on the journal tighten its bolts or nuts (as applicable) to the specified torque. The connecting rod and bearings are then disassembled and the crushed Plastigauge examined.

3.15 Plastigauge placed across shaft journal

● Using the scale provided in the Plastigauge kit, measure the width of the material to determine the oil clearance **(see illustration 3.16)**. Always remove all traces of Plastigauge after use using your fingernails.

Caution: Arriving at the correct clearance demands that the assembly is torqued correctly, according to the settings and sequence (where applicable) provided by the motorcycle manufacturer.

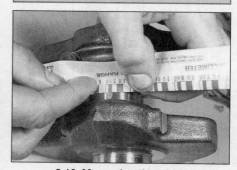

3.16 Measuring the width of the crushed Plastigauge

Dial gauge or DTI (Dial Test Indicator)

● A dial gauge can be used to accurately measure small amounts of movement. Typical uses are measuring shaft runout or shaft endfloat (sideplay) and setting piston position for ignition timing on two-strokes. A dial gauge set usually comes with a range of different probes and adapters and mounting equipment.

● The gauge needle must point to zero when at rest. Rotate the ring around its periphery to zero the gauge.

● Check that the gauge is capable of reading the extent of movement in the work. Most gauges have a small dial set in the face which records whole millimetres of movement as well as the fine scale around the face periphery which is calibrated in 0.01 mm divisions. Read off the small dial first to obtain the base measurement, then add the measurement from the fine scale to obtain the total reading.

In the example shown the gauge reads 1.48 mm (see illustration 3.17):

Base measurement	1.00 mm
Fine measurement	0.48 mm
Total figure	1.48 mm

3.17 Dial gauge reading of 1.48 mm

● If measuring shaft runout, the shaft must be supported in vee-blocks and the gauge mounted on a stand perpendicular to the shaft. Rest the tip of the gauge against the centre of the shaft and rotate the shaft slowly whilst watching the gauge reading (see illustration 3.18). Take several measurements along the length of the shaft and record the

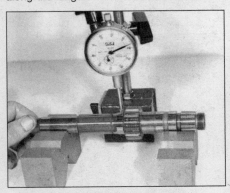

3.18 Using a dial gauge to measure shaft runout

maximum gauge reading as the amount of runout in the shaft. **Note:** *The reading obtained will be total runout at that point - some manufacturers specify that the runout figure is halved to compare with their specified runout limit.*

● Endfloat (sideplay) measurement requires that the gauge is mounted securely to the surrounding component with its probe touching the end of the shaft. Using hand pressure, push and pull on the shaft noting the maximum endfloat recorded on the gauge (see illustration 3.19).

3.19 Using a dial gauge to measure shaft endfloat

● A dial gauge with suitable adapters can be used to determine piston position BTDC on two-stroke engines for the purposes of ignition timing. The gauge, adapter and suitable length probe are installed in the place of the spark plug and the gauge zeroed at TDC. If the piston position is specified as 1.14 mm BTDC, rotate the engine back to 2.00 mm BTDC, then slowly forwards to 1.14 mm BTDC.

Cylinder compression gauges

● A compression gauge is used for measuring cylinder compression. Either the rubber-cone type or the threaded adapter type can be used. The latter is preferred to ensure a perfect seal against the cylinder head. A 0 to 300 psi (0 to 20 Bar) type gauge (for petrol/gasoline engines) will be suitable for motorcycles.

● The spark plug is removed and the gauge either held hard against the cylinder head (cone type) or the gauge adapter screwed into the cylinder head (threaded type) (see illustration 3.20). Cylinder compression is measured with the engine turning over, but not running. The

3.20 Using a rubber-cone type cylinder compression gauge

gauge will hold the reading until manually released.

Oil pressure gauge

● An oil pressure gauge is used for measuring engine oil pressure. Most gauges come with a set of adapters to fit the thread of the take-off point (see illustration 3.21). If the take-off point specified by the motorcycle manufacturer is an external oil pipe union, make sure that the specified replacement union is used to prevent oil starvation.

3.21 Oil pressure gauge and take-off point adapter (arrow)

● Oil pressure is measured with the engine running (at a specific rpm) and often the manufacturer will specify pressure limits for a cold and hot engine.

Straight-edge and surface plate

● If checking the gasket face of a component for warpage, place a steel rule or precision straight-edge across the gasket face and measure any gap between the straight-edge and component with feeler gauges (see illustration 3.22). Check diagonally across the component and between mounting holes (see illustration 3.23).

3.22 Use a straight-edge and feeler gauges to check for warpage

3.23 Check for warpage in these directions

● Checking individual components for warpage, such as clutch plain (metal) plates, requires a perfectly flat plate or piece or plate glass and feeler gauges.

4 Torque and leverage

What is torque?

● Torque describes the twisting force about a shaft. The amount of torque applied is determined by the distance from the centre of the shaft to the end of the lever and the amount of force being applied to the end of the lever; distance multiplied by force equals torque.

● The manufacturer applies a measured torque to a bolt or nut to ensure that it will not slacken in use and to hold two components securely together without movement in the joint. The actual torque setting depends on the thread size, bolt or nut material and the composition of the components being held.

● Too little torque may cause the fastener to loosen due to vibration, whereas too much torque will distort the joint faces of the component or cause the fastener to shear off. Always stick to the specified torque setting.

Using a torque wrench

● Check the calibration of the torque wrench and make sure it has a suitable range for the job. Torque wrenches are available in Nm (Newton-metres), kgf m (kilograms-force metre), lbf ft (pounds-feet), lbf in (inch-pounds). Do not confuse lbf ft with lbf in.

● Adjust the tool to the desired torque on the scale (see illustration 4.1). If your torque wrench is not calibrated in the units specified, carefully convert the figure (see Conversion Factors). A manufacturer sometimes gives a torque setting as a range (8 to 10 Nm) rather than a single figure - in this case set the tool midway between the two settings. The same torque may be expressed as 9 Nm ± 1 Nm. Some torque wrenches have a method of locking the setting so that it isn't inadvertently altered during use.

4.1 Set the torque wrench index mark to the setting required, in this case 12 Nm

● Install the bolts/nuts in their correct location and secure them lightly. Their threads must be clean and free of any old locking compound. Unless specified the threads and flange should be dry - oiled threads are necessary in certain circumstances and the manufacturer will take this into account in the specified torque figure. Similarly, the manufacturer may also specify the application of thread-locking compound.

● Tighten the fasteners in the specified sequence until the torque wrench clicks, indicating that the torque setting has been reached. Apply the torque again to double-check the setting. Where different thread diameter fasteners secure the component, as a rule tighten the larger diameter ones first.

● When the torque wrench has been finished with, release the lock (where applicable) and fully back off its setting to zero - do not leave the torque wrench tensioned. Also, do not use a torque wrench for slackening a fastener.

Angle-tightening

● Manufacturers often specify a figure in degrees for final tightening of a fastener. This usually follows tightening to a specific torque setting.

● A degree disc can be set and attached to the socket (see illustration 4.2) or a protractor can be used to mark the angle of movement on the bolt/nut head and the surrounding casting (see illustration 4.3).

4.2 Angle tightening can be accomplished with a torque-angle gauge . . .

4.3 . . . or by marking the angle on the surrounding component

Loosening sequences

● Where more than one bolt/nut secures a component, loosen each fastener evenly a little at a time. In this way, not all the stress of the joint is held by one fastener and the components are not likely to distort.

● If a tightening sequence is provided, work in the REVERSE of this, but if not, work from the outside in, in a criss-cross sequence (see illustration 4.4).

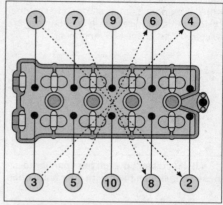

4.4 When slackening, work from the outside inwards

Tightening sequences

● If a component is held by more than one fastener it is important that the retaining bolts/nuts are tightened evenly to prevent uneven stress build-up and distortion of sealing faces. This is especially important on high-compression joints such as the cylinder head.

● A sequence is usually provided by the manufacturer, either in a diagram or actually marked in the casting. If not, always start in the centre and work outwards in a criss-cross pattern (see illustration 4.5). Start off by securing all bolts/nuts finger-tight, then set the torque wrench and tighten each fastener by a small amount in sequence until the final torque is reached. By following this practice,

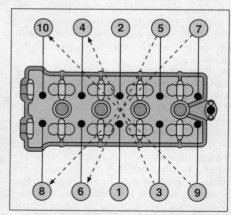

4.5 When tightening, work from the inside outwards

the joint will be held evenly and will not be distorted. Important joints, such as the cylinder head and big-end fasteners often have two- or three-stage torque settings.

Applying leverage

● Use tools at the correct angle. Position a socket wrench or spanner on the bolt/nut so that you pull it towards you when loosening. If this can't be done, push the spanner without curling your fingers around it **(see illustration 4.6)** - the spanner may slip or the fastener loosen suddenly, resulting in your fingers being crushed against a component.

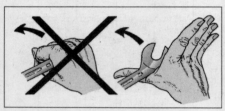

4.6 If you can't pull on the spanner to loosen a fastener, push with your hand open

● Additional leverage is gained by extending the length of the lever. The best way to do this is to use a breaker bar instead of the regular length tool, or to slip a length of tubing over the end of the spanner or socket wrench.
● If additional leverage will not work, the fastener head is either damaged or firmly corroded in place (see Fasteners).

5 Bearings

Bearing removal and installation

Drivers and sockets

● Before removing a bearing, always inspect the casing to see which way it must be driven out - some casings will have retaining plates or a cast step. Also check for any identifying markings on the bearing and if installed to a certain depth, measure this at this stage. Some roller bearings are sealed on one side - take note of the original fitted position.
● Bearings can be driven out of a casing using a bearing driver tool (with the correct size head) or a socket of the correct diameter. Select the driver head or socket so that it contacts the outer race of the bearing, not the balls/rollers or inner race. Always support the casing around the bearing housing with wood blocks, otherwise there is a risk of fracture. The bearing is driven out with a few blows on the driver or socket from a heavy mallet. Unless access is severely restricted (as with wheel bearings), a pin-punch is not recommended unless it is moved around the bearing to keep it square in its housing.

● The same equipment can be used to install bearings. Make sure the bearing housing is supported on wood blocks and line up the bearing in its housing. Fit the bearing as noted on removal - generally they are installed with their marked side facing outwards. Tap the bearing squarely into its housing using a driver or socket which bears only on the bearing's outer race - contact with the bearing balls/rollers or inner race will destroy it **(see illustrations 5.1 and 5.2)**.
● Check that the bearing inner race and balls/rollers rotate freely.

5.1 Using a bearing driver against the bearing's outer race

5.2 Using a large socket against the bearing's outer race

Pullers and slide-hammers

● Where a bearing is pressed on a shaft a puller will be required to extract it **(see illustration 5.3)**. Make sure that the puller clamp or legs fit securely behind the bearing and are unlikely to slip out. If pulling a bearing

5.3 This bearing puller clamps behind the bearing and pressure is applied to the shaft end to draw the bearing off

off a gear shaft for example, you may have to locate the puller behind a gear pinion if there is no access to the race and draw the gear pinion off the shaft as well **(see illustration 5.4)**.

> **Caution: Ensure that the puller's centre bolt locates securely against the end of the shaft and will not slip when pressure is applied. Also ensure that puller does not damage the shaft end.**

5.4 Where no access is available to the rear of the bearing, it is sometimes possible to draw off the adjacent component

● Operate the puller so that its centre bolt exerts pressure on the shaft end and draws the bearing off the shaft.
● When installing the bearing on the shaft, tap only on the bearing's inner race - contact with the balls/rollers or outer race with destroy the bearing. Use a socket or length of tubing as a drift which fits over the shaft end **(see illustration 5.5)**.

5.5 When installing a bearing on a shaft use a piece of tubing which bears only on the bearing's inner race

● Where a bearing locates in a blind hole in a casing, it cannot be driven or pulled out as described above. A slide-hammer with knife-edged bearing puller attachment will be required. The puller attachment passes through the bearing and when tightened expands to fit firmly behind the bearing **(see illustration 5.6)**. By operating the slide-hammer part of the tool the bearing is jarred out of its housing **(see illustration 5.7)**.
● It is possible, if the bearing is of reasonable weight, for it to drop out of its housing if the casing is heated as described opposite.

5.6 Expand the bearing puller so that it locks behind the bearing . . .

5.7 . . . attach the slide hammer to the bearing puller

If this method is attempted, first prepare a work surface which will enable the casing to be tapped face down to help dislodge the bearing - a wood surface is ideal since it will not damage the casing's gasket surface. Wearing protective gloves, tap the heated casing several times against the work surface to dislodge the bearing under its own weight **(see illustration 5.8)**.

5.8 Tapping a casing face down on wood blocks can often dislodge a bearing

● Bearings can be installed in blind holes using the driver or socket method described above.

Drawbolts

● Where a bearing or bush is set in the eye of a component, such as a suspension linkage arm or connecting rod small-end, removal by drift may damage the component. Furthermore, a rubber bushing in a shock absorber eye cannot successfully be driven out of position. If access is available to a engineering press, the task is straightforward. If not, a drawbolt can be fabricated to extract the bearing or bush.

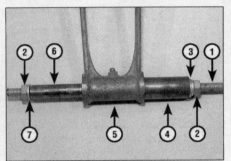

5.9 Drawbolt component parts assembled on a suspension arm

1 *Bolt or length of threaded bar*
2 *Nuts*
3 *Washer (external diameter greater than tubing internal diameter)*
4 *Tubing (internal diameter sufficient to accommodate bearing)*
5 *Suspension arm with bearing*
6 *Tubing (external diameter slightly smaller than bearing)*
7 *Washer (external diameter slightly smaller than bearing)*

5.10 Drawing the bearing out of the suspension arm

● To extract the bearing/bush you will need a long bolt with nut (or piece of threaded bar with two nuts), a piece of tubing which has an internal diameter larger than the bearing/bush, another piece of tubing which has an external diameter slightly smaller than the bearing/bush, and a selection of washers **(see illustrations 5.9 and 5.10)**. Note that the pieces of tubing must be of the same length, or longer, than the bearing/bush.

● The same kit (without the pieces of tubing) can be used to draw the new bearing/bush back into place **(see illustration 5.11)**.

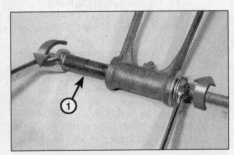

5.11 Installing a new bearing (1) in the suspension arm

Temperature change

● If the bearing's outer race is a tight fit in the casing, the aluminium casing can be heated to release its grip on the bearing. Aluminium will expand at a greater rate than the steel bearing outer race. There are several ways to do this, but avoid any localised extreme heat (such as a blow torch) - aluminium alloy has a low melting point.

● Approved methods of heating a casing are using a domestic oven (heated to 100°C) or immersing the casing in boiling water **(see illustration 5.12)**. Low temperature range localised heat sources such as a paint stripper heat gun or clothes iron can also be used **(see illustration 5.13)**. Alternatively, soak a rag in boiling water, wring it out and wrap it around the bearing housing.

> ⚠ *Warning: All of these methods require care in use to prevent scalding and burns to the hands. Wear protective gloves when handling hot components.*

5.12 A casing can be immersed in a sink of boiling water to aid bearing removal

5.13 Using a localised heat source to aid bearing removal

● If heating the whole casing note that plastic components, such as the neutral switch, may suffer - remove them beforehand.

● After heating, remove the bearing as described above. You may find that the expansion is sufficient for the bearing to fall out of the casing under its own weight or with a light tap on the driver or socket.

● If necessary, the casing can be heated to aid bearing installation, and this is sometimes the recommended procedure if the motorcycle manufacturer has designed the housing and bearing fit with this intention.

● Installation of bearings can be eased by placing them in a freezer the night before installation. The steel bearing will contract slightly, allowing easy insertion in its housing. This is often useful when installing steering head outer races in the frame.

Bearing types and markings

● Plain shell bearings, ball bearings, needle roller bearings and tapered roller bearings will all be found on motorcycles (see illustrations 5.14 and 5.15). The ball and roller types are usually caged between an inner and outer race, but uncaged variations may be found.

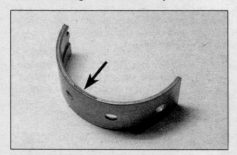

5.14 Shell bearings are either plain or grooved. They are usually identified by colour code (arrow)

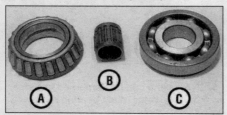

5.15 Tapered roller bearing (A), needle roller bearing (B) and ball journal bearing (C)

● Shell bearings (often called inserts) are usually found at the crankshaft main and connecting rod big-end where they are good at coping with high loads. They are made of a phosphor-bronze material and are impregnated with self-lubricating properties.
● Ball bearings and needle roller bearings consist of a steel inner and outer race with the balls or rollers between the races. They require constant lubrication by oil or grease and are good at coping with axial loads. Taper roller bearings consist of rollers set in a tapered cage set on the inner race; the outer race is separate. They are good at coping with axial loads and prevent movement along the shaft - a typical application is in the steering head.
● Bearing manufacturers produce bearings to ISO size standards and stamp one face of the bearing to indicate its internal and external diameter, load capacity and type (see illustration 5.16).
● Metal bushes are usually of phosphor-bronze material. Rubber bushes are used in suspension mounting eyes. Fibre bushes have also been used in suspension pivots.

5.16 Typical bearing marking

Bearing fault finding

● If a bearing outer race has spun in its housing, the housing material will be damaged. You can use a bearing locking compound to bond the outer race in place if damage is not too severe.
● Shell bearings will fail due to damage of their working surface, as a result of lack of lubrication, corrosion or abrasive particles in the oil (see illustration 5.17). Small particles of dirt in the oil may embed in the bearing material whereas larger particles will score the bearing and shaft journal. If a number of short journeys are made, insufficient heat will be generated to drive off condensation which has built up on the bearings.

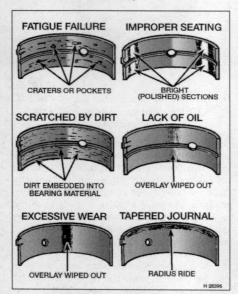

5.17 Typical bearing failures

● Ball and roller bearings will fail due to lack of lubrication or damage to the balls or rollers. Tapered-roller bearings can be damaged by overloading them. Unless the bearing is sealed on both sides, wash it in paraffin (kerosene) to remove all old grease then allow it to dry. Make a visual inspection looking to dented balls or rollers, damaged cages and worn or pitted races (see illustration 5.18).
● A ball bearing can be checked for wear by listening to it when spun. Apply a film of light oil to the bearing and hold it close to the ear - hold the outer race with one hand and spin the

5.18 Example of ball journal bearing with damaged balls and cages

5.19 Hold outer race and listen to inner race when spun

inner race with the other hand (see illustration 5.19). The bearing should be almost silent when spun; if it grates or rattles it is worn.

6 Oil seals

Oil seal removal and installation

● Oil seals should be renewed every time a component is dismantled. This is because the seal lips will become set to the sealing surface and will not necessarily reseal.
● Oil seals can be prised out of position using a large flat-bladed screwdriver (see illustration 6.1). In the case of crankcase seals, check first that the seal is not lipped on the inside, preventing its removal with the crankcases joined.

6.1 Prise out oil seals with a large flat-bladed screwdriver

● New seals are usually installed with their marked face (containing the seal reference code) outwards and the spring side towards the fluid being retained. In certain cases, such as a two-stroke engine crankshaft seal, a double lipped seal may be used due to there being fluid or gas on each side of the joint.

● Use a bearing driver or socket which bears only on the outer hard edge of the seal to install it in the casing - tapping on the inner edge will damage the sealing lip.

Oil seal types and markings

● Oil seals are usually of the single-lipped type. Double-lipped seals are found where a liquid or gas is on both sides of the joint.
● Oil seals can harden and lose their sealing ability if the motorcycle has been in storage for a long period - renewal is the only solution.
● Oil seal manufacturers also conform to the ISO markings for seal size - these are moulded into the outer face of the seal (see illustration 6.2).

6.2 These oil seal markings indicate inside diameter, outside diameter and seal thickness

7 Gaskets and sealants

Types of gasket and sealant

● Gaskets are used to seal the mating surfaces between components and keep lubricants, fluids, vacuum or pressure contained within the assembly. Aluminium gaskets are sometimes found at the cylinder joints, but most gaskets are paper-based. If the mating surfaces of the components being joined are undamaged the gasket can be installed dry, although a dab of sealant or grease will be useful to hold it in place during assembly.
● RTV (Room Temperature Vulcanising) silicone rubber sealants cure when exposed to moisture in the atmosphere. These sealants are good at filling pits or irregular gasket faces, but will tend to be forced out of the joint under very high torque. They can be used to replace a paper gasket, but first make sure that the width of the paper gasket is not essential to the shimming of internal components. RTV sealants should not be used on components containing petrol (gasoline).
● Non-hardening, semi-hardening and hard setting liquid gasket compounds can be used with a gasket or between a metal-to-metal joint. Select the sealant to suit the application: universal non-hardening sealant can be used on virtually all joints; semi-hardening on joint faces which are rough or damaged; hard setting sealant on joints which require a permanent bond and are subjected to high temperature and pressure. **Note:** *Check first if the paper gasket has a bead of sealant*

impregnated in its surface before applying additional sealant.
● When choosing a sealant, make sure it is suitable for the application, particularly if being applied in a high-temperature area or in the vicinity of fuel. Certain manufacturers produce sealants in either clear, silver or black colours to match the finish of the engine. This has a particular application on motorcycles where much of the engine is exposed.
● Do not over-apply sealant. That which is squeezed out on the outside of the joint can be wiped off, whereas an excess of sealant on the inside can break off and clog oilways.

Breaking a sealed joint

● Age, heat, pressure and the use of hard setting sealant can cause two components to stick together so tightly that they are difficult to separate using finger pressure alone. Do not resort to using levers unless there is a pry point provided for this purpose (see illustration 7.1) or else the gasket surfaces will be damaged.
● Use a soft-faced hammer (see illustration 7.2) or a wood block and conventional hammer to strike the component near the mating surface. Avoid hammering against cast extremities since they may break off. If this method fails, try using a wood wedge between the two components.

Caution: If the joint will not separate, double-check that you have removed all the fasteners.

7.1 If a pry point is provided, apply gently pressure with a flat-bladed screwdriver

7.2 Tap around the joint with a soft-faced mallet if necessary - don't strike cooling fins

Removal of old gasket and sealant

● Paper gaskets will most likely come away complete, leaving only a few traces stuck

Most components have one or two hollow locating dowels between the two gasket faces. If a dowel cannot be removed, do not resort to gripping it with pliers - it will almost certainly be distorted. Install a close-fitting socket or Phillips screwdriver into the dowel and then grip the outer edge of the dowel to free it.

on the sealing faces of the components. It is imperative that all traces are removed to ensure correct sealing of the new gasket.
● Very carefully scrape all traces of gasket away making sure that the sealing surfaces are not gouged or scored by the scraper (see illustrations 7.3, 7.4 and 7.5). Stubborn deposits can be removed by spraying with an aerosol gasket remover. Final preparation of

7.3 Paper gaskets can be scraped off with a gasket scraper tool . . .

7.4 . . . a knife blade . . .

7.5 . . . or a household scraper

REF•18 **Tools and Workshop Tips**

7.6 Fine abrasive paper is wrapped around a flat file to clean up the gasket face

7.7 A kitchen scourer can be used on stubborn deposits

the gasket surface can be made with very fine abrasive paper or a plastic kitchen scourer (see illustrations 7.6 and 7.7).

● Old sealant can be scraped or peeled off components, depending on the type originally used. Note that gasket removal compounds are available to avoid scraping the components clean; make sure the gasket remover suits the type of sealant used.

8 Chains

Breaking and joining final drive chains

● Drive chains for all but small bikes are continuous and do not have a clip-type connecting link. The chain must be broken using a chain breaker tool and the new chain securely riveted together using a new soft rivet-type link. Never use a clip-type connecting link instead of a rivet-type link, except in an emergency. Various chain breaking and riveting tools are available, either as separate tools or combined as illustrated in the accompanying photographs - read the instructions supplied with the tool carefully.

⚠ **Warning: The need to rivet the new link pins correctly cannot be overstressed - loss of control of the motorcycle is very likely to result if the chain breaks in use.**

● Rotate the chain and look for the soft link. The soft link pins look like they have been

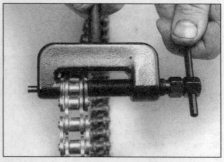

8.1 Tighten the chain breaker to push the pin out of the link . . .

8.2 . . . withdraw the pin, remove the tool . . .

8.3 . . . and separate the chain link

deeply centre-punched instead of peened over like all the other pins (see illustration 8.9) and its sideplate may be a different colour. Position the soft link midway between the sprockets and assemble the chain breaker tool over one of the soft link pins (see illustration 8.1). Operate the tool to push the pin out through the chain (see illustration 8.2). On an O-ring chain, remove the O-rings (see illustration 8.3). Carry out the same procedure on the other soft link pin.

> *Caution: Certain soft link pins (particularly on the larger chains) may require their ends to be filed or ground off before they can be pressed out using the tool.*

● Check that you have the correct size and strength (standard or heavy duty) new soft link - do not reuse the old link. Look for the size marking on the chain sideplates (see illustration 8.10).

● Position the chain ends so that they are engaged over the rear sprocket. On an O-ring

8.4 Insert the new soft link, with O-rings, through the chain ends . . .

8.5 . . . install the O-rings over the pin ends . . .

8.6 . . . followed by the sideplate

chain, install a new O-ring over each pin of the link and insert the link through the two chain ends (see illustration 8.4). Install a new O-ring over the end of each pin, followed by the sideplate (with the chain manufacturer's marking facing outwards) (see illustrations 8.5 and 8.6). On an unsealed chain, insert the link through the two chain ends, then install the sideplate with the chain manufacturer's marking facing outwards.

● Note that it may not be possible to install the sideplate using finger pressure alone. If using a joining tool, assemble it so that the plates of the tool clamp the link and press the sideplate over the pins (see illustration 8.7). Otherwise, use two small sockets placed over

8.7 Push the sideplate into position using a clamp

8.8 Assemble the chain riveting tool over one pin at a time and tighten it fully

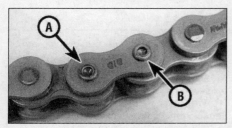

8.9 Pin end correctly riveted (A), pin end unriveted (B)

the rivet ends and two pieces of the wood between a G-clamp. Operate the clamp to press the sideplate over the pins.

● Assemble the joining tool over one pin (following the maker's instructions) and tighten the tool down to spread the pin end securely **(see illustrations 8.8 and 8.9)**. Do the same on the other pin.

> **Warning: Check that the pin ends are secure and that there is no danger of the sideplate coming loose. If the pin ends are cracked the soft link must be renewed.**

Final drive chain sizing

● Chains are sized using a three digit number, followed by a suffix to denote the chain type **(see illustration 8.10)**. Chain type is either standard or heavy duty (thicker sideplates), and also unsealed or O-ring/X-ring type.

● The first digit of the number relates to the pitch of the chain, ie the distance from the centre of one pin to the centre of the next pin **(see illustration 8.11)**. Pitch is expressed in eighths of an inch, as follows:

8.10 Typical chain size and type marking

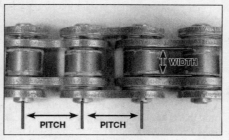

8.11 Chain dimensions

| Sizes commencing with a 4 (eg 428) have a pitch of 1/2 inch (12.7 mm) |
| Sizes commencing with a 5 (eg 520) have a pitch of 5/8 inch (15.9 mm) |
| Sizes commencing with a 6 (eg 630) have a pitch of 3/4 inch (19.1 mm) |

● The second and third digits of the chain size relate to the width of the rollers, again in imperial units, eg the 525 shown has 5/16 inch (7.94 mm) rollers **(see illustration 8.11)**.

9 Hoses

Clamping to prevent flow

● Small-bore flexible hoses can be clamped to prevent fluid flow whilst a component is worked on. Whichever method is used, ensure that the hose material is not permanently distorted or damaged by the clamp.

a) A brake hose clamp available from auto accessory shops *(see illustration 9.1)*.

b) A wingnut type hose clamp *(see illustration 9.2)*.

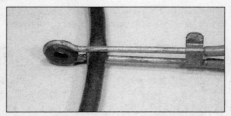

9.1 Hoses can be clamped with an automotive brake hose clamp . . .

9.2 . . . a wingnut type hose clamp . . .

c) Two sockets placed each side of the hose and held with straight-jawed self-locking grips *(see illustration 9.3)*.

d) Thick card each side of the hose held between straight-jawed self-locking grips *(see illustration 9.4)*.

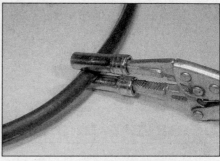

9.3 . . . two sockets and a pair of self-locking grips . . .

9.4 . . . or thick card and self-locking grips

Freeing and fitting hoses

● Always make sure the hose clamp is moved well clear of the hose end. Grip the hose with your hand and rotate it whilst pulling it off the union. If the hose has hardened due to age and will not move, slit it with a sharp knife and peel its ends off the union **(see illustration 9.5)**.

● Resist the temptation to use grease or soap on the unions to aid installation; although it helps the hose slip over the union it will equally aid the escape of fluid from the joint. It is preferable to soften the hose ends in hot water and wet the inside surface of the hose with water or a fluid which will evaporate.

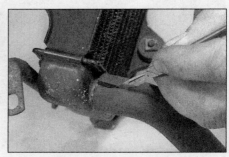

9.5 Cutting a coolant hose free with a sharp knife

Introduction

In less time than it takes to read this introduction, a thief could steal your motorcycle. Returning only to find your bike has gone is one of the worst feelings in the world. Even if the motorcycle is insured against theft, once you've got over the initial shock, you will have the inconvenience of dealing with the police and your insurance company.

The motorcycle is an easy target for the professional thief and the joyrider alike and the official figures on motorcycle theft make for depressing reading; on average a motor-cycle is stolen every 16 minutes in the UK!

Motorcycle thefts fall into two categories, those stolen 'to order' and those taken by opportunists. The thief stealing to order will be on the look out for a specific make and model and will go to extraordinary lengths to obtain that motorcycle. The opportunist thief on the other hand will look for easy targets which can be stolen with the minimum of effort and risk.

Whilst it is never going to be possible to make your machine 100% secure, it is estimated that around half of all stolen motorcycles are taken by opportunist thieves. Remember that the opportunist thief is always on the look out for the easy option: if there are two similar motorcycles parked side-by-side, they will target the one with the lowest level of security. By taking a few precautions, you can reduce the chances of your motorcycle being stolen.

Security equipment

There are many specialised motorcycle security devices available and the following text summarises their applications and their good and bad points.

Once you have decided on the type of security equipment which best suits your needs, we recommended that you read one of the many equipment tests regularly carried out by the motorcycle press. These tests compare the products from all the major manufacturers and give impartial ratings on their effectiveness, value-for-money and ease of use.

No one item of security equipment can provide complete protection. It is highly recommended that two or more of the items described below are combined to increase the security of your motorcycle (a lock and chain plus an alarm system is just about ideal). The more security measures fitted to the bike, the less likely it is to be stolen.

will be supplied with a carry bag which can be strapped to the pillion seat.

● Heavy-duty chains and locks are an excellent security measure **(see illustration 1)**. Whenever the motorcycle is parked, use the lock and chain to secure the machine to a solid, immovable object such as a post or railings. This will prevent the machine from being ridden away or being lifted into the back of a van.

● When fitting the chain, always ensure the chain is routed around the motorcycle frame or swingarm **(see illustrations 2 and 3)**. Never merely pass the chain around one of the wheel rims; a thief may unbolt the wheel and lift the rest of the machine into a van, leaving you with just the wheel! Try to avoid having excess chain free, thus making it difficult to use cutting tools, and keep the chain and lock off the ground to prevent thieves attacking it with a cold chisel. Position the lock so that its lock barrel is facing downwards; this will make it harder for the thief to attack the lock mechanism.

Ensure the lock and chain you buy is of good quality and long enough to shackle your bike to a solid object

Lock and chain

Pros: *Very flexible to use; can be used to secure the motorcycle to almost any immovable object. On some locks and chains, the lock can be used on its own as a disc lock (see below).*

Cons: *Can be very heavy and awkward to carry on the motorcycle, although some types*

Pass the chain through the bike's frame, rather than just through a wheel . . .

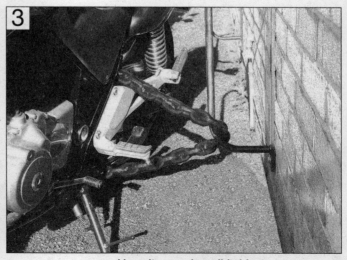

. . . and loop it around a solid object

U-locks

Pros: *Highly effective deterrent which can be used to secure the bike to a post or railings. Most U-locks come with a carrier which allows the lock to be easily carried on the bike.*

Cons: *Not as flexible to use as a lock and chain.*

● These are solid locks which are similar in use to a lock and chain. U-locks are lighter than a lock and chain but not so flexible to use. The length and shape of the lock shackle limit the objects to which the bike can be secured **(see illustration 4)**.

Disc locks

Pros: *Small, light and very easy to carry; most can be stored underneath the seat.*

Cons: *Does not prevent the motorcycle being lifted into a van. Can be very embarrassing if*

A typical disc lock attached through one of the holes in the disc

U-locks can be used to secure the bike to a solid object – ensure you purchase one which is long enough

you forget to remove the lock before attempting to ride off!

● Disc locks are designed to be attached to the front brake disc. The lock passes through one of the holes in the disc and prevents the wheel rotating by jamming against the fork/ brake caliper **(see illustration 5)**. Some are equipped with an alarm siren which sounds if the disc lock is moved; this not only acts as a theft deterrent but also as a handy reminder if you try to move the bike with the lock still fitted.

● Combining the disc lock with a length of cable which can be looped around a post or railings provides an additional measure of security **(see illustration 6)**.

Alarms and immobilisers

Pros: *Once installed it is completely hassle-free to use. If the system is 'Thatcham' or 'Sold Secure-approved', insurance companies may give you a discount.*

Cons: *Can be expensive to buy and complex to install. No system will prevent the motorcycle from being lifted into a van and taken away.*

● Electronic alarms and immobilisers are available to suit a variety of budgets. There are three different types of system available: pure alarms, pure immobilisers, and the more expensive systems which are combined alarm/immobilisers **(see illustration 7)**.
● An alarm system is designed to emit an audible warning if the motorcycle is being tampered with.
● An immobiliser prevents the motorcycle being started and ridden away by disabling its electrical systems.
● When purchasing an alarm/immobiliser system, check the cost of installing the system unless you are able to do it yourself. If the motorcycle is not used regularly, another consideration is the current drain of the system. All alarm/immobiliser systems are powered by the motorcycle's battery; purchasing a system with a very low current drain could prevent the battery losing its charge whilst the motorcycle is not being used.

A disc lock combined with a security cable provides additional protection

A typical alarm/immobiliser system

Indelible markings can be applied to most areas of the bike – always apply the manufacturer's sticker to warn off thieves

Chemically-etched code numbers can be applied to main body panels . . .

. . . again, always ensure that the kit manufacturer's sticker is applied in a prominent position

Security marking kits

Pros: *Very cheap and effective deterrent. Many insurance companies will give you a discount on your insurance premium if a recognised security marking kit is used on your motorcycle.*

Cons: *Does not prevent the motorcycle being stolen by joyriders.*

● There are many different types of security marking kits available. The idea is to mark as many parts of the motorcycle as possible with a unique security number **(see illustrations 8, 9 and 10)**. A form will be included with the kit to register your personal details and those of the motorcycle with the kit manufacturer. This register is made available to the police to help them trace the rightful owner of any motorcycle or components which they recover should all other forms of identification have been removed. Always apply the warning stickers provided with the kit to deter thieves.

Ground anchors, wheel clamps and security posts

Pros: *An excellent form of security which will deter all but the most determined of thieves.*

Cons: *Awkward to install and can be expensive.*

● Whilst the motorcycle is at home, it is a good idea to attach it securely to the floor or a solid wall, even if it is kept in a securely locked garage. Various types of ground anchors, security posts and wheel clamps are available for this purpose **(see illustration 11)**. These security devices are either bolted to a solid concrete or brick structure or can be cemented into the ground.

Permanent ground anchors provide an excellent level of security when the bike is at home

Security at home

A high percentage of motorcycle thefts are from the owner's home. Here are some things to consider whenever your motorcycle is at home:
● Where possible, always keep the motorcycle in a securely locked garage. Never rely solely on the standard lock on the garage door, these are usual hopelessly inadequate. Fit an additional locking mechanism to the door and consider having the garage alarmed. A security light, activated by a movement sensor, is also a good investment.

● Always secure the motorcycle to the ground or a wall, even if it is inside a securely locked garage.
● Do not regularly leave the motorcycle outside your home, try to keep it out of sight wherever possible. If a garage is not available, fit a motorcycle cover over the bike to disguise its true identity.
● It is not uncommon for thieves to follow a motorcyclist home to find out where the bike is kept. They will then return at a later date. Be aware of this whenever you are returning

home on your motorcycle. If you suspect you are being followed, do not return home, instead ride to a garage or shop and stop as a precaution.
● When selling a motorcycle, do not provide your home address or the location where the bike is normally kept. Arrange to meet the buyer at a location away from your home. Thieves have been known to pose as potential buyers to find out where motorcycles are kept and then return later to steal them.

Security away from the home

As well as fitting security equipment to your motorcycle here are a few general rules to follow whenever you park your motorcycle.
● Park in a busy, public place.
● Use car parks which incorporate security features, such as CCTV.

● At night, park in a well-lit area, preferably directly underneath a street light.
● Engage the steering lock.
● Secure the motorcycle to a solid, immovable object such as a post or railings with an additional lock. If this is not possible,

secure the bike to a friend's motorcycle. Some public parking places provide security loops for motorcycles.
● Never leave your helmet or luggage attached to the motorcycle. Take them with you at all times.

Lubricants and fluids

A wide range of lubricants, fluids and cleaning agents is available for motor-cycles. This is a guide as to what is available, its applications and properties.

Four-stroke engine oil

● Engine oil is without doubt the most important component of any four-stroke engine. Modern motorcycle engines place a lot of demands on their oil and choosing the right type is essential. Using an unsuitable oil will lead to an increased rate of engine wear and could result in serious engine damage. Before purchasing oil, always check the recommended oil specification given by the manufacturer. The manufacturer will state a recommended 'type or classification' and also a specific 'viscosity' range for engine oil.

● The oil 'type or classification' is identified by its API (American Petroleum Institute) rating. The API rating will be in the form of two letters, e.g. SG. The S identifies the oil as being suitable for use in a petrol (gasoline) engine (S stands for spark ignition) and the second letter, ranging from A to J, identifies the oil's performance rating. The later this letter, the higher the specification of the oil; for example API SG oil exceeds the requirements of API SF oil. **Note:** *On some oils there may also be a second rating consisting of another two letters, the first letter being C, e.g. API SF/CD. This rating indicates the oil is also suitable for use in a diesel engines (the C stands for compression ignition) and is thus of no relevance for motorcycle use.*

● The 'viscosity' of the oil is identified by its SAE (Society of Automotive Engineers) rating. All modern engines require multigrade oils and the SAE rating will consist of two numbers, the first followed by a W, e.g. 10W/40. The first number indicates the viscosity rating of the oil at low temperatures (W stands for winter – tested at –20ºC) and the second number represents the viscosity of the oil at high temperatures (tested at 100ºC). The lower the number, the thinner the oil. For example an oil with an SAE 10W/40 rating will give better cold starting and running than an SAE 15W/40 oil.

● As well as ensuring the 'type' and 'viscosity' of the oil match the recommendations, another consideration to make when buying engine oil is whether to purchase a standard mineral-based oil, a semi-synthetic oil (also known as a synthetic blend or synthetic-based oil) or a fully-synthetic oil. Although all oils will have a similar rating and viscosity, their cost will vary considerably; mineral-based oils are the cheapest, the fully-synthetic oils the most expensive with the semi-synthetic oils falling somewhere in-between. This decision is very much up to the owner, but it should be noted that modern synthetic oils have far better lubricating and cleaning qualities than traditional mineral-based oils and tend to retain these properties for far longer. Bearing in mind the operating conditions inside a modern, high-revving motorcycle engine it is highly recommended that a fully synthetic oil is used. The extra expense at each service could save you money in the long term by preventing premature engine wear.

● As a final note always ensure that the oil is specifically designed for use in motorcycle engines. Engine oils designed primarily for use in car engines sometimes contain additives or friction modifiers which could cause clutch slip on a motorcycle fitted with a wet-clutch.

Two-stroke engine oil

● Modern two-stroke engines, with their high power outputs, place high demands on their oil. If engine seizure is to be avoided it is essential that a high-quality oil is used. Two-stroke oils differ hugely from four-stroke oils. The oil lubricates only the crankshaft and piston(s) (the transmission has its own lubricating oil) and is used on a total-loss basis where it is burnt completely during the combustion process.

● The Japanese have recently introduced a classification system for two-stroke oils, the JASO rating. This rating is in the form of two letters, either FA, FB or FC – FA is the lowest classification and FC the highest. Ensure the oil being used meets or exceeds the recommended rating specified by the manufacturer.

● As well as ensuring the oil rating matches the recommendation, another consideration to make when buying engine oil is whether to purchase a standard mineral-based oil, a semi-synthetic oil (also known as a synthetic blend or synthetic-based oil) or a fully-synthetic oil. The cost of each type of oil varies considerably; mineral-based oils are the cheapest, the fully-synthetic oils the most expensive with the semi-synthetic oils falling somewhere in-between. This decision is very much up to the owner, but it should be noted that modern synthetic oils have far better lubricating properties and burn cleaner than traditional mineral-based oils. It is therefore recommended that a fully synthetic oil is used. The extra expense could save you money in the long term by preventing premature engine wear, engine performance will be improved, carbon deposits and exhaust smoke will be reduced.

● Always ensure that the oil is specifically designed for use in an injector system. Many high quality two-stroke oils are designed for competition use and need to be pre-mixed with fuel. These oils are of a much higher viscosity and are not designed to flow through the injector pumps used on road-going two-stroke motorcycles.

Transmission (gear) oil

● On a two-stroke engine, the transmission and clutch are lubricated by their own separate oil bath which must be changed in accordance with the Maintenance Schedule.
● Although the engine and transmission units of most four-strokes use a common lubrication supply, there are some exceptions where the engine and gearbox have separate oil reservoirs and a dry clutch is used.
● Motorcycle manufacturers will either recommend a monograde transmission oil or a four-stroke multigrade engine oil to lubricate the transmission.
● Transmission oils, or gear oils as they are often called, are designed specifically for use in transmission systems. The viscosity of these oils is represented by an SAE number, but the scale of measurement applied is different to that used to grade engine oils. As a rough guide a SAE90 gear oil will be of the same viscosity as an SAE50 engine oil.

Shaft drive oil

● On models equipped with shaft final drive, the shaft drive gears are will have their own oil supply. The manufacturer will state a recommended 'type or classification' and also a specific 'viscosity' range in the same manner as for four-stroke engine oil.
● Gear oil classification is given by the number which follows the API GL (GL standing for gear lubricant) rating, the higher the number, the higher the specification of the oil, e.g. API GL5 oil is a higher specification than API GL4 oil. Ensure the oil meets or

exceeds the classification specified and is of the correct viscosity. The viscosity of gear oils is also represented by an SAE number but the scale of measurement used is different to that used to grade engine oils. As a rough guide an SAE90 gear oil will be of the same viscosity as an SAE50 engine oil.
● If the use of an EP (Extreme Pressure) gear oil is specified, ensure the oil purchased is suitable.

Fork oil and suspension fluid

● Conventional telescopic front forks are hydraulic and require fork oil to work. To ensure the forks function correctly, the fork oil must be changed in accordance with the Maintenance Schedule.
● Fork oil is available in a variety of viscosities, identified by their SAE rating; fork oil ratings vary from light (SAE 5) to heavy (SAE 30). When purchasing fork oil, ensure the viscosity rating matches that specified by the manufacturer.
● Some lubricant manufacturers also produce a range of high-quality suspension fluids which are very similar to fork oil but are designed mainly for competition use. These fluids may have a different viscosity rating system which is not to be confused with the SAE rating of normal fork oil. Refer to the manufacturer's instructions if in any doubt.

Brake and clutch fluid

● All disc brake systems and some clutch systems are hydraulically operated. To ensure correct operation, the hydraulic fluid must be changed in accordance with the Maintenance Schedule.
● Brake and clutch fluid is classified by its DOT rating with most motorcycle manufacturers specifying DOT 3 or 4 fluid. Both fluid types are glycol-based and

can be mixed together without adverse effect; DOT 4 fluid exceeds the requirements of DOT 3

fluid. Although it is safe to use DOT 4 fluid in a system designed for use with DOT 3 fluid, never use DOT 3 fluid in a system which specifies the use of DOT 4 as this will adversely affect the system's performance. The type required for the system will be marked on the fluid reservoir cap.
● Some manufacturers also produce a DOT 5 hydraulic fluid. DOT 5 hydraulic fluid is silicone-based and is not compatible with the glycol-based DOT 3 and 4 fluids. Never mix DOT 5 fluid with DOT 3 or 4 fluid as this will seriously affect the performance of the hydraulic system.

Coolant/antifreeze

● When purchasing coolant/antifreeze, always ensure it is suitable for use in an aluminium engine and contains corrosion inhibitors to prevent possible blockages of the internal coolant passages of the system. As a general rule, most coolants are designed to be used neat and should not be diluted whereas antifreeze can be mixed with distilled water to provide

a coolant solution of the required strength. Refer to the manufacturer's instructions on the bottle.
● Ensure the coolant is changed in accordance with the Maintenance Schedule.

Chain lube

● Chain lube is an aerosol-type spray lubricant specifically designed for use on motorcycle final drive chains. Chain lube has two functions, to minimise friction between the final drive chain and sprockets and to prevent corrosion of the chain. Regular use of a good-quality chain lube will extend the life of the drive chain and sprockets and thus maximise the power being transmitted from the transmission to the rear wheel.
● When using chain lube, always allow some time for the solvents in the lube to evaporate before riding the motorcycle. This will minimise the amount of lube which will

'fling' off from the chain when the motorcycle is used. If the motorcycle is equipped with an 'O-ring' chain, ensure the chain lube is labelled as being suitable for use on 'O-ring' chains.

Degreasers and solvents

● There are many different types of solvents and degreasers available to remove the grime and grease which accumulate around the motorcycle during normal use. Degreasers and solvents are usually available as an aerosol-type spray or as a liquid which you apply with a brush. Always closely follow the manufacturer's instructions and wear eye protection during use. Be aware that many solvents are flammable and may give off noxious fumes; take adequate precautions when using them (see Safety First!).

● For general cleaning, use one of the many solvents or degreasers available from most motorcycle accessory shops. These solvents are usually applied then left for a certain time before being washed off with water.

Brake cleaner is a solvent specifically designed to remove all traces of oil, grease and dust from braking system components. Brake cleaner is designed to evaporate quickly and leaves behind no residue.

Carburettor cleaner is an aerosol-type solvent specifically designed to clear carburettor blockages and break down the hard deposits and gum often found inside carburettors during overhaul.

Contact cleaner is an aerosol-type solvent designed for cleaning electrical components. The cleaner will remove all traces of oil and dirt from components such as switch contacts or fouled spark plugs and then dry, leaving behind no residue.

Gasket remover is an aerosol-type solvent designed for removing stubborn gaskets from engine components during overhaul. Gasket remover will minimise the amount of scraping required to remove the gasket and therefore reduce the risk of damage to the mating surface.

Spray lubricants

● Aerosol-based spray lubricants are widely available and are excellent for lubricating lever pivots and exposed cables and switches. Try to use a lubricant which is of the dry-film type as the fluid evaporates, leaving behind a dry-film of lubricant. Lubricants which leave behind an oily residue will attract dust and dirt which will increase the rate of wear of the cable/lever.

● Most lubricants also act as a moisture dispersant and a penetrating fluid. This means they can also be used to 'dry out' electrical components such as wiring connectors or switches as well as helping to free seized fasteners.

Greases

● Grease is used to lubricate many of the pivot-points. A good-quality multi-purpose grease is suitable for most applications but some manufacturers will specify the use of specialist greases for use on components such as swingarm and suspension linkage bushes. These specialist greases can be purchased from most motorcycle (or car) accessory shops; commonly specified types include molybdenum disulphide grease, lithium-based grease, graphite-based grease, silicone-based grease and high-temperature copper-based grease.

Gasket sealing compounds

● Gasket sealing compounds can be used in conjunction with gaskets, to improve their sealing capabilities, or on their own to seal metal-to-metal joints. Depending on their type, sealing compounds either set hard or stay relatively soft and pliable.

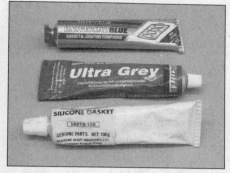

● When purchasing a gasket sealing compound, ensure that it is designed specifically for use on an internal combustion engine. General multi-purpose sealants available from DIY stores may appear visibly similar but they are not designed to withstand the extreme heat or contact with fuel and oil encountered when used on an engine (see 'Tools and Workshop Tips' for further information).

Thread locking compound

● Thread locking compounds are used to secure certain threaded fasteners in position to prevent them from loosening due to vibration. Thread locking compounds can be purchased from most motorcycle (and car) accessory shops. Ensure the threads of the both components are completely clean and dry before sparingly applying the locking compound (see 'Tools and Workshop Tips' for further information).

Fuel additives

● Fuel additives which protect and clean the fuel system components are widely available. These additives are designed to remove all traces of deposits that build up on the carburettors/injectors and prevent wear, helping the fuel system to operate more efficiently. If a fuel additive is being used, check that it is suitable for use with your motorcycle, especially if your motorcycle is equipped with a catalytic converter.

● Octane boosters are also available. These additives are designed to improve the performance of highly-tuned engines being run on normal pump-fuel and are of no real use on standard motorcycles.

Conversion factors

Length (distance)

Inches (in)	x 25.4	= Millimetres (mm)	x 0.0394	=	Inches (in)
Feet (ft)	x 0.305	= Metres (m)	x 3.281	=	Feet (ft)
Miles	x 1.609	= Kilometres (km)	x 0.621	=	Miles

Volume (capacity)

Cubic inches (cu in; in³)	x 16.387	= Cubic centimetres (cc; cm³)	x 0.061	Cubic inches (cu in; in³)
Imperial pints (Imp pt)	x 0.568	= Litres (l)	x 1.76	Imperial pints (Imp pt)
Imperial quarts (Imp qt)	x 1.137	= Litres (l)	x 0.88	Imperial quarts (Imp qt)
Imperial quarts (Imp qt)	x 1.201	= US quarts (US qt)	x 0.833	Imperial quarts (Imp qt)
US quarts (US qt)	x 0.946	= Litres (l)	x 1.057	US quarts (US qt)
Imperial gallons (Imp gal)	x 4.546	= Litres (l)	x 0.22	Imperial gallons (Imp gal)
Imperial gallons (Imp gal)	x 1.201	= US gallons (US gal)	x 0.833	Imperial gallons (Imp gal)
US gallons (US gal)	x 3.785	= Litres (l)	x 0.264	US gallons (US gal)

Mass (weight)

Ounces (oz)	x 28.35	= Grams (g)	x 0.035	= Ounces (oz)
Pounds (lb)	x 0.454	= Kilograms (kg)	x 2.205	= Pounds (lb)

Force

Ounces-force (ozf; oz)	x 0.278	= Newtons (N)	x 3.6	= Ounces-force (ozf; oz)
Pounds-force (lbf; lb)	x 4.448	= Newtons (N)	x 0.225	= Pounds-force (lbf; lb)
Newtons (N)	x 0.1	= Kilograms-force (kgf; kg)	x 9.81	= Newtons (N)

Pressure

Pounds-force per square inch (psi; lbf/in²; lb/in²)	x 0.070	= Kilograms-force per square centimetre (kgf/cm²; kg/cm²)	x 14.223	= Pounds-force per square inch (psi; lbf/in²; lb/in²)
Pounds-force per square inch (psi; lbf/in²; lb/in²)	x 0.068	= Atmospheres (atm)	x 14.696	= Pounds-force per square inch (psi; lbf/in²; lb/in²)
Pounds-force per square inch (psi; lbf/in²; lb/in²)	x 0.069	= Bars	x 14.5	= Pounds-force per square inch (psi; lbf/in²; lb/in²)
Pounds-force per square inch (psi; lbf/in²; lb/in²)	x 6.895	= Kilopascals (kPa)	x 0.145	= Pounds-force per square inch (psi; lbf/in²; lb/in²)
Kilopascals (kPa)	x 0.01	= Kilograms-force per square centimetre (kgf/cm²; kg/cm²)	x 98.1	= Kilopascals (kPa)
Millibar (mbar)	x 100	= Pascals (Pa)	x 0.01	= Millibar (mbar)
Millibar (mbar)	x 0.0145	= Pounds-force per square inch (psi; lbf/in²; lb/in²)	x 68.947	= Millibar (mbar)
Millibar (mbar)	x 0.75	= Millimetres of mercury (mmHg)	x 1.333	= Millibar (mbar)
Millibar (mbar)	x 0.401	= Inches of water (inH₂O)	x 2.491	= Millibar (mbar)
Millimetres of mercury (mmHg)	x 0.535	= Inches of water (inH₂O)	x 1.868	= Millimetres of mercury (mmHg)
Inches of water (inH₂O)	x 0.036	= Pounds-force per square inch (psi; lbf/in²; lb/in²)	x 27.68	= Inches of water (inH₂O)

Torque (moment of force)

Pounds-force inches (lbf in; lb in)	x 1.152	= Kilograms-force centimetre (kgf cm; kg cm)	x 0.868	= Pounds-force inches (lbf in; lb in)
Pounds-force inches (lbf in; lb in)	x 0.113	= Newton metres (Nm)	x 8.85	= Pounds-force inches (lbf in; lb in)
Pounds-force inches (lbf in; lb in)	x 0.083	= Pounds-force feet (lbf ft; lb ft)	x 12	= Pounds-force inches (lbf in; lb in)
Pounds-force feet (lbf ft; lb ft)	x 0.138	= Kilograms-force metres (kgf m; kg m)	x 7.233	= Pounds-force feet (lbf ft; lb ft)
Pounds-force feet (lbf ft; lb ft)	x 1.356	= Newton metres (Nm)	x 0.738	= Pounds-force feet (lbf ft; lb ft)
Newton metres (Nm)	x 0.102	= Kilograms-force metres (kgf m; kg m)	x 9.804	= Newton metres (Nm)

Power

Horsepower (hp)	x 745.7	= Watts (W)	x 0.0013	= Horsepower (hp)

Velocity (speed)

Miles per hour (miles/hr; mph)	x 1.609	= Kilometres per hour (km/hr; kph)	x 0.621	= Miles per hour (miles/hr; mph)

Fuel consumption*

Miles per gallon, Imperial (mpg)	x 0.354	= Kilometres per litre (km/l)	x 2.825	= Miles per gallon, Imperial (mpg)
Miles per gallon, US (mpg)	x 0.425	= Kilometres per litre (km/l)	x 2.352	= Miles per gallon, US (mpg)

Temperature

Degrees Fahrenheit = (°C x 1.8) + 32   Degrees Celsius (Degrees Centigrade; °C) = (°F - 32) x 0.56

It is common practice to convert from miles per gallon (mpg) to litres/100 kilometres (l/100km), where mpg x l/100 km = 282

About the MOT Test

In the UK, all vehicles more than three years old are subject to an annual test to ensure that they meet minimum safety requirements. A current test certificate must be issued before a machine can be used on public roads, and is required before a road fund licence can be issued. Riding without a current test certificate will also invalidate your insurance.

For most owners, the MOT test is an annual cause for anxiety, and this is largely due to owners not being sure what needs to be checked prior to submitting the motorcycle for testing. The simple answer is that a fully roadworthy motorcycle will have no difficulty in passing the test.

This is a guide to getting your motorcycle through the MOT test. Obviously it will not be possible to examine the motorcycle to the same standard as the professional MOT tester, particularly in view of the equipment required for some of the checks. However, working through the following procedures will enable you to identify any problem areas before submitting the motorcycle for the test.

It has only been possible to summarise the test requirements here, based on the regulations in force at the time of printing. Test standards are becoming increasingly stringent, although there are some exemptions for older vehicles. More information about the MOT test can be obtained from the TSO publications, *How Safe is your Motorcycle* and *The MOT Inspection Manual for Motorcycle Testing*.

Many of the checks require that one of the wheels is raised off the ground. If the motorcycle doesn't have a centre stand, note that an auxiliary stand will be required. Additionally, the help of an assistant may prove useful.

Certain exceptions apply to machines under 50 cc, machines without a lighting system, and Classic bikes - if in doubt about any of the requirements listed below seek confirmation from an MOT tester prior to submitting the motorcycle for the test.

Check that the frame number is clearly visible.

Electrical System

Lights, turn signals, horn and reflector

● With the ignition on, check the operation of the following electrical components. **Note:** *The electrical components on certain small-capacity machines are powered by the generator, requiring that the engine is run for this check.*

a) *Headlight and tail light. Check that both illuminate in the low and high beam switch positions.*

b) *Position lights. Check that the front position light (or sidelight) and tail light illuminate in this switch position.*

c) *Turn signals. Check that all flash at the correct rate, and that the warning light(s) function correctly. Check that the turn signal switch works correctly.*

d) *Hazard warning system (where fitted). Check that all four turn signals flash in this switch position.*

e) *Brake stop light. Check that the light comes on when the front and rear brakes are independently applied. Models first used on or after 1st April 1986 must have a brake light switch on each brake.*

f) *Horn. Check that the sound is continuous and of reasonable volume.*

● Check that there is a red reflector on the rear of the machine, either mounted separately or as part of the tail light lens.

● Check the condition of the headlight, tail light and turn signal lenses.

Headlight beam height

● The MOT tester will perform a headlight beam height check using specialised beam setting equipment **(see illustration 1)**. This equipment will not be available to the home mechanic, but if you suspect that the headlight is incorrectly set or may have been maladjusted in the past, you can perform a rough test as follows.

● Position the bike in a straight line facing a brick wall. The bike must be off its stand, upright and with a rider seated. Measure the height from the ground to the centre of the headlight and mark a horizontal line on the wall at this height. Position the motorcycle 3.8 metres from the wall and draw a vertical

Headlight beam height checking equipment

line up the wall central to the centreline of the motorcycle. Switch to dipped beam and check that the beam pattern falls slightly lower than the horizontal line and to the left of the vertical line **(see illustration 2)**.

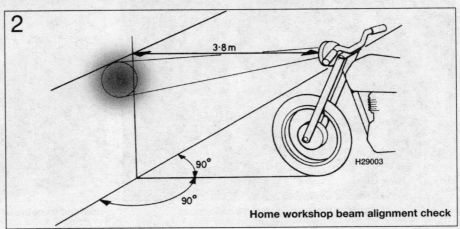

Home workshop beam alignment check

Exhaust System and Final Drive

Exhaust

● Check that the exhaust mountings are secure and that the system does not foul any of the rear suspension components.
● Start the motorcycle. When the revs are increased, check that the exhaust is neither holed nor leaking from any of its joints. On a linked system, check that the collector box is not leaking due to corrosion.

● Note that the exhaust decibel level ("loudness" of the exhaust) is assessed at the discretion of the tester. If the motorcycle was first used on or after 1st January 1985 the silencer must carry the BSAU 193 stamp, or a marking relating to its make and model, or be of OE (original equipment) manufacture. If the silencer is marked NOT FOR ROAD USE, RACING USE ONLY or similar, it will fail the MOT.

Final drive

● On chain or belt drive machines, check that the chain/belt is in good condition and does not have excessive slack. Also check that the sprocket is securely mounted on the rear wheel hub. Check that the chain/belt guard is in place.
● On shaft drive bikes, check for oil leaking from the drive unit and fouling the rear tyre.

Steering and Suspension

Steering

● With the front wheel raised off the ground, rotate the steering from lock to lock. The handlebar or switches must not contact the fuel tank or be close enough to trap the rider's hand. Problems can be caused by damaged lock stops on the lower yoke and frame, or by the fitting of non-standard handlebars.
● When performing the lock to lock check, also ensure that the steering moves freely without drag or notchiness. Steering movement can be impaired by poorly routed cables, or by overtight head bearings or worn bvearings. The tester will perform a check of the steering head bearing lower race by mounting the front wheel on a surface plate, then performing a lock to lock check with the weight of the machine on the lower bearing (see illustration 3).
● Grasp the fork sliders (lower legs) and attempt to push and pull on the forks

3
Front wheel mounted on a surface plate for steering head bearing lower race check

(see illustration 4). Any play in the steering head bearings will be felt. Note that in extreme cases, wear of the front fork bushes can be misinterpreted for head bearing play.
● Check that the handlebars are securely mounted.
● Check that the handlebar grip rubbers are secure. They should by bonded to the bar left end and to the throttle cable pulley on the right end.

Front suspension

● With the motorcycle off the stand, hold the front brake on and pump the front forks up and down (see illustration 5). Check that they are adequately damped.

4
Checking the steering head bearings for freeplay

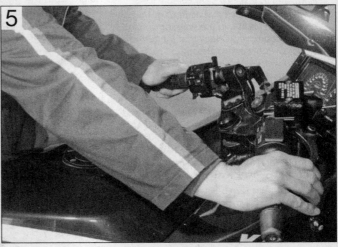

5
Hold the front brake on and pump the front forks up and down to check operation

Inspect the area around the fork dust seal for oil leakage (arrow)

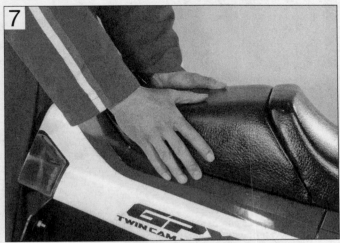

Bounce the rear of the motorcycle to check rear suspension operation

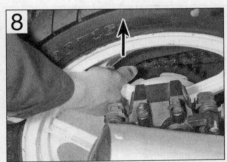

Checking for rear suspension linkage play

● Inspect the area above and around the front fork oil seals (see illustration 6). There should be no sign of oil on the fork tube (stanchion) nor leaking down the slider (lower leg). On models so equipped, check that there is no oil leaking from the anti-dive units.

● On models with swingarm front suspension, check that there is no freeplay in the linkage when moved from side to side.

Rear suspension

● With the motorcycle off the stand and an assistant supporting the motorcycle by its handlebars, bounce the rear suspension (see illustration 7). Check that the suspension components do not foul on any of the cycle parts and check that the shock absorber(s) provide adequate damping.

● Visually inspect the shock absorber(s) and check that there is no sign of oil leakage from its damper. This is somewhat restricted on certain single shock models due to the location of the shock absorber.

● With the rear wheel raised off the ground, grasp the wheel at the highest point and attempt to pull it up (see illustration 8). Any play in the swingarm pivot or suspension linkage bearings will be felt as movement. **Note:** *Do not confuse play with actual suspension movement.* Failure to lubricate suspension linkage bearings can lead to bearing failure (see illustration 9).

● With the rear wheel raised off the ground, grasp the swingarm ends and attempt to move the swingarm from side to side and forwards and backwards - any play indicates wear of the swingarm pivot bearings (see illustration 10).

Worn suspension linkage pivots (arrows) are usually the cause of play in the rear suspension

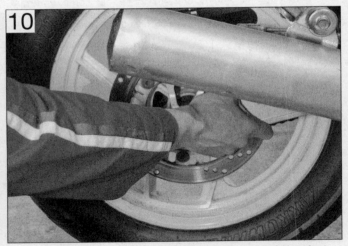

Grasp the swingarm at the ends to check for play in its pivot bearings

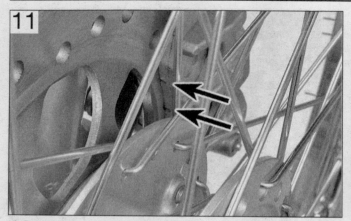

Brake pad wear can usually be viewed without removing the caliper. Most pads have wear indicator grooves (arrowed) and some also have indicator tangs or cut-outs.

On drum brakes, check the angle of the operating lever with the brake fully applied. Most drum brakes have a wear indicator pointer or scale.

Brakes, Wheels and Tyres

Brakes

● With the wheel raised off the ground, apply the brake then free it off, and check that the wheel is about to revolve freely without brake drag.

● On disc brakes, examine the disc itself. Check that it is securely mounted and not cracked.

● On disc brakes, view the pad material through the caliper mouth and check that the pads are not worn down beyond the limit **(see illustration 11)**.

● On drum brakes, check that when the brake is applied the angle between the operating lever and cable or rod is not too great **(see illustration 12)**. Check also that the operating lever doesn't foul any other components.

● On disc brakes, examine the flexible hoses from top to bottom. Have an assistant hold the brake on so that the fluid in the hose is under pressure, and check that there is no sign of fluid leakage, bulges or cracking. If there are any metal brake pipes or unions, check that these are free from corrosion and damage. Where a brake-linked anti-dive system is fitted, check the hoses to the anti-dive in a similar manner.

● Check that the rear brake torque arm is secure and that its fasteners are secured by self-locking nuts or castellated nuts with split-pins or R-pins **(see illustration 13)**.

● On models with ABS, check that the self-check warning light in the instrument panel works.

● The MOT tester will perform a test of the motorcycle's braking efficiency based on a calculation of rider and motorcycle weight. Although this cannot be carried out at home, you can at least ensure that the braking systems are properly maintained. For hydraulic disc brakes, check the fluid level, lever/pedal feel (bleed of air if its spongy) and pad material. For drum brakes, check adjustment, cable or rod operation and shoe lining thickness.

Wheels and tyres

● Check the wheel condition. Cast wheels should be free from cracks and if of the built-up design, all fasteners should be secure. Spoked wheels should be checked for broken, corroded, loose or bent spokes.

● With the wheel raised off the ground, spin the wheel and visually check that the tyre and wheel run true. Check that the tyre does not foul the suspension or mudguards.

● With the wheel raised off the ground, grasp the wheel and attempt to move it about the axle (spindle) **(see illustration 14)**. Any play felt here indicates wheel bearing failure.

Brake torque arm must be properly secured at both ends

Check for wheel bearing play by trying to move the wheel about the axle (spindle)

Checking the tyre tread depth

Tyre direction of rotation arrow can be found on tyre sidewall

Castellated type wheel axle (spindle) nut must be secured by a split pin or R-pin

Two straightedges are used to check wheel alignment

● Check the tyre tread depth, tread condition and sidewall condition (see illustration 15).
● Check the tyre type. Front and rear tyre types must be compatible and be suitable for road use. Tyres marked NOT FOR ROAD USE, COMPETITION USE ONLY or similar, will fail the MOT.

● If the tyre sidewall carries a direction of rotation arrow, this must be pointing in the direction of normal wheel rotation (see illustration 16).
● Check that the wheel axle (spindle) nuts (where applicable) are properly secured. A self-locking nut or castellated nut with a split-pin or R-pin can be used (see illustration 17).
● Wheel alignment is checked with the motorcycle off the stand and a rider seated. With the front wheel pointing straight ahead, two perfectly straight lengths of metal or wood and placed against the sidewalls of both tyres (see illustration 18). The gap each side of the front tyre must be equidistant on both sides. Incorrect wheel alignment may be due to a cocked rear wheel (often as the result of poor chain adjustment) or in extreme cases, a bent frame.

General checks and condition

● Check the security of all major fasteners, bodypanels, seat, fairings (where fitted) and mudguards.

● Check that the rider and pillion footrests, handlebar levers and brake pedal are securely mounted.

● Check for corrosion on the frame or any load-bearing components. If severe, this may affect the structure, particularly under stress.

Sidecars

A motorcycle fitted with a sidecar requires additional checks relating to the stability of the machine and security of attachment and swivel joints, plus specific wheel alignment (toe-in) requirements. Additionally, tyre and lighting requirements differ from conventional motorcycle use. Owners are advised to check MOT test requirements with an official test centre.

Preparing for storage

Before you start

If repairs or an overhaul is needed, see that this is carried out now rather than left until you want to ride the bike again.

Give the bike a good wash and scrub all dirt from its underside. Make sure the bike dries completely before preparing for storage.

Engine

● Remove the spark plug(s) and lubricate the cylinder bores with approximately a teaspoon of motor oil using a spout-type oil can (see illustration 1). Reinstall the spark plug(s). Crank the engine over a couple of times to coat the piston rings and bores with oil. If the bike has a kickstart, use this to turn the engine over. If not, flick the kill switch to the OFF position and crank the engine over on the starter (see illustration 2). If the nature on the ignition system prevents the starter operating with the kill switch in the OFF position, remove

the spark plugs and fit them back in their caps; ensure that the plugs are earthed (grounded) against the cylinder head when the starter is operated (see illustration 3).

⚠ **Warning: It is important that the plugs are earthed (grounded) away from the spark plug holes otherwise there is a risk of atomised fuel from the cylinders igniting.**

HAYNES HINT *On a single cylinder four-stroke engine, you can seal the combustion chamber completely by positioning the piston at TDC on the compression stroke.*

● Drain the carburettor(s) otherwise there is a risk of jets becoming blocked by gum deposits from the fuel (see illustration 4).

● If the bike is going into long-term storage, consider adding a fuel stabiliser to the fuel in the tank. If the tank is drained completely, corrosion of its internal surfaces may occur if left unprotected for a long period. The tank can be treated with a rust preventative especially for this purpose. Alternatively, remove the tank and pour half a litre of motor oil into it, install the filler cap and shake the tank to coat its internals with oil before draining off the excess. The same effect can also be achieved by spraying WD40 or a similar water-dispersant around the inside of the tank via its flexible nozzle.

● Make sure the cooling system contains the correct mix of antifreeze. Antifreeze also contains important corrosion inhibitors.

● The air intakes and exhaust can be sealed off by covering or plugging the openings. Ensure that you do not seal in any condensation; run the engine until it is hot,

Squirt a drop of motor oil into each cylinder

Flick the kill switch to OFF . . .

. . . and ensure that the metal bodies of the plugs (arrows) are earthed against the cylinder head

Connect a hose to the carburettor float chamber drain stub (arrow) and unscrew the drain screw

Exhausts can be sealed off with a plastic bag

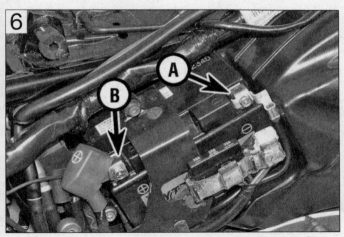

Disconnect the negative lead (A) first, followed by the positive lead (B)

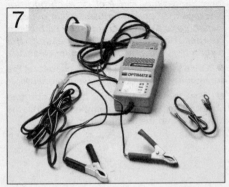

Use a suitable battery charger - this kit also assess battery condition

then switch off and allow to cool. Tape a piece of thick plastic over the silencer end(s) **(see illustration 5)**. Note that some advocate pouring a tablespoon of motor oil into the silencer(s) before sealing them off.

Battery

● Remove it from the bike - in extreme cases of cold the battery may freeze and crack its case **(see illustration 6)**.

● Check the electrolyte level and top up if necessary (conventional refillable batteries). Clean the terminals.
● Store the battery off the motorcycle and away from any sources of fire. Position a wooden block under the battery if it is to sit on the ground.
● Give the battery a trickle charge for a few hours every month **(see illustration 7)**.

Tyres

● Place the bike on its centrestand or an auxiliary stand which will support the motorcycle in an upright position. Position wood blocks under the tyres to keep them off the ground and to provide insulation from damp. If the bike is being put into long-term storage, ideally both tyres should be off the ground; not only will this protect the tyres, but will also ensure that no load is placed on the steering head or wheel bearings.
● Deflate each tyre by 5 to 10 psi, no more or the beads may unseat from the rim, making subsequent inflation difficult on tubeless tyres.

Pivots and controls

● Lubricate all lever, pedal, stand and footrest

pivot points. If grease nipples are fitted to the rear suspension components, apply lubricant to the pivots.
● Lubricate all control cables.

Cycle components

● Apply a wax protectant to all painted and plastic components. Wipe off any excess, but don't polish to a shine. Where fitted, clean the screen with soap and water.
● Coat metal parts with Vaseline (petroleum jelly). When applying this to the fork tubes, do not compress the forks otherwise the seals will rot from contact with the Vaseline.
● Apply a vinyl cleaner to the seat.

Storage conditions

● Aim to store the bike in a shed or garage which does not leak and is free from damp.
● Drape an old blanket or bedspread over the bike to protect it from dust and direct contact with sunlight (which will fade paint). This also hides the bike from prying eyes. Beware of tight-fitting plastic covers which may allow condensation to form and settle on the bike.

Getting back on the road

Engine and transmission

● Change the oil and replace the oil filter. If this was done prior to storage, check that the oil hasn't emulsified - a thick whitish substance which occurs through condensation.
● Remove the spark plugs. Using a spout-type oil can, squirt a few drops of oil into the cylinder(s). This will provide initial lubrication as the piston rings and bores comes back into contact. Service the spark plugs, or fit new ones, and install them in the engine.

● Check that the clutch isn't stuck on. The plates can stick together if left standing for some time, preventing clutch operation. Engage a gear and try rocking the bike back and forth with the clutch lever held against the handlebar. If this doesn't work on cable-operated clutches, hold the clutch lever back against the handlebar with a strong elastic band or cable tie for a couple of hours **(see illustration 8)**.
● If the air intakes or silencer end(s) were blocked off, remove the bung or cover used.
● If the fuel tank was coated with a rust

Hold clutch lever back against the handlebar with elastic bands or a cable tie

preventative, oil or a stabiliser added to the fuel, drain and flush the tank and dispose of the fuel sensibly. If no action was taken with the fuel tank prior to storage, it is advised that the old fuel is disposed of since it will go off over a period of time. Refill the fuel tank with fresh fuel.

Frame and running gear

● Oil all pivot points and cables.
● Check the tyre pressures. They will definitely need inflating if pressures were reduced for storage.
● Lubricate the final drive chain (where applicable).
● Remove any protective coating applied to the fork tubes (stanchions) since this may well destroy the fork seals. If the fork tubes weren't protected and have picked up rust spots, remove them with very fine abrasive paper and refinish with metal polish.
● Check that both brakes operate correctly. Apply each brake hard and check that it's not possible to move the motorcycle forwards, then check that the brake frees off again once released. Brake caliper pistons can stick due to corrosion around the piston head, or on the sliding caliper types, due to corrosion of the slider pins. If the brake doesn't free after repeated operation, take the caliper off for examination. Similarly drum brakes can stick due to a seized operating cam, cable or rod linkage.
● If the motorcycle has been in long-term storage, renew the brake fluid and clutch fluid (where applicable).
● Depending on where the bike has been stored, the wiring, cables and hoses may have been nibbled by rodents. Make a visual check and investigate disturbed wiring loom tape.

Battery

● If the battery has been previously removal and given top up charges it can simply be reconnected. Remember to connect the positive cable first and the negative cable last.
● On conventional refillable batteries, if the battery has not received any attention, remove it from the motorcycle and check its electrolyte level. Top up if necessary then charge the battery. If the battery fails to hold a charge and a visual checks show heavy white sulphation of the plates, the battery is probably defective and must be renewed. This is particularly likely if the battery is old. Confirm battery condition with a specific gravity check.
● On sealed (MF) batteries, if the battery has not received any attention, remove it from the motorcycle and charge it according to the information on the battery case - if the battery fails to hold a charge it must be renewed.

Starting procedure

● If a kickstart is fitted, turn the engine over a couple of times with the ignition OFF to distribute oil around the engine. If no kickstart is fitted, flick the engine kill switch OFF and the ignition ON and crank the engine over a couple of times to work oil around the upper cylinder components. If the nature of the ignition system is such that the starter won't work with the kill switch OFF, remove the spark plugs, fit them back into their caps and earth (ground) their bodies on the cylinder head. Reinstall the spark plugs afterwards.
● Switch the kill switch to RUN, operate the choke and start the engine. If the engine won't start don't continue cranking the engine - not only will this flatten the battery, but the starter motor will overheat. Switch the ignition off and try again later. If the engine refuses to start, go through the fault finding procedures in this manual. **Note:** *If the bike has been in storage for a long time, old fuel or a carburettor blockage may be the problem. Gum deposits in carburettors can block jets - if a carburettor cleaner doesn't prove successful the carburettors must be dismantled for cleaning.*

● Once the engine has started, check that the lights, turn signals and horn work properly.

● Treat the bike gently for the first ride and check all fluid levels on completion. Settle the bike back into the maintenance schedule.

This Section provides an easy reference-guide to the more common faults that are likely to afflict your machine. Obviously, the opportunities are almost limitless for faults to occur as a result of obscure failures, and to try and cover all eventualities would require a book. Indeed, a number have been written on the subject.

Successful troubleshooting is not a mysterious 'black art' but the application of a bit of knowledge combined with a systematic and logical approach to the problem. Approach any troubleshooting by first accurately identifying the symptom and then checking through the list of possible causes, starting with the simplest or most obvious and progressing in stages to the most complex.

Take nothing for granted, but above all apply liberal quantities of common sense.

The main symptom of a fault is given in the text as a major heading below which are listed the various systems or areas which may contain the fault. Details of each possible cause for a fault and the remedial action to be taken are given, in brief, in the paragraphs below each heading. Further information should be sought in the relevant Chapter.

1 Engine doesn't start or is difficult to start
- [ ] Starter motor doesn't rotate
- [ ] Starter motor rotates but engine does not turn over
- [ ] Starter works but engine won't turn over (seized)
- [ ] No fuel flow
- [ ] Engine flooded
- [ ] No spark or weak spark
- [ ] Compression low
- [ ] Stalls after starting
- [ ] Rough idle

2 Poor running at low speed
- [ ] Spark weak
- [ ] Fuel/air mixture incorrect
- [ ] Compression low
- [ ] Poor acceleration

3 Poor running or no power at high speed
- [ ] Firing incorrect
- [ ] Fuel/air mixture incorrect
- [ ] Compression low
- [ ] Knocking or pinking
- [ ] Miscellaneous causes

4 Overheating
- [ ] Engine overheats
- [ ] Firing incorrect
- [ ] Fuel/air mixture incorrect
- [ ] Compression too high
- [ ] Engine load excessive
- [ ] Lubrication inadequate
- [ ] Miscellaneous causes

5 Clutch problems
- [ ] Clutch slipping
- [ ] Clutch not disengaging completely

6 Gearchanging problems
- [ ] Doesn't go into gear, or lever doesn't return
- [ ] Jumps out of gear
- [ ] Overselects

7 Abnormal engine noise
- [ ] Knocking or pinking
- [ ] Piston slap or rattling
- [ ] Valve noise
- [ ] Other noise

8 Abnormal driveline noise
- [ ] Clutch noise
- [ ] Transmission noise
- [ ] Final drive noise

9 Abnormal frame and suspension noise
- [ ] Front end noise
- [ ] Shock absorber noise
- [ ] Brake noise

10 Oil pressure warning light comes on
- [ ] Engine lubrication system
- [ ] Electrical system

11 Excessive exhaust smoke
- [ ] White smoke
- [ ] Black smoke
- [ ] Brown smoke

12 Poor handling or stability
- [ ] Handlebar hard to turn
- [ ] Handlebar shakes or vibrates excessively
- [ ] Handlebar pulls to one side
- [ ] Poor shock absorbing qualities

13 Braking problems
- [ ] Brakes are spongy, don't hold
- [ ] Brake lever or pedal pulsates
- [ ] Brakes drag

14 Electrical problems
- [ ] Battery dead or weak
- [ ] Battery overcharged

1 Engine doesn't start or is difficult to start

Starter motor doesn't rotate

- [ ] Engine kill switch OFF.
- [ ] Fuse blown. Check main fuse and FI fuse (Chapter 8).
- [ ] Battery voltage low. Check and recharge battery (Chapter 8).
- [ ] Starter motor defective. Make sure the wiring to the starter is secure. Make sure the starter relay clicks when the start button is pushed. If the relay clicks, then the fault is in the wiring or motor (Chapter 8).
- [ ] Starter switch not contacting. The contacts could be wet, corroded or dirty. Disassemble and clean the switch (Chapter 8).
- [ ] Wiring open or shorted. Check all wiring connections and harnesses to make sure that they are dry, tight and not corroded. Also check for broken or frayed wires that can cause a short to ground (earth) (see *Wiring diagrams*, Chapter 8).
- [ ] Ignition switch defective. Check the switch and replace with a new one if it is defective (Chapter 8).
- [ ] Engine kill switch defective. Check for wet, dirty or corroded contacts. Clean or replace the switch with a new one as necessary (Chapter 8).
- [ ] Faulty gear position switch, sidestand switch or clutch switch. Check the wiring to each switch and the switch itself (Chapter 8).
- [ ] Faulty diode (Chapter 8).
- [ ] Fuel injection system shutdown due to system fault (Chapter 4).

Starter motor rotates but engine does not turn over

- [ ] Starter clutch defective. Inspect and repair or replace with a new one (Chapter 2).
- [ ] Damaged idler or starter gears. Inspect and replace the damaged parts (Chapter 2).

Starter works but engine won't turn over (seized)

- [ ] Seized engine caused by one or more internally damaged components. Failure due to wear, abuse or lack of lubrication. Damage can include seized valves, followers, camshafts, pistons, crankshaft, connecting rod bearings, or transmission gears or bearings. Refer to Chapter 2 for engine disassembly.

No fuel flow

- [ ] No fuel in tank.
- [ ] Fuel tank breather hose obstructed.
- [ ] Faulty fuel pump relay. Check the relay (Chapter 4).
- [ ] Fuel pump faulty or blocked (Chapter 4).
- [ ] Fuel hose clogged. Remove the fuel hose and carefully blow through it.
- [ ] Fuel injector clogged. For both of the injectors to be clogged, either a very bad batch of fuel with an unusual additive has been used, or some other foreign material has entered the tank. In some cases, if a machine has been unused for several months, the fuel turns to a varnish-like liquid that can cause an injector needle to stick to its seat. Drain the tank and fuel system (Chapter 4).

Engine flooded

- [ ] Injector needle valve worn or stuck open causing excess fuel to be admitted to the throttle body. In this case, the injectors should be renewed.
- [ ] Starting technique incorrect. Under normal circumstances (i.e. if all the components of the fuel injection system are good) the machine should start with the throttle closed.

No spark or weak spark

- [ ] Ignition switch OFF.
- [ ] Engine kill switch turned to the OFF position.
- [ ] Ignition or kill switch shorted. This is usually caused by water, corrosion, damage or excessive wear. The switches can be disassembled and cleaned with electrical contact cleaner. If cleaning does not help, replace the switches (Chapter 8).
- [ ] Battery voltage low. Check and recharge the battery as necessary (Chapter 8).
- [ ] Spark plug caps not making good contact. Make sure that the caps fit snugly over the plug ends.
- [ ] Spark plugs dirty, defective or worn out. Locate reason for fouled plugs using spark plug condition chart on the inside back cover and follow the plug maintenance procedures (Chapter 1).
- [ ] Incorrect spark plugs. Wrong type or heat range. Check and install correct plugs (Chapter 1).
- [ ] Ignition coil or spark plug cap defective. Test and replace if necessary (Chapter 4).
- [ ] Fuel injection system shutdown due to system fault (Chapter 4).
- [ ] Crankshaft position (CKP) sensor defective (Chapter 4).
- [ ] Faulty tip-over sensor (Chapter 4).
- [ ] Engine control module (ECM) defective (Chapter 4).
- [ ] Wiring shorted or broken between:
    - a)   *Ignition switch and engine kill switch (or blown fuse)*
    - b)   *ECM and engine kill switch*
    - c)   *ECM and ignition coils*
    - d)   *ECM and CKP sensor*
- [ ] Make sure that all wiring connections are clean, dry and tight. Look for chafed and broken wires (Chapters 4 and 8).

Compression low

- [ ] Spark plug loose. Remove the plugs and inspect their threads. Reinstall and tighten securely (Chapter 1).
- [ ] Cylinder head not sufficiently tightened down. If a cylinder head is suspected of being loose, then there's a chance that the gasket or head is damaged if the problem has persisted for any length of time. The head bolts should be tightened to the proper torque and in the correct sequence (Chapter 2).
- [ ] Improper valve clearance. This means that the valve is not closing completely and compression pressure is leaking past the valve. Check and adjust the valve clearances (Chapter 1).
- [ ] Cylinder and/or piston worn. Excessive wear will cause compression pressure to leak past the rings. This is usually accompanied by worn rings as well. A top-end overhaul is necessary (Chapter 2).
- [ ] Piston rings worn, weak, broken, or sticking. Broken or sticking piston rings usually indicate a lubrication or fuelling problem that causes excess carbon deposits to form on the pistons and rings. Top-end overhaul is necessary (Chapter 2).
- [ ] Piston ring-to-groove clearance excessive. This is caused by excessive wear of the piston ring lands. Piston renewal is necessary (Chapter 2).
- [ ] Cylinder head gasket damaged. If a head is allowed to become loose, or if excessive carbon build-up on the piston crown and combustion chamber causes extremely high compression, the head gasket may leak. Retorquing the head is not always sufficient to restore the seal, so a new gasket is necessary (Chapter 2).
- [ ] Cylinder head warped. This is caused by overheating or improperly tightened head bolts. Machine shop resurfacing or head renewal is necessary (Chapter 2).
- [ ] Valve spring broken or weak. Caused by component failure or wear; the springs must be renewed (Chapter 2).
- [ ] Valve not seating properly. This is caused by a bent valve (from over-revving or improper valve adjustment), burned valve or seat (improper fuelling) or an accumulation of carbon deposits on the seat. The valves must be cleaned and/or renewed and the seats serviced (Chapter 2).

1 Engine doesn't start or is difficult to start (continued)

Stalls after starting

- ☐ Engine idle speed incorrect. Faulty idle speed control system (Chapter 4).
- ☐ Ignition malfunction (Chapter 4).
- ☐ Fuel injection system malfunction (Chapter 4).
- ☐ Fuel contaminated. The fuel can be contaminated with either dirt or water, or can change chemically if the machine has been unused for several months. Drain the tank and fuel system (Chapter 4).
- ☐ Intake air leak. Check for loose throttle body-to-intake duct connections or a loose or damaged vacuum hose (Chapter 4).

Rough idle

- ☐ Idle speed incorrect (Chapter 4).
- ☐ Ignition fault (Chapter 4).
- ☐ Fuel injection system malfunction (Chapter 4).
- ☐ Fuel contaminated. The fuel can be contaminated with either dirt or water, or can change chemically if the machine has been unused for several months. Drain the tank and the fuel system (Chapter 4).
- ☐ Intake air leak. Check for loose throttle body-to-intake duct connections or a loose or damaged vacuum hose (Chapter 4).
- ☐ Air filter clogged. Clean the air filter element or replace it with a new one (Chapter 1).

2 Poor running at low speeds

Spark weak

- ☐ Battery voltage low. Check and recharge battery (Chapter 8).
- ☐ Spark plug caps not making good contact. Make sure that the caps fit snugly over the plug ends.
- ☐ Spark plugs dirty, defective or worn out. Locate reason for fouled plugs using spark plug condition chart on the inside back cover and follow the plug maintenance procedures (Chapter 1).
- ☐ Incorrect spark plugs. Wrong type or heat range. Check and install correct plugs (Chapter 1).
- ☐ Ignition coil or spark plug cap defective. Test and renew if necessary (Chapter 4).

Fuel/air mixture incorrect

- ☐ Fuel tank breather hose obstructed.
- ☐ Fuel pump faulty or blocked (Chapter 4).
- ☐ Fuel hose clogged. Remove the fuel hose and carefully blow through it.
- ☐ Fuel injector clogged. For both of the injectors to be clogged, either a very bad batch of fuel with an unusual additive has been used, or some other foreign material has entered the tank. In some cases, if a machine has been unused for several months, the fuel turns to a varnish-like liquid which can cause an injector needle to stick to its seat. Drain the tank and fuel system (Chapter 4).
- ☐ Intake air leak. Check for loose throttle body-to-intake duct connections, or loose or damaged vacuum hoses (Chapter 4).
- ☐ Air filter clogged. Clean the air filter element or replace it with a new one (Chapter 1).

Compression low

- ☐ Spark plug loose. Remove the plugs and inspect their threads. Reinstall and tighten securely (Chapter 1).
- ☐ Cylinder head not sufficiently tightened down. If a cylinder head is suspected of being loose, then there's a chance that the gasket or head is damaged if the problem has persisted for any length of time. The head bolts should be tightened to the proper torque and in the correct sequence (Chapter 2).
- ☐ Improper valve clearance. This means that the valve is not closing completely and compression pressure is leaking past the valve. Check and adjust the valve clearances (Chapter 1).

- ☐ Cylinder and/or piston worn. Excessive wear will cause compression pressure to leak past the rings. This is usually accompanied by worn rings as well. A top-end overhaul is necessary (Chapter 2).
- ☐ Piston rings worn, weak, broken, or sticking. Broken or sticking piston rings usually indicate a lubrication or fuelling problem that causes excess carbon deposits to form on the pistons and rings. Top-end overhaul is necessary (Chapter 2).
- ☐ Piston ring-to-groove clearance excessive. This is caused by excessive wear of the piston ring lands. Piston renewal is necessary (Chapter 2).
- ☐ Cylinder head gasket damaged. If the head is allowed to become loose, or if excessive carbon build-up on the piston crown and combustion chamber causes extremely high compression, the head gasket may leak. Retorquing the head is not always sufficient to restore the seal, so a new gasket is necessary (Chapter 2).
- ☐ Cylinder head warped. This is caused by overheating or improperly tightened head bolts. Machine shop resurfacing or head renewal is necessary (Chapter 2).
- ☐ Valve spring broken or weak. Caused by component failure or wear; the springs must be renewed (Chapter 2).
- ☐ Valve not seating properly. This is caused by a bent valve (from over-revving or improper valve adjustment), burned valve or seat (improper fuelling) or an accumulation of carbon deposits on the seat (from fuelling or lubrication problems). The valves must be cleaned and/or renewed and the seats serviced (Chapter 2).

Poor acceleration

- ☐ Timing not advancing. The crankshaft position sensor (CKP) or the engine control module (ECM) may be defective (Chapter 4). If so, they must be renewed.
- ☐ Engine oil viscosity too high. Using heavier oil than that recommended in Chapter 1 can damage the oil pump or lubrication system and cause drag on the engine.
- ☐ Brakes dragging. Usually caused by debris that has entered the brake caliper piston seals, or from a warped disc or bent axle (Chapter 6).

3 Poor running or no power at high speed

Firing incorrect

☐ Spark plug caps not making good contact. Make sure that the caps fit snugly over the plug ends and that the wiring is secure.

☐ Spark plugs dirty, defective or worn out. Locate reason for fouled plugs using spark plug condition chart on the inside back cover and follow the plug maintenance procedures (Chapter 1).

☐ Incorrect spark plugs. Wrong type or heat range. Check and install correct plugs (Chapter 1).

☐ Ignition coil or spark plug cap defective. Test and renew if necessary (Chapter 4).

☐ Faulty ECM (engine control module) (Chapter 4).

Fuel/air mixture incorrect

☐ Fuel tank breather hose obstructed.

☐ Fuel pump faulty or blocked (Chapter 4).

☐ Fuel hose clogged. Remove the fuel hose and carefully blow through it.

☐ Fuel injector clogged. For both of the injectors to be clogged, either a very bad batch of fuel with an unusual additive has been used, or some other foreign material has entered the tank. In some cases, if a machine has been unused for several months, the fuel turns to a varnish-like liquid that can cause an injector needle to stick to its seat. Drain the tank and fuel system (Chapter 4).

☐ Intake air leak. Check for loose throttle body-to-intake duct connections, or loose or damaged vacuum hoses (Chapter 4).

☐ Air filter clogged. Clean the air filter element or replace it with a new one (Chapter 1).

Compression low

☐ Spark plug loose. Remove the plugs and inspect their threads. Reinstall and tighten securely (Chapter 1).

☐ Cylinder head not sufficiently tightened down. If a cylinder head is suspected of being loose, then there's a chance that the gasket or head is damaged if the problem has persisted for any length of time. The head bolts should be tightened to the proper torque and in the correct sequence (Chapter 2).

☐ Improper valve clearance. This means that the valve is not closing completely and compression pressure is leaking past the valve. Check and adjust the valve clearances (Chapter 1).

☐ Cylinder and/or piston worn. Excessive wear will cause compression pressure to leak past the rings. This is usually accompanied by worn rings as well. A top-end overhaul is necessary (Chapter 2).

☐ Piston rings worn, weak, broken, or sticking. Broken or sticking piston rings usually indicate a lubrication or fuelling problem that causes excess carbon deposits to form on the pistons and rings. Top-end overhaul is necessary (Chapter 2).

☐ Piston ring-to-groove clearance excessive. This is caused by excessive wear of the piston ring lands. Piston renewal is necessary (Chapter 2).

☐ Cylinder head gasket damaged. If a head is allowed to become loose, or if excessive carbon build-up on the piston crown and combustion chamber causes extremely high compression, the head gasket may leak. Retorquing the head is not always sufficient to restore the seal, so a new gasket is necessary (Chapter 2).

☐ Cylinder head warped. This is caused by overheating or improperly tightened head bolts. Machine shop resurfacing or head renewal is necessary (Chapter 2).

☐ Valve spring broken or weak. Caused by component failure or wear; the springs must be replaced with new ones (Chapter 2).

☐ Valve not seating properly. This is caused by a bent valve (from over-revving or improper valve adjustment), burned valve or seat (improper fuelling) or an accumulation of carbon deposits on the seat (from fuelling or lubrication problems). The valves must be cleaned and/or renewed and the seats serviced (Chapter 2).

Knocking or pinking

☐ Carbon build-up in combustion chamber. Use of a fuel additive that will dissolve the adhesive bonding the carbon particles to the piston crown and chamber is the easiest way to remove the build-up. Otherwise, the cylinder head will have to be removed and decarbonised (Chapter 2).

☐ Incorrect or poor quality fuel. Old or improper grades of fuel can cause detonation. This causes the piston to rattle, thus the knocking or pinking sound. Drain old fuel and always use the recommended fuel grade.

☐ Spark plug heat range incorrect. Uncontrolled detonation indicates the plug heat range is too hot. The plug in effect becomes a glow plug, raising cylinder temperatures. Install the proper heat range plug (Chapter 1).

☐ Improper air/fuel mixture. This will cause the cylinders to run hot, which leads to detonation. A blockage in the fuel system or an air leak can cause this imbalance (Chapter 4).

Miscellaneous causes

☐ Throttle valve doesn't open fully. Adjust the throttle twistgrip freeplay (Chapter 1).

☐ Clutch slipping due loose or worn clutch components (Chapter 2).

☐ Timing not advancing. The crankshaft position sensor (CKP) or the engine control module (ECM) may be defective (Chapter 4). If so, they must be replaced with new ones.

☐ Engine oil viscosity too high. Using a heavier oil than the one recommended in Chapter 1 can damage the oil pump or lubrication system and cause drag on the engine.

☐ Brakes dragging. Usually caused by debris which has entered the brake caliper piston seals, or from a warped disc or bent axle (Chapter 6).

4 Overheating

Engine overheats

☐ Coolant level low. Check the level and add coolant (see *Pre-ride checks*).
☐ Leak in cooling system. Check cooling system hoses and radiator for leaks and other damage. Repair or renew parts as necessary (Chapter 3).
☐ Faulty thermostat. Check and renew as described in Chapter 3.
☐ Faulty pressure cap. Remove the cap and have it pressure tested.
☐ Coolant passages clogged. Have the entire system drained and flushed, then refill with fresh coolant.
☐ Water pump defective. Remove the pump and check the components (Chapter 3).
☐ Clogged or damaged radiator fins (Chapter 3).
☐ Faulty cooling fan, relay or ECT sensor (Chapter 3).

Firing incorrect

☐ Wrongly connected ignition coil wiring or plug leads.
☐ Spark plugs dirty, defective or worn out. Locate reason for fouled plugs using spark plug condition chart on the inside back cover and follow the plug maintenance procedures (Chapter 1).
☐ Incorrect spark plugs. Wrong type or heat range. Check and install correct plugs (Chapter 1).
☐ Ignition coil or spark plug cap defective. Test and replace with a new one if necessary (Chapter 4).
☐ Faulty ECM (engine control module) (Chapter 4).

Fuel/air mixture incorrect

☐ Fuel tank breather hose obstructed.
☐ Fuel pump faulty or blocked (Chapter 4).
☐ Fuel hose clogged. Remove the fuel hose and carefully blow through it.
☐ Fuel injector clogged. For both of the injectors to be clogged, either a very bad batch of fuel with an unusual additive has been used, or some other foreign material has entered the tank. In some cases, if a machine has been unused for several months, the fuel turns to a varnish-like liquid that can cause an injector needle to stick to its seat. Drain the tank and fuel system (Chapter 4).
☐ Intake air leak. Check for loose throttle body-to-intake duct connections, or loose or damaged vacuum hoses (Chapter 4).
☐ Air filter clogged. Clean the air filter element or replace it with a new one (Chapter 1).

Compression too high

☐ Carbon build-up in combustion chamber. Use of a fuel additive that will dissolve the adhesive bonding the carbon particles to the piston crown and chamber is the easiest way to remove the build-up. Otherwise, the cylinder head will have to be removed and decarbonised (Chapter 2).
☐ Improperly machined head surface or installation of incorrect gasket during engine assembly.

Engine load excessive

☐ Clutch slipping due to loose or worn clutch components (Chapter 2).
☐ Engine oil level too high. Too much oil will cause pressurisation of the crankcase and inefficient engine operation. Check Specifications and drain to proper level (Chapter 1 and *Pre-ride checks*).
☐ Engine oil viscosity too high. Using a heavier oil than the one recommended in Chapter 1 can damage the oil pump or lubrication system as well as cause drag on the engine.
☐ Brakes dragging. Usually caused by debris which has entered the brake caliper piston seals, or from a warped disc or bent axle (Chapter 6).

Lubrication inadequate

☐ Engine oil level too low. Friction caused by intermittent lack of lubrication or from oil that is overworked can cause overheating. The oil provides a definite cooling function in the engine. Check the oil level (see *Pre-ride checks*).
☐ Low engine oil pressure. Check the pressure (Chapter 2).
☐ Blocked oil filter (Chapter 1). Blocked oil cooler on 2004 to 2011 DL models (Chapter 2).
☐ Poor quality engine oil or incorrect viscosity or type. Oil is rated not only according to viscosity but also according to type. Some oils are not rated high enough for use in this engine. Check the Specifications section and change to the correct oil (Chapter 1).

Miscellaneous causes

☐ Modification to exhaust system. Most aftermarket exhaust systems cause the engine to run leaner, which make them run hotter. When installing an accessory exhaust system, always check with the manufacturer/supplier as to whether the ECM requires re-mapping.

5 Clutch problems

Clutch slipping

☐ Insufficient clutch cable freeplay. Check and adjust (Chapter 1).
☐ Clutch plates worn or warped. Overhaul the clutch assembly (Chapter 2).
☐ Clutch springs broken or weak. Old or heat-damaged (from slipping clutch) springs should be renewed (Chapter 2).
☐ Faulty clutch release mechanism. Replace any defective parts with new ones (Chapter 2).
☐ Clutch centre or housing unevenly worn. This causes improper engagement of the plates. Replace the damaged or worn parts (Chapter 2).

Clutch not disengaging completely

☐ Excessive clutch cable freeplay. Check and adjust (see Chapter 1).
☐ Faulty clutch release mechanism. Replace any defective parts with new ones (Chapter 2).
☐ Clutch plates warped or damaged. This will cause clutch drag, which in turn will cause the machine to creep. Overhaul the clutch assembly (Chapter 2).
☐ Clutch springs fatigued or broken. Check and renew the springs (Chapter 2).
☐ Engine oil deteriorated. Old, thin oil will not provide proper lubrication for the plates, causing the clutch to drag. Renew the oil and filter (Chapter 1).
☐ Engine oil viscosity too high. Using a heavier oil than recommended in Chapter 1 can cause the plates to stick together. Change to the correct weight oil.
☐ Clutch housing guide seized on the transmission input shaft. Lack of lubrication, severe wear or damage can cause the bearing to seize. Overhaul of the clutch, and perhaps transmission, may be necessary to repair the damage (Chapter 2).
☐ Loose clutch centre nut. Causes housing and centre misalignment putting a drag on the engine. Engagement adjustment continually varies. Overhaul the clutch assembly (Chapter 2).

6 Gearchanging problems

Doesn't go into gear or lever doesn't return

- [ ] Clutch not disengaging (above).
- [ ] Gearchange mechanism stopper arm spring weak or broken, or arm roller broken or worn. Replace the spring or arm with a new one (Chapter 2).
- [ ] Selector fork(s) bent, worn or seized. Overhaul the transmission (Chapter 2).
- [ ] Gear(s) stuck on shaft. Most often caused by a lack of lubrication or excessive wear in transmission bearings and bushes. Overhaul the transmission (Chapter 2).
- [ ] Selector drum binding. Caused by lubrication failure or excessive wear. Replace the drum and/or its bearing with a new one (Chapter 2).
- [ ] Gearchange mechanism return spring weak or broken (Chapter 2).
- [ ] Gearchange lever or linkage broken. Splines stripped out of arm or shaft, caused by a loose linkage arm pinch bolt or from dropping the machine (Chapter 2).

Jumps out of gear

- [ ] Selector fork(s) worn (Chapter 2).
- [ ] Selector fork groove(s) in selector drum worn (Chapter 2).
- [ ] Gear pinion dogs or dog slots worn or damaged. The gear pinions should be inspected and renewed. No attempt should be made to repair the worn parts.

Overselects

- [ ] Gearchange mechanism stopper arm spring weak or broken, or arm roller broken or worn. Renew the spring or arm (Chapter 2).
- [ ] Gearchange mechanism return spring weak or broken (Chapter 2).

7 Abnormal engine noise

Knocking or pinking

- [ ] Carbon build-up in combustion chambers. Use of a fuel additive that will dissolve the adhesive bonding the carbon particles to the piston crown and chamber is the easiest way to remove the build-up. Otherwise, the cylinder heads will have to be removed and decarbonised (Chapter 2).
- [ ] Incorrect or poor quality fuel. Old or improper grades of fuel can cause detonation. This causes the pistons to rattle, thus the knocking or pinking sound. Drain old fuel and always use the recommended fuel grade.
- [ ] Spark plug heat range incorrect. Uncontrolled detonation indicates the plug heat range is too hot. The plug in effect becomes a glow plug, raising cylinder temperatures. Install the proper heat range plug (Chapter 1).
- [ ] Improper air/fuel mixture. This will cause the cylinders to run hot, which leads to detonation. A blockage in the fuel system or an air leak can cause this imbalance (Chapter 4).

Piston slap or rattling

- [ ] Cylinder-to-piston clearance excessive. Cylinder and/or piston worn, usually accompanied by worn rings as well. A top-end overhaul is necessary (Chapter 2).
- [ ] Piston ring(s) worn, broken or sticking. Overhaul the top-end (Chapter 2).
- [ ] Piston pin, piston pin bore or connecting rod small-end worn from high mileage or seized due to lack of lubrication (Chapter 2).
- [ ] Piston seizure damage. Usually from lack of lubrication or overheating. Replace the pistons and cylinders, as necessary (Chapter 2). Note that the cylinders can be rebored on 2004 to 2011 DL models and oversize pistons fitted.
- [ ] Connecting rod big-end clearance excessive. Caused by excessive wear or lack of lubrication. Replace worn parts.

- [ ] Connecting rod bent. Caused by over-revving, trying to start a badly flooded engine or from ingesting a foreign object into the combustion chamber. Replace the damaged parts (Chapter 2).

Valve noise

- [ ] Incorrect valve clearances – check and adjust (Chapter 1).
- [ ] Valve spring broken or weak. Check and replace weak valve springs with new ones (Chapter 2).
- [ ] Camshaft or camshaft journals in the cylinder head worn or damaged. Lubrication failure at high rpm is usually the cause of damage due to insufficient oil or failure to change the oil at the recommended intervals. Since there are no replaceable bearings in the head, the head itself will have to be replaced with a new one (Chapter 2).

Other noise

- [ ] Cylinder head gasket leaking. Check around the joint for blowing with the engine running.
- [ ] Exhaust pipe leaking at cylinder head connection. Caused by incorrect fit of pipe(s), loose exhaust flange or damaged gasket. All exhaust system fasteners should be tightened evenly and carefully to avoid leaks (Chapter 4).
- [ ] Crankshaft runout excessive. Caused by a bent crankshaft (from over-revving) or damage from an upper cylinder component failure. Can also be attributed to dropping the machine on either of the crankshaft ends.
- [ ] Engine mounting bolts loose – ensure all the bolts are tightened to the specified torque settings (Chapter 2).
- [ ] Crankshaft bearings worn (Chapter 2).
- [ ] Cam chain rattle, due to worn chain or defective tensioner. Also worn chain tensioner/guide blades (Chapter 2).

8 Abnormal driveline noise

Clutch noise

☐ Clutch housing/friction plate clearance excessive (Chapter 2).
☐ Wear between the clutch housing splines and input shaft splines (Chapter 2).
☐ Worn release bearing (Chapter 2).

Transmission noise

☐ Bearings worn. Also includes the possibility that the shafts are worn. Overhaul the transmission (Chapter 2).
☐ Gears worn or chipped (Chapter 2).
☐ Metal chips jammed in gear teeth. Probably pieces from a broken

clutch, gear or selector mechanism that were picked up by the gears. This will cause early bearing failure (Chapter 2).
☐ Engine oil level too low. Causes a howl from transmission. Also affects engine power and clutch operation (see *Pre-ride checks*).

Final drive noise

☐ Chain not adjusted properly (Chapter 1).
☐ Front or rear sprocket loose. Tighten fasteners (Chapter 6).
☐ Sprockets and/or chain worn. Fit new sprockets and chain (Chapter 6).
☐ Rear sprocket warped. Fit a new sprocket (Chapter 6).
☐ Rubber dampers worn in sprocket coupling (Chapter 6).

9 Abnormal frame and suspension noise

Front end noise

☐ Low fluid level or improper viscosity oil in forks. This can sound like spurting and is usually accompanied by irregular fork action (Chapter 5).
☐ Spring weak or broken. Makes a clicking or scraping sound. Fork oil, when drained, will have a lot of metal particles in it (Chapter 5).
☐ Steering head bearings loose or damaged. Clicks when braking. Check and adjust or replace with new ones as necessary (Chapters 1 and 5).
☐ Fork yoke clamp bolts loose – ensure all the bolts are tightened to the specified torque (Chapter 6).
☐ Forks bent. Good possibility if machine has been dropped. Replace the inner and outer tubes with new ones as required (Chapter 5).
☐ Front axle or axle pinch bolts loose. Tighten them to the specified torque (Chapter 6).
☐ Loose or worn wheel bearings. Check and replace with new ones as needed (Chapters 1 and 6).

Rear end noise

☐ Shock absorber fluid level incorrect. Indicates a leak caused by defective seal. Shock will be covered with oil. Replace shock with a new one or seek advice on repair from a suspension specialist (Chapter 5).
☐ Defective shock absorber with internal damage. This is in the body of the shock and can't be remedied. The shock must be replaced with a new one or rebuilt (Chapter 5).

☐ Bent or damaged shock body. Replace the shock with a new one (Chapter 5).
☐ Loose or worn swingarm bearings. Check and replace with new ones as necessary (Chapter 5).
☐ Loose or worn suspension linkage bearings. Check and replace with new ones as necessary (Chapter 5).

Brake noise

☐ Squeal caused by pad shim not installed or positioned correctly (where fitted) (Chapter 6).
☐ Squeal caused by dust on brake pads. Usually found in combination with glazed pads. Clean using brake cleaning solvent (Chapter 6).
☐ Pads glazed. Caused by excessive heat from prolonged hard use or from contamination. DO NOT use sandpaper, emery cloth, carborundum cloth or any other abrasive to roughen the pad surfaces as abrasives will stay in the pad material and damage the disc. A very fine flat file can be used, but new pads is the best remedy (Chapter 6).
☐ Contamination of brake pads. Oil or brake fluid can cause the brake pads to chatter or squeal. Fit new pads. Identify the cause of the contamination, especially check the caliper piston seals for leaking fluid. Clean disc thoroughly with brake system cleaner (Chapter 6).
☐ Disc warped. Can cause a chattering, clicking or intermittent squeal. Usually accompanied by a pulsating lever and uneven braking. Replace the disc with new one (Chapter 6).
☐ Loose or worn wheel bearings. Check and replace with new ones as needed (Chapters 1 and 6).

10 Oil pressure warning light comes on

Engine lubrication system

☐ Engine oil level low. Inspect for leak or other problem causing low oil level and add recommended oil (see *Pre-ride checks*).
☐ Engine oil pump defective, blocked oil strainer gauze or failed pressure relief valve. Carry out an oil pressure check (Chapter 2).
☐ Engine oil viscosity too low. Very old, thin oil or an improper weight of oil used in the engine. Change to correct oil (Chapter 1).
☐ Camshaft or crankshaft journals worn. Excessive wear causing drop in oil pressure. Abnormal wear could be caused by oil

starvation at high rpm from low oil level or improper weight or type of oil (Chapter 1).

Electrical system

☐ Oil pressure switch defective. Check the switch according to the procedure in Chapter 8. Replace it with a new one it if is defective.
☐ Oil pressure warning LED defective. Check for pinched, shorted, disconnected or damaged wiring (Chapter 8).

11 Excessive exhaust smoke

White smoke

☐ Piston rings worn or broken, causing oil from the crankcase to be pulled past the piston into the combustion chamber. Replace the rings with new ones (Chapter 2).
☐ Cylinders worn or scored. Caused by overheating or oil starvation. Rebore cylinders on 2004 to 2011 DL models and renew them on all others (Chapter 2).
☐ Valve stem oil seal damaged or worn. Replace the oil seals with new ones (Chapter 2).
☐ Valve guide worn. Perform a complete valve job (Chapter 2).
☐ Engine oil level too high, which causes the oil to be forced past the rings. Drain oil to the proper level (see *Pre-ride checks*).

☐ Head gasket broken between oil return and cylinder. Causes oil to be pulled into the combustion chamber. Replace the head gasket with a new ones and check the head for warpage (Chapter 2).
☐ Abnormal crankcase pressurisation which forces oil past the rings, usually caused by a clogged breather.

Black smoke

☐ Air filter clogged. Clean the air filter element or replace it with a new one (Chapter 1).
☐ Fuel injection system malfunction (Chapter 4).

Brown smoke

☐ Air filter poorly sealed or not installed (Chapter 1).
☐ Fuel injection system malfunction (Chapter 4).

12 Poor handling or stability

Handlebar hard to turn

☐ Steering head bearing adjuster nut too tight. Check adjustment as described in Chapter 1.
☐ Bearings damaged. Roughness can be felt as the bars are turned from side-to-side. Replace the bearings with new ones (Chapter 5).
☐ Races dented or worn. Denting results from wear in only one position (e.g., straight ahead), from a collision or hitting a pothole or from dropping the machine. Replace the bearings with new ones (Chapter 5).
☐ Steering stem lubrication inadequate. Causes are grease getting hard from age or being washed out by high pressure car washes. Disassemble steering head and repack bearings (Chapter 5).
☐ Steering stem bent. Caused by a collision, hitting a pothole or by dropping the machine. Replace damaged part. Don't try to straighten the steering stem (Chapter 5).
☐ Front tyre air pressure too low (see *Pre-ride checks*).

Handlebar shakes or vibrates excessively

☐ Tyres worn or out of balance (Chapter 6).
☐ Swingarm bearings worn. Replace the bearings with new ones (Chapter 5).
☐ Wheel rim(s) warped or damaged. Inspect wheels for runout (Chapter 6).
☐ Wheel bearings worn. Worn front or rear wheel bearings can cause poor tracking. Worn front bearings will cause wobble (Chapters 1 and 6).
☐ Fork yoke clamp bolts or handlebar clamp bolts loose. Tighten them to the specified torque (Chapter 5).
☐ Engine mounting bolts loose. Will cause excessive vibration with increased engine rpm – ensure all the bolts are tightened to the specified torque settings (Chapter 2).

Machine pulls to one side

☐ Frame bent. Definitely suspect this if the machine has been dropped. May or may not be accompanied by cracking near the steering head, swingarm mountings or engine mountings. Replace the frame with a new one (Chapter 5).
☐ Wheels out of alignment. Caused by poor chain adjustment, improper location of axle spacers or from bent steering stem or frame (Chapters 1 and 5).
☐ Forks bent. Disassemble the forks and replace the damaged parts (Chapter 5).
☐ Swingarm bent or twisted. Replace the arm with a new one (Chapter 5).
☐ Fork oil level uneven. Check and add or drain as necessary (Chapter 5).

Poor shock absorbing qualities

☐ Too hard:
a) *Suspension adjustment incorrect (Chapter 5).*
b) *Fork oil level excessive (Chapter 5).*
c) *Fork oil viscosity too high. Use a lighter oil (see the Specifications in Chapter 5).*
d) *Fork tube bent. Causes a harsh, sticking feeling (Chapter 5).*
e) *Fork internal damage (Chapter 5).*
f) *Shock shaft or body bent or damaged (Chapter 5).*
g) *Shock internal damage (Chapter 5).*
h) *Swingarm bearings or suspension linkage bearings seized (Chapter 5).*
i) *Tyre pressure too high (see Pre-ride checks).*
☐ Too soft:
a) *Suspension adjustment incorrect (Chapter 5).*
b) *Fork oil level too low (Chapter 5).*
c) *Fork oil viscosity too light (Chapter 5).*
d) *Fork springs weak or broken (Chapter 5).*
e) *Fork or shock oil leaking (Chapter 5).*
f) *Shock internal damage (Chapter 5).*

13 Braking problems

Brakes are spongy, don't hold

- ☐ Low brake fluid level (see *Pre-ride checks*).
- ☐ Air in hydraulic system. Caused by inattention to master cylinder fluid level or by leakage. Locate problem and bleed brakes (Chapter 6).
- ☐ Pad or disc worn (Chapters 1 and 6).
- ☐ Contaminated pads. Caused by contamination with oil, grease, brake fluid, etc. Fit new pads. Identify the cause of the contamination, especially check the caliper piston seals for leaking fluid. Clean disc thoroughly with brake system cleaner (Chapter 6).
- ☐ Brake fluid deteriorated. Fluid is old or contaminated. Drain system, replenish with new fluid and bleed the system (Chapter 6).
- ☐ Master cylinder internal seals worn or damaged causing fluid to bypass (Chapter 6).
- ☐ Master cylinder bore scratched by foreign material or broken spring. Fit a new master cylinder (Chapter 6).
- ☐ Disc warped. Replace disc with new one (Chapter 6).
- ☐ ABS system faulty (where fitted – Chapter 6).

Brake lever or pedal pulsates

- ☐ Disc warped. Replace disc with new one (Chapter 6).

- ☐ Axle bent. Replace axle with new one (Chapter 6).
- ☐ Brake caliper bolts loose – tighten the bolts to the specified torque (Chapter 6).
- ☐ Wheel warped or otherwise damaged (Chapter 6).
- ☐ Wheel bearings damaged or worn (Chapters 1 and 6).
- ☐ ABS system faulty (where fitted – Chapter 6).

Brakes drag

- ☐ Master cylinder piston seized. Caused by wear or damage to piston or cylinder bore (Chapter 6).
- ☐ Lever balky or stuck. Check pivot and lubricate (Chapter 6).
- ☐ Brake caliper piston seized in bore. Caused by corrosion or ingestion of dirt past deteriorated seal (Chapter 6).
- ☐ Brake caliper slider pins sticking. Clean and lubricate the pins and check that the dust boots are in good condition (Chapter 6).
- ☐ Brake pad damaged. Pad material separated from backing plate. Usually caused by faulty manufacturing process or from contact with chemicals. Fit new pads (Chapter 6).
- ☐ Pads improperly installed (Chapter 6).
- ☐ Brake caliper incorrectly installed (Chapter 6).
- ☐ ABS system faulty (where fitted – Chapter 6).

14 Electrical problems

Battery dead or weak

- ☐ Battery faulty. Caused by sulphated plates which are shorted through sedimentation. Confirm with battery condition check (Chapter 8).
- ☐ Broken battery terminal making only occasional contact.
- ☐ Battery leads making poor contact (Chapter 8).
- ☐ Load excessive. Caused by addition of high wattage lights or other electrical accessories.
- ☐ Ignition switch defective. Switch either grounds (earths) internally or fails to shut off system. Renew the switch (Chapter 8).
- ☐ Regulator/rectifier defective (Chapter 8).
- ☐ Alternator stator coil open or shorted (Chapter 8).

- ☐ Charging system fault. Check for excessive current leakage (Chapter 8).
- ☐ Wiring faulty. Wiring grounded (earthed) or connections loose in ignition, charging or lighting circuits (Chapter 8).

Battery overcharged

- ☐ Regulator/rectifier defective. Overcharging is noticed when battery gets excessively warm (Chapter 8).
- ☐ Battery faulty. Confirm with battery condition check (Chapter 8).
- ☐ Battery amperage too low, wrong type or size of battery. Install manufacturer's specified amp-hour battery to handle charging load (Chapter 8).

A

ABS (Anti-lock braking system) A system, usually electronically controlled, that senses incipient wheel lockup during braking and relieves hydraulic pressure at wheel which is about to skid.

Aftermarket Components suitable for the motorcycle, but not produced by the motorcycle manufacturer.

Allen key A hexagonal wrench which fits into a recessed hexagonal hole.

Alternating current (ac) Current produced by an alternator. Requires converting to direct current by a rectifier for charging purposes.

Alternator Converts mechanical energy from the engine into electrical energy to charge the battery and power the electrical system.

Ampere (amp) A unit of measurement for the flow of electrical current. Current = Volts ÷ Ohms.

Ampere-hour (Ah) Measure of battery capacity.

Angle-tightening A torque expressed in degrees. Often follows a conventional tightening torque for cylinder head or main bearing fasteners **(see illustration)**.

Angle-tightening con-rod bolts

Antifreeze A substance (usually ethylene glycol) mixed with water, and added to the cooling system, to prevent freezing of the coolant in winter. Antifreeze also contains chemicals to inhibit corrosion and the formation of rust and other deposits that would tend to clog the radiator and coolant passages and reduce cooling efficiency.

Anti-dive System attached to the fork lower leg (slider) to prevent fork dive when braking hard.

Anti-seize compound A coating that reduces the risk of seizing on fasteners that are subjected to high temperatures, such as exhaust clamp bolts and nuts.

API American Petroleum Institute. A quality standard for 4-stroke motor oils.

Asbestos A natural fibrous mineral with great heat resistance, commonly used in the composition of brake friction materials. Asbestos is a health hazard and the dust created by brake systems should never be inhaled or ingested.

ATF Automatic Transmission Fluid. Often used in front forks.

ATU Automatic Timing Unit. Mechanical device for advancing the ignition timing on early engines.

ATV All Terrain Vehicle. Often called a Quad.

Axial play Side-to-side movement.

Axle A shaft on which a wheel revolves. Also known as a spindle.

B

Backlash The amount of movement between meshed components when one component is held still. Usually applies to gear teeth.

Ball bearing A bearing consisting of a hardened inner and outer race with hardened steel balls between the two races.

Bearings Used between two working surfaces to prevent wear of the components and a build-up of heat. Four types of bearing are commonly used on motorcycles: plain shell bearings, ball bearings, tapered roller bearings and needle roller bearings.

Bevel gears Used to turn the drive through 90°. Typical applications are shaft final drive and camshaft drive **(see illustration)**.

Bevel gears are used to turn the drive through 90°

BHP Brake Horsepower. The British measurement for engine power output. Power output is now usually expressed in kilowatts (kW).

Bias-belted tyre Similar construction to radial tyre, but with outer belt running at an angle to the wheel rim.

Big-end bearing The bearing in the end of the connecting rod that's attached to the crankshaft.

Bleeding The process of removing air from an hydraulic system via a bleed nipple or bleed screw.

Bottom-end A description of an engine's crankcase components and all components contained there-in.

BTDC Before Top Dead Centre in terms of piston position. Ignition timing is often expressed in terms of degrees or millimetres BTDC.

Bush A cylindrical metal or rubber component used between two moving parts.

Burr Rough edge left on a component after machining or as a result of excessive wear.

C

Cam chain The chain which takes drive from the crankshaft to the camshaft(s).

Canister The main component in an evaporative emission control system (California market only); contains activated charcoal granules to trap vapours from the fuel system rather than allowing them to vent to the atmosphere.

Castellated Resembling the parapets along the top of a castle wall. For example, a castellated wheel axle or spindle nut.

Catalytic converter A device in the exhaust system of some machines which converts certain pollutants in the exhaust gases into less harmful substances.

Charging system Description of the components which charge the battery, ie the alternator, rectifier and regulator.

Circlip A ring-shaped clip used to prevent endwise movement of cylindrical parts and shafts. An internal circlip is installed in a groove in a housing; an external circlip fits into a groove on the outside of a cylindrical piece such as a shaft. Also known as a snap-ring.

Clearance The amount of space between two parts. For example, between a piston and a cylinder, between a bearing and a journal, etc.

Coil spring A spiral of elastic steel found in various sizes throughout a vehicle, for example as a springing medium in the suspension and in the valve train.

Compression Reduction in volume, and increase in pressure and temperature, of a gas, caused by squeezing it into a smaller space.

Compression damping Controls the speed the suspension compresses when hitting a bump.

Compression ratio The relationship between cylinder volume when the piston is at top dead centre and cylinder volume when the piston is at bottom dead centre.

Continuity The uninterrupted path in the flow of electricity. Little or no measurable resistance.

Continuity tester Self-powered bleeper or test light which indicates continuity.

Cp Candlepower. Bulb rating commonly found on US motorcycles.

Crossply tyre Tyre plies arranged in a criss-cross pattern. Usually four or six plies used, hence 4PR or 6PR in tyre size codes.

Cush drive Rubber damper segments fitted between the rear wheel and final drive sprocket to absorb transmission shocks **(see illustration)**.

Cush drive rubbers dampen out transmission shocks

D

Decarbonisation The process of removing carbon deposits - typically from the combustion chamber, valves and exhaust port/system.

Degree disc Calibrated disc for measuring piston position. Expressed in degrees.

Detonation Destructive and damaging explosion of fuel/air mixture in combustion chamber instead of controlled burning.

Dial gauge Clock-type gauge with adapters for measuring runout and piston position. Expressed in mm or inches.

Diaphragm The rubber membrane in a master cylinder or carburettor which seals the upper chamber.

Diaphragm spring A single sprung plate often used in clutches.

Direct current (dc) Current produced by a dc generator.

Diode An electrical valve which only allows current to flow in one direction. Commonly used in rectifiers and starter interlock systems.

Disc valve (or rotary valve) A induction system used on some two-stroke engines.

Double-overhead camshaft (DOHC) An engine that uses two overhead camshafts, one for the intake valves and one for the exhaust valves.

Drivebelt A toothed belt used to transmit drive to the rear wheel on some motorcycles. A drivebelt has also been used to drive the camshafts. Drivebelts are usually made of Kevlar.

Driveshaft Any shaft used to transmit motion. Commonly used when referring to the final driveshaft on shaft drive motorcycles.

E

Earth return The return path of an electrical circuit, utilising the motorcycle's frame.

ECU (Electronic Control Unit) A computer which controls (for instance) an ignition system, or an anti-lock braking system.

EGO Exhaust Gas Oxygen sensor. Sometimes called a Lambda sensor.

Electrolyte The fluid in a lead-acid battery.

EMS (Engine Management System) A computer controlled system which manages the fuel injection and the ignition systems in an integrated fashion.

Endfloat The amount of lengthways movement between two parts. As applied to a crankshaft, the distance that the crankshaft can move side-to-side in the crankcase.

Endless chain A chain having no joining link. Common use for cam chains and final drive chains.

EP (Extreme Pressure) Oil type used in locations where high loads are applied, such as between gear teeth.

Evaporative emission control system Describes a charcoal filled canister which stores fuel vapours from the tank rather than allowing them to vent to the atmosphere. Usually only fitted to California models and referred to as an EVAP system.

Expansion chamber Section of two-stroke engine exhaust system so designed to improve engine efficiency and boost power.

F

Feeler blade or gauge A thin strip or blade of hardened steel, ground to an exact thickness, used to check or measure clearances between parts.

Final drive Description of the drive from the transmission to the rear wheel. Usually by chain or shaft, but sometimes by belt.

Firing order The order in which the engine cylinders fire, or deliver their power strokes, beginning with the number one cylinder.

Flooding Term used to describe a high fuel level in the carburettor float chambers, leading to fuel overflow. Also refers to excess fuel in the combustion chamber due to incorrect starting technique.

Free length The no-load state of a component when measured. Clutch, valve and fork spring lengths are measured at rest, without any preload.

Freeplay The amount of travel before any action takes place. The looseness in a linkage, or an assembly of parts, between the initial application of force and actual movement. For example, the distance the rear brake pedal moves before the rear brake is actuated.

Fuel injection The fuel/air mixture is metered electronically and directed into the engine intake ports (indirect injection) or into the cylinders (direct injection). Sensors supply information on engine speed and conditions.

Fuel/air mixture The charge of fuel and air going into the engine. See Stoichiometric ratio.

Fuse An electrical device which protects a circuit against accidental overload. The typical fuse contains a soft piece of metal which is calibrated to melt at a predetermined current flow (expressed as amps) and break the circuit.

G

Gap The distance the spark must travel in jumping from the centre electrode to the side electrode in a spark plug. Also refers to the distance between the ignition rotor and the pickup coil in an electronic ignition system.

Gasket Any thin, soft material - usually cork, cardboard, asbestos or soft metal - installed between two metal surfaces to ensure a good seal. For instance, the cylinder head gasket seals the joint between the block and the cylinder head.

Gauge An instrument panel display used to monitor engine conditions. A gauge with a movable pointer on a dial or a fixed scale is an analogue gauge. A gauge with a numerical readout is called a digital gauge.

Gear ratios The drive ratio of a pair of gears in a gearbox, calculated on their number of teeth.

Glaze-busting see **Honing**

Grinding Process for renovating the valve face and valve seat contact area in the cylinder head.

Gudgeon pin The shaft which connects the connecting rod small-end with the piston. Often called a piston pin or wrist pin.

H

Helical gears Gear teeth are slightly curved and produce less gear noise that straight-cut gears. Often used for primary drives.

Helicoil A thread insert repair system. Commonly used as a repair for stripped spark plug threads **(see illustration).**

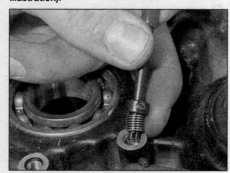

Installing a Helicoil thread insert

Honing A process used to break down the glaze on a cylinder bore (also called glaze-busting). Can also be carried out to roughen a rebored cylinder to aid ring bedding-in.

HT (High Tension) Description of the electrical circuit from the secondary winding of the ignition coil to the spark plug.

Hydraulic A liquid filled system used to transmit pressure from one component to another. Common uses on motorcycles are brakes and clutches.

Hydrometer An instrument for measuring the specific gravity of a lead-acid battery.

Hygroscopic Water absorbing. In motorcycle applications, braking efficiency will be reduced if DOT 3 or 4 hydraulic fluid absorbs water from the air - care must be taken to keep new brake fluid in tightly sealed containers.

I

Ibf ft Pounds-force feet. An imperial unit of torque. Sometimes written as ft-lbs.

Ibf in Pound-force inch. An imperial unit of torque, applied to components where a very low torque is required. Sometimes written as in-lbs.

IC Abbreviation for Integrated Circuit.

Ignition advance Means of increasing the timing of the spark at higher engine speeds. Done by mechanical means (ATU) on early engines or electronically by the ignition control unit on later engines.

Ignition timing The moment at which the spark plug fires, expressed in the number of crankshaft degrees before the piston reaches the top of its stroke, or in the number of millimetres before the piston reaches the top of its stroke.

Infinity (∞) Description of an open-circuit electrical state, where no continuity exists.

Inverted forks (upside down forks) The sliders or lower legs are held in the yokes and the fork tubes or stanchions are connected to the wheel axle (spindle). Less unsprung weight and stiffer construction than conventional forks.

J

JASO Quality standard for 2-stroke oils.

Joule The unit of electrical energy.

Journal The bearing surface of a shaft.

K

Kickstart Mechanical means of turning the engine over for starting purposes. Only usually fitted to mopeds, small capacity motorcycles and off-road motorcycles.

Kill switch Handebar-mounted switch for emergency ignition cut-out. Cuts the ignition circuit on all models, and additionally prevent starter motor operation on others.

km Symbol for kilometre.

kmh Abbreviation for kilometres per hour.

L

Lambda (λ) sensor A sensor fitted in the exhaust system to measure the exhaust gas oxygen content (excess air factor).

Technical Terms Explained REF•47

Lapping see Grinding.

LCD Abbreviation for Liquid Crystal Display.

LED Abbreviation for Light Emitting Diode.

Liner A steel cylinder liner inserted in a aluminium alloy cylinder block.

Locknut A nut used to lock an adjustment nut, or other threaded component, in place.

Lockstops The lugs on the lower triple clamp (yoke) which abut those on the frame, preventing handlebar-to-fuel tank contact.

Lockwasher A form of washer designed to prevent an attaching nut from working loose.

LT Low Tension Description of the electrical circuit from the power supply to the primary winding of the ignition coil.

M

Main bearings The bearings between the crankshaft and crankcase.

Maintenance-free (MF) battery A sealed battery which cannot be topped up.

Manometer Mercury-filled calibrated tubes used to measure intake tract vacuum. Used to synchronise carburettors on multi-cylinder engines.

Micrometer A precision measuring instrument that measures component outside diameters (see illustration).

Tappet shims are measured with a micrometer

MON (Motor Octane Number) A measure of a fuel's resistance to knock.

Monograde oil An oil with a single viscosity, eg SAE80W.

Monoshock A single suspension unit linking the swingarm or suspension linkage to the frame.

mph Abbreviation for miles per hour.

Multigrade oil Having a wide viscosity range (eg 10W40). The W stands for Winter, thus the viscosity ranges from SAE10 when cold to SAE40 when hot.

Multimeter An electrical test instrument with the capability to measure voltage, current and resistance. Some meters also incorporate a continuity tester and buzzer.

N

Needle roller bearing Inner race of caged needle rollers and hardened outer race. Examples of uncaged needle rollers can be found on some engines. Commonly used in rear suspension applications and in two-stroke engines.

Nm Newton metres.

NOx Oxides of Nitrogen. A common toxic pollutant emitted by petrol engines at higher temperatures.

O

Octane The measure of a fuel's resistance to knock.

OE (Original Equipment) Relates to components fitted to a motorcycle as standard or replacement parts supplied by the motorcycle manufacturer.

Ohm The unit of electrical resistance. Ohms = Volts ÷ Current.

Ohmmeter An instrument for measuring electrical resistance.

Oil cooler System for diverting engine oil outside of the engine to a radiator for cooling purposes.

Oil injection A system of two-stroke engine lubrication where oil is pump-fed to the engine in accordance with throttle position.

Open-circuit An electrical condition where there is a break in the flow of electricity - no continuity (high resistance).

O-ring A type of sealing ring made of a special rubber-like material; in use, the O-ring is compressed into a groove to provide the sealing action.

Oversize (OS) Term used for piston and ring size options fitted to a rebored cylinder.

Overhead cam (sohc) engine An engine with single camshaft located on top of the cylinder head.

Overhead valve (ohv) engine An engine with the valves located in the cylinder head, but with the camshaft located in the engine block or crankcase.

Oxygen sensor A device installed in the exhaust system which senses the oxygen content in the exhaust and converts this information into an electric current. Also called a Lambda sensor.

P

Plastigauge A thin strip of plastic thread, available in different sizes, used for measuring clearances. For example, a strip of Plastigauge is laid across a bearing journal. The parts are assembled and dismantled; the width of the crushed strip indicates the clearance between journal and bearing.

Polarity Either negative or positive earth (ground), determined by which battery lead is connected to the frame (earth return). Modern motorcycles are usually negative earth.

Pre-ignition A situation where the fuel/air mixture ignites before the spark plug fires. Often due to a hot spot in the combustion chamber caused by carbon build-up. Engine has a tendency to 'run-on'.

Pre-load (suspension) The amount a spring is compressed when in the unloaded state. Preload can be applied by gas, spacer or mechanical adjuster.

Premix The method of engine lubrication on older two-stroke engines. Engine oil is mixed with the petrol in the fuel tank in a specific ratio. The fuel/oil mix is sometimes referred to as "petroil".

Primary drive Description of the drive from the crankshaft to the clutch. Usually by gear or chain.

PS Pfedestärke - a German interpretation of BHP.

PSI Pounds-force per square inch. Imperial measurement of tyre pressure and cylinder pressure measurement.

PTFE Polytetrafluroethylene. A low friction substance.

Pulse secondary air injection system A process of promoting the burning of excess fuel present in the exhaust gases by routing fresh air into the exhaust ports.

Q

Quartz halogen bulb Tungsten filament surrounded by a halogen gas. Typically used for the headlight (see illustration).

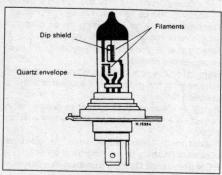

Quartz halogen headlight bulb construction

R

Rack-and-pinion A pinion gear on the end of a shaft that mates with a rack (think of a geared wheel opened up and laid flat). Sometimes used in clutch operating systems.

Radial play Up and down movement about a shaft.

Radial ply tyres Tyre plies run across the tyre (from bead to bead) and around the circumference of the tyre. Less resistant to tread distortion than other tyre types.

Radiator A liquid-to-air heat transfer device designed to reduce the temperature of the coolant in a liquid cooled engine.

Rake A feature of steering geometry - the angle of the steering head in relation to the vertical (see illustration).

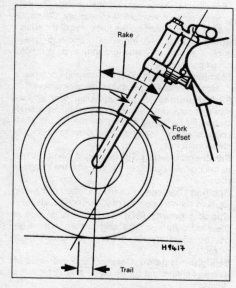

Steering geometry

Rebore Providing a new working surface to the cylinder bore by boring out the old surface. Necessitates the use of oversize piston and rings.

Rebound damping A means of controlling the oscillation of a suspension unit spring after it has been compressed. Resists the spring's natural tendency to bounce back after being compressed.

Rectifier Device for converting the ac output of an alternator into dc for battery charging.

Reed valve An induction system commonly used on two-stroke engines.

Regulator Device for maintaining the charging voltage from the generator or alternator within a specified range.

Relay A electrical device used to switch heavy current on and off by using a low current auxiliary circuit.

Resistance Measured in ohms. An electrical component's ability to pass electrical current.

RON (Research Octane Number) A measure of a fuel's resistance to knock.

rpm revolutions per minute.

Runout The amount of wobble (in-and-out movement) of a wheel or shaft as it's rotated. The amount a shaft rotates 'out-of-true'. The out-of-round condition of a rotating part.

S

SAE (Society of Automotive Engineers) A standard for the viscosity of a fluid.

Sealant A liquid or paste used to prevent leakage at a joint. Sometimes used in conjunction with a gasket.

Service limit Term for the point where a component is no longer useable and must be renewed.

Shaft drive A method of transmitting drive from the transmission to the rear wheel.

Shell bearings Plain bearings consisting of two shell halves. Most often used as big-end and main bearings in a four-stroke engine. Often called bearing inserts.

Shim Thin spacer, commonly used to adjust the clearance or relative positions between two parts. For example, shims inserted into or under tappets or followers to control valve clearances. Clearance is adjusted by changing the thickness of the shim.

Short-circuit An electrical condition where current shorts to earth (ground) bypassing the circuit components.

Skimming Process to correct warpage or repair a damaged surface, eg on brake discs or drums.

Slide-hammer A special puller that screws into or hooks onto a component such as a shaft or bearing; a heavy sliding handle on the shaft bottoms against the end of the shaft to knock the component free.

Small-end bearing The bearing in the upper end of the connecting rod at its joint with the gudgeon pin.

Spalling Damage to camshaft lobes or bearing journals shown as pitting of the working surface.

Specific gravity (SG) The state of charge of the electrolyte in a lead-acid battery. A measure of the electrolyte's density compared with water.

Straight-cut gears Common type gear used on gearbox shafts and for oil pump and water pump drives.

Stanchion The inner sliding part of the front forks, held by the yokes. Often called a fork tube.

Stoichiometric ratio The optimum chemical air/fuel ratio for a petrol engine, said to be 14.7 parts of air to 1 part of fuel.

Sulphuric acid The liquid (electrolyte) used in a lead-acid battery. Poisonous and extremely corrosive.

Surface grinding (lapping) Process to correct a warped gasket face, commonly used on cylinder heads.

T

Tapered-roller bearing Tapered inner race of caged needle rollers and separate tapered outer race. Examples of taper roller bearings can be found on steering heads.

Tappet A cylindrical component which transmits motion from the cam to the valve stem, either directly or via a pushrod and rocker arm. Also called a cam follower.

TCS Traction Control System. An electronically-controlled system which senses wheel spin and reduces engine speed accordingly.

TDC Top Dead Centre denotes that the piston is at its highest point in the cylinder.

Thread-locking compound Solution applied to fastener threads to prevent slackening. Select type to suit application.

Thrust washer A washer positioned between two moving components on a shaft. For example, between gear pinions on gearshaft.

Timing chain See **Cam Chain**.

Timing light Stroboscopic lamp for carrying out ignition timing checks with the engine running.

Top-end A description of an engine's cylinder block, head and valve gear components.

Torque Turning or twisting force about a shaft.

Torque setting A prescribed tightness specified by the motorcycle manufacturer to ensure that the bolt or nut is secured correctly. Undertightening can result in the bolt or nut coming loose or a surface not being sealed. Overtightening can result in stripped threads, distortion or damage to the component being retained.

Torx key A six-point wrench.

Tracer A stripe of a second colour applied to a wire insulator to distinguish that wire from another one with the same colour insulator. For example, Br/W is often used to denote a brown insulator with a white tracer.

Trail A feature of steering geometry. Distance from the steering head axis to the tyre's central contact point.

Triple clamps The cast components which extend from the steering head and support the fork stanchions or tubes. Often called fork yokes.

Turbocharger A centrifugal device, driven by exhaust gases, that pressurises the intake air. Normally used to increase the power output from a given engine displacement.

TWI Abbreviation for Tyre Wear Indicator. Indicates the location of the tread depth indicator bars on tyres.

U

Universal joint or U-joint (UJ) A double-pivoted connection for transmitting power from a driving to a driven shaft through an angle. Typically found in shaft drive assemblies.

Unsprung weight Anything not supported by the bike's suspension (ie the wheel, tyres, brakes, final drive and bottom (moving) part of the suspension).

V

Vacuum gauges Clock-type gauges for measuring intake tract vacuum. Used for carburettor synchronisation on multi-cylinder engines.

Valve A device through which the flow of liquid, gas or vacuum may be stopped, started or regulated by a moveable part that opens, shuts or partially obstructs one or more ports or passageways. The intake and exhaust valves in the cylinder head are of the poppet type.

Valve clearance The clearance between the valve tip (the end of the valve stem) and the rocker arm or tappet/follower. The valve clearance is measured when the valve is closed. The correct clearance is important - if too small the valve won't close fully and will burn out, whereas if too large noisy operation will result.

Valve lift The amount a valve is lifted off its seat by the camshaft lobe.

Valve timing The exact setting for the opening and closing of the valves in relation to piston position.

Vernier caliper A precision measuring instrument that measures inside and outside dimensions. Not quite as accurate as a micrometer, but more convenient.

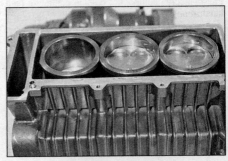

Wet liner arrangement

VIN Vehicle Identification Number. Term for the bike's engine and frame numbers.

Viscosity The thickness of a liquid or its resistance to flow.

Volt A unit for expressing electrical "pressure" in a circuit. Volts = current x ohms.

W

Water pump A mechanically-driven device for moving coolant around the engine.

Watt A unit for expressing electrical power. Watts = volts x current.

Wear limit see **Service limit**

Wet liner A liquid-cooled engine design where the pistons run in liners which are directly surrounded by coolant **(see illustration)**.

Wheelbase Distance from the centre of the front wheel to the centre of the rear wheel.

Wiring harness or loom Describes the electrical wires running the length of the motorcycle and enclosed in tape or plastic sheathing. Wiring coming off the main harness is usually referred to as a sub harness.

Woodruff key A key of semi-circular or square section used to locate a gear to a shaft. Often used to locate the alternator rotor on the crankshaft.

Wrist pin Another name for gudgeon or piston pin.

Note: *References throughout this index are in the form - "Chapter number" • "Page number"*

Preserving Our Motoring Heritage

< The Model J Duesenberg Derham Tourster. Only eight of these magnificent cars were ever built – this is the only example to be found outside the United States of America

Almost every car you've ever loved, loathed or desired is gathered under one roof at the Haynes Motor Museum. Over 300 immaculately presented cars and motorbikes represent every aspect of our motoring heritage, from elegant reminders of bygone days, such as the superb Model J Duesenberg to curiosities like the bug-eyed BMW Isetta. There are also many old friends and flames. Perhaps you remember the 1959 Ford Popular that you did your courting in? The magnificent 'Red Collection' is a spectacle of classic sports cars including AC, Alfa Romeo, Austin Healey, Ferrari, Lamborghini, Maserati, MG, Riley, Porsche and Triumph.

A Perfect Day Out

Each and every vehicle at the Haynes Motor Museum has played its part in the history and culture of Motoring. Today, they make a wonderful spectacle and a great day out for all the family. Bring the kids, bring Mum and Dad, but above all bring your camera to capture those golden memories for ever. You will also find an impressive array of motoring memorabilia, a comfortable 70 seat video cinema and one of the most extensive transport book shops in Britain. The Pit Stop Cafe serves everything from a cup of tea to wholesome, home-made meals or, if you prefer, you can enjoy the large picnic area nestled in the beautiful rural surroundings of Somerset.

> John Haynes O.B.E., Founder and Chairman of the museum at the wheel of a Haynes Light 12.

< The 1936 490cc sohc-engined International Norton — well known for its racing success

The Museum is situated on the A359 Yeovil to Frome road at Sparkford, just off the A303 in Somerset. It is about 40 miles south of Bristol, and 25 minutes drive from the M5 intersection at Taunton.
Open 9.30am - 5.30pm (10.00am - 4.00pm Winter) 7 days a week, *except Christmas Day, Boxing Day and New Years Day*
Special rates available for schools, coach parties and outings Charitable Trust No. 292048